CLEMEN

OB PARTUM CELEBRANDUM

DONO DEDIT   W. W.

MMXXII.

THE CAMBRIDGE EDITION
OF THE NOVELS OF

THOMAS LOVE PEACOCK

MELINCOURT

THE CAMBRIDGE EDITION
OF THE NOVELS OF

THOMAS LOVE PEACOCK

GENERAL EDITOR: Freya Johnston, *University of Oxford*

SENIOR EDITORIAL ADVISOR: Nicholas A. Joukovsky,
Pennsylvania State University

VOLUMES IN THIS SERIES

1. *Headlong Hall*

2. *Melincourt*

3. *Nightmare Abbey*

4. *Maid Marian*

5. *The Misfortunes of Elphin*

6. *Crotchet Castle*

7. *Gryll Grange*

THOMAS LOVE PEACOCK

MELINCOURT

Edited by
Gary Dyer

CAMBRIDGE
UNIVERSITY PRESS

CAMBRIDGE
UNIVERSITY PRESS

University Printing House, Cambridge CB2 8BS, United Kingdom

One Liberty Plaza, 20th Floor, New York, NY 10006, USA

477 Williamstown Road, Port Melbourne, VIC 3207, Australia

314–321, 3rd Floor, Plot 3, Splendor Forum, Jasola District Centre,
New Delhi – 110025, India

103 Penang Road, #05-06/07, Visioncrest Commercial, Singapore 238467

Cambridge University Press is part of the University of Cambridge.

It furthers the University's mission by disseminating knowledge in the pursuit of
education, learning, and research at the highest international levels of excellence.

www.cambridge.org
Information on this title: www.cambridge.org/9781107032262
DOI: 10.1017/9781139424806

© Cambridge University Press 2022

First published 2022

Printed in the United Kingdom by TJ Books Limited, Padstow Cornwall

A catalogue record for this publication is available from the British Library.

ISBN 978-1-107-03226-2 Hardback

CONTENTS

Contents

ILLUSTRATIONS

The editor thanks Nicholas A. Joukovsky and the Pforzheimer Collection for kind permission to reproduce these images, and for supplying photographs.

GENERAL EDITOR'S PREFACE

'That Peacock is a classic', declared the scholar and editor R. W. Chapman in 1924, 'now needs no proof; he has passed his century, and his reputation grows'. Such a judgement might have appeared sanguine even in the year in which *The Works of Thomas Love Peacock*, edited by H. F. B. Brett-Smith and C. E. Jones (1924–34), also known as the Halliford Edition, began to be published. During the early 1920s, Oxford University Press steadfastly resisted proposals for works by and about Peacock. But Chapman – learned, urbane Secretary to Delegates of the Press from 1920 to 1942 – was eager to see the novels back in print. He remarked in his Introduction to the World's Classics texts of *The Misfortunes of Elphin and Crotchet Castle* that the 'experiment' of publishing them, shortly after the initial five volumes of his ground-breaking edition of Jane Austen (1923) had appeared, might transform Peacock into a 'popular classic'.[1]

The present editors hope, in part, to realize that frustrated ambition. It seems fitting that the Cambridge Edition of the Novels of Thomas Love Peacock should appear not long after the Cambridge Edition of the Works of Jane Austen (2005–8). That the decades since the 1920s have been kinder to Austen than to Peacock is no surprise; unlike Austen, Peacock is habitually, wilfully arcane. Nora

---

[1] Thomas Love Peacock, *The Misfortunes of Elphin and Crotchet Castle*, introd. R. W. Chapman, World's Classics, CCXLIV (1924), pp. ix, x. On Oxford University Press and proposals for works relating to Peacock, see *Register of the Orders of the Delegates of the Clarendon Press* (Nov. 1913 – June 1924), p. 308 (21 Oct. 1921), item 5227; p. 315 (4 Nov. 1921), item 5314. An edition of *Headlong Hall and Nightmare Abbey* was published as World's Classics, CCCXXXIX in 1929.

Crook and Derek Guiton observe that 'His writings contain references as inaccessible to the common reader as medieval graffiti in cathedral towers'; the historical and architectural contexts are appropriate, as is the flavour of irreverence suggested by 'graffiti'.[2] Even if his comic fictions abound, like Austen's, with clever, good-looking women and with sparkling dialogue that culminates in marriage, Peacock's repartee can be hard to follow. On a first, unmediated encounter with him, many readers will feel, with Captain Fitzchrome (in Chapter 6 of *Crotchet Castle*), that 'the pleasantry and the obscurity go together'. Peacock does not aspire to the portrayal of interiority – perhaps the most cherished aspect of Austen's novels. Rather, his characters, both male and female, exist primarily in order to share, voice and test the limits of their ideas. His fictions, rebuffing intimacy, are inescapably political and intellectual. To approach the nineteenth-century novel via Peacock is therefore to see it as an outward-facing genre indebted to philosophical tracts, lectures, classical dialogues and the rhythms of parliamentary debate.

It would have amused Peacock, who tended to write contemptuously of academics and their institutions, that in 1921 Professor Herbert G. Wright's proposal for a new edition of *The Misfortunes of Elphin* was rejected by Oxford University Press, whereas the Snowdon Mountain Tramroad and Hotels Company, 'being desirous to provide holiday reading for visitors to the Principality', successfully lobbied for the same work's appearance in the World's Classics series, alongside *Crotchet Castle*, three years later.[3] Making the case for Peacock can be a tricky, unpredictable business. According to J. B. Priestley, he is 'a treacherous subject for criticism'.[4] An erudite,

[2] Nora Crook and Derek Guiton, *Shelley's Venomed Melody* (Cambridge: Cambridge University Press, 1986), p. 13.

[3] *Register of the Orders of the Delegates of the Clarendon Press* (Nov. 1913 – June 1924), p. 308 (21 Oct. 1921), item 5227.

[4] J. B. Priestley, *Thomas Love Peacock* [1927], reissued with an introduction by J. I. M. Stewart (London, Melbourne, Toronto: Macmillan; New York: St Martin's Press, 1966), p. 195.

eclectic and fastidious reader, possessed of an excellent memory, Peacock is a daunting prospect for editors, too; as Stephen Gill puts it, 'he was a bibliographer of sorts and a textual critic of some severity'.[5] One of the most striking things about his fastidious and omnivorous novels is just how many ancient and modern writers they lightly touch upon, in such a way as to reveal their author's delighted saturation in literature. To gloss his works judiciously therefore requires more than a few notes. 'Doing so much', thought Chapman, the Halliford editors 'might well have done a little more' in this regard: 'In the process of verification they must have traced many of Peacock's adespotic quotations; readers would have been grateful if they had given the references. It would be interesting, too, to know if Peacock often misquoted.'[6] 'Adespotic', in the hyper-abstruse sense in which Chapman uses it here (i.e. relating to classical, especially Greek, literature which is not attributed to any particular author), is so rare as not to appear in the *Oxford English Dictionary*, or indeed in Peacock's fiction, but there are plenty of other terms and allusions in his novels that will baffle the modern reader. Peacock's head, like Taliesin's (in Chapter 16 of *The Misfortunes of Elphin*), was 'brimfull of Pagan knowledge', sometimes misquoted. Volume editors have tried to keep in view the reader's need for information about and explanation of Peacock's myriad sources, and his relationship to them, while remaining conscious that annotations of his works are potentially limitless. Peacock wrote in a letter to Lord Broughton that he believed 'the author of an inscription always knows what he means, however difficult of apprehension his meaning may be to others'.[7] His comment suggests a puzzling quality to the epigraphs and other forms of quotation in the novels and elsewhere; but it also suggests that we might recover the author's meanings, if we will only

[5] Stephen Gill, review of Nicholas A. Joukovsky, ed., *The Letters of Thomas Love Peacock*, *The Review of English Studies*, New Series, 53 (2002), 449–51 (p. 449).

[6] R. W. Chapman, review of the Halliford Edition of *The Works of Thomas Love Peacock*, vols. 2–5 (1924), *The Review of English Studies*, 1 (1925), 239–42 (p. 241).

[7] Peacock to Lord Broughton (13 May 1861), *Letters*, 2.413.

persist in hunting for them. The Cambridge Edition aims to reveal his locally apposite, imaginative use of out-of-the-way sources and analogues. The appearance in 2001 of Nicholas A. Joukovsky's definitive edition of Peacock's *Letters*, incorporating details of the books Peacock read while composing his fiction, has paved the way for many new attributions. The seven novels he wrote between 1815 and 1861 have been enriched in the present edition by ampler cross-referencing to his other works, published and unpublished, and to their relevant literary, historical and cultural contexts, than has previously been attempted.

In his essay on 'French Comic Romances', Peacock remarked of Pigault-Lebrun that 'his successive works are impressed with the political changes of the day: they carry their eras in their incidents'.[8] The same might be said of Peacock's fiction, but he was equally interested in the capacity of his works to outlive their moment. Looking back on *Melincourt* some thirty-nine years after the novel first appeared in print, its author pointed out that 'Many of the questions, discussed in the dialogues, have more of general than of temporary application, and still have their advocates on both sides'. Some things might not be true, some decades later, but they had 'worthy successors' in the present. As Alexander Pope reflected with malicious complacency that his dunces would be perennially replaced with a fresh stock of dud writers, generation after generation, so Peacock envisaged his satires living beyond their original moment, as well as being marked by it (and needing some explanation accordingly).[9]

---

[8] Halliford, 9.255.

[9] Peacock's reflections on the changes appeared in his Preface to the 1856 edition of *Melincourt*, while the reference to 'worthy successors' appeared in his Preface of 1837. In 'The Publisher to the Reader', Pope asserts of *The Dunciad* that 'the *Poem was not made for these Authors, but these Authors for the Poem*. And I should judge that they were clapp'd in as they rose, fresh and fresh, and chang'd from day to day, in like manner as when the old boughs wither, we thrust new ones into a chimney.' The Twickenham Edition of the Poems of Alexander Pope, ed. John Butt et al., 11 vols. (London: Methuen;

The numerous quotations from and allusions to other writers in Peacock's fiction suggest the company he chose to keep and in which he wished to be recorded. He would have agreed with Samuel Johnson that citing ancient writers, far from being mere pedantry, 'is a good thing; there is a community of mind in it. Classical quotation is the *parole* of literary men all over the world.'[10] That phrase, 'community of mind', sums up the sociable disputes to which Peacock's novels play host, and explains the gravitation within them towards the library as well as to the dining table. In *Crotchet Castle*, for instance, the library is a suite of interlinked apartments in which games, words and music are shown to be continuous with one another. The library is therefore structurally representative of the novel, revealing adjacency, sequence, continuity and difference between play, talk, literature and song.

There is a further sense in which Peacock's books might be viewed as miniature libraries: they share certain characteristics with commonplace books of quotation gathered around different subjects. It can be hard to differentiate a quotation from an allusion in Peacock; to tell why certain sources are named and flagged while others are left more implicit or indeed almost entirely submerged. But one way of reading the novels might be as anthologies of classical material, as well as of the state of political life and reviewing culture at a given nineteenth-century moment (at one point in Chapter 18, *Melincourt* quotes an issue of the *Edinburgh Review* in place of a character's speech). A definitive edition of Peacock's fiction therefore requires attentiveness to old and contemporary orthodoxies, and to the bridges between them. He is a writer who manages to rehearse highly acrimonious debates without himself becoming either angry or jaded.

New Haven, CT: Yale University Press, 1939–69), vol. 5: *The Dunciad*, ed. James Sutherland, 3rd ed., revised (1963), pp. 205–6.

[10] James Boswell, *Boswell's Life of Johnson*, ed. George Birkbeck Hill, rev. L. F. Powell, 6 vols. (Oxford: Clarendon Press, 1934–50), vol. 4, p. 102.

Quotations serve, too, as forms of evidence, anchoring the claims made in the text, so that they contribute to the kind of authority and probability that Peacock, following in Henry Fielding's wake, claimed was necessary in all kinds of fiction – however outrageous – and in the teeth of such historically incoherent works as Thomas Moore's *The Epicurean* (1827), which Peacock reviewed with majestic scorn.[11] In nineteenth-century reviews, lengthy quotations are often provided in order to ridicule and condemn a work, as well as to offer a representative selection from it. Perhaps the long footnotes quoting (for instance) Lord Monboddo in *Melincourt* combine these roles. They serve to establish a genuine basis for Sylvan Forester's arguments about his captured creature in Monboddo's own outlandish claims about orangutans, and in so doing they also poke fun at the nature of those arguments. In fact, the quotations are so substantial that, like the *Edinburgh Review*, they invade the text, forming part of Forester's italicized speech in Chapter 6 – a chapter which amounts to a miniature encyclopaedia of arguments in favour of natural man. Such quotations are both seriously meant – they show attentive fidelity to source material – and satirically driven, since they show how far from common sense such arguments may be taken. In other words, they resemble the notes to Pope's *Dunciad*.

Having said all this, and acknowledging Peacock's remarkable allusiveness, scholarly editing is not only about commentary and explanatory annotation. We have benefited handsomely from more than a century of sophisticated textual enquiry into Peacock, and from the formidable legacy of earlier bibliographical investigators. The Cambridge Edition is indebted to the diligence and skill of H. F. B. Brett-Smith and C. E. Jones, who set a very high standard in terms of the accuracy and completeness of their work. The first collected edition of Peacock, published in 1874 (dated 1875), was in three volumes; the Halliford editors oversaw the publication of ten. Their bibliographical retrievals and discoveries were legion; the

---

[11] See Halliford, 9.3–4.

dearth of explanatory notes accompanying the texts was dictated by prevailing trends in editorial practice, rather than by their own preferences. Supplemented by David Garnett's two-volume edition of the novels (1948, 1963), and by Nicholas A. Joukovsky's numerous textual, critical and biographical gleanings, Halliford continues to offer the best and fullest selection of Peacock's writings as a whole.

Unlike Brett-Smith and Jones, who, in accordance with editorial thinking at the time, gave the preference to Peacock's revised lifetime texts, the Cambridge Edition of the Novels of Thomas Love Peacock employs as copytexts the first editions, in book-length form, of his fictions. This policy has been adopted partly because it seems better to accord with Peacock's authorial character; when given the opportunity to do so, he made few revisions to his novels. The first editions of those works also serve as the best witnesses of Peacock's satirical topicality, a vital source of his appeal and interest, and a distinctive aspect of his contribution to nineteenth-century fiction. In the case of *Nightmare Abbey*, for instance, now Peacock's best-known and most widely studied work, the text as first published in 1818 not only reflected but also directly participated in the literary and political debates of his time.

Our texts remain as close to the copytexts as possible. Spelling and punctuation have not been modernized and inconsistencies in presentation, titles (such as Dr. and Doctor) and grammatical forms have generally been left as they were found. Peacock's own footnotes are an essential part of his mock-explicatory, Scriblerian style; they are also a means, like his epigraphs, of displaying his literary allegiances and antagonisms. In this edition they remain at the bottom of the page – signalled by asterisks and daggers – as in the copytexts. The presence of editorial endnotes is contrastingly indicated by superscript numbers in the text.

The few corrections and emendations we have made to the texts, other than replacing dropped or missing letters, have been permitted only when an error is very plain, or where its retention might impede comprehension of the passage. For instance, missing quotation marks have been supplied, run-on words have been separated, repeated words have been excised and unclosed parentheses have been closed. Occasionally, where the copytext is corrupt and clearly does not reflect Peacock's intentions at the time of writing, it has been emended. For instance, at the beginning of Chapter 13 of *Nightmare Abbey*, the 1818 text reads 'or of a waggon, or of a weighing-bridge'. In this case, the 1837 correction 'or of a waggon on a weighing-bridge' appears to be a restoration of what he must have originally written or intended to write. All such changes to the texts have been noted in the final apparatus. Where relevant, in each volume surviving draft manuscript fragments have been transcribed, with explanatory headnotes indicating both their nature and their relationship to the printed text, in an appendix or series of appendices. All manuscript materials have been transcribed with their changes or erasures either reproduced or noted. Variant readings of such materials are not incorporated into the textual apparatus.

Peacock appears to have been sparing in the changes he made to the four novels (*Headlong Hall, Nightmare Abbey, Maid Marian* and *Crotchet Castle*) that were re-published by Richard Bentley in his Standard Novels series in 1837, but countless tiny alterations were introduced to this text. For many of those, Peacock is unlikely to have been responsible, although the concern he showed when correcting or altering orthography in the cases of characters' names, locations, dialect and pronunciation makes it generally unwise to attempt to determine which are his, and which are not. In the case of *Headlong Hall*, for instance, along with a number of misprints, there are some new substantive readings in 1837, one of which appears to be authorial. The Cambridge Edition accepts that many decisions about spelling, punctuation, capitalization, spacing, italicizing and paragraphing may not have been Peacock's, either in the copytexts or in subsequent lifetime texts, but we have no way of knowing for certain that they were not. All volume editors have therefore undertaken a complete collation of the copytext with other lifetime editions, but not all the accidental variants have been printed. Instead, we have reproduced all substantive variants between the copytext and other lifetime editions, and a number of variants in accidentals, including all those in the spelling of proper names.

Introductions to each volume are substantial and have a common basic structure. They incorporate original discussion of each work's genesis and composition, its publication history, reception and after-life. An extensive chronology of Peacock's life, revised by Nicholas A. Joukovsky from his edition of the *Letters*, is also provided in every volume.

Modern readers may ask what Peacock hoped to achieve through the elegant representation of opposing views in his imaginative, dia-logic and dramatic prose. The answer is probably something akin to what he admired in French comic fiction: its capacity, by 'presenting or embodying opinion' through characters that are 'abstractions or embodied classifications', or representatives 'of actual life', to direct 'the stream of opinion against the mass of delusions and abuses' in the public arena.[12] Peacock commented of Paul de Kock that the author very rarely expressed a political opinion ('never', he says in 'French Comic Romances', modified to a 'very slight' indication of such opinion in 'The Épicier'); this elusive quality evidently puzzled and interested him.[13] What sort of a writer pursues opinion with-out committing himself? Does it make him tantamount to a mere reviewer? What kind of public is interested in opinions, and why? What is the status of literature in relation to public opinion? In a letter to Thomas L'Estrange (11 July 1861), Peacock wrote that: 'In the questions which have come within my scope, I have endeavoured to be impartial, and to say what could be said on both sides'. Around the same time (June 1861), he suggested to Lord Broughton what talking heads might, at their best, have to offer:

[12] Halliford, 9.259.   [13] Halliford, 9.256.

The dialogues of Plato and Cicero are made up of discussions among persons who differed in opinion. Neither they nor their heroes would have been content to pass eternity in the company of persons who merely thought as they did. They were enquirers. They did not profess to have found truth. They might have expected to find it in another life: but then they would no longer think, as they had thought, with those who agreed with them in this.[14]

Freya Johnston

[14] *Letters*, 2.425, 419.

ACKNOWLEDGEMENTS

I wish to thank Cleveland State University for a Faculty Scholarship Initiative grant that funded research for this project. For help and suggestions, I thank Rachel Carnell, William Galperin, Michael Gamer, Freya Johnston, Nicholas A. Joukovsky, James J. Marino, Barbara Riebling and Susan Wolfson.

CHRONOLOGY
THOMAS LOVE PEACOCK, 1785–1866
NICHOLAS A. JOUKOVSKY

1785

18 Oct. — Born at Weymouth, or Melcombe Regis, Dorset, the only child of Samuel Peacock (born 1722/3), a London glass merchant whose father, Josiah Peacock, had been a linen draper and grocer at Taunton, Somerset, and Sarah Love (born 10 Nov. 1754), daughter of Thomas Love, a retired master in the Royal Navy from Topsham, Devon, who lost a leg as Master of HMS *Prothée* in the battle of the Saints, Rodney's great victory off Dominica, on 12 Apr. 1782. (His parents were married at St Luke's, Chelsea, on 29 Mar. 1780.)

?Dec.–Jan. 1786 — Baptized by Henry Hunter, DD, minister of the Scots Presbyterian church, London Wall. (The Loves were Presbyterians, while the Peacocks were Independents.)

1786

Autumn–Winter 1787 — His father stops attending the Court of the Pewterers' Company (of which he is an Assistant) and apparently transfers his interest in his glass warehouse at 46 Holborn Bridge to his brother George (his brother Thomas having previously become a junior partner in the firm).

1791

before 31 Dec.   His mother and her parents take separate houses at Chertsey. (His uncle William Love also settles his family at Chertsey in 1793.)

1792

Winter–Spring   Sent to a private school kept by John Harris Wicks at Englefield Green, where he remains for six and a half years, spending his vacations at Chertsey and often visiting a schoolfellow named Charles at the Abbey House.

1793

early Feb.   Death of his father (buried 5 Feb. at the Elim Baptist Chapel, Fetter Lane), after the purchase of two small annuities for his widow and one for his son.

1 Mar.   Birth of his cousin Henry Ommanney Love (died 16 Sept. 1872) at Chertsey.

1794

Apr.   His uncle William Love (born early Apr. 1764) promoted to the rank of lieutenant in the Royal Navy, having been a midshipman since 1778.

1 June   His uncle Thomas Love (born 29 May 1752) serves as Master of HMS *Alfred* in Howe's great victory over the French.

Nov.   Death of his uncle Richard Love (baptized 1 Mar. 1761) at Bombay, after having served in the Russian navy.

1795

4–14 Feb.   Writes his first known poem, an epitaph for a schoolfellow named Hamlet Wade.

1797

before 24 Apr.   Birth of his cousin Harriet Blagrave Deane Love (died 14 Feb. 1881) at Chertsey.

1798

June	Writes a poem on his 'Midsummer Holidays'.
before 18 Oct.	Removed from school, possibly due to failure of one of his mother's annuities. From this time he is entirely self-educated.

1800

before 11 Feb.–?1805 or 1806	Employed as a clerk for Ludlow, Fraser & Company, merchants in the City of London, while residing with his mother on the firm's premises at 4 Angel Court, Throgmorton Street. During these years he has a circle of friends in the neighbourhood of Hackney, including William de St Croix of Homerton and, perhaps later, Thomas Forster of Lower Clapton.
Feb.	Receives an 'Extra Prize' from the *Monthly Preceptor, or Juvenile Library* for his first publication, a verse 'Answer to the Question: "Is History or Biography the More Improving Study?"'

1803

16 Nov.	Presents a (lost) manuscript volume of poems to Lucretia Oldham, 'the beauty of Shacklewell Green', with a dedicatory poem on the first leaf.

1804

Sept.	Writes 'The Monks of St. Mark' (later privately printed as a leaflet, probably in connection with the printing of the *Palmyra* volume in the autumn of 1805).
?Sept.–Oct.	Collects most of his juvenile verse, except the Lucretia Oldham poems, in a manuscript volume of 'Poems, by T. L. Peacock'.

?Autumn	Writes a verse drama entitled 'The Circle of Loda'.

1805

Nov.–Dec.	*Palmyra, and Other Poems* published by W. J. & J. Richardson, with title page post-dated 1806.
10 Dec.	Death of his grandfather, Thomas Love, at Chertsey (buried 20 Dec. at the Presbyterian meeting-house).

1806

Autumn	Solitary walking tour in Scotland.
18 Oct.	The annuity purchased for him by his father expires on his coming of age.

1807

Feb.	His uncle William Love promoted to the rank of commander.
?Spring	Returns to live with his mother at Chertsey.
3 Aug.	Accepts a 'generous offer' of Edward Thomas Hookham and his brother Thomas Hookham, Junior, to supply him with books from their father's extensive circulating library at 15 Old Bond Street and to publish a projected poem, apparently in the same vein as *Palmyra*.
?Summer–Autumn	Brief engagement to Fanny Falkner broken off by the interference of one of her relations. She marries another man and dies the next year.

1808

14 May–2 Apr. 1809	Serves as Captain's Clerk to Sir Home Riggs Popham and, after 18 Dec., to Capt. Andrew King, aboard HMS *Venerable* in the Downs – 'this floating Inferno'. During this period he writes several prologues and epilogues for the officers' amateur theatricals as well as 'Stanzas Written at Sea' (published with *The Genius of the Thames*).

1809

13 Mar.   Sends Edward Hookham a 'little poem of the Thames' and mentions 'a classical ballad or two now in embryo', perhaps 'Romance' and 'Remember Me'.

after 2 Apr.   Having left the *Venerable*, walks from Deal to Ramsgate and around the North Foreland to Margate, before proceeding to Canterbury and London, then eventually returning to live at Chertsey.

?Apr.–Dec.   Expands his 'little poem on the Thames' into *The Genius of the Thames*.

29 May   Begins a two-week expedition to trace the course of the Thames on foot from its source to Chertsey, with a stay of two or three days at Oxford.

1810

Jan.   Travels to North Wales, visiting Tremadoc before settling at Maentwrog, Merionethshire.

after 20 Jan.   Sends Edward Hookham the Prooemium to *The Genius of the Thames* while the poem is being printed.

Apr.–May   Attracted to the Maentwrog parson's daughter Jane Gryffydh, 'the Caernarvonshire nymph', but by 12 June 'Richard is himself again'.

late May–early June   *The Genius of the Thames: A Lyrical Poem, in Two Parts* published by Thomas and Edward Hookham.

late June–?early Oct.   Affair with an unidentified 'Caernarvonshire charmer' ('not a parson's daughter'), ending in disillusionment.

27 Dec.   Death of his grandmother, Sarah Love, at Chertsey (buried 3 Jan. 1811 at the Presbyterian meeting-house).

1811

7 Apr.   Leaves Maentwrog, after bidding farewell to Jane Gryffydh, 'the most innocent, the most amiable, the most beautiful girl in existence'. On his walk home by way of South Wales, he climbs Cadair Idris and calls on Edward Scott at Bodtalog, near Towyn, before proceeding to Aberystwyth and the Devil's Bridge, near Hafod.

?May–July   A 'long abode in Covent-Garden'.

Autumn   His mother's remaining annuity having expired at Michaelmas, she is forced by creditors to leave Chertsey. He and his mother are enabled by friends to occupy Morven Cottage, Wyrardisbury, near Staines.

?Autumn   Writes *The Philosophy of Melancholy* – 'in ten days', according to Edward Hookham.

before 14 Nov.   Revises *The Genius of the Thames, Palmyra* and 'Fiolfar, King of Norway' for a new edition, to which he adds 'Inscription for a Mountain Dell'. Consigns all his other poems 'to the tomb of the Capulets'.

18 Dec.   Grant of £21 from the Literary Fund.

1812

Winter–Spring   Writes a (lost) farce entitled 'Mirth in the Mountains', which is read by James Grant Raymond, the actor-manager of the Drury Lane Company.

?Winter–Autumn   Translates passages from Greek tragedies, which he thinks of publishing under the title 'Fragments of Greek Tragedy'. Around this time he probably also writes and privately prints his Aristophanic Greek anapaests on Christ (no known copy).

late Feb.	*The Philosophy of Melancholy: A Poem in Four Parts, with a Mythological Ode* published by Thomas and Edward Hookham.
early Apr.	Second edition of *The Genius of the Thames, Palmyra, and Other Poems* published by Thomas and Edward Hookham.
before 20 May	Forced temporarily to leave Morven Cottage, Wyrardisbury, by his inability to pay local tradesmen's bills.
20 May	Grant of £30 from the Literary Fund. Edward Hookham, in his letter of application, expresses fears that 'the fate of Chatterton might be that of Peacock'.
20 May	Cosigns an East India Company bond for Peter Auber in the amount of £500.
?Summer–Spring 1813	Writes, with Raymond's encouragement, two more farces, 'The Dilettanti' and 'The Three Doctors', but neither is performed at Drury Lane. Other dramatic projects of this period include two Roman tragedies entitled 'Otho' and 'Virginia'.
July–Aug.	Thomas Forster visits him for a week at Wyrardisbury.
before 18 Aug.	Thomas Hookham sends Peacock's two recent volumes of poetry to Shelley at Lynmouth, Devon.
late Aug.–early Sept.	Visits Thomas Forster at Tunbridge Wells.
?Sept.–Dec.	In love with Clarinda Knowles at Englefield Green – 'this goddess of my idolatry'.
17–30 Sept.	Walking and sailing tour of the Isle of Wight with Joseph Gulston of Englefield Green, during which he visits his uncle William Love at Yarmouth and finds his cousin Harriet 'grown into a fine girl'.

4 Oct.–13 Nov.	Introduced to Shelley by Thomas Hookham in London.
late Nov.	Thomas Hookham sends Peacock's poem 'Farewell to Meirion' to Shelley at Tan-yr-allt, near Tremadoc.

1813

?Winter–Spring	Writes, and possibly prints, a prospectus outlining his educational theories and proposing 'to receive eight pupils, in a beautiful retirement in the county of Westmoreland'.
?Winter–Spring	Writes *Sir Hornbook*, which is illustrated by Henry Corbould before 1 June.
12 Mar.	Writes the poem 'Al mio primiero amore!' to an unidentified 'first love'.
?Apr.–June	Sees Shelley several times in London and meets Thomas Jefferson Hogg and William Godwin.
11 June	His epilogue to Lumley Skeffington's comedy *Lose No Time* is recited at Drury Lane, then printed in the *Morning Post* on 14 June.
16 June	Grant of £10 from the Literary Fund.
late June–late Aug.	Second visit to Wales, during which he wanders through Radnorshire, Cardiganshire and Merionethshire. Tentatively engages 'a very beautiful place in Radnorshire'. Returns by way of Bath.
Sept.	Visits Shelley at Bracknell, where he meets John Frank Newton, Harriet de Boinville and their circle.
4 Oct.–early Dec.	Accompanies Shelley and his family to the Lake District and Edinburgh.

Nov.–Dec.	*Sir Hornbook; or, Childe Launcelot's Expedition: A Grammatico-Allegorical Ballad* published by Sharpe & Hailes, with plates dated 1 June 1813 and title page post-dated 1814. (Second and third editions follow in 1815, fourth edition in 1817, fifth edition in 1818.)

1814

Mar.	*Sir Proteus: A Satirical Ballad* published under the pseudonym of P. M. O'Donovan, Esq. by Thomas and Edward Hookham.
8 Apr.	Letter signed 'P.', pointing out a resemblance between *Hamlet* and Euripides' *Hippolytus*, published in the *Morning Chronicle*.
?Spring–Spring 1815	Begins and outlines two versions of 'Ahrimanes', an unfinished romantic epic in Spenserian stanzas.
12 July	Writes gloomy 'Lines to a Favorite Laurel in the Garden at Ankerwyke Cottage'.
28 July	After having consulted Peacock about his marital crisis, Shelley elopes to the Continent with Mary Godwin and Claire Clairmont. During his absence, he writes to ask Peacock 'to superintend money affairs'. Peacock does not meet the two girls until after their return on 13 Sept.
?Aug.	Proposes marriage to Cecilia Knowles at Englefield Green, having previously proposed to her sister Clarinda.
?Sept.	Watches the driving of the deer, by two regiments of cavalry, from Windsor Forest into the Park – 'the most beautiful sight I ever witnessed'.

25 Sept.–15 Nov.	Helps Shelley to raise money and to elude bailiffs, while residing with his mother in Southampton Buildings, Chancery Lane.
30 Sept.	Becomes involved in a plan to liberate Shelley's sisters from boarding school and run away to the west of Ireland, a scheme that would somehow enable him to marry Marianne de St Croix.
20 Oct.	Calls on Godwin in an unsuccessful attempt to effect a reconciliation between Godwin and Shelley.
?late Nov.–late Feb. 1815	Visits Zipporah Simpson, mother of John Arthur Roebuck, at Gumley, Leicestershire.

1815

9–10 Jan.	Arrested for debt in Liverpool and lodged in a 'sponging house', after a mysterious affair with a supposed heiress named Charlotte.
Apr.	Considers emigrating to Canada and taking Marianne de St Croix.
13 May	Shelley reaches a financial settlement with his father, giving him an annuity of £1000 a year, from which he allows Peacock £120 a year.
?Summer	Settles with his mother at Marlow, near his uncle Thomas Love.
3 Aug.	Shelley takes a house at Bishopsgate, where Peacock is a frequent visitor throughout the autumn and winter months. Hogg later describes the winter at Bishopsgate as 'a mere Atticism'.
late Aug.–early Sept.	Excursion up the Thames from Old Windsor to beyond Lechlade with Shelley, Mary Godwin and Charles Clairmont.

early Dec.	*Headlong Hall* published by Thomas Hookham, with title page post-dated 1816.
?Dec.	Suggests the title for Shelley's *Alastor; or, The Spirit of Solitude.*
1816	
3 May	Shelley leaves England for Switzerland with Mary Godwin and Claire Clairmont. During his absence he asks Peacock to take custody of his books and furniture at Bishopsgate and to find another house for him and Mary.
late July	Second edition of *Headlong Hall* published by Thomas Hookham.
13/14–25 Sept.	Shelley visits him at Marlow.
5 Nov.	His prologue to John Tobin's comedy *The Faro Table; or, The Guardians* is recited at Drury Lane, then printed in both the *Morning Chronicle* and the *Morning Post* on 6 Nov.
5–9/10 Dec.	Shelley takes a house at Marlow and commissions him to supervise the fitting up of the house and the laying out of the grounds.
10 Dec.	Harriet Shelley's body discovered in the Serpentine.
30 Dec.	Shelley marries Mary Godwin.
1817	
27 Feb.–18 Mar.	The Shelleys stay with him while waiting to occupy their house at Marlow, where their spring visitors include Godwin and Leigh Hunt.
early Mar.	*Melincourt* published in three volumes by Thomas Hookham.
?Spring–Summer	Writes the unfinished tale known as 'Calidore'.

?Aug.–Nov.	*The Round Table; or, King Arthur's Feast* published by John Arliss.
before 28 Nov.	Completes *Rhododaphne*, which Mary Shelley copies on 4–10 Dec.
Dec.	Two of Shelley's letters from Switzerland 'To T.P., Esq.' published in revised form in *History of a Six Weeks' Tour*.
14–16 Dec.	Assists Shelley in revising *Laon and Cythna* for reissue as *The Revolt of Islam*.
1818	
?Jan.	Proposes marriage to Claire Clairmont, who has been living with the Shelleys at Marlow with her illegitimate daughter by Lord Byron.
29 Jan.	Goes to London, where he sees the Shelleys and Claire Clairmont almost daily until their departure for Italy.
early Feb.	*Rhododaphne* published anonymously by Thomas Hookham.
11 Feb.	Dines at Leigh Hunt's with the Shelleys and Claire, Hogg and Keats.
mid-Feb.	Shelley writes a review of *Rhododaphne*, which he gives to Leigh Hunt after Mary copies it on 20–3 Feb., but Hunt does not publish it in *The Examiner*.
11 Mar.	The Shelleys and Claire Clairmont leave London for Italy. During their absence Peacock sends them quarterly parcels and acts as Shelley's agent in business and literary matters.
20 Mar.	Back at Marlow, plans to write a novel set in London.
late Mar.–June	Writes *Nightmare Abbey*.

?17–24 June	Hogg visits him for a week at Marlow, during which they walk to Virginia Water and to Chequers.
7 July	Moves, with his mother, to a new house in West Street, Marlow.
7 July–26 Sept.	Keeps a journal.
16 July–23 Aug.	Writes, but does not finish, 'An Essay on Fashionable Literature'.
18–26 Sept.	Begins writing a political pamphlet.
early Oct.–early Nov.	On the recommendation of Peter Auber, goes to London as a candidate for a position in the Examiner's Office of the East India Company. Writes an examination paper on 'Ryotwar & Zemindarry Settlements', dated 2 Nov.
16 Oct.	Death of his uncle Thomas Love at Marlow.
mid-Nov.	*Nightmare Abbey* published by Thomas Hookham.
?Nov.–Dec.	Writes all but the last three chapters of *Maid Marian.*

1819

early Jan.	Begins regular attendance at the East India House, while living with his mother, and later his cousin Harriet Love, in lodgings at 5 York Street, Covent Garden.
Jan.	Begins reading proofs of Shelley's *Rosalind and Helen* volume.
18 May	Provisional appointment as Assistant to the Examiner of India Correspondence, with a salary of £600. His colleagues in the Examiner's Office include James Mill and Edward Strachey. Through Mill he subsequently meets Jeremy Bentham and other leading philosophical radicals.

1 July	Moves into his house at 17 Upper Stamford Street (later 18 Stamford Street), Blackfriars, where Harriet Love probably continues as a member of his household at least through Nov.
after 25 Sept.	Submits Shelley's tragedy *The Cenci* to Thomas Harris, manager and proprietor of Covent Garden Theatre, who finds the play objectionable on account of its subject.
20 Nov.	Writes a letter proposing marriage to Jane Gryffydh, with whom he has had no contact since Apr. 1811. According to Harriet Love, the letter was written under a 'feeling of bitter disappointment', at the suggestion of 'an old acquaintance' who called unexpectedly at the India House.

1820

22 Mar.	Marriage to Jane Gryffydh at Eglwysfach Chapel, Cardiganshire, while staying with his friends George and Justina Jeffreys at nearby Glandyfi Castle.
June–?July	Reads proofs of Shelley's *Prometheus Unbound* volume.
late June–early July	'The Four Ages of Poetry' published in *Olliers Literary Miscellany*, No. I.
?Sept.–Oct.	Holiday with his wife at Marlow.

1821

late Feb.–21 Mar.	In response to 'The Four Ages of Poetry', Shelley writes the first part of 'A Defence of Poetry' and sends it to Charles Ollier for publication in *Olliers Literary Miscellany*, but the essay remains unpublished because the Olliers fail to issue a second number.
10 Apr.	Appointment as Assistant to the Examiner confirmed, with a raise in salary to £800.

9 July	His poem 'Rich and Poor; or, Saint and Sinner' published in *The Traveller*, then reprinted in *The Examiner* on 22 July.
29 July	Birth of his daughter Mary Ellen in London (baptized 31 May 1822 at Christ Church, Southwark).
8 or 9 Sept.– ?1 Oct.	Holiday alone in Wales.

1822

late Mar.	*Maid Marian* published by Thomas Hookham.
late Mar.	Third edition of *Headlong Hall* published by Thomas Hookham.
8 July	Shelley drowns off Viareggio, leaving Byron and Peacock as joint executors of his will, dated 18 Feb. 1817. Peacock learns of his death on 6 Aug. in a letter from Leigh Hunt and writes to inform Sir Timothy Shelley.
?late Aug.– 16 Sept.	Holiday with his wife and daughter at Combe, near Wendover, in the Chiltern Hills.
3 Dec.	James Robinson Planché's opera *Maid Marian; or, The Huntress of Arlingford*, with music by Henry Rowley Bishop, first performed at Covent Garden, with Charles Kemble as Friar Tuck and Anna Maria Tree as Maid Marian.

1823

23 Mar.	Birth of his daughter Margaret Love in London (baptized 11 July 1823 at Christ Church, Southwark).
9 Apr.	Salary raised to £1000.
14 Apr.	Obtains a reader's ticket for the British Museum Library on the recommendation of a Mr Banks.

21 May	John Stuart Mill appointed as a junior clerk in the Examiner's Office.
28 June	After a quarrel with Mary Shelley, Byron declines to act as joint executor of Shelley's will, leaving Peacock as sole executor.
25 Aug.	Mary Shelley returns to London but does not see Peacock until after 18 Oct. because he is on holiday in the country.
before Nov.	Takes a cottage for his mother on the Thames at Lower Halliford.
6 Nov.	Begins protracted negotiations with Sir Timothy Shelley's solicitor, William Whitton, respecting financial provision for Mary Shelley and her son Percy Florence.

1824

5 June	Joins the Cymmrodorion, or Metropolitan Cambrian Institution.
24 June	Starts separate negotiations with William Whitton and others respecting the purchase of an annuity for Mary Shelley.
July–Aug.	Arranges for the suppression of Shelley's *Posthumous Poems* and an intended companion volume of prose works, at the insistence of Sir Timothy Shelley, who threatens to cut off Mary Shelley's allowance.

1825

30 July	Birth of his son Edward Gryffydh in London (baptized 14 Jan. 1832 at Shepperton).
before 26 Dec.	Intervenes to prevent the publication of Leigh Hunt's article on Shelley's *Posthumous Poems* in the *Westminster Review*.
?Dec.–Feb. 1826	Writes *Paper Money Lyrics*, but does not publish them, in order to avoid giving offence to James Mill.

1826

13 Jan.   Death of his daughter Margaret Love in London (buried 21 Jan. at Shepperton). He later quarrels with William Russell, Rector of Shepperton, over the wording of his verse epitaph on her tombstone. His wife's grief gradually leads to mental illness.

Mar.   Takes the cottage adjoining his mother's and moves his family to Lower Halliford.

15 Apr.   Lets his house at 18 Stamford Street to Capt. Henry Robert Cole, retaining the use of two rooms and taking a friendly interest in Cole's son Henry.

?Spring–Summer   Informally adopts Mary Ann ('May') Rosewell (baptized 20 July 1823, died 1 June 1883) because of her resemblance to his dead daughter.

June   His poem 'Llyn-y-dreiddiad-vrawd; or, The Pool of the Diving Friar' published in the *New Monthly Magazine*.

1827

May–June   Completes negotiations with William Whitton and Sir Timothy Shelley for a financial settlement for Mary Shelley and her son Percy Florence.

19 Sept.   Birth of his daughter Rosa Jane at Lower Halliford (baptized 14 Jan. 1832 at Shepperton).

Oct.   Article on 'Moore's Epicurean' published in the *Westminster Review*.

1828

?Feb.   Begins an article on Leigh Hunt's *Lord Byron and Some of His Contemporaries* for the *Westminster Review*.

1829

?Jan.   The East India Company's Chairman asks him 'to look into the whole question' of steam navigation.

24 Jan.   His poem 'Touchandgo' published in the *Globe and Traveller*.

early Mar.   *The Misfortunes of Elphin* published by Thomas Hookham.

Sept.   Completes a long 'Memorandum respecting the Application of Steam Navigation to the Internal and External Communication of India' (printed in 1834).

21 Dec.   Lord Ellenborough, as President of the Board of Control, sends Peacock's memorandum on steam navigation to the Duke of Wellington, the Prime Minister.

1830

?Feb.–Aug.   Serves as opera critic for the *Globe and Traveller*.

Apr.   Article on the first volume of 'Moore's Letters and Journals of Lord Byron' published in the *Westminster Review*. Moore's protests apparently induce the editor, John Bowring, to change his mind about publishing Peacock's intended review of the second volume.

May   Capt. Francis Rawdon Chesney begins his reconnaissance of overland routes to India, stimulated by Peacock's questionnaires, sent the previous year through the Foreign Office to the British embassy at Constantinople and the British consulate at Alexandria.

Oct.   Articles on 'Randolph's Memoirs, &c. of Thomas Jefferson' and 'London Bridge' published in the *Westminster Review*.

12 Oct.	Birth of his natural daughter Susan Mary Abbott (died 4 Mar. 1921), probably to Alice Bunce Abbott. Susan is baptized on 1 Nov. at St Pancras Old Church as the daughter of Alice's brother John Abbott and Emmeline Spencer, but there is no other record of Emmeline's existence. Susan is raised by John and Alice as John's daughter.
8 Dec.	Appointed Senior Assistant to the Examiner, with a salary of £1,200. James Mill succeeds William McCulloch as Examiner.

1831

Feb.–Aug. 1834	Serves as opera critic for *The Examiner*.
mid-Feb.	*Crotchet Castle* published by Thomas Hookham.
28 Feb.	Completes a long memorandum on 'Steam Navigation of the Ganges'.
Apr.–Mar. 1833	With Capt. James Henry Johnston, the Bengal Government's Controller of Steam Vessels, supervises the design and construction of iron steamers for the Ganges.
14 Aug.	His poem 'The Fate of a Broom: An Anticipation', a satire on Lord Brougham dated Mar. 1831, published in *The Examiner*.
Oct.	Holiday in Wales with his daughter Mary Ellen.

1832

9 Feb. and 17 Mar.	Gives evidence before the House of Commons Select Committee on the Affairs of the East India Company.
early Oct.	Death of his mother (buried 11 Oct. at Shepperton).

1833

Jan.   Meets Chesney and induces him to print his *Reports on the Navigation of the Euphrates.*

10 Apr.   Signs an agreement by which his landlord, Thomas Nettleship, undertakes to pay for extensive reconstruction to connect his two cottages at Lower Halliford and convert them into a comfortable residence, while he undertakes to sign a twenty-one-year lease.

2 Dec.   Completes a long memorandum on 'Steam Navigation in India, and between Europe and India' (printed in 1834).

1834

16 Apr.   Submits a 'Corrected Estimate of the Probable Expense of Placing Two Iron Steam Vessels on the River Euphrates at Bussora, and Navigating the Same from Bussora to Bir and Back' to Charles Grant, President of the Board of Control.

9 and 20 June   Gives evidence as the leading witness before the House of Commons Select Committee on Steam Navigation to India, which accepts his estimate in recommending a Parliamentary grant of £20,000 for the Euphrates Expedition. The Appendix to the Committee's *Report* includes his memoranda of Sept. 1829 and 2 Dec. 1833, his estimate of 16 Apr. 1834 and other papers submitted by him.

11, 15, 17 and 31 July   Gives evidence for the East India Company before the House of Commons Select Committee on the Suppression of the *Calcutta Journal.*

Sept.–June 1837	Supervises the design, construction, fitting and outward voyages of the *Atalanta* and the *Berenice*, the first vessels to steam the entire distance to India.

1835

Jan.	Article 'On Steam Navigation to India' published in the *Edinburgh Review*.
Jan.–Mar.	Seriously ill with inflammation of the lungs.
10 Feb.	The Euphrates Expedition sails from Liverpool under Chesney's command.
Apr.	Article on 'Lord Mount Edgcumbes's Musical Reminiscences' published in the *London Review*.
Oct.	Article on 'French Comic Romances' published in the *London Review*.

1836

Jan.	Articles on 'The Épicier' and 'Bellini' published in the *London Review*.
17 Feb.	Appointed Assistant Examiner, with a salary of £1,500.
4–7 and 21 July	Gives evidence for the East India Company before the House of Commons Select Committee on Salt, British India.
27 July	Appointed to succeed James Mill as Examiner, with a salary of £2,000.

1837

Jan.	'The Legend of Manor Hall' published in *Bentley's Miscellany*.
Feb.	'Recollections of Childhood: The Abbey House' published in *Bentley's Miscellany*.
24 Mar.	*Headlong Hall, Nightmare Abbey, Maid Marian* and *Crotchet Castle* reprinted as No. LVII in Richard Bentley's series of Standard Novels, with a Preface dated 4 Mar.

22 Apr.–18 June	Seven of his *Paper Money Lyrics*, as well as 'Promotion BY Purchase and by NO Purchase' and 'Rich and Poor; or, Saint and Sinner', published by Henry Cole in *The Guide, a new weekly newspaper.*
26 June	Gives evidence before the House of Commons Select Committee on Steam Communication with India.
July–Sept.	*Paper Money Lyrics, and Other Poems* privately printed by Henry Cole, with a Preface dated 20 July.
July–Apr. 1838	Supervises the purchase, refitting and outward voyage of the *Semiramis* (originally the *Waterford*).

1838

Jan.	'The New Year: Lines on George Cruikshank's Illustration of January, in the Comic Almanack for 1838' published in *Bentley's Miscellany.*
Aug.–Sept.	Two of his *Paper Money Lyrics* published in *Bentley's Miscellany.*
Sept.–Oct. 1841	As Clerk to the Secret Committee, supervises the procurement and shipment of iron steamers for the Euphrates, the Tigris and the Indus. Also supervises the design, construction, fitting and trials of a new class of iron steamers with sliding keels for sea or river service, four of which are finished in England and sent around the Cape (*Nemesis, Phlegethon, Pluto* and *Proserpine*), while two others are shipped in pieces to India (*Ariadne* and *Medusa*). Five of his 'iron chickens' see service in the later phases of the Opium War of 1839–42, the *Nemesis* winning great renown under Capt. William Hutcheon Hall.

3 and 7 Nov.	Two letters signed 'Philatmos', on the failure of the *Semiramis* to make the passage from Bombay to the Red Sea against the South-West Monsoon in July, published in *The Times*.

1839

Jan.	James Spedding's article on 'Tales by the Author of Headlong Hall' published anonymously in the *Edinburgh Review*.
21 Jan.	Recommends that the Board of Control employ Arthur Conolly for a mission to Khiva and Bokhara, with a view to placing British steamers on the Aral Sea and the Oxus and Jaxartes rivers.
17 Apr.	Death of his uncle William Love at Yarmouth, Isle of Wight.
mid-Dec.	Thirteen of Shelley's letters from Italy 'To T.L.P., Esq.' published in Mary Shelley's edition of his *Essays, Letters from Abroad, Translations, and Fragments* (post-dated 1840), which also contains an edited version of 'A Defence of Poetry', without Shelley's references to 'The Four Ages of Poetry'.

1840

?Summer	Takes his two daughters and his cousin Harriet Love on a trial voyage of the *Proserpine*, whose Second Officer is Edward Nicolls.
24 Oct.–4 Nov.	Pays the first of many visits to Sir John Cam Hobhouse at Erle Stoke Park, near Westbury, Wilts. (Hobhouse was Byron's friend and executor, but Peacock knew him officially as President of the Board of Control, 1835–41 and 1846–52.)

1841

19 May	His son Edward Gryffydh appointed as a midshipman in the Indian Navy. He arrives in India on 2 Oct., but returns on a medical furlough granted on 22 Apr. 1842.
11–16 Sept.	Keeps a log of a trial voyage of the *Pluto*, during which he lands briefly at Cherbourg, the only time he is known to have stepped on foreign soil.

1842

14 May	Letter signed 'Philatmos', on steamboat explosions and railway accidents, published in *The Times*.
late June	Makes 'proposals' of an unknown nature to Miss Jane Fotheringhame, perhaps for her to serve as Susan Abbott's governess and/or piano teacher.
Aug.	Writes 'Newark Abbey' (published in 1860).

1843

?Spring	*Sir Hornbook* reprinted by Henry Cole in the Home Treasury series.
?Autumn–Autumn 1844	Gives up his house in Stamford Street and takes chambers at 22 John Street, Adelphi.

1844

8 Jan.	Marriage of his daughter Mary Ellen to Lt Edward Nicolls of the Royal Navy (baptized 13 July 1817) at Shepperton.
11 Mar.	Edward Nicolls drowns in the Shannon estuary, while in command of HMS *Dwarf*.
24 Apr.	Death of Sir Timothy Shelley, allowing Shelley's will to be proved and executed.
21 Aug.	His son Edward Gryffydh becomes a clerk in the Examiner's Office.

27 Oct.	Birth of his granddaughter Edith Nicolls (died 20 Aug. 1926) at Shooters Hill.
1 Nov.	Proves Shelley's will at Doctors' Commons.
12 Dec.	Accepts legacies of £2,000 and £500 under Shelley's will.

1845

June	Visits the Isle of Wight, possibly for reasons of health.
6 Oct.	Death of his aunt Jane Love, probably the widow of his uncle Thomas, at Chertsey.

1846

?Mar.	His Greek anapaests on Christ (probably written and privately printed in 1812–13) published anonymously at Bruges in the Prolegomena (dated 27 Feb. 1846) to Thomas Forster's *Philosophia Musarum* (title page dated 1845).
9 Oct.	Sends Hobhouse a manuscript satire on Sir Robert Peel entitled 'Ancient Examples of Modern Political Virtue, I.'

1847

8 Oct.	His daughter Mary Ellen Nicolls writes to inform Hobhouse that Peacock is severely depressed by 'a heavy pressure of debt' under which he has been labouring 'for some years'.

1848

22 Dec.	Meets Disraeli at Erle Stoke Park.

1849

?Winter–Summer	Projects a series of 'Tales for Three Sisters', inspired by Hobhouse's daughters.
9 Aug.	Marriage of his daughter Mary Ellen Nicolls to George Meredith (born 12 Feb. 1828, died 18 May 1909) at St George's, Hanover Square.

5 Sept.	Death of Hobhouse's daughter Julia, whom he commemorates in lines sent to Hobhouse on 18 Sept.
20 Sept.	Marriage of his daughter Rosa Jane to Henry Collinson (born 16 Nov. 1811, died 13 Jan. 1877) at St Martin's in the Fields.
17 Nov.	Marriage of his son Edward Gryffydh to Mary Hall (born 19 Aug. 1830) at St Marylebone.

1850

16 Oct.	Birth of his granddaughter Rosa Collinson (died 31 Aug. 1899) at Hurcott, near Kidderminster. (Three younger Collinson children die in infancy or early childhood.)
?Autumn–Spring 1851	Takes a house at 1 Torrington Street, Russell Square.
24 Dec.	Meets Thackeray at Erle Stoke.

1851

?Winter–Spring	Begins working on an edition of Aeschylus' *Supplices*.
Feb.	Writes 'A Goodlye Ballade of Little John', satirizing Lord John Russell's attacks on 'Papal Aggression' (circulated in manuscript with illustrations by P. A. Daniel).
1 Feb.	Death of Mary Wollstonecraft Shelley.
26 Feb.	Hobhouse created Baron Broughton of Broughton-de-Gyfford.
1 May–15 Oct.	After initially disliking the idea of the Great Exhibition and staying away for the first few weeks, he eventually 'became fascinated with it, and after his first visit haunted Paxton's glass Palace daily', according to Henry Cole.
late May–early June	Meredith's first volume of *Poems* published by John W. Parker & Son, with a dedication to Peacock, dated May.

?before 6 June	Writes 'A New Order of Chivalry' (circulated in manuscript and later published in *Gryll Grange*).
23 July–19 Nov.	Writes and privately prints his Greek lines on 'A White-Bait Dinner, at Lovegrove's, at Blackwall. July, 1851'. Also writes and lithographs a literal Latin translation. Lord Broughton translates the poem into English verse.
31 July	Marriage of Lord Broughton's daughter Sophia Hobhouse to John Strange Jocelyn (afterwards fifth Earl of Roden).
Autumn	The Merediths move into his house at Lower Halliford.
?Autumn	Begins collaborating with his daughter Mary Ellen Meredith on a projected revision of William Kitchiner's *Apicius Redivivus; or, The Cook's Oracle*, to be published by John W. Parker & Son.
Dec.	Article on 'Gastronomy and Civilization', written in collaboration with his daughter Mary Ellen Meredith and signed with the initials M.M., published in *Fraser's Magazine*.
23 Dec.	Death of his wife at Southend, Essex (buried 30 Dec. at St Mary's, Prittlewell, Southend). He learns of her death on Christmas morning at Erle Stoke but does not leave to attend her funeral.

1852

?early Mar.	*Letters of Percy Bysshe Shelley* published by Edward Moxon with an Introductory Essay by Robert Browning. After examining the manuscripts and declaring them to be clever forgeries, Peacock gives Moxon permission

	to publish his own unedited letters from Shelley in their place, but nothing comes of the scheme.
Mar.	'Horæ Dramaticæ [No. I]: Querolus; or, The Buried Treasure' published in *Fraser's Magazine*.
Apr.	'Horæ Dramaticæ [No. II]: The Phaëthon of Euripides' published in *Fraser's Magazine*.
?May–Oct.	After the deaths of John and Alice Abbott (27 Mar. and 16 Apr.), his natural daughter Susan Mary Abbott comes to live with the Merediths in his house at Lower Halliford.
?Summer–Autumn	Proposes marriage to Claire Clairmont's twenty-seven-year-old niece, Pauline Clairmont, who 'looked daggers at the dear old man'.

1853

13 June	Birth of his grandson Arthur Gryffydh Meredith (died 3 Sept. 1890) at Lower Halliford.
11 July	Gives evidence for the East India Company before the House of Commons Select Committee on Indian Territories.
?Autumn	Takes Vine Cottage for the Merediths, across the green from his house at Lower Halliford. Susan Abbott also leaves his house around this time.
?Autumn–Autumn 1854	Gives up his London quarters at 1 Torrington Street, Russell Square.

1854

27 July	Marriage of Lord Broughton's daughter Charlotte Hobhouse to Dudley Wilmot Carleton (afterwards fourth Baron Dorchester).

before 25 Sept.	His 'little book' of scatological Latin inscriptions *In Statuam Roberti Peel, Baronetti . . . Epigrammata Anathematica ad Singula Baseos Latera* privately printed on a friend's press.

1856

Mar.	Writes a Preface for a yellowback edition of *Melincourt* published by Chapman & Hall.
12 Mar.	Tenders his resignation of the Examinership.
28 Mar.	Granted a superannuation allowance of £1,333.6.8. John Stuart Mill appointed to succeed him as Examiner.

1857

12 Mar.	Sends Lord Broughton a Latin squib on the parliamentary coalition against Lord Palmerston's government. Broughton translates it into English verse.
before 29 Sept.	His daughter Mary Ellen, pregnant by Henry Wallis, asks Meredith for a separation.
Oct.	'Horæ Dramaticæ [No. III]: The "Flask" of Cratinus' published in *Fraser's Magazine*.
5 Oct.	Death of his daughter Rosa Jane Collinson at 13 Cambridge Terrace, Paddington (buried 10 Oct. at Shepperton).

1858

24 Jan.	Has his portrait painted by Henry Wallis.
late Jan.	Two of Shelley's letters to Peacock from Switzerland published in revised form in Charles S. Middleton's *Shelley and his Writings*.
Apr.	The first two volumes of Thomas Jefferson Hogg's *The Life of Percy Bysshe Shelley* published. Hogg caricatures Peacock in 1813 as the poor poet 'Otho' – a 'professor of suicide' who made a strong impression on Harriet Shelley.

Apr.	Article on 'Chapelle and Bachaumont' published in *Fraser's Magazine*.
18 Apr.	Birth of his grandson Harold ('Felix') Wallis (died 4 Feb. 1933) to Mary Ellen Meredith and Henry Wallis (born 21 Feb. 1830, died 20 Dec. 1916) at Elm Cottage, Redland, near Bristol.
June	'Memoirs of Percy Bysshe Shelley' [Part I] published in *Fraser's Magazine*.
Autumn–Winter 1859	His daughter Mary Ellen Meredith goes to Capri with Henry Wallis for the sake of her health.
Nov.	Article on 'Demetrius Galanus: Greek Translations from Sanskrit' published in *Fraser's Magazine*.
22 Nov.	Marriage of his natural daughter Susan Mary Abbott to William Mayne Neill at All Souls, St Marylebone.
25 Dec.	His son Edward Gryffydh receives a pension on the demise of the East India Company. He subsequently studies law.
1859	
Mar.	Article on 'Müller and Donaldson's History of Greek Literature' published in *Fraser's Magazine*.
2–20 Aug.	Visits Lord Broughton at Corsham Court, near Chippenham, Wilts.
1860	
Jan.	'Memoirs of Percy Bysshe Shelley', [Part II], published in *Fraser's Magazine*.
Mar.	'Unpublished Letters of Percy Bysshe Shelley: From Italy – 1818 to 1822' published in *Fraser's Magazine* (followed by a 'Postscript to the Shelley Letters' in the May issue).

Apr.–Dec.	*Gryll Grange* serialized in *Fraser's Magazine*.
?Spring–Summer 1861	Writes 'A Dialogue on Idealities' and gives the manuscript to Charlotte Carleton.
June	Richard Garnett's article 'Shelley in Pall Mall', contradicting Peacock's account of the separation of Shelley and Harriet, published in *Macmillan's Magazine*.
21 Aug.–10 Sept.	Visits Lord Broughton at Tedworth House, near Andover, Hants. This proves to be the last of many visits.
Nov.	'Newark Abbey, August 1842, with a Reminiscence of August 1807' published in *Fraser's Magazine*.

1861

late Feb.	*Gryll Grange* published in book form by Parker, Son & Bourn.
early Aug.	Onset of his daughter Mary Ellen Meredith's fatal illness, during which he visits her daily at Grotto Cottage, Oatlands Park, Weybridge.
22 Oct.	Death of his daughter Mary Ellen Meredith (buried 26 Oct. at Weybridge). He does not attend her funeral.
?Nov.–Dec.	Clari Leigh Hunt comes to live as a member of his family at Lower Halliford. She remains at least until Dec. 1863.

1862

?Winter–Spring	Writes 'The Last Day of Windsor Forest' (published in the *National Review*, Sept. 1887).
Mar.	'Percy Bysshe Shelley: Supplementary Notice' published in *Fraser's Magazine*.
June	Richard Garnett's 'Shelley, Harriet Shelley, and Mr. T. L. Peacock', dated 6 Mar., published in his *Relics of Shelley*.

?Summer	Robert Buchanan is a frequent visitor at Lower Halliford.
mid-Aug.	*Gl'Ingannati, The Deceived: A Comedy Performed at Siena in 1531: and Aelia Laelia Crispis* published by Chapman & Hall.
27 Aug.	Death of Thomas Jefferson Hogg.

1863

?Winter–Spring	Suffers a decline in health and spirits, from which he never fully recovers.

1864

22 Oct.	Makes a simple will, leaving his entire estate to his adopted daughter, Mary Rosewell.

1865

Oct.–Dec.	His son Edward Gryffydh qualifies as a solicitor during Michaelmas Term. (He died 4 Jan. 1867 at 45 Hunter Street, Bloomsbury.)
?Dec.	Refuses to leave his library when his house is threatened by fire, saying, 'By the immortal gods, I will not move!'

1866

23 Jan.	Dies while sleeping. Cause of death is certified as 'Climacteric'.
29 Jan.	Buried in the New Cemetery at Shepperton. His grave is later marked by a horizontal slab placed there by his cousins Henry and Harriet Love.
7 Mar.	His will is proved in London by Mary Rosewell, his sole executrix. The value of his effects is sworn under £1,500.
11–12 June	His library is sold at Sotheby's.

ABBREVIATIONS

References to Greek and Latin texts, unless otherwise stated, are to the editions in the Loeb Classical Library.

Quotations from the Bible come from the King James Version.

References to Shakespeare are to *The Riverside Shakespeare: The Complete Works*, ed. G. Blakemore Evans et al., 2nd ed. (Boston: Houghlin Mifflin, 1997). All quotations from Samuel Butler's *Hudibras* in the explanatory notes conform to *Hudibras, in Three Parts; Written in the Time of the Late Wars; Corrected and Amended. With Large Annotations, and a Preface, by Zachary Grey, LL. D.*, 3rd ed., 2 vols. (C. Bathurst, et al., 1772), which is one of the two editions of *Hudibras* TLP owned when he died (*Sale Catalogue* 97).

References to Peacock's novels are given by chapter number and, unless otherwise stated, are to the texts as they appear in the Cambridge Edition of the Novels of Thomas Love Peacock, gen. ed. Freya Johnston, 7 vols. (Cambridge: Cambridge University Press, 2016–). References to editorial materials in the Cambridge Edition are given by page number, or by chapter and note number, as appropriate. References to 'An Essay on Fashionable Literature' and 'The Four Ages of Poetry' are to the Cambridge edition of *Nightmare Abbey*. References to Peacock's other works are to *The Works of Thomas Love Peacock* (Halliford Edition), ed. H. F. B. Brett-Smith and C. E. Jones, 10 vols. (Constable, 1924–34).

Quotations from Peacock's correspondence are accompanied by the date of the relevant letter or letters and by the volume and page number in Nicholas A. Joukovsky's edition.

Throughout the text and notes, the place of publication, unless otherwise stated, is London.

1817	The Author of Headlong Hall [Thomas Love Peacock], *Melincourt*, 3 vols. (T. Hookham, Jun. and Co., and Baldwin, Cradock and Joy, 1817)
1856	The Author of 'Headlong Hall' [Thomas Love Peacock], *Melincourt or Sir Oran Haut-ton* (Chapman and Hall, 1856)
AM	[James Burnett, Lord Monboddo], *Antient Metaphysics: or, The Science of Universals*, 6 vols. (Edinburgh: J. Balfour, 1779–99)
Buffon 1799	[George Louis LeClerc, Comte de Buffon], *Histoire naturelle générale et particulière, par Leclerc de Buffon; Nouvelle Edition, accompagnée de notes, et dans laquelle les supplémens sont insérés dans le premier texte, à la place qui leur convient . . . Rédigé par C. S. Sonnini, Membre de Plusieurs Sociétés Savantes*, 127 vols. (Paris: F. Dufart, [1799]–1808)
Butler, *Peacock*	Marilyn Butler, *Peacock Displayed: A Satirist in His Context* (Routledge and Kegan Paul, 1979)
Cal	*Calidore*
CC	*Crotchet Castle*
Drummond	Sir William Drummond, *Academical Questions* (Cadell and Davies, 1805)
Garnett, *Novels*	David Garnett, ed., *The Novels of Thomas Love Peacock* (Hart-Davis, 1948; 2nd impression corrected in 2 vols., 1963)
GG	*Gryll Grange*

Halliford | *The Works of Thomas Love Peacock* (Halliford Edition), ed. H. F. B. Brett-Smith and C. E. Jones, 10 vols. (Constable, 1924–34)

HH | *Headlong Hall*

Johnson-Steevens | *The Plays of William Shakspeare: In Twenty-One Volumes, With the Corrections and Illustrations of Various Commentators, to Which are Added Notes, by Samuel Johnson and George Steevens, Revised and Augmented by Isaac Reed with a Glossarial Index*, 6th ed. (J. Nichols and Son, 1813)

Letters | *The Letters of Thomas Love Peacock*, ed. Nicholas A. Joukovsky, 2 vols. (Oxford: Clarendon Press, 2001)

LS | Samuel Taylor Coleridge, *Lay Sermons*, ed. R. J. White (Princeton: Princeton University Press, 1972)

Malthus, *Essay* | T. R. Malthus, *An Essay on the Principle of Population; or, A View of Its Past and Present Effects on Human Happiness; with An Inquiry into Our Prospects Respecting the Future Removal or Mitigation of the Evils Which It Occasions. A New Edition, Very Much Enlarged* (J. Johnson, 1803)

ME | *The Misfortunes of Elphin*

Mel | *Melincourt*

MM | *Maid Marian*

MWS Journals | *The Journals of Mary Shelley, 1814–1844*, ed. Paula R. Feldman and Diana Scott-Kilvert, 2 vols. (Oxford and New York: Clarendon Press and Oxford University Press, 1987;

	repr. Baltimore: Johns Hopkins University Press, 1995)
MWS Letters	*The Letters of Mary Wollstonecraft Shelley*, ed. Betty T. Bennett, 3 vols. (Baltimore: Johns Hopkins University Press, 1980–88)
NA	*Nightmare Abbey*
ODEP	*The Oxford Dictionary of English Proverbs*, 3rd ed. (Oxford: Clarendon Press, 1970)
OED	*The Oxford English Dictionary*, 2nd ed., 20 vols. (Oxford: Oxford University Press, 1989), along with revisions for the 3rd ed. in the online edition up to 2019
Origin	James Burnet (*sic*), Lord Monboddo, *Of the Origin and Progress of Language*, vol. 1, 2nd ed. (Edinburgh: J. Balfour and T. Cadell, 1774)
PBS Letters	*The Letters of Percy Bysshe Shelley*, ed. Frederick L. Jones, 2 vols. (Oxford: Clarendon Press, 1964)
PBS Prose	*The Prose Works of Percy Bysshe Shelley*, ed. E. B. Murray, vol. 1 (Oxford: Clarendon Press, 1993)
Paris-1818	[Thomas Love Peacock], *Anthélia Mélincourt, ou Les enthousiastes. Roman satyrique, traduit de l'anglais sur la cinquième édition de l'auteur de La Maison de Head Long-Hall. Par M.ᴵˡᵉ Al. de L**. Traducteur des Frères-Hongrois*, [trans. Aline de Verdier de Lacoste], 2 vols. (Paris: Béchet, 1818)
Raven-Garside	Peter Garside, James Raven and Rainer Schöwerling, gen. eds., *The English Novel*

	1770–1829: A Bibliographical Survey of Prose Fiction Published in the British Isles, 2 vols. (Oxford: Oxford University Press, 2000)
Sale Catalogue	*Catalogue of the Library of the Late Thos. Love Peacock, Esq. . . . which will be Sold by Auction, by Messrs. Sotheby, Wilkinson & Hodge . . . on Monday, the 11th of June, 1866, and Following Day*, reprinted in *Sale Catalogues of Libraries of Eminent Persons*, ed. A. N. L. Munby, vol. 1 (Mansell, with Sotheby Parke-Bernet, 1971)
Shelley and His Circle	*Shelley and His Circle, 1773–1822*, ed. Kenneth Neill Cameron, Donald H. Reiman and Doucet Devin Fischer, 10 vols. to date (Cambridge, MA: Harvard University Press, 1961–2002)
Thomas	The Author of Headlong Hall [Thomas Love Peacock], *Melincourt*, 2 vols. (Philadelphia: Moses Thomas, 1817)
Times	*The Times* (London)
TLP	Thomas Love Peacock
TNA	The National Archives, Kew
WPR	Cobbett's *Weekly Political Register*

INTRODUCTION

In March 1817, Thomas Hookham Jr. and Baldwin, Cradock and Joy published *Melincourt* in three duodecimo volumes, with each title page attributing the work to 'the Author of Headlong Hall'. *Melincourt* has not been published separately in a new edition since 1896, and it may need re-editing more than Thomas Love Peacock's other novels. On the one hand, preparing a reading text of *Melincourt* is straightforward: no manuscript of the novel itself survives; there is no reason to believe that Peacock ever considered revising it after it first appeared; and, when a second edition appeared, thirty-nine years after initial publication, the author added only a brief preface. On the other hand, the extraordinary range of *Melincourt* means that readers require an unusual amount of background knowledge in order to appreciate it fully. When *Melincourt* is interpreted in its historical and literary context, it is one of Peacock's most stimulating works. Even though it did not achieve popular success, such figures as Percy Shelley and Lord Byron praised it, and it deserved this recognition.

The present edition aims to provide a better view of Peacock's most ambitious work of fiction than has been available before. Ambitious it is. In 1829 the *Monthly Magazine* recognized that *Melincourt* was 'more original and elevated' than its predecessor, *Headlong Hall*, and in 1839 James Spedding commented that 'Its purposes appear to be graver' and 'its pretensions loftier' than those of Peacock's other novels.[1] *Melincourt* is not just Peacock's longest work (his only novel

---

[1] Anon., 'Novels by the Author of Headlong Hall', *Monthly Magazine*, vol. 7, no. 40 (Apr. 1829), 381–92 (p. 382); [James Spedding], review of *Headlong*

in three volumes) but also his most comprehensive, surveying and exploring the widest range of controversies: the dangers of 'paper money' (a topic Peacock returned to in *CC* and in *Paper Money Lyrics*); the complicity of British consumers in slavery; the inequities of the current system of parliamentary representation; the value of 'chivalry' for modern society; the boundary between human beings and other animals; and, most centrally, the questions of whether and how the human condition might be improved. *Melincourt's* form is similarly comprehensive, subsuming elements of the quest romance, the symposium and the domestic novel. The narrative is framed by a courtship plot: the first sentence describes the heiress Anthelia Melincourt, who is soon besieged by suitors, and the third volume concludes with her marriage to Sylvan Forester. Though conversation often dominates, as it does in most of Peacock's fiction, the action is not restricted to a single country house, as in *Headlong Hall* or *Nightmare Abbey*. The second volume involves a journey across England, and, in the third, Forester, Mr Fax and Sir Oran Haut-ton traverse the byways of the Lake District, coming upon scenes that illustrate the novel's themes.

Though *Melincourt* emphasizes debate and courtship, the most memorable character neither talks nor seeks to marry the heroine. Sir Oran Haut-ton is an 'oran outang' from 'the woods of Angola' (Chapter 6) whom Forester adopts and provides with an estate, a baronetcy and a seat in the House of Commons representing the rotten borough 'Onevote'. Sir Oran is not an orangutan, the red-haired ape unique to Sumatra and Borneo, but one of the 'Orang Outangs' described by James Burnet (*sic*), Lord Monboddo (1714–99), a capacious species that Monboddo's twenty-first century readers will recognize includes orangutans, gorillas, chimpanzees and baboons. (Throughout this edition of *Melincourt*, 'oran outang' will be used to refer to the animal Monboddo described, and 'orangutan' to mean

---

Hall, Nightmare Abbey, Maid Marian, and *Crotchet Castle, Edinburgh Review*, vol. 68 (Jan. 1839), 432–59 (p. 447).

the animal today called by that name.)[2] Monboddo was notorious for arguing that the oran outang 'is an animal of the human form, inside as well as outside',[3] and Forester adopts Sir Oran to prove Monboddo right: not only is the oran outang 'a variety of the human species' but 'the civilized world' should be convinced of this fact (Chapter 6).

GENESIS AND COMPOSITION

As Nicholas A. Joukovsky points out, 'Any account of the genesis and composition of *Melincourt* must be largely conjectural'.[4] Direct evidence is scanty. No letters Peacock wrote between 10 January 1815 and 15 July 1817 survive, nor any letters written to him between 2 August 1816 and 14 July 1817. The publication of *Headlong Hall* in December 1815 establishes a *terminus a quo*. Shelley said nothing about *Melincourt* when he wrote to Peacock from Switzerland on 17 July 1816.[5] In summer 1816, the second edition of *Headlong Hall* appeared, in which Thomas Hookham and Baldwin, Cradock and Joy advertised a three-volume novel titled *Melincourt*, 'by the same author', 'in the press'.[6] On 20 September, Claire Claremont, in Bath, asked Mary Wollstonecraft Shelley, who had left to join Percy Shelley and Peacock at Marlow, to 'Tell Peacock from me to

---

[2] The spelling 'oran outang' in the first edition of *Melincourt* may be the printer's preference: in an 1809 letter, Peacock used the spelling 'Ourang-Outang' (*Letters*, 2.40).

[3] *Origin*, 1.89.

[4] Nicholas A. Joukovsky, 'The Composition of Peacock's *Melincourt* and the Date of the "Calidore" Fragment', *English Language Notes*, 12 (1975), 18–25 (p. 19).

[5] Joukovsky, 'Composition', 20; *PBS Letters*, 1.488–91.

[6] *Headlong Hall*, 2nd ed. (Hookham and Baldwin, Cradock and Joy, 1816). In the copy owned by the Library Company of Philadelphia, O Eng Peac 2591.D.1., the advertisement for *Mel* is on 2Lr (or [219]), with advertisements for other works co-published by Hookham and Baldwin on the verso. The second edition of *HH* was published 'by 1 August 1816' (Joukovsky, 'Composition', 18).

make his Book "funny"'.[7] On 8 December, Percy, visiting Peacock again, wrote to Leigh Hunt that Peacock was pleased to learn that Hunt admired *Headlong Hall*, and he recorded that Peacock 'is now writing "Melincourt" in the same style, but, as I judge, far superior to Headlong Hall'.[8] On 25 January 1817, the *Literary Gazette* and *Journal of Belles Lettres* announced that *Melincourt* was 'in the press', and similar notices appeared in other publications.[9] A month later, on 24 February, an advertisement in the *Morning Chronicle* announced publication on 5 March. On 8 March the *Literary Gazette* advertised that *Melincourt* was published and on sale.[10] It was also advertised in the *Morning Chronicle*, on 18 and 20 March 1817.[11] On 18 March Mary Shelley wrote to Leigh and Marianne Hunt, saying that 'I hope Hunt will criticise Melincourt next week'.[12] Mary's father, William Godwin, read the first volume of *Melincourt* in London on 19 March 1817, the second volume on 20 March, and the third on 23 March, according to his journal.[13] On 22 March *Melincourt* was reviewed for the first time, by the *Literary Gazette*.[14]

So, external evidence reveals merely that Peacock had a title and format by July 1816, that Percy Shelley had read parts of *Melincourt* by 8 December, and that by 24 February preparations were far

---

[7] *The Clairmont Correspondence: Letters of Claire Clairmont, Charles Clairmont, and Fanny Imlay Godwin*, ed. Marion Kingston Stocking, 2 vols. (Baltimore: Johns Hopkins University Press, 1995), vol. 1, p. 73.

[8] *PBS Letters*, 1.518, 'not' corrected to 'now'.

[9] *Literary Gazette* (25 Jan. 1817), 15. No publisher was mentioned.

[10] *Literary Gazette* (8 Mar. 1817), 112. This advertisement included both of the book's epigraphs (from Horace and Rousseau) and gave the publishers as 'T. and E. T. Hookham, Old Bond Street; and Baldwin and Co. Paternoster Row'.

[11] Joukovsky, 'Composition', 21, n. 14.

[12] *MWS Letters*, 1.35. Hunt's newspaper, *The Examiner*, never reviewed *Mel*, probably in part because so much space at this time needed to be devoted to pressing political news.

[13] http://godwindiary.bodleian.ox.ac.uk/index2.html. On 22 Mar., Shelley asked if Godwin had read *Mel*, promising that 'it would entertain you' (*PBS Letters*, 1.537).

[14] Anon., *Literary Gazette* (22 Mar. 1817), 132.

enough advanced that the book might be put on sale within nine days. Perhaps enough of *Melincourt* was in the printer's hands in January that publication appeared imminent. Internal evidence is scarcely more helpful. In Chapter 16 (the second chapter of volume 2) Fax quotes from the *Edinburgh Review* that appeared on 12 November 1816.[15] Chapter 31, early in volume 3, relies upon a work published in December 1816, Coleridge's *The Statesman's Manual or The Bible the Best Guide to Political Skill and Foresight: A Lay Sermon Addressed to the Higher Classes of Society.* Chapter 39, taking place at Mainchance Villa, alludes to a speech George Canning made in the House of Commons on 29 January 1817, and it makes extensive use of an article in the *Quarterly Review* (by Robert Southey) that did not appear until 11 February 1817. Indeed, much of Chapter 39, the fourth from the end, could not have been written until that date, about three weeks before *Melincourt* was put on sale.[16] Peacock was writing the final volume in February, though by that time he must have sent copy for the first two volumes to the printer and must have read proofs for much of those volumes.[17]

---

[15] As Joukovsky observes, Fax's statement 'may or may not have been a late addition' ('Composition', 22).

[16] [Robert Southey], 'Parliamentary Reform', *Quarterly Review*, vol. 16, no. 31 (Oct. 1816), 225–78. *Mel* is not the only novel in which Peacock inserts a topical reference late in the narrative. In the final pages of *CC*, news arrives that the 'learned friend' has taken office and been granted a title (ch. 18, p. 139). Henry Brougham became Lord Chancellor only three months before the novel's publication.

[17] Joukovsky suggests that Southey's article in the *Quarterly Review* may have inspired 'Mr Vamp's remarks on political corruption' that appear in ch. 13, and because TLP could not have read the article before mid Feb., 'any allusion to it at this point in the novel must have been added in the course of revision'. These revisions may have been made in the proofs, although it would be surprising if TLP was correcting proofs for vol. 1 as late as mid Feb., given that on 24 Feb. *Mel* was advertised for 5 Mar. Joukovsky makes another point about internal evidence that is more speculative: 'Mr. Killthedead's line about his salary in the Quintetto at the end of Chapter xxxix . . . was probably inspired by the debate in the House of Commons on 17 February 1817 over John Wilson Croker's demand for a quarter's war salary as Secretary to the Admiralty during Lord Exmouth's expedition against the Algerine pirates

Melincourt echoes other recent texts. On 28 November 1816, the Court of Common Council of the City of London passed a resolution calling for parliamentary reform, but Sir William Curtis, MP for the city, declared during the debate that his response to arguments for reform was that 'I am quite satisfied with things as they are'.[18] Perhaps Peacock had read of Curtis's statement before he wrote Chapter 24 (in the middle of the second volume), where the narrator comments that 'political economists' have argued money, food or drink 'will induce the friends of *things as they are* to submit to any thing'. Peacock did not need assistance in order to see how he might apply the phrase 'things as they are' – best known from the title of Godwin's *Things as They Are; or, The Adventures of Caleb Williams* (1794) – but Curtis may still have helped him along. Curtis's remark is echoed directly late in volume 3 when Mr Anyside Antijack advocates 'appropriating as much as possible of the public money; and saying to those from whose pockets it is taken, "I am perfectly satisfied with things as they are"' (Chapter 39).[19]

Ultimately, we can infer only that '*Melincourt* was written more or less consecutively in the eight or nine months preceding its publication'.[20] Throughout this period, Peacock was living with his

---

("the triumph of Algiers"), but the allusion is not absolutely certain since the question of Croker's salary had previously been raised in March 1816' ('Composition', 22). On 13 Mar. 1816, Henry Brougham mentioned in the Commons that the government had raised the salaries of the two Secretaries to the Admiralty, and Croker provided a justification; *Times* (14 Mar. 1816), 3. For the 17 Feb. 1817 debate, see *Times* (18 Feb. 1817), 2; *The Examiner* (23 Feb. 1817), 117.

[18] *Times* (29 Nov. 1816), 3.

[19] An allusion to Curtis in ch. 39 cannot affect the dating of the chapter, which alludes to texts that appeared as late as Feb. 1817.

[20] Joukovsky, 'Composition', 22–3. 'Assuming that the quotation from the *Edinburgh Review* in Chapter xvi was not a late addition, it would appear that the second volume was begun early in November, and the third volume completed late in February. But even if Peacock began Volume II earlier than this isolated quotation would suggest, it seems most unlikely, in view of the numerous references to current literature and politics in Chapters xxxi and xxxix, that he began Volume III much before the beginning of December

mother at Great Marlow, on the Thames, about 32 miles west of Charing Cross. We have no evidence that he visited London, where his publisher was located.[21] In fact, nothing indicates that Peacock went far from Marlow, and he evidently did not go to London at all in February.[22] In September 1816, Percy Shelley, having returned from the Continent, visited Marlow in order to secure a house, and Peacock years later recalled that 'The first fortnight of September was a period of unbroken sunshine' (July and August had brought 'perpetual rain'), and the two men 'took every day a long excursion, either on foot or on the water'.[23] Perhaps Peacock devoted less time to *Melincourt* during these weeks. By 8 December, Shelley, who was again visiting Peacock, had read some of *Melincourt*. Shelley's life was troubled between his return to England in September and moving into at Albion House in Marlow in March: he continually had to connive to avoid his creditors, Mary's half-sister Fanny Imlay killed herself, his estranged wife Harriet Westbrook killed herself and then Harriet's sister initiated proceedings in the Court

---

1816. This would still leave the period from July to November for the composition of Volumes I and II' ('Composition', 22).

[21] Thirty-two miles is TLP's figure. After Shelley moved permanently to Marlow, he and TLP often walked to London (Halliford, 8.107).

[22] The King's Theatre announced a performance of Mozart's *Le Nozze di Figaro* for 4 Mar. (*Times* (3 Mar. 1817), 2), but then a different work had to be substituted 'in consequence of the continued indisposition of Signor Ambrogetti' (*Times* (4 Mar. 1817), 3), and on 5 Mar. Mary Shelley informed Leigh Hunt that 'Peacock will be disappointed by the alteration this week as he wished very much to see Figaro' (*MWS Letters*, 1.32–3). On 5 Mar. TLP had not seen the opera, and he would have seen it if he had travelled to London since its season debut. So, he had not been in London when *Le Nozze di Figaro* had its debut on 1 Feb. (*Times* (31 Jan. 1817), 2) – Mary Shelley went with Leigh and Marianne Hunt and was 'very much pleased' (*MWS Journals*, p. 161) – nor when it was performed on 4 Feb. (*Times* (4 Feb. 1817), 3), 8 Feb. (*Times* (8 Feb. 1817), 3), 15 Feb. (*Times* (14 Feb. 1817), 2), 18 Feb. (*Times* (18 Feb. 1817), 3), or 22 Feb. (*Times* (22 Feb. 1817), 3).

[23] Halliford, 8.105–6. On 8 Dec. 1816, Shelley wrote to Hunt from Marlow, telling him of TLP and *Mel*, and commenting that he was about to lease 'a house among these woody hills, these sweet green fields & this delightful river' (*PBS Letters*, 2.518).

of Chancery. Her objective, Shelley informed Byron, was 'to deprive me of my unfortunate children, now more than ever dear to me; of my inheritance, & to throw me into prison & expose me in the pillory on the ground of my being a <u>Revolutionist</u> & an <u>Atheist</u>'.[24] Throughout this period, Shelley presumably was meditating the long poem *Laon and Cythna*, on which he set to work as soon as he settled at Albion House.

Peacock cites recent numbers of the *Edinburgh Review* and *Quarterly Review* (and even if he had not, we could safely assume that he followed the major quarterlies), yet he apparently depended most on two weekly publications whose political orientation resembled his own: *The Examiner* for news and William Cobbett's *Weekly Political Register* for commentary. (Only one daily newspaper is mentioned in *Melincourt*, and Peacock had no reason to read the Tory *Morning Post* regularly.) In 1818 he wrote that 'the periodical press . . . has many ultras on the side of power, but none on the side of liberty', with the exception of 'one or two *weekly* publications'; presumably, he was thinking of *The Examiner* and Cobbett.[25] The journal he kept in 1818 suggests that his practice when in Marlow was to read *The Examiner* each Tuesday, which may have been the day when the paper – which was published in London each Sunday – usually arrived from the metropolis.[26] When Peacock could not get the *Weekly Political Register* in Marlow, he relied upon visitors from London, on several occasions asking T. J. Hogg to bring a copy or copies with him.[27] In September 1818 he became so 'absorbed' in the *Weekly Political Register* and in Cobbett's book on America that he neglected his journal for more than a week.[28] Even after Peacock

---

[24] *Shelley and His Circle*, 5.82.   [25] Halliford, 8.273.

[26] He read *The Examiner* on 28 July, 11 Aug. and 8 Sept., all Tuesdays (*Letters*, 1.136, 138, 139). On Sunday, 2 Mar. 1817, Mary Shelley, staying with the Peacocks at Marlow, had not seen that day's *Examiner* (*MWS Letters*, 1.29), but on Tuesday 18 Mar. she had read the number published two days before (*MWS Letters*, 1.34).

[27] 15 July 1817, 12 June 1818 and 15 Dec. 1818 (*Letters*, 1.115, 1.125, 1.163).

[28] *Letters*, 1.140.

assumed his post at the East India Office, he kept up with *The Examiner* and *Weekly Political Register*: in October 1819 his non-Indian reading was limited to 'some articles in the Quarterly and one or two fashionable books which every body reads and the Examiner and, ὕστερος πρότερος, Cobbett', the Greek phrase means 'putting the first thing last'.[29] On 19 September 1822, he informed Hogg that his reading during his vacation included the *Weekly Political Register*, 'as usual'.[30] *Melincourt* provides evidence that some other texts were on his mind, perhaps because he had been reading them with an eye to how they illuminated problems of his own day. The allusions to Milton's prose, for example, suggest that Peacock was taking an interest in the republican cause in the English Civil War.

Melincourt was Peacock's first – and last – three-volume novel. Each volume contains fourteen chapters.[31] It was advertised as comprising three volumes eight months before publication, when it surely was only begun, which suggests that Peacock and his publishers always planned for it to take this form. The three-volume format was becoming standard: twenty-four of the fifty-five new novels published in Britain in 1817 were in three volumes, while only ten were in Peacock's usual one-volume format. In 1819, for the first time, more three-volume novels appeared in a calendar year than novels in all other formats combined – thirty-eight of the seventy-three new novels were 'three-deckers'.[32] In 1816, *Headlong Hall*'s Philomela Poppyseed is writing a four-volume novel (Chapter 6), but fifteen years later, in *Crotchet Castle*, Lady

---

[29] *Letters*, 1.167.

[30] *Letters*, 1.192. At his death, TLP's set of Cobbett's Weekly Political Register went from Jan. 1802 to Dec. 1814, and from 1821 to 1835. He still owned a copy of Cobbett's *Paper Against Gold, and Glory against Prosperity* (1815) (*Sale Catalogue* 128).

[31] Butler is mistaken when she writes that 'The first edition is . . . bound up with thirteen chapters in the first volume and fifteen in the second' (*Peacock Displayed: A Satirist in His Context* (Routledge and Kegan Paul, 1979), p. 84). She recognizes, though, that the *intention* was to have fourteen chapters in each volume.

[32] Raven-Garside, 2.439–54, 91.

Clarinda's 'fashionable novel' will fill only three (Chapter 5). Presumably Peacock wished to attempt something more ambitious after *Headlong Hall*, and Hookham (and perhaps co-publishers Baldwin, Cradock and Joy) may have thought three-volume novels were more marketable. Yet the experiences of writing *Melincourt* and seeing the response probably discouraged Peacock from trying to extend a narrative beyond one volume again.

The design of *Melincourt* is such that the author cannot ever have intended the novel's action to conclude near the point at which the action of the published second volume concludes; however, in 1924 H. F. B. Brett-Smith speculated that *Melincourt* was originally designed to end there. Noting that *Melincourt* was claimed to be 'in the press' in summer 1816, Brett-Smith concluded that the publisher 'may be presumed to have had a complete manuscript of it in his hands by the end of July 1816, and to have passed it on to his printers'.[33] Recognizing that parts of volume 3 were written as late as January, Brett-Smith hypothesized that in summer 1816 Peacock completed a version of the novel that concluded, 'more naturally than the published version, with the marriage of Anthelia and Forester', and this marriage occurred 'shortly after' the events recounted at the end of the second volume, as published. The printer, Brett-Smith speculated, realized 'that the tale was too short for three volumes . . . and too long for one'. Peacock 'chose to lengthen his work', and 'at the point where a happy conclusion might have been expected there was substituted the lame device of a second and successful attempt to abduct Anthelia; current literature and politics provided plenty of scope for fresh satiric commentary, and additions must have continued up to the last moment'.[34] As Marilyn Butler noted, the theory 'seems gratuitous', having been devised to respond to Brett-Smith's 'subjective response, to the last part in particular'.[35] Joukovsky observes that both of Brett-Smith's premises can easily be

[33] Halliford, 1.lxx.   [34] Halliford, 1.lxx.   [35] Butler, *Peacock*, p. 84.

refuted: the phrase 'in the press' should not be interpreted literally, and Hookham would have been willing to publish a two-volume novel.[36] Brett-Smith appears to have been unaware that the earliest advertisement for *Melincourt* promised three volumes.[37] Hookham and Baldwin would not have specified three volumes unless Peacock had agreed to that length, and he could hardly have intended to produce three normal-sized duodecimo volumes yet written only enough to fill two.

Brett-Smith's theory has provoked others to examine *Melincourt*'s structure. As Joukovsky and Butler have observed, the novel's remarkable symmetry suggests that the three volumes were always planned to be constituted in the manner of the published version.[38] Peacock began, then, with the premise that *Melincourt* would consist of three volumes, each about the length of *Headlong Hall*. As Joukovsky points out, 'the major developments of the rambling plot—the meeting of Anthelia and Forester in Chapter xv and the disappearance of Anthelia in Chapter xxix—correspond to the physical divisions of the first edition'. Moreover, Anthelia's 'disappearance is carefully foreshadowed by the unsuccessful abduction scheme of Chapter xviii and its comic aftermath in Chapter xxiii, both of which would have been rather pointless without the sequel'.[39] Lord Anophel's final, successful abduction is necessary, even if Peacock did place Anthelia in danger too many times. The finished novel, Butler writes, suggests that 'Peacock thought of his

[36] Joukovsky, 'Composition', 18–19.

[37] He was also wrong to assume that novels had to be in either one or three volumes. In 1817 there were seven two-volume novels published in Britain, along with the twenty-four three-volume novels and ten one-volume novels (Raven-Garside, 2.439–54), and in 1819 Hookham himself co-published Mrs M. M. Busk's *Zeal and Experience: A Tale in Two Volumes*.

[38] Joukovsky, 'Composition', 19; Butler, *Peacock*, pp. 84–7. However, *Mel* need not be printed as three volumes (or a single volume) in order to be effective. Both the Philadelphia edition and the French translation divided it into two, with twenty-one chapters in each volume, and the break occurring between ch. 21 (at Novote) and ch. 22 (at Onevote).

[39] Joukovsky, 'Composition', 19.

forty-two chapters as dividing equally', and she presents a diagram showing that 'each volume is symmetrically laid out, but also formally linked with the other two.[40] Volume 2, for example, 'has four very distinct movements', and the presence of 'a fifth section', the chapters dealing with the election at Onevote, as 'a centrepiece' makes it 'hard to believe that it was not designed from the beginning as the centrepiece to the entire book'.[41]

Butler writes that any roughness in the novel's execution can be blamed on 'two events [that] could be accommodated within his original plan, but at a cost to its simplicity of outline', namely, the publication of Coleridge's *Statesman's Manual* and the 'Tory campaign against the liberty or licence of the press'.[42] Peacock's design was probably not disrupted much when he responded to these provocative new publications in the Cimmerian Lodge and Mainchance Villa episodes. Allusions to the most recent number of the (Tory) *Quarterly Review* are so extensive in the Mainchance Villa chapter that most of this chapter, fourth from the end, must have been written within a few weeks before *Melincourt* was published. Although this chapter ended up as the longest in the novel, the final volume is a few pages shorter than either of the first two. Peacock must have had his forty-two chapters mapped out before *The Statesman's Manual* appeared in December (and provided material for his chapter devoted to Coleridge) and before the *Quarterly* containing Robert Southey's article appeared in February (and gave him new ideas for the Mainchance Villa visit). Though Peacock might have benefited from additional time to polish his critique of Coleridge or to refine his satire on Canning and the

---

[40] Butler, *Peacock*, p. 84. 'For example, the first volume introduces the topic of marriage, and its fourteen chapters are divided in a markedly regular fashion into four sections: three chapters with Anthelia at Melincourt, four with Forester at Redrose, and again three with Anthelia, four with Forester. Broadly, Anthelia's chapters, romantically set in her castle, establish her challenge to her suitors' (Butler, *Peacock*, pp. 84–5).

[41] Butler, *Peacock*, pp. 85–6.   [42] Butler, *Peacock*, p. 87.

Tory press, he surely knew all along that he was going to satirize them in some way. Mr Mystic and his home Cimmerian Lodge are mentioned in volume 1 when Mr Feathernest relies upon his friend's tutelage in 'the mysteries of the transcendental philosophy' (Chapter 8), and Peacock must have written this passage, alluding to Coleridge's jargon and immersion in transcendental mysteries, before *The Statesman's Manual* appeared in December. He probably planned to have Forester, Fax and Sir Oran visit Mystic in the final volume; by stressing 'the mysteries of transcendental philosophy', he took the approach that also was chosen by William Hazlitt in his preemptive review of *The Statesman's Manual*, which appeared in September.[43] Peacock could not know in summer 1816 that Southey's 'Parliamentary Reform' would appear in the *Quarterly* the next February and provide so much useful material, but he may have intended from the first that Forester, Fax and Sir Oran would encounter Mr Vamp and other representatives of the Tory press. When he first decided to set the action in the Lake District, he surely anticipated that his main characters would visit Wordsworth, Southey or both. Indeed, those poets' association with the region was probably a major reason Peacock selected this setting.

Volume 3 shows signs of hasty composition, such as the continuity error at the opening of Chapter 40 that was noted by the *Monthly Review*.[44] With additional revision, some late thoughts (both late in the composition process and late in the published text) could have been incorporated fully into the novel. References to paper money are surprisingly rare until the third volume. In the final chapter, Peacock alludes extensively to John Fletcher's play *The Faithful*

---

[43] 'Mr. Coleridge's Lay Sermon', *The Examiner* (8 Sept. 1816), 571–3.

[44] The chapter begins, 'THE mountain-roads being now buried in snow, they were compelled, on leaving Mainchance Villa', and the *Monthly Review* pointed out that 'the persons who were last mentioned in the chapter preceding are certainly not among the travellers'; Anon., *Monthly Review*, new ser., vol. 83 (July 1817), 322–3 (p. 323). TLP could have polished his prose more thoroughly; he tends to repeat figures and allusions for no good reason, such as 'mind's eye'.

Shepherdess (c. 1609), and it is odd that such a good analogue for Sir Oran's relationship to Anthelia appears so late. Peacock's title suggests that Melincourt Castle will figure in this novel much as Headlong Hall figured in that novel, yet only about a quarter of *Melincourt* takes place at Anthelia's residence.[45] The title had been chosen by August 1816, and perhaps at this point Peacock had written so little that he still could imagine Melincourt Castle would be more prominent than it became.

PUBLICATION

Melincourt, like *Headlong Hall* and *Maid Marian*, was printed by Samuel Gosnell.[46] The three crown duodecimo volumes were printed on paper without watermarks.[47] Three leaves are cancels: volume 1, B12 (pp. 23–4, Chapter 2, containing from 'cient to' to 'do not think I'); volume 1, D6 (pp. 59–60, Chapter 5, from 'other men's' to 'the practice of'); and volume 2, E2 (pp. 75–6, Chapter 19,

[45] The first few pages reveal that 'Melincourt' means the house; TLP surely never intended this title to refer to Anthelia Melincourt or her family. When novels in the early nineteenth century have titles that refer primarily to a character's surname, the character is the male protagonist, and the male protagonist in particular is meant, rather than his family. If TLP had conformed to the pattern exemplified by Scott's *Waverley*, Godwin's *St. Leon* and *Mandeville*, Percy Bysshe Shelley's *Zastrozzi* and *St. Irvyne* and, later, Mary Wollstonecraft Shelley's *Frankenstein*, then *Mel* would have been called *Forester*.

[46] Gosnell was based at 8 Little Queen St. in Holborn from 1799 to 1827 (William B. Todd, *A Directory of Printers and Other Allied Trades in London and Vicinity, 1800–1840* (Printing Historical Society, 1972), p. 82). He was occasionally employed by John Murray, for whom he printed Lord Byron's *Waltz* (1813). Gosnell also printed the catalogue of Hookham's library.

[47] Each of the first six of the twelve leaves in each gathering is signed ('B', 'B2', and so on). Signing all leaves in the first half of a gathering was standard for Gosnell, to judge from the fact that he numbered the first six leaves of each gathering in the duodecimo *Headlong Hall* and the first four leaves of each gathering in the octavo edition of J. B. Sumner's *Apostolic Preaching Considered, in An Examination of St. Paul's Epistles*, 2nd ed. (J. Hatchard, 1817).

from 'riage was' to 'the lake. The'). No copy of the first edition that retains any of the original leaves has been located. As Joukovsky has observed, the cancels probably correct printer's errors; they occur in scenes involving uncontroversial subjects, so the substitutions cannot be explained by worries about legal attacks.[48] None of the three cancel leaves appears in the final volume, and one might speculate that readings in copies of the last volume would have been emended if time had permitted, but obvious errors are no more frequent in the third than in earlier volumes.

Peacock probably delivered the manuscript to the printer piecemeal – by volume, or in smaller units – and he may have received proofs one gathering at a time, or several gatherings at once. He was not always able to modify earlier portions of the novel when writing later portions. Indeed, the inconsistencies that occur when Peacock directs readers to passages in a previous volume are a sign that Gosnell was printing as Peacock wrote. At certain moments during composition of the second or third volumes, he evidently was unable to refer to printed sheets of passages in a previous volume. Early in volume 2, the narrator refers to 'reasons we have given in the ninth chapter' (Chapter 18; *1817*, 2.55–6); to be precise, the reasons appear on pp. 121–2 of the first volume, in gathering G. Later in the second volume, Forester displays a skull, and Peacock's footnote suggests that the reader 'See Chap. IV' (Chapter 19; *1817*, 2.67n); the skull first appears on p. 43 of volume 1, in gathering C. In both instances Peacock refers back to a chapter in the previous volume and not to the page, so he probably had yet to see proofs of gatherings C or G in volume 1, or he no longer had access to the proofs.[49] He preferred to give

---

[48] Joukovsky also points out that all three cancels are present in the copy (now in the British Library, pressmark 1206.b.22) that was sent to the *Critical Review*, presumably as soon as *Melincourt* was available ('Composition', 21, n. 13).

[49] TLP did not add the page numbers before he sent the manuscript of chs. 18 and 19 to the printer, or when he read the two passages in the proof of vol. 2's gathering D.

references in the form of page numbers in earlier volumes if he could.[50] Later in the second volume, in Chapter 24, a footnote points the reader to 'Vol. I. page 156' (*1817*, 2.158n); by this time, Peacock had clearly received and consulted the proof of gathering H of volume 1. In volume 3, he cites volume 1, gathering E, when a footnote advises the reader to 'See vol. i. p. 73, note' (*1817*, 3.63n). In volume 3, Peacock twice refers to the preceding volume, here volume 2, without giving page numbers: he mentions events 'detailed in the eighteenth Chapter' (*1817*, 3.4), the chapter that occupies pp. 54–63 (D3v–D8r) in volume 2. Later, he writes that Mr Paperstamp first appeared 'in the twenty-eighth Chapter' (*1817*, 3.119), a chapter to be found on pp. 200–15 (K4v–K12v) of the second volume.

The arrangements that publishers made with authors of new novels fall into four catagories: a book could be published by subscription; the publisher could take a commission, with the author being responsible for all losses; the publisher and writer could split the profits; or the publisher could buy the entire copyright (in *Melincourt*, Chapter 13, Desmond offers Mr Foolscap the copyright of his treatise).[51] A variant of the last option would be for a publisher to buy the exclusive right to print and sell an edition or editions.[52] Peacock apparently retained the copyrights of his early novels, while

---

[50] When TLP referred to an earlier volume, he knew a reader might not have the necessary books to hand (circulating libraries lent out multi-volume novels piecemeal). He is content to be vague when referring to a passage earlier in the volume he is writing. The opening of ch. 23 returns to Grovelgrub and Lord Anophel, 'whom we left perched on the summit of the rock, where Sir Oran had placed them', but TLP sees no need to specify that the two were left there at the end of ch. 18.

[51] See Raven-Garside, 2.80–2.

[52] William St Clair notes that one 'common type of contract involved the publisher buying the copyright [sic] for an edition of a certain agreed size, say 500 or 1,000 copies, another fee to be negotiated if a second edition was agreed'; *The Reading Nation in the Romantic Period* (Cambridge: Cambridge University Press, 2004), p. 163.

granting Hookham the right to print and sell either a specific number of editions or a specific number of copies.[53]

When *Melincourt* was offered for sale by 'T. Hookham, Jun. and Co. / Old Bond Street; and Baldwin, Cradock, and Joy, Paternoster Row', it cost 18 shillings in boards, the standard price for a three-volume novel from 1813 to 1817.[54] We do not know how large the print run was, how many copies were sold or how the distribution of *Melincourt* was affected by the fact that the Hookham family's primary business at 15 Old Bond Street was not publishing or bookselling but running a circulating library. The Hookhams' library contained a wide range of recent fiction; in *Melincourt*, Peacock uses it as a metonym for contemporary fiction when he writes that the 'virtues' with which Miss Danaretta endows her imaginary future husband can be found 'in our good friend Hookham's library' (Chapter 2). The role of Baldwin, Cradock and Joy, Thomas Hookham's co-publishers for *Melincourt* and the second edition of *Headlong Hall*, is unclear, and perhaps they put up no money, but simply sold the novels.[55] *Headlong Hall*, *Melincourt* and *Nightmare Abbey* were the only novels Hookham published between 1813 (when he and his brother E. T. Hookham were responsible for *A*

---

[53] This is a logical inference from the letters Thomas Hookham wrote to Richard Bentley when Bentley wished to buy the copyrights of *Headlong Hall*, *Nightmare Abbey* and *Maid Marian* (*Letters*, 2.232–3, 239).

[54] Raven-Garside, 2.93.

[55] Apparently in summer 1816 Hookham had agreed to sell books in cooperation with them, including leftover copies of novels Hookham had published earlier (alone or with his brother E. T. Hookham). The advertisement for *Mel* in the second edition of *HH* appeared on the recto of a leaf, and the verso contained advertisements for three 'Modern Works' that were 'published by' Hookham and Baldwin: *Faulconstein Forest: A Romantic Tale* (1810), *A Picture of Society, or, The Misanthropist* (1813) and the second edition of Étienne de Jouy, *Paris Chit-Chat; or, A View of the Society, Manners, Customs, Literature and Amusements of the Parisians* (1816). However, none of these works was ever published with Baldwin's name. Evidently copies remained in 1816 of *Faulconstein Forest* and *A Picture of Society*, but not of Hogg's *Memoirs of Prince Alexy Haimatoff* (1813), all of which Thomas Hookham had originally published with his brother.

Picture of Society, or, The Misanthropist and T. J. Hogg's *Memoirs of Prince Alexy Haimatoff*) and 1819 (when he published Mrs M. M. Busk's *Zeal and Experience*).[56] In contrast, Baldwin, Cradock and Joy put out ten novels in 1817 alone.

RECEPTION

Although *Melincourt* was appreciated by those whom Shelley called 'the chosen spirits of the time', book reviews in early nineteenth-century Britain were often perfunctory, and they characteristically reflected contemporary political divisions.[57] Hookham's edition of *Melincourt* received six reviews, the same number as *Headlong Hall*. On 22 March, the *Literary Gazette* praised the novel, congratulating its author for 'singular, and we may add, original work'.[58] The May *New Monthly Magazine and Universal Register* found that Peacock's new 'extravagant romance' suffered by comparison with *Headlong Hall*: it seemed 'to be constructed for the purpose of trying how far human credulity can be outraged with impunity', and, beyond the 'attack upon probability' posed by Peacock's gentlemanly oran outang, *Melincourt* possessed a fault that was 'still worse': a pattern of 'insult upon religion'.[59] In May, John Payne Collier in the *Critical Review* found the book's quality inconsistent: parts were 'shrewd, ingenious, and humorous', but the novel 'opens better than it proceeds: the descriptions are more easy, lively, and varied, and the characters seem to possess an originality which they do not afterwards keep up; the second volume is therefore more dull than the first,

---

[56] Hookham did not publish much in other genres, either. His productions include a few volumes of poetry by TLP, and he co-published the Shelleys' *History of a Six Weeks' Tour* with Charles Ollier.

[57] P. B. Shelley, 'Letter to Maria Gisborne' (wr. 1820), l.244, in *The Poems of Shelley, 1819–1820*, ed. Jack Donovan, Cian Duffy, Kelvin Everest and Michael Rossington (Harlow: Longman/Pearson, 2011), vol. 3, p. 455.

[58] Anon., *Literary Gazette* (22 Mar. 1817), 132.

[59] Anon., *The New Monthly Magazine*, vol. 7, no. 40 (1 May 1817), 349.

and the third than the second'.[60] Reviewers imagined the author of *Melincourt* as a young man, intemperate in his views and expressions, who had been emboldened by his success with *Headlong Hall*. The *Critical Review* preferred the parts of *Melincourt* that concerned politics to those that concerned 'literary and critical' matters.[61] Yet the political portions were marred by Peacock's enthusiasm for ridicule: although he favoured reform and scoffed at 'virtual representation', he could not 'restrain himself' and so 'he represents the population of the town of Novote as so servile and contemptible, so thoughtless and so drunken, as to be unworthy of a respectable representative'.[62] In June, the *Monthly Magazine* praised this 'satirical novel' 'as the best of its class that has for some years met our notice'. The author was obviously 'a philosopher, a patriot, and a man of taste'.[63] In July, the *Monthly Review* offered bland praise: 'for quaint burlesque, for characteristic satire, and for ingenious discussion', *Melincourt* 'will stand high among the lighter productions of the present day'.[64]

While Collier thought the 'best portion' of *Melincourt* was 'that which related to politics', the Tory *British Critic* in its October number objected to the author's '*reforming* notions', and, not surprisingly, deemed *Melincourt* 'miserable trash'.[65] Sounding like a Church-and-King man of the 1790s condemning Godwin's *Things as They Are; or, The Adventures of Caleb Williams* or Robert Bage's *Hermsprong; or, Man as He is Not* (1796), the *British Critic* reviewer called Forester a 'philosopher, reformer, and infidel', and indeed saw

---

[60] [John Payne Collier], *Critical Review*, 5th ser., vol. 5 (May 1817), 494–502 (pp. 496, 495). As Nicholas A. Joukovsky has pointed out, one of the British Library's two copies of the first edition was evidently the review copy of *Melincourt*: it is inscribed 'For the Editor of / The Critical Review' (British Library, pressmark 1206. b. 22.) (Joukovsky, 'Composition', p. 21 n. 13).

[61] [Collier], *Critical Review*, 5th ser., vol. 5 (May 1817), 500.

[62] [Collier], *Critical Review*, 5th ser., vol. 5 (May 1817), 501.

[63] Anon., *Monthly Magazine*, vol. 43 (June 1817), 453.

[64] Anon., *Monthly Review*, new ser., vol. 83 (July 1817), 323.

[65] Anon., *British Critic*, new ser., vol. 8 (Oct. 1817), 430–42 (p. 430).

'the cloven foot of infidelity' throughout.[66] The author's satire upon clergymen they blamed on 'some personal spite'.[67] The author of *Melincourt* 'mistakes sound for sense, and taking the leading idea in a passage for the whole, quotes it boldly, without troubling [himself] with the meaning or construction of any particular word, much less with the bearing of the passage as relating to the context'.[68]

The most striking characteristics of the reviews are, first, that they judge *Melincourt* on its ability to amuse, more than on its insight; second, that they approach *Melincourt* anticipating a typical novel, only to discover that it is not one. The *Monthly Review* expected no more from *Melincourt* than from any of 'the lighter productions of the present day'. The reviewers continually assume that plausibility is the author's objective and complain that the story is implausible: the *Literary Gazette* mentioned that an ape's election to parliament was 'rather an outrageous improbability' (though they enjoyed the 'poignant burlesque').[69]

If the consensus of critics over the years has been 'that *Melincourt* is Peacock's failure', as Marilyn Butler wrote in 1979, such a consensus was not apparent in 1817, when some critics saw it as equal to *Headlong Hall*, although others objected to the author's change of direction.[70] While *Headlong Hall* could be called 'a pleasant evening's amusement',[71] a reader would need more than one evening for *Melincourt* (Godwin needed three), and it would challenge or provoke more than amuse. The *Monthly Review* said *Melincourt* displayed 'equal pleasantry' but 'more argument' than *Headlong Hall*.[72] The *New Monthly Magazine* wrote that the action of *Melincourt* was so implausible that 'The praise which we bestowed upon

---

[66] Anon., *British Critic*, new ser., vol. 8 (Oct. 1817), 431, 437.

[67] Anon., *British Critic*, new ser., vol. 8 (Oct. 1817), 437.

[68] Anon., *British Critic*, new ser., vol. 8 (Oct. 1817), 430.

[69] Anon., *Literary Gazette*, 22 Mar. 1817, 132.

[70] Butler, *Peacock*, p. 97.

[71] Anon., *Monthly Review*, new ser., vol. 82 (Mar. 1817), 330.

[72] Anon., *Monthly Review*, new ser., vol. 83 (July 1817), 322.

Headlong Hall cannot be extended to this extravagant romance' – as though a novel featuring a woman named Cephalis Cranium is not extravagant.

One item that may be treated as a review is the poem 'The German Professor and the Ape', written by 'P.W.', which appeared in Rudolph Ackermann's *Repository of Arts, Literature, Fashions, Manufactures, &c.* on 1 March 1822.

> The author of a novel lately written,
>   Entitled 'Melincourt',
>   ('Tis very sweet and short,)
> Seems indeed by some wond'rous madness bitten,
>   Thinking it good
>   To take his hero from the wood:
> And though I own there's nothing treasonable
> In making ouran-outangs reasonable,
>   I really do not think he should
> Go quite the length that he has done,
> Whether for satire or for fun,
> To make this creature an M.P.
> As if mankind no wiser were than he.

The author goes on to say that readers of *Melincourt* 'Must give the author credit / For skill and ingenuity'.[73]

Anonymous fiction naturally elicited speculation about its authorship. One reviewer of *Headlong Hall* had suspected that the author was 'D*****' – presumably Edward DuBois, author of the anonymous satires *St. Godwin: A Tale of the Sixteenth, Seventeenth, and Eighteenth Century* (1800) and *My Pocket Book; or, Hints for 'A Ryghte Merrie and Conceitede' Tour, in Quarto; To Be Called 'The Stranger in Ireland', in 1805* (1808). Seeing the footnote in *Melincourt* that recommends sources on Kant, the *British Critic* claimed to be

---

[73] P.W., 'The German Professor and the Ape', *The Repository of Arts, Literature, Fashions, Manufactures, &c.*, 2nd ser., vol. 12 (1 Mar. 1822), 133.

struck by the inclusion of the book *Academical Questions*, written by someone of whom they had never heard, Sir William Drummond, and accused 'the author of Headlong Hall' of self-advertisement: Drummond was responsible for *Melincourt*.[74] Knowledge of the real identity of 'the author of Headlong Hall' spread, at least through literary London. Eleven months after *Melincourt* appeared, the *Literary Gazette* attributed *Rhododaphne* to 'Mr. Peacock, known to the world, if not generally by name, at least pretty generally as the author of "The Genius of the Thames", "Headlong Hall", and 'Melincourt'".[75] Although the novel-reading world knew that *Headlong Hall* and *Melincourt* were by the same author, not everyone possessed the inside information to know that the author was the Thomas Love Peacock whose name had appeared on the title page of *The Genius of the Thames*. By 3 February 1819, Mary Russell Mitford knew to attribute *Melincourt*, *Rhododaphne* and *Nightmare Abbey* to 'Mr Peacock'.[76] The 'P.W.' who wrote the poem 'The German Professor and the Ape' in 1822 was aware that Peacock was the author of *Melincourt*, and alluded to Peacock's new career in the East India office:

> In Leadenhall he gives a close attendance,
>   Where, if I not mistake
>   He now contrives to make

---

[74] The *British Critic* had attacked *Academical Questions* years earlier; see Van Doren, *The Life of Thomas Love Peacock* (Dent, 1911), p. 94. Perhaps the reviewer of *Mel* was being disingenuous; perhaps he remembered *Academical Questions*, discerned kinship between the two books, and suspected that Drummond was responsible for *Mel*; or perhaps the reviewer simply wished to lump together two infidels. The *Port Folio*, reviewing the Philadelphia edition of *Mel*, probably relied upon the *British Critic* when it nominated Drummond on the basis of 'internal evidence'; *The Port Folio* (Philadelphia), vol. 5, no. 4 (Apr. 1818), 321. See Carl Van Doren, *The Life of Thomas Love Peacock* (Dent, 1911), p. 94.

[75] *Literary Gazette* (21 Feb. 1818), 114.

[76] *Letters of Mary Russell Mitford, Second Series*, ed. Henry Chorley, 2 vols. (Bentley, 1872), vol. 1, p. 41.

A very comfortable *India*-pendence:
But be it known,
Or good or bad, this pun is not my own.[77]

Two songs from *Melincourt*, 'The Morning of Love' and 'The Flower of Love', were set to music by George Kiallmark before the end of 1817.[78] *The British Lady's Magazine* commented that 'The airs of these songs are extremely well adapted to the words; and the plan of a varied accompaniment according with the sentiment of each verse is a great improvement.'[79] Songs from *Melincourt* were reprinted in newspapers and periodicals.[80]

According to information collected by Peter Garside, *Melincourt* made its way into five out of fifteen possible circulating libraries, and three out of five possible subscription libraries.[81] In 1839 James Spedding wrote that 'The popularity of [Peacock's] works has been just sufficient to make them scarce; which implies that they are highly esteemed, but by a limited circle of readers'; in 1856 Henry Chorley remembered in *The Athenaeum* that these novels 'found a few readers, though rather in the circles of Philosophical Radicalism than among the general public'.[82] In November 1820 Shelley told Peacock that discerning readers preferred *Melincourt* to his other

---

[77] P.W., 'The German Professor and the Ape', 133.

[78] *The Morning of Love, a Song, from Melincourt, The Music Composed & Dedicated to Miss Gale*, by G. Kiallmark (Chappell, [1817]), and *The Flower of Love, a Song, from Melincourt, The Music Composed by G. Kiallmark* (Chappell [1817]).

[79] *The British Lady's Magazine*, vol. 1, no. 6 (Nov. 1817), 309. On 13 Sept. 1859, Captain John Walker wrote a letter 'To the Author of "Melincourt"' asking permission to set the 'Terzetto' to music for tenor, soprano and contralto (*Letters*, 2.495).

[80] 'The Flower of Love' was printed in the *Literary Gazette* (15 Mar. 1817), 18, and in the *Weekly Entertainer* (31 Mar. and 9 June 1817).

[81] See www.british-fiction.cf.ac.uk/. *NA* made it into four out of thirteen circulating libraries and three out of five subscription libraries, and *MM* into three out of eleven and one out of four.

[82] [Spedding], review, *Edinburgh Review*, vol. 68 (Jan. 1839), 435; [Chorley], *The Athenæum* (19 Apr. 1856), 486–8 (p. 486).

works, but he was generalizing from a tiny sample. On 22 March Shelley asked if Godwin had read *Melincourt* and said 'it would entertain you'.[83] By February 1819 Mary Russell Mitford had read *Melincourt*; she later decided that *Nightmare Abbey* was more 'pleasant'.[84] Claire Clairmont read *Melincourt* in Italy on 25 June 1821.[85] On 8 November 1820 Shelley wrote to Peacock that *Melincourt* was 'exceedingly admired, and I think much more so than any of your other writings'. Shelley thought that 'In this respect the world judges rightly.' (To whom might Shelley have been speaking in Pisa who admired *Melincourt* – Maria Gisborne?) *Melincourt* was superior to *Headlong Hall* and *Nightmare Abbey* insofar as it had 'more of the true spirit, and an object less indefinite'. Concerned that Peacock was so absorbed by the East India Company that he was neglecting his writing, Shelley hoped that Peacock would 'give us another "Melincourt"'.[86]

Lord Byron had read *Melincourt* by June 1821, perhaps because Shelley had drawn his attention to it. *A Letter to the Right Hon. Lord Byron* by 'John Bull' had appeared, and Byron, finding it 'diabolically *well* written', told publisher John Murray that Peacock, 'a very clever fellow', was one of four men he suspected might be responsible, the other candidates being John Cam Hobhouse, Isaac D'Israeli and Washington Irving.[87] (The *Letter* has been attributed to John Gibson Lockhart.) In August 1821, Shelley informed Peacock that Byron claimed he attributed the *Letter* to Peacock because of 'the style resembling "Melincourt", of which he is a

---

[83] *PBS Letters*, 1.537. Godwin had indeed finished *Mel* by the time this letter reached London.

[84] *Letters of Mary Russell Mitford, Second Series*, vol. 1, p. 41.

[85] *The Journals of Claire Clairmont*, ed. Marion Kingston Stocking, with the assistance of David Mackenzie Stocking (Cambridge, MA: Harvard University Press, 1968), 238.

[86] *PBS Letters*, 2.244.

[87] Byron to Murray, 29 June 1821, *Byron's Letters and Journals*, ed. Leslie A. Marchand, 13 vols. (Cambridge, MA: Harvard University Press, 1973–94), vol. 8, p. 145.

great admirer'.[88] (Peacock responded that he had never heard of *A Letter to the Right Hon. Lord Byron.*)[89] Commenting years later on this letter, Peacock suggested that 'Shelley's partiality for me and my book put too favourable a construction on what Lord Byron may have said'.[90] If Thomas Medwin's account of his conversations with Byron can be trusted, the poet referred to *Melincourt* as 'a witty satire' written by a 'friend of Shelley's', and he said that the novel was 'founded on my bear' – that is, the pet bear he kept when at Cambridge.[91] In 1860, Peacock summarized Medwin's account and commented that he 'thought neither of Lord Byron's bear nor of Caligula's horse' when he created Sir Oran (Halliford, 8.501).

Melincourt sold out in a few years, and critical discussions of the novel before 1856 were hindered by its unavailability. In April 1822, an advertisement in the first edition of *Maid Marian* indicated that Hookham had copies of *Melincourt* available for purchase, but an advertisement for the third edition of *Headlong Hall* which appeared in the *Literary Gazette* for 12 February 1825 did not mention *Melincourt*, and when *Crotchet Castle* first appeared, in 1831, Hookham's inserted advertisements stated explicitly that, among the author's earlier novels, only *Headlong Hall* and *The Misfortunes of Elphin* (1829) remained in print. So, enough copies were sold that Hookham had none left in 1831, although, again, we do not know how many he printed or offered for sale.[92] *Melincourt* was discussed in an article on the 'Novels by the Author of Headlong

---

[88] Shelley to Peacock, 10 Aug. 1821, *PBS Letters*, 2.331.   [89] *Letters*, 1.186.

[90] Halliford, 8.500.

[91] *Medwin's Conversations of Lord Byron: Revised with a New Preface by the Author for a New Edition and Annotated by Lady Byron, et al.*, ed. Ernest J. Lovell, Jr. (Princeton: Princeton University Press, 1966), p. 67. Medwin supplied the title of *Melincourt* in a footnote. Medwin was in contact with Byron from 20 Nov. 1821 until c. 11 Mar. 1822, and from 16 Aug. 1822 until the fourth week of Aug. (p. xvi, n. 2). See Nicholas A. Joukovsky, 'Peacock's Sir Oran Haut-ton: Byron's Bear or Shelley's Ape?', *Keats–Shelley Journal*, 29 (1980), 173–90.

[92] Henry Cole acquired a copy eleven years after publication; it is now in the Pforzheimer Collection of the New York Public Library.

Hall' that appeared in the *Monthly Magazine* for April 1829, and at moments the writer revealed that he had not re-read *Melincourt*. Fax is 'a Malthusian philosopher, if we remember rightly', while Forester becomes 'Forster' and 'Redrose' is 'Red Rose' (yet this article reproduces the entire 'Cimmerian Lodge' chapter).[93] In 1839 James Spedding wrote one of the best analyses of *Melincourt*, but he had apparently been unable to re-read it: his commentary might be different if *Melincourt* were 'fresher in [his] memory'.[94] The novel had not been reprinted for twenty-two years.

Two early unauthorized editions testify to the initial appeal of *Melincourt*: one published in 1817 by Moses Thomas in Philadelphia, and the French translation, entitled *Anthélia Mélincourt, ou Les enthousiastes*, published in 1818 by Béchet in Paris. *Melincourt* was in select company: of the fifty-five new novels that appeared in Britain in 1817, the only others that were both reprinted in the United States and translated into either French or German were Godwin's *Mandeville*, Maria Edgeworth's *Harrington*, Anna Maria Porter's *The Knight of St. John*, Mrs Ross's *The Balance of Comfort* (all translated into French), Elizabeth B. Lester's *The Bachelor and the Married Man* (German) and Jane Porter's *The Pastor's Fire-Side* (French and German).[95]

Moses Thomas's *Melincourt. By the Author of Headlong Hall* splits the work into two volumes, the first volume printed by J. Maxwell, the second by William Fry.[96] One reviewer mentioned Kirk & Mercein, in New York, as co-publishers.[97] Because Thomas's edition divides

---

[93] Anon., 'Novels', *Monthly Magazine*, vol. 7, no. 40 (Apr. 1829), 385–8.

[94] [Spedding], review, *Edinburgh Review*, vol. 68 (Jan. 1839), 447.

[95] See Raven-Garside, 2.439–54.

[96] The volumes are evidently octodecimos, albeit with six leaves per signature (the recto of the third leaf of each signature is numbered '2' – e.g. 'F2'). On printing 'A Sheet of Eighteens, with Three Signatures', see C[aleb] Stower, *The Printer's Grammar; or, Introduction to the Art of Printing: Containing a Concise History of the Art* (B. Crosby, 1808), p. 180.

[97] *The American Monthly Magazine and Critical Review*, vol. 1, no. 3 (July 1817), 235.

the forty-two chapters evenly, the break occurs between the Novote chapter (Chapter 21) and the Onevote chapter (Chapter 22). Only sixteen of the fifty-five new novels published in Britain in 1817 were reprinted by publishers in the United States.[98] Moses Thomas published four of these sixteen: *Harrington*, *Mandeville* and Catharine Hutton's *The Welsh Mountaineer*, along with *Melincourt*.[99] (He also published many editions of Byron.) Mary Shelley's *Frankenstein* (1818), in contrast, was not picked up by an American publisher until Bentley's 1831 London edition was reprinted in the United States in 1833.

The Philadelphia edition had three reviews, all brief. The *North American Review* commented merely that 'This little work has not a high character as a novel, but derives interest from the introduction of Scott, Southey, Gifford, Coleridge, and Wordsworth among its characters; under the names of Derrydown, Feathernest, Vamp, Paperstamp and Mystic.' ('Paperstamp' and 'Mystic' should have been transposed.)[100] *The American Monthly Magazine and Critical Review* wrote that *Melincourt* was 'extremely tedious', the work of someone who knew 'nothing of the art of writing in a popular manner'. The novel was 'a jumble, from which the reader can extract no interest, and very little information'. *Melincourt* was a *roman* in need of a *clef*: it 'has an air of mystery, and may contain stores of recondite knowledge, which our vision, bedimmed by its powerful soporific influence, had not the keenness to detect'.[101] *The Port Folio*, published in Philadelphia, disliked *Melincourt* on political grounds: the author was 'one of the Jack Cade philosophers, who would commence the establishment of the rights of man by the summary pro-

---

[98] On United States reprints of British novels, see Raven-Garside, 2.98–9.

[99] The well-known Philadelphia publisher Mathew Carey had published *HH*, and he later published *NA*. No American publisher picked up *MM* or *ME*, even though their romance dimensions would seem to give them wide appeal.

[100] *North American Review*, vol. 5 (Sept. 1817), 437.

[101] *The American Monthly Magazine and Critical Review*, vol. 1, no. 3 (July 1817), 235.

cess of that celebrated reformist'.[102] The *Port Folio* reviewer repeats the attribution to Sir William Drummond, and this is not the only indication that he had read the *British Critic*'s review.

Melincourt became Peacock's first novel to become available in another language when Béchet published *Anthélia Mélincourt, ou Les enthousiastes*, a 'roman satyrique' written by the author of 'Maison de Head Long-Hall'. The translator was 'Mlle Al. de L**' – 'ostensibly Aline de Lacoste, daughter of Henri Verdier, comte de Lacoste (c. 1770–1821)'.[103] The title page claims that the text was based on that of 'la cinquième édition', but Hookham never put out even a second edition. Of the fifty-one new novels published in Britain in 1817 that were not already translations from foreign languages, eight were translated into French within the next few years. (*Maid Marian* appeared in French in 1826; *Nightmare Abbey* and *Maid Marian* appeared in German in 1819 and 1823 respectively.) Foreign publishers were apt to revise an English novel's title – so, for example, *Nightmare Abbey* became *Die Burg Alphausen, oder, Ziprians Frauenwahl*. By directing attention to 'Anthélia Mélincourt' (the running heads read simply 'Anthélia'), Béchet underscored the novel's courtship plot, and by referring to Peacock's characters as 'les enthousiastes' he reduced their ideas to eccentricities (this sub-title would befit *Headlong Hall* more than *Melincourt*). The French translation of *Melincourt* leaves the characters' names as they are, whereas the German *Nightmare Abbey*

---

[102] *The Port Folio* (Philadelphia), vol. 5, no. 4 (Apr. 1818), 321. This reviewer was careless, writing that Peacock 'had conjured into his brain some strange figures, and affixed to them the names of Southey, Gifford, and Wordsworth', though Peacock's characters are not named as such, and that the author 'believes, with lord Monboddo, of whom he is an ardent admirer, that men formerly had tails'.

[103] Nicholas A. Joukovsky, 'The French Translation of Peacock's *Melincourt*', *Notes and Queries*, 23 (1976), 110–12 (p. 111). Joukovsky writes that 'it is not unlikely that [the elder Lacoste] had a hand in . . . *Anthélia Melincourt*' (p. 111). On the translation of British novels into French or German, see Raven-Garside, 2.99–102.

tried to find German equivalents. Like Thomas's edition, the French translation split *Melincourt* into two volumes, with the break coming between Chapters 21 and 22. The translation is generally faithful, with a conspicuous exception, the Béchet edition's oddest feature: it omits the footnotes, and so the Cimmerian Lodge chapter never refers to Drummond or Coleridge, the relation between Sir Oran's behaviour and Monboddo's writings is concealed, and the speeches at Mainchance Villa lose much of their point. The preface addressed 'Au Lecteur' stated that the author is 'connu pour être l'un des membres les plus ardens du parti de l'opposition' (1: [i]), but it is unclear what grounds the translator had for this assertion. Although *Melincourt* supposedly needed to be understood as the work of a member of the Opposition, this edition, by leaving out the footnotes, obscured some of Peacock's topicality.

One crucial event in *Melincourt*'s history is a non-event: its absence from the Peacock volume which appeared in 1837 in Richard Bentley's Standard Novels series. Examining this book, which contained *Headlong Hall*, *Nightmare Abbey*, *Maid Marian* and *Crotchet Castle*, Spedding assumed that the author, not Bentley, had excluded *Melincourt*, and he speculated that Peacock did so out of 'a consciousness of [its] defects'.[104] *Melincourt* was the most topical among Peacock's fictions, and it had not been one of the most popular, but its length alone surely must have proved fatal. Each of the four novels Bentley included had originally been published in a single volume, and he would have been unlikely to consider trying to fit in Peacock's only triple-decker.[105] As William St Clair has argued, Bentley's series established certain novels as common reading for the Victorian era and thereafter, while 'Novels such as [James] Hogg's [*The Private Memoirs and Confessions of a*] *Justified*

---

[104] [Spedding], review, *Edinburgh Review*, vol. 68 (Jan. 1839), 446.

[105] Although Bentley usually fitted into a single volume those novels that, like *Frankenstein*, were originally published in three, he had no reason to reprint one long Peacock work when he could choose three or four short ones.

Sinner and Godwin's *Mandeville*, which failed to be selected, disappeared from public attention until the twentieth century'.[106] *Headlong Hall*, *Nightmare Abbey*, *Maid Marian* and *Crotchet Castle* were readily available, while *Melincourt* and *The Misfortunes of Elphin* were not. (The inclusion of *Crotchet Castle*, one of Peacock's best-crafted works, was an afterthought.) The 1837 Bentley volume inspired reevaluations of Peacock, such as Spedding's, reevaluations from which *Melincourt* was largely omitted.

Melincourt was reprinted only once in Britain during Peacock's lifetime: in 1856 it appeared, renamed *Melincourt, or Sir Oran Haut-ton*, as the fourteenth title in Chapman and Hall's 'Select Library of Fiction', a series of single-volume reprints (or 'yellowbacks') that sold for only 2 shillings apiece.[107] The Chapman and Hall *Melincourt* had appeared by 1 April 1856.[108] Whereas Bentley's Standard Novels series emphasized older works originally published by others (for several years, none of the novels included were less than seven years old), the Select Library of Fiction concentrated on more recent novels that Chapman and Hall had published previously. This series began in 1854 with Nathaniel Hawthorne's *The Blithedale Romance* and Elizabeth Gaskell's *Mary Barton*, which Chapman and Hall had first published in more expensive editions in 1852 and 1848 respectively. *Melincourt* was a step in a new direction, the first work in the Select Library of Fiction that predated 1845 and the first that Chapman and Hall had not published before. Indeed, the decision to publish *Melincourt* suggests that Chapman and Hall were willing to make their series more akin to Bentley's Standard Novels. At 2 shillings, this *Melincourt* sold for one-ninth of the original price (yellowbacks were even less expensive than the

---

[106] St Clair, *The Reading Nation in the Romantic Period*, p. 361.
[107] See Chester W. Topp, *Victorian Yellowbacks and Paperbacks, 1849–1905*, 9 vols. (Denver: Hermitage Antiquarian Bookshop, 1993), vol. 3, pp. xxiii–iv, 297.
[108] *Times* (1 Apr. 1856), 13.

Standard Novels; Chapman and Hall's *Melincourt* cost one-third of the price of Bentley's 1837 Peacock collection).

Presumably Peacock sold Chapman and Hall the copyright of *Melincourt* in 1856, and not just the right to publish an edition or editions. If, as seems to be the case, Peacock had granted Hookham only the exclusive right to print and sell a specific number of copies, then Peacock controlled all rights to *Melincourt* by 1831 because Hookham's copies were gone.[109] In 1856, the copyright was certain to last until seven years after the author's death; if the entire copyright had belonged to Peacock on 1 July 1842, which seems to have been the case, then it could expire no sooner than 1863 (it actually lasted until 1873 because he lived until 1866).[110] Peacock may not have been savvy about these considerations: in 1861 he noted that he was unfamiliar with 'the present law of copyright', and indeed he was unaware that a copyright could not expire while the author was alive, even though this had been the law since 1814.[111]

---

[109] Again, see *Letters*, 2.232–3, 239.

[110] The 1842 copyright statute declared that an existing copyright would now last either for the author's lifetime plus seven years, or for forty-two years, whichever was longer. The one qualification was that if all or part of the copyright belonged on 1 July 1842 to a publisher or anyone else who had acquired this property in exchange 'for other consideration than that of natural love and affection', then the copyright would be limited to the term authorized by the 1814 statute unless, before this term expired, the copyright-owner reached an agreement either with the author (if alive) or with the author's representatives to the effect that the copyright would last as long as permitted by the 1842 statute. See Peter Burke, *A Treatise on the Law of Copyright* (J. Richards, 1842), pp. 7–9.

[111] *Letters*, 2.423. The 1814 copyright statute law, 54 Geo. III. c. 156 (1814), said that copyrights for new works would last for twenty-eight years, and, if the author were alive after twenty-eight years, for the remainder of his or her lifetime. See Robert Maugham, *A Treatise on the Laws of Literary Property, Comprising the Statutes and Cases Relating to Books, Manuscripts, Lectures, Dramatic and Musical Compositions; Engravings, Sculpture, Maps, Etc. Including the Piracy and Transfer of Copyright; with an Historical View, and Disquisitions on the Principles and Effects of the Law* (Longman, Rees, Orme, Brown and Green, 1828), pp. 66, 68–9.

Peacock's only contribution to Chapman and Hall's *Melincourt* was a 418-word preface, which was probably seen as desirable because after thirty-nine years this novel needed to be re-introduced to the public. Bentley often asked authors to write new prefaces when their works were included in his Standard Novels, for two reasons: additions and improvements were a selling point (the title page of Bentley's Peacock edition mentioned 'corrections, and a preface, by the author') and readers often needed to be supplied with context, because most of the Standard Novels were at least ten years old. Neither objective applied to Chapman and Hall's 'Select Library', which provided inexpensive editions of newer fiction; probably the only reason Peacock wrote a preface was that the publishers thought that they needed to follow Bentley's model in this one instance, to help readers understand the concerns of *Melincourt*. If Peacock's *Melincourt* preface resembles the one he wrote for the 1837 edition of *Headlong Hall*, *Nightmare Abbey*, *Maid Marian* and *Crotchet Castle*, that is because *Melincourt* demanded the same kind of contextualization. Rather than offer *Melincourt* as a document of the past, Peacock emphasized how little had changed since 1817, regardless of whatever people in the 1850s might assume. 'Many of the questions, discussed in the dialogues, have more of general than of temporary application', he wrote in the preface, and, despite the 1832 Reform Bill, some boroughs were still rotten enough that an oran outang might be elected. In 1817 Peacock criticized Coleridge for distrusting the 'reading public'; in 1856 he observed that this public had 'increased its capacity of swallow, in a proportion far exceeding that of its digestion'. Peacock notes some dubious innovations (beards, trains, cigars) without pointing to any counterparts in the world of 1817. In 1837 he emphasized how much had remained the same in the twenty-two years since *Headlong Hall*, and in 1856 he said that things were much the same as in 1817. The *Melincourt* preface has similarities to *Gryll Grange* and might even be thought to foreshadow that 1861 novel, when Peacock observes that 'new questions have arisen, which furnish abundant argument for similar conversations, and of which I may yet, perhaps, avail myself on some future occasion'.

Peacock probably played no role in preparing Chapman and Hall's edition other than contributing the preface (his surviving letters are silent on the matter). The 1856 edition repeats apparent mistakes, including the reference to creatures like Sir Oran being found in 'South America', a mistake that the author probably would have wished to correct. The 1856 text, printed by Bradbury and Evans, conforms to that of 1817 so closely that the compositor surely worked directly from a copy of the Hookham edition.[112]

Two of the three reviews of the Chapman and Hall *Melincourt* treated 'the author of Headlong Hall' as an old acquaintance whose works they were pleased to see made available again. Years after the conflicts of 1817 were past, *The Athenaeum* and *The Examiner* could reflect upon his works with a certain distance. Henry Chorley in *The Athenaeum* did find Peacock's new preface too dismissive of the progress that had occurred since 1817.[113] The *Literary Gazette* thought *Melincourt*'s interest was primarily historical: though 'not a book of great literary ability', it would interest readers simply because it 'recall[ed] scenes of English social and political life of the past generation'.[114] In April 1857 *Household Words* cited *Melincourt* in an article on elections, yet seemed unaware that this novel which first appeared 'forty years ago' had recently been reissued.[115]

The Select Library of Fiction was later taken over by Ward & Lock, who reissued *Melincourt*, now numbered 759, in 1884.[116] The title on the decorated cover of the 1884 edition, *Miss Melincourt or Ten Thousand a Year*, placed Peacock's work in the tradition of the courtship novel:

---

112 See the Note on the Text.
113 [Chorley], *The Athenæum* (19 Apr. 1856), 486.
114 Anon., *Literary Gazette* (19 Apr. 1856), 180.
115 Anon., *Household Words* (11 Apr. 1857), 337–40 (p. 338).
116 See Topp, *Victorian Yellowbacks and Paperbacks*, vol. 2, p. 268.

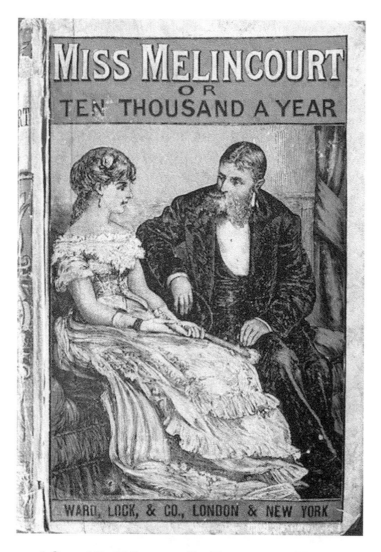

1 Cover, *Miss Melincourt; or, Ten Thousand a Year* (Ward &
Lock, 1884), collection of Nicholas A. Joukovsky

The novel was next published separately in 1896: *Melincourt; or,
Sir Oran Haut-ton*, with an introduction by George Saintsbury, and
with illustrations by F. H. Townsend that are of interest for how

the artist visualizes Sir Oran (London and New York: Macmillan, 1896). *Melincourt* also was included in the three-volume *Works of Thomas Love Peacock, Including His Novels, Poems, Fugitive Pieces, Criticisms, Etc.*, ed. Henry Cole, with a preface by Lord Houghton, and a biographical notice by Edith Nichols (R. Bentley, 1875). [117]

OVERVIEW OF THE NOVEL

Melincourt is Peacock's most ambitious novel, and a recurrent question has been how well his ambitions were fulfilled. Critics have deemed it his weakest completed work of fiction 'virtually without a dissenting voice', as Butler noted. [118] Sometimes they have valued the picture it provides of what Peacock might have wished to achieve in his fiction. Spedding commented that although *Melincourt* was 'a comparative failure', it displayed 'indications of a capacity for a better and a higher strain than he has yet attempted' (a strain that Peacock might yet, in 1839, still achieve). [119] Carl Dawson writes that '*Melincourt* is . . . to a few readers Peacock's most intriguing [novel], for it has its own riches—they are closely related to its flaws—and it offers a complexity of detail and reference missing in the other stories'. Dawson calls *Melincourt* 'a kind of satiric intellectual odyssey, full of incident and wonderfully improbable happenings'; 'Some of its scenes and characters are among Peacock's most inventive, and the boldest of the creations is, doubtless, Sir Oran Haut-ton, Bart.' [120] Among all Peacock's fictional works, *Melincourt*

[117]   The election scene was reprinted in W. H. D. Rouse, ed., *Election Scenes in Fiction* (London and Glasgow: Blackie and Son, 1929) and H. G. Nicholas, ed., *To the Hustings: Election Scenes from English Fiction* (Cassell, 1956). Chapter 31 was reprinted as *Cimmerian Lodge*, ill. Frances Butler (Berkeley, CA: Poltroon Press, 1976).

[118]   Butler, *Peacock*, p. 97. *Mel* is 'in the opinion of most readers his least successful' novel (Garnett, *Novels*, 2.645). It 'is usually considered the least interesting of Peacock's novels', according to George Saintsbury, and he adds that this judgment is correct (*Melincourt; or, Sir Oran Haut-ton*, introd. Saintsbury, p. vii).

[119]   [Spedding], review, *Edinburgh Review*, vol. 68 (Jan. 1839), 447.

[120]   Carl Dawson, *His Fine Wit: A Study of Thomas Love Peacock* (Berkeley: University of California Press, 1970), p. 194.

is 'closest to conventional novel form and to the conventional plots and characters of the "modern novel"', as Gary Kelly points out, and one might predict that *Melincourt* therefore would be popular.[121]

One weakness twentieth-century critics perceived was ephemerality. Dawson notes that 'Successful satire often manages . . . to speak beyond its own generation', and *Melincourt* 'falters' when we ask 'whether as a literary work it holds together'.[122] According to J. B. Priestley, the fact that *Melincourt* is 'the more definitely satirical in intention and the most topical' among Peacock's novels is the reason it has 'lost force with every succeeding year since its first appearance' and 'from being the most admired of all his novels it had gradually come to be the least admired'.[123] Carl Van Doren writes that, 'More than any other of Peacock's novels, *Melincourt* has lost force and appeal with the passage of time, for the reason that the objects of its satire were in many cases of ephemeral interest.'[124] Perhaps the topics with which *Melincourt* deals were too transient to interest later readers; perhaps *Headlong Hall* or *Nightmare Abbey* are more appealing because their topics and characters can more easily be uncoupled from their immediate context and subordinated to concerns that seem permanent, so that, for example, Scythrop Glowry can represent gloomy young men of any decade.

It was unusual in 1817 for 'an avowed satire' to fill 'about 700 pages'.[125] Yet, even if Lionel Madden is correct that *Melincourt*'s great flaw is 'that it is too long', the more frequent complaint is that it 'goes on too long', that Peacock failed to devise enough original incidents or enough variety of action to justify three volumes.[126] One early

---

[121] Gary Kelly, *English Fiction of the Romantic Period, 1789–1830* (Longman, 1989), p. 231.

[122] Dawson, *His Fine Wit*, p. 193.

[123] J. B. Priestley, *Thomas Love Peacock* (1927; repr. Macmillan, 1966), p. 36.

[124] Van Doren, *Life*, p. 95.

[125] [Collier], *Critical Review*, 5th ser., vol. 5 (May 1817), 494.

[126] Lionel Madden, *Thomas Love Peacock* (Evans Bros., 1967), pp. 99–100; Garnett, *Novels*, 2.97.

reviewer commented that 'the author has allowed himself sufficient room to be tedious, and he has not neglected to avail himself of it', while another objected that *Melincourt*'s tediousness was 'the worst of all faults, in a work designed for amusement'.[127] Later critics have expressed similar views. Characters 'talk beyond the point where their comments remain witty', and the narrator, too, 'is seldom willing enough to let his characters carry the burden of implication'.[128] The novel as a whole overstays the reader's patience. The problem 'is not that the later chapters are inferior, but merely that the reader has had enough'.[129] The weakness of the final volume is that Peacock writes 'only one type of chapter—the rambling episodic sort, directed at a specific evil—without, as in the early part of the novel, balancing them with a "percussion of ideas"'.[130] Spedding, surveying Peacock's fiction up to 1839, saw *Melincourt* as a turning point for its author, and inferred that its obvious weaknesses taught him a lesson: Peacock recognized that he had failed to integrate the conversations into the quest romance plot (a fault particularly conspicuous in the third volume), and he saw that he had tried to do too much.[131]

The obvious political alignment of *Melincourt* affected the earliest responses: while Percy Shelley praised it because Peacock revealed himself to be 'an enemy to every shape of tyranny & superstitious imposture', the *British Critic* saw in *Melincourt* 'the cloven foot of infidelity'.[132] Twentieth-century critics saw it as brazenly partisan. Madden and Priestley observe that its readers are too aware of the

---

[127] [Collier], *Critical Review*, 5th ser., vol. 5 (May 1817), 494; *The American Monthly Magazine and Critical Review*, 235.

[128] Dawson, *His Fine Wit*, p. 215.

[129] Ian Jack, *English Literature, 1815–1832* (Oxford: Clarendon Press, 1963), p. 216.

[130] Dawson, *His Fine Wit*, p. 204.

[131] [Spedding], review, *Edinburgh Review*, vol. 68 (Jan. 1839), 446–7. For Butler, 'the essentially prosaic, epigrammatic spirit of the philosophic dialogue does not merge easily into a tradition of romance which requires both extension and mystery' (*Peacock*, p. 98).

[132] *PBS Letters*, 1.518; Anon., *British Critic*, new ser., vol. 8 (Oct. 1817), 437.

author's views, unlike in *Headlong Hall*.[133] David Garnett writes that 'nowhere else does he so obviously take sides, reserving most of his satire for members of the opposite political party' (though Peacock's taking sides brings rewards; *Melincourt* 'in some ways tells us more about the author than any of his other novels').[134] Yet if *Melincourt* tells us about Peacock, it also tells us about his friend Shelley, the inspiration for Sylvan Forester: Madden writes that the author's clarity about his beliefs can be traced to Shelley's influence, an influence conspicuous 'in the social concern about slavery and poverty and the emphasis on the necessity for the rich to display disinterested benevolence towards those less fortunate than themselves'.[135] Madden observes that *Melincourt* is most significant insofar as it reflects 'the author's thought during the period of his closest friendship with Shelley'.[136] According to Mills, Shelley's influence is both good and bad: while *Melincourt* 'is fruitfully engaged with the wider world and newer ideas', it also 'seems strained or constricted at the moments when the author's *attitude* is inseparable from Forester's'. The root of the problem is that Peacock differed too much from his friend: his 'attempt at close intellectual sympathy with Shelley' seems 'false and forced'.[137] When the implied author seems to think as Forester thinks, the congruity appears contrived, as though Peacock has not convinced himself that Shelley's views are correct. Ian Jack observes that Peacock 'was too angry at the political situation, and was seeing too much of Shelley, to give his genius for comedy a free rein'.[138] Van Doren writes that Peacock, recognizing that *Headlong Hall* had tended to be 'purely negative', erred when he tried to add affirmative elements. The fault may lie in Shelley's influence, or in

---

[133] Madden, *Thomas Love Peacock*, p. 85; Priestley, *Thomas Love Peacock*, pp. 35–6.

[134] Garnett, *Novels*, 2.97.

[135] Madden, *Thomas Love Peacock*, pp. 85–6.

[136] Madden, *Thomas Love Peacock*, p. 85.

[137] Howard Mills, *Peacock: His Circle and His Age* (Cambridge: Cambridge University Press, 1969), p. 97.

[138] Jack, *English Literature 1815–1832*, p. 217.

Peacock's 'own failure to perceive how much his real power lay in mockery'. Van Doren, pointing to Forester's boycotting sugar, comments that 'Peacock seems not yet to have been willing to pay the cynic's penalty by laughing at what he secretly admired, sustained by the consciousness that in the cynic branch of comedy all things are folly, in a sense, and fit for nothing so much as laughter'. Van Doren believes *Melincourt* would be better if it were free from 'partisanship', and David Garnett complains, as we have seen, that Peacock concentrates too much on 'the opposite political party',[139] although Peacock was not committed to any party as such: Desmond applies to write for various newspapers and journals, but 'every one was the organ of some division or subdivision of a faction', and he refuses 'to imprison myself in any one of these magical rings' (Chapter 13).

Except for the excursion to Onevote, the action of *Melincourt* takes place in or near the Lake District, which Peacock had visited with the Shelleys in autumn 1813.[140] The author seems interested in this region as a whole, not in specific places.[141] The Lake District's picturesque qualities make it suitable for Anthelia's castle and for her

---

[139] Van Doren, *Life*, p. 96; Garnett, *Novels*, 2.97.

[140] See Nicholas A. Joukovsky, 'Peacock before *Headlong Hall*: A New Look at His Early Years', *Keats–Shelley Review*, 36 (1985), 1–40 (p. 33). Joukovsky comments that 'Little is known about the journey to the Lakes and Edinburgh' (p. 33).

[141] Melincourt Castle and Redrose Abbey are in Westmoreland; Melincourt Castle lies within riding distance of both Keswick and the Low-Wood Inn (ch. 8), which were about 30 miles apart. Sir Telegraph's barouche covers the distance between Melincourt Castle and Redrose Abbey before breakfast, and, after the party dawdles at Forester's home, arrives at the Low-Wood Inn well before the early sunset of a day in late autumn (ch. 19). Alga Castle, on the coast, is only a few hours' journey from Melincourt Castle (ch. 41). When Forester, Fax and Sir Oran debate the effect of mountains, they have crossed into Cumberland (ch. 37). An unnamed inn that the characters visit lies on the route to Gretna Green (ch. 38), but this is true of many inns in Cumberland or Westmoreland. Mr Paperstamp's 'new residence', Mainchance Villa, is not made to resemble Wordsworth's Rydal Mount. The narrator seems uninterested in locales outside the Lake District. The journey across England to Onevote is described vaguely, unlike the journey up the Thames and into Wales that Peacock recounts in *CC*. Mr Hippy lives somewhere in Durham.

abduction (unlike, say, the Lincolnshire fens of *Nightmare Abbey*). Only a few pages into the novel, Peacock describes how Anthelia's mind is affected by 'The majestic forms and wild energies of Nature that surrounded her from her infancy' (Chapter 1). Cumberland and Westmoreland also suggest the Lake Poets – Wordsworth, Coleridge and Southey – who Peacock surely imagined from the start would figure in his narrative. Anthelia's 'splendid visions of chivalry and enchantment' (Chapter 1) instil virtue in her, but communing with waterfalls and mountains does not always have this benefit: Forester acknowledges the 'little horde of poets' who, after settling in the Lake District, shifted their energies to 'the praise of luxurious power, to the strains of courtly sycophancy, and to the hymns of exploded superstition' (Chapter 37).

The action is not compressed as in *Headlong Hall* and *Nightmare Abbey*, but rather extends from autumn to winter, beginning when 'the last flowers of Autumn' can be seen at Melincourt Castle (Chapter 2) and ending in January, at the time of the opening of parliament (Chapter 42). Only changes in the weather and the commencement of the parliamentary and opera seasons mark the passing of time: *Headlong Hall* and *Crotchet Castle* feature Christmas balls, yet the holiday passes unmentioned in *Melincourt*.[142] (Anthelia is kidnapped in November.) The passage of seasons in *Melincourt* perhaps mirrors their passage as Peacock wrote, but, in any case, autumn, a season in which the social elite sojourned in the country, was an apt location for a novel set in Westmoreland. Anthelia's father spent his summers at Melincourt Castle and his winters in London (Chapter 1), but the fashion now, Mrs Pinmoney notes, is to remain in the country as late as November (and then stay in London 'till the end of the dog-days'; Chapter 2).[143] Forester, Fax and Sir Oran's

---

[142] Unless we count the 'Christmas pie' in the song at Mainchance Villa (ch. 39). TLP used a similar time scheme in *CC*, the action of which begins in May and proceeds 'to the middle of autumn', when the narrator jumps forward to Christmas (see beginning of ch. 17).

[143] In 'An Essay on Fashionable Literature' TLP writes that '[t]he fashionable

mid-winter quest in search of Anthelia means that Sir Oran cannot take his seat in Westminster – and misses the opening of the opera. A winter setting befits Peacock's characteristic emphasis on conversation simply because shorter days and colder weather obliged people to spend more time indoors. In *Melincourt*, this advantage might be negated by the characters' long walks, were it not for the fact that walking in the Lake District gives them plenty of time for talk. The action is more mobile in *Melincourt* than in *Headlong Hall* or *Nightmare Abbey*, and various works from the period could have served as pedestrian muses. William Wordsworth's long poem *The Excursion* appeared in 1814. In John Thelwall's *The Peripatetic* (1793), Sylvanus Theophrastus and various friends make excursions around London's southern suburbs and to Rochester and St Albans, meditating on poetry, the poor, wars past and present, gypsies, slavery, Charlotte Smith's sonnets, and the competing merits of Dryden and Pope. (Obviously, Sylvan Forester's name resembles that of Sylvanus Theophrastus.) In Peacock's other 'conversation novels', the master of a country house brings together assorted intellectuals or dilettantes, his role being, as Priestley says, 'to issue invitations to all the eccentrics of [his] acquaintance and then to see that the bottle is kept moving' (Priestley 153–4). But Anthelia Melincourt's visitors settle there to court her, to lay siege to the castle, and so Mr Hippy's only function is to play the role of host, a role that contemporary mores said that only a male relation could fill.

The contemporary context of *Melincourt* that is most challenging to reconstruct is literary: no one else was writing fiction like this. The *Literary Gazette*, reviewing *Nightmare Abbey*, observed that 'It would be difficult to say what [Peacock's] books are, for they are neither romances, novels, tales, nor treatises, but a mixture of all these

metropolitan winter which begins in spring and ends in autumn is the season of happy re-union to those ornamental varieties of the human species who live to be amused for the benefit of social order' (p. 107).

combined.'[144] He drew upon each of the three classes of prose fiction recognized most frequently at the time – the romance, the novel, the tale – and a genre of non-fiction, the treatise, a genre that is discursive and argumentative.[145] The *Monthly Magazine* called *Melincourt* a 'satirical novel' and praised it as the best recent representative of this 'class'.[146] The *Monthly Magazine* in 1829 called *Melincourt* 'a satirical allegory', which was 'a species of writing of unusual rarity in the writings of modern times, as distinguished from those of Greece and Rome'.[147] Peacock's novels also draw on the satirical tradition that originates in the dialogues of Lucian of Samosata and continues in eighteenth-century dialogues such as Clara Reeve's *The Progress of Romance* (1785).

One way to read Peacock in 1817 was to see him as not merely strange but new. The *Literary Gazette* wrote that *Melincourt* exemplified 'a new species of humourous writing', one that, 'taking the novel for its foundation, and the drama for its superstructure, should superadd to both, the learning and enquiry of the Essay'. Upon the conventions that governed the novel, Peacock built an edifice resembling drama, and the whole was suffused with the intellectual content usually reserved for essays. Peacock adopted the forms of the English novel of his own era. The *Critical Review*'s Collier speculated that the author of *Melincourt* had 'given it the appearance of a novel' because readers will be loath to persist reading 'an avowed satire' for 'about 700 pages'.[148] Wishing to write a long, comprehensive satirical work, Peacock recognized that, in order to be read, it must be endowed with the trappings of a novel, such as a plot and characters.

In many respects Peacock's fictional works are Menippean satires, focusing upon ideas and featuring stylized, rather than naturalistic,

---

[144] Anon., *Literary Gazette*, 99 (12 Dec. 1818), 787–8 (p. 787).
[145] On how the terms 'romance', 'novel' and 'tale' were employed in the period, see Raven-Garside, 2.50–1.
[146] Anon., *Monthly Magazine*, 43 (June 1817), 453.
[147] Anon., 'Novels', *Monthly Magazine*, 382.
[148] [Collier], *Critical Review*, 5th ser., vol. 5 (May 1817), 494.

characters. Northrop Frye observed that critics who overlook the Menippean tradition will inevitably view Peacock as 'a slapdash eccentric'.[149] *Melincourt's* fanciful and evocative names declare we are in Menippean territory, even if they are less fantastic than in *Headlong Hall* (the guest list for Forester's Anti-Saccharine Fête does not include Mr Chromatic). Collier remarked that most of the names in *Melincourt* referred 'to the individual, his pursuits, or disposition'.[150] Some names evoke personal traits in such a way that the names would be practical impossibilities. Readers know what they are meant to think of 'the Reverend Mr. Simony' (Chapter 13), and they may wonder why people within Peacock's fictional world do not look askance at his name.

In 1835 Peacock divided fictional narratives which deal with ideas into two categories: narratives in which 'the characters are abstractions or embodied classifications, and the implied or embodied opinions the main matter of the work', and narratives in which 'the characters are individuals, and the events and the action those of actual life—the opinions, however prominent they may be made, being merely incidental'. As Richard Cronin observes, Peacock's 'speakers are not so much embodied opinions as embodied texts'.[151] His footnotes repeatedly attribute ideas and phrases to sources,

---

[149] Northrop Frye's description of the Menippean satire recalls *HH* more than any other TLP narratives: the focus is upon 'Pedants, bigots, cranks, parvenus, virtuosi, enthusiasts, rapacious and incompetent professional men of all kinds', all 'handled in terms of their occupational approach to life as distinct from their social behavior'. *Anatomy of Criticism: Four Essays* (Princeton: Princeton University Press, 1957), p. 309.

[150] Collier noted that some were 'etymological', some 'compounded of cant-phrases'; *Critical Review*, 5th ser., vol. 5 (May 1817), 497. Some names rely upon the Greek language (Lord Anophel Achthar, the Marquis of Agaric, Sir Telegraph Paxarett, Humphrey Hippy), and one relies upon Italian (Danaretta Contantina Pinmoney), but most are simple English. Some are slang, like Dr Bosky. Many placenames, too, are both suggestive and implausible: Onevote, Novote, Gullgudgeon, Mainchance Villa, Alga Castle, Cimmerian Lodge.

[151] Richard Cronin, *Paper Pellets: British Literary Culture after Waterloo* (Oxford University Press, 2010), p. 165.

often providing lengthy quotations. Nowhere else in his fiction does he cite and quote published sources as frequently and fully as he does when Sir Oran Haut-ton is around. The footnotes demonstrate that almost every act of Sir Oran's reflects a claim Monboddo made for the skills and proclivities of oran outangs in either *Of the Origin and Progress of Language* (1773–92), particularly the first volume, or *Antient Metaphysics: or, The Science of Universals* (1779–99), particularly the third volume, published in 1784.[152]

In the first edition, underneath the word 'Melincourt', the half-title leaf prints the epigraph 'vocem comœdia tollit', which would have suggested to readers who remembered the context in Horace's *Ars Poetica* that *Melincourt* was a hybrid of genres. Horace admitted that although comedy and tragedy each has a distinct 'voice', a comic writer sometimes ought to assume the voice usually reserved for the most serious subjects. The author of *Melincourt* promised (or warned) that it was not always comic. If a reader assumed that the proper noun 'Melincourt' on the half-title page was merely the short title and expected elaboration on the title page, he or she would be disappointed. The title page repeats the word, attributes *Melincourt* to 'the author of Headlong Hall', and quotes Jean-Jacques Rousseau on the value of knights-errant, without translation. The word 'Melincourt' would be meaningless to readers who had never heard of Melincourt Falls in Wales. The only other novel published in 1817 with a title this sparse and uninformative was the anonymous *Ponsonby: In Two Volumes*, though 'Ponsonby' was the name of a prominent Irish family, and so the title at least promised a setting among the aristocracy. *Melincourt* is not called *Melincourt Castle*, even though every other Peacock title that refers to a country house contains its entire name – Headlong *Hall*, Nightmare *Abbey*, Crotchet *Castle*, Gryll *Grange*. Perhaps Peacock omitted

---

[152] At his death, TLP owned this first edition of *Antient Metaphysics*, six volumes bound as three, in half calf (*Sale Catalogue* 650). On Monboddo, see E. L. Cloyd, *James Burnett, Lord Monboddo* (Oxford: Clarendon Press, 1972).

'castle' because readers would anticipate gothic fiction, the kind of romance offered by the Minerva Press rather than the kind found in Ariosto.[153] The only 1817 novel with 'castle' in its primary title was *Howard Castle; or A Romance from the Mountains*, written by 'A North Briton', and although *Melincourt* is a romance set amid mountains, it is a romance in the mode of Spenser, and misleading readers about Peacock's satirical purposes would ultimately hurt sales. The title was at least suggestive, yet the *Literary Gazette* averred that the promises made by the title were not kept. 'Melincourt' was 'the most inveterate Novel-name that we have latterly found in a title-page', but the work itself was not a novel, having 'little love, less incident, and . . . not even the common etiquette of a single swoon'.[154]

The Pavilion, or A Month in Brighton, written by 'Humphrey Hedgehog' and published at the same time as *Melincourt*, had the secondary title 'A Satirical Novel'.[155] This phrase was used repeatedly in the period; seven years earlier, Thomas Hookham and E. T. Hookham had offered *Romance Readers and Romance Writers: A Satirical Novel*. The *Monthly Magazine* termed *Melincourt* a 'satirical novel', and a reader's experience might be different if he or she encountered 'Melincourt: A Satirical Novel' at the outset.[156] But Peacock eschewed the secondary titles (such as 'A Romance from the Mountains') that commonly identified a work's subgenre.[157]

---

[153] Five years earlier the Hookhams published Ann Doherty's *The Castles of Wolfnorth and Mont Eagle*.

[154] Anon., *Literary Gazette* (22 Mar. 1817), 132.

[155] The example of *The Pavilion* underscores how the phrase 'A Satirical Novel' had been diluted by its being applied to scandal fiction.

[156] Anon., *Monthly Magazine*, 43 (June 1817), 453.

[157] Prose fiction published in 1817 might be 'A Novel'; 'A Narrative'; 'A Romance'; 'An Historical Romance' (Anne Ker's *Edric*); 'A Romantic Legend' (Anne Julia Kemble Hatton's *Gonzalo de Baldivia*); 'A Tale'; 'A Domestic Tale'; 'A Spanish Tale'; 'A Scottish Tale' (the anonymous *Reft Rob*); 'A Moral Tale' (the anonymous *Conirdan*); or 'A New Story upon an Old Foundation' (the anonymous *The Revealer of Secrets*). Edward Moore's *The Mysteries of Hungary* was 'A Romantic History, of the Fifteenth Century', and Godwin's *Mandeville* was 'A Tale of the Seventeenth Century in England'.

Whereas Scott's *Ivanhoe* (published in December 1819) was disambiguated by the sub-title 'A Romance of the Twelfth Century', the title page of Peacock's *Maid Marian*, closely akin to *Ivanhoe*, does not even call it a 'romance', and readers knew what to expect only if they remembered legends of Robin Hood. The French edition of *Melincourt* termed it a 'roman satyrique', much as the *Monthly Magazine* would. The clearest indication on the title page of the kind of fiction to be expected was the phrase 'By the Author of Headlong Hall', which encouraged anyone who had read Peacock's first novel (or seen reviews) to anticipate in *Melincourt* a satire upon contemporary intellectual foibles.[158] Subsequent editions re-interpreted the novel by changing the title, and re-interpreted it by singling out a character who would be the focus of interest. The French publisher moved Peacock's heroine to centre stage by calling the book *Anthélia Mélincourt*. In 1856, Chapman and Hall published *Melincourt, or Sir Oran Haut-ton*, yet the 1884 reprint of Chapman and Hall's edition chose the same path as the French edition by devising the title *Miss Melincourt or Ten Thousand a Year*.

The *Literary Gazette* divided the characters in *Nightmare Abbey* into two classes: while some represent a 'fashionable folly or doctrine' (Mr Listless is 'a dandy'), others represent specific 'originals' who are 'easily recognizable in the literary world'.[159] Some *Melincourt*

---

[158] With *Mel*, TLP became 'The Author of Headlong Hall', although in Mar. 1817 he could not know that this would remain his signature for all his fictional works. The absence of quotation marks around the title of TLP's first novel – he was 'The Author of Headlong Hall', not 'The Author of "Headlong Hall"' – meant that a phrase which pointed to the author's previous novel was elevated into a proper name. The words 'Headlong Hall' never appeared within quotation marks in a work by TLP before Bentley's Standard Novels edition in 1837, the preface of which was signed 'The Author of "Headlong Hall"', and never appeared within quotation marks on a title page before the 1856 *Mel*.

[159] *Literary Gazette* 99 (12 Dec. 1818), 787. This second class includes Flosky, the 'disciple of Kant', who is 'we suppose aimed at Mr. Coleridge', and Asterias, whose pursuit of mermaids makes a reader think of 'that worthy baronet Sir J. Sinclair' (p. 787). See *NA*, p. lxxxiv.

characters, such as Mrs Pinmoney, represent contemporary follies; others represent identifiable originals. Collier in the *Critical Review* wrote that readers would discern that many characters were 'meant to be representatives of living characters', who might be recognized easily.[160] *The New Monthly Magazine* predicted that 'the likenesses will be instantly recognized by those who are conversant with their history and works'; Collier in the *Critical Review* declined 'to supply a key, partly because it is often not worth explanation, and partly because the extracts we shall proceed to furnish will generally sufficiently explain themselves'.[161] Work remains to be done on the ways in which contemporary readers interpreted Peacock's characters. A copy of the American edition of *Melincourt* now owned by the Library Company of Philadelphia contains pencil notations that identify Feathernest as Southey and Derrydown as Scott.[162]

When Peacock explained *Melincourt* to Victorian readers, he mentioned that the 'opinions and public characters' of well-known figures 'were shadowed in some of the persons of the story'. Fax, Feathernest and Anyside Antijack only 'shadowed' certain men's utterances and acts, and all the utterances and acts were 'public'; they were visible to the public and they affected the public good. Peacock added that he 'never trespassed on private life'; it is also true that he never claimed to draw upon privileged information. In his 1837 preface to *Headlong Hall* and three other novels, he wrote that he had 'never intruded on the personality of others, nor taken any liberties but with public conduct and public opinions' (*CC*, p. 161). For example, when he accuses people of mercenary motives (for example, accusing Southey of aiming only to feather his nest), he restricts himself to evidence that is commonly known and to actions

---

[160] [Collier], *Critical Review*, 5th ser., vol. 5 (May 1817), 498.

[161] Anon., *The New Monthly Magazine*, vol. 7, no. 40 (1 May 1817), 349; [Collier], *Critical Review*, 5th ser., vol. 5 (May 1817), 498.

[162] Library Company of Philadelphia, Am 1817 Pea 2572.D., verso of vol. 2 title page.

that bear consequences for the public. Peacock could have adopted the eighteenth-century political motto 'Measures, not men'.[163]

Some characters in *Melincourt* appear designed to connote one man in particular, even if the reader is unsure which man. Unfortunately, critics of satirical fiction are often eager to say that a character *is* a particular individual. But it is misleading to assert, for example, that Fax 'is based on Malthus' when Fax simply takes positions that conform to those of Thomas Malthus.[164] Saintsbury, who objected to Peacock's treatment of the Lake Poets, assumed that Paperstamp could be equated with Wordsworth and Mystic with Coleridge; he therefore complained that the scenes at Mainchance Villa and Cimmerian Lodge misrepresent the two poets' modes of living.[165] Mr Paperstamp reflects upon Wordsworth, but readers in 1817 would not necessarily infer that Paperstamp's daughter Celandina was meant to reflect on Wordsworth's daughter, if they even knew he had one. Critics seem to wish for Derrydown to represent one man rather than a class, and this desire can lead them into trouble. It seemingly inspires David Garnett to write that Derrydown is 'Based upon Sir Walter Scott',[166] although Scott was not the only man who collected ancient ballads, and Derrydown can hardly be 'based upon' Scott if Derrydown sneers at the *Legitimate Review* (Chapter 17), which clearly represents the *Quarterly Review*, and if Derrydown has not written a book recently (Chapter 17) – Scott had published many. *The British Critic* wrote that the 'phantoms' Vamp, Feathernest and Derrydown represent 'Gifford, Southey, and Wordsworth', but if Derrydown is a phantasmal Wordsworth, who is Paperstamp? Ian Jack asserts that Derrydown's opinions 'represent' Scott's just

---

[163] Lord Chesterfield, letter to the Rev. Dr Chenevix, 6 Mar. 1742: 'I have opposed measures not men'. Bonamy Dobrée, ed. and introd., *The Letters of Philip Dormer Stanhope, 4th Earl of Chesterfield*, 6 vols. (Eyre & Spottiswoode, 1932), vol. 2, p. 490.

[164] Garnett, *Novels*, 2.140.

[165] *Melincourt; or, Sir Oran Haut-ton*, introd. Saintsbury, pp. ix–x.

[166] Garnett, *Novels*, 2.145.

as Feathernest's represent Southey's or Mystic's Coleridge's.[167] Carl Dawson calls Derrydown 'a curious mixture of Scott and Burns', while Howard Mills writes that Derrydown 'reminds us partly of Scott, partly of Coleridge'.[168] If he is a specific person, Derrydown must be someone who collects ballads among the peasantry; he does indeed resemble Scott insofar as Scott did field work when he gathered ballads, but none of the critics explains why Derrydown could not be George Ellis or Joseph Ritson.

The most persistent caricature in *Melincourt* is Mr Feathernest, the poet. Peacock may not have known how closely his critique fitted Southey; it is uncertain when or if he knew that the *Quarterly Review* article he pilloried in the Mainchance Villa chapter had been written by the poet laureate. In early March 1817, Hazlitt implied that it was common knowledge that the author of the Jacobinical play *Wat Tyler*, Southey, was the same man who had composed the recent *Quarterly* attack on reformers.[169] Yet Hazlitt also acknowledged that, at first, many had thought that Canning was responsible for the *Quarterly* article.[170] Antijack, Peacock's Canning figure, is the first person in the Mainchance Villa scene to echo that article, and it is possible that Peacock thought Canning was its author.

The lesson these critics teach us is not that we should resist looking for personal allusions, but that we should be precise about our claims. Critics often fail to distinguish between imitation and allusion: a novelist can model a character upon a real person without

---

[167] Jack, *English Literature 1815–1832*, p. 215.

[168] Dawson, *His Fine Wit*, p. 198; Mills, *Peacock*, p. 123.

[169] Hazlitt wrote: 'if we were told that both performances were literally and *bonâ fide* by the same person, we should have little hesitation in saying to Mr Southey, "Thou art the man"'. *The Examiner* (9 Mar. 1817), 157.

[170] At the end of March, Hazlitt wrote, 'What a squeeze must that be which Mr. Canning gives the hand that wrote the Sonnet to Old Sarum, and the Defence of Rotten Boroughs in the *Quarterly Review!* Mr. Canning was at first suspected of being the author of this last article: no one has attributed *Wat Tyler* to the classical pen of that glib orator and consistent anti-jacobin.' *The Examiner* (30 Mar. 1817), 195.

alluding to that person; an allusion, by definition, is designed to be recognized, but such is not true of all copying. *Melincourt's* Captain Hawltaught probably developed from Peacock's memories of his grandfather, Thomas Love (see Chapter 6, note 10), but few (if any) readers outside the author's family would see the connection, and even if Forester's mythologist friend is 'Thomas Taylor, the Platonist, who called Peacock "Greeky Peaky"', few readers in 1817 would recognize the debt.[171]

Melincourt is a transitional work between the comparative awkwardness of *Headlong Hall* and the polish of *Nightmare Abbey*. Peacock had been developing some conceptions that became prominent in *Melincourt*: Mr Escot in *Headlong Hall* is a preliminary version of Sylvan Forester.[172] Similarly, some satire in *Melincourt* becomes more concise and more vivid in his next book, so that, for example, Mr Flosky is a better caricature of Coleridge than Mr Mystic. While *Melincourt* was a departure for Peacock, in some respects it was a dead end: never again did he range so widely over his contemporary society in this way. Yet certain traits that make their first appearance here became central to his fiction: as Butler observed, Peacock introduces 'his most typical and important idea: the satiric portrait of contemporary intellectuals as a complete class, measured against a single idealised figure, the type of the poet'.[173] *Melincourt* is as close as Peacock gets to 'conventional novel form', as Gary Kelly mentions, and someone who had read no Peacock other than *Headlong Hall* would notice the difference: the action moves across locales, and a courtship plot becomes central.[174] Whereas *Headlong Hall* shows what happens after Squire Headlong decides to bring together a range of 'philosophers

---

[171] Garnett, *Novels*, 2.135.

[172] Spedding wrote that 'Forester, though in some respects only a reproduction of Escot, is a character far more life-like and earnest'; review, *Edinburgh Review*, vol. 68 (Jan. 1839), 449.

[173] Butler, *Peacock*, p. 98.

[174] Kelly, *English Fiction of the Romantic Period*, p. 231.

and dilettanti', *Melincourt* focuses on the question of who will display enough of the spirit of chivalry to attract Anthelia.

Melincourt was the first of Peacock's novels in which the chapters had titles; in 1822, titles were added to the third edition of *Headlong Hall*; *The Misfortunes of Elphin* and *Crotchet Castle* had chapter titles in their first edition.[175] Footnotes are only slightly more frequent than in *Headlong Hall* (which has 29 footnotes in 216 pages, while the first volume of *Melincourt* has 32 in 224 pages) but the notes in *Melincourt* are usually much longer, partly because Peacock quotes Monboddo and others at length whenever Sir Oran is involved. In *Headlong Hall*, Escot's assertions often echo Monboddo's, but Monboddo is cited only once, and there Peacock refers simply to 'Lord Monboddo's Ancient Metaphysics' (Chapter 4), without specifying one of the six volumes. Peacock often leaves Greek untranslated in *Melincourt*, whereas he provided English translations or paraphrases for almost all the Greek in *Headlong Hall*. Although *Melincourt* is in some respects more conventionally novelistic than his other works of fiction, it also relies more on one of Peacock's least novelistic practices, dialogue set up with speech tags. This form of dialogue appears first in *Melincourt* on p. 21 of the first volume, whereas in *Headlong Hall* or *Nightmare Abbey* it does not occur until nearly a quarter of the way through the book.[176]

One recurrent complaint about *Melincourt* over the last hundred years is that the author never should have endorsed specific opinions, even implicitly, and certainly should never have endorsed opinions so much like Shelley's. Critics have suggested that Peacock's taking sides is one reason *Melincourt* has become the least admired among his novels. Priestley writes that the satire in *Melincourt* is 'not, like so

---

[175] TLP increasingly favoured paratextual features: in *MM* (1822) he started giving the chapters epigraphs, and continued the practice through *GG*.

[176] Dramatic dialogue becomes less frequent in *Mel* after ch. 24, as if Peacock forgot about this option, and some conversations that could be printed as dramatic dialogue are not. There is no such dialogue between p. 163 of vol. 2 and p. 63 of vol. 3 of the first edition.

much of Peacock's satire, double-edged': 'Openly declaring himself to be of one party, he proceeds to attack the other.' Forester and Anthelia 'are there to represent a point of view that is meant to be seriously accepted', Priestley writes, and such partisanship is a poor match for Peacock's talents.[177] Carl Dawson writes that, 'Like Escot, Forester is partly ridiculous, but since he is even more of an intellectual and more of a prig, he should have been, at least at the beginning of the story, a more obvious butt of comedy.'[178] Priestley thought that Peacock was doomed to fail when he devised characters whose opinions the reader was expected to accept, and doomed to fail because he 'had not the right kind of imagination'.[179] David Garnett comments that *Melincourt* 'is shrill in tone, and one suspects that in places the shrillness is an echo of Shelley's voice'.[180] Most of these criticisms predated Butler's *Peacock Displayed*, which demonstrates how fully the author immersed himself in substantial controversies of his time. *Melincourt* will always disappoint readers who cannot take these controversies seriously.[181] Critics who write as though Forester will inevitably bore readers may be suspected of bias. One reason *Melincourt* takes opinions so seriously is that it deals with pressing issues, such as slavery, taxation and parliamentary reform, that had an urgency and had consequences which debates over degenerationism often lack. Peacock's satire on Vamp, Feathernest, Anyside Antijack and

---

[177] Priestley, *Thomas Love Peacock*, p. 36.

[178] Dawson, *His Fine Wit*, p. 197. Saintsbury suggests that every reader will 'sometimes put up a prayer for the excision, extinction, expulsion, and general extermination of Mr. Fax' (*Melincourt* [1896], p. viii).

[179] Priestley, *Thomas Love Peacock*, p. 36.

[180] Garnett, *Novels*, 2.99. *Melincourt*'s politics were one reason Shelley preferred it: it was superior to *HH* and *NA* because it has 'more of the true spirit, and an object less indefinite' (*PBS Letters*, 2.244), and the spirit and object apparently involved advancing the cause of reform.

[181] See e.g. Priestley, who writes that, in *Mel*, 'this satirist of the crotchet has now become a crotcheteer himself' and points to 'the frequent references to West Indian sugar and paper money', but opposing paper money was not a 'crotchet' and shunning West Indian products was not eccentric (*Thomas Love Peacock*, p. 37).

Killthedead may be just as simplistic or contrived as his satire on Gall, Treacle, Mac Laurel and Nightshade in the earlier novel, but Peacock emphasizes what is at stake. Shunning horses, sugar or waltzing was unusual, but none of these choices was absurd.

In fact, one of *Melincourt*'s merits is its acknowledgement that opinions can actually be correct. Where *Headlong Hall* targets its characters' dedication to their opinions, and the epigraph announces that the topic is the philosopher's insistence that nature conform to a 'favourite system', *Melincourt* targets the absurdity of opinions – only when they *are* absurd. In *Melincourt*, people can reject conventional wisdom without being silly, so, for example, Forester's deteriorationism is taken more seriously than Escot's in *Headlong Hall*. Furthermore, in *Melincourt* the disputants respond to each other's arguments (even when their views are as antithetical as Forester's and Feathernest's), whereas in *Headlong Hall* people usually talk past each other. Although one theme of *Melincourt* is the question whether events will vindicate the optimism of Godwin's *Enquiry Concerning Political Justice* (1793) or the pessimism of Malthus's *An Essay on the Principle of Population* (1798), Forester and Fax are not just spokesmen for optimism and pessimism.[182] They cannot be reduced to two opposite predispositions, and their discussions are more compelling than the disputes among *Headlong Hall*'s perfectabilian, deteriorationist and 'statu-quo-ite'. In Chapter 24 ('The Barouche'), Forester and Fax act as different voices of a Greek chorus, supplementing each other.[183]

---

[182] See Gary Dyer, *British Satire and the Politics of Style, 1789–1832* (Cambridge: Cambridge University Press, 1997), p. 117. Escot is identified as a 'deteriorationist'; his name implies that he 'is always looking into the dark side of the question' (ch. 1). But he turns out to be complex. Though a pessimist, he can sound Godwinian: he echoes *Political Justice* by boasting that he 'make[s] a point of speaking the truth on all occasions' (ch. 5). When Escot endorses 'disinterested virtue—active benevolence—self-oblivion—universal philanthropy' (ch. 4), he might look good in Anthelia's eyes.

[183] '[U]nlike the immovable *opionés* of *Headlong Hall*, Fax and Forester meet in mutual respect, through which one can influence the other and fresh

Perhaps *Melincourt* anticipates readers such as Sir Telegraph, who, though 'thoughtless', have the advantages of 'a good heart and a good natural capacity' (Chapter 7) – those who are willing to be convinced by a strong argument. What is the relation between the implied author and the narrator, who does not always articulate every message the text seems designed to convey?[184] Where does the implied author stand amid the characters' debates, and where does he stand amid the real-life disputes which these debates 'shadow'? Fax and Forester, the two speakers whose opinions appear to be central, and who even get the last word (in Chapter 40, 'The Hopes of the World'), are sometimes shown to be wrong, so they do not stand in for the implied author. Readers could be fooled when an author declines to reject a position explicitly: the *British Critic* thought that Peacock 'seems to be enamoured of all the absurdities of Lord Monboddo', and the American *Port Folio* said the author 'believes, with lord Monboddo . . . that men formerly had tails'.[185]

Readers are aware of Peacock's narrator, who refers to himself and acknowledges the readers he anticipates. In this respect he resembles Scott's self-conscious story-teller rather than, for example, the vanishing narrator of Jane Austen's *Emma* (1816). Certainly, Peacock's mastery of metaphor is on display. When the narrator notes Mrs

thoughts can be developed' (Mills, *Peacock*, p. 100); 'Certainly Forester and Fax discuss more pressing matters, go into more detail, and argue with more of an eye to nuances than the three philosophers of *Headlong Hall*; unlike Foster, Escot, and Jenkison, they seldom push their convictions to ridiculous extremes' (Dyer, *British Satire and the Politics of Style*, p. 118).

[184] Dawson writes that, when TLP 'footnotes both the narrator and the characters', he thereby distinguishes the narrator from the implied author; he 'calls into question the narrator's judgment, and he implies throughout the novels a standard of values almost as much beyond the narrator's as it is beyond the characters' understanding' (*His Fine Wit*, pp. 161–2). But even though the footnotes make points that the main narrative leaves unstated, that is a difference between modes of reporting, not between degrees of knowledge. The footnotes do not undermine the narrator's judgment.

[185] *British Critic*, new ser., vol. 8 (Oct. 1817), 437; *The Port Folio* (Philadelphia), vol. 5, no. 4 (April 1818), 321.

Desmond's modesty of dress, he explains that in regard to clothing, people fall into 'two classes':

Nature makes the first herself, for the beauty of her own creation: her journeymen cut out the second for tailors and mantua-makers to finish. The first, when apparelled, may be called dressed people—the second, peopled dresses: the first bear the same relation to their clothes as an oak to its foliage—the second, the same as a wig-block bears to a wig: the first may be compared to cocoa-nuts, in which the kernel is more valuable than the shell—the second, to some varieties of the *Testaceous Mollusca*, where a shell of infinite value covers a stupid fish that is good for nothing.   (Chapter 14)

Using more metaphors than would be tolerable if they were deployed with less skill, the narrator shifts back-and-forth four times between the 'classes' until the polysyllabic, Latinate 'varieties of the *Testaceous Mollusca*' is followed by short Anglo-Saxon words: 'a stupid fish that is good for nothing'. *Melincourt* exemplifies Peacock's enthusiasms for archaic vocabulary and for coining words as needed, most of which are used by the narrator. Unusual words include 'circumvallation' (Chapter 9), 'adoperation' (Chapter 18), 'consentaneous to' (used to mean 'suited to', Chapter 31), 'nubilous' (Chapter 31), 'fuliginous' (Chapter 31) and 'irruption' (Chapter 38). Words for which *Melincourt* provides the earliest appearance noted by the *OED*, or the first with a particular sense, include 'titubant' (Chapter 5), 'noometry' (Chapter 13, the only occurrence recognized in the *OED*), 'duplex' (Chapter 17), 'peirastically' (Chapter 18), 'cooper' (Chapter 19, the first occurrence with this sense), 'veridicous' (Chapter 19, only occurrence), 'incipiency' (Chapter 26), 'compotatory' (Chapter 27), 'dialled' (Chapter 32, only occurrence), to 'knock off' (Chapter 34, first use to mean 'to carry out hastily'), 'œnogen' (Chapter 39, only occurrence), 'critico-poetical' (only occurrence cited, 'criticopoetical' in Chapter 39). Words such as 'meteorosophist' (Chapter 31), 'opticothaumaturgical' (Chapter 31), 'pseudolatreiological' (Chapter 31) or 'deisidæmoniacoparadoxographical' (Chapter 31) belong in their own category.

The narrator articulates his opinions. He does so most explicitly in the footnotes, such as those in the Mainchance Villa chapter (Chapter 39), but in the main narration he introduces Feathernest and the Reverend Mr Grovelgrub as Lord Anophel's 'two parasites' (Chapter 8), and he refers to 'a happy medium between the days of feudality, commonly called the dark ages, and the nineteenth century, commonly called the enlightened age: *why*, I could never discover' (Chapter 2). In the first paragraph, the narrator supposes that at least one of Anthelia's suitors must have valued her 'personal qualifications' more than her 'rent-roll and her old castle', and he then asks any reader who finds this supposition too improbable to grant him some 'poetical license' (Chapter 1). When the narrator refers to the 'notion that women are, or at least may be, rational beings' as 'heretical' (Chapter 1), he is criticizing the view that this is a heresy. Sometimes when the narrator uses verbal irony his import is ambiguous. When he refers sarcastically to 'the admirable doctrine, that the positive representation of one individual is a virtual representation of fifty thousand' (Chapter 21), he notes that 'it seemed as if' the people of Novote 'were satisfied of [its] truth', and the reader may wonder to whom this 'seemed' true; perhaps only those who think virtual representation is valid would conclude that the people of Novote agreed.

The narrator's forthrightness is less remarkable, however, than his reticence. He often stays neutral and refrains from evaluating facts or opinions that he reports. He expresses his judgments, but he is more remarkable for how often he withholds them, and how often we are uncertain where he stands. His sarcasm seldom reflects directly on the major characters. And the reader often is on shaky ground trying to discern if the narrator is being ironical. One illustration of the fact that the narrator is less conspicuous than in *Nightmare Abbey* is that *Melincourt* has few of the carefully crafted, sarcastic character sketches that enrich Peacock's next novel, such as the initial portrait of Mr Flosky, or the succinct summary of Scythrop's education.[186] The narrator does not summarize Sylvan Forester's or Sir Oran's traits or histories, but instead lets them emerge naturally, while Anthelia's character is described in Chapter 1 simply because it is necessary for setting the stage.

The *Monthly Review* objected to Peacock's 'giving his own powerful diction' to women such as Anthelia and Mrs Pinmoney, but his diction is given to everyone.[187] Every character in a Peacock novel sounds like the narrator, except for those rare people who use regional dialects, and the narrator, in turn, sounds like the author of 'The Four Ages of Poetry' (1820). The narrator's favoured authors and quotations are adopted by his characters, as well, even by those with disparate viewpoints and disparate views: for example, Samuel Butler's *Hudibras* is quoted by Forester, Feathernest and Mr Sarcastic, along with the narrator. *1 Henry IV*'s Falstaff is quoted four times in *Mel*, by four different characters: Forester (Chapter 7); Feathernest (Chapter 16); Sarcastic (Chapter 21, with no quotation marks); and Sir Telegraph (Chapter 24). This is Peacock's distinctive kind of stylization. When a character's speech resembles a third-person narrator's, the similarity makes the character's sentiments appear worthier of consideration than they otherwise might (this method is one of the most common by which a character is made to seem authoritative). The effect is diluted, however, when all characters sound alike.

Spedding recognized that in *Headlong Hall* the question whether Foster or Escot is correct 'is dissolved, rather than solved; it disappears, and the action closes over it'.[188] The same is true in *Melincourt*, particularly in some of the discussions between Forester and Fax. The debates involving Mr Sarcastic are ambiguous: yes, Forester and Anthelia get the last word with their optimism, but Sarcastic is not

---

[186] The main exception is TLP's introduction of Derrydown in ch. 8.
[187] Anon., *Monthly Review*, new ser., vol. 83 (July 1817), 323.
[188] [Spedding], review, *Edinburgh Review*, vol. 68 (Jan. 1839), 448.

clearly wrong when he argues that human improvement must wait until self-interest brings it about (Chapters 21, 27). Furthermore, the authorities Peacock has cited to buttress pessimism on this question cannot be brushed away; how wrong can Milton's *Doctrine and Discipline of Divorce* (1643) be (Chapter 27)? Some guests at the Fête resolve to boycott sugar only because they recoil from the arguments on the other side. Fax attributes their decisions to 'associated sympathies', which serve to 'give an impulse of co-operation to any good and generous feeling' (Chapter 27).

Some propositions which Peacock appears to satirize may be valid within the novel's imaginary world. For example, Sir Oran behaves as Monboddo's oran outangs would behave if placed in Sir Oran's situation. The point may be that the novel's fictitious world is not the world inhabited by *Melincourt*'s purchasers. Even if Sir Oran's behaviour does not show that Forester and Monboddo are correct about oran outangs, it does not undermine their claims, either.

INTELLECTUAL AND ARTISTIC CONTEXTS

Melincourt invites the reader to situate it within two historical contexts: the years and months immediately before and during its composition, and the wider Enlightenment. Clearly *Melincourt* responds to debates occurring as Peacock wrote, yet most of the texts to which he alludes date from the eighteenth century. *Melincourt* announces itself to be a product of 1816 and 1817, and a product of the era that began with Rousseau. Oddly, it also makes itself a product of the 1790s.

Melincourt was written amid the tumult of late 1816 and early 1817. On 20 November 1816, Shelley reported to Byron that 'The whole fabric of society presents a most threatning aspect.'[189] The harvest of 1816 was the worst in years, in part because temperatures

---

[189] *Shelley and His Circle*, 5.16–17.

were lower after the explosion of Tambora, in April 1815.[190] In the wake of Napoleon's defeat at Waterloo in June 1815, the transition from a wartime economy caused unrest in the British Isles, as soldiers and sailors returned from the war and could not find employment. Mr Anyside Antijack boasts that the victory over Napoleon has benefited 'legitimacy, divine right, the Jesuits, the Pope, the Inquisition, and the Virgin Mary's petticoat' (Chapter 39), and Peacock was not alone in doubting that there was cause for celebration. Cobbett objected that the British 'found the Pope dethroned, the Jesuits scattered, the Bourbons driven out, and the Inquisition put down', and then '*our success* has caused them all to be *restored*'.[191] Parliament was not in session between early July and late January, and the public discussed which steps parliament should take when it reconvened. Shelley noted that the people 'meet, resolve & petition', and until parliament met, 'all classes will probably remain in a sullen & moody expectation of what the session will produce'.[192]

Melincourt was published just as parliament cracked down on dissent, suspending habeas corpus and suppressing 'seditious meetings'.[193] On 29 January 1817, George Canning assured the Commons that habeas corpus must be suspended because of the threats to social order which supposedly were posed by followers of Thomas Spence. Peacock responded in *Melincourt*: when Mr Anyside Antijack refers to 'the *Spencean* blunderbuss', Peacock observes sarcastically in a footnote that despite the dangers attributed to the 'Spencean chimæra', this chimæra had been 'till lately

---

[190] See Gillen D'Arcy Wood, *Tambora: The Eruption That Changed the World* (Princeton: Princeton University Press, 2014).

[191] *WPR* (28 Dec. 1816), 829–30.   [192] *Shelley and His Circle*, 5.17.

[193] The Habeas Corpus Suspension Act, 57 Geo. III. c. 3; The Seditious Meetings Act, 57 Geo. III. c. 19. The main provision of the Suspension Act was that a person accused of 'high treason, suspicion of high treason, or treasonable practices' might be detained until 1 July 1817 if the detention was authorized by a warrant signed either by six privy councillors or by any of the three secretaries of state. See Gary Dyer, '1817: The Year Without Habeas Corpus', *Keats–Shelley Journal* 66 (2017), 136–54.

invisible to the naked eye of the political entomologist' (Chapter 39). In March, Cobbett fled to the United States because people could no longer 'write on political subjects according to the dictates of truth and reason, without drawing down upon our heads certain and swift destruction'.[194] To the extent that *Melincourt* mimics Cobbett, it was mimicking propositions that might be deemed criminal if disseminated in a popular form (the attorney general was too busy prosecuting T. J. Wooler's *The Black Dwarf* and William Hone's 'parodies' to bother with novels, much less with novels that cost 18 shillings).

Was the present economic distress the result of unusual events (the harvest, the transition to a peacetime economy), or was it an inevitable consequence of an illegitimate and unjust political and economic system? Sir William Curtis blamed 'the badness of the harvest, not in this country only, but in others also', and he thought that the people should see their sufferings as 'a dispensation of Providence'.[195] On 2 July 1816, the Prince Regent, addressing parliament, referred only to 'the Pressure and Distress which the circumstances of the Country, at the close of so long a War, have unavoidably entailed'; and to the 'difficulties, which will, I trust, be found to have arisen from causes of a temporary nature'.[196] In late August the weather improved, and Cobbett wrote hopefully that 'a good average crop of wheat' would keep food prices down enough to prevent riots. If riots occurred, the government's 'supporters would impute all the miseries of the country to the rain and the cold', though the real cause was 'that intolerable load of taxes, which takes from the gentleman, the farmer, the manufacturer and the tradesman, the means of giving employment to, and bestowing a sufficiency of wages upon, the labourers and the journeymen'.[197]

---

[194] *WPR* (5 Apr. 1817), 418.
[195] *Times* (29 Nov. 1816), 3.   [196] *The Examiner* (7 July 1816), 420.
[197] *WPR* (31 Aug. 1816), 286. In 1860 TLP remembered that '[t]he first fortnight of September was a period of unbroken sunshine', after the 'perpetual rain' of July and August (Halliford, 8.105).

The author of *Melincourt* was among those who blamed the miseries of the country upon longstanding social and political realities. Peacock's method is complex, however: while *Melincourt* reenacts the debates that dominated 1815–17, it neglects the specific events of those years. Although the controversies are often those of late 1816, the novel might take place in 1810, 1815 or 1825. There are echoes of Cobbett, Canning and Sir William Curtis, and quotations from Coleridge's *Statesman's Manual*, but no references to the bad harvest or petitions for parliamentary reform or the peace – the only recent war mentioned is 'the Antijacobin war' (Chapter 39). By ignoring these realities, Peacock dismisses the immediate causes on which the government and its supporters blamed the people's sufferings, so that those sufferings must appear to be predictable consequences of a bad system – just as Cobbett, *The Examiner* and petitioners to parliament had claimed. No one in *Melincourt* mentions the Spa Fields riots that occurred on 2 December 1816; Peacock declined to draw attention to a complex series of events that had been interpreted so as to delegitimize reformers.[198]

The *British Critic* sneered that the '*reforming* notions' which dominated *Melincourt* were 'much better done in Cobbett, [Henry] Hunt, or [William] Hone' (the reviewer believed that these notions were best not done at all), and Peacock certainly was influenced by Cobbett, whose views on paper money, taxation and parliamentary reform are reiterated by Forester, Fax, Sarcastic, Desmond and even Sir Telegraph.[199] Cobbett blamed the country's sufferings on

---

[198] Spa Fields is alluded to by the narrator in *NA*. The nearest TLP comes to an alternative perspective on Spa Fields is when Forester asks what the views of 'an obscure herd of fanatics' like the Spenceans had to do with 'the great national question of parliamentary reform' (ch. 39).

[199] In May 1818 Peacock updated Shelley (who was in Europe) on the *Weekly Political Register*, commenting that Cobbett was 'indefatigable. He gives us a close-printed sheet every week which is something surprising if we only consider the quantity, more especially if we take into account the number of his other avocations' (*Letters*, 1.123). '[B]y and large, the political goals of *Melincourt* are identifiably Cobbett's goals', Butler has argued, 'and his

'*Paper-Money, National Debts, Standing Armies, Enormous Sinecures, Pensions* and *Grants to East-India Companies, French Emigrants*, &c.', all of which, he insisted, were 'quite NEW THINGS'.[200] Rather than set tenant farmers against landowners or labourers against tenants, as many writers would do, Cobbett argued that all these groups were victims of a parasitical class composed of army officers, lawyers, government officials and hired journalists. (Squire Openhand's misfortunes, which Mr Hawthorn describes for Forester, Fax and Sir Oran in Chapter 32, encapsulate Cobbett's portraits of the problems landowners faced.) The roots of society's problems were sinecures and pensions, and, indeed, all regular payments of government money that did not award merit and labour. (A few years later, John Wade's *The Black Book* attempted to list all government offices and pensions, and how much each of them paid.) For Cobbett, sinecures were not a partisan issue, any more than rotten boroughs were: 'the attack upon *sinecures*, &c. levels itself against the Opposition as well as against the ministry'.[201] Forester and Fax share common ground even though they often disagree, and much of that common ground is Cobbett. Fax, not Forester, proclaims that 'All the arts and eloquence of corruption may be overthrown by the enumeration of these simple words: boroughs, taxes, and paper-money' (Chapter 39).

Melincourt satirizes the unreformed system of parliamentary representation: how could this system *not* be the target, if an ape is elected to the Commons? Before the 1832 Reform Act, 139 of the 203 English boroughs had fewer than 500 voters, and some had far fewer: in 1801, Buckingham had thirteen, Malmesbury thirteen, Marlborough no more than twelve and Winchelsea fewer than ten.[202] When *Melincourt* was written, seven men chose the two

---

presence is felt powerfully in the last volume, which Peacock was finishing just as Cobbett's dispute with the government press came to a head' (*Peacock*, p. 93).

[200] *WPR* (28 Dec. 1816), 805.   [201] *WPR* (3 Aug. 1816), 154–5.

[202] R. G. Thorne, *History of Parliament: The House of Commons, 1790–1820*, 5 vols. (Secker and Warburg, 1986), vol. 1, p. 43; vol. 2, pp. 22, 422, 424, 480.

representatives for St Germans.[203] In a 'rotten' borough, only a few men were entitled to vote to elect the borough's representatives; in a proprietary (or 'pocket') borough, one man or one family by right dictated who the electors chose.[204] Onevote is both rotten and proprietary: Christopher Corporate is the only voter, and he votes as the landowner directs. As Peacock was aware, oddities like proprietary boroughs could benefit the Opposition as well as the Ministry. Winchelsea, which (as mentioned above) had fewer than ten voters, and was controlled by the Earl of Darlington, was represented by the prominent Whig Henry Brougham (later to figure in *Crotchet Castle* as 'the learned friend').[205] The harm of the current system was not only that it aided the ministry presently in office, but also that it restricted representation to a narrow range of political positions.

Money corrupted parliamentary representation in several ways. First, the wealthiest men could purchase a borough. In 1800, Sir Mark Wood paid £90,000 for Gatton Park in Surrey, and, with it, the pocket borough of Gatton, which had no more than seven voters.[206] In 1802 Lord Caledon paid £43,000 for the most notorious rotten borough, Old Sarum.[207] Perhaps Onevote has belonged to the Dukes of Rottenburgh for centuries, perhaps not. Second, a smaller but still substantial sum would buy a seat from the man who controlled the borough. Prices in the first decades of the nineteenth century usually ranged from £4,000 to £6,000; in 1819, David Ricardo bought an Irish seat from Lord Portarlington for four years with a payment of £4,000 and a loan of £25,000.[208] Forester must have sacrificed a huge sum to put Sir Oran in the House of

---

[203] Thorne, *History of Parliament*, vol. 1, p. 21.

[204] See ch. 6, n. 33, pp. 375–6. According to R. G. Thorne, in the period 1790 to 1820, 'Of the 203 English boroughs, 101 duly returned Members sponsored by a patron or patrons in this period, 39 of them . . . without giving patrons the trouble of a contest' (*History of Parliament*, vol. 1, p. 43).

[205] Thorne, *History of Parliament*, vol. 2, p. 480; *CC*, ch. 2, n. 3.

[206] Thorne, *History of Parliament*, vol. 2, p. 380.

[207] Thorne, *History of Parliament*, vol. 2, p. 425.

[208] Thorne, *History of Parliament*, vol. 1, p. 58; vol. 2, p. 682.

Commons. Third, in those boroughs where electors were at liberty to vote as they pleased, they might be bribed. Mr Sarcastic observes that 'A burgess will hold up one hand for purity of election, while the price of his own vote is slily dropped into the other' (Chapter 21). Everyone in *Melincourt* seems preoccupied with electoral and parliamentary corruption: Forester contrasts Feathernest with 'the poorest barber in the poorest borough in England, who will not sell his vote' (Chapter 16); Sir Telegraph will give up his barouche only when 'borough-electors will not sell their suffrage, nor their representatives their votes' (Chapter 24).

After the Duke of Richmond's 1780 proposal for parliamentary reform failed, reform remained a constant theme in radical circles, but it was deemphasized by the Whigs, the main opposition to the Pittite ministries that governed for most of the period from 1783 to 1830. Only one motion in favour of reform went to a vote in the Commons in the five years before *Melincourt* appeared, and that not until 11 February 1817, when Peacock was finishing the novel.[209] Parliament convened on 28 January 1817, and in the first debate in the House of Commons, Lord Cochrane presented several petitions calling for reform, and Sir Francis Burdett announced that in February he would move on this subject.[210] *The Examiner* and Cobbett's *Political Register* demanded reform, and in mid February 1817 Shelley wrote the pamphlet *A Proposal for Putting Reform to the*

---

[209] Thorne, *History of Parliament*, vol. 1, pp. 251–2. On the movement for reform in 1816–17, see in particular John Cannon, *Parliamentary Reform, 1640–1832* (Cambridge: Cambridge University Press, 1973), pp. 167–75. Some reformers favoured annual parliaments and manhood suffrage. In Jan. 1817 Cobbett abruptly converted from householder suffrage to universal suffrage (*WPR* [22 Feb. 1817], 235–7), but many would not go so far. The City of London's Court of Common Council favoured 'shortening the duration of Parliaments, and a fair and equal distribution of the elective franchise among all Freeholders, Copyholders, and Householders paying taxes'; *The Examiner* (26 Jan. 1817), 58. Lord Cochrane told the House of Commons that all who might serve in militias should vote; then he said that suffrage should be extended at least to all householders; *The Examiner* (16 Feb. 1817), 104.

[210] *Times* (29 Jan. 1817), 2.

Vote Throughout the Kingdom, in which he objected that the people must not 'be governed by laws and impoverished by taxes originating in the edicts of an assembly which represents somewhat less than a thousandth part of the intire community'.[211]

One subject of public controversy was how much blame for the present distresses belonged to the rotten and proprietary boroughs. Whereas Peacock's Fax and Forester see human improvement as a long-term project at best, Cobbett argued that annual parliaments and manhood suffrage would quickly transform society. Reform on its own would restore prosperity, while prosperity could not be restored without reform. A reformed parliament 'would instantly put an end to that accursed thing, called *Parliamentary Interest*', so that 'Promotions and rewards and honours in the army, the navy, the church, the law, and in all other departments, would follow *merit*, and not be bestowed and measured out according to the number of votes that the party, or his friends, were able to bring to the poll in support of this or that set of people in power'.[212] A reformed parliament would trim 'the long list of Sinecures, Pensions, grants, and other emoluments'; it 'would remove all disabilities from Catholics and Dissenters'.[213] A reformed parliament would relieve the people of £1 million a year in taxes by reducing payments to the civil list and to the royal family.[214] However, these steps would never be taken by 'the representatives of Old Sarum, Gatton, Queenborough, Corfe Castle, Winchelsea, &c. &c'.[215] On 28 November 1816, the Court of Common Council of the City of London approved resolutions calling for reform, using reasoning much the same as Cobbett's. Although the people's sufferings had many causes, all of these causes must be blamed in turn on '*the corrupt and inadequate state of the*

---

[211] *PBS Prose*, 171. According to E. B. Murray, 'evidence, concrete and circumstantial, suggests that S[helley] drafted the pamphlet some time between 10 and 21 Feb.' (*PBS Prose*, 414).

[212] *WPR* (12 Oct. 1816), 453–4.   [212] *WPR* (12 Oct. 1816), 456–7, 478.

[213] *WPR* (12 Oct. 1816), 468.   [215] *WPR* (12 Oct. 1816), 472.

Representation of the People in Parliament.[216] Peacock's Mr Sarcastic lampoons the claim that MPs who were chosen by a few men might provide 'virtual representation', voting on behalf of those excluded from the franchise. Cobbett wrote that 'The people of Manchester and Birmingham and Sheffield have no inclination to have Members chosen for them by Old Sarum, Gatton, and Winchelsea',[217] and Sarcastic implies that the people of Novote should not rely upon the goodwill of the representatives of Onevote. In 'On the Game Laws', written at some point between March 1816 and February 1818, Shelley commented that the members of the House of Commons 'virtually represent none but the powerful and the rich'.[218]

The Onevote election, which occurs precisely halfway through the novel (in the twenty-first and twenty-second of the forty-two chapters), is arguably the high point of *Melincourt*.[219] While Novote's 'fifty thousand inhabitants' have 'no representative in the Honourable House' (Chapter 21), Onevote's sole resident, Christopher Corporate, is empowered to elect two men. Peacock's description is vivid: 'The borough of Onevote stood in the middle of a heath, and consisted of a solitary farm, of which the land was so poor and untractable, that it would not have been worth the while of any human being to cultivate it, had not the Duke of Rottenburgh found it very well worth his to pay his tenant for living there, to keep the honourable borough in existence' (Chapter 22). Onevote would vanish if some king, centuries earlier, had not made it a parliamentary borough. While many borough proprietors sent to parliament only men who committed themselves to a specific political line, the Duke of Rottenburgh asks nothing of Mr Sarcastic or Sir Oran, but

---

[216] *The Examiner* (1 Dec. 1816), 765.   [217] *WPR* (18 Jan. 1817), 88.

[218] *PBS Prose*, 487, 280.

[219] The election has been called '[t]he best chapters in the whole book' (Priestley, *Thomas Love Peacock*, p. 37); 'the most memorable part of the book' and one of 'the best passages Peacock ever wrote' (Madden, *Thomas Love Peacock*, p. 99). The election at Onevote might be compared to the Eatanswill election in *The Pickwick Papers*. On TLP and *Pickwick*, see *CC*, pp. cxiii–v.

simply sells each seat to the highest bidder. Sarcastic and Sir Oran are obliged to wait for a general election, so neither seat is vacant and two MPs are being displaced – perhaps because they were outbid.

By 1817, it had long been conventional to cite rotten boroughs to convey how small and unrepresentative the electorate was, and it was conventional to contrast them with large, newly expanded cities that remained unrepresented. In *The Rights of Man* (1791), Thomas Paine complained that 'old Sarum, which contains not three houses, sends two members; [while] the town of Manchester, which contains upwards of sixty thousand souls, is not admitted to send any'; in 1792, William Playfair wrote that 'Every one can perceive it to be unjust that Old Sarum should send up two members to Parliament, while Manchester and Birmingham do not send up one' (Playfair added that 'the same injustice takes place, in a greater or less degree, in the election for every borough and county in England').[220] Novote and Onevote are ten days' journey from Westmoreland, 'almost at the extremity of the kingdom' (Chapter 19), and therefore they must lie in southernmost England. While rotten boroughs were plentiful in the southern counties, which contained over half the boroughs that were abolished in 1832, *Melincourt*'s original readers would have thought of one southern borough in particular, Old Sarum, which, like Onevote, lies 'on a barren plain' not far from a city. Tiny electorates could be found throughout the country, and Newton, 15 miles from unrepresented Manchester, had about fifty voters in 1801, but Newton was not infamous like the borough that had lost its inhabitants to Salisbury back in Henry III's reign. [221] Peacock dramatizes the contrast between unenfranchised cities and rotten boroughs by placing his fictionalized Manchester or Birmingham 'a short distance' from his fictionalized Old Sarum (Chapter 21), and

---

[220] Thomas Paine, *Rights of Man: Being an Answer to Mr. Burke's Attack on the French Revolution* (J. Johnson, 1791), p. 57; and William Playfair, *Inevitable Consequences of a Reform in Parliament* (John Stockdale, 1792) p. 7.

[221] Thorne, *History of Parliament*, vol. 2, p. 234.

by inviting the city's inhabitants to attend the borough's election. And just as Peacock put a large industrial city at a spot near Old Sarum, he transported to Old Sarum the loud, boisterous elections, with crowds and speeches, that occurred only in the boroughs with the broadest electorates. Westminster had approximately 12,000 voters and Westminster elections were public spectacles: unruly behaviour was common at the hustings, erected in Covent Garden, and candidates might be physically assaulted.[222] In 1818 Peacock informed Shelley that 'We have been very tranquil in our rotten borough amidst the bustle of the general election which has been attended in one or two places with very riotous proceedings'; the proprietary borough Great Marlow was quieter than Westminster.[223]

In the *Critical Review*, John Payne Collier complained that *Melincourt*'s election scene sent contradictory messages, because the author satirized so indiscriminately and so impulsively: even while Peacock critiques Corruption's apologists, the misbehaviour of Novote's citizens suggests that the common people are too unsophisticated to take a role in governing.[224] The contradiction might be illusory, however: the author might believe that universal suffrage would be premature. Although Shelley endorsed annual parliaments, citing Cobbett's arguments, he thought that abruptly giving the franchise to all adult males would empower those 'who have been rendered brutal and torpid and ferocious by ages of slavery', and therefore voting should be restricted to men who pay 'a certain small sum in *direct taxes*'.[225]

When Sir Telegraph learns that Sir Oran will represent Onevote, he suspects that Forester's goal is 'irresistible exposure of the universality and omnipotence of corruption' (Chapter 6). For Forester, however, this exposure is tangential at most; he is not, like Sarcastic, 'determined to amuse himself at the expense of this most "venerable

---

[222] Thorne, *History of Parliament*, vol. 2, p. 266.   [223] *Letters*, 1.130.
[224] [Collier], *Critical Review*, 5th ser., vol. 5 (May 1817), 501.
[225] *PBS Prose*, 175–6.

feature" in our old constitution' (Chapter 22). Forester's professed motive is to guarantee for Sir Oran the 'respect' which 'attends on rank and fortune' (Chapter 6): he bought Sir Oran a seat for the same reason he supplied him with an estate and a baronetcy, society's esteem (rude behaviour can kill an oran outang). Forester's desire to show that the oran outang is '*one of us*' (Chapter 6) is secondary at most. Forester never considers that society would be better served if he purchased the Onevote seat for himself. Ricardo, in contrast, bought his way into parliament in 1819 so he could advocate for social and economic changes, including resumption of cash payments and parliamentary reform. When Peacock describes the subsequent lives of his characters at the conclusion of *Melincourt*, he seems to forget that Sir Oran is now an MP.

Peacock's critique of 'interest' is paramount whenever he mentions Edmund Burke's pension, Southey's laureateship or Wordsworth's post as Stamp Collector. Forester despises the 'self-satisfied dealer in courtly poetry' who writes 'well-paid eulogiums of licentiousness and corruption', which are repeated by 'hireling gazetteers and pensioned reviewers' (Chapter 16). Sir Gregory Greenmould wants his daughter to marry Sir Bonus Mac Scrip not only because Mac Scrip is MP for 'Threevotes' but also because he has 'two places, three pensions, and a sinecure' (Chapter 38). And there were sinecures. *The Examiner* reprinted a report that George Canning collected a salary of £160 as Receiver-General of the Alienation Office, even though 'the whole of the business is executed by Deputy'.[226] William Gifford received £600 as Comptroller of the Lottery Office and £300 as Paymaster of Gentlemen Pensioners; Southey received £100 annually for being poet laureate, in addition to his pension of £200; Wordsworth's position as Distributor of Stamps brought him £400.[227] (For comparison, Peacock's annual allowance from Shelley

---

[226] *The Examiner* (26 Jan. 1817), 54.
[227] [John Wade], *The Black Book; or, Corruption Unmasked!* (John Fairburn, 1820), pp. 43, 78–9, 89.

was £120.) Cobbett wrote that a reformed parliament would not tolerate 'sinecures given to such men as Canning and Gifford'.[228]

When Peacock was working on *Melincourt*, Cobbett repeatedly arraigned 'paper money' – 'that fictitious trash', 'those despicable and dirty rags' – as a main cause of the present distress.[229] This paper money, like heavy taxation, oppressed landowners, and thus, indirectly, oppressed the labouring classes. In 1797, the Bank of England, the privately owned institution in Threadneedle Street that served as the government's bank, suspended cash payments – that is, they would no longer redeem their banknotes ('promises to pay') with gold or silver – and parliament passed the Bank Restriction Act, exempting the Bank from penalties for their refusal. After the Napoleonic Wars ended, the question of resuming cash payments arose, but the chancellor of the exchequer, Nicholas Vansittart, and others opposed this step because of the war debt.[230] Payments were not resumed until 1821. Cobbett complained that 'fresh bales of paper money' were issued not only by 'the Old Lady in Threadneedle Street', the Bank of England, but also by 'her more than thousand children'.[231] The Old Lady's children were the provincial banks, and the distress in the town of 'Gullgudgeon', which Peacock describes in Chapter 30 of *Melincourt*, reflects the unreliability of country bankers, who, unlike the Bank of England, might abscond.[232] Although slavery,

---

[228] *WPR* (12 Oct. 1816), 466.

[229] *WPR* (1 Feb. 1817), 141. Cobbett had criticized the entire financial and monetary system in his *Paper Against Gold and Glory Against Prosperity*, 2 vols. (M'Creery, 1815), and at the time *Mel* was being written he kept up his assault in the *WPR*. On these monetary issues, see Alexander Dick, *Romanticism and the Gold Standard: Money, Literature, and Economic Debate in Britain 1790–1830* (New York: Palgrave, 2013). On Peacock's *Paper Money Lyrics*, see Dick, pp. 146–9.

[230] In May 1818 TLP informed Shelley that 'The renewal of the Bank Restriction Act . . . is now generally acknowledged must be an annual measure as long as "the system" lasts' (*Letters*, 1.123).

[231] *WPR* (1 Feb. 1817), 139.

[232] In Aug. 1816 *The Examiner* reported that banks in Huddersfield, Chipping Norton and Tamworth had ceased making payments; *The Examiner* (4 Apr. 1816), 491. In TLP's *Paper Money Lyrics*, 'Newspaper Man' announces

population and reform figure in the first chapters involving Forester and Fax, paper money is not mentioned until halfway through *Melincourt* (Chapter 21), and it is possible that Peacock suddenly was inspired to address this issue. In his fragmentary *Calidore*, the title character brings gold coins to Britain from his home on Terra Incognita, and the gold astonishes a Welsh vicar 'who had seen nothing but paper-money for twenty years' (Halliford, 8.316). When Mr Chainmail in *Crotchet Castle* discovers that Susanna's father is a banker who absconded, he rationalizes the offence by saying that he has 'always understood, from Mr Mac Quedy, who is a great oracle in this way, that promises to pay ought not to be kept; the essence of a safe and economical currency being an interminable series of broken promises' (pp. 259–60). When the *Paper Money Lyrics* were published, in 1837, Peacock wrote in his preface that the poems, though over ten years old, would remain relevant as long as the currency 'consists of a series of paper promises, made with the deliberate purpose, that the promise shall always be a payment, and the payment shall always be a promise' (Halliford, 7.100).

Because sugar was provided by slave labour, Forester shuns it himself and urges others to boycott it.[233] The *Literary Gazette* thought this aspect of *Melincourt* was dated: Peacock's 'Antisaccharine fête has become obsolete' because of 'the abolition of the Slave-Trade'. Indeed, after 1807, the slave trade was illegal throughout the British Empire. Ending the British slave trade did not end slavery, however. The trade continued under other flags, and slavery itself remained legal in British colonies until 1833. Nor did the 1807 Act stop slavery from appearing in fiction – the example of Austen's *Mansfield Park*,

---

that 'The respectable old firm, / (We have much concern in saying,) / Kite, Grubbings, and Muckworm, / Have been forced to leave off paying' (Halliford, 7.107). Elsewhere in the *Paper Money Lyrics*, 'R— S—, Esq., Poet Laureate' presents an epic poem relating the 'wild and wondrous tale' of what occurred when 'Fly-by-Night went down, / And set a bank up in a country town' (Halliford, 7.111).

[233] This is one issue that did not interest Cobbett, as Butler notes (*Peacock*, p. 93).

published in May 1814, is evidence enough. In 1815 the Treaty of Paris committed its signatories to worldwide abolition of the slave trade, but it gave no timetable.[234] In this context, Peacock's focus on products of the West Indies shows that he is interested in concentrating people's attention on slavery itself.

Mr Mystic repeatedly voices sentiments that Peacock attributes to 'Coleridge's Lay Sermon', meaning Coleridge's new intervention into the state of the nation, *The Statesman's Manual or The Bible the Best Guide to Political Skill and Foresight: A Lay Sermon Addressed to the Higher Classes of Society*. This short treatise was published in December 1816, although it had been announced earlier, and in September *The Examiner* had published Hazlitt's anticipatory review condemning it.[235] Peacock neglects now-famous elements of *The Statesman's Manual* such as the distinction between symbol and allegory in favour of an attack upon Coleridge's obfuscation and reactionary politics. *The Statesman's Manual* was 'Addressed to the Higher Classes of Society', and Coleridge thought that every book should be directed 'to its appropriate class of Readers', although this discrimination had been ruled out by the emergence of a 'reading public' – for him, an oxymoron.[236] Mystic's devotion to 'the immortal Kant' is remarkable because Kant's name appears only once in *The Statesman's Manual* (in one of the appendices), and Hazlitt's writings, which appear to have influenced Peacock, did not emphasize Coleridge's interest

---

[234] For this provision of the Treaty of Paris, see *The Parliamentary Debates from the Year 1803 to the Present Time*, vol. 32 (printed T. C. Hansard, 1816), pp. 200–1.

[235] See n. 43, above. Godwin read *The Statesman's Manual* on 26 Dec. 1816, and Mary Shelley read it on 2 and 3 Jan. 1817 in Bath, perhaps enjoying a copy that she and her husband had brought with them from London the day before (*MWS Journal*, 153). Percy Shelley read it before the end of 1816, and it appears in his reading list for that year (*MWS Journal*, 98). Coleridge's most recent volume of poetry, *Christabel, Kubla Khan, The Pains of Sleep*, plays no role in *Melincourt*, despite Hazlitt's memorable critique of it in *The Examiner* for 2 June 1816 (348–9).

[236] Samuel Taylor Coleridge, *Lay Sermons*, ed. R. J. White (Princeton: Princeton University Press, 1972), p. 36.

in the philosopher.[237] (Kant is prominent in Coleridge's *Biographia Literaria*, but that work was not published until July 1817.) Kant was a byword for obscurity in Peacock's mind, so he was the ideal choice to be Mystic's hero. Peacock was not 'a German scholar', and someone who did not read German could have only superficial knowledge of Kant in 1816.[238] The *Critique of Pure Reason* was not translated into English until 1838. In a footnote Peacock cites various sources on Kant (none by Coleridge), including the source that clearly influenced *Melincourt* most, *Academical Questions* (1805) by William Drummond, who misunderstood Kant's ideas. By the time of *Nightmare Abbey*, Peacock had more material from which to work, and his next Coleridge figure, Mr Flosky, benefits.

Despite this immersion in the controversies and writings of 1816–17, most of the texts that figure in *Melincourt* appeared between 1762 and 1799.[239] Some (Godwin, Malthus, Condorcet, Weld, Louvet) first reached print in the 1790s, though some (Monboddo, Buffon, Rousseau, Junius) come from earlier in the period. *Melincourt* is in many ways an eighteenth-century book. Consider the use of keywords such as 'corruption' or 'disinterested'. These two words are mutually exclusive in eighteenth-century civic republican thinking: corruption is the failure to be disinterested, and disinterested action is not corrupt. The adjective 'disinterested' appears as a term of praise throughout *Melincourt*, where Peacock's main target is the selfish insistence on individual benefit that prevents people from acting virtuously. The first paragraph of *Melincourt* celebrates the suitor who might experience 'disinterested passion'. The causes of a man's 'passion' for a woman and the causes behind political commitments may seem too different for comparison, but Peacock's point is that they all are corrupted by avarice. Readers in 1817 might have

---

[237] For Kant's name, see *Lay Sermons*, p. 114.

[238] *Letters*, 2.284; René Wellek, *Immanuel Kant in England, 1793–1838* (Princeton: Princeton University Press, 1931).

[239] Early modern literature is clearly prominent, too: Ariosto, Tasso and Fletcher, along with Shakespeare and Milton.

been surprised that *Melincourt* refers so often to Monboddo, whose works were curiosities of the Enlightenment (the volumes that Peacock cites most frequently date from 1773 and 1784). Because Monboddo's writings were so old, readers were less likely to see Peacock as satirizing his ideas and more likely to see Peacock as simply needing to have a gentlemanly oran outang.[240]

The two most vocal debaters in *Melincourt*, Forester and Fax, often echo Monboddo and Malthus. Forester endorses two of Monboddo's contentions. The first is the thesis that the 'Orang Outang' (a class that comprises most or all kinds of anthropoid apes) represents man in his natural state, and Peacock's main source is the first volume of *The Origin and Progress of Language*, published in 1773, particularly chapters four and five. The second is the conviction that the human species has degenerated physically, and here Forester and Peacock rely upon the third volume of Monboddo's *Antient Metaphysics*, published in 1784. Malthus was a pessimist of a different kind, arguing that misery and vice play a regrettable but necessary role in keeping population down: one of 'the causes that have hitherto impeded the progress of mankind towards happiness' was 'the constant tendency in all animated life to increase beyond the nourishment prepared for it'.[241] When Fax first appears, he seems purely Malthusian. The chapter that introduces him borrows from the title of Malthus's famous *Essay on the Principle of Population*, and Fax soon blames 'all the evils of human society' upon 'the tendency of population to

---

[240] See Joukovsky, 'Peacock's Sir Oran Haut-ton', 185–9, for the argument that Peacock thought of Monboddo because of Shelley.

[241] T[homas] R[obert] Malthus, *An Essay on the Principle of Population; or, A View of Its Past and Present Effects on Human Happiness; with An Inquiry into Our Prospects Respecting the Future Removal or Mitigation of the Evils Which It Occasions. A New Edition, Very Much Enlarged* (J. Johnson, 1803), pp. 1–2. We know what edition TLP had access to because *Mel* quotes a passage that Malthus omitted after 1803; see ch. 42, n. 16. On Malthus, see James Huzel, *The Popularization of Malthus in Early Nineteenth-Century England: Martineau, Cobbett and the Pauper Press* (Burlington, VT: Ashgate, 2006); Robert Mayhew, *Malthus: The Life and Legacies of an Untimely Prophet* (Cambridge, MA: Harvard University Press, 2014).

increase beyond the means of subsistence' (Chapter 7). Fax argues that these evils can be prevented by 'an universal social compact' which commits everyone to celibacy until society can be sure of people's 'maintaining the average number of six children' (Chapter 7). Yet Fax later supplements his Malthusian concern about overpopulation with a critique of the highest classes that evokes Cobbett. Cobbett had complained that when Malthus contemplated the poor's sufferings, he ignored 'the *real cause*, the *taxes*',[242] but Fax repeatedly notes the damage caused by heavy taxation, and when he says that 'All the arts and eloquence of corruption' can be refuted simply by pointing to 'boroughs, taxes, and paper-money' (Chapter 39), his rhetoric is not Malthus's but Cobbett's. Fax acknowledges the danger of overpopulation, but sees that the danger would be less, were it not for abuses such as rotten boroughs. Fax does find it unfortunate that the lower classes 'marry by wholesale . . . and commit the future care of their family to Providence and the overseer' (Chapter 7). Cobbett, addressing labourers, argued that Malthus's views on marriage were merely another instance of the poor being oppressed by privileged men: some of 'the Corrupt', he argued, view 'your *early marriages* as a great evil, and a *Clergyman*, named MALTHUS, has seriously proposed measures for *checking* you in this respect'.[243]

Peacock finds Malthus more reasonable than some others did; never does *Melincourt* suggest that Malthus is one of 'the Corrupt', as Cobbett asserted, or that ideas like Malthus's must be 'those of a eunuch & of a tyrant', as Shelley proclaimed.[244] Fax's arguments

---

[242] *WPR* (4 Jan. 1817), 27.   [243] *WPR* (2 Nov. 1816), 562.

[244] *Shelley and His Circle*, 6.1023. In the preface to *The Revolt of Islam*, written shortly after *Melincourt*, Shelley suggested that Malthus's 'sophisms' were 'calculated to lull the oppressors of mankind into a security of everlasting triumph' (Percy Bysshe Shelley, *The Revolt of Islam; A Poem, in Twelve Cantos* [C. and J. Ollier], 1818), pp. xi–xii). In *A Philosophical View of Reform* (written between Nov. 1819 and Jan. 1820) Shelley stated that Malthus argued that the poor ought to be 'required to abstain from marrying under penalty of starvation'. After these people 'have been stript naked by the tax gatherer & reduced to bread & tea & fourteen hours of hard labour by their masters', they should

when debating with Forester in Chapter 11 (on love) are not absurd or groundless, even though the Malthusian proposition Peacock emphasizes, celibacy, is the one that so offended Shelley. While Malthus's critics claimed he was detached from humanity, Fax's analysis is put in service of a progressive utilitarianism. He pays Desmond's debt. Fax is not a 'priest', and he appears to have no ulterior motive in advocating population control, which he favours only because it can reduce human suffering. Cobbett was indignant that Malthus would perceive 'a young man, arm-in-arm with a rosy-cheeked girl' as 'a spectacle of evil omen',[245] and *Melincourt* envisions Malthusian arguments being addressed to a peasant couple arriving at a church to be married – a young man named Robin Ruddyface and, grasping his arm, 'a strong, healthy-looking country girl' named Susan. Fax's frustrations in trying to get Robin to recognize the demands made by 'general reason' are played for laughs (Chapter 35), yet the author's point is ambiguous: obviously Fax's efforts are futile, given his audience and the occasion, but his warnings are well-founded: did a person need to be a Malthusian in order to think that Robin and Susan ought to plan for the future?

In 1816, British culture might have seemed to be re-living the 1790s. On 28 November, Sir William Curtis said that his reply to arguments for parliamentary reform was simple: 'I am quite satisfied with things as they are.' The comment was met with 'great laughter'.[246] One cause of the hilarity may have been that hearers were startled by the phrase 'things as they are'. In the 1790s, this phrase was used frequently by people of reformist sympathies when they contrasted regrettable actuality with potential improvement; 'things as they are' needed to be distinguished from things as they might be. Godwin's *Enquiry Concerning Political Justice* had warned of danger if the public heard only 'praise of things as they are'. The phrase was most familiar

---

now, according to Malthus, be forced to relinquish 'the one thing which made it impossible to degrade them below the beasts' (*Shelley and His Circle*, 6.1024). [245] *WPR* (2 Nov. 1816), 563.   [246] *Times* (29 Nov. 1816), 3.

to Peacock's generation because of Godwin's novel *Things as They Are; or, The Adventures of Caleb Williams*, designed to address 'The question now afloat in the world respecting THINGS AS THEY ARE': 'While one party pleads for reformation and change, the other extols in the warmest terms the existing constitution of society.'[247] In Mary Wollstonecraft's *Maria; or, The Wrongs of Woman* (1798), Darnford says smugly that 'If the poor are happy, or can be happy, *things are very well as they are*.'[248] Curtis echoed the villains of 1790s fiction, even if he was unaware he did so, and one of Peacock's villains, Anyside Antijack, echoes Curtis when he advocates taking 'the public money' and telling the public, 'I am perfectly satisfied with things as they are' (Chapter 39).[249] An even more notorious catchphrase from the 1790s appears in *Melincourt* when Mr Sarcastic promises to ignore 'the whole swinish multitude' (Chapter 21), when Mr Mystic regrets that the reading public includes 'the swinish multitude' (Chapter 31) and when Anyside Antijack is sorry to see Forester 'taking the part of the swinish multitude' (Chapter 39). The obvious source was Burke's *Reflections on the Revolution in France* (1790), in which he predicted that 'learning will be . . . trodden down under the hoofs of a swinish multitude'.[250] Radicals in the 1790s threw the term back

---

[247] William Godwin, *An Enquiry Concerning Political Justice, and Its Influence on General Virtue and Happiness*, 2 vols. (G. G. and J. Robinson, 1793), vol. 2, p. 643; William Godwin, *Things as They Are; or, The Adventures of Caleb Williams*, 2nd ed., 3 vols. (G. G. and J. Robinson, 1796), vol. 1, [p. v]. In 1809 TLP received a copy of *Political Justice* from E. T. Hookham (*Letters*, 1.36).

[248] [Mary Wollstonecraft], *Posthumous Works of the Author of Vindication of the Rights of Woman*, 4 vols. (J. Johnson and G. G. and J. Robinson, 1798), vol. 1, p. 114.

[249] The narrator elsewhere comments that 'political economists' have argued that money, food or drink will placate 'the friends of *things as they are*' (ch. 24). *NA* suggests how reactions against things as they are can become inefficacious: Scythrop proclaims that 'Ardent spirits cannot but be dissatisfied with things as they are'; they 'rush into the extremes of either hope or despair', into either 'enthusiasm' or 'misanthropy' (p. 51).

[250] *The Writings and Speeches of Edmund Burke*, gen. ed. Paul Langford, 9 vols. (Oxford: Clarendon Press, 1981–2015), vol. 8: *The French Revolution, 1790–1794*, ed. L. G. Mitchell (1989), p. 130.

in Burke's face, acknowledging, sarcastically, that the lower orders were swine: the title of Thomas Spence's *Pig's Meat* (1793–4) is one of the best-known instances. In February 1817 Cobbett wrote that there still might be, 'as there have been, men to call us the "*Swinish Multitude*"'.[251]

Phrases such as 'things as they are' and 'the swinish multitude' suggest how much the political and intellectual battles of the 1790s shape *Melincourt*. One reason the 1790s are so conspicuous is that the ideological conflicts of that decade had been revivified in the year and a half since Waterloo. Certainly, contemporary writers (Shelley, Cobbett, Coleridge) drew upon the ideas and the terms used in earlier debates. Curtis's tone-deaf endorsement of 'things as they are' fitted into a pattern. Anyside Antijack's name reminds the reader of *The Anti-Jacobin*, the newspaper to which Canning contributed in 1797 and 1798, and Antijack echoes a speech Canning made a few weeks before *Melincourt*'s appearance, a speech suggesting that he thought the 1790s had never ended. Because some of the men behind the Spa Fields gathering in December 1816 were inspired by the late Thomas Spence, Canning linked all calls for parliamentary reform to Spencean ideas; from Peacock's perspective, such an appeal to fears of a discredited doctrine from the 1790s looked merely paranoid. At this time, Cobbett and *The Examiner* repeatedly reminded Southey and Dr John Stoddart (writer for *The Times*) of their radical pasts, and in August and September 1816 *The Examiner* reprinted several early Southey poems under the title 'Acanthologia. Specimens of Early Jacobin Poetry', attributing them to 'Robert Southey, Esq. Poet-Laureate'.[252] Southey himself was apt to return to the 1790s, as in his *Quarterly Review* article that Peacock exploits in the Mainchance Villa episode. Like Forester and Shelley, Peacock admired Southey's poetry but despised him for abandoning his early progressive politics

---

[251] *WPR* (1 Feb. 1817), 150.
[252] See *The Examiner* (11 Aug. 1816), 504; (18 Aug. 1816), 521; (25 Aug. 1816), 538; (1 Sept. 1816), 552; (15 Sept. 1816), 586.

and for his recent defences of the *status quo*. Serendipity decreed that at nearly the time when *Melincourt* appeared, Southey suffered the embarrassment of seeing his radical play *Wat Tyler*, written in the 1790s, published without authorization.[253] Anthelia's sentiments often echo those of Mary Wollstonecraft, and her final confrontation with Lord Anophel Achthar closely resembles a scene in Thomas Holcroft's *Anna St. Ives* (1792).[254] Godwin would certainly have admired Anthelia's 'uniform sincerity' (Chapter 42).[255]

Anthelia announces that she requires in a husband 'the spirit of the age of chivalry, manifested in the forms of modern life' (Chapter 8), and, like *Crotchet Castle*, *Melincourt* is an important as well as idiosyncratic contribution to the nineteenth-century resurgence of interest in the Middle Ages. Burke complained in 1790 that 'the age of chivalry is gone', but Britain seemed intent on reviving aspects of that age.[256] One of Peacock's objections to the contemporary cult of medievalism might have been that its adherents disregarded knightly selflessness in favour of trifling or absurd medieval practices.[257] When Harum O'Scarum hears Anthelia endorse chivalry, he envisions challenging his rivals to duels; for Derrydown, chivalry suggests imitations of old ballads; Sir Telegraph Paxarett looks for the modern-day equivalent of 'tilts and tournaments, and trials of skill and courage' and finds it in a 'four-in-hand race' (Chapter 8).

---

[253] See *Robert Southey: Later Poetical Works, 1811–1838*, gen. ed. Tim Fulford and Lynda Pratt, 4 vols. (Pickering & Chatto, 2012), vol. 3: *Poems from the Laureate Period, 1813–1823*, ed. Lynda Pratt, Daniel E. White, Ian Packer, Tim Fulford and Carol Bolton, pp. 441–60.

[254] Butler observes that Anthelia's 'abduction and threatened rape' reads like *Anna St. Ives* (*Peacock*, p. 80). Anthelia's insistence that nothing Achthar might do can shame her (ch. 42) would be commended by Wollstonecraft, who wrote that 'miserable beyond all names of misery is the condition of a being, who could be degraded without its own consent!'; Mary Wollstone-craft, *A Vindication of the Rights of Woman: with Strictures on Political and Moral Subjects* (J. Johnson, 1792), p. 157.

[255] See Godwin, *Political Justice*, vol. 1, p. 96; vol. 2, pp. 494–5.

[256] *The French Revolution, 1790–1794*, p. 127.

[257] TLP would depict the Middle Ages in *MM* and *ME*; in chs. 9 and 10 of *CC*, Chainmail and Mac Quedy debate Scott's version of the Middle Ages.

But there is a chivalric 'spirit' that is far from trivial. It had even become conventional to differentiate the spirit of medieval chivalry from its form, and to applaud the spirit's endurance. In his *View of the State of Europe During the Middle Ages* (1818), Henry Hallam wrote that 'The spirit of chivalry left behind it a more valuable successor' when 'The character of knight gradually subsided in that of gentleman',[258] and Scott in his *Encyclopaedia Britannica* article 'Chivalry' (written in 1817) wrote that 'from the wild and over-strained courtesies of chivalry has been derived our present system of manners'.[259]

Indeed, one thesis of *Melincourt*, articulated by Anthelia early in the novel and developed throughout, is that within medieval chivalry lay a set of values that ought to be cultivated in any era. Mrs Pinmoney says, echoing Burke, that 'The age of chivalry is gone', and she is indifferent to its passing and replacement by a commercial era. Anthelia responds that 'its spirit survives', the spirit of 'disinterested benevolence'. It is chivalrous 'To protect the feeble—to raise the fallen—to liberate the captive—to be the persevering foe of tyrants', and therefore one can 'find as true a knight-errant in a brown coat in the nineteenth century, as in a suit of golden armour in the days of Charlemagne' (Chapter 2). (In the quotation Peacock placed on each title page of *Melincourt*, Rousseau chastises his own age for laughing at knights errant.) Mr Feathernest further associates chivalry with 'disinterested benevolence', even though he has abandoned it (Chapter 8). Peacock has crossbred Romantic medievalism with the radical ethics of Godwin, who wished to replace chivalry with the 'system of disinterested benevolence' he celebrated in *Political Justice*.[260] *Melincourt* re-imagines this benevolence

---

[258] Henry Hallam, *View of the State of Europe During the Middle Ages*, 4 vols. (Philadelphia: Thomas Dobson, 1821), vol. 4, p. 364.

[259] [Scott], 'Chivalry', *Supplement to the Fourth, Fifth, and Sixth Editions of the Encyclopaedia Britannica: With Preliminary Dissertations on the History of the Sciences* (Edinburgh: Archibald Constable, 1824), vol. 3, p. 126.

[260] Godwin, *Political Justice*, vol. 1, p. 359. Though often critical of medieval

as constituting, in Anthelia's words, 'the mainspring of all that is really admirable in the days of chivalry' (Chapter 2). Peacock's chivalry is not neutral politically, and when Lord Anophel Achthar hears chivalry defined in terms of 'truth and liberty—disinterested benevolence—self-oblivion—heroic devotion to love and honour—protection of the feeble, and subversion of tyranny', he exclaims that these things are 'All the ingredients of a rank Jacobin'. To the hireling poet Feathernest, the word 'chivalry' seems like a 'spectre of his youthful integrity' (Chapter 8). The narrator and the characters refer repeatedly to romance narrative – Spenser, Ariosto, Tasso – thereby giving the reader the sense that *Melincourt* is a quest romance in which the participants know they are in a quest romance.[261] Peacock identifies his protagonists with the heroes and heroines of medieval and Renaissance romance, and he affiliates their reformist, enlightened ideas with chivalry to which his unsympathetic characters are cold.

Sir Oran is one of the most intertextual characters in literature: Peacock's footnotes repeatedly cite Monboddo in order to authenticate Sir Oran's characteristics, such as his strength, his bravery, his loyalty and his enthusiasm for music.[262] Years later, Peacock wrote

chivalry or its modern remnants, Godwin did write in his *Life of Geoffrey Chaucer* (1803) that chivalry and romance were the origins of 'the principle of modern honour in the best sense of that term, the generosity of disinterested adventure, and the more persevering and successful cultivation of the private affections'. William Godwin, *Life of Geoffrey Chaucer, the Early English Poet: Including Memoirs of His Near Friend and Kinsman, John of Gaunt, Duke of Lancaster: with Sketches of the Manners, Opinions, Arts and Literature of England in the Fourteenth Century*, 2 vols. (Richard Phillips, 1803), vol. 1, p. 361.

[261] See Butler's account of the role of romance in *Mel* (*Peacock*, pp. 67–9). For TLP's acerbic account of medieval romance, see 'The Four Ages of Poetry', *NA*, Appendix C, p. 146.

[262] Not surprisingly, Sir Oran has received attention from scholars who examine relations of the human and the non-human. Laura Brown, for example, argues that 'Sir Oran provides an object lesson in the flexibility of the representation of animal-kind in the modern period. In this single imaginary animal we can find an anthropomorphic projection of human virtue as well as a fearful vision of violent alterity'; Brown, *Homeless Dogs and Melancholy*

that he 'condensed Lord Monboddo's views of the humanity of the Oran Outang into the character of *Sir Oran Haut-ton*'.[263] Sir Oran encapsulates Monboddo's thesis that the oran outang 'is an animal of the human form, inside as well as outside'.[264] He possesses several traits that Forester or Monboddo claims are unique to humanity, such as love of music and 'a sense of honour' (Chapter 6). Indeed, Sir Oran represents what would happen if one of Monboddo's oran outangs were to be integrated into English society. Furthermore, Peacock takes from Buffon and others the idea that oran outangs were the originals of mythological figures like pans and satyrs, and Sir Oran is compared to a range of figures from literature: Ajax, Orson, the Satyr in Fletcher's *The Faithful Shepherdess*.

Sir Oran's true place in the natural order remains ambiguous because the narrator never describes him in any detail. He stands erect like a man; he walks as a man walks; and, after he drinks too much wine, his gait, though unsteady, still appears human (Chapter 5). His hands are such that he can hold a candle (see Chapter 33, explanatory note 4). Mrs Pinmoney describes Sir Oran as '*very* tall', which no one would say of a gorilla or orangutan, but Monboddo's 'pongos', a subspecies of oran outangs, reached 7 to 9 feet (and walked upright), while one 'young' oran outang was 'six feet and a half tall'.[265] The physician who accompanied Lord Amherst's diplomatic mission which in 1817 brought back an 'Orang-Outang of Borneo' explained that this species had been confused with the African ape 'which has also been called Orang-Outang, but is more

---

Apes: Humans and Other Animals in the Modern Literary Imagination (Ithaca: Cornell University Press, 2010), p. 6. See also Jonathan Bate, *The Song of the Earth* (Cambridge, MA: Harvard University Press, 2000).

[263] Halliford, 8.500–1.

[264] *Origin*, 1.89. One of TLP's few indications of where he thought oran outangs fit in the animal world occurs in his letter to Thomas Forster (12 Oct. 1809). TLP drew a chart meant to illustrate 'The general connection of the chain of terrestrial being', and the last five animals in the chart are 'Ourang-Outang', 'Albino', 'Negro', 'Red Man', 'White Man' (*Letters*, 1.39–40).

[265] *Origin*, 1.281n, 1.287.

correctly known by the name of Pongo' (one difference is that the pongo has 'large ears and black hair').[266] Like Monboddo's pongo and 'chimpenza', Sir Oran comes from Africa; his height indicates he is a pongo; and, indeed, most of Monboddo's pronouncements upon oran outangs that are quoted by Peacock concern pongos. Forester identifies Sir Oran as 'the wild man of the woods; called, in the language of the more civilized and sophisticated natives of Angola, *Pongo*, and in that of the Indians of South America, *Oran Outang*' (Chapter 6). That is, Sir Oran was called a pongo in his home country, but if he were transported to 'South America' (almost surely a printer's error for Peacock's 'Sumatra'), the natives there would call him by a different name.[267] Forester cares little about nomenclature; Sir Oran simply represents a point on the spectrum of humanity. Peacock's vagueness about Sir Oran's appearance means that readers must use their imaginations, although their imaginations have sometimes gone further than the text authorizes. Part of the reason is the danger of confusing oran outangs with orangutans, and the greater familiarity that later readers have had with the various species of apes. Twentieth-century readers have envisioned Sir Oran as an orangutan, with reddish hair and disproportionately long arms; in F. H. Townsend's illustrations for the 1896 edition, Sir Oran has an orangutan's whiskers but a chimpanzee's face, while his body appears human. Unlike Peacock, Townsend would have seen orangutans or accurate images of them, and he could have drawn an orangutan, although he chose to treat Sir Oran as a hybrid produced by Peacock's imagination to serve artistic ends.

---

[266] Clarke Abel, *Narrative of a Journey in the Interior of China, and of a Voyage to and from That Country, in the Years 1816 and 1817, Containing An Account of the Most Interesting Transactions of Lord Amherst's Embassy to the Court of Pekin, and Observations on the Countries Which it Visited* (Longman, 1818), p. 319.

[267] 'Since Peacock must have known from his reading of Lord Monboddo that the orang-utan was native to the East Indies, it seems likely that the compositor of the first edition misread the unfamiliar "Sumatra" as "S. America".' Joukovsky, 'Peacock's Sir Oran Haut-ton', 173, n. 1.

Sir Oran Haut-ton.

2 Frontispiece, *Melincourt; or, Sir Oran Haut-ton,* introd. George Saintsbury, ill. F. H. Townsend (Macmillan, 1896), The Carl H. Pforzheimer Collection of Shelley and His Circle, New York Public Library, Astor, Lenox, and Tilden Foundation

Peacock and his readers could have consulted sources of information on apes other than those which he quotes. As Nicholas A. Joukovsky has pointed out, a character in Isaac D'Israeli's *Flim-Flams! or, the Life and Errors of My Uncle, and the Amours of My Aunt!* (1805) trains an 'orang-outang'.[268] Debating eighteenth-century philosophy with the local curate, the narrator's uncle 'espoused a notion of Lord MONBODDO'S, that MEN once wore *tails!* and going on with this fascinating system, asserted with [Erasmus] DARWIN and other Philos of this enlightened æra, that MEN are only *educated monkies!*'.[269] The uncle, in fact, 'had long been secretly boarding and educating an orang-outang'.[270] The narrator goes on to say that 'the monkey . . . certainly turned out a gentleman! and dressed as fashionably, and in every other respect rivalled the accomplishments and the talents of a *Bond-street Lounger!*'.[271] This gentleman might pass unnoticed among the fashionable men who frequent Bond Street in the West End, much as Sir Oran might. The family is nonetheless troubled by the oran outang's 'animality', including 'his amazing *swallow* for all kinds of dainties, the easiness with which you might put him into a passion, and his fits of tenderness to our maids'.[272] Later, the narrator's aunt becomes pregnant, and his uncle is convinced that her mood and thoughts will determine the foetus's development. Overcome by strange longings, 'she resolved, being fair time, to give sixpence to look at a rope-dancing ape'.[273] The

---

[268] See Joukovsky, 'Peacock's Sir Oran Haut-ton'. Joukovsky was the first to suggest that Peacock had read *Flim-Flams!* (180–1).

[269] [Isaac D'Israeli], *Flim-Flams! or, the Life and Errors of My Uncle, and the Amours of My Aunt! with Illustrations and Obscurities, By Messieurs Tag, Rag, and Bobtail. With an Illuminating Index!*, 3 vols. (John Murray, 1805), vol. 2, pp. 160–1.

[270] D'Israeli, *Flim-Flams!*, vol. 2, p. 161.

[271] D'Israeli, *Flim-Flams!*, vol. 2, p. 161.

[272] D'Israeli, *Flim-Flams!*, vol. 2, p. 163.

[273] D'Israeli, *Flim-Flams!*, vol. 3, p. 135.

narrator's uncle insists, 'I am cuckolded by an ape!'[274] Sure enough, the baby is born looking like the ape.[275]

Peacock's first published poem appeared in 1800 in *The Juvenile Library, Including a Complete Course of Instruction on Every Useful Subject*, and elsewhere in the same issue was an article on 'The Ourang Outang; or, Wild Man of the Wood'.[276] The accompanying illustration may have implanted in Peacock's mind a sense of what an oran outang looked like (see ill. 3). The 'chimpanzee' in the left foreground appears to be a hybrid of chimpanzee and human, but the 'ourang-outang' to the right is harder to classify. Political prints also remind us that the culture in which Peacock lived did not always differentiate between apes. Sir Murray Maxwell's ship brought to England a Bornean orangutan that had been collected by Lord Amherst's party. When Maxwell stood for parliament, a print titled 'Ourang Outang Candidate for Westminster' (July 1818) transformed the candidate into a skinny, tailless monkey, even though Maxwell's orangutan was on display a short walk from the Covent Garden hustings.[277] In the print 'The Orang Outang— The *Beast* that *Violates Every Thing*' (1830), the king's disreputable younger brother, the Duke of Cumberland, is covered with the hair typical of a gorilla, but he has a man's height and a man's posture (as well as feet unlike those of any primate).[278]

---

[274] D'Israeli, *Flim-Flams!*, vol. 3, p. 135.

[275] As Joukovsky has also pointed out, Mr Perriwinkle in *Six Weeks at Long's* (1817), who resembles Shelley in many respects, has 'brought up an ape in the country, with the idea of making it speak and act as a human creature'; A Late Resident [William Jerdan and Michael Nugent], *Six Weeks at Long's*, 2nd ed., 3 vols. (for the author, 1817), vol. 2, p. 200. See Joukovsky, 'Peacock's Sir Oran Haut-ton', 181–6. Joukovsky argues that Perriwinkle is related to Forester as a portrait of Shelley.

[276] *The Juvenile Library, Including a Complete Course of Instruction on Every Useful Subject* (R. Phillips, 1800), pp. 8–17.

[277] *A Catalogue of Political and Personal Satires in the British Museum*, ed. Frederic G. Stephens and M. Dorothy George, 11 vols. (British Museum, 1870–1954), vol. 9, no. 13000. TLP mentioned Maxwell's candidacy in a letter to Shelley (*Letters*, 1.130–1).

[278] *Catalogue of Political and Personal Satires*, vol. 11, no. 16026.

CHIMPANZEE,1. OURANG-OUTANG,2.

3 Illustration from *The Juvenile Library, Including a Complete Course of Instruction on Every Useful Subject* (1800), The Carl H. Pforzheimer Collection of Shelley and His Circle, New York Public Library, Astor, Lenox, and Tilden Foundation

Londoners had the opportunity to see an actual orangutan a few months after *Melincourt* appeared, when Lord Amherst's 'Ourang Outang' was exhibited at Exeter Change in the Strand. An advertisement claimed that 'one of his kind has not been seen in England (if we are correctly informed) for the last 80 years'. The 'formation, habits, and motions' of this creature 'so strongly resemble man, and its actions are so much the apparent result of thought, that it may be truly said to be the connecting link in the chain of nature uniting the human species with the brute creation'.[279] A subsequent advertisement described this 'distinguished stranger' in terms that might inspire Sir Oran's admirers to travel to the Strand: 'He holds his levee every day at Exeter Change, which is very numerously attended', and 'All ranks retire from his presence highly gratified with his condescension and politeness.'[280] The Exeter Change orangutan might not be 'of the human form, inside as well as outside', as Monboddo said of the oran outang, but he at least represented 'the connecting link' between the human and the non-human.

The two most notable apes who appear in literature later in the nineteenth century are oran outangs. In Scott's novel *Count Robert of Paris* (1832), 'Sylvan' serves the jailor in a medieval prison. He is from 'Taprobana', meaning Sumatra.[281] He has 'the form of a human being', but 'a stranger shape than human'.[282] More than 7 feet tall, with 'a dreadful grin' and 'hideous eyes', Sylvan is 'covered, all but the face, with a reddish-dun fur'.[283] His hands, like Sir Oran's, evidently

---

[279] *Times* (30 Aug. 1817), 3. For an account of this orangutan's appearance and behaviour, see Abel, *Narrative*, pp. 318–30. Could TLP have seen this orangutan?

[280] *Times* (24 Dec. 1817), 4.

[281] *Count Robert of Paris*, ed. J. H. Alexander (Edinburgh: Edinburgh University Press, 2006), *The Edinburgh Edition of the Waverley Novels*, ed.-in-chief David Hewitt, 25 vols. in 30 (Edinburgh: Edinburgh University Press, 1993–2012), vol. 23a, p. 271.

[282] Scott, *Count Robert*, pp. 169, 206.

[283] Scott, *Count Robert*, pp. 169, 170, 172, 206.

grasp objects just as human hands do.[284] When Sylvan first appears, Scott narrates from the eleventh-century protagonist's point of view, but then comments that the reader must have deduced that Sylvan is 'a specimen of that gigantic species of ape—if it is not indeed some animal more nearly allied to ourselves—to which, I believe, naturalists have given the name of the Ourang Outang'.[285] This species is 'more docile and serviceable' than other apes, and its 'power of imitation' is directed by 'a desire of improvement and instruction perfectly unknown to its brethren', though none of these creatures has 'the gift of speech'.[286] The most famous anthropoid ape in nineteenth-century literature, the Bornean 'Ourang-Outang' who kills two women in Edgar Allan Poe's 'The Murders in the Rue Morgue' (1841), is an inversion of Scott's docile Sylvan. Poe's 'gigantic' oran outang is imitative, but his impulse to imitate causes him to kill one woman, and he then strangles another and shoves her corpse up a chimney.[287]

The novelty of finding an oran outang in a novel meant that Sir Oran became central to readers' responses to *Melincourt*, and the tradition of focusing upon, even exaggerating, Sir Oran's importance began immediately upon publication. He was 'the most conspicuous character', and perhaps even 'the hero' of *Melincourt*, according to the *Literary Gazette*. If he was the hero, this was 'the first time' an oran outang had assumed such a role, the *Critical Review* observed.[288] Reportedly, Lord Byron also referred to Sir Oran as the novel's 'hero'.[289] A silent character must be at a disadvantage in a novel of talk, and, when conversation dominates, Sir

---

[284] Scott, *Count Robert*, p. 170.   [285] Scott, *Count Robert*, p. 171.

[286] Scott, *Count Robert*, p. 171.

[287] Edgar Allan Poe, *Poetry, Tales, and Selected Essays* (New York: Library of America, 1996), pp. 397–431. For 'gigantic', see p. 424. Poe's ape is an example of 'the large fulvous Ourang-Outang of the East Indian Islands' (p. 424).

[288] Anon., *Literary Gazette* (22 Mar. 1817), 132; [Collier], *Critical Review*, 5th ser., vol. 5 (May 1817), 494.

[289] Lovell, ed., *Medwin's Conversations of Lord Byron*, p. 67.

Oran often fades into the background; there is little for him to do until his strength is called upon. Peacock seemingly forgets about Sir Oran for most of Chapter 31, until the oran outang is needed to extinguish a fire. Although the plot focuses on courtship, Sir Oran is never a candidate for the heroine's hand. While deeming Sir Oran 'the real hero', Henry Chorley in *The Athenaeum* admitted that Forester 'is the lover who is to carry off the fair Anthelia'.[290] At the beginning of Chapter 10, the narrator records Anthelia's disappointment with 'her present suitors'; just when literary convention dictates that a better alternative must emerge, she meets Sir Oran, although, within a few chapters, his friend Forester will travel to Melincourt Castle and bond with Anthelia over Italian poetry.

Peacock's example of the 'natural man' blends into fashionable English society, at home amid the civilization of the *ton*, wearing a very natural 'green coat and nankins' (Chapter 4). Unlike Forester and Anthelia, Sir Oran loves the West End. His peculiarities do not impede him: when Mrs Pinmoney learns that the 'ugly gentleman' is a wealthy baronet who soon will have a seat in Parliament, she reevaluates his appearance, noting that 'he has a very fashionable air'. The name 'Haut-ton' is of 'French extraction', and she now perceives that 'there is something very French in his physiognomy' (Chapter 15). There was an English tradition of depicting the French as simian: Louis Simond, who visited Britain in 1811–12, complained that caricaturists always depicted men of his nation 'as diminutive, starved beings, of monkey-mien'.[291] However, during the Regency, the highest classes had adopted French and German fashions, a trend to which Sir Oran seems to conform. Mrs

---

[290] When Chorley said that Sir Oran 'is the real hero', he was encouraged to take this view because this edition elevated Sir Oran to the sub-title. *The Athenæum* (19 Apr. 1856), 486.

[291] [Louis Simond], *Journal of a Tour and Residence in Great Britain, during the Years 1810 and 1811, by a French Traveller: with Remarks on the Country, its Arts, Literature, and Politics, and on the Manners and Customs of its Inhabitants*, 2 vols. (Edinburgh: Constable, 1815) vol. 1, p. 21. In *NA* Scythrop says that 'A Frenchman is a monstrous compound of monkey, spaniel, and tiger' (p. 73).

Pinmoney mentions the fashion for 'German whiskers' (Chapter 2), and Sir Oran's 'enormous whiskers' (Chapter 4) ally him with many fashionable men of the Regency, including the Prince Regent.[292] Moreover, Mrs Pinmoney's identifying Sir Oran as French reminds us further of the French associations of 'chivalry'. If 'the spirit of the age of chivalry' can be 'manifested in the forms of modern life', as Anthelia says (Chapter 8), then Sir Oran's innate chivalry and sense of justice can be consistent with his conformity to the style of the haut monde.

No one simply recognizes that Sir Oran is an oran outang; people need to be told, and only Forester, Mr Fax and Sir Telegraph know the truth, while everyone else assumes he is an odd-looking, mute man.[293] (One wonders if Forester eventually illuminates Anthelia.) When people apply human standards to Sir Oran, he is deemed ugly (Chapters 4, 15); Mr Hippy concludes Sir Oran is 'no great beauty' and 'manifestly dumb', though obviously 'a man of consequence' (Chapter 10).[294] Lord Anophel assumes that Sir Oran can read and write, and therefore assumes that he can point to Grovelgrub and himself as the men who attempted to abduct Anthelia (Chapter 23). The citizens of Novote who witness Sir Oran's election apparently never notice anything unusual about him (and most of them belong to the lower and middling classes from whose tactlessness Forester wishes to shield Sir Oran).

---

[292] As Byron remarked in *Waltz*, 'whiskers' were one of the German imports that arrived at the time the Regency commenced, along with 'the new Government' and 'Waltz' itself; Lord Byron, *The Complete Poetical Works*, ed. Jerome J. McGann, 7 vols. (Oxford: Clarendon Press, 1980–93), vol. 3 (1981), p. 401n.

[293] Though Forester aims to show that the oran outang is 'a variety of the human species', 'the civilized world' cannot be persuaded of this (ch. 6) unless they know Sir Oran is an oran outang. Yet in the course of the novel Forester reveals Sir Oran's history only to Sir Telegraph.

[294] Monboddo wrote that 'in general . . . it will be very difficult, or rather impossible, for a man, who is accustomed to divide things according to specific marks, not individual differences, to draw the line betwixt the Orang Outang and the dumb persons among us' (*Origin*, 1.297). Peacock quotes this passage in a footnote in ch. 6.

Peacock leaves open the possibility that when Sir Oran responds to others he is merely imitating them, but the author does not insist on this interpretation. At times, Sir Oran merely replicates others' actions: Hippy gives him a bow, and he 'return[s] it with great politeness' (Chapter 15). Sometimes, however, Sir Oran seems to respond to words alone: Sir Telegraph says, 'I shall trouble Sir Oran for a slice of fish', and then the oran outang 'helped him with great dexterity' (Chapter 4). Sir Oran's bow when Sir Telegraph invites him to share the madeira seems to indicate assent (Chapter 4). When Anthelia 'renewed the expressions of her gratitude to Sir Oran, and bade him welcome to Melincourt', he 'bowed in silence' (Chapter 15). Sir Oran also bows as though he understands what Sarcastic says about him (Chapter 21), and taps glasses with Sarcastic in a similar situation (earlier in Chapter 21). At times, he obviously relies upon Forester's indications (presumably gestures): Sir Oran gives the artist 'a polite bow' and returns his portfolio after 'a hint' from Forester (Chapter 14), and, when Forester wishes to see the place where Anthelia was rescued from the deluge, he 'made Sir Oran understand his desire' (Chapter 18). The narrator neither confirms nor denies that the speaker's gestures alone could indicate to Sir Oran what was expected.

At one point, Peacock draws attention to whether Sir Oran's behaviour reveals that he understands speech. Forester says that Sir Telegraph witnessed Sir Oran's actions after 'you asked him to take wine, and applied to him for fish and partridge', and Sir Telegraph observes that Sir Oran may have responded to 'The gestures, however slight, that accompany the expression of the ordinary forms of intercourse'. Forester replies that Sir Oran 'understands many things addressed to him, on occasions of very unfrequent occurrence' (Chapter 6). At times, the narrator indicates that the natural man is imitating others: Forester offers his hand to Anthelia to lead her in to dinner, and when Sir Oran presents his to Mrs Pinmoney, he is 'following the example' (Chapter 15). Hearing the word 'bumper, *with which Captain Hawltaught had made him very familiar*', Sir Oran grabs Miss Danaretta's tea, the wine having been removed from the table when the ladies arrived (Chapter 21).

Like Monboddo, Forester contends that oran outangs are practically human, and *Melincourt* does not refute this contention, although it is treated as humorous. When the narrator is read literally, he accepts that Sir Oran is human; when the narrator is read with an eye for verbal irony, Sir Oran's humanity is not denied. That is, the narrator never undermines Forester's claim that Sir Oran represents 'a variety of the human species' (Chapter 6). After Forester reveals to Sir Telegraph that Sir Oran is a pongo or oran outang, Peacock's readers know that Sir Oran belongs to a class of creatures whose humanity they are predisposed to deny, and because readers assume that no oran outang is human, they may discern verbal irony when the narrator writes about Sir Oran: the narrator must be sarcastic, even if he does not sound sarcastic. Yet the narrator does not sneer at Forester for believing Sir Oran is human, or laugh at Anthelia for treating him as such.

Perhaps narratorial statements which imply that Sir Oran is human reflect the perceptions of actual or hypothetical observers who assume he is such, and the result is a kind of free indirect discourse; the narrator may not be expressing an opinion but simply reporting one. When 'Sir Oran testified, by a copious draught, that he found much virtue in home-brewed ale' (Chapter 14), the narrator may doubt that drinking qualifies as 'testimony' or perhaps he is merely conveying neutrally the interpretation of those present. When Sir Oran 'preserve[s] an inflexible silence' during one dinner or remains quiet after Mr Sarcastic inquires about joining his party, the narrator writes as though Sir Oran might be 'flexible' and speak (Chapters 4, 21). When Sir Oran 'maintain[s] a grave and dignified silence' (Chapter 16), readers may wonder what trait makes his (inevitable) silence appear to have this gravity and dignity, but they will also suspect that people at the table perceive these attributes.

In 1797 Southey wrote that 'man is a Beast, and an ugly Beast, and Monboddo libels the Ouran-outangs, by suspecting them of the same family'.[295] Peacock does not employ Sir Oran only to underscore the absurdity of Monboddo's theories, or to amuse by envisioning the results that would ensue if one of Monboddo's oran outangs adapted to civilization; Sir Oran also serves as a standard by which the human characters fall short. Peacock satirizes both Monboddo's elevation of the oran outang *and* humanity's inability to be as virtuous as Monboddo's oran outangs.[296] The shortcomings of contemporary society become vivid when *Melincourt* imagines a reality in which an oran outang displays many of the best attributes commonly believed to be unique to humans. Whether or not noble savages exist, an author can conjure them up so they can embody the nobility too often lacking in human society. Sir Oran is the gentleman that Lord Anophel is not. The *Literary Gazette* wrote that Peacock satirized not only 'over-brained philosophers' like Monboddo, but also 'those brainless fops, who would degrade men into monkies by their example'.[297] D'Israeli's oran outang in *Flim-Flams!* 'dressed as fashionably, and in every other respect rivalled the accomplishments and the talents of a *Bond-street Lounger*'; the point of the comparison is to degrade the Bond Street loungers.[298]

---

[295] Robert Southey, *Letters Written During a Short Residence in Spain and Portugal* (Bristol: Joseph Cottle, 1797), p. 63.

[296] Priestley is one of those who views *Mel* this way: 'Peacock takes [Monboddo and others] at their word by' giving Sir Oran 'all the virtues and accomplishments variously ascribed to the animal.' Yet Peacock's satire is 'double-edged': 'Sir Oran is at once seen to be superior, in all the qualities that matter most, to the members of the new society in which he finds himself' (Priestley, *Thomas Love Peacock*, p. 202). Bate writes that 'Peacock's central comic device is to give what he regards as the highest characteristics of mankind . . . not to a well-born human, but to the highest of the apes' (*Song of the Earth*, pp. 196–7). Bate finds that *Melincourt* implies something about actual non-human animals: it 'forc[es] us to begin to rethink our relations to our non-human cousins' (pp. 198–9). He goes far beyond the text when he writes that Sir Oran 'has the capacity for language, but he chooses not to use it' (p. 198); this capacity is not at all certain.

[297] Anon., *Literary Gazette* (22 Mar. 1817), 132.

[298] D'Israeli, *Flim-Flams!*, vol. 2, p. 161. The comparison of 'dandies' to monkeys was conventional. In Thomas Moore's *The Fudge Family in Paris* (1818), the dandies of the French capital wear hats that are 'fit for monkies';

A Romantic-era library patron, hearing of a novel with an oran outang as a major character, might suspect that the ape was an ingenuous visitor from whose viewpoint English society's practices were defamiliarized and satirized. In the long eighteenth century, narratives of this kind most often focused upon a visitor from a foreign culture. In Voltaire's *L'Ingenu* (1767), a Huron Indian visits France; in Robert Bage's *Hermsprong; or, Man as He is Not* (1796), the visitor to England is a man who has lived among American Indians. Elizabeth Hamilton's *Letters of a Hindoo Rajah* (1796) examines English life using the device of an Asian observer, a device familiar from Giovanni Marana's *Letters Writ by a Turkish Spy* (1687–94), Montesquieu's *Lettres Persanes* (1721) or Oliver Goldsmith's *The Citizen of the World* (1762). Hamilton's 'Sheermaal' interprets card-playing as 'poojah', which means religious worship.[299] Soon after finishing *Melincourt*, Peacock began a satirical narrative in which Britain is visited by a native of Terra Incognita, and Calidore's conclusion that paper money is the work of a 'great magician' (Halliford, 8.338) resembles Sheermaal's interpretation of card games. In these novels, society is seen not merely from the outsider's viewpoint, but through the outsider's consciousness, his interpretations and misinterpretations. Satirical narratives attributed thoughts to the observer even when that observer was an animal or object: Charles Johnstone's *Chrysal: or, The Adventures of a Guinea* (1760), one of many such tales, is narrated by a coin.

Yet whereas Hamilton's 'Hindoos' or Peacock's Calidore remain aliens, Sir Oran has already blended into the English landed gentry

Thomas Brown the Younger, ed. [Thomas Moore], *The Fudge Family in Paris*, 5th ed. (Longman, Hurst, Rees, Orme and Brown, 1818), p. 27. Mr Perriwinkle's elegy on his ape in *Six Weeks at Long's* (see Joukovsky, 'Peacock's Sir Oran Haut-ton', 183) compares fashionable men to monkeys.

299 Eliza[beth] Hamilton, *Translation of the Letters of a Hindoo Rajah; Written Previous to, and During the Period of his Residence in England*, 2 vols. (G. G. and J. Robinson, 1796), vol. 1, p. 96. William Beckford wrote a novel about a native of Turkey who ends up in England: *Azemia: A Descriptive and Sentimental Novel. Interspersed with Pieces of Poetry* (Sampson Low, 1797).

when he first appears. Though more virtuous than most of English society, he is able to function within it and to be accepted as 'a man of consequence' (Chapter 10). Sir Oran seems 'to feel himself completely at home' amid the fashionable world (Chapter 6) as soon as he is introduced to it. Moreover, Peacock's narrator never assumes Sir Oran's viewpoint, much less describes his thoughts. The reader never knows what Sir Oran thinks, and although Bate writes that he 'is the most philanthropic of creatures', the most that can be conceded is that his actions have the same effects that philanthropy would have.[300] His actions are, like the Exeter Change orangutan's, 'the apparent result of thought',[301] but the narrator seldom clarifies whether these appearances should be trusted. When raging waters trap Anthelia on a rock, Sir Oran makes 'gestures' that are 'expressive of a design to assist her' (Chapter 10), and here he seems capable of deliberate communicative acts: his gestures express his design, and he evidently intends to communicate this design to Anthelia. The scene is narrated from her viewpoint, however, and the assertion about Sir Oran's gestures may be free indirect discourse – *Anthelia believes that* his movements are his way of communicating his plan, but the narrator does not confirm that her belief is correct. Next, Sir Oran 'paused a moment, as if measuring with his eyes the breadth of the chasm' (Chapter 10), and this claim is qualified: he pauses *as if* estimating the breadth. Either Anthelia is aware that she is inferring Sir Oran's thoughts, and the narrator conveys her awareness to us, or the narrator independently suggests that any resemblance between the oran outang's pause and human computation may be misleading. Sir Oran then rips out the pine 'deliberately'.

If *Melincourt* is a quest romance, then Sir Oran is the chief quest-knight, and chivalry traditionally involved male protection of women. He acts chivalrously when women are concerned, whether by offering Mrs Pinmoney his arm or by rescuing Anthelia; apparently, he feels 'a most chivalrous sympathy with females in distress'

---

[300] Bate, *Song of the Earth*, p. 197.   [301] *Times* (30 Aug. 1817), 3.

(Chapter 38). According to Burke, writing to Philip Francis, chivalrous men venerate and defend women 'without any consideration whatsoever of enjoying them',[302] and it is therefore intriguing that Sir Oran seems to lack one trait that is conspicuous in Monboddo's oran outangs: sexual desire.[303] Most of Monboddo's evidence for male oran outangs' libido involves their pursuing female humans. According to the travellers he cites, male oran outangs are 'very fond of women, whom they always attack when they meet with them in the woods'; they 'frequently carry away young girls'; they 'have a great desire for women'; Brosses's 'Quimpezes' 'carry away young negroe girls, and keep them for their pleasure', and 'one negroe girl ... had been with them three years'. Not only is it true that the oran outang 'copulates with our females', but also there is 'the greatest reason to believe, that there is offspring'.[304] We should recall that the oran outang in D'Israeli's *Flim-Flams!* displays 'tenderness to our maids'. Mrs Pinmoney seems to weigh Sir Oran's potential as a husband for her daughter or for some other fortunate young woman, yet the only woman who interests him is Anthelia, and his affection seems chaste, a 'reverential attachment' (Chapter 42). Peacock, by not endowing Sir Oran with any discernible sexual drives, renders him truly disinterested: the most effective knight in the novel is a creature who has no desire to possess Anthelia. He is an ideal natural man, invested in Anthelia's safety but desiring nothing from her.

Yet the sexuality of Monboddo's oran outangs makes Sir Oran's disinterest all the more utopian. The manner of Anthelia's final rescue shows that even while Peacock tries to envision a non-oppressive chivalry, he has to resort to desperate measures to resolve his plot,

---

[302] *The Correspondence of Edmund Burke*, ed. Alfred Cobban and Robert A. Smith, 10 vols. (Cambridge: Cambridge University Press, 1958), vol. 6, pp. 90–1.

[303] On the hypersexuality attributed to male apes in the Enlightenment, see Londa L. Schiebinger, *Nature's Body: Gender in the Making of Modern Science* (Boston: Beacon Press, 1993), pp. 95–8. In *Mel* Sir Oran is compared to Pan and to satyrs, all known for their libido.

[304] *Origin*, 1.274–7, 334.

and his reliance on them undercuts his vision. After days of frustration, Lord Anophel Achthar announces to the captive Anthelia that he will assault her so that she must marry him in order to prevent a scandal. She responds that 'false shame would [not] induce me to conceal what both truth and justice would command me to make known'. Lord Anophel then indignantly 'seize[s] her hand with violence, and thr[ows] his arm round her waist' (Chapter 42). At this moment Sir Oran bursts in, holding the Reverend Mr Grovelgrub, and seizes Lord Anophel. The narrator backtracks to explain that Sir Oran, Forester and Mr Fax were walking on the beach when Sir Oran spotted Grovelgrub, whom he remembered from the time he foiled the first attempt to abduct Anthelia.

Two facts about Anthelia's final rescue are significant. First, Sir Oran deserves all the credit, while Forester and Fax do nothing but follow him. Second, it is implausible that the three wander onto the beach near the villain's Alga Castle just as Grovelgrub is walking there, and just as Lord Anophel, within the castle, is about to threaten Anthelia with assault.[305] As Spedding remarked, Forester 'meets with no trace whatever of the heroine; till at length, by the most fortunate accident in the world, he suddenly stumbles upon her, at that precise moment when, if he had not,—the author must have found some difficulty in going on'.[306] This implausibility makes the wish-fulfilment blatant; there can be no protection against a villain who will simply assault the woman, and no narrative resolution is available other than that of an *oran outang ex machina*.

If Peacock's disinterested benevolence constitutes an attempt to reinvent chivalry in a form that does not sustain men's domination,

---

[305] The scene in Alga Castle seems to have been transferred from more hackneyed works: the *Monthly Review* complained that Anthelia's abduction was 'too common-place an incident, in novels particularly' (*Monthly Review*, new ser., vol. 83 (July 1817), 323. Twenty-two years later, Spedding regretted that TLP had 'borrowed on this one occasion the common-place book of a melodramatist'; *Edinburgh Review*, vol. 68 (Jan. 1839), 446. See n. 254, above.

[306] [Spedding], review, *Edinburgh Review*, vol. 68 (Jan. 1839), 446.

it fails. The issue becomes still more complex, however. At the conclusion, Anthelia misrepresents her rescue: she says that Forester 'emancipate[d] a captive damsel', but she really was emancipated by Sir Oran. The fact that the 'knight' who twice rescues Anthelia is an oran outang may be Peacock's way of burlesquing the medieval revival, but it also serves to expose the inadequacy of all the alternatives that are available to resolve Anthelia's dilemma. Sir Oran evidently feels 'a most chivalrous sympathy with females in distress' (Chapter 38); his chivalry emerges not from the baronetcy that transforms him into 'Sir' Oran but from his natural impulses. These impulses, moreover, are apparently divorced from any hope of sexual gain or the other benefits of human patriarchy. While the implausibility of Anthelia's rescue seems to underscore the author's desperation, *Melincourt*'s dependence on Sir Oran reflects a failure on another level.

At the conclusion, Anthelia says to Sylvan Forester that after he has 'emancipate[d] a captive damsel', herself, she will 'but change the mode of her durance, and become your captive for life' (Chapter 42). Anthelia appears satisfied with this outcome, and so, perhaps, does Peacock, but the imagery she uses makes her victory seem hollow. The marriage plot that provides the framework of almost all Peacock's fictions becomes ugly here. After Lord Anophel's unsuccessful attempt to abduct Anthelia, she gives up her habitual 'solitary rambles', and looks forward to revisiting 'her favourite haunts' with Forester, whose 'presence would . . . restore to them that feeling of security which her late adventure had destroyed' (Chapter 41). The attempted abduction reveals a problem only marriage can solve.

MELINCOURT.

BY THE AUTHOR OF

HEADLONG HALL.

" Nous nous moquons des Paladins! quand ces maximes romanesques commencerent à devenir ridicules, ce changement fut moins l'ouvrage de la raison que celui des mauvaises mœurs."—ROUSSEAU.

IN THREE VOLUMES.

VOL. I.

LONDON:

PRINTED FOR T. HOOKHAM, JUN. AND CO.
OLD BOND STREET;
AND BALDWIN, CRADOCK, AND JOY,
PATERNOSTER ROW.

1817.

4 Title page of *Melincourt* (1817), vol. 1, The Carl H. Pforzheimer
Collection of Shelley and His Circle, New York Public Library,
Astor, Lenox, and Tilden Foundation

"Nous nous moquons des Paladins! quand ces maximes
romanesques commencerent à devenir ridicules,
ce changement fut moins l'ouvrage de la raison
que celui des mauvaises mœurs."—ROUSSEAU.

CHAPTER I.

ANTHELIA.[1]

ANTHELIA MELINCOURT, at the age of twenty-one, was mistress of herself and of ten thousand a year, and of a very ancient and venerable castle in one of the wildest valleys in Westmoreland.[2] It follows of course, without reference to her personal qualifications, that she had a very numerous list of admirers, and equally of course that there were both Irishmen and clergymen[3] among them. The young lady nevertheless possessed sufficient attractions to kindle the flames of disinterested passion;[4] and accordingly we shall venture to suppose, that there was at least one in the number of her sighing swains with whom her rent-roll and her old castle were secondary considerations; and if the candid reader should esteem this supposition too violent for the probabilities of daily experience in this calculating age,[5] he will at least concede it to that degree of poetical license which is invariably accorded to a tale founded on facts.

Melincourt Castle[6] had been a place of considerable strength in those golden days of feudal and royal prerogative, when no man was safe in his own house unless he adopted every possible precaution for shutting out all his neighbours. It is, therefore, not surprising, that a rock, of which three sides were perpendicular, and which was only accessible on the fourth by a narrow ledge,[7] forming a natural bridge over a tremendous chasm, was considered a very enviable situation for a gentleman to build on. An impetuous torrent boiled through the depth of the chasm, and after eddying round the base of the castle-rock, which it almost insulated, disappeared in the obscurity of a woody glen, whose mysterious recesses, by popular superstition formerly consecrated to the devil, are now fearlessly explored by the solitary angler, or laid open to view by the more profane hand of the picturesque tourist,[8] who contrives, by the magic of his pencil, to transport their romantic terrors from the depths of mountain-solitude to the gay and crowded, though not very wholesome atmosphere of a metropolitan exhibition.

The narrow ledge, which formed the only natural access to the castle-rock, had been guarded by every impediment which the genius of fortification could oppose to the progress of the hungry Scot, who might be disposed, in his neighbourly way, to drop in without invitation and carouse at the expense of the owner, rewarding him, as usual, for his extorted hospitality, by cutting his throat and setting fire to his house. A drawbridge over the chasm, backed by a double portcullis, presented the only mode of admission. In this secure retreat, thus strongly guarded both by nature and art, and always plentifully victualled for a siege, lived the lords of Melincourt in all the luxury of rural seclusion, throwing open their gates on occasional halcyon days to regale all the peasants and mountaineers of the vicinity with roasted oxen and vats of October.[9]

When these times of danger and turbulence had passed, Melincourt Castle was not, as most of its brother edifices were, utterly deserted. The drawbridge, indeed, became gradually divorced from its chains; the double portcullis disappeared; the turrets and battlements were abandoned to the owl and the ivy; and a very spacious wing was left free to the settlement of a colony of ghosts, which, according to the report of the peasantry and the domestics, very soon took possession, and retained it most pertinaciously, notwithstanding the pious incantations of the neighbouring vicar, the Reverend Mr. Portpipe,[10] who often passed the night in one of the dreaded apartments over a blazing fire with the same invariable exorcising apparatus of a large venison pasty, a little prayer-book, and three bottles of Madeira:[11] for the reverend gentleman sagaciously observed, that as he had always found the latter an infallible charm against blue devils, he had no doubt of its proving equally efficacious against black, white, and grey.[12] In this opinion experience seemed to confirm him; for though he always maintained a becoming silence as to the mysteries of which he was a witness during his spectral vigils, yet a very correct inference might be drawn from the fact, that he was always found in the morning comfortably asleep in his large arm-chair, with the dish scraped clean, the three bottles empty, and the prayer-book clasped and folded precisely in the same state and place in which it had lain the preceding night.

But the larger and more commodious part of the castle continued still to be inhabited; and while one half of the edifice was fast improving into a picturesque ruin, the other was as rapidly degenerating, in its interior at least, into a comfortable modern dwelling.

In this romantic seclusion Anthelia was born. Her mother died in giving her birth. Her father, Sir Henry Melincourt, a man of great acquirements, and of a retired disposition, devoted himself in solitude to the cultivation of his daughter's understanding; for he was one of those who maintained the heretical notion that women are, or at least may be, rational beings;[13] though, from the great pains usually taken in what is called education to make them otherwise, there are unfortunately very few examples to warrant the truth of the theory.

The majestic forms and wild energies of Nature[14] that surrounded her from her infancy, impressed their character on her mind, communicating to it all their own wildness, and more than their own beauty. Far removed from the pageantry of courts and cities, her infant attention was awakened to spectacles more interesting and more impressive: the misty mountain-top, the ash-fringed precipice, the gleaming cataract, the deep and shadowy glen, and the fantastic magnificence of the mountain clouds. The murmur of the woods, the rush of the winds, and the tumultuous dashing of the torrents, were the first music of her childhood. A fearless wanderer among these romantic solitudes, the spirit of mountain liberty diffused itself through the whole tenour of her feelings, modelled the symmetry of her form, and illumined the expressive but feminine brilliancy of her features: and when she had attained the age at which the mind expands itself to the fascinations of poetry, the muses of Italy[15] became the chosen companions of her wanderings, and nourished a naturally susceptible imagination by conjuring up the splendid visions of chivalry and enchantment in scenes so congenial to their developement.

It was seldom that the presence of a visitor dispelled the solitude of Melincourt; and the few specimens of the living world with whom its inmates held occasional intercourse, were of the usual character of country acquaintance, not calculated to leave behind them any very lively regret, except for the loss of time during the period of their stay. One of these was the Reverend Mr. Portpipe, whom we have already celebrated for his proficiency in the art of exorcising goblins by dint of venison and Madeira. His business in the ghost line had, indeed, declined with the progress of the human understanding, and no part of his vocation was in very high favour with Sir Henry, who, though an unexceptionable moral character, was unhappily not one of the children of grace, in the theological sense of the word: but the vicar, adopting St. Paul's precept of being all things to all men,[16] found it on this occasion his interest to be liberal; and observing that no man could coerce his opinions, repeated with great complacency the line of Virgil:

Tros Tyriusque mihi nullo discrimine agetur;[17]

though he took especial care that this heterodox concession should not reach the ears of his bishop, who would infallibly have unfrocked him for promulgating a doctrine so subversive of the main pillar of all orthodox establishments.

When Anthelia had attained her sixteenth year, her father deemed it necessary to introduce her to that human world of which she had hitherto seen so little, and for this purpose took a journey to London, where he was received by the surviving portion of his old acquaintance as a ghost returned from Acheron.[18] The impression which the gay scenes of the metropolis made on the mind of Anthelia—to what illustrious characters she was introduced—"and all she thought of all she saw,"[19]—it would be foreign to our present purpose to detail: suffice it to say, that from this period Sir Henry regularly passed the winter in London and the summer in Westmoreland, till his daughter attained the age of twenty, about which period he died.

Anthelia passed twelve months from this time in total seclusion at Melincourt, notwith-standing many pressing invitations from various match-making dowagers in London, who were solicitous to dispose of her according to their views of her advantage; in which how far their own was lost sight of, it may not be difficult to determine.

Among the numerous lovers who had hitherto sighed at her shrine, not one had succeeded in making the slightest impression on her heart; and during the twelve months of seclusion which elapsed from the death of her father to the commencement of this authentic history, they had all completely vanished from the tablet of her memory.[20] Her knowledge of love was altogether theoretical; and her theory, being formed by the study of Italian poetry in the bosom of mountain solitude, naturally and necessarily pointed to a visionary model of excellence which it was very little likely the modern world could realize.

The dowagers at length despairing of drawing her from her retirement, respectively came to various resolutions for the accomplishment of their ends; some resolving to go in person to Melincourt, and exert all their powers of oratory to mould her to their wishes, and others instigating their several *protégés* to set boldly forward in search of fortune, and lay siege to the castle and its mistress together.

CHAPTER II.

FASHIONABLE ARRIVALS.[1]

It was late in the afternoon of an autumnal day, when the elegant post-chariot[2] of the Honourable Mrs. Pinmoney,[3] a lady of high renown in the annals of match-making, turned the corner of a stupendous precipice in the narrow pass which formed the only access to the valley of Melincourt. This Honourable lady was accompanied by her only daughter Miss Danaretta Contantina;[4] which names, by the by, appear to be female diminutives of the Italian words *danaro contante*, signifying *ready money*, and genteelly hinting to all fashionable Strephons,[5] the only terms on which the *commodity*[6] so denominated would be disposed of, according to the universal practice of this liberal and enlightened generation, in that most commercial of all bargains, marriage.

The ivied battlements and frowning towers of Melincourt Castle, as they burst at once upon the sight, very much astonished the elder and delighted the younger lady; for the latter had cultivated a great deal of theoretical romance— in taste, not in feeling—an important distinction — which enabled her to be most liberally sentimental in words, without at all influencing her actions; to talk of heroic affection and self-sacrificing enthusiasm, without incurring the least danger of forming a disinterested attachment, or of erring in any way whatever on the score of practical generosity. Indeed, in all respects of practice the young lady was the true counterpart of her mother, though they sometimes differed a little in the forms of sentiment: thus, for instance, when any of their dear friends happened to go, as it is called, down hill in the world, the old lady was generally very severe on their *imprudence*, and the young lady very pathetic on their *misfortune:* but as to holding any further intercourse with, or rendering any species of assistance to, any dear friend so circumstanced, neither the one nor the other was ever suspected of conduct so very unfashionable. In the main point, therefore, of both their lives, that of making a *good match* for Miss Danaretta, their views perfectly coincided; and though Miss Danaretta, in her speculative conversations on this subject, among her female acquaintance, talked as young ladies always talk, and laid down very precisely *the only kind of man she would ever think of marrying,* endowing him, of course, with all the virtues in our good friend Hookham's Library;[7] yet it was very well understood, as it usually is on similar occasions, that no other proof of the possession of the aforesaid virtues would be required from any individual, who might present himself in the character of *Corydon sospiroso,*[8] than a satisfactory certificate from the old lady in Threadneedle Street,[9] that the bearer was a *good man,*[10] and could be proved so in the *Alley.*[11]

Such were the amiable specimens of worldly wisdom and affected romance, that prepared to invade the retirement of the mountain-enthusiast, the really romantic unworldly Anthelia.

"What a strange-looking old place!" said Mrs. Pinmoney: "it seems like any thing but the dwelling of a young heiress. I am afraid the rascally postboys[12] have joined in a plot against us, and intend to deliver us to a gang of thieves!"

"Banditti,[13] you should say, mamma," said Miss Danaretta: "thieves is an odious word."

"Pooh, child!" said Mrs. Pinmoney. "The reality is odious enough, let the word be what it will. Is not a rogue a rogue, call him by what name you may?"

"O, certainly not," said Miss Danaretta; "for in that case a poor rogue without a title, would not be more a rogue than a rich rogue with one; but that he is so in a most infinite proportion, the whole experience of the world demonstrates."

"True," said the old lady; "and as our reverend friend Dr. Bosky[14] observes, to maintain the contrary would be to sanction a principle utterly subversive of all social order and aristocratical privilege."

The carriage now rolled over the narrow ledge, which connected the site of the castle with the neighbouring rocks. A furious peal at the outer bell brought forth a venerable porter, who opened the gates with becoming gravity, and the carriage entered a spacious court, of much more recent architecture than the exterior of the castle, and built in a style of modern Gothic,[15] that seemed to form a happy medium between the days of feudality, commonly called the dark ages, and the nineteenth century, commonly called the enlightened age: *why*, I could never discover.[16]

The inner gates were opened by another grave and venerable domestic, who with all the imperturbable decorum and formality of the old school, assisted the ladies to alight, and ushered them along an elegant colonnade into the library, which we shall describe no farther than by saying, that the apartment was Gothic and the furniture Grecian:[17] whether this be an unpardonable incongruity calculated to disarrange all legitimate associations, or a judicious combination of solemnity and elegance, most happily adapted to the purposes of study, we must leave to the decision, or rather discussion, of picturesque and antiquarian disputants.[18]

The windows, which were of stained glass, were partly open to a shrubbery, which admitting the meditative mind into the recesses of nature, and excluding all view of distant scenes, heightened the deep seclusion and repose of the apartment. It consisted principally of evergreens; but the parting beauty of the last flowers of autumn, and the lighter and now fading tints of a few deciduous shrubs, mingled with the imperishable verdure of the cedar and the laurel.

The old domestic went in search of his young mistress, and the ladies threw themselves on a sofa in graceful attitudes.[19] They were shortly joined by Anthelia, who welcomed them to Melincourt with all the politeness which the necessity of the case imposed.

The change of dress, the dinner, the dessert, seasoned with the *newest news* of the fashionable world, which the visitors thought must be of all things the most delightful to the mountain-recluse, filled up a portion of the evening. When they returned from the dining-room to the library, the windows were closed, the curtains drawn, and the tea and coffee urns bubbling on the table, and sending up their steamy columns: an old fashion, to be sure, and sufficiently rustic, for which we apologize in due form to the reader, who prefers his tea and coffee brought in cool by the butler in little cups on a silver salver, and handed round to the simpering company till it is as cold as an Iceland spring. There is no disputing about taste, and the taste of Melincourt Castle on this subject had been always very poetically unfashionable; for the tea would have satisfied Johnson, and the coffee enchanted Voltaire.[20]

"I must confess, my dear," said the Honourable Mrs. Pinmoney, "there is a great deal of comfort in your way of living, that is, there would be in good company; but you are so solitary——"[21]

"Here is the best of company," said Anthelia smiling, and pointing to the shelves of the library.

THE HONOURABLE MRS. PINMONEY.[22]

Very true: books are very good things in their way; but an hour or two at most is quite enough of them for me: more can serve no purpose but to muddle one's head. If I were to live such a life for a week as you have done for the last twelve months, I should have more company than I like, in the shape of a whole legion of blue devils.[23]

MISS DANARETTA.

Nay, I think there is something delightfully romantic in Anthelia's mode of life: but I confess I should like now and then, peeping through the ivy of the battlements, to observe a *preux chevalier*[24] exerting all his eloquence to persuade the inflexible porter to open the castle gates, and allow him one opportunity of throwing himself at the feet of the divine lady of the castle, for whom he had been seven years dying a lingering death.

THE HONOURABLE MRS. PINMONEY.

And growing fatter all the while.—Heaven defend me from such hypocritical fops! Seven years indeed! It did not take as many weeks to bring me and poor dear dead Mr. Pinmoney together.

ANTHELIA.

I should have been afraid that so short an acquaintance would scarcely have been sufficient to acquire that mutual knowledge of each other's tastes, feelings, and character, which I should think the only sure basis of matrimonial happiness.

THE HONOURABLE MRS. PINMONEY.

Tastes, feelings, and character! Why, my love, you really do seem to believe yourself in the age of chivalry, when those words certainly signified very essential differences. But now the matter is very happily simplified. Tastes:—they depend on the fashion. There is always a fashionable taste: a taste for driving the mail[25]—a taste for acting Hamlet[26]—a taste for philosophical lectures[27]—a taste for the marvellous—a taste for the simple—a taste for the brilliant—a taste for the sombre—a taste for the tender—a taste for the grim[28]—a taste for banditti[29]—a taste for ghosts[30]—a taste for the devil—a taste for French dancers and Italian singers, and German whiskers[31] and tragedies—a taste for enjoying the country in November, and wintering in London till the end of the dog-days[32]—a taste for making shoes[33]—a taste for picturesque tours[34]—a taste for taste itself, or for essays on taste:[35]—but no gentleman would be so rash as to have a taste of his own, or his last winter's taste, or any taste, my love, but the fashionable taste. Poor dear Mr. Pinmoney was reckoned a man of exquisite taste among all his acquaintance; for the new taste, let it be what it would, always fitted him as well as his new coat, and he was the very pink[36] and mirror of fashion, as much in the one as the other.—So much for tastes, my dear.

ANTHELIA.

I am afraid I shall always be a very unfashionable creature; for I do not think I should have sympathized with any one of the tastes you have just enumerated.

THE HONOURABLE MRS. PINMONEY.

You are so contumacious, such a romantic heretic from the orthodox supremacy of fashion. Now, as for feelings, my dear, you know there are no such things in the fashionable world; therefore that difficulty vanishes even more easily than the first.

ANTHELIA.

I am sorry for it.

THE HONOURABLE MRS. PINMONEY.

Sorry!—Feelings are very troublesome things, and always stand in the way of a person's own interests. Then, as to character—a gentleman's character[37] is usually in the keeping of his banker, or his agent, or his steward, or his solicitor; and if they can certify and demonstrate that he has the means of keeping a handsome equipage,[38] and a town and country house,[39] and of giving routs[40] and dinners, and of making a good settlement[41] on the happy object of his choice—what more of any gentleman's character would you desire to know?

ANTHELIA.

A great deal more. I would require him to be free in all his thoughts, true in all his words, generous in all his actions—ardent in friendship, enthusiastic in love, disinterested in both—prompt in the conception, and constant in the execution, of benevolent enterprise—the friend of the friendless, the champion of the feeble, the firm opponent of the powerful oppressor—not to be enervated by luxury, nor corrupted by avarice, nor intimidated by tyranny, nor enthralled by superstition—more desirous to distribute wealth than to possess it, to disseminate liberty than to appropriate power, to cheer the heart of sorrow than to dazzle the eyes of folly.

THE HONOURABLE MRS. PINMONEY.

And do you really expect to find such a knight-errant? The age of chivalry is gone.[42]

ANTHELIA.

It is, but its spirit survives.[43] Disinterested benevolence,[44] the mainspring of all that is really admirable in the days of chivalry, will never perish for want of some minds calculated to feel its influence, still less for want of a proper field of exertion. To protect the feeble—to raise the fallen—to liberate the captive—to be the persevering foe of tyrants (whether the great tyrant of an overwhelming empire, the petty tyrant of the fields, or the "little tyrant of a little corporation"*),[45] it is not necessary to wind the bugle before enchanted castles, or to seek adventures in the depths of mountain-caverns and forests of pine: there is no scene of human life but presents sufficient scope to energetic generosity: the field of action, though less splendid in its accompaniments, is not less useful in its results, nor less attractive to a liberal spirit:[46] and I believe it possible

* Junius.

to find as true a knight-errant in a brown coat in the nineteenth century, as in a suit of golden armour in the days of
Charlemagne.

THE HONOURABLE MRS. PINMONEY.

Well! well! my dear, when you have seen a little more of the
world, you will get rid of some of your chivalrous whimsies;
and I think you will then agree with me, that there is not,
in the whole sphere of fashion, a more elegant, fine-spirited,
dashing, generous fellow than my nephew Sir Telegraph[47]
Paxarett,[48] who by the by will be driving[49] his barouche[50] this
way shortly, and if you do not absolutely forbid it, will call on
me in his route.

These words seemed to portend that the Honourable Mrs.
Pinmoney's visit would be a visitation, and at the same time
threw a clear light on its motive; but they gave birth in the
mind of Anthelia to a train of ideas which concluded in a
somewhat singular determination.

CHAPTER III.

HYPOCON HOUSE.[1]

ANTHELIA had received intimations, from various quarters, of
similar intentions on the part of various individuals, not less
valuable than Sir Telegraph Paxarett in the scale of moral utility;[2] and though there was not one among them for whom she
felt the slightest interest, she thought it would be too uncour-
teous in a pupil of chivalry, and too inhospitable in the mistress of an old English castle, to bar her gates against them.
At the same time she felt the want of a lord seneschal[3] to
receive and entertain visitors so little congenial to her habits
and inclinations: and it immediately occurred to her, that no
one would be more fit for this honourable office, if he could be
prevailed on to undertake it, than an old relation, a medium, as
it were, between cousin and great uncle; who had occasionally
passed a week or a month with her father at Melincourt. The
name of this old gentleman was Hippy: Humphrey Hippy,[4]
Esquire, of Hypocon House, in the county of Durham. He was
a bachelor, and his character exhibited a singular compound
of kind-heartedness, spleen, and melancholy, which governed
him by turns, and sometimes in such rapid succession that
they seemed almost co-existent. To him Anthelia determined
on sending an express, with a letter entreating him to take on
himself, for a short time, the superintendence of Melincourt
Castle, and giving as briefly as possible her reasons for the
request. In pursuance of this determination, old Peter Gray, a
favourite domestic of Sir Henry, and I believe a distant relation of little Lucy,*[5] was dispatched the following morning to
Hypocon House, where the gate was opened to him by old
Harry Fell, a distant relation of little Alice,* who, as the reader

---

* For Lucy Gray and Alice Fell, see Mr. Wordsworth's Lyrical Ballads.

well knows, "belonged to Durham."[6] Old Harry had become, by long habit, a curious species of animated mirror, and reflected all the humours of his master with wonderful nicety. When Mr. Hippy was in a rage, old Harry looked fierce: when Mr. Hippy was in a good humour, old Harry was the picture of human kindness: when Mr. Hippy was blue-devilled,[7] old Harry was vapourish:[8] when Mr. Hippy was as melancholy as a gib cat,[9] old Harry was as dismal as a screech-owl. The latter happened to be the case, when old Peter presented himself at the gate, and old Harry accordingly opened it with a most rueful elongation of visage. Peter Gray was ready with a warm salutation for his old acquaintance Harry Fell; but the lamentable cast of expression in the physiognomy of the latter froze it on his lips, and he contented himself with asking in a hesitating tone, "Is Mr. Hippy at home?"

"He is," slowly and sadly articulated Harry Fell, shaking his head.

"I have a letter for him," said Peter Gray.

"Ah!" said Harry Fell, taking the letter, and stalking off with it as solemnly as if he had been following a funeral.

"A pleasant reception," thought Peter Gray, "instead of the old ale and cold sirloin I dreamed of."

Old Harry tapped three times at the door of his master's chamber, observing the same interval between each tap as is usual between the sounds of a muffled drum: then, after a due pause, he entered the apartment. Mr. Hippy was in his night-gown and slippers, with one leg on a cushion, suffering under an imaginary attack of the gout, and in the last stage of despondency. Old Harry walked forward in the same slow pace till he found himself at the proper distance from his master's chair. Then putting forth his hand as deliberately as if it had been the hour-hand of the kitchen-clock, he presented the letter. Mr. Hippy took it in the same manner, sunk back in his chair as if exhausted with the effort, and cast his eyes languidly on the seal. Immediately his eyes brightened, he tore open the letter, read it in an instant, sprang up, flung his night-gown one way, his night-cap another, kicked off his slippers, kicked away his cushion, kicked over his chair, and bounced down stairs, roaring for his coat and boots, and his travelling chariot,[10] with old Harry capering at his heels, and re-echoing all his requisitions. Harry Fell was now a new man: Peter Gray was seized by the hand and dragged into the buttery, where a cold goose and a flagon of ale were placed before him; to which he immediately proceeded to do ample justice; while old Harry rushed off with a cold fowl and ham, for the refection of Mr. Hippy, who had been too seriously indisposed in the morning, to touch a morsel of breakfast. Having placed these and a bottle of Madeira in due form and order before his master, he flew back to the buttery to assist old Peter in the demolition of the goose and ale, his own appetite in the morning having sympathized with his master's, and being now equally disposed to make up for lost time.

Mr. Hippy's travelling chariot was rattled up to the door by four high-mettled posters[11] from the nearest inn. Mr. Hippy sprang into the carriage, old Harry vaulted into the dicky, the postillions cracked their whips,[12] and away they went,

> "Over the hills and the plains,
> Over the rivers and rocks,"[13]

leaving old Peter gaping after them at the gate, in profound astonishment at their sudden metamorphosis, and in utter despair of being able, by any exertions of his own, to be their forerunner and announcer at Melincourt. Considering, therefore, that when the necessity of being too late is inevitable, hurry is manifestly superfluous, he mounted his galloway[14] with great gravity and deliberation, and trotted slowly off towards the mountains, philosophizing all the way in the usual poetical style of a Cumberland peasant.[15] Our readers will of course feel much obliged to us for not presenting them with his meditations. But instead of jogging back with old Peter Gray, or travelling post with Humphrey Hippy, Esquire, we shall avail ourselves of the four-in-hand barouche[16] which is just coming in view, to take a seat on the box by the side of Sir Telegraph Paxarett, and proceed in his company to Melincourt.

CHAPTER IV.

REDROSE ABBEY.

Sir Telegraph Paxarett had entered the precincts of the mountains of Westmoreland, and was bowling his barouche along a romantic valley, looking out very anxiously for an inn, as he had now driven his regular diurnal allowance of miles, and was becoming very impatient for his equally regular diurnal allowance of fish, fowl, and Madeira. A wreath of smoke ascending from a thick tuft of trees at a distance, and in a straight direction before him, cheered up his spirits, and induced him to cheer up those of his horses with two or three of those technical terms of the road, which we presume to have formed part of the genuine language of the ancient Houhynnhmns,[1] since they seem not only much better adapted to equine than human organs of sound, but are certainly much more generally intelligible to four-footed than to two-footed animals. Sir Telegraph was doomed to a temporary disappointment; for when he had attained the desired point, the smoke proved to issue from the chimneys of an ancient abbey which appeared to have been recently converted from a pile of ruins into the habitation of some variety of the human species, with very singular veneration for the relics of antiquity, which, in their exterior aspect, had suffered little from the alteration. There was something so analogous between the state of this building and what he had heard of Melincourt, that if it had not been impossible to mistake an abbey for a castle, he might almost have fancied himself arrived at the dwelling of the divine Anthelia. Under a detached piece of ruins near the road, which appeared to have been part of a chapel, several workmen were busily breaking the ground with spade and pickaxe: a gentleman was superintending their operations, and seemed very eager to arrive at the object of his search. Sir Telegraph stopped his barouche to inquire the distance to the nearest inn: the gentleman replied, six miles. "That is just five miles and a half too far," said Sir Telegraph, and was proceeding to drive on, when, on turning round to make his parting bow to the stranger, he suddenly recognised him for an old acquaintance and fellow-collegian.

"Sylvan Forester!"[2] exclaimed Sir Telegraph; "who should have dreamed of meeting you in this uncivilized part of the world?"

"I am afraid," said Mr. Forester, "this part of the world does not deserve the compliment implied in the epithet you have bestowed on it. Within no very great distance from this spot are divers towns, villages, and hamlets, in any one of which, if you have money, you may make pretty sure of being cheated, and if you have none, quite sure of being starved—strong evidences of a state of civilization."

"Aha!" said Sir Telegraph, "your old way, now I recollect—always fond of railing at civilized life, and holding forth in praise of savages and what you called original men. But what, in truth, make you in Westmoreland?"[3]

"I have purchased this old abbey," said Mr. Forester, "(anciently called the abbey of Rednose,[4] which I have altered to Redrose, as being more analogous to my notions of beauty, whatever the reverend Fellows of our old college might have thought of it), and have fitted it up for my habitation, with the view of carrying on in peace and seclusion some peculiar experiments on the nature and progress of man.[5] Will you dine with me, and pass the night here? and I will introduce you to an original character."[6]

"With all my heart," said Sir Telegraph; "I can assure you, independently of the pleasure of meeting an old acquaintance, it is a great comfort to dine in a gentleman's house, after living from inn to inn, and being poisoned with bad wine for a month."

Sir Telegraph descended from his box, and directed one of his grooms to open the carriage-door and emancipate the coachman,[7] who was fast asleep inside. Sir Telegraph gave him the reins, and Mr. Forester sent one of his workmen to show him the way to the stables.

"And pray," said Sir Telegraph, as the barouche disappeared among the trees, "what may be the object of your researches in this spot?"

"You know," said Mr. Forester, "it is a part of my tenets that the human species is gradually decreasing in size and strength,[8] and I am digging in the old cemetery for bones and skulls to establish the truth of my theory."

"Have you found any?" said Sir Telegraph.

"Many," said Mr. Forester. "About three weeks ago we dug up a very fine skeleton, no doubt of some venerable father, who must have been, in more senses than one, a pillar of the church. I have had the skull polished and set in silver. You shall drink your wine out of it,[9] if you please, to-day."

"I thank you," said Sir Telegraph, "but I am not particular: a glass will suit me as well as the best skull in Europe. Besides, I am a moderate man: one bottle of Madeira and another of claret[10] are enough for me at any time; so that the quantity of wine a reverend sconce can carry would be just treble my usual allowance."

They walked together towards the abbey. Sir Telegraph earnestly requested, that, before they entered, he might be favoured with a peep at the stable. Mr. Forester of course complied. Sir Telegraph found this important part of the buildings capacious and well adapted to its purpose, but did not altogether approve its being totally masked by an old ivied wall, which had served in former times to prevent the braw and bonny Scot from making too free with the beeves[11] of the pious fraternity.

The new dwelling-house was so well planned, and fitted in so well between the ancient walls, that very few vestiges of the modern architect were discernible; and it was obvious that the growth of the ivy, and of numerous trailing and twining plants, would soon over-run all vestiges of the innovation, and blend the whole exterior into one venerable character of antiquity.

"I do not think," said Mr. Forester, as they proceeded through part of the grounds, "that the most determined zealot of the picturesque would quarrel with me here. I found the woods around the abbey matured by time and neglect into a fine state of wildness and intricacy, and I think I have left enough of them to gratify their most ardent admirer."

"Quite enough, in all conscience," said Sir Telegraph, who was in white jean trowsers, with very thin silk stockings and pumps.[12] "I do not generally calculate on being, as an old song I have somewhere heard expresses it,

> "Forced to scramble,
> When I ramble,
> Through a copse of furze and bramble;"[13]

which would be all very pleasant perhaps, if the fine effect of picturesque roughness were not unfortunately, as Macbeth says of his dagger, 'sensible to feeling as to sight.'[14] But who is that gentleman, sitting under the great oak yonder in the green coat and nankins?[15] He seems very thoughtful."

"He is of a contemplative disposition," said Mr. Forester: "you must not be surprised if he should not speak a word during the whole time you are here. The politeness of his manner makes amends for his habitual taciturnity. I will introduce you."

The gentleman under the oak had by this time discovered them, and came forward with great alacrity to meet Mr. Forester, who cordially shook hands with him, and introduced him to Sir Telegraph as Sir Oran Haut-ton,[16] Baronet.

Sir Telegraph looked earnestly at the stranger, but was too polite to laugh,[17] though he could not help thinking there was something very ludicrous in Sir Oran's physiognomy, notwithstanding the air of high fashion which characterized his whole deportment, and which was heightened by a pair of enormous whiskers,[18] and the folds of a vast cravat.[19] He therefore bowed to Sir Oran with becoming gravity, and Sir Oran returned the bow with very striking politeness.

"Possibly," thought Sir Telegraph,[20] "possibly I may have seen an uglier fellow."

The trio entered the abbey, and shortly after sate down to dinner.

Mr. Forester and Sir Oran Haut-ton took the head and foot of the table. Sir Telegraph sate between them. "Some soup, Sir Telegraph?" said Mr. Forester. "I rather think," said Sir Telegraph, "I shall trouble Sir Oran for a slice of fish." Sir Oran helped him with great dexterity, and then performed the same office for himself. "I think you will like this Madeira?" said Mr. Forester. "Capital!" said Sir Telegraph: "Sir Oran, shall I have the pleasure of taking wine with you?" Sir Oran Haut-ton bowed gracefully to Sir Telegraph Paxarett, and the glasses were tossed off with the usual ceremonies. Sir Oran preserved an inflexible silence during the whole duration of dinner, but showed great proficiency in the dissection of game.[21]

When the cloth was removed, the wine circulated freely, and Sir Telegraph, as usual, filled a numerous succession of glasses. Mr. Forester, not as usual, did the same; for he was generally very abstemious in this respect: but, on the present occasion, he relaxed from his severity, quoting the *Placari genius festis impune diebus*, and the *Dulce est desipere in loco*, of Horace.[22] Sir Oran likewise approved, by his practice, that he thought the wine particularly excellent, and *Beviamo tutti tre*[23] appeared to be the motto of the party. Mr Forester inquired into the motives which had brought Sir Telegraph to Westmoreland; and Sir Telegraph entered into a rapturous encomium of the heiress of Melincourt, which was suddenly cut short by Sir Oran, who having taken a glass too much, rose suddenly from table, took a flying leap through the window, and went dancing along the woods like a harlequin.[24]

"Upon my word," said Sir Telegraph, "a devilish lively, pleasant fellow! Curse me, if I know what to make of him."

"I will tell you his history," said Mr. Forester, "by and by. In the mean time I must look after him, that he may neither do nor receive mischief. Pray take care of yourself till I return." Saying this, he sprang through the window after Sir Oran, and disappeared by the same track among the trees.

"Curious enough!" soliloquized Sir Telegraph; "however, not much to complain of, as the best part of the company is left behind: videlicet,[25] the bottle."

CHAPTER V.

SUGAR.

SIR Telegraph was tossing off the last heeltap[1] of his regular diurnal allowance of wine, when Mr. Forester and Sir Oran Haut-ton re-appeared, walking past the window arm in arm; Sir Oran's mode of progression being very vacillating, indirect, and titubant;[2] enough so, at least, to show that he had not completely danced off the effects of the Madeira. Mr. Forester shortly after entered; and Sir Telegraph inquiring concerning Sir Oran, "I have persuaded him to go to bed," said Mr. Forester, "and I doubt not he is already fast asleep." A servant now entered with tea. Sir Telegraph proceeded to help himself, when he perceived there was no sugar, and reminded his host of the omission.

MR. FORESTER.

If I had anticipated the honour of your company, Sir Telegraph, I would have provided myself with a small quantity of that nefarious ingredient: but in this solitary situation, these things are not to be had at a moment's notice. As it is, seeing little company, and regulating my domestic arrangements on philosophical principles, I never suffer an atom of West Indian produce to pass my threshold. I have no wish to resemble those pseudo-philanthropists, those miserable declaimers against slavery, who are very liberal of words which cost them nothing, but are not capable of advancing the object they profess to have at heart, by submitting to the smallest personal privation. If I wish seriously to exterminate an evil, I begin by examining how far I am myself, in any way whatever, an accomplice in the extension of its baleful influence. My reform commences at home. How can I unblushingly declaim against thieves, while I am a receiver of stolen goods? How can I seriously call myself an enemy to slavery, while I indulge in the luxuries that slavery acquires? How can the consumer of sugar pretend to throw on the grower of it the exclusive burden of their participated criminality? How can he wash his hands, and say with Pilate: "*I am innocent of this blood, see ye to it?*"[3]

Sir Telegraph poured some cream into his unsweetened tea, drank it, and said nothing. Mr. Forester proceeded:

If every individual in this kingdom, who is truly and conscientiously an enemy to the slave-trade, would subject himself to so very trivial a privation as abstinence from colonial produce, I consider that a mortal blow would be immediately struck at the roots of that iniquitous system.

SIR TELEGRAPH PAXARETT.

If every individual enemy to the slave-trade would follow your example, the object would no doubt be much advanced; but the practice of one individual, more or less, has little or no influence on general society; most of us go on with the tide, and the dread of the single word *quiz*[4] has more influence in keeping the greater part of us within the pale of custom, fashion, and precedent, than all the moral reasonings and declamations in the world will ever have in persuading us to break through it. As to the diffusion of liberty, and the general happiness of mankind, which used to be your favourite topics when we were at College together, I should have thought your subsequent experience would have shown you, that there is not one person in ten thousand, who knows what liberty means, or cares a single straw for any happiness but his own——

MR. FORESTER.

Which his own miserable selfishness must estrange from him for ever. He whose heart has never glowed with a generous resolution, who has never felt the conscious triumph of a disinterested sacrifice, who has never sympathized with human joys or sorrows, but when they have had a direct and palpable reference to himself, can never be acquainted with even the semblance of happiness. His utmost enjoyment must be many degrees inferior to that of a pig, inasmuch as the sordid mire of selfish and brutal stupidity is more defiling to the soul, than any coacervation[5] of mere material mud can possibly be to the body. The latter may be cleared away with two or three ablutions, but the former cleaves and accumulates into a mass of impenetrable corruption, that bids defiance to the united powers of Hercules and Alpheus.[6]

SIR TELEGRAPH PAXARETT.

Be that as it may, every man will continue to follow his own fancy. The world is bad enough, I dare say; but it is not for you or me to mend it.

MR. FORESTER.

There is the key-stone of the evil—mistrust of the influence of individual example. "We are bad ourselves, because we despair of the goodness of others."[*][7] Yet the history of the world abounds with sudden and extraordinary revolutions in the opinions of mankind, which have been effected by single enthusiasts.

SIR TELEGRAPH PAXARETT.

Speculative opinions have been sometimes changed by the efforts of roaring fanatics. Men have been found very easily permutable into *ites* and *onians*, *avians* and *arians*, Wesleyites or Whitfieldites, Huntingtonians or Muggletonians, Moravians, Trinitarians, Unitarians, Anythingarians:[8] but the metamorphosis only affects a few obscure notions concerning types, symbols, and mysteries,[9] which have scarcely any effect on

* Coleridge's Friend.

moral theory, and of course, *à fortiori*,[10] none whatever on moral practice: the latter is for the most part governed by the general habits and manners of the society we live in. One man may twang responses in concert with the parish-clerk; another may sit silent in a Quakers' meeting, waiting for the inspiration of the Spirit; a third may groan and howl in a tabernacle;[11] a fourth may breakfast, dine, and sup, in a Sandemonian chapel:[12] but meet any of the four in the common intercourse of society, you will scarcely know one from another. The single adage, *Charity begins at home*,[13] will furnish a complete key to the souls of all four: for I have found, as far as my observation has extended, that men carry their religion*[14] in other men's heads, and their morality in their own pockets.

MR. FORESTER.

I think it will be found that individual example has in many instances produced great moral effects on the practice of society. Even if it were otherwise, is it not better to be Abdiel

---

* "There is not any burden that some would gladlier post off to another than the charge and care of their religion. There be of Protestants and professors who live and die in as arrant and implicit faith as any lay Papist of Loretto. A wealthy man, addicted to his pleasure and to his profits, finds religion to be a traffic so entangled and of so many peddling accounts, that, of all mysteries, he cannot skill to keep a stock going upon that trade. What should he do? Fain would he have the name to be religious: fain would he bear up with his neighbours in that. What does he, therefore, but resolves to give over toiling, and to find himself out some factor, to whose care and credit he may commit the whole management of his religious affairs; some divine of note and estimation that must be. To him he adheres, resigns the whole warehouse of his religion, with all the locks and keys, into his custody, and, indeed, makes the very person of that man his religion, esteems his associating with him a sufficient evidence and commendatory of his own piety. So that a man may say, his religion is now no more within himself, but is become a dividual moveable, and goes and comes near him according as that good man frequents the house. He entertains him, gives him gifts, feasts him, lodges him: his religion comes home at night, prays, is liberally supped, and sumptuously laid to sleep, rises, is saluted, and after the malmsey, or some well-spiced bruage, and better breakfasted than he whose morning appetite would have gladly fed on green figs between Bethany and Jerusalem, his religion walks abroad at eight, and leaves his kind entertainer in the shop, trading all day without his religion." —MILTON's *Speech for the Liberty of unlicensed Printing*.

among the fiends,[15] than to be lost and confounded in the legion of imps grovelling in the train of the evil power?

SIR TELEGRAPH PAXARETT.

There is something in that.

MR. FORESTER.

To borrow an allegory from Homer:[16] I would say society is composed of two urns, one of good, and one of evil. I will suppose, that every individual of the human species receives from his natal genius a little phial, containing one drop of a fluid, which shall be evil, if poured into the urn of evil, and good if into that of good. If you were proceeding to the station of the urns with ten thousand persons, every one of them predetermined to empty his phial into the urn of evil, which I fear is too true a picture of the practice of society, should you consider their example, if you were hemmed in in the centre of them, a sufficient excuse for not breaking from them, and approaching the neglected urn? Would you say, "The urn of good will derive little increase from my solitary drop, and one more or less will make very little difference in the urn of ill: I will spare myself trouble, do as the world does, and let the urn of good take its chance, from those who can approach it with less difficulty?" No: you would rather say, "That neglected urn contains the hopes of the human species: little, indeed, is the addition I can make to it, but it will be good as far as it goes;" and if, on approaching the urn, you should find it not so empty as you had anticipated, if the genius appointed to guard it should say to you, "There is enough in this urn already to allow a reasonable expectation that it will one day be full, and yet it has only accumulated drop by drop through the efforts of individuals, who broke through the pale and pressure of the multitude, and did not despair of human virtue;" would you not feel ten thousand times repaid for the difficulties you had overcome, and the scoffs of the fools and slaves you had abandoned, by the single reflection that would then rush upon your mind, *I am one of these?*

SIR TELEGRAPH PAXARETT.

Gad,[17] very likely: I never considered the subject in that light. You have made no allowance for the mixture of good and evil, which I think the fairest state of the case. It seems to me, that the world always goes on pretty much in one way. People eat, drink, and sleep, make merry with their friends, get as much money as they can, marry when they can afford it, take care of their children because they are their own, are thought well of while they live in proportion to the depth of their purse, and when they die, are sure of as good a character on their tombstones as the bellman and stonemason can afford for their money.

MR. FORESTER.

Such is the multitude; but there are noble exceptions to this general littleness.

SIR TELEGRAPH PAXARETT.

Now and then an original genius strikes out of the common track; but there are two ways of doing that—into a worse as well as a better.

MR. FORESTER.

There are some assuredly, who strike into a better; and these are the ornaments of their age, and the lights of the world.[18] You must admit too, that there are many, who, though without energy or capacity to lead, have yet virtue enough to follow an illustrious example.

SIR TELEGRAPH PAXARETT.

One or two.

MR. FORESTER.

In every mode of human action there are two ways to be pursued—a good and a bad one. It is the duty of every man to ascertain the former, as clearly as his capacity will admit, by an accurate examination of general relations; and to act upon it rigidly, without regard to his own previous habits, or the common practice of the world.

SIR TELEGRAPH PAXARETT.

And you infer from all this, that it is my duty to drink my tea without sugar.

MR. FORESTER.

I infer, that it is the duty of every one, thoroughly penetrated with the iniquity of the slave-trade, to abstain entirely from the use of colonial produce.

SIR TELEGRAPH PAXARETT.

I may do that, without any great effort of virtue. I find the difference in this instance, more trivial than I could have supposed. In fact, I never thought of it before.

MR. FORESTER.

I hope I shall before long have the pleasure of enrolling you a member of the Anti-saccharine Society,[19] which I have had the happiness to organize, and which is daily extending its numbers. Some of its principal members will shortly pay a visit to Redrose Abbey; and I purpose giving a festival, to which I shall invite all that is respectable and intelligent in this part of the country, and in which I intend to demonstrate practically, that a very elegant and luxurious entertainment may be prepared without employing a single particle of that abominable ingredient, and theoretically, that the use of sugar is economically superfluous, physically pernicious, morally atrocious, and politically abominable.

SIR TELEGRAPH PAXARETT.

I shall be happy to join the party, and I may possibly bring with me one or two inside passengers,[20] who will prove both ornamental and attractive to your festival. But you promised me an account of Sir Oran.

CHAPTER VI.

SIR ORAN HAUT-TON.

MR. FORESTER.

Sir Oran Haut-ton was caught very young in the woods of Angola.

SIR TELEGRAPH PAXARETT.

Caught!

MR. FORESTER.

Very young. He is a specimen of the natural and original man—the wild man of the woods; called, in the language of the more civilized and sophisticated natives of Angola, *Pongo*, and in that of the Indians of South America,[1] *Oran Outang*.

SIR TELEGRAPH PAXARETT.

The devil he is!

MR. FORESTER.

Positively. Some presumptuous naturalists have refused his species the honours of humanity; but the most enlightened and illustrious philosophers agree in considering him in his true light as the natural and original man.*[2] One French

---

* "I think I have established his humanity by proof that ought to satisfy every one who gives credit to human testimony."—*Ancient Metaphysics,* vol. iii. p. 40.[3]

"I have brought myself to a perfect conviction that the oran outang is a human creature as much as any of us."—*Ibid.* p. 133.[4]

"Nihil humani ei deesse diceres præter loquelam."—Bontius.[5]

"The fact truly is, that the man is easily distinguishable in him; nor are there any differences betwixt him and us, but what may be accounted for in so satisfactory a manner, that it would be extraordinary and unnatural if they were not to be found. His body, which is of the same shape as ours, is bigger and stronger than ours, ... according to that general law of nature above observed *(that all animals thrive best in their natural state).* His mind is such as that of a man must be, uncultivated by arts and sciences, and living wild in the woods. . . . . . . One thing, at least, is certain: that if ever men were in that state which I call natural, it must have been in such a country and climate as Africa, where they could live without art upon the natural fruits of the earth. 'Such countries,' Linnæus says,

36

philosopher, indeed, has been guilty of an inaccuracy, in considering him as a degenerated man:*[7] degenerated he cannot be; as his prodigious physical strength, his uninterrupted health, and his amiable simplicity of manners demonstrate. He is, as I have said, a specimen of the natural and original man—a genuine fac simile of the philosophical Adam.

He was caught by an intelligent negro very young, in the woods of Angola; and his gentleness and sweet temper†[8] winning the hearts of the negro and negress, they brought him up in their cottage as the playfellow of their little boys and girls, where, with the exception of speech, he acquired the practice of such of the simpler arts of life as the degree of civilization in that part of Africa admits. In this way he lived till he was about seventeen years of age——

SIR TELEGRAPH PAXARETT.

By his own reckoning?

'are the native country of man; there he lives naturally; in other countries, *non nisi coactè*, that is, by force of art.' If this be so, then, the short history of man is, that the race having begun in those fine climates, and having, as is natural, multiplied there so much that the spontaneous productions of the earth could not support them, they migrated into other countries, where they were obliged to invent arts for their subsistence; and with such arts, language, in process of time, would necessarily come........ That my facts and arguments are so convincing as to leave no doubt of the humanity of the oran outang, I will not take upon me to say; but thus much I will venture to affirm, that I have said enough to make the philosopher consider it as problematical, and a subject deserving to be inquired into. *For, as to the vulgar, I can never expect that they should acknowledge any relation to those inhabitants of the woods of Angola;* but that they should continue, through a false pride, to think highly derogatory from human nature what the philosopher, on the contrary, will think the greatest praise of man, that from the savage state in which the oran outang is, he should, by his own sagacity and industry, have arrived at the state in which we now see him."—*Origin and Progress of Language*, book ii. chap. 5.[6]

* "L'Oran outang, ou l'homme des bois, est un être particulier à la zone torride de notre hémisphere: le Pline de la nation qui l'a rangé dans la classe de singes ne me paroît pas conséquent; car il résulte des principaux traits de sa description que c'est un homme dégénéré."—*Philosophie de la Nature.*

† "The dispositions and affections of his mind are mild, gentle, and humane."—*Origin and Progress of Language*, book ii. chap. 4.
"The oran outang whom Buffon himself saw was of a sweet temper."—*Ibid.*

MR. FORESTER.

By analogical computation. At this period, my old friend Captain Hawltaught[9] of the Tornado frigate, being driven by stress of weather to the coast of Angola, was so much struck with the contemplative cast of Sir Oran's countenance,[*][10] that he offered the negro an irresistible bribe to surrender him to his possession. The negro brought him on board, and took an opportunity to leave him slily, but with infinite reluctance and sympathetic grief. When the ship weighed anchor, and Sir Oran found himself separated from the friends of his youth, and surrounded with strange faces, he wept bitterly,[†][11] and fell into such deep grief that his life was despaired of.[‡][12] The surgeon of the ship did what he could for him; and a much better doctor, Time, completed his cure. By degrees a very warm friendship for my friend Captain Hawltaught extinguished his recollection of his negro friends. Three years they cruised

---

[*] "But though I hold the oran outang to be of our species, it must not be supposed that I think the monkey or ape, with or without a tail, participates of our nature: on the contrary, I maintain that, however much his form may resemble man's, yet he is, as Linnæus says of the Troglodyte, *nec nostri generis nec sanguinis*. For as the mind, or internal principle, is the chief part of every animal, it is by it principally that the ancients have distinguished the several species. Now, it is laid down by Mr. Buffon, and I believe it to be a fact that cannot be contested, that neither monkey, ape, nor baboon, have any thing mild or gentle, tractable or docile, benevolent or humane in their dispositions; but, on the contrary, are malicious and untractable, to be governed only by force and fear, and without any *gravity or composure in their gait or behaviour, such as the oran outang has.*" —*Origin and Progress of Language*, book ii. chap. 4.

[†] "He is capable of the greatest affection, not only to his brother oran outangs, but to such among us as use him kindly. And it is a fact well attested to me by a gentleman who was an eye-witness of it, that an oran outang on board his ship conceived such an affection for the cook, that when upon some occasion he left the ship to go ashore, the gentleman saw the oran outang shed tears in great abundance."—*Origin and Progress of Language*, book ii. chap. 4.

[‡] "One of them was taken, and brought with some negro slaves to the capital of the kingdom of Malemba. He was a young one, but six feet and a half tall. Before he came to this city, he had been kept some months in company with the negro slaves, and during that time was tame and gentle, and took his victuals very quietly; but when he was brought into the town, such crowds of people came about him to gaze at him, that he could not bear it, but grew sullen, abstained from food, and died in four or five days."—*Origin and Progress of Language*, book ii. chap. 4.

together in the Tornado, when a dangerous wound compelled the old Captain to renounce his darling element, and lay himself up in ordinary[13] for the rest of his days. He retired on his half-pay and the produce of his prize-money,[14] to a little village in the west of England,[15] where he employed himself very assiduously in planting cabbages and watching the changes of the wind. Mr. Oran, as he was then called, was his inseparable companion, and became a very expert practical gardener. The old Captain used to observe, he could always say he had an honest man in his house, which was more than could be said of many honourable houses[16] where there was much vapouring[17] about honour.

Mr. Oran had long before shown a taste for music, and, with some little instruction from a marine officer in the Tornado, had become a proficient on the flute and French horn*.[18] He could never be brought to understand the notes; but from hearing any simple tune played or sung two or three times, he never failed to perform it with great exactness and brilliancy of execution. I shall merely observe, *en passant*,[19] that music appears, from this and several similar circumstances, to be more natural to man than speech.[20] The old Captain was fond of his bottle of wine after dinner, and his glass of grog[21] at night. Mr. Oran was easily brought to sympathize

---

* "He has the capacity of being a musician, and has actually learned to play upon the pipe and harp: a fact attested, not by a common traveller, but by a man of science, Mr. Peiresc, and who relates it, not as a hearsay, but as a fact consisting with his own knowledge. And this is the more to be attended to, as it shows that the oran outang has a perception of numbers, measure, and melody, which has always been accounted peculiar to our species. But the learning to speak, as well as the learning music, must depend upon particular circumstances; and men, living, as the oran outangs do, upon the natural fruits of the earth, with few or no arts, are not in a situation that is proper for the invention of language. The oran outangs who played upon the pipe had certainly not invented this art in the woods, but they had learned it from the negroes or the Europeans; and that they had not at the same time learned to speak, may be accounted for in one or other of two ways: either the same pains had not been taken to teach them articulation; or, secondly, music is more natural to man, and more easily acquired than speech."—*Origin and Progress of Language*, book ii. chap. 5.

in this taste;*[22] and they have many times sat up together half the night over a flowing bowl, the old Captain singing Rule Britannia, True Courage, or Tom Tough,[23] and Sir Oran accompanying him on the French horn.

During a summer tour in Devonshire, I called on my old friend Captain Hawltaught, and was introduced to Mr. Oran. You, who have not forgotten my old speculations on the origin and progress of man, may judge of my delight at this happy *rencontre*.[24] I exerted all the eloquence I was master of to persuade Captain Hawltaught to resign him to me, that I might give him a philosophical education.†[25] Finding this point unattainable, I took a house in the neighbourhood, and the intercourse which ensued was equally beneficial and agreeable to all three.

SIR TELEGRAPH PAXARETT.

And what part did you take in their nocturnal concerts, with Tom Tough and the French horn?

MR. FORESTER.

I was seldom present at them, and often remonstrated, but ineffectually, with the Captain, on his corrupting the amiable simplicity of the natural man by this pernicious celebration of vinous and spiritous orgies; but the only answer I could ever get from him was a hearty damn against all water-drinkers, accompanied with a reflection that he was sure every enemy to wine and grog must have clapped down the hatches of

---

* "Ces animaux," dit M. de la Brosse, "ont l'instinct de s'asseoir à table comme les hommes; ils mangent de tout sans distinction; ils se servent du couteau, de la cuiller, et de la fourchette, pour prendre et couper ce qu'on sert sur l'assiette: *ils boivent du vin et d'autres liqueurs:* nous les portames à bord; quaud ils étoient à table, ils se faisoient entendre des mousses lorsqu'ils avoient besoin de quelque chose."—BUFFON

† "If I can believe the newspapers, there was an oran outang of the great kind, that was some time ago shipped aboard a French East India ship. I hope he has had a safe voyage to Europe, and that his education will be taken care of." —*Ancient Metaphysics*, vol. iii. p. 40.

his conscience on some secret villany,[26] which he feared good liquor would pipe ahoy: and he usually concluded by striking up *Nothing like Grog, Saturday Night,* or *Swing the flowing Bowl,*[27] his friend Oran's horn ringing in sympathetic symphony.

The old Captain used to say, that grog was the elixir of life;[28] but it did not prove so to him; for one night he tossed off his last bumper,[29] sung his last stave,[30] and heard the last flourish of his Oran's horn. I thought poor Oran would have broken his heart; and had he not been familiarized to me, and conceived a very lively friendship for me before the death of his old friend, I fear the consequences would have been fatal.

Considering that change of scene would divert his melancholy, I took him with me to London. The theatres delighted him, particularly the opera, which not only accorded admirably with his taste for music; but where, as he looked round on the ornaments of the fashionable world, he seemed to be particularly comfortable, and to feel himself completely at home.

There is to a stranger something ludicrous in a first view of his countenance, which led me to introduce him only into the best society, where politeness would act as a preventive to the propensity to laugh; for he has so nice a sense of honour (which I shall observe, by the way, is peculiar to man), that if he were to be treated with any kind of contumely, he would infallibly die of a broken heart, as has been seen in some of his species.*[31] With a view of ensuring him the respect of society, which always attends on rank and fortune, I have purchased him a baronetcy,[32] and made over to him an estate. I have also purchased of the Duke of Rottenburgh[33] one half of the elective franchise vested in the body of Mr. Christopher

---

* Origin and Progress of Language, book ii. chap. 4.

Corporate,[34] the free, fat, and dependent burgess of the ancient and honourable borough of Onevote, who returns two members to Parliament, one of whom will shortly be Sir Oran. *(Sir Telegraph gave a long whistle.)* But before taking this important step, I am desirous that he should *finish his education.*[35] *(Sir Telegraph whistled again.)* I mean to say, that I wish, if possible, to put a few words into his mouth, which I have hitherto found impracticable, though I do not entirely despair of ultimate success. But this circumstance, for reasons which I will give you by and by, does not at all militate against the proofs of his being a man.

SIR TELEGRAPH PAXARETT.

If he be but half a man, he will be the fitter representative of half an elector; for as that "large body corporate of one,"[36] the free, fat, and dependent burgess of Onevote, returns two members to the honourable house, Sir Oran can only be considered as the representative of half of him. But, seriously, is not your principal object an irresistible exposure of the universality and omnipotence of corruption by purchasing for an oran outang one of those seats, the sale of which is unblushingly acknowledged to be *as notorious as the sun at noon-day?*[37] or do you really think him *one of us?*

MR. FORESTER.

I really think him a variety of the human species; and this is a point which I have it much at heart to establish in the acknowledgment of the civilized world.

SIR TELEGRAPH PAXARETT.

Buffon, whom I dip into now and then in the winter, ranks him, with Linnæus,[38] in the class of *Simiæ*.

MR. FORESTER.

Linnæus has given him the curious denominations of *Troglodytes, Homo nocturnus,* and *Homo silvestris:* but he evidently thought him a man: he describes him as having a hissing speech, thinking, reasoning, believing that the earth was made for him, and that he will one day be its sovereign.*[39]

SIR TELEGRAPH PAXARETT.

God save King Oran! By the by, you put me very much in mind of Valentine and Orson.[40] This wild man of yours will turn out some day to be the son of a king, lost in the woods, and suckled by a lioness:—"No waiter, but a knight templar:"[41]—no Oran, but a true prince.

MR. FORESTER.

As to Buffon, it is astonishing how that great naturalist could have placed him among the *singes*, when the very words of his description give him all the characteristics of human nature.†[42] It is still more curious to think that modern trav-

---

* "Homo nocturnus, Troglodytes, Silvestris, orang outang Bontii. Corpus album, incessu erectum. . . . . Loquitur sibilo, cogitat, ratiocinatur, credit sui causâ factam tellurem, se aliquando iterum fore imperantem."—LINNÆUS.

† "Il n'a point de queue: ses bras, ses mains, ses doigts, ses ongles, sont pareils aux nôtres: il marche toujours debout: il a des traits approchans de ceux de l'homme, des oreilles de la même forme, des cheveux sur la tête, de la barbe au menton, et du poil ni plus ni moins que l'homme en a dans l'état de nature. Aussi les habitans de son pays, les Indiens policés, n'ont pas hésité de l'associer à l'espèce humaine, par le nom d'oran outang, *homme sauvage*. Si l'on ne faisoit attention qu'à la figure, on pourroit regarder l'oran outang comme le premier des singes ou le dernier des hommes, parce qu'à l'exception de l'ame, il ne lui manque rien de tout ce que nous avons, et parce qu'il diffère moins de l'homme pour le corps qu'il ne diffère des autres animaux auxquels on a donné le même nom de singe. —S'il y avoit un degré par lequel on pût descendre de la nature humaine à celle des animaux, si l'essence de cette nature consistoit en entier dans la forme du corps et dépendoit de son organisation, l'oran outang se trouveroit plus près de l'homme que d'aucun animal: assis au second rang des êtres, s'il ne pouvoit commander en premier, il feroit au moins sentir aux autres sa supériorité, et s'efforceroit à ne pas obéir: si l'imitation qui semble copier de si près la pensée en étoit le vrai signe ou l'un des résultats, il se trouveroit encore à une plus grande distance des animaux et plus voisin de l'homme."—BUFFON.

"On est tout étonné, d'après tous les aveux, que M. de Buffon ne fasse de l'oran outang qu'une espèce de magot, essentiellement circonscrit dans les bornes de l'animalité: il falloit, où infirmer les relations des voyageurs, ou s'en tenir à leurs résultats. —Quand on lit dans ce naturaliste, l'histoire du Nègre blanc, on voit que ce bipède diffère de nous bien plus que l'oran outang, soit par l'organisation, soit par l'intelligence, et cependent on ne balance pas à le mettre dans la classe des hommes."
—*Philosophie de la Nature.*

ellers should have made beasts, under the names of Pongos, Mandrills, and Oran Outangs, of the very same beings whom the ancients worshipped as divinities under the names of Fauns and Satyrs, Silenus and Pan.[*][43]

SIR TELEGRAPH PAXARETT.

Your Oran rises rapidly in the scale of being:—from a Baronet and M. P. to a king of the world, and now to a god of the woods.

MR. FORESTER.

When I was in London last winter, I became acquainted with a learned mythologist,[44] who has long laboured to rebuild the fallen temple of Jupiter. I introduced him to Sir Oran, for whom he immediately conceived a high veneration, and would never call him by any name but Pan. His usual salutation to him was in the following words:

Ελθε, μακαρ, σκιρτητα, φιλενθεος, αντροδιαιτε,

Ἁρμονιην κοσμοιο κρεκων φιλοπαιγμονι μολπη,

Κοσμοκρατωρ, βακχευτα![†][45]

---

[*] "Les jugemens précipités, et qui ne sont point le fruit d'une raison éclairée, sont sujets à donner dans l'excès. Nos voyageurs font sans façon des bêtes, sous les noms de pongos, de mandrills, d'oran outangs, de ses mêmes êtres, dont, sous le nom de satyres, de faunes, de sylvains, les anciens fassoient des divinités. Peut-être, après des recherches plus exacts, trouvera-t-on que ce sont des hommes."—ROUSSEAU, *Discours sur l'Inégalité*, note 8.

"Il est presque démontré que les faunes, les satyres, les sylvains, les ægipans, et toute cette foule de demi-dieux, difformes et libertins, à qui les filles des Phocion et des Paul Emile s'aviserent de rendre hommage, ne furent dans l'origine que des oran outangs. Dans la suite, les poëtes chargerent le portrait de l'homme des bois, en lui donnant des pieds de chèvre, une queue et des cornes; mais le type primordial resta, et le philosophe l'apperçoit dans les monumens les plus défigurés par l'imagination d'Ovide et le ciseau de Phidias. Les anciens, très embarrassés de trouver la filiation de leurs sylvains, et de leurs satyres, se tirerent d'affaire en leur donnant des dieux pour pères: les dieux étoient d'un grand secours aux philosophes des tems reculés, pour résoudre les problèmes d'histoire naturelle; ils leur servoient comme les cycles et les épicycles dans le système planétaire de Ptolomée: avec des cycles et des dieux on répond à tout, quoiqu'on ne satisfasse personne."—*Philosophie de la Nature.*

[†] Orphica, Hymn. XI. (X. *Gesn.*)

Which he thus translated:

> King of the world! enthusiast free,
> Who dwell'st in caves of liberty!
> And on thy wild pipe's notes of glee
> Respondest Nature's harmony!
> Leading beneath the spreading tree
> The Bacchanalian revelry!

"This," said he, "is part of the Orphic invocation of Pan. It alludes to the happy existence of the dancing Pans, Fauns, Orans, *et id genus omne*,[46] whose dwellings are the caves of rocks and the hollows of trees, such as undoubtedly was, or would have been, the natural mode of life of our friend Pan among the woods of Angola. It alludes, too, to their musical powers, which in our friend Pan it gives me indescribable pleasure to find so happily exemplified. The epithet *Bacchic*, our friend Pan's attachment to the bottle demonstrates to be very appropriate; and the epithet Κοσμοκρατωρ, king of the world, points out a striking similarity between the Orphic Pan and the Troglodyte of Linnæus, *who believes that the earth was made for him, and that he will again be its sovereign.*"[47] He laid great stress on the word AGAIN, and observed, if he were to develope all the ideas to which this word gave rise in his mind, he should find ample matter for a volume. Then repeating several times, Παν κοσμοκρατωρ, and *iterum fore telluris imperantem*,[48] he concluded by saying, he had known many profound philosophical and mythological systems founded on much slighter analogies.

SIR TELEGRAPH PAXARETT.

Your learned mythologist appears to be *non compos*.[49]

MR. FORESTER.

By no means. He has a system of his own, which only appears in the present day more absurd than other systems, because it has fewer followers. The manner in which the spirit of system twists every thing to its own views is truly wonderful. I believe that in every nation of the earth the system which has most followers will be found the most absurd in the eye of an enlightened philosophy.

SIR TELEGRAPH PAXARETT.

But if your Oran be a man, how is it that his long intercourse with other varieties of the human species has not taught him to speak?

MR. FORESTER.

Speech is a highly artificial faculty. Civilized man is a highly artificial animal. The change from the wild to the civilized state, affects not only his moral but his physical nature, and this not rapidly and instantly, but in a long process of generations. The same change is obvious in domestic animals, and in cultivated plants. You know not where to look for the origin of the common dog or the common fowl. The wild and tame hog, and the wild and tame cat, are marked by more essential differences than the oran and the civilized man. The origin of corn is as much a mystery to us, as the source of the Nile was to the ancients. Innumerable flowers have been so changed from their original simplicity, that the art of horticulture may almost lay claim to the magic of a new creation. Is it then wonderful, that the civilized man should have acquired some physical faculties, which the natural man has not? It is demonstrable that speech is one. I do not, however, despair of seeing him make some progress in this art. Comparative anatomy shows that he has all the organs of articulation. Indeed, he has in every essential particular, the human form and the human anatomy. *Now I will only observe, that if an animal who walks upright—is of the human form, both outside and inside—uses a weapon for defence and attack—associates with his kind—makes huts to defend himself from the weather, better I believe than those*

of the New Hollanders—is tame and gentle—and instead of kill-
ing men and women, as he could easily do, takes them prisoners,
and makes servants of them—who has what I think essential to
the human kind, a sense of honour, which is shown by breaking
his heart, if laughed at, or made a show, or treated with any
kind of contumely—*who, when he is brought into the company*
of civilized men, behaves (as you have seen) *with dignity and*
composure, altogether unlike a monkey; from whom he differs like-
wise in this material respect, that he is capable of great attachment
to particular persons, of which the monkey is altogether incapa-
ble; and also in this respect, that a monkey never can be so tamed,
that we may depend on his not doing mischief when left alone, by
breaking glasses or china within his reach; whereas the oran outang
is altogether harmless;—who has so much of the docility of a man,
that he learns not only to do the common offices of life, but also to
play on the flute and French horn; *which shows that he must have*
an idea of melody, and concord of sounds, which no brute animal
has;—and lastly, if joined to all these qualities, he has the organ of
pronunciation, and consequently the capacity of speech, though not
the actual use of it; if, I say, such an animal be not a man, I should
desire to know in what the essence of a man consists, and what it is
that distinguishes a natural man from the man of art.*[50] That he

* The words in italics are from the Ancient Metaphysics, vol. iii. p. 41, 42.
Lord Monboddo adds: "I hold it to be impossible to convince any philosopher
or any man of common sense, who has bestowed any time to consider the mechanism of speech, that such various actions and configurations of the organs of
speech as are necessary for articulation can be natural to man. Whoever thinks
this possible, should go and see, as I have done, Mr. Braidwood of Edinburgh, or
the Abbé de l'Epée in Paris, teach the dumb to speak; and when he has observed
all the different actions of the organs, which those professors are obliged to
mark distinctly to their pupils with a great deal of pains and labour, so far from
thinking articulation natural to man, he will rather wonder how, by any teaching
or imitation, he should attain to the ready performance of such various and
complicated operations."
    "Quoique l'organe de la parole soit naturel à l'homme, la parole elle-même
ne lui est pourtant pas naturelle."—ROUSSEAU, *Discours sur l'Inégalité*, note 8.
    "The oran outang, so accurately dissected by Tisson, had exactly the same
organs of voice that a man has." —*Ancient Metaphysics*, vol. iii. p. 44.

understands many words, though he does not yet speak any, I think you may have observed, when you asked him to take wine, and applied to him for fish and partridge.[*][52]

SIR TELEGRAPH PAXARETT.

The gestures, however slight, that accompany the expression of the ordinary forms of intercourse, may possibly explain that.

MR. FORESTER.

You will find that he understands many things addressed to him, on occasions of very unfrequent occurrence. *With regard to his moral character, he is undoubtedly a man, and a much better man than many that are to be found in civilized countries,*[†][53] as, when you are better acquainted with him, I feel very confident you will readily acknowledge.[‡][54]

"I have been told that the oran outang who is to be seen in Sir Ashton Lever's collection had learned before he died to articulate some words."—*Ibid.* p. 40.

[*] "I desire any philosopher to tell me the specific difference between an oran outang, sitting at table, and behaving as M. de la Brosse or M. Buffon himself has described him, and one of our dumb persons; and in general I believe it will be very difficult, or rather impossible, for a man who is accustomed to divide things according to specific marks, not individual differences, to draw the line betwixt the oran outang and the dumb persons among us: they have both their organs of pronunciation, and both show signs of intelligence by their actions."—*Origin and Progress of Language,* book ii. chap. 4.[51]

[†] Ancient Metaphysics, vol. iv. p. 55.

[‡] "Toute la terre est couverte de nations, dont nous ne connoissons que les noms, et nous nous mêlons de juger le genre humain! Supposons un Montesquieu, un Buffon, un Diderot, un Duclos, un D'Alembert, un Condillac, ou des hommes de cette trempe, voyageant pour instruire leurs compatriotes, observant et décrivant comme ils sçavent faire, la Turquie, l'Egypte, la Barbarie, l'Empire de Maroc, la Guinée, le pays des Caffres, l'interieur de l'Afrique et ses côtes orientales, les Malabares, le Mogol, les rives du Gange, les royaumes de Siam, de Pégu et d'Ava, la Chine, la Tartarie, et sur-tout le Japon; puis dans l'autre hémisphere le Mexique, le Pérou, le Chili, les Terres Magellaniques, sans oublier les Patagons vrais ou faux, le Tucuman, le Paraguai, s'il étoit possible, le Brésil, enfin les Caraïbes, la Floride, et toutes les contrées sauvages, voyage le plus important de tous, et celui qu'il faudroit faire avec le plus de soin; supposons que ces nouveaux Hercules, de retour de ces courses mémorables, fissent ensuite à loisir l'histoire naturelle, morale, et politique de ce qu'ils auroient vus, nous verrions nous-mêmes sortir un monde nouveau de dessous leur plume, et nous apprendrions ainsi à connoître le nôtre: je dis que quand de pareils observateurs affirmeront d'un tel animal que c'est un homme, et d'un autre que c'est une bête,

SIR TELEGRAPH PAXARETT.

I shall be very happy, when his election comes on for Onevote, to drive him down in my barouche to the ancient and honourable borough.

Mr. Forester promised to avail himself of this proposal; when the iron tongue of midnight[55] tolling twelve induced them to separate for the night.

il faudra les en croire; mais ce seroit une grande simplicité de s'en rapporter là-dessus à des voyageurs grossiers, sur lesquels on seroit quelquefois tenté de faire la même question qu'ils se mêlent de résoudre sur d'autres animaux."
—ROUSSEAU, *Discours sur l'Inégalité*, note 8.

CHAPTER VII.

THE PRINCIPLE OF POPULATION.[1]

THE next morning, while Sir Telegraph, Sir Oran, and Mr. Forester, were sitting down to their breakfast, a post-chaise[2] rattled up to the door; the glass was let down, and a tall, thin, pale, grave-looking personage peeped from the aperture. "This is Mr. Fax,"[3] said Mr. Forester, "the champion of calm reason, the indefatigable explorer of the cold clear springs of knowledge, the bearer of the torch of dispassionate truth, that gives more light than warmth. He looks on the human world, the world of mind, the conflict of interests, the collision of feelings, the infinitely diversified developements of energy and intelligence, as a mathematician looks on his diagrams, or a mechanist on his wheels and pulleys, as if they were foreign to his own nature, and were nothing more than subjects of curious speculation."

Mr. Forester had not time to say more; for Mr. Fax entered, and shook hands with him, was introduced in due form to Sir Telegraph, and sate down to assist in the demolition of the *matériel* of breakfast.

MR. FAX.

Your Redrose Abbey is a beautiful metamorphosis.—I can scarcely believe that these are the mouldering walls of the pious fraternity of Rednose, which I contemplated two years ago.

MR. FORESTER.

The picturesque tourists will owe me no good will for the metamorphosis, though I have endeavoured to leave them as much mould, mildew, and weather-stain[4] as possible.

MR. FAX.

The exterior has suffered little; it still retains a truly venerable monastic character.

SIR TELEGRAPH PAXARETT.

Something monastic in the interior too.—Very orthodox old wine in the cellar, I can tell you. And the Reverend Father Abbot there, as determined a bachelor as the Pope.

MR. FORESTER.

If I am so, it is because, like the Squire of Dames,[5] I seek and cannot find. I see in my mind's eye[6] the woman I would choose, but I very much fear that is the only mode of optics, in which she will ever be visible.

MR. FAX.

No matter. Bachelors and spinsters I decidedly venerate.[7] The world is overstocked with featherless bipeds.[8] More men than corn, is a fearful pre-eminence, the sole and fruitful cause of penury, disease, and war, plague, pestilence, and famine.[9]

SIR TELEGRAPH PAXARETT.

I hope you will not long have cause to venerate me. What is life without love? A rose-bush in winter, all thorns, and no flowers.

MR. FAX.

And what is it with love? A double-blossomed cherry, flowers without fruit; if the blossoms last a month, it is as much as can be expected: they fall, and what comes in their place? Vanity, and vexation of spirit.

SIR TELEGRAPH PAXARETT.

Better vexation, than stagnation: marriage may often be a stormy lake, but celibacy is almost always a muddy horsepond.

MR. FAX.

Rather a calm clear river——

MR. FORESTER.

Flowing through a desert, where it moves in loneliness, and reflects no forms of beauty.

MR. FAX.

That is not the way to consider the case. Feelings and poetical images are equally out of place in a calm philosophical view of human society. Some must marry, that the world may be peopled:[10] many must abstain, that it may not be overstocked. *Little and good*, is very applicable in this case. It is better that the world should have a smaller number of peaceable and rational inhabitants, living in universal harmony and social intercourse, than the disproportionate mass of fools, slaves, coxcombs, thieves, rascals, liars, and cut-throats, with which its surface is at present encumbered. It is in vain to declaim about the preponderance of physical and moral evil, and attribute it, with the Manicheans, to a mythological principle,[11] or, with some modern philosophers, to the physical constitution of the globe. The cause of all the evils of human society is single, obvious, reducible to the most exact mathematical calculation; and of course susceptible not only of remedy, but even of utter annihilation. The cause is the tendency of population to increase beyond the means of subsistence.[12] The remedy is an universal social compact, binding both sexes to equally rigid celibacy, till the prospect of maintaining the average number of six children be as clear as the arithmetic of futurity can make it.

MR. FORESTER.

The arithmetic of futurity has been found in a more than equal number of instances to baffle human skill. The rapid and sudden mutations of fortune are the inexhaustible theme of history, poetry, and romance; and they are found in forms as various and surprising, in the scenes of daily life, as on the stage of Drury Lane.[13]

MR. FAX.

That the best prospects are often overshadowed, is most certainly true; but there are degrees and modes of well-grounded reliance on futurity, sufficient to justify the enterprises of prudence, and equally well-grounded prospiciencies[14] of hopelessness and helplessness, that should check the steps of rashness and passion, in their headlong progress to perdition.

MR. FORESTER.

You have little cause to complain of the present age. It is calculating enough to gratify the most determined votary of moral and political arithmetic. This certainly is not the time,

"When unrevenged stalks Cocker's injured ghost."[15]

What is friendship—except in some most rare and miraculous instances—but the fictitious bond of interest, or the heartless intercourse of idleness and vanity? What is love, but the most venal of all venal commodities? What is marriage, but the most sordid of bargains, the most cold and slavish of all the forms of commerce? We want no philosophical ice-rock, towed into the Dead Sea of modern society, to freeze that which is too cold already. We want rather the torch of Prometheus[16] to revivify our frozen spirits. We are a degenerate race,[17] half-reasoning developements of the principle of infinite littleness, "with hearts in our bodies, no bigger than pins' heads."[18] We are in no danger of forgetting that two and two make four. There is no fear that the warm impulses of feeling will ever overpower, with us, the tangible eloquence of the pocket.

MR. FAX.

With relation to the middle and higher classes, you are right in a great measure as to fact, but wrong, as I think, in the asperity of your censure. But among the lower orders the case is quite different. The baleful influence of the poor laws[19] has utterly destroyed the principle of calculation in them. They marry by wholesale, without scruple or compunction, and commit the future care of their family to Providence and the overseer. They marry even in the workhouse, and convert the intended asylum of age and infirmity, into a flourishing manufactory of young beggars and vagabonds.

Sir Telegraph's barouche rolled up gracefully to the door. Mr. Forester pressed him to stay another day, but Sir Telegraph's plea of urgency was not to be overcome. He promised very shortly to revisit Redrose Abbey, shook hands with Mr. Forester and Sir Oran, bowed politely to Mr. Fax, mounted his box, and disappeared among the trees.

"Those four horses," said Mr. Fax, as the carriage rolled away, "consume the subsistence of eight human beings, for the foolish amusement of one.[20] As Solomon observes: 'This is vanity, and a great evil.'"[21]

"Sir Telegraph is thoughtless," said Mr. Forester, "but he has a good heart and a good natural capacity. I have great hopes of him. He had some learning, when he went to college; but he was cured of it before he came away.[22] Great, indeed, must be the zeal for improvement, which an academical education cannot extinguish."

CHAPTER VIII.

THE SPIRIT OF CHIVALRY.

SIR Telegraph was welcomed to Melincourt in due form by Mr. Hippy,[1] and in a private interview with the Honourable Mrs. Pinmoney, was exhorted to persevere in his suit to Anthelia, though she could not flatter him with very strong hopes of immediate success, the young lady's notions being, as she observed, extremely outré[2] and fantastical, but such as she had no doubt time and experience would cure. She informed him at the same time, that he would shortly meet a formidable rival, no less a personage than Lord Anophel Achthar,[*3] son and heir of the Marquis of Agaric,[†4] who was somewhat in favour with Mr. Hippy, and seemed determined at all hazards to carry his point; "and with any other girl than Anthelia," said Mrs. Pinmoney, "considering his title and fortune, I should pronounce his success infallible, unless a Duke were to make his appearance." She added, the[5] young lord would be accompanied by his tutor, the Reverend Mr. Grovelgrub,[6] and by a celebrated poet, Mr. Feathernest,[7] to whom the Marquis had recently given a place in exchange for his conscience. It was thought by Mr. Feathernest's friends, that he had made a very good bargain. The poet had, in consequence, burned his old Odes to Truth and Liberty,[8] and had published a volume of Panegyrical Addresses "to all the crowned heads in Europe,"[9] with the motto, "Whatever is at court, is right."[10]

The dinner party that day at Melincourt Castle consisted of Mr. Hippy, in the character of lord of the mansion; Anthelia,

---

[*] ΑΝΩΦΕΛον ΑΧΘος ΑΡουρας, *Terræ pondus inutile.*
[†] AGARICUS, in Botany, a genus of plants of the class Cryptogamia, comprehending the mushroom, and a copious variety of toadstools.

in that of his inmate;[11] Mrs. and Miss Pinmoney, as her visitors; and Sir Telegraph, as the visitor of Mrs. Pinmoney, seconded by Mr. Hippy's invitation to stay. Nothing very luminous passed on this occasion.

The fame of Mr. Hippy, and his hospitable office, was rapidly diffused by Dr. Killquick, the physician of the district; who thought a draught or pill could not possibly be efficacious, unless administered with an anecdote, and who was called in, in a very few hours after Mr. Hippy's arrival, to cure the hypochondriacal old gentleman of an imaginary swelling in his elbow. The learned doctor, who had studied with peculiar care the symptoms, diagnostics, prognostics, sedatives, lenitives, and sanatives of hypochondriasis, had arrived at the sagacious conclusion, that the most effectual method of curing an imaginary disease was to give the patient a real one; and he accordingly sent Mr. Hippy a pint bottle of mixture, to be taken by a table-spoonful every two hours, which would have infallibly accomplished the purpose, but that the bottle was cracked over the head of Harry Fell, for treading on his master's toe, as he presented the composing potion, which would perhaps have composed him in the Roman sense.[12]

The fashionable attractions of Low-wood and Keswick[13] afforded facilities to some of Anthelia's lovers to effect a *logement*[14] in her neighbourhood, from whence occasionally riding over to Melincourt Castle, they were hospitably received by the lord seneschal Humphrey Hippy, Esquire, who often made them fixed stars in the circumference of that jovial system, of which the bottle and glasses are the sun and planets, till it was too late to dislodge for the night; by which means they sometimes contrived to pass several days together at the Castle.

The gentlemen in question were Lord Anophel Achthar, with his two parasites, Mr. Feathernest, and the Reverend Mr. Grovelgrub; Harum O'Scarum,[15] Esquire, the sole proprietor of a vast tract of undrained bog in the county of Kerry; and Mr. Derrydown,[16] the only son of an old lady in London, who having in vain solicited a visit from Anthelia, had sent off her hopeful progeny to try his fortune in Westmoreland. Mr. Derrydown had received a laborious education, and had consumed a great quantity of midnight oil, over ponderous tomes of ancient and modern learning, particularly of moral, political, and metaphysical philosophy, ancient and modern. His lucubrations in the latter branch of science having conducted him, as he conceived, into the central opacity of utter darkness,[17] he formed a hasty conclusion "that all human learning is vanity;"[18] and one day in a listless mood, taking down a volume of the Reliques of Ancient Poetry,[19] he found, or fancied he found, in the plain language of the old English ballad, glimpses of the truth of things,[20] which he had vainly sought in the vast volumes of philosophical disquisition. In consequence of this luminous discovery, he locked up his library, purchased a travelling chariot,[21] with a shelf in the back, which he filled with collections of ballads, and popular songs; and passed the greater part of every year in posting about the country, for the purpose, as he expressed it, of studying together poetry and the peasantry, unsophisticated nature and the truth of things.

Mr. Hippy introduced Lord Anophel, and his two learned friends, to Sir Telegraph, and Mrs. and Miss Pinmoney. Mr. Feathernest whispered to the Reverend Mr. Grovelgrub, "This Sir Telegraph Paxarett has some good livings in his gift:"[22] which bent the plump figure of the reverend gentleman into a very orthodox right angle.

Anthelia, who felt no inclination to show particular favour to any one of her Strephons,[23] was not sorry to escape the evil of a solitary persecutor, more especially as they so far resembled the suitors of Penelope,[24] as to eat and drink together with great cordiality. She could have wished, when she left them to the congenial society of Bacchus, to have retired to

57

company more congenial to her, than that of Mrs. Pinmoney and Miss Danaretta: but she submitted to the course of necessity with the best possible grace.

She explicitly made known to all her suitors her ideas on the subject of marriage. She had never perverted the simplicity of her mind, by indulging in the usual cant[25] of young ladies, that she should prefer a single life: but she assured them that the spirit of the age of chivalry, manifested in the forms of modern life,[26] would constitute the only character on which she could fix her affections.

Lord Anophel was puzzled, and applied for information to his tutor. "Grovelgrub," said he, "what is the spirit of the age of chivalry?"

"Really, my Lord," said the Reverend Mr. Grovelgrub, "my studies never lay that way."

"True," said Lord Anophel; "it was not necessary to your degree."

His Lordship's next recourse was to Mr. Feathernest. "Feathernest, what is the spirit of the age of chivalry?"

Mr. Feathernest was taken by surprise. Since his profitable metamorphosis into an *ami du prince*,[27] he had never dreamed of such a question. It burst upon him like the spectre of his youthful integrity, and he mumbled a half-intelligible reply, about truth and liberty—disinterested benevolence—self-oblivion—heroic devotion to love and honour—protection of the feeble, and subversion of tyranny.

"All the ingredients of a rank Jacobin, Feathernest, 'pon honour!" exclaimed his Lordship.

There was something in the word Jacobin very grating to the ears of Mr. Feathernest, and he feared he had thrown himself between the horns of a dilemma;[28] but from all such predicaments he was happily provided with an infallible means of extrication. His friend Mr. Mystic,[29] of Cimmerian Lodge,[30] had initiated him in some of the mysteries of the transcendental philosophy,[31] which on this, as on all similar occasions, he called in to his assistance; and overwhelmed his Lordship with a volley of ponderous jargon,[32] which left him in profound astonishment at the depth of Mr. Feathernest's knowledge.

"The spirit of the age of chivalry!" soliloquized Mr. O'Scarum; "I think I know what that is: I'll shoot all my rivals, one after another, as fast as I can find a decent pretext for picking a quarrel.[33] I'll write to my friend Major O'Dogskin[34] to come to Low-wood Inn, and hold himself in readiness. He is the neatest hand in Ireland at delivering a challenge."

"The spirit of the age of chivalry!" soliloquized Mr. Derrydown: "I think I am at home there. I will be a knight of the round table. I will be Sir Lancelot, or Sir Gawaine, or Sir Tristram. No: I will be a troubadour—a love-lorn minstrel. I will write the most irresistible ballads in praise of the beautiful Anthelia. She shall be my lady of the lake.[35] We will sail about Ulleswater[36] in our pinnace,[37] and sing duets about Merlin, and King Arthur, and Fairyland. I will develope the idea to her in a ballad: it cannot fail to fascinate her romantic spirit." And down he sate to put his scheme in execution.

Sir Telegraph's head ran on tilts and tournaments, and trials of skill and courage. How could they be resolved into the forms of modern life? A four-in-hand race[38] he thought would be a pretty substitute: Anthelia to be arbitress of the contest, and place the Olympic wreath on the head of the victor, which he had no doubt would be himself, though Harum O'Scarum, Esquire, would dash through neck or nothing,[39] and Lord Anophel Achthar was reckoned one of the best coachmen in England.

CHAPTER IX.

THE PHILOSOPHY OF BALLADS.

THE very indifferent success of Lord Anophel did not escape the eye of his abject slave, the Reverend Mr. Grovelgrub, whose vanity led him to misinterpret Anthelia's general sweetness of manner into the manifestation of something like a predilection for himself. Having made this notable discovery, he sate down to calculate the probability of his chance of Miss Melincourt's fortune on the one hand, and the certainty of church-preferment, through the patronage of the Marquis of Agaric, on the other. The sagacious reflection, that a bird in the hand was worth two in the bush, determined him not to risk the loss of the Marquis's favour for the open pursuit of a doubtful success; but he resolved to carry on a secret attack on the affections of Anthelia, and not to throw off the mask to Lord Anophel till he could make sure of his prize.

It would have totally disconcerted the schemes of the Honourable Mrs. Pinmoney, if Lord Anophel had made any progress in the favour of Anthelia—not only because she had made up her mind that her young friend should be her niece and Lady Paxarett, but because, from the moment of Lord Anophel's appearance, she determined on drawing lines of circumvallation[1] round him, to compel him to surrender at discretion to her dear Danaretta, who was very willing to second her views. That Lord Anophel was both a fool and a coxcomb, did not strike her at all as an objection; on the contrary, she considered them as very favourable circumstances for the facilitation of her design.

As Anthelia usually passed the morning in the seclusion of her library, Lord Anophel and the Reverend Mr. Grovelgrub killed the time in shooting; Sir Telegraph, in driving Mrs. and

Miss Pinmoney in his barouche, to astonish the natives of the mountain-villages; Harum O'Scarum, Esquire, in riding full gallop along the best roads, looking every now and then at his watch, to see how time went; Mr. Derrydown, in composing his troubadour ballad; Mr. Feathernest, in writing odes to all the crowned heads in Europe; and Mr. Hippy, in getting very ill after breakfast every day of a new disease, which came to its climax at the intermediate point of time between break-fast and dinner, showed symptoms of great amendment at the ringing of the first dinner-bell, was very much alleviated at the butler's summons, vanished entirely at the sight of Anthelia, and was consigned to utter oblivion after the ladies retired from table, when the Reverend Mr. Grovelgrub lent his clerical assistance to lay its ghost in the Red Sea of a copious libation of claret.

Music and conversation consumed the evenings. Mr. Feathernest and Mr. Derrydown were both zealous admirers of old English literature; but the former was chiefly enraptured with the ecclesiastical writers and the translation of the Bible; the latter admired nothing but ballads, which he maintained to be, whether ancient or modern, the only manifestations of feeling and thought containing any vestige of truth and nature.

"Surely," said Mr. Feathernest one evening, "you will not maintain that Chevy Chase² is a finer poem than Paradise Lost?"

MR. DERRYDOWN.

I do not know what you mean by a fine poem; but I will maintain that it gives a much deeper insight into the truth of things.

MR. FEATHERNEST.

I do not know what you mean by the truth of things.

THE REVEREND MR. GROVELGRUB.

Define, gentlemen, define: let the one explain what he means by a fine poem, and the other what he means by the truth of things.

MR. FEATHERNEST.

A fine poem is a luminous developement of the complicated machinery of action and passion, exalted by sublimity, softened by pathos, irradiated with scenes of magnificence, figures of loveliness and characters of energy, and harmonized with infinite variety of melodious combination.

LORD ANOPHEL ACHTHAR.

Admirable!

MISS DANARETTA CONTANTINA PINMONEY.

Admirable, indeed, my Lord! *(With a sweet smile at his Lordship, which unluckily missed fire.)*

THE REVEREND MR. GROVELGRUB.

Now, Sir, for the truth of things.

MR. O'SCARUM.

Troth, Sir, that is the last point about which I should expect a gentleman of your cloth to be very solicitous.

THE REVEREND MR. GROVELGRUB.

I must say, Sir, that is a very uncalled for, and very illiberal observation.

MR. O'SCARUM.

Your coat is your protection, Sir.[3]

THE REVEREND MR. GROVELGRUB.

I will appeal to his Lordship if——

MR. O'SCARUM.

I shall be glad to know his Lordship's opinion.

LORD ANOPHEL ACHTHAR.

Really, Sir, I have no opinion on the subject.

MR. O'SCARUM.

I am sorry for it, my Lord.

MR. DERRYDOWN.

The truth of things is nothing more than an exact view of the necessary relations between object and subject, in all the modes of reflection and sentiment which constitute the reciprocities of human association.

THE REVEREND MR. GROVELGRUB.

I must confess I do not exactly comprehend——

MR. DERRYDOWN.

I will illustrate. You all know the ballad of Old Robin Gray.[4]

Young Jamie loved me well, and asked me for his bride;
But saving a crown, he had nothing else beside.
To make the crown a pound my Jamie went to sea,
And the crown and the pound they were both for me.

He had not been gone a twelvemonth and a day,
When my father broke his arm, and our cow was stolen away;
My mother she fell sick, and Jamie at the sea,
And old Robin Gray came a courting to me.

In consequence whereof, as you all very well know, old Robin being rich, the damsel married the aforesaid old Robin.

THE REVEREND MR. GROVELGRUB.

In the heterodox kirk of the north?[5]

MR. DERRYDOWN.

Precisely. Now, in this short space, you have a more profound view than the deepest metaphysical treatise or the most elaborate history can give you of the counteracting power of opposite affections, the conflict of duties and inclinations, the omnipotence of interest, tried by the test of extremity, and the supreme and irresistible dominion of universal moral necessity.

"Young Jamie loved me well, and asked me for his bride;"

and would have had her, it is clear, though she does not explicitly say so, if there had not been a necessary moral motive
counteracting what would have been otherwise the plain free
will of both. "Young Jamie loved me well." She does not say
that she loved young Jamie; and here is a striking illustration
of that female decorum which forbids young ladies to speak
as they think on any subject whatever: an admirable political
institution, which has been found by experience to be most
happily conducive to that ingenuousness of mind and simplicity of manner which constitutes so striking a charm in the
generality of the fair sex.

"But saving a crown, he had nothing else beside."

Here is the quintessence of all that has been said and written on the subject of love and prudence, a decisive refuta-
tion of the stoical doctrine that poverty is no evil, a very
clear and deep insight into the nature of the preventive or
prudential check to population, and a particularly luminous view of the respective conduct of the two sexes on
similar occasions. The poor love-stricken swain, it seems,
is ready to sacrifice all for love. He comes with a crown
in his pocket, and asks her for his bride. The damsel is a
better arithmetician. She is fully impressed with the truth
of the old proverb about poverty coming in at the door,[6]
and immediately stops him short, with "What can you settle on me, Master Jamie?" or, as Captain Bobadil would
express it, "How much money ha' you about you, Master
Matthew?"[7] Poor Jamie looks very foolish—fumbles in
his pocket—produces his crown-piece—and answers like
Master Matthew, with a remarkable elongation of visage,
"'Faith, I ha' n't past a five shillings or so." "Then," says
the young lady, in the words of another very admirable

ballad—where you will observe it is also the damsel who asks the question:

> "Will the love that you're so rich in,
> Make a fire in the kitchen?"[8]

On which the poor lover shakes his head, and the lady gives him leave of absence. Hereupon Jamie falls into a train of reflections.

MR. O'SCARUM.

Never mind his reflections.

MR. DERRYDOWN.

The result of which is, that he goes to seek his fortune at sea; intending, with the most perfect and disinterested affection, to give all he can get to his mistress, who seems much pleased with the idea of having it. But when he comes back, as you will see in the sequel, he finds his mistress married to a rich old man. The detail of the circumstances abounds with vast and luminous views of human nature and society, and striking illustrations of the truth of things.

MR. FEATHERNEST.

I do not yet see that the illustration throws any light on the definition, or that we are at all advanced in the answer to the question concerning Chevy Chase and Paradise Lost.

MR. DERRYDOWN.

We will examine Chevy Chase, then, with a view to the truth of things, instead of Old Robin Gray:

> "God prosper long our noble king,
> Our lives and safeties all."[9]

MR. O'SCARUM.

God prosper us all, indeed! if you are going through Chevy Chase at the same rate as you were through Old Robin Gray, there is an end of us all for a month. The truth of things, now!—is it that you're looking for? Ask Miss Melincourt to touch the harp. The harp is the great key to the truth of things; and in the hand of Miss Melincourt it will teach you the music of the spheres, the concord of creation, and the harmony of the universe.

ANTHELIA.

You are a libeller of our sex, Mr. Derrydown, if you think the truth of things consists in showing it to be more governed by the meanest species of self-interest than yours. Few, indeed, are the individuals of either in whom the spirit of the age of chivalry survives.

MR. DERRYDOWN.

And yet, a man distinguished by that spirit would not be in society what Miss Melincourt is—a phœnix. Many knights can wield the sword of Orlando,[10] but only one nymph can wear the girdle of Florimel.[11]

THE HONOURABLE MRS. PINMONEY.

That would be a very pretty compliment, Mr. Derrydown, if there were no other ladies in the room.

Poor Mr. Derrydown looked a little disconcerted: he felt conscious that he had on this occasion lost sight of his usual politeness by too close an adherence to the truth of things.

ANTHELIA.

Both sexes, I am afraid, are too much influenced by the spirit of mercenary calculation. The desire of competence is prudence; but the desire of more than competence is avarice: it is against the latter only that moral censure should be directed: but I fear that in ninety-nine cases out of an hundred in which the course of true love is thwarted by considerations of fortune, it will be found that avarice rather than prudence is to be considered as the cause. Love in the age of chivalry, and love in the age of commerce, are certainly two very different deities; so much so, that the former may almost be regarded as a departed power; and, perhaps, the little ballad I am about to sing does not contain too severe an allegory in placing the tomb of chivalric love among the ruins of the castles of romance.

THE TOMB OF LOVE.

By the mossy weed-flowered column,
  Where the setting moonbeam's glance
Streams a radiance cold and solemn
  On the haunts of old romance:
Know'st thou what those shafts betoken,
  Scattered on that tablet lone,
Where the ivory bow lies broken
  By the monumental stone?
When true knighthood's shield, neglected,
  Mouldered in the empty hall;
When the charms that shield protected
  Slept in death's eternal thrall
When chivalric glory perished
  Like the pageant of a dream,
Love in vain its memory cherished,
  Fired in vain the minstrel's theme.

Falsehood to an elvish minion
  Did the form of Love impart:
Cunning plumed its vampire pinion;
  Avarice tipped its golden dart.
Love, the hideous phantom flying,
  Hither came, no more to rove:
There his broken bow is lying
  On that stone——the tomb of Love!

CHAPTER X.

THE TORRENT.

ANTHELIA did not wish to condemn herself to celibacy, but in none of her present suitors could she discover any trace of the character she had drawn in her mind of the companion of her life: yet she was aware of the rashness of precipitate judgments, and willing to avail herself of this opportunity of studying the kind of beings that constitute modern society. She was happy in the long interval between breakfast and dinner, to retire to the seclusion of her favourite apartment; whence she sometimes wandered into the shades of her shrubbery: sometimes passing onward through a little postern door, she descended a flight of rugged steps,[1] which had been cut in the solid stone, into the gloomy glen of the torrent that dashed round the base of the castle rock; and following a lonely path through the woods that fringed its sides, wandered into the deepest recesses of mountain solitude. The sunshine of a fine autumnal day, the solemn beauty of the fading woods, the thin grey mist, that spread waveless over the mountains, the silence of the air, the deep stillness of nature, broken only by the sound of the eternal streams, tempted her on one occasion beyond her usual limits.

Passing over the steep and wood-fringed hills of rock that formed the boundary of the valley of Melincourt, she descended through a grove of pines, into a romantic chasm, where a foaming stream was crossed by a rude and ancient bridge, consisting of two distinct parts, each of which rested against a columnar rock, that formed an island in the roaring waters. An ash had fixed its roots in the fissures of the rock, and the knotted base of its aged trunk offered to the passenger a natural seat, over-canopied with its beautiful branches, and leaves, now tinged with their autumnal yellow. Anthelia rested awhile in this delightful solitude. There was no breath of wind, no song of birds, no humming of insects, only the dashing of the waters beneath. She felt the presence of the genius of the scene.[2] She sate absorbed in a train of contemplations, dimly defined, but infinitely delightful: emotions rather than thoughts, which attention would have utterly dissipated, if it had paused to seize their images.

She was roused from her reverie by sounds of music, issuing from the grove of pines, through which she had just passed, and which skirted the hollow. The notes were wild and irregular, but their effect was singular and pleasing. They ceased. Anthelia looked to the spot from which they had proceeded, and saw, or thought she saw, a face peeping at her through the trees; but the glimpse was momentary. There was in the expression of the countenance, something so extraordinary, that she almost felt convinced her imagination had created it; yet her imagination was not in the habit of creating such physiognomies. She could not, however, apprehend that this remarkable vision portended any evil to her; for, if so, alone and defenceless as she was, why should it be deferred? She rose, therefore, to pursue her walk, and ascended, by a narrow winding path, the brow of a lofty hill, which sunk precipitously on the other side, to the margin of a lake, that seemed to slumber in the same eternal stillness as the rocks that bordered it. The murmur of the torrent was inaudible at that elevation. There was an almost oppressive silence in the air. The motion and life of nature seemed suspended. The grey mist that hung on the mountains spreading its thin transparent uniform veil over the whole surrounding scene, gave a deeper impression to the mystery of loneliness, the predominant feeling that pressed on the mind of Anthelia, to seem the only thing that lived and moved in all that wide and awful scene of beauty.

Suddenly the grey mist fled before the rising wind, and a deep black line of clouds appeared in the west, that rising rapidly, volume on volume, obscured in a few minutes the whole face of the heavens. There was no interval of preparation, no notice for retreat. The rain burst down in a sheeted cataract, comparable only to the bursting of a water-spout. The sides of the mountains gleamed at once with a thousand torrents. Every little hollow and rain-worn channel, which but a few minutes before was dry, became instantaneously the bed of a foaming stream. Every half-visible rivulet swelled to a powerful and turbid river. Anthelia glided down the hill like an Oread, but the wet and slippery footing of the steep descent necessarily retarded her progress. When she regained the bridge, the swollen torrent had filled the chasm beneath, and was still rising like a rapid and impetuous tide, rushing and roaring along with boiling tumult and inconceivable swiftness. She had passed one half of the bridge—she had gained the insular rock—a few steps would have placed her on the other side of the chasm—when a large trunk of an oak, which months, perhaps years before had baffled the woodman's skill, and fallen into the dingle above, now disengaged by the flood, and hurled onward with irresistible strength, with large and projecting boughs towering high above the surface, struck the arch she had yet to pass, which, shattered into instant ruin, seemed to melt like snow into the torrent, leaving scarcely a vestige of its place.

Anthelia followed the trunk with her eyes till it disappeared among the rocks, and stood gazing on the torrent with feelings of awful delight. The contemplation of the mighty energies of nature, energies of liberty and power[3] which nothing could resist or impede, absorbed, for a time, all considerations of the difficulty of regaining her home. The water continued to rise, but still she stood rivetted to the spot, watching with breathless interest its tumultuous revolutions. She dreamed not, that its increasing pressure was mining the foundation of the arch she had passed. She was roused from her reverie only by the sound of its dissolution. She looked back, and found herself on the solitary rock insulated by the swelling flood.

Would the flood rise above the level of the rock? The ash must in that case be her refuge. Could the force of the torrent rend its massy roots from the rocky fissures which grasped them with giant strength? Nothing could seem less likely: yet it was not impossible. But she had always looked with calmness on the course of necessity: she felt that she was always in the order of nature. Though her life had been a series of uniform prosperity, she had considered deeply the changes of things, and *the nearness of the paths of night and day*[*4] in every pursuit and circumstance of human life. She sate on the stem of the ash. The torrent rolled almost at her feet. Could this be the calm sweet scene of the morning, the ivied bridges, the romantic chasm, the stream far below, bright in its bed of rocks, chequered by the pale sunbeams through the leaves of the ash?

She looked towards the pine-grove, through which she had descended in the morning; she thought of the wild music she had heard, and of the strange face that had appeared among the trees. Suddenly it appeared again: and shortly after, a stranger issuing from the wood, ran with surprising speed to the edge of the chasm.

Anthelia had never seen so singular a physiognomy; [5] but there was nothing in it to cause alarm. The stranger seemed interested for her situation, and made gestures expressive of a design to assist her. He paused a moment, as if measuring with his eyes the breadth of the chasm, and then returning to the grove, proceeded very deliberately to pull up a pine.[†6] Anthelia

---

[*] Εγγυς γαρ νυκτος τε και ηματος εισι κελευθοι.

[†] "Ils sont si robustes, dit le traducteur de l'Histoire des Voyages, que dix hommes ne suffiroient pas pour les arrêter."—ROUSSEAU.

"The oran outang is prodigiously strong."—*Ancient Metaphysics*, vol. iv. p. 51.; vol. v. p. 4.

"I have heard the natives say, he can throw down a palm-tree, by his amazing

thought him mad; but infinite was her astonishment to see the tree sway and bend beneath the efforts of his incredible strength, till at length he tore it from the soil, and bore it on his shoulders to the chasm: where placing one end on a high point of the bank, and lowering the other on the insulated rock, he ran like a flash of lightning along the stem, caught Anthelia in his arms, and carried her safely over in an instant: not that we should wish the reader to suppose, our heroine, a mountaineer from her infancy, could not have crossed a pine-bridge without such assistance; but the stranger gave her no time to try the experiment.

The remarkable physiognomy and unparalleled strength of the stranger, caused much of surprise, and something of apprehension, to mingle with Anthelia's gratitude: but the air of high fashion, which characterized his whole deportment, diminished her apprehension, while it increased her surprise at the exploit he had performed.

Shouts were now heard in the wood, from which shortly emerged Mr. Hippy, Lord Anophel Achthar, and the Reverend Mr. Grovelgrub. Anthelia had been missed at Melincourt at the commencement of the storm, and Mr. Hippy had been half distracted on the occasion. The whole party had in consequence dispersed in various directions in search of her, and accident had directed these three gentlemen to the spot where Anthelia was just set down by her polite deliverer, Sir Oran Haut-ton, Baronet.

Mr. Hippy ran up with great alacrity to Anthelia, assuring her that at the time when Miss Danaretta Contantina Pinmoney informed him his dear niece was missing, he was suffering under a complete paralysis of his right leg, and was on the point of swallowing a potion sent to him by Dr.

strength, to come at the wine."—*Letter of a Bristol Merchant, in a note to the Origin and Progress of Language,* book ii. c. 4.

Killquick, which, on receiving the alarming intelligence, he had thrown out of the window, and he believed it had alighted on the doctor's head, as he was crossing the court. Anthelia communicated to him the particulars of the signal service she had received from the stranger, whom Mr. Hippy stared at heartily, and shook hands with cordially.

Lord Anophel now came up, and surveyed Sir Oran through his quizzing-glass,[7] who making him a polite bow, took his quizzing-glass from him, and examined him through it, in the same manner. Lord Anophel flew into a furious passion; but receiving a gentle hint from Mr. Hippy, that the gentleman to whom he was talking, had just pulled up a pine, he deemed it prudent to restrain his anger within due bounds.

The Reverend Mr. Grovelgrub now rolled up to the party, muffled in a ponderous great coat, and surmounted with an enormous umbrella, humbly soliciting Miss Melincourt to take shelter. Anthelia assured him that she was so completely wet through, as to render all shelter superfluous, till she could change her clothes. On this, Mr. Hippy, who was wet through himself, but had not till that moment been aware that he was so, voted for returning to Melincourt with all possible expedition; adding, that he feared it would be necessary, immediately on their arrival, to send off an express for Dr. Killquick, for his dear Anthelia's sake, as well as his own. Anthelia disclaimed any intention or necessity on her part, of calling in the services of the learned doctor, and, turning to Sir Oran, requested the favour of his company to dinner at Melincourt. This invitation was warmly seconded by Mr. Hippy, with gestures as well as words.[8] Sir Oran bowed acknowledgment, but pointing in a direction different from that of Melincourt, shook his head, and took a respectful farewell.

"I wonder who he is," said Mr. Hippy, as they walked rapidly homewards: "manifestly dumb, poor fellow! a man of consequence, no doubt: no great beauty, by the by; but as strong as

Hercules, quite an Orlando Furioso.[9] He pulled up a pine, my Lord, as you would a mushroom."[10]

"Sir," said Lord Anophel, "I have nothing to do with mush-rooms: and as to this gentleman, whoever he is, I must say, not-withstanding his fashionable air, his taking my quiz-zing-glass was a piece of impertinence, for which I shall feel necessitated to require gentlemanly satisfaction."[11]

A long, toilsome, and slippery walk, brought the party to the castle-gate.

CHAPTER XI.

LOVE AND MARRIAGE.

Sɪʀ Oran Haut-ton, as we conjecture, had taken a very long ramble beyond the limits of Redrose Abbey, and had sat down in the pine-grove to solace himself with his flute, when Anthelia, bursting upon him like a beautiful vision, rivetted him in silent admiration to the spot whence she departed, about which he lingered in hopes of her reappearance, till the accident which occurred on her return enabled him to exert his extraordinary physical strength, in a manner so remarkably advantageous to her. On parting from her and her companions, he ran back all the way to the Abbey, a formidable distance, and relieved the anxious apprehensions which his friend Mr. Forester entertained respecting him.

A few mornings after this occurrence, as Mr. Forester, Mr. Fax, and Sir Oran were sitting at breakfast, a letter was brought in, addressed to *Sir Oran Haut-ton, Baronet, Redrose Abbey;* a circumstance which very much surprised Mr. Forester, as he could not imagine how Sir Oran had obtained a correspondent, seeing that he could neither write nor read. He accordingly took the liberty of opening the letter himself.

It proved to be from a limb of the law, signing himself Richard Ratstail,[1] and purported to be a notice[2] to Sir Oran to defend himself in an action[3] brought against him by the said Richard Ratstail, solicitor, in behalf of his client, Lawrence Litigate, Esquire, lord of the manor of Muckwormsby,[4] for that he the said Sir Oran Haut-ton did, with force and arms, videlicet, swords, pistols, daggers, bludgeons, and staves,[5] break into the manor of the said Lawrence Litigate, Esquire, and did then and there, with malice aforethought, and against the peace of our sovereign lord the King, his crown and dignity, cut down, root up, hew, hack, and cut in pieces sundry and several pine-trees, of various sizes and dimensions, to the utter ruin, havoc, waste, and devastation of a large tract of pine-land; and that he had wilfully, maliciously, and with intent to injure the said Lawrence Litigate, Esquire, carried off with force and arms, namely, swords, pistols, bludgeons, daggers, and staves, fifty cart-loads of trunks, fifty cart-loads of bark, fifty cart-loads of loppings, and fifty cart-loads of toppings.

This was a complete enigma to Mr. Forester; and his surprise was increased when, on reading further, he found that Miss Melincourt, of Melincourt Castle, was implicated in the affair, as having aided and abetted Sir Oran in devastating the pine-grove, and carrying it off by cart-loads with force and arms.

It immediately occurred to him, that the best mode he could adopt of elucidating the mystery would be, to call on Miss Melincourt, whom, besides, Sir Telegraph's enthusiastic description had given him some curiosity to see; and the present appeared a favourable opportunity to indulge it.

He therefore asked Mr. Fax if he were disposed for a very long walk. Mr. Fax expressed a cordial assent to the proposal, and no time was lost in preparation.

Mr. Forester, though he had built stables for the accommodation of his occasional visitors, kept no horses himself, for reasons which will appear hereafter.[6]

They set forth accordingly, accompanied by Sir Oran, who joined them without waiting for an invitation.

"We shall see Sir Telegraph Paxarett," said Mr. Forester, "and, perhaps, his phœnix, Miss Melincourt."

MR. FAX.

If a woman be the object, and a lover's eyes the medium, I should say there is nothing in nature so easily found as a phœnix.

MR. FORESTER.

My eyes have no such magical property. I am not a lover, it is true, but it is because I have never found a phœnix.

MR. FAX.

But you have one in your mind, a *beau idéal*,[7] I doubt not.

MR. FORESTER.

Not too ideal to exclude the possible existence of its material archetype,[8] though I have never found it yet.

MR. FAX.

You will, however, find a female who has some one at least of the qualities of your imaginary damsel, and that one quality will serve as a peg on which your imagination will suspend all the others. This is the usual process of mental hallucination. A little truth forms the basis, and the whole superstructure is falsehood.

MR. FORESTER.

I shall guard carefully against such self-deception; though, perhaps, a beautiful chimæra[9] is better than either a hideous reality or a vast and formless void.

MR. FAX.

As an instrument of transitory pleasure, probably; but very far from it as a means of permanent happiness, which is only consistent with perfect mental tranquillity, which again is only consistent with the calm and dispassionate contemplation of truth.

MR. FORESTER.

What say you, then, to the sentiment of Voltaire?[10]

"Le raisonneur tristement s'accrédite:
On court, dit-on, après la vérité,
Ah! croyez-moi, l'erreur à son mérite."

MR. FAX.

You will scarcely coincide with such a sentiment, when you consider how much this doctrine of happy errors, and pleasing illusions, and salutary prejudices, has tended to rivet the chains of superstition on the necks of the grovelling multitude.

MR. FORESTER.

And yet, if you take the colouring of imagination from the objects of our mental perception, and pour the full blaze of daylight into all the dark recesses of selfishness and cunning, I am afraid a refined and enthusiastic benevolence will find little to interest or delight in the contemplation of the human world.

MR. FAX.

That should rather be considered the consequence of morbid feelings, and exaggerated expectations of society and human nature. It is the false colouring in which youthful enthusiasm depicts the scenes of futurity that throws the gloom of disappointment so deeply on their actual presence. You have formed to yourself, as you acknowledge, a visionary model of female perfection, which has rendered you utterly insensible to the real attractions of every woman you have seen. This exaggerated imagination loses more than it gains. It has not made a fair calculation of the mixture of good and evil in every constituent portion of the world of reality. It has utterly excluded the latter from the objects of its hope, and has magnified the former into such gigantic proportions, that the real goodness and beauty which would be visible and delightful to simpler optics, vanish into imperceptibility in the infinity of their diminution.

MR. FORESTER.

I desire no phantasm of abstract perfection—no visionary creation of a romantic philosophy: I seek no more than I know to have existed—than, I doubt not, does exist, though in such lamentable rarity, that the calculations of probability make the search little better than desperate. I would have a woman that can love and feel poetry, not only in its harmony and decorations, which limit the admiration of ordinary mortals, but in the deep sources of love, and liberty, and truth, which are its only legitimate springs, and without which, well-turned periods and glittering images are nothing more nor less than the vilest and most mischievous tinsel. She should be musical, but she should have music in her soul as well as her fingers: her voice and her touch should have no one point in common with that mechanical squalling and jingling which are commonly dignified with the insulted name of music: they should be modes of the harmony of her mind.

MR. FAX.

I do not very well understand that; but I think I have a glimpse of your meaning. Pray proceed.

MR. FORESTER.

She should have charity—not penny charity—

MR. FAX.

I hope not.[11]

MR. FORESTER.

But a liberal discriminating practical philanthropy, that can select with justice the objects of its kindness, and give that kindness a form of permanence equally delightful and useful to its object and to society, by increasing the aggregate mass of intelligence and happiness.

MR. FAX.

Go on.

MR. FORESTER.

She should have no taste for what are called public pleasures. Her pleasures should be bounded in the circle of her family, and a few, a very few congenial friends, her

books, her music, her flowers—she should delight in flowers—the uninterrupted cheerfulness of domestic concord,
the delightful effusions of unlimited confidence. The rocks,
and woods, and mountains, boundaries of the valley of her
dwelling, she should be content to look on as the boundaries
of the world.

MR. FAX.

Any thing more?

MR. FORESTER.

She should have a clear perception of the beauty of truth.
Every species of falsehood, even in sportiveness, should be
abhorrent to her.[12] The simplicity of her thoughts should shine
through the ingenuousness of her words. Her testimony should
convey as irresistible conviction as the voice of the personified
nature of things. And this ingenuousness should comprise in
its fullest extent, that perfect conformity of feelings and opinions, which ought to be the most common, but is unfortunately the most rare of the qualities of the female mind.

MR. FAX.

You say nothing of beauty.

MR. FORESTER.

As to what is usually called beauty, mere symmetry of form
and features, it would be an object with me in purchasing a
statue, but none whatever in choosing a wife. Let her countenance be the mirror of such qualities as I have described,
and she cannot be otherwise than beautiful. I think with the
Athenians, that beauty and goodness are inseparable. I need
not remind you of the perpetual $\kappa\alpha\lambda o\varsigma$ $\kappa'\alpha\gamma\alpha\vartheta o\varsigma$.[13]

MR. FAX.

You have said nothing of the principal, and, indeed, almost
the only usual consideration in marriage—fortune.

MR. FORESTER.

I am rich enough myself to dispense with such considerations. Even were I not so, I doubt if worldly wisdom would ever influence me to bend my knee with the multitude, at the shrine of the omnipotence of money. Nothing is more uncertain, more transient, more perishable, than riches. How many prudent marriages of interest and convenience were broken to atoms by the French revolution! Do you think there was one couple, among all those calculating characters that acted in those trying times, like Louvet and his Lodoiska?[*][14] But without looking to periods of public convulsion, in no state of society is any individual secure against the changes of fortune. What becomes of those ill-assorted unions, which have no basis but money, when, as is very often the case, the money departs, and the persons remain? The qualities of the heart and of the mind are alone out of the power of accident; and by these, and these only, shall I be guided in the choice of the companion of my life.

MR. FAX.

Are there no other indispensable qualities, that you have omitted in your enumeration?

MR. FORESTER.

None, I think, but such as are implied in those I have mentioned, and must necessarily be coexistent with them: an endearing sensibility, an agreeable cheerfulness, and that serenity of temper which is truly the balm of being, and the absence of which, in the intercourse of domestic life, obliterates all the radiance of beauty, all the splendour of talent, and all the dignity of virtue.

[*] See Louvet's "Récit de mes Périls."

MR. FAX.

I presume, then, you seriously purpose to marry, when you can find such a woman as this you have described?

MR. FORESTER.

Seriously I do.

MR. FAX.

And not till then?

MR. FORESTER.

Certainly not.

MR. FAX.

Then your present heir presumptive has nothing to fear for his reversion.[15]

CHAPTER XII.

LOVE AND POVERTY.

"WE shall presently," said Mr. Fax, as they pursued their walk, "come in sight of a cottage, which I remarked two years ago: a deplorable habitation! A picture of its exterior and interior suspended in some public place, in every town in the kingdom, with a brief commentary subjoined, would operate *in terrorem*[1] in favour of the best interests of political economy,[2] by placing before the eyes of the rising generation, the lamentable consequences of imprudent marriage, and the necessary result of attachment, of which romance is the foundation, and marriage the superstructure, without the only cement which will make it wind-and-water-tight—money."

MR. FORESTER.

Nothing but money! The resemblance Fluellen found between Macedon and Monmouth, because both began with an M,[3] holds equally true of money and marriage: but there seems to be a much stronger connexion in the latter case; for marriage is but a body, of which money is the soul.

MR. FAX.

It is so. It must be so. The constitution of society imperiously commands it to be so. The world of reality is not the world of romance. When a lover talks of lips of coral, teeth of pearl, tresses of gold, and eyes of diamonds, he knows all the while that he is lying by wholesale; and that no baker in England would give him credit for a penny roll, on all this display of his Utopian treasury. All the aërial castles that are founded in the contempt of worldly prudence, have not half the solidity of the cloud-built towers that surround the setting of the autumnal sun.

MR. FORESTER.

I maintain, on the contrary, that, *let all possible calamities be accumulated on two affectionate and congenial spirits, they will find more true happiness in weeping together, than they would have found in all the riches of the world, poisoned by the disunion of hearts.*[*4]

MR. FAX.

The disunion of hearts is an evil of another kind. It is not a comparison of evils I wish to institute. That two rich people fettered by the indissoluble bond of marriage, and hating each other cordially, are two as miserable animals as any on the face of the earth, is certain; but that two poor ones, let them love each other ever so fondly, starving together in a garret, are therefore in a less positively wretched condition, is an inference which no logic, I think, can deduce. For the picture you must draw in your mind's eye,[5] is not that of a neatly-dressed, young, healthy-looking couple, weeping in each other's arms in a clean, however homely cottage, in a fit of tender sympathy; but you must surround them with all the squalid accompaniments of poverty, rags, and famine, the contempt of the world, the dereliction of friends, half a dozen hungry squalling children, all clothed perhaps in the cutting up of an old blanket, duns in presence, bailiffs in prospect, and the long perspective of hopelessness closed by the workhouse or the gaol.

MR. FORESTER.

You imagine an extreme case, which something more than the original want of fortune seems requisite to produce.

MR. FAX.

I have heard you declaim very bitterly against those who maintain the necessary connexion between misfortune and imprudence.

---

* Rousseau, Emile, liv. 5.

MR. FORESTER.

Certainly. To assert that the unfortunate must necessarily have been imprudent, is to furnish an excuse to the cold-hearted and illiberal selfishness of a state of society, which needs no motive superadded to its own miserable narrow-mindedness, to produce the almost total extinction of benevolence and sympathy. Good and evil fortune depend so much on the combinations of external circumstances, that the utmost skill and industry cannot command success; neither is the result of the most imprudent actions always fatal:

> Our indiscretions sometimes serve us well,
> When our deep plots do pall.[*][6]

MR. FAX.

Sometimes, no doubt; but not so often as to equalize the probable results of indiscretion and prudence. "Where there is prudence," says Juvenal, "fortune is powerless;"[8] and this doctrine, though liable to exceptions, is replete with general truth. We have a nice balance to adjust. To check the benevolence of the rich, by persuading them that all misfortune is the result of imprudence, is a great evil; but it would be a much greater evil to persuade the poor, that indiscretion may have a happier result than prudence; for where this appears to be true in one instance, it is manifestly false in a thousand. It is certainly not enough to possess industry and talent; there must be means for exerting them; and in a redundant population

---

[*] "L'issuë aucthorise souvent une très-inepte conduitte. Nostre entremise n'est quasy qu'une routine, et plus communement consideration d'usage et d'exemple que de raison . . . . L'heur et le mal-heur sont à mon gré deux souveraines puissances. C'est imprudence d'estimer que l'humaine prudence puisse remplir le roolle de la fortune. Et vaine est l'entreprinse de celuy qui presume, d'embrasser et causes et consequences, et meiner par la main le progrez de son faict. . . . . . Qu'on reguarde qui sont les plus puissans aux villes, et qui font mieulx leurs besongues, on trouvera ordinairement que ce sont les moins habiles. . . . . . Nous attribuons les effects de leur bonne fortune à leur prudence. . . . . Parquoy je dy bien, en toutes façons, que les evenements sont maigres tesmoings de nostre prix et capacité."—MONTAIGNE, liv. iii. chap. 8.[7]

these means are often wanting, even to the most skilful and the most industrious: but though Calamity sometimes seizes those who use their best efforts to avoid her, yet she seldom disappoints the intentions of those who leap headlong into her arms.

MR. FORESTER.

It seems, nevertheless, peculiarly hard, that all the blessings of life should be confined to the rich. If you banish the smiles of love from the cottage of poverty, what remains to cheer its dreariness? The poor man has no friends, no amusements, no means of exercising benevolence, nothing to fill up the gloomy and desolate vacancy of his heart, if you banish love from his dwelling. "There is one alone, and there is not a second," says one of the greatest poets and philosophers of antiquity:[9] "there is one alone, and there is not a second: yea, he hath neither child nor brother; yet is there no end of all his labour: . . . . . neither saith he, For whom do I labour and bereave my soul of good? . . . . Two are better than one . . . . . for if they fall, the one will lift up his fellow; but woe to him that is alone when he falleth, for he hath not another to help him up*." Society in poverty, is better than solitude in wealth; but solitude and poverty together, it is scarcely in human nature to tolerate.

MR. FAX.

This, if I remember rightly, is the cottage of which I was speaking.

The cottage was ruined and uninhabited. The roof had fallen in. The garden was choked with weeds. "What," said Mr. Fax, "can have become of its unfortunate inhabitants?"

MR. FORESTER.

What were they?

---

* Ecclesiastes, chap. iv.

MR. FAX.

A couple for whom nature had done much, and fortune nothing. I took shelter in their cottage from a passing storm. The picture which you called the imagination of an extreme case, falls short of the reality of what I witnessed here. It was the utmost degree of misery and destitution compatible with the preservation of life. A casual observer might have passed them by, as the most abject of the human race. But their physiognomy showed better things. It was with the utmost difficulty I could extract a word from either of them: but when I at last succeeded, I was astonished, in garments so mean and a dwelling so deplorable, to discover feelings so generous and minds so enlightened. The semblance of human sympathy seemed strange to them; little of it as you may suppose could be discovered through my saturnine complexion, and the habitual language of what you call my frosty philosophy. By degrees I engaged their confidence, and he related to me his history, which I will tell you as nearly as I can remember, in his own words.

CHAPTER XIII.

DESMOND.[1]

My name is Desmond. My father was a naval officer, who
in the prime of life was compelled by wounds to retire from
the service on his half-pay, and a small additional pension. I
was his only son, and he submitted to the greatest personal
privations, to procure me a liberal education, in the hope that
by these means he should live to see me making my way in
the world: but he always accompanied his wishes for this
consummation, with a hope that I should consider money
as a means, and not as an end, and that I should remember
the only real treasures of human existence were truth, health,
and liberty. You will not wonder, that, with such principles,
the father had been twenty years a lieutenant, and that the
son was looked on at College as a fellow that would come to
nothing.

I profited little at the University, as you will easily suppose. The system of education pursued there, appeared to
me the result of a deep-laid conspiracy against the human
understanding, a mighty effort of political and ecclesiastical
machiavelism,[2] to turn the energies of inquiring minds into
channels, where they will either stagnate in disgust, or waste
themselves in nugatory labour. To discover or even to illustrate a single moral truth, to shake the empire of a single prejudice, to apply a single blow of the axe of philosophy to the
wide-spreading roots of superstition and political imposture,[3]
is to render a real service to the best hopes of mankind; but
all this is diametrically opposed to the selfish interests of the
hired misleaders of society, the chosen few, as they are called,
before whom the wretched multitude grovel in the dust as
before

"The children of a race,
Mightier than they, and wiser, and by heaven
Beloved and favoured more."[4]

Moral science, therefore, moral improvement, the doctrines of benevolence, the amelioration of the general condition of mankind, will not only never form a part of any public institution, for the performance of that ridiculous and mischievous farce called the *Finishing of Education;* but every art of clerical chicanery and fraudulent misrepresentation will be practised, to render odious the very names of philosophy and philanthropy, and to extinguish, by ridicule and persecution, that enthusiastic love of truth, which never fails to conduct its votaries to conclusions very little compatible with the views of those who have built, or intend to build, their own worldly prosperity, on the foundations of hypocrisy and servility in themselves, and ignorance and credulity in others.

The study of morals and of mind occupied my exclusive attention. I had little taste for the science of lines and numbers, and still less for verbal criticism, the pinnacle of academical glory.

I delighted in the poets of Greece and Rome, but I thought that the *igneus vigor et cœlestis origo*[5] of their conceptions and expressions was often utterly lost sight of, in the microscopic inspection of philological minutiæ. I studied Greek, as the means of understanding Homer and Æschylus: I did not look on them as mere secondary instruments to the attainment of a knowledge of their language. I had no conception of the taste that could prefer Lycophron[6] to Sophocles, because he had the singular advantage of being obscure; and should have been utterly at a loss to account for such a phænomenon, if I had not seen that the whole system of public education was purposely calculated to make inferior minds recoil in disgust and terror from the vestibule of knowledge, and superior minds consume their dangerous energies in the *difficiles nugæ* and *labor ineptiarum* of its adytum.[7]

I did not *finish*, as it is called, my college *education*. My father's death compelled me to leave it before the expiration of the usual period, at the end of which the same distinction is conferred on all capacities, by the academical noometry,[8] not of merit but of time. I found myself almost destitute; but I felt the consciousness of talents, that I doubted not would amply provide for me in that great centre of intellect and energy, London. To London I accordingly went, and became a boarder in the humble dwelling of a widow, who maintained herself and an only daughter by the perilous and precarious income derived from lodgers.

My first application was to a bookseller in Bond Street,[9] to whom I offered the copyright[10] of a treatise on the Elements of Morals. "My dear Sir," said he, with an air of supercilious politeness, "only take the trouble of sitting a few hours in my shop, and if you detect any one of my customers in the fact of pronouncing the word *morals*, I will give any price you please to name for your copyright." But, glancing over the manuscript, "I perceive," said he, "there are some smart things here; and though they are good for nothing where they are, they would cut a pretty figure in a Review. My friend Mr. Vamp,[11] the editor, is in want of a hand for the moral department of his Review: I will give you a note to him." I thanked him for his kindness, and, furnished with the note, proceeded to the lodgings of Mr. Vamp, whom I found in an elegant first floor, lounging over a large quarto, which he was marking with a pencil. A number of books and pamphlets, and fragments of both curiously cut up, were scattered on the table before him, together with a large pot of paste, and an enormous pair of scissars.[12]

He received me with great hauteur, read the note, and said, "Mr. Foolscap[13] has told you we are in want of a hand, and he thinks you have a turn in the moral line: I shall not be sorry if it prove so, for we have been very ill provided in that way a long while; and though morals are not much in demand among our patrons and customers, and will not do, by any means, for a standing dish, they make, nevertheless, a very pretty seasoning for our politics, in cases where they might otherwise be rather unpalatable and hard of digestion. You see this pile of pamphlets, these volumes of poetry, and this rascally quarto: all these, though under very different titles, and the productions of very different orders of mind, have, either openly or covertly, only one object; and a most impertinent one it is. This object is two-fold: first, to prove the existence, to an immense extent, of what these writers think proper to denominate political corruption; secondly, to convince the public that this corruption ought to be extinguished. Now, we are anxious to do away[14] the effect of all these incendiary clamours. As to the existence of corruption (it is a villanous[15] word, by the by—we call it *persuasion in a tangible shape):* as to the existence, then, of *persuasion in a tangible shape*,[16] we do not wish to deny it; on the contrary, we have no hesitation in affirming that it is *as notorious as the sun at noon-day:*[17] but as to the inference that it ought to be extinguished—that is the point against which we direct the full fire of our critical artillery; we maintain that it ought to exist; and here is the leading article of our next number, in which we confound in one mass all these obnoxious publications, putting the weakest at the head of the list, that if any of our readers should feel inclined to judge for themselves (I must do them the credit to say I do not suspect many of them of such a democratical propensity), they may be stopped *in limine,* by finding very little temptation to proceed. The political composition of this article is beautiful: it is the production of a gentleman high in office, who is indebted to *persuasion in a tangible shape* for his present income of several thousands per annum;[18] but it wants, as I have hinted, a little moral seasoning; and there, as ill-luck will have it, we are all thrown out. We have several reverend gentlemen in our corps, but morals are unluckily quite out of their way. We have, on some occasions, with their assistance, substituted theology for morals: they manage this very cleverly, but, I am sorry to say, it only takes among the old women; and though the latter are our best and most numerous customers, yet we have some very obstinate and hard-headed readers who will not, as I have observed, swallow our politics without a little moral seasoning; and, as I told Mr. Foolscap, if we did not contrive to pick up a spice of morals somewhere or other, all the eloquence of *persuasion in a tangible shape* would soon become of little avail. Now, if you will undertake the seasoning of this article in such a manner as to satisfy my employers, I will satisfy you: you understand me."

I observed, that I hoped he would allow me the free exercise of my own opinion; and that I should wish to season his article in such a manner as to satisfy myself, which I candidly told him would not be in such a manner as seemed likely to satisfy him.

On this he flew into a rage, and vowed vengeance against Mr. Foolscap for having sent him a Jacobin.[19] I strenuously disclaimed this appellation; and being then quite a novice in the world, I actually endeavoured to reason with him, as if the conviction of general right and wrong could have any influence upon him; but he stopped me short, by saying, that till I could reason him out of his pension, I might spare myself the trouble of interfering with his opinions; as the logic from which they were deduced had presented itself to him in a much more *tangible shape* than any abstract notions of truth and liberty. He had thought, from Mr. Foolscap's letter, that I had a talent for moral theory, and that I was inclined to turn it to account; as for moral practice, he had nothing to do with it, desired to know nothing about it, and wished me a good morning.

I was not yet discouraged, and made similar applications to the editors and proprietors of several daily, weekly, monthly, and quarterly publications, but I found every where the same indifference or aversion to general principles, the same partial and perverted views: every one was the organ of some division or subdivision of a faction; and had entrenched himself in a narrow circle, within the pale of which all was honour, consistency, integrity, generosity, and justice; while all without it was villany, hypocrisy, selfishness, corruption, and lies. Not being inclined to imprison myself in any one of these magical rings, I found all my interviews terminate like that with Mr. Vamp.

By the advice and introduction of a college acquaintance, I accepted the situation of tutor in the family of Mr. Dross,[20] a wealthy citizen, who had acquired a large fortune by contracts with Government, in the execution of which he had not forgotten to charge for his vote and interest. His conscience, indeed, of all the commodities he dealt in, was that which he had brought to the best market; though, among his more fair dealing, and consequently poorer neighbours, it was thought he had made the ministry pay too dearly for so very rotten an article. They seemed not to be aware that a corrupt administration estimates conscience and Stilton cheese by the same criterion, and that its rottenness was its recommendation.

Mr. Dross was a tun of man,[21] with the soul of a hazelnut: his wife was a tun of woman, without any soul whatever. The principle that animated her bulk was composed of three ingredients—arrogance, ignorance, and the pride of money. They were, in every sense of the word, what the world calls respectable people.[22]

Mrs. Dross aspired to be *somebody*, aped the nobility, and gave magnificent routs, which were attended by many noble personages, and by all that portion of the fashionable world that will go anywhere for a crowd and a supper.

Their idea of virtue consisted in having no debts, going regularly to church, and feeding the parson; their idea of charity, in paying the poor-rates,[23] and putting down their names to public subscriptions: and they had a profound contempt for every species of learning, which they associated indissolubly with rags and famine, and with that neglect of the main chance,[24] which they regarded as the most deadly of all deadly sins. But as they had several hopeful children, and as Mrs. Dross found it was fashionable to have a governess and a *tutorer*,[25] they had looked out for two pieces of human furniture under these denominations, and my capricious destiny led me to their splendid dwelling in the latter capacity.

I found the governess, Miss Pliant, very admirably adapted to her situation. She did not presume to have a will of her own. Suspended like Mahomet's coffin[26] between the mistress and the housekeeper, despising the one, and despised by the other, her mind seemed unconscious of its vacancy, and her heart of its loneliness. She had neither feelings nor principles, either of good or ill: perfectly selfish, perfectly cold-hearted, and perfectly obsequious, she was contented with her situation, because it seemed likely to lead to an advantageous establishment; for if ever she thought of marriage, it was only in the light of a system of bargain, in which youth and beauty were very well disposed of when bartered for age and money. She was highly accomplished: a very scientific musician, without any soul in her performance; a most skilful copier of landscapes, without the least taste for the beauties of nature; and a proficient in French grammar, though she had read no book in that language but *Télémaque*,[27] and hated the names of Rousseau and Voltaire, because she had heard them called rascals by her father, who had taken his opinion on trust from the Reverend Mr. Simony, who had never read a page of either of them.

I very soon found that I was regarded as an upper servant—as a person of more pretension, but less utility, than the footman. I was expected to be really more servile, in mind especially. If I presumed to differ in opinion from Mr. or Mrs.

Dross, they looked at each other and at me with the most profound astonishment, wondering at so much audacity in one of their moveables.[28] I really envied the footman, living as he did among his equals, where he might have his own opinion, as far as he was capable of forming one, and express it without reserve or fear; while all my thoughts were to be those of a mirror, and my motions those of an automaton. I soon saw that I had but the choice of alternatives: either to mould myself into a slave, liar, and hypocrite, or to take my leave of Mr. Dross. I therefore embraced the latter, and determined from that moment never again to live under the roof of a superior, if my own dwelling were to be the most humble and abject of human habitations.

I returned to my old lodgings, and, after a short time, procured some employment in the way of copying for a lawyer. My labour was assiduous, and my remuneration scanty; but my habits were simple, my evenings were free, and in the daughter of the widow with whom I lodged, I found a congenial mind: a desire for knowledge, an ardent love of truth, and a capacity that made my voluntary office of instruction at once easy and delightful.

The widow died embarrassed:[29] her creditors seized her effects, and her daughter was left destitute. I was her only friend: to every other human being, not only her welfare, but even her existence, were matters of total indifference. The course of necessity seemed to have thrown her on my protection, and if I before loved her, I now regarded her as a precious trust, confided to me by her evil fate. Call it what you may, imprudence, madness, frenzy—we were married.

The lawyer who employed me, had chosen his profession very injudiciously, for he was an honest and benevolent man. He interested himself for me, acquainted himself with my circumstances, and, without informing me of his motives, increased my remuneration; though, as I afterwards found, he

could very ill afford to do so. By this means we lived twelve
months in comfort, I may say, considering the simplicity of
our habits, in prosperity. The birth of our first child was an
accession to our domestic happiness. We had no pleasures
beyond the limits of our humble dwelling. Our circumstances
and situation were much below the ordinary level of those of
well-educated people: we had, therefore, no society, but we
were happy in each other: our evenings were consecrated to
our favourite authors; and the din of the streets, the tumult
of crowds and carriages thronging to parties of pleasure and
scenes of public amusement, came to us like the roar of a
stormy ocean, on which we had neither wish nor power to
embark.

One evening we were surprised by an unexpected visitor:
it was the lawyer my employer. "Desmond!" said he, "I am a
ruined man. For having been too scrupulous to make beggars
of others, I have a fair prospect of becoming one myself. You
are shocked and astonished. Do not grieve on my account. I
have neither wife nor children. Very trivial and very remedi-
able is the evil that can happen to me. 'The valiant by himself, what can he suffer?'[30] You will think a lawyer has as little
business with poetry as he has with justice. Perhaps so. I have
been too partial to both."

I was glad to see him so cheerful, and expressed a hope that
his affairs would take a better turn than he seemed to expect.
"You shall know more," said he, "in a few days; in the mean
time here are the arrears I owe you."

When he came again, he said: "My creditors are neither
numerous nor cruel. I have made over to them all my property, but they allow me to retain possession of a small house
in Westmoreland, with an annuity for my life, sufficient to
maintain me in competence. I could propose a wild scheme to
you if I thought you would not be offended."

"That," said I, "I certainly will not, propose what you may."

"Tell me," said he, "which do you think the most useful and uncontaminating implement, the quill or the spade?"

"The spade," said I, "generally speaking, unquestionably: the quill, in some most rare and solitary instances."

"In the hand of Homer and Plutarch, of Seneca and Tacitus, of Shakespeare and Rousseau? I am not speaking of them, or of those who, however humbly, reflect their excellencies. But in the hands of the slaves of commerce, the minions of law, the venal advocates of superstition, the sycophants of corruption, the turnspits of literature, the paragraph-mongers of prostituted journals, the hireling compounders of party praise and censure, under the name of periodical criticism, what say you to it?"

"What can I say," said I, "but that it is the curse of society, and the bane of the human mind?"

"And yet," said he, "in some of these ways must you employ it, if you wish to live by it. Literature is not the soil in which truth and liberty can flourish, unless their cultivators be independent of the world. Those who are not so, whatever be the promise of their beginning, will end either in sycophants or beggars. As mere mechanical instruments, in pursuits unconnected with literature, what say you to the comparison?"

"What Cincinnatus[31] would have said," I answered.

"I am glad," said he, "to hear it. You are not one of the multitude, neither I believe am I. I embraced my profession, I assure you, from very disinterested motives. I considered that the greater the powers of mischief with which that profession is armed, and I am sorry to add, the practice of mischief in the generality of its professors, the greater might be the scope of philanthropy, in protecting weakness, and counteracting oppression. Thus I have passed my life in an attempt to reconcile philanthropy and law. I had property sufficient to enable me to try the experiment. The natural consequence is, my property has vanished. I do not regret it, for I have done some good. But I can do no more. My power is annulled. I must retire from the stage of life. If I retire alone, I must have servants; I had much rather have friends. If you will accompany me to Westmoreland, we will organize a little republic of our own. Your wife shall be our housekeeper. We will cultivate our garden.[32] We shall want little more, and that my annuity will amply supply. We will select a few books, and we will pronounce eternal banishment on pen and ink."

I could not help smiling at the earnestness with which he pronounced the last clause. The change of a lawyer into a Roman republican appeared to me as miraculous as any metamorphosis in Ovid.[33] Not to weary you with details, we carried this scheme into effect, and passed three years of natural and healthy occupation, with perfect simplicity and perfect content. They were the happiest of our lives. But at the end of this period, our old friend died. His annuity died with him. He left me his heir, but his habitation and its furniture were all he had to leave. I procured a tenant for the house, and we removed to this even yet more humble dwelling. The difference of the rent, a very trifling sum indeed, constituted our only income. The increase of our family, and the consequent pressure of necessity, compelled us to sell the house. From the same necessity we have become strict Pythagoreans.[34] I do not complain that we live hardly: it is almost wonderful that we live at all. The produce of our little garden preserves us from famine: but this is all it does. I consider myself a mere rustic, and very willingly engage in agricultural labour, when the neighbouring farmers think proper to employ me: but they feel no deficiency of abler hands. There are more labourers than means of labour. In the cities it is the same. If all the modes of human occupation in this kingdom, from the highest to the lowest, were to require at once a double number of persons, there would not remain one of them twelve hours unfilled.

With what views could I return to London? Of the throng continually pressing onward, to spring into the vacancies of employment, the foremost ranks are unfortunately composed of the selfish, the servile, the intriguing; of those to whose ideas general justice is a chimæra, liberty an empty name, and truth at best a verbal veil for the sycophantic falsehood of a mercenary spirit. To what end could a pupil of the ancient Romans mingle with such a multitude? To cringe, to lie, to flatter? To bow to the insolence of wealth, the superciliousness of rank, the contumely of patronage, that, while it exacts the most abject mental prostration, in return for promises never meant to be performed, despises the servility it fosters, and laughs at the credulity it betrays?

The wheel of fortune is like a water-wheel, and human beings are like the waters it disturbs. Many are thrown into the channels of action, many are thrown back to be lost for ever in the stream. I am one of the latter: but I shall not consider it disgraceful to me that I am so, till I see that candour, simplicity, integrity, and intellectual power directed by benevolence and liberty, have a better claim to worldly estimation, than either venal talent prostituted to the wages of corruption, or ignorance, meanness, and imbecility, exalted by influence and interest.

CHAPTER XIV.

THE COTTAGE.

MR. FAX *(In continuation).*

"I CANNOT help thinking," said I, when Desmond had done speaking, "that you have formed too hasty an estimate of the world. Mr. Vamp and Mr. Dross are bad specimens of human nature: but there are many good specimens of it in both those classes of men. The world is, indeed, full of prejudices and superstitions, which produce ample profit to their venal advocates, who consequently want neither the will nor the power to calumniate and persecute the enlightened and the virtuous. The rich, too, are usually arrogant and exacting, and those feelings will never perish for want of sycophants to nourish them. An ardent love of truth and liberty will, therefore, always prove an almost insuperable barrier to any great degree of worldly advancement. A celebrated divine, who turned his theological morality to very excellent account, and died *en bonne odeur,*[1] used to say, *he could not afford to have a conscience, for it was the most expensive luxury a man could indulge in.*[2] So it certainly is: but though a conscientious man, who has his own way to make in the world, will very seldom flourish in the sunshine of prosperity, it is not, therefore, necessary that he should sit quietly down and starve." He said he would think of it, and if he could find any loop-hole in the great feudal fortress of society, at which poverty and honesty could creep in together, he would try to effect an entrance. I made more particular inquiry into their circumstances, and they at length communicated to me, but with manifest reluctance, that they were in imminent danger of being deprived of their miserable furniture, and turned out of their wretched habitation, by Lawrence Litigate, Esquire, their landlord, for arrears of rent amounting to five pounds.

MR. FORESTER.

Which of course you paid?

MR. FAX.

I did so: but I do not see that it is of course.

Mr. Forester, Mr. Fax, and Sir Oran, were still leaning over the gate of the cottage, when a peasant came whistling along the road. "Pray, my honest friend," said Mr. Fax, "can you inform me what has become of the family which inhabited this cottage two years ago?"—"Ye'll voind[3] them," said the peasant, "about a mile vurther an, just by the lake's edge like, wi' two large elms by the door, and a vir tree." He resumed his tune and his way.

The philosophical trio proceeded on their walk.

MR. FORESTER.

You have said little of his wife.

MR. FAX.

She was an interesting creature. With her the feelings of misfortune had subsided into melancholy silence, while with him they broke forth in misanthropical satire.

MR. FORESTER.

And their children?

MR. FAX.

They would have been fine children, if they had been better clothed and fed.

MR. FORESTER.

Did they seem to repent their marriage?

MR. FAX.

Not for themselves. They appeared to have no wish but to live and die together. For their children, indeed, I could easily perceive they felt more grief than they expressed.

MR. FORESTER.

You have scarcely made out your case. Poverty had certainly come in at the door, but Love does not seem to have flown out at the window.[4] You would not have prevailed on them to separate at the price of living in palaces. The energy of intellect was not deadened; the independence of spirit was not broken. The participation of love communicates a luxury to sorrow, that all the splendour of selfishness can never bestow. If, as has been said, a friend is more valuable than the elements of fire and water, how much more valuable must be the one only associate, the more than friend, to him whom in affliction and in poverty all other friends have abandoned! If the sun shines equally on the palace and the cottage, why should not love, the sun of the intellectual world, shine equally on both? More needful, indeed, is its genial light to the latter, where there is no worldly splendour to diminish or divide its radiance.

With a sudden turn of the road, a scene of magnificent beauty burst upon their view: the still expanse of a lake, bordered with dark precipices and fading woods, and mountains rising above them, height on height, till the clouds rested on their summits. A picturesque tourist[5] had planted his travelling chair under the corner of a rock, and was intently occupied in sketching the scene. The process attracted Sir Oran's curiosity: he walked up to the tourist, who was too deeply engaged to notice his approach, and peeped over his shoulder. Sir Oran, after looking at the picture, then at the landscape, then at the picture, then at the landscape again; at length suddenly expressed his delight in a very loud and very singular shout, close in the painter's ear, that re-echoed from rock to rock. The tourist sprang up in violent alarm, and seeing the extraordinary physiognomy of the personage at his elbow, drew a sudden conclusion of evil intentions, and ran off with great rapidity, leaving all his apparatus behind him. Sir Oran sate down in the artist's seat, took up the drawing utensils, placed the unfinished drawing on his knee, and sate in an attitude of deep contemplation, as if meditating on the means to be pursued for doing the same thing himself.

The flying tourist encountered Messieurs Fax and Forester, who had observed the transaction, and were laughing at it as heartily as Democritus himself could have done.[6] They tranquillized his apprehensions, and led him back to the spot. Sir Oran, on a hint from his friend Mr. Forester, rose, made the tourist a polite bow, and restored to him his beloved portfolio. They then wished him a good morning, and left him in a state of nervous trepidation, which made it very obvious that he would draw no more that day.

MR. FAX.

Can Sir Oran draw?

MR. FORESTER.

No: but I think he would easily acquire the art. It is very probable, that in the nation of the Orans,[7] which I take to be *a barbarous nation, that has not yet learned the use of speech*,*[8] drawing, as a means of communicating ideas, may be in no contemptible state of forwardness.†

* Origin and Progress of Language, book ii. chap. 4.
† "I have endeavoured to support the ancient definition of man, and to show that it belongs to the oran outang, though he have not the use of speech. And indeed it appears surprising to me, that any man, pretending to be a philosopher, should not be satisfied with the expression of intelligence in the most useful way, for the purposes of life; I mean by actions; but should require likewise the expression of them, by those signs of arbitrary institution we call *words*, before they will allow an animal to deserve the name of *man*. Suppose that, upon inquiry, it should be found, that the oran outangs have not only invented the art of building huts, and of attacking and defending with sticks, *but also have contrived a way of communicating to the absent, and recording their ideas by the method of painting or drawing*, as is practised by many barbarous nations (and the supposition is not at all impossible, or even improbable); and suppose they should have contrived some form of government, and should elect kings or rulers, which is possible, and, according to the information of the Bristol merchant above mentioned, is reported to be actually the case, what would Mr. Buffon then say? Must they still be accounted brutes, because they have not yet fallen upon the method of communication by articulate sounds?"—*Ibid.*[9]

MR. FAX.

He has of course seen many drawings, since he has been among civilized men: what so peculiarly delighted and surprised him in this?

MR. FORESTER.

I suspect this is the first opportunity he has had, of comparing the natural original with the artificial copy; and his delight was excited by seeing the vast scene before him, transferred so accurately into so small a compass, and growing as it were into a distinct identity under the hand of the artist.

They now arrived at the elms and the fir-tree, which the peasant had pointed out as the landmarks of the dwelling of Desmond. They were surprised to see a very pretty cottage standing in the midst of a luxuriant garden, one part of which sloped down to the edge of the lake. Every thing bore the air of comfort and competence. They almost doubted if the peasant had been correct in his information. Three rosy children, plainly but neatly dressed, were sitting on the edge of the shallow water, watching with intense delight and interest the manœuvres of a paper flotilla which they had committed to the mercy of the waves.

MR. FAX.

What is the difference between these children, and Xerxes on the shores of Salamis?[10]

MR. FORESTER.

None, but that where they have pure and unmingled pleasure, his feelings began in selfish pride, and ended in slavish fear: their amusement is natural and innocent; his was unnatural, cruel, and destructive, and, therefore, more unworthy of a rational being. *Better is a poor and wise child, than a foolish king that will not be admonished.*[11]

A female came from the cottage. Mr. Fax recognised Mrs. Desmond. He was surprised at the change in her appearance. Health and content animated her countenance. The simple neatness of her dress derived an appearance of elegance from its interesting wearer; contrary to the fashionable process in which dress, neither neat nor simple, but a heterogeneous mixture of all the fripperies of Europe, gives what the world calls elegance, where less partial nature has denied it. There are in this respect two classes of human beings: Nature makes the first herself, for the beauty of her own creation: her journeymen cut out the second for tailors and mantua-makers[12] to finish. The first, when apparelled, may be called dressed people—the second, peopled dresses: the first bear the same relation to their clothes as an oak bears to its foliage—the second, the same as a wig-block bears to a wig: the first may be compared to cocoa-nuts, in which the kernel is more valuable than the shell—the second, to some varieties of the *Testaceous Mollusca*,[13] where a shell of infinite value covers a stupid fish that is good for nothing.

Mrs. Desmond recognised Mr. Fax. "O Sir!" said she, "I rejoice to see you."—"And I rejoice," said Mr. Fax, "to see you as you now are: Fortune has befriended you."—"You rendered us great service, Sir, in our wretched condition; but the benefit, of course, was transient. With the next quarter-day Mr. Litigate, our landlord, resumed his persecutions; and we should have been turned out of our wretched dwelling to perish in the roads, had not some happy accident made Miss Melincourt acquainted with our situation. To know what it was, and to make it what it is, were the same thing to her. So suddenly, when the extremity of evil was impending over us, to be placed in this little Paradise in competence—nay, to our simple habits, in affluence, and in such a manner, as if we were bestowing, not receiving, favours——O Sir! there cannot be two Miss Melincourts! But will you not walk in, and take some refreshment?—We can offer you refreshment now. My husband is absent at present, but he will very soon return."

While she was speaking he arrived. Mr. Fax congratulated him. At his earnest solicitation, they entered the cottage, and were delighted with the beautiful neatness that predominated in every part of it. The three children ran in to see the strangers. Mr. Forester took up the little girl, Mr. Fax a boy, and Sir Oran Haut-ton another. The latter took alarm at the physiognomy of his new friend, and cried, and kicked, and struggled for release; but Sir Oran producing a flute from his pocket, struck up a lively air, which reconciled the child, who then sate very quietly on his knee.

Some refreshment was placed before them, and Sir Oran testified, by a copious draught, that he found much virtue in home-brewed ale.

"There is a farm attached to this cottage," said Mr. Desmond; "and Miss Melincourt, by having placed me in it, enabled me to maintain my family in comfort and independence, and to educate them in a free, healthy, and natural occupation. I have ever thought agriculture the noblest of human pursuits:[14] to the theory and practice of it I now devote my whole attention, and I am not without hopes that the improvement of this part of my benefactress's estate will justify her generous confidence in a friendless stranger: but what can repay her benevolence?"

"I will answer for her," said Mr. Forester, "though she is as yet personally unknown to me, that she loves benevolence for its own sake, and is satisfied with its consummation."

After a short conversation, and a promise soon to revisit the now happy family, Mr. Forester, Mr. Fax, and Sir Oran Haut-ton resumed their walk. Mr. Forester, at parting, put unobserved into the hand of the little boy a folded paper, telling him to give it to his father. It was a leaf which he had torn from his pocket-book: he had enclosed in it a bank-note, and had written on it with a pencil, "Do not refuse to a stranger the happiness of reflecting that he has, however tardily and slightly, co-operated with Miss Melincourt in a work of justice."

THE END OF VOL. I.

CHAPTER XV.

THE LIBRARY.

Mr. Forester, Mr. Fax, and Sir Oran Haut-ton arrived at Melincourt Castle. They were shown into a parlour, where they were left alone a few minutes; when Mr. Hippy made his appearance, and recognising Sir Oran, shook hands with him very cordially. Mr. Forester produced the letter he had received from Mr. Ratstail, which Mr. Hippy having read, vented a string of invectives against the impudent rascal, and explained the mystery of the adventure, though he seemed to think it strange that Sir Oran could not have explained it himself. Mr. Forester shook his head significantly;[1] and Mr. Hippy affecting to understand the gesture, exclaimed, "Ah! poor gentleman!"—He then invited them to stay to dinner. "I won't be refused," said he; "I am lord and master of this castle at present, and here you shall stay till to-morrow. Anthy[2] will be delighted to see her friend here" (bowing to Sir Oran, who returned it with great politeness), "and we will hold a council of war how to deal with this pair of puppies, Lawrence Litigate, Esquire, and Richard Ratstail, Solicitor. I have several visitors here already: lords, baronets, and squires, all Corydons,[3] sighing for Anthy; but it seems *Love's Labour Lost*[4] with all of them. However, love and wine,[5] you know! Anthy won't give them the first, so I drench them with the second: there will be more bottles than hearts cracked in the business, for all Anthy's beauty. *Men die, and worms eat them*, as usual, *but not for love*."[6]

Mr. Forester inquired for Sir Telegraph Paxarett. "An excellent fellow after dinner!" exclaimed Mr. Hippy. "I never see him in the morning; nor any one else, but my rascal Harry Fell, and now and then Doctor Killquick. The moment breakfast is over, one goes one way, and another another. Anthy locks herself up in the library."

"Locks herself up in the library!" said Mr. Fax: "a young lady, a beauty, and an heiress, in the nineteenth century, think of cultivating her understanding!"

"Strange but true," said Mr. Hippy; "and here am I, a poor invalid, left alone all the morning to prowl about the castle like a ghost; that is, when I am well enough to move, which is not always the case. But the library is opened at four, and the party assembles there before dinner; and as it is now about the time, come with me, and I will introduce you."

They followed Mr. Hippy to the library, where they found Anthelia alone.

"Anthy," said Mr. Hippy, after the forms of introduction, "do you know you are accused of laying waste a pine-grove, and carrying it off by cart-loads, with force and arms?"

Anthelia read Mr. Ratstail's letter. "This is a very strange piece of folly," she said: "I hope it will not be a mischievous one." She then renewed the expressions of her gratitude to Sir Oran, and bade him welcome to Melincourt. Sir Oran bowed in silence.

"Folly and mischief," said Mr. Fax, "are very nearly allied;[7] and no where more conspicuously than in the forms of the law."

MR. FORESTER.

You have an admirable library, Miss Melincourt: and I judge from the great number of Italian books, you are justly partial to the poets of that exquisite language. The apartment itself seems singularly adapted to the genius of their poetry, which combines the magnificent simplicity of ancient Greece with the mysterious grandeur of the feudal ages. Those windows of stained glass would recall to an enthusiastic mind the attendant spirit of Tasso;[8] and the waving of the cedars beyond, when the wind makes music in their boughs, with the birds singing in their shades and the softened dash of the torrent from the dingle below, might, with little aid from fancy, be modulated into that exquisite combination of melody which flowed from the enchanted wood at the entrance of Rinaldo, and which Tasso has painted with a degree of harmony not less magical than the music he describes. Italian poetry is all fairyland: I know not any description of literature so congenial to the tenderness and delicacy of the female mind, which, however opposite may be the tendency of modern education, Nature has most pre-eminently adapted to be 'a mansion for all lovely forms: a dwelling-place for all sweet sounds and harmonies'.[*][9] Of these, Italian poetry is a most inexhaustible fountain; and for that reason I could wish it to be generally acknowledged a point of the very first importance in female education.

ANTHELIA.

You have a better opinion of the understandings of women, Sir, than the generality of your lordly sex seems disposed to entertain.

MR. FORESTER.

The conduct of men, in this respect, is much like that of a gardener who should plant a plot of ground with merely ornamental flowers, and then pass sentence on the soil for not bearing substantial fruit. If women are treated only as pretty dolls,[10] and dressed in all the fripperies of irrational education; if the vanity of personal adornment and superficial accomplishments be made from their very earliest years to suppress all mental aspirations, and to supersede all thoughts of intellectual beauty,[11] is it to be inferred that they are incapable of better things? But such is the usual logic of tyranny, which first places its extinguisher on the flame, and then argues that it cannot burn.

[*] Wordsworth's Tintern Abbey.

MR. FAX.

Your remark is not totally just: for though custom, how justly I will not say, banishes women from the fields of classical literature, yet the study of Italian poetry, of which you think so highly, is very much encouraged among them.

MR. FORESTER.

You should rather say it is not discouraged. They are permitted to know it: but in very few instances is the permission accompanied by any practical aid. The only points practically enforced in female education are sound, colour, and form,—music, dress, drawing, and dancing. The mind is left to take care of itself.

MR. FAX.

And has as much chance of doing so as a horse in a pound, circumscribed in the narrowest limits, and studiously deprived of nourishment.

ANTHELIA.

The simile is, I fear, too just. To think is one of the most unpardonable errors a woman can commit in the eyes of society. In our sex a taste for intellectual pleasures is almost equivalent to taking the veil; and though not absolutely a vow of perpetual celibacy, it has almost always the same practical tendency. In that universal system of superficial education which so studiously depresses the mind of women, a female who aspires to mental improvement will scarcely find in her own sex a congenial associate; and the other will regard her as an intruder on its prescriptive authority, its legitimate and divine right over the dominion of thought and reason: and the general consequence is, that she remains insulated between both, in more than cloistered loneliness. Even in its effect on herself, the ideal beauty which she studies will make her fastidious, too fastidious, perhaps, to the world of realities, and deprive her of the happiness that might be her portion, by fixing her imagination on chimæras of unattainable excellence.

MR. FORESTER.

I can answer for men, Miss Melincourt, that there are some, many I hope, who can appreciate justly that most heavenly of earthly things, an enlightened female mind; whatever may be thought by the pedantry that envies, the foppery that fears, the folly that ridicules, or the wilful blindness that will not see its loveliness. I am afraid your last observation approaches most nearly to the truth, and that it is owing more to their own fastidiousness than to the want of friends and admirers, that intelligent women are so often alone in the world. But were it otherwise, the objection will not apply to Italian poetry, a field of luxuriant beauty, from which women are not interdicted even by the most intolerant prejudice of masculine usurpation.

ANTHELIA.

They are not interdicted, certainly; but they are seldom encouraged to enter it. Perhaps it is feared, that, having gone thus far, they might be tempted to go farther: that the friend of Tasso might aspire to the acquaintance of Virgil, or even to an introduction to Homer and Sophocles.

MR. FORESTER.

And why should she not? Far from desiring to suppress such a noble ambition, how delightful should I think the task of conducting the lovely aspirant through the treasures of Grecian genius!—to wander hand-in-hand with such a companion among the valleys and fountains of Ida, and by the banks of the eddying Scamander;* [12] through the island of Calypso and the gardens of Alcinous;† [13] to the rocks of

---

* The Iliad.
† The Odyssey.

the Scythian desert;* 14 to the caverned shores of the solitary Lemnos;† 15 and to the fatal sands of Trœzene.‡ 16—to kindle in such scenes the enthusiasm of such a mind, and to see the eyes of love and beauty beaming with their reflected inspiration! Miserably perverted, indeed, must be the selfishness of him who, having such happiness in his power, would,

> Like the base Indian, throw a pearl away,
> Richer than all his tribe."17

MR. FAX.

My friend's enthusiasm, Miss Melincourt, usually runs away with him when any allusion is made to ancient Greece.

Mr. Forester had spoken with ardour and animation; for the scenes of which he spoke rose upon his mind as depicted in the incomparable poetry to which he had alluded; the figurative idea of wandering among them with a young and beautiful female aspirant, assumed for a moment a visionary reality; and when he subsequently reflected on it, it appeared to him very singular that the female figure in the mental picture had assumed the form and features of Anthelia Melincourt.

Anthelia, too, saw in the animated countenance of Sylvan Forester traces of more than common feeling, generosity, and intelligence: his imaginary wanderings through the classic scenes of antiquity assumed in her congenial mind the brightest colours of intellectual beauty; and she could not help thinking that if he were what he appeared, such wanderings, with such a guide, would not be the most unenviable of earthly destinies.

The other guests dropped in by ones and twos. Sir Telegraph was agreeably surprised to see Mr. Forester: "By the bye," said

---

* The Prometheus of Æschylus.
† The Philoctetes of Sophocles.
‡ The Hippolytus of Euripides.

he, "have you heard that a general election[18] is to take place immediately?"

"I have," said Mr. Forester, "and was thinking of putting you and your barouche in requisition very shortly."

"As soon as you please," said Sir Telegraph.

The Honourable Mrs. Pinmoney took Sir Telegraph aside, to make inquiry concerning the new-comers.

THE HONOURABLE MRS. PINMONEY.

Who is that very bright-eyed wild-looking young man?

SIR TELEGRAPH PAXARETT.

That is my old acquaintance and fellow-collegian, Sylvan Forester, now of Redrose Abbey, in this county.

THE HONOURABLE MRS. PINMONEY.

Is he respectable?

SIR TELEGRAPH PAXARETT.

He has a good estate, [19] if you mean that.

THE HONOURABLE MRS. PINMONEY.

To be sure I mean that. And who is that tall thin saturnine personage?

SIR TELEGRAPH PAXARETT.

I know nothing of him but that his name is Fax, and that he is now on a visit to Mr. Forester at Redrose Abbey.

THE HONOURABLE MRS. PINMONEY.

And who is that *very* tall and remarkably ugly gentleman?[20]

SIR TELEGRAPH PAXARETT.

That is Sir Oran Haut-ton, Baronet; to which designation you may shortly add M. P. for the ancient and honourable borough of Onevote.

THE HONOURABLE MRS. PINMONEY.

A Baronet! and M. P.! Well, now I look at him again, I certainly do not think him so very plain: he has a very fashionable air. Haut-ton! French extraction, no doubt. And now I think of it, there is something very French in his physiognomy.[21]

Dinner was announced, and the party adjourned to the dining-room. Mr. Forester offered his hand to Anthelia; and Sir Oran Haut-ton, following the example, presented his to the Honourable Mrs. Pinmoney.*

---

* "Je l'ai vu présenter sa main pour reconduire les gens qui venoient le visiter; se promener gravement avec eux et comme de compagnie, &c."—BUFFON, *H. N. de l' Oran-Outang.*[22]

CHAPTER XVI

THE SYMPOSIUM.

THE dinner passed off with great harmony. The ladies withdrew. The bottle revolved with celerity, under the presidency of Mr. Hippy, and the vice-presidency of Sir Telegraph Paxarett. The Reverend Mr. Portpipe, who was that day of the party, pronounced an eulogium on the wine, which was echoed by the Reverend Mr. Grovelgrub, Mr. O'Scarum, Lord Anophel Achthar, Mr. Feathernest, and Mr. Derrydown. Mr. Forester and Mr. Fax showed no disposition to destroy the unanimity of opinion on this interesting subject. Sir Oran Haut-ton maintained a grave and dignified silence, but demonstrated by his practice that his taste was orthodox. Mr. O'Scarum sate between Sir Oran and the Reverend Mr. Portpipe, and kept a sharp look-out on both sides of him; but did not, during the whole course of the sitting, detect either of his supporters in the heinous fact of a heeltap.[1]

MR. HIPPY.

Doctor Killquick may say what he pleases

> "Of mithridate, cordials, and elixirs;
> But from my youth this was my only physic.—
> Here's a colour! what lady's cheek comes near it?
> It sparkles, hangs out diamonds! O my sweet heart!
> Mistress of merry hearts! they are not worth thy favours
> Who number thy moist kisses in these crystals!"* [2]

THE REVEREND MR. PORTPIPE.

An excellent text!—sound doctrine, plain and practical. When I open the bottle, I shut the book of Numbers. There are two reasons for drinking: one is, when you are thirsty,

---

* Fletcher's Sea Voyage.

to cure it; the other, when you are not thirsty, to prevent it. The first is obvious, mechanical, and plebeian; the second is most refined, abstract, prospicient,[3] and canonical. I drink by anticipation of thirst that may be. Prevention is better than cure. Wine is the elixir of life. "The soul," says St. Augustine,[4] "cannot live in drought."* What is death? Dust and ashes. There is nothing so dry. What is life? Spirit. What is spirit? Wine.

MR. O'SCARUM.

And whisky.

THE REVEREND MR. PORTPIPE.

Whisky is hepatic, phlogistic, and exanthematous.[5] Wine is the hierarchical and archiepiscopal[6] fluid. Bacchus is said to have conquered the East,[7] and to have returned loaded with its spoils. "Marry how? tropically."[8] The conquests of Bacchus are the victories of imagination, which, sublimated[9] by wine, puts to rout care, fear, and poverty, and revels in the treasures of Utopia.

MR. FEATHERNEST.

The juice of the grape is the liquid quintessence of concentrated sun-beams. Man is an exotic, in this northern climate, and must be nourished like a hot-house plant, by the perpetual adhibition of artificial heat.

LORD ANOPHEL ACHTHAR.

You were not always so fond of wine,[10] Feathernest?

MR. FEATHERNEST.

Oh, my Lord! no allusion, I beseech you, to my youthful errors. Demosthenes being asked what wine he liked best, answered, that which he drank at the expense of others.[11]

---

* Anima certè, quia spiritus est, in sicco habitare non potest.

THE REVEREND MR. PORTPIPE.

Demosthenes was right. His circumstance, or qualification, is an accompaniment of better relish than a devilled biscuit or an anchovy toast.[12]

MR. FEATHERNEST.

In former days, my Lord, I had no experience that way; therefore I drank water against my will.

LORD ANOPHEL ACHTHAR.

And wrote Odes upon it, to Truth and Liberty.[13]

MR. FEATHERNEST.

"Ah, no more of that, an thou lovest me."[14] Now that I can get it for a song, I take my pipe of wine[15] a year: and what is the effect? Not cold phlegmatic lamentations over the sufferings of the poor, but high-flown, jovial, reeling dithyrambics[16] "to all the crowned heads in Europe."[17] I had then a vague notion that all was wrong. Persuasion has since appeared to me in a tangible shape, and convinced me that all is right, especially at court.[18] Then I saw darkly through a glass—of water.[19] Now I see clearly through a glass of wine.

THE REVEREND MR. PORTPIPE.

(Looking through his glass, at the light.)

An infallible telescope!

MR. FORESTER.

I am unfortunately one of those, Sir, who very much admired your Odes to Truth and Liberty, and read your royal lyrics with very different sensations.

MR. FEATHERNEST.

I presume, Sir, every man has a right to change his opinions.

MR. FORESTER.

From disinterested conviction undoubtedly: but when it is obviously from mercenary motives, the apostacy[20] of a public man is a public calamity. It is not his single loss to the cause he supported, that is alone to be lamented: the deep shade of mistrust which his conduct throws on that of all others, who embark in the same career, tends to destroy all sympathy with the enthusiasm of genius, all admiration for the intrepidity of truth, all belief in the sincerity of zeal for public liberty: if their advocates drop one by one into the vortex of courtly patronage, every new one that arises will be more and more regarded as a hollow-hearted hypocrite, a false and venal angler for pension and place; for there is in these cases no criterion, by which the world can distinguish the baying of a noble dog that will defend his trust till death, from the yelping of a political cur, that only infests the heels of power to be silenced with the offals of corruption.

LORD ANOPHEL ACHTHAR.
Cursed severe, Feathernest, 'pon honour.

MR. FAX.
The gradual falling off of prudent men from unprofitable virtues, is perhaps too common an occurrence to deserve much notice, or justify much reprobation. *[21]

MR. FORESTER.
If it were not common, it would not need reprobation. Vices of unfrequent occurrence stand sufficiently self-exposed in the insulation of their own deformity. The vices that call for the scourge of satire, are those which pervade the whole frame of society, and which, under some specious pretence of private duty, or the sanction of custom and precedent, are almost permitted to assume the semblance of virtue, or at least to pass unstigmatized in the crowd of congenial transgressions.

MR. FEATHERNEST.
You may say what you please, Sir. I am accustomed to this language, and am quite callous to it, I assure you. I am in

---

* Edinburgh Review, No. LIII. p. 10.

good odour at court,[22] Sir; and you know, *Non cuivis homini contingit adire Corinthum.*[23] While I was out, Sir, I made a great noise till I was let in. There was a pack of us, Sir, to keep up your canine metaphor: two or three others got in at the same time:[24] we knew very well that those who were shut out, would raise a hue and cry after us: it was perfectly natural: we should have done the same in their place: mere envy and malice, nothing more. Let them bark on: when they are either wanted or troublesome, they will be let in, in their turn. If there be any man, who prefers a crust and water, to venison and sack, I am not of his mind. It is pretty and politic to make a virtue of necessity: but when there is an end of the necessity I am very willing that there should be an end of the virtue. *If you could live on roots*, said Diogenes to Aristippus, *you would have nothing to do with kings.—If you could live on kings*, replied Aristippus, *you would have nothing to do with roots.*[25]—Every man for himself, Sir, and God for us all.

MR. DERRYDOWN.

The truth of things on this subject, is contained in the following stave:[26]

> "This world is a well-furnished table,
> Where guests are promiscuously set:
> We all fare as well as we're able,
> And scramble for what we can get."

SIR TELEGRAPH PAXARETT.

Buz the bottle.[27]

MR. O'SCARUM.

Over, by Jupiter!

SIR TELEGRAPH PAXARETT.

No.

MR. O'SCARUM.

Yes.

THE REVEREND MR. PORTPIPE.

No. The Baronet has a most mathematical eye. Buzzed to a drop!

MR. FORESTER.

Fortunately, Sir, for the hopes of mankind, every man does not bring his honour and conscience to market, though I admit the majority do: there are some who dare be honest in the worst of times.

MR. FEATHERNEST.

Perhaps, Sir, you are one of those who can *afford to have a conscience*,[28] and are therefore under no necessity of bringing it to market. If so, you should "give God thanks, and make no boast of it."[29] It is a great luxury certainly, and well worth keeping, *cæteris paribus*.[30] But it is neither meat, clothes, nor fire. It becomes a good coat well; but it will never make one. Poets are verbal musicians, and, like other musicians, they have a right to sing and play, where they can be best paid for their music.

MR. FORESTER.

There could be no objection to that, if they would be content to announce themselves as dealers and chapmen:[31] but the poetical character is too frequently a combination of the most arrogant and exclusive assumption of freedom and independence in theory, with the most abject and unqualified venality, servility, and sycophancy in practice.

MR. FEATHERNEST.

It is *as notorious*, Sir, *as the sun at noon-day*,[32] that theory and practice are never expected to coincide. If a West Indian planter declaims against the Algerines,[33] do you expect him to lose any favourable opportunity of increasing the number of his own slaves? If an invaded country cries out against spoliation, do you suppose, if the tables were turned, it would show its weaker neighbours the forbearance it required? If an Opposition orator clamours for a reform in Parliament, does any one dream, that, if he gets into office, he will ever say another word about it? If one of your reverend friends should display his touching eloquence on the subject of temperance, would you therefore have the barbarity to curtail him of one drop of his three bottles? Truth and liberty, Sir, are pretty words, very pretty words—a few years ago they were the gods of the day—they superseded in poetry the agency of mythology and magic: they were the only passports into the poetical market: I acted accordingly the part of a prudent man: I took my station, became my own crier, and vociferated Truth and Liberty, till the noise I made brought people about me, to bid for me: and to the highest bidder I knocked myself down, at less than I am worth certainly; but when an article is not likely to keep, it is by no means prudent to postpone the sale.

> "What makes all doctrines plain and clear?
> About two hundred pounds a year.—
> And that which was proved true before,
> Prove false again?—Two hundred more."[34]

MR. HIPPY.

A dry discussion! Pass the bottle, and moisten it.

MR. O'SCARUM.

Here's half of us fast asleep. Let us make a little noise to wake us. A glee[35] now: I'll be one: who'll join?

SIR TELEGRAPH PAXARETT.

I.

THE REVEREND MR. PORTPIPE.

And I.

MR. HIPPY.

Strike up then. Silence!

GLEE—THE GHOSTS.

In life three ghostly friars were we,
And now three friarly ghosts we be.
Around our shadowy table placed,
The spectral bowl before us floats:
With wine that none but ghosts can taste,
We wash our unsubstantial throats.
Three merry ghosts—three merry ghosts—three merry ghosts are we:
Let the ocean be Port, and we'll think it good sport
To be laid in that Red Sea.

With songs that jovial spectres chaunt,
Our old refectory still we haunt.
The traveller hears our midnight mirth:
"O list!"[36] he cries, "the haunted choir!
"The merriest ghost that walks the earth,
"Is sure the ghost of a ghostly friar."
Three merry ghosts—three merry ghosts—three merry ghosts are we:
Let the ocean be Port, and we'll think it good sport
To be laid in that Red Sea.

MR. HIPPY.

Bravo! I should like to have my house so haunted. The deuce is in it, if three such ghosts would not keep the blue devils at bay. Come, we'll lay them in a bumper of claret.

(Sir Oran Haut-ton took his flute from his pocket, and played over the air of the glee. The company was at first extremely surprised, and then joined in applauding his performance. Sir Oran bowed acknowledgment, and returned his flute to his pocket.)

MR. FORESTER.

It is, perhaps, happy for yourself, Mr. Feathernest, that you can treat with so much levity a subject that fills me with the deepest grief. Man under the influence of civilization has fearfully diminished in size and deteriorated in strength.[37] The intellectual are confessedly nourished at the expense of the physical faculties. Air, the great source and fountain of health and life, can scarcely find access to civilized man, muffled as he is in clothes, pent in houses, smoke-dried in cities, half-roasted by artificial fire, and parboiled in the hydrogen of crowded apartments. Diseases multiply upon him in compound proportion. Even if the prosperous among us enjoy some comforts unknown to the natural man, yet what is the poverty of the savage, compared with that of the lowest classes in civilized nations? The specious aspect of luxury and abundance in one, is counterbalanced by the abject penury and circumscription of hundreds. Commercial prosperity is a golden surface, but all beneath it is rags and wretchedness. It is not in the splendid bustle of our principal streets—in the villas and mansions that sprinkle our valleys—for those who enjoy these things (even if they did enjoy them—even if they had health and happiness—and the rich have seldom either), bear but a small proportion to the whole population:—but it is in the mud hovel of the labourer—in the cellar of the artizan—in our crowded prisons—our swarming hospitals—our overcharged workhouses—in those narrow districts of our overgrown cities, which the affluent never see—where thousands and thousands of families are compressed within limits not sufficient for the pleasure-ground of a simple squire,— that we must study the true mechanism of political society. When the philosopher turns away in despair from this dreadful accumulation of moral and physical evil, where is he to look for consolation, if not in the progress of science, in the enlargement of mind, in the diffusion of philosophical truth? But if truth is a chimæra—if virtue is a name—if science is not the handmaid of moral improvement, but the obsequious minister of recondite luxury, the specious appendage of vanity and power—then indeed, *that man has fallen never to* *rise again,*[*38] is as much the cry of nature as the dream of superstition.

THE REVEREND MR. PORTPIPE.

Man has fallen, certainly, by the fruit of the tree of knowledge: which shows that human learning is vanity and a great evil, and therefore very properly discountenanced by all bishops, priests, and deacons.

MR. FAX.

The picture which you have drawn of poverty is not very tempting; and you must acknowledge that it is most galling to the most refined feelings. You must not, therefore, wonder that it is peculiarly obnoxious to the practical notions of poets. If the radiance of gold and silver gleam not through the foliage of the Pierian laurel,[39] there is something to be said in their excuse if they carry their chaplet[40] to those who will gild its leaves; and in that case they will find their best customers and patrons among those who are ambitious of acquiring panegyric by a more compendious method than the troublesome practice of the virtues that deserve it.

MR. FORESTER.

You have quoted Juvenal, but you should have completed the sentence: "If you see no glimpse of coin in the Pierian shade, you will prefer the name and occupation of a barber or an auctioneer."[†41] This is most just: if the pursuits of literature, conscientiously conducted, condemn their votary to famine, let him live by more humble, but at least by honest, and therefore honourable occupations: he may still devote his leisure to his favourite pursuits. If he produce but a single volume

---

* See the preface to the third volume of the Ancient Metaphysics. See also Rousseau's Discourse on Inequality, and that on the Arts and Sciences.
† "Nam si Pieriâ quadrans tibi nullus in umbrâ
Ostendatur, ames nomen victumque Machæræ,
Et vendas potius commissa quod auctio vendit, &c."
JUV.

consecrated to moral truth, its effect must be good as far as it goes; but if he purchase leisure and luxury by the prostitution of talent to the cause of superstition and tyranny, every new exertion of his powers is a new outrage to reason and virtue, and in precise proportion to those powers is he a curse to his country, and a traitor to mankind.

MR. FEATHERNEST.

A barber, Sir!—a man of genius turn barber!

MR. O'SCARUM.

Troth, Sir, and I think it is better he should be in the suds[42] himself, than help to bring his country into that situation.

MR. FORESTER.

I can perceive, Sir, in your exclamation the principle that has caused so enormous a superabundance in the number of bad books over that of good ones. The objects of the majority of men of talent seem to be exclusively two: the first, to convince the world of their transcendent abilities; the second, to convert that conviction into a source of the greatest possible pecuniary benefit to themselves. But there is no class of men more resolutely indifferent to the moral tendency of the means by which their ends are accomplished. Yet this is the most extensively pernicious of all modes of dishonesty; for that of a private man can only injure the pockets of a few individuals (a great evil, certainly, but light in comparison); while that of a public writer, who has previously taught the multitude to respect his talents, perverts what is much more valuable, the mental progress of thousands; misleading, on the one hand, the shallow believers in his sincerity; and on the other, stigmatizing the whole literary character in the opinions of all who see through the veil of his venality.

MR. FEATHERNEST.

All this is no reason, Sir, why a man of genius should condescend to be a barber.

MR. FORESTER.

He condescends much more in being a sycophant. The poorest barber in the poorest borough in England, who will not sell his vote, is a much more honourable character in the estimate of moral comparison than the most self-satisfied dealer in courtly poetry, whose well-paid eulogiums of licentiousness and corruption were ever re-echoed by the "most sweet voices"[43] of hireling gazetteers and pensioned reviewers.

The summons to tea and coffee put a stop to the conversation.

CHAPTER XVII.

MUSIC AND DISCORD.

THE evenings were beginning to give symptoms of winter, and a large fire was blazing in the library. Mr. Forester took the opportunity of stigmatizing the use of sugar, and had the pleasure of observing that the practice of Anthelia in this respect was the same as his own. He mentioned his intention of giving an anti-saccharine festival at Redrose Abbey, and invited all the party at Melincourt to attend it. He observed that his aunt, Miss Evergreen, who would be there at the time, would send an invitation in due form to the ladies, to remove all scruples on the score of propriety; and added, that if he could hope for the attendance of half as much moral feeling as he was sure there would be of beauty and fashion, he should be satisfied that a great step would be made towards accomplishing the object of the Anti-saccharine Society.

The Reverend Mr. Grovelgrub felt extremely indignant at Mr. Forester's notion "of every real enemy to slavery being bound by the strictest moral duty to practical abstinence from the luxuries which slavery acquires;" but when he found that the notion was to be developed in the shape of a festival, he determined to suspend his judgment till he had digested the solid arguments that were to be brought forward on the occasion.

Mr. O'Scarum was, as usual, very clamorous for music, and was seconded by the unanimous wish of the company, with which Anthelia readily complied, and sung as follows:

THE FLOWER OF LOVE.[1]

'T is said the rose is Love's own flower,
Its blush so bright, its thorns so many;
And winter on its bloom has power,
But has not on its sweetness any.

For though young Love's ethereal rose
Will droop on Age's wintry bosom,
Yet still its faded leaves disclose
The fragrance of their earliest blossom.

But ah! the fragrance lingering there
Is like the sweets that mournful duty
Bestows with sadly-soothing care,
To deck the grave of bloom and beauty.
For when its leaves are shrunk and dry,
Its blush extinct, to kindle never,
That fragrance is but Memory's sigh,
That breathes of pleasures past for ever.

Why did not Love the amaranth choose,
That bears no thorns, and cannot perish?
Alas! no sweets its flowers diffuse,
And only sweets Love's life can cherish.
But be the rose and amaranth twined,
And Love, their mingled powers assuming,
Shall round his brows a chaplet bind,
For ever sweet, for ever blooming.

"I am afraid," said Mr. Derrydown, "the flower of modern love is neither the rose nor the amaranth, but the *chrysanthemum*, or *gold-flower*. If Miss Danaretta and Mr. O'Scarum will accompany me, we will sing a little harmonized ballad, something in point, and rather more conformable to the truth of things." Mr. O'Scarum and Miss Danaretta consented, and they accordingly sung the following

BALLAD TERZETTO.[2]

THE LADY, THE KNIGHT, AND THE FRIAR.
THE LADY.
O cavalier! what dost thou here,
Thy tuneful vigils keeping;

While the northern star looks cold from far,
And half the world is sleeping?

THE KNIGHT.

O lady! here, for seven long year,
Have I been nightly sighing,
Without the hope of a single tear
To pity me were I dying.

THE LADY.

Should I take thee to have and to hold,
Who hast nor lands nor money?
Alas! 't is only in flowers of gold
That married bees find honey.

THE KNIGHT.

O lady fair! to my constant prayer
Fate proves at last propitious;
And bags of gold in my hand I bear,
And parchment scrolls delicious.

THE LADY.

My maid the door shall open throw,
For we too long have tarried:
The friar keeps watch in the cellar below,
And we will at once be married.

THE FRIAR.

My children! great is Fortune's power;
And plain this truth appears,
That gold thrives more in a single hour,
Than love in seven long years.

During this terzetto, the Reverend Mr. Portpipe fell asleep,
and accompanied the performance with rather a deeper bass
than was generally deemed harmonious.

Sir Telegraph Paxarett took Mr. Forester aside, to consult
him on the subject of the journey to Onevote.

"I have asked," said he, "my aunt and cousin, Mrs. and Miss
Pinmoney, to join the party, and have requested them to exert

their influence with Miss Melincourt to induce her to accompany them."

"That would make it a delightful expedition, indeed," said Mr. Forester, "if Miss Melincourt could be prevailed on to comply."

"*Nil desperandum*,"[3] said Sir Telegraph.

The Honourable Mrs. Pinmoney drew Anthelia into a corner, and developed all her eloquence in enforcing the proposition. Miss Danaretta joined in it with great earnestness; and they kept up the fire of their importunity till they extorted from Anthelia a promise that she would consider of it.

Mr. Forester took down a splendid edition of Tasso, printed by Bodoni at Parma,[4] and found it ornamented with Anthelia's drawings. In the magic of her pencil the wild and wonderful scenes of Tasso seemed to live under his eyes: he could not forbear expressing to her the delight he experienced from these new proofs of her sensibility and genius, and entered into a conversation with her concerning her favourite poet, in which the congeniality of their tastes and feelings became more and more manifest to each other.

Mr. Feathernest and Mr. Derrydown got into a hot dispute over Chapman's Homer and Jeremy Taylor's Holy Living:[5] Mr. Derrydown maintaining that the ballad metre which Chapman had so judiciously chosen, rendered his volume the most divine poem in the world; Mr. Feathernest asserting that Chapman's verses were mere doggrel: which vile aspersion Mr. Derrydown revenged by depreciating Mr. Feathernest's favourite Jeremy. Mr. Feathernest said he could expect no better judgment from a man who was mad enough to prefer Chevy Chase to Paradise Lost; and Mr. Derrydown retorted, that it was idle to expect either taste or justice from one who had thought fit to unite in himself two characters so anomalous as those of a poet and a critic, in which duplex[6] capacity he had first deluged the world with torrents of execrable verses, and then written anonymous criticisms to prove them divine. "Do you think, Sir," he continued, "that it is possible for the same man to be both Homer and Aristotle? No, Sir; but it is very possible to be both Dennis and Colley Cibber,[7] as in the melancholy example before me."

At this all the blood of the *genus irritabile*[8] boiled in Mr. Feathernest's veins, and uplifting the ponderous folio, he seemed inclined to bury his antagonist under Jeremy's *weight of words*, by applying them in a *tangible shape:* but wisely recollecting that this was not the time and place

> "To prove his doctrine orthodox,
> By apostolic blows and knocks,"[9]

he contented himself with a point-blank denial of the charge that he wrote critiques on his own works, protesting that all the articles on his poems were written either by his friend Mr. Mystic, of Cimmerian Lodge, or by Mr. Vamp, the amiable editor of the Legitimate Review.[10] "Yes," said Mr. Derrydown, "on the '*Tickle me Mr. Hayley*' principle;[11] by which a miserable cabal of doggrel rhymesters and worn-out paragraph-mongers of bankrupt gazettes[12] ring the eternal changes of panegyric on each other, and on every thing else that is either rich enough to buy their praise, or vile enough to deserve it: like a gang[13] in a country steeple, paid for being a public nuisance, and maintaining that noise is melody."

Mr. Feathernest on this became perfectly outrageous;[14] and waving Jeremy Taylor in the air, exclaimed, "*Oh that mine enemy had written a book!*[15] Horrible should be the vengeance of the Legitimate Review!"

Mr. Hippy now deemed it expedient to interpose for the restoration of order, and entreated Anthelia to throw in a little musical harmony as a sedative to the ebullitions[16] of poetical discord. At the sound of the harp the antagonists turned away, the one flourishing his Chapman and the other his Jeremy with looks of lofty defiance.

CHAPTER XVIII.

THE STRATAGEM.

THE Reverend Mr. Grovelgrub, who had acquired a great proficiency in the art of hearing without seeming to listen, had overheard Mrs. Pinmoney's request to Anthelia;[1] and, notwithstanding the young lady's hesitation, he very much feared she would ultimately comply. He had seen, much against his will, a great congeniality in feelings and opinions, between her and Mr. Forester, and had noticed some unconscious external manifestations of the interior mind on both sides, some outward and visible signs of the inward and spiritual sentiment, which convinced him that a more intimate acquaintance with each other would lead them to a conclusion, which, for the reasons we have given in the ninth chapter,[2] he had no wish to see established. After long and mature deliberation, he determined to rouse Lord Anophel to a sense of his danger, and spirit him up to an immediate *coup-de-main*.[3] He calculated, that, as the young Lord was a spoiled child, immoderately vain, passably foolish, and totally unused to contradiction, he should have little difficulty in moulding him to his views. His plan was, that Lord Anophel, with two or three confidential[4] fellows, should lie in ambush for Anthelia in one of her solitary rambles, and convey her to a lonely castle of his Lordship's on the sea-coast, with a view of keeping her in close custody, till fair means or foul should induce her to regain her liberty, in the character of Lady Achthar. This was to be Lord Anophel's view of the subject; but the Reverend Mr. Grovelgrub had in the inner cave of his perceptions a very promising image of a different result. As he would have free access to Anthelia in her confinement, he intended to worm himself into her favour, under the cover of friendship and sympathy, with the most ardent professions of devotion to her cause, and promises of endeavours to effect her emancipation, involving the accomplishment of this object in a multitude of imaginary difficulties, which it should be his professed study to vanquish. He deemed it very probable, that, by a skilful adoperation[5] of these means, and by moulding Lord Anophel, at the same time, into a system of conduct as disagreeable as possible to Anthelia, he might himself become the lord and master of the lands and castle of Melincourt, when he would edify the country with the example of his truly orthodox life, faring sumptuously every day, raising the rents of his tenants, turning out all who were in arrear, and occasionally treating the rest with discourses on temperance and charity.

With these ideas in his head, he went in search of Lord Anophel, and proceeding *pedetentim,*[6] and opening the subject *peirastically,*[7] he managed so skilfully, that his Lordship became himself the proposer of the scheme, with which the Reverend Mr. Grovelgrub seemed unwillingly to acquiesce.

Mr. Forester, Mr. Fax, and Sir Oran Haut-ton took leave of the party at Melincourt Castle; the former having arranged with Sir Telegraph Paxarett, that he was to call for them at Redrose Abbey in the course of three days, and reiterated his earnest hopes that Anthelia would be persuaded to accompany Mrs. Pinmoney and her beautiful daughter, in the expedition to Onevote.

Lord Anophel Achthar and the Reverend Mr. Grovelgrub also took leave, as a matter of policy, that their disappearance at the same time with Anthelia, might not excite surprise. They pretended a pressing temporary engagement in a distant part of the country, and carried off with them Mr. Feathernest the poet, whom, nevertheless, they did not deem it prudent to let into the secret of their scheme.

The next day Anthelia, still undecided on this subject, wandered alone to the ruined bridge, to contemplate the scene

of her former misadventure. As she ascended the hill that
bounded the valley of Melincourt, a country-man crossed
her path, and touching his hat passed on. She thought there
was something peculiar in his look, but had quite forgotten
him, when, on looking back as she descended on the other
side, she observed him making signs, as if to some one at
a distance: she could not, however, consider that they had
any relation to her. The day was clear and sunny; and when
she entered the pine-grove, the gloom of its tufted foliage,
with the sunbeams chequering the dark-red soil, formed a
grateful contrast to the naked rocks and heathy mountains
that lay around it, in the full blaze of daylight. In many
parts of the grove was a luxuriant laurel underwood, glittering like silver in the partial sunbeams that penetrated the
interstices of the pines. Few scenes in nature have a more
mysterious solemnity than such a scene as this. Anthelia
paused a moment. She thought she heard a rustling in the
laurels, but all was again still. She proceeded: the rustling
was renewed. She felt alarmed, yet she knew not why, and
reproached herself for such idle and unaccustomed apprehensions. She paused again to listen: the soft tones of a flute
sounded from a distance: these gave her confidence, and she
again proceeded. She passed by the tuft of laurels in which
she had heard the rustling. Suddenly a mantle was thrown
over her. She was wrapped in darkness, and felt that she
was forcibly seized by several persons, who carried her rapidly along. She screamed, but the mantle was immediately
pressed on her mouth, and she was hurried onward. After a
time the party stopped: a tumult ensued: she found herself
at liberty, and threw the mantle from her head. She was on
a road at the verge of the pine-grove: a chaise and four was
waiting. Two men were running away in the distance: two
others, muffled and masked, were rolling on the ground, and
roaring for mercy, while Sir Oran Haut-ton was standing

over them with a stick,* and treating them as if he were a thresher, and they were sheaves of corn. By her side was Mr. Forester, who, taking her hand, assured her that she was in safety, while at the same time he endeavoured to assuage Sir Oran's wrath, that he might raise and unmask the fallen foes. Sir Oran, however, proceeded in his summary administration of natural justice[9] till he had dispensed what was to his notion a *quantum sufficit*[10] of the application: then throwing his stick aside, he caught them both up, one under each arm, and climbing with great dexterity a high and precipitous rock, left them perched upon its summit, bringing away their masks in his hand, and making them a profound bow at taking leave.†

Mr. Forester was anxious to follow them to their aërial seat, that he might ascertain who they were, which Sir Oran's precipitation had put it out of his power to do; but Anthelia begged him to return with her immediately to the Castle, assuring him that she thought them already sufficiently punished, and had no apprehension that they would feel tempted again to molest her.

Sir Oran now opened the chaise-door, and drew out the post-boys[12] by the leg, who, at the beginning of the fray, had concealed themselves from his fury under the seat. Mr. Forester succeeded in rescuing them from Sir[13] Oran, and endeavoured to extract from them information as to their

---

* "They use an artificial weapon for attack and defence, viz. a stick, which no animal merely brute is known to do."—*Origin and Progress of Language*, book ii. chap. 4.[8]

† "There is a story of one of them, which seems to show they have a sense of justice as well as honour. For a negro having shot a female of this kind, that was feeding among his Indian corn, the male, whom our author calls the husband of this female, pursued the negro into his house, of which having forced open the door, he seized the negro and dragged him out of the house to the place where his wife lay dead or wounded, and the people of the neighbourhood could not rescue the negro, nor force the oran to quit his hold of him, till they shot him likewise."—*Origin and Progress of Language*, book ii. chap. 4.[11]

employers: but the boys declared that they knew nothing of them, the chaise having been ordered by a strange man to be in waiting at that place, and the hire paid in advance.

Anthelia, as she walked homeward, leaning on Mr. Forester's arm, inquired to what happy accident she was indebted for the timely intervention of himself and Sir Oran Haut-ton. Mr. Forester informed her, that having a great wish to visit the scene which had been the means of introducing him to her acquaintance, he had made Sir Oran understand his desire, and they had accordingly set out together, leaving Mr. Fax at Redrose Abbey, deeply engaged in the solution of a problem in political arithmetic.

CHAPTER XIX.

THE EXCURSION.

ANTHELIA found, from what Mr. Forester had said, that she had excited a much greater interest in his mind than she had previously supposed; and she did not dissemble to herself that the interest was reciprocal. The occurrence of the morning, by taking the feeling of safety from her solitary walks, and unhinging her long associations with the freedom and security of her native mountains, gave her an inclination to depart for a time at least from Melincourt Castle; and this inclination combining with the wish to see more of one who appeared to possess so much intellectual superiority to the generality of mankind, rendered her very flexible to Mrs. Pinmoney's wishes, when that Honourable lady renewed her solicitations to her to join the expedition to Onevote. Anthelia, however, desired that Mr. Hippy might be of the party, and that her going in Sir Telegraph's carriage should not be construed in any degree into a reception of his addresses. The Honourable Mrs. Pinmoney, delighted to carry her point, readily complied with the condition, trusting to the influence of time and intimacy to promote her own wishes, and the happiness of her dear nephew.

Mr. Hippy was so overjoyed at the project, that, in the first ebullitions of his transport, meeting Harry Fell on the landing-place, with a packet of medicine from Dr. Killquick, he seized him by the arm, and made him dance a *pas de deux:*[1] the packet fell to the earth, and Mr. Hippy, as he whirled old Harry round to the tune of *La Belle Laitière*,[2] danced over that which, but for this timely demolition, might have given his heir an opportunity of dancing over him.

It was accordingly arranged that Sir Telegraph Paxarett, with the ladies and Mr. Hippy, should call on the appointed day at Redrose Abbey for Mr. Forester, Mr. Fax, and Sir Oran Haut-ton.

Mr. Derrydown and Mr. O'Scarum were inconsolable on the occasion, notwithstanding Mr. Hippy's assurance that they should very soon return, and that the hospitality of Melincourt Castle should then be resumed under his supreme jurisdiction. Mr. Derrydown determined to consume the interval at Keswick, in the composition of dismal ballads; and Mr. O'Scarum to proceed to Low-wood Inn, and drown his cares in claret with Major O'Dogskin.

We shall pass over the interval till the arrival of the eventful day on which Mr. Forester, from the windows of Redrose Abbey, watched the approach of Sir Telegraph's barouche. The party from Melincourt arrived, as had been concerted, to breakfast: after which, they surveyed the Abbey, and perambulated the grounds. Mr. Forester produced the Abbot's skull,[*3] and took occasion to expatiate very largely on the diminution of the size of mankind; illustrating his theory by quotations and anecdotes from Homer,[†4] Herodotus,[‡5] Arrian,[6]

---

[*] See Chap. IV.

[†] "Homer has said nothing positively, of the size of any of his heroes, but only comparatively, as I shall presently observe: nor is this to be wondered at; for I know no historian ancient or modern, that says any thing of the size of the men of his own nation, except comparatively with that of other nations. But in that fine episode of his, called by the ancient critics the Τειχοσκοπια, or *Prospect from the Walls*, he has given us a very accurate description of the persons of several of the Greek heroes; which I am persuaded he had from very good information. In this description he tells us, that Ulysses was shorter than Agamemnon by the head, shorter than Menelaus by the head and shoulders, and that Ajax was taller than any of the Greeks by the head and shoulders; consequently, Ulysses was shorter than Ajax by two heads and shoulders, which we cannot reckon less than four feet. Now, if we suppose these heroes to have been no bigger than we, then Ajax must have been a man about six feet and a half, or at most seven feet; and if so, Ulysses must have been most contemptibly short, not more than three feet, which is certainly not the truth, but a most absurd and ridiculous fiction, such as we cannot suppose in Homer: whereas, if we allow Ajax to have been twelve or thirteen feet high, and, much more, if we suppose him to have been eleven cubits, as Philostratus makes him, Ulysses, though four feet short of him, would have been of a good size, and, with the extraordinary breadth which Homer observes he had, may have been as strong a man as Ajax."—*Ancient Metaphysics*, vol. iii. p. 146.

[‡] "It was only in after-ages, when the size of men was greatly decreased, that the bodies of those heroes, if they happened to be discovered, were, as was natural, admired and exactly measured. Such a thing happened in Laconia, where the body of Orestes was discovered, and found to be of length seven cubits, that is, ten feet

Plutarch,[7] Philostratus, Pausanias,[8] and Solinus Polyhistor.[9]
He asked, if it were possible that men of such a stature as they

and a half. The story is most pleasantly told by Herodotus, and is to this effect: The Lacedemonians were engaged in a war with the Tegeatæ, a people of Arcadia, in which they were unsuccessful. They consulted the oracle at Delphi, what they should do in order to be more successful. The oracle answered, 'That they must bring to Sparta the bones of Orestes, the son of Agamemnon.' But these bones they could not find, and therefore they sent again to the oracle to inquire where Orestes lay buried. The God answered in hexameter verse, but so obscurely and enigmatically, that they could not understand what he meant. They went about inquiring every where for the bones of Orestes, till at last a wise man among them, called by Herodotus *Liches*, found them out, partly by good fortune, and partly by good understanding; for, happening to come one day to a smith's shop in the country of the Tegeatæ, with whom at that time there was a truce and intercourse betwixt the two nations, he looked at the operations of the smith, and seemed to admire them very much; which the smith observing, stopped his work, and, 'Stranger,' says he, 'you that seem to admire so much the working of iron, would have wondered much more if you had seen what I saw lately; for, as I was digging for a well in this court here, I fell upon a coffin that was seven cubits long; but *believing that there never were at any time bigger men than the present*, I opened the coffin, and found there a dead body as long as the coffin, which having measured, I again buried.' Hearing this, the Spartan conjectured that the words of the oracle would apply to a smith's shop, and to the operations there performed; but taking care not to make this discovery to the smith, he prevailed on him, with much difficulty, to give him a lease of the court; which having obtained, he opened the coffin, and carried the bones to Sparta. After which, says our author, the Spartans were upon every occasion superior in fight to the Tegeatæ."—*Ancient Metaphysics*, vol. iii. p. 146.

"The most of our philosophers at present are, I believe, of the opinion of the smith in Herodotus, who might be excused for having that opinion at a time when perhaps no other heroic body had been discovered. But in later times, I believe there was not the most vulgar man in Greece, who did not believe that those heroes were very much superior, both in mind and body, to the men of after-times. Indeed, they were not considered as mere men, but as something betwixt gods and men, and had *heroic* honours paid them, which were next to the *divine*. On the stage they were represented as of extraordinary size, both as to length and breadth; for the actor was not only raised upon very high shoes, which they called *cothurns*, but he was put into a case that swelled his size prodigiously (and I have somewhere read a very ridiculous story of one of them, who, coming upon the stage, fell and broke his case, so that all the trash with which it was stuffed, came out and was scattered upon the stage in the view of the whole people). This accounts for the high style of ancient tragedy, in which the heroes speak a language so uncommon, that, if I considered them as men nowise superior to us, I should think it little better than fustian, and should be apt to apply to it what Falstaff says to Pistol: 'Pr'ythee, Pistol, speak like a man of this world.' And I apply the same observation to Homer's poems. If I considered his heroes as no more than men of this world, I should consider the things he relates of them as quite ridiculous; but believing them to be men very much superior to us, I read Homer with the highest admiration, not only as a poet, but as the historian of the noblest race of men that ever existed. Thus, by having right notions of the superiority of men in former times, we both improve our philosophy of man, and our taste in poetry."—*Ancient Metaphysics*, vol. iii. p. 150.

have dwindled to in the present age, could have erected that stupendous monument of human strength, Stonehenge? In the vicinity of which, he said, a body had been dug up, measuring fourteen feet ten inches in length.* [10]

* "But though we should give no credit to those ancient authors, there are monuments still extant, one particularly to be seen in our own island, which I think ought to convince every man that the men of ancient times were much superior to us, at least in the powers of the body. The monument I meant is well known by the name of Stonehenge, and there are several of the same kind to be seen in Denmark and Germany. I desire to know where are the arms now, that, with so little help of machinery as they must have had, could have raised and set up on end such a number of prodigious stones, and put others on the top of them, likewise of very great size? Such works are said by the peasants in Germany to be the works of giants, and I think they must have been giants compared with us. And, indeed, the men who erected Stonehenge could not, I imagine, be of size inferior to that man whose body was found in a quarry near to Salisbury within a mile of which Stonehenge stands. The body of that man was fourteen feet ten inches. The fact is attested by an eye-witness, one Elyote, who writes, I believe, the first English-Latin Dictionary that ever was published. It is printed in London in 1542, in folio, and has, under the word *Gigas*, the following passage: 'About thirty years passed and somewhat more, I myself beynge with my father Syr Rycharde Elyote, at a monastery of regular canons, called Juy Churche, two myles from the citie of Sarisburye, beholde the bones of a deade man founde deep in the grounde, where they dygged stone, which being joined together, was in length xiiii feet and ten ynches, there beynge mette; whereof one of the teethe my father hadde, whych was of the quantytie of a great walnutte. This have I wrytten, because some menne wylle believe nothynge that is out of the compasse of theyre owne knowledge, and yet some of them presume to have knowledge, above any other, contempnynge all men but themselfes or suche as they favour.'It is for the reason mentioned by this author, that I have given so many examples of the greater size of men than is to be seen in our day, to which I could add several others concerning bodies that have been found in this our island, particularly one mentioned by Hector Boece in his *Description of Scotland*, prefixed to his Scotch History, where he tells us that in a certain church which he names in the shire of Murray, the bones of a man of much the same size as those of the man mentioned by Elyote, viz. fourteen feet, were preserved. One of these bones Boece himself saw, and has particularly described."—*Ancient Metaphysics*, vol. iii. p. 156.

"But without having recourse to bones or monuments of any kind, if a man has looked upon the world as long as I have done with any observation, he must be convinced that the size of man is diminishing. I have seen such bodies of men, as are not now to be seen: I have observed in families, of which I have known three generations, a gradual decline in that, and I am afraid in other respects. Others may think otherwise; but for my part I have so great a veneration for our ancestors, that I have much indulgence for that ancient superstition among the Etrurians, and from them derived to the Romans, of worshipping the *manes* of their ancestors under the names of *Lares* or domestic gods, which undoubtedly proceeded upon the supposition that they were men superior to themselves, and their departed souls such genii as Hesiod has described,

Εσθλοι, αλεξικακοι, Φυλακες θνητων ανθρωπων.

The barouche bowled off from the Abbey gates, carrying four inside and eight out; videlicet, the Honourable Mrs. Pinmoney, Miss Danaretta, Mr. Hippy, and Anthelia, inside; Sir Telegraph Paxarett and Sir Oran Haut-ton on the box, the former with his whip and the latter with his French horn, in the characters of coachman and guard; Mr. Forester and Mr. Fax in the front of the roof; and Sir Telegraph's two grooms, with Peter Gray and Harry Fell, behind. Sir Telegraph's coachman, as the inside of the carriage was occupied, had been left at Melincourt.[11]

In addition to Sir Telegraph's travelling library (which consisted of a single quarto volume, magnificently bound: videlicet, a Greek Pindar,[12] which Sir Telegraph always carried with him; not that he ever read a page of it, but that he thought such a classical inside passenger would be a perpetual tacit vindication of his tethrippharmatelasipedioploctypophilous[13] pursuits), Anthelia and Mr. Forester had taken with them a few of their favourite authors; for, as the ancient and honourable borough of Onevote was situated almost at the extremity of the kingdom,[14] and as Sir Telegraph's diurnal stages were necessarily limited, they had both conjectured that

"the poet's page, by one
Made vocal for the amusement of the rest,"[15]

might furnish an agreeable evening employment in the dearth of conversation. Anthelia also, in compliance with the general

And if antiquity and the universal consent of nations can give a sanction to any opinion, it is to this, that our forefathers were better men than we. Even as far back as the Trojan war, the best age of men, of which we have any particular account, Homer has said that few men were better than their fathers, and the greater part worse:

Οι πλεονες κακιους, παυροι δε τε πατρος αρειους.

And this he puts into the mouth of the Goddess of Wisdom ...... But when I speak of the universal consent of nations, I ought to except the men, and particularly the young men, of this age, who generally believe themselves to be better men than their fathers, or than any of their predecessors."—*Ancient Metaphysics*, vol. iii. p. 161.

desire, had taken her lyre, by which the reader may understand, if he pleases, the *harp-lute-guitar;* which, whatever be
its merit as an instrument, has so unfortunate an appellation,
that we cannot think of dislocating our pages with such a
cacophonous compound.

They made but a short stage from Redrose Abbey, and
stopped for the first evening at Low-wood Inn, to the great
joy of Mr. O'Scarum and Major O'Dogskin. Mr. O'Scarum
introduced the Major; and both offered their services to assist
Mr. Hippy and Sir Telegraph Paxarett in the council they
were holding with the landlady on the eventful subject of
dinner. This being arranged, and the hour and minute punc-
tually specified, it was proposed to employ the interval in a
little excursion on the lake.[16] The party was distributed in two
boats: Sir Telegraph's grooms rowing the one, and Peter Gray
and Harry Fell the other. They rowed to the middle of the lake,
and rested on their oars. The sun sunk behind the summits
of the western mountains: the clouds that, like other mountains, rested motionless above them, crested with the towers
and battlements of aërial castles, changed by degrees from
fleecy whiteness to the deepest hues of crimson. A solitary
cloud, resting on an eastern pinnacle, became tinged with the
reflected splendour of the west: the clouds over-head spreading, like an uniform veil of network, through the interstices of
which the sky was visible, caught in their turn the radiance,
and reflected it on the lake, that lay in its calm expanse like
a mirror, imaging with such stillness and accuracy the forms
and colours of all around and above it, that it seemed as if
the waters were withdrawn by magic, and the boats floated in
crimson light between the mountains and the sky.

The whole party was silent, even the Honourable Mrs.
Pinmoney, till Mr. O'Scarum entreated Anthelia to sing
"something neat and characteristic; or a harmony now for
three voices, would be the killing thing; eh! Major?"—"Indeed

and it would," said Major O'Dogskin: "there's something very soft and pathetic in a cool evening on the water, to sit still, doing nothing at all but listening to pretty words and tender melodies." And lest the sincerity of his opinion should be questioned, he accompanied it with an emphatical oath, to show that he was in earnest; for which the Honourable Mrs. Pinmoney called him to order.

Major O'Dogskin explained.

Anthelia, accompanied by Miss Danaretta and Mr. O'Scarum, sung the following

TERZETTO.[17]

1. Hark! o'er the silent waters stealing,
   The dash of oars sounds soft and clear:
   Through night's deep veil, all forms concealing,
   Nearer it comes, and yet more near.

2. See! where the long reflection glistens,
   In yon lone tower her watch-light burns:
3. To hear our distant oars she listens,
   And, listening, strikes the harp by turns.

1. The stars are bright, the skies unclouded;
   No moonbeam shines; no breezes wake:
   Is it my love, in darkness shrouded,
   Whose dashing oar disturbs the lake?

2. O haste, sweet maid, the cords unrolling;
   The holy hermit chides our stay!
1.2.3. Hark! from his lonely islet tolling,
   His midnight bell shall guide our way.

Sir Oran Haut-ton now produced his flute, and treated the company with a solo. Another pause succeeded. The contemplative silence was broken by Major O'Dogskin, who began to fidget about in the boat, and drawing his watch from his fob, held it up to Mr. Hippy, and asked him if he did not think the partridges would be spoiled? "To be sure they will," said Mr. Hippy, "unless we make the best of our way. Cold comfort this, after all: sharp air and water:—give me a roaring fire and a six-bottle cooper[18] of claret."

The oars were dashed into the water, and the fairy reflections of clouds, rocks, woods, and mountains were mingled in the confusion of chaos. The reader will naturally expect, that, having two lovers on a lake, we shall not lose the opportunity of throwing the lady into the water, and making the gentleman fish her out; but whether that our Thalia[19] is too veridicous[20] to permit this distortion of facts, or that we think it the more original incident to return them to the shore as dry as they left it, the reader must submit to the disappointment, and be content to see the whole party comfortably seated, without let, hindrance, or molestation, at a very excellent dinner, served up under the judicious inspection of mine hostess of Low-wood.

The heroes and heroines of Homer used to eat and drink all day till the setting sun*;[21] and, by dint of industry, contrived to finish that important business by the usual period at which modern beaux and belles begin it—who are, therefore, necessitated, like Penelope, to sit up all night:[22] not, indeed, to destroy the works of the day, for how can nothing be annihilated? This does not apply to all our party, and we hope not to many of our readers.

---

* Ἡμεις μεν προπαν ημαρ, ες ηελιον καταδυντα,
  Ἡμεθα, δαινυμενοι κρεα τ' ασπετα και μεθυ ἡδυ κτλ.

CHAPTER XX.

THE SEA-SHORE.

THEY stopped the next evening at a village on the sea-shore. The wind rose in the night, but without rain. Mr. Forester was up before the sun, and descending to the beach, found Anthelia there before him, sitting on a rock, and listening to the dash of the waves, like a Nereid to Triton's shell.[1]

MR. FORESTER.

You are an early riser, Miss Melincourt.

ANTHELIA.

I always was so. The morning is the infancy of the day, and, like the infancy of life, has health and bloom, and cheerfulness and purity, in a degree unknown to the busy noon, which is the season of care, or the languid evening, which is the harbinger of repose. Perhaps the song of the nightingale is not in itself less cheerful than that of the lark: it is the season of her song that invests it with the character of melancholy. It is the same with the associations of infancy: it is all cheerfulness, all hope: its path is on the flowers of an untried world. The daisy has more beauty in the eye of childhood than the rose in that of maturer life. The spring is the infancy of the year: its flowers are the flowers of promise and the darlings of poetry. The autumn too has its flowers; but they are little loved, and little praised: for the associations of autumn are not with ideas of cheerfulness, but with yellow leaves and hollow winds, heralds of winter, and emblems of dissolution.

MR. FORESTER.

These reflections have more in them of the autumn than of the morning. But the mornings of autumn participate in the character of the season.

ANTHELIA.

They do so: yet even in mists and storms the opening must be always more cheerful than the closing day.

MR. FORESTER.

But this morning is fine and clear, and the wind blows over the sea. Yet this, to me at least, is not a cheerful scene.

ANTHELIA.

Nor to me. But our long habits of association with the sound of the winds and the waters, have given them to us a voice of melancholy majesty: a voice not audible by those little children who are playing yonder on the shore. To them all scenes are cheerful. It is the morning of life: it is infancy that makes them so.

MR. FORESTER.

Fresh air and liberty are all that is necessary to the happiness of children. In that blissful age "when nature's self is new,"[2] the bloom of interest and beauty is found alike in every object of perception—in the grass of the meadow, the moss on the rock, and the sea-weed on the sand. They find gems and treasures in shells and pebbles; and the gardens of fairyland in the simplest flowers. They have no melancholy associations with autumn or with evening. The falling leaves are their playthings; and the setting sun only tells them that they must go to rest as he does, and that he will light them to their sports in the morning. It is this bloom of novelty, and the pure, unclouded, unvitiated feelings with which it is contemplated, that throw such an unearthly radiance on the scenes of our infancy, however humble in themselves, and give a charm to their recollections which not even Tempe[3] can compensate. It is the force of first impressions. The first meadow in which we gather cowslips, the first stream on which we sail, the first home in which we awake to the sense of human sympathy, have all a peculiar and exclusive charm, which we shall never find again in richer meadows, mightier rivers, and more magnificent dwellings; nor even in themselves, when we revisit them after the lapse of years, and the sad realities of noon have dissipated the illusions of sunrise. It is the same, too, with first love, whatever be the causes that render it unsuccessful: the second choice may have just preponderance in the balance of moral estimation; but the object of first affection, of all the perceptions of our being, will be most divested of the attributes of mortality. The magical associations of infancy are revived with double power in the feelings of first love; but when they too have departed, then, indeed, the light of the morning is gone.

Pensa che questo di mai non raggiorna![4]

ANTHELIA.

If this be so, let me never be the object of a second choice: let me never love, or love but once.

MR. FORESTER.

The object of a second choice you cannot be, with any one who will deserve your love: for to have loved any other woman, would show a heart too lightly captivated to be worthy of yours. The only mind that can deserve to love you, is one that would never have known love, if it never had known you.

Anthelia and Mr. Forester were both so unfashionably sincere, that they would probably, in a very few minutes, have confessed to each other, more than they had till that morning, perhaps, confessed to themselves, but that their conversation was interrupted by the appearance of Mr. Hippy fuming for his breakfast, accompanied by Sir Telegraph cracking his whip, and Sir Oran blowing the Reveillée on his French horn.

"So ho!" exclaimed Sir Telegraph; "Achilles and Thetis,[5] I protest, consulting on the sea-shore."

ANTHELIA.

Do you mean to say, Sir Telegraph, that I am old enough to be Mr. Forester's mother?

SIR TELEGRAPH PAXARETT.

No, no; that is no part of the comparison: but we are the ambassadors of Agamemnon[6] (videlicet, Mr. Fax, whom we left very busily arranging the urns, not of lots by the by, but of tea and coffee): here is old Phœnix on one side of me, and Ajax on the other.

MR. FORESTER.

And you, of course, are the wise Ulysses.

SIR TELEGRAPH PAXARETT.

There the simile fails again. *Comparatio non urgenda,* as I think Heyne used to say,[7] before I was laughed out of reading at college.

MR. FORESTER.

You should have found me too, if you call me Achilles, solacing my mind with music, φρενα τερπομενον φορμιγγι λιγειη:[8] but, to make amends for the deficiency, you have brought me a musical Ajax.

SIR TELEGRAPH PAXARETT.

You have no reason to wish even for the golden lyre of my old friend Pindar himself:[9] you have been listening to the music of the winds and the waters, and to what is more than music, the voice of Miss Melincourt.

MR. HIPPY.

And there is a very pretty concert waiting for you at the inn—the tinkling of cups and spoons, and the divine song of the tea-urn.

CHAPTER XXI.

THE CITY OF NOVOTE.

On the evening of the tenth day, the barouche rattled triumphantly into the large and populous city of Novote, which was situated at a short distance from the ancient and honourable borough of Onevote.[1] The city contained fifty thousand inhabitants, and had no representative in the Honourable House, the deficiency being virtually supplied[2] by the two members for Onevote; who, having no affairs to attend to for the borough, or rather the burgess,[3] that did return them, were supposed to have more leisure for those of the city which did not: a system somewhat analogous to that which the learned author of *Hermes* calls *a method of supply by negation.*[4]

Sir Oran signalized[5] his own entrance by playing on his French horn, *See the conquering hero comes!*[6] Bells were ringing, ale was flowing, mobs were huzzaing,[7] and it seemed as if the inhabitants of the large and populous city were satisfied of the truth of the admirable doctrine, that the positive representation of one individual is a virtual representation of fifty thousand.[8] They[9] found afterwards, that all this festivity had been set in motion by Sir Oran's brother candidate, Simon Sarcastic, Esquire, to whom we shall shortly introduce our readers.

The barouche stopped at the door of a magnificent inn, and the party was welcomed with some scores of bows from the whole *corps d'hôtel*,[10] with the fat landlady in the van, and Boots in the rear.[11] They were shown into a splendid apartment, a glorious fire was kindled in a minute, and while Mr. Hippy looked over the bill of fare, and followed mine hostess to inspect the state of the larder, Sir Telegraph proceeded to *peel*,[12] and emerged from his four *benjamins*,[13] like a butterfly from its chrysalis.

After dinner they formed, as usual, a semicircle round the fire, with the table in front supported by Mr. Hippy and Sir Telegraph Paxarett.

"Now this," said Sir Telegraph, rubbing his hands, "is what I call devilish comfortable after a cold day's drive—an excellent inn, a superb fire, charming company, and better wine than has fallen to our lot since we left Melincourt Castle."

The waiter had picked up from the conversation at dinner, that one of the destined members for Onevote was in company; and communicated this intelligence to Mr. Sarcastic, who was taking his solitary bottle in another apartment. Mr. Sarcastic sent his compliments to Sir Oran Haut-ton, and hoped he would allow his future colleague the honour of being admitted to join his party. Mr. Hippy, Mr. Forester, and Sir Telegraph, undertook to answer for Sir Oran, who was silent on the occasion: Mr. Sarcastic was introduced, and took his seat in the semicircle.

SIR TELEGRAPH PAXARETT.

Your future colleague, Mr. Sarcastic, is *a man of few words;* but he will join in a bumper to your better acquaintance.—*(The collision of glasses ensued between Sir Oran and Mr. Sarcastic.)*

MR. SARCASTIC.

I am proud of the opportunity of this introduction. The day after to-morrow is fixed for the election. I have made some preparations to give a little *éclat* to the affair, and have begun by intoxicating half the city of Novote, so that we shall have a great crowd at the scene of election, whom I intend to harangue from the hustings, on the great benefits and blessings of virtual representation.

MR. FORESTER.

I shall, perhaps, take the opportunity of addressing them also, but with a different view of the subject.

MR. SARCASTIC.

Perhaps our views of the subject are not radically different, and the variety is in the mode of treatment. In my ordinary intercourse with the world, I reduce practice to theory: it is a habit, I believe, peculiar to myself, and a source of inexhaustible amusement.

SIR TELEGRAPH PAXARETT.

Fill and explain.

MR. SARCASTIC.

Nothing, you well know, is so rare as the coincidence of theory and practice. A man who "will go through fire and water to serve a friend"[14] in words, will not give five guineas to save him from famine. A poet will write Odes to Independence, and become the obsequious parasite of any great man who will hire him. A burgess will hold up one hand for purity of election, while the price of his own vote is slily dropped into the other. I need not accumulate instances.

MR. FORESTER.

You would find it difficult, I fear, to adduce many to the contrary.

MR. SARCASTIC.

This then is my system. I ascertain the practice of those I talk to, and present it to them as from myself, in the shape of theory: the consequence of which is, that I am universally stigmatized as a promulgator of rascally doctrines. Thus I said to Sir Oliver Oilcake,[15] "When I get into Parliament I intend to make the sale of my vote as notorious as the sun at noon-day.[16] I will have no rule of right, but my own pocket. I will support every measure of every administration, even if they ruin half the nation for the purpose of restoring the Great Lama, or of subjecting twenty millions of people to be hanged, drawn, and quartered at the pleasure of the man-milliner of

Mahomet's mother.[17] I will have ship-loads of turtle[18] and rivers of Madeira for myself, if I send the whole swinish multitude[19] to draff and husks."[20] Sir Oliver flew into a rage, and swore he would hold no further intercourse with a man who maintained such infamous principles.

MR. HIPPY.

Pleasant enough, to show a man his own picture, and make him damn the ugly rascal.

MR. SARCASTIC.

I said to Miss Pennylove, whom I knew to be *laying herself out* for a *good match*,[21] "When my daughter becomes of marriageable age, I shall commission Christie[22] to put her up to auction, 'the highest bidder to be the buyer; and if any dispute arise between two or more bidders, the lot to be put up again and resold.'" Miss Pennylove professed herself utterly amazed and indignant, that any man, and a father especially, should imagine a scheme so outrageous to the dignity and delicacy of the female mind.

THE HONOURABLE MRS. PINMONEY, AND MISS DANARETTA.

A most horrid idea certainly.

MR. SARCASTIC.

The fact, my dear ladies, the fact: how stands the fact? Miss Pennylove afterwards married a man old enough to be her grandfather, for no other reason, but because he was rich; and broke the heart of a very worthy friend of mine, to whom she had been previously engaged, who had no fault but the folly of loving her, and was quite rich enough for all purposes of matrimonial happiness. How the dignity and delicacy of such a person could have been affected, if the preliminary negotiation with her hobbling Strephon had been conducted through the instrumentality of honest Christie's hammer, I cannot possibly imagine.

MR. HIPPY.

Nor I, I must say. All the difference is in the form, and not in the fact. It is a pity the form does not come into fashion: it would save a world of trouble.

MR. SARCASTIC.

I irreparably offended the Reverend Doctor Vorax[23] by telling him, that having a nephew, whom I wished to shine in the church, I was on the look-out for a luminous butler, and a cook of solid capacity, under whose joint tuition he might graduate. "Who knows," said I, "but he may immortalize himself at the University, by giving his name to a pudding?"—I lost the acquaintance of Mrs. Cullender, by saying to her, when she had told me a piece of gossip as a very particular secret, that there was nothing so agreeable to me as to be in possession of a secret, for I made a point of telling it to all my acquaintance;

Intrusted under solemn vows,
Of Mum, and Silence, and the Rose,
To be retailed again in whispers,
For the easy credulous to disperse.*[24]

Mrs. Cullender left me in great wrath, protesting she would never again throw away *her* confidence on so leaky a vessel.

SIR TELEGRAPH PAXARETT.

Ha! ha! ha! Bravo! Come, a bumper to Mrs. Cullender.

MR. SARCASTIC.

With all my heart; and another if you please to Mr. Christopher Corporate, the free, fat, and dependent[25] burgess of Onevote, of which "plural unit"[26] the Honourable Baronet and myself are to be the joint representatives.—(*Sir Oran Haut-ton bowed.*)

---

* Hudibras: Part III. ii. 1493.

MR. HIPPY.

And a third, by all means, to His Grace the Duke of Rottenburgh.

MR. SARCASTIC.

And a fourth, to crown all, to *the blessings of virtual representation*, which I shall endeavour to impress on as many of the worthy citizens of Novote, as shall think fit to be present the day after to-morrow, at the proceedings of the borough of Onevote.

SIR TELEGRAPH PAXARETT.

And now for tea and coffee. Touch the bell for the waiter.

The bottles and glasses vanished, and the beautiful array of urns and cups succeeded. Sir Telegraph and Mr. Hippy seceded from the table, and resigned their stations to Mrs. and Miss Pinmoney.

MR. FORESTER.

Your system is sufficiently amusing, but I much question its utility. The object of moral censure is reformation, and its proper vehicle is plain and fearless sincerity: VERBA ANIMI PROFERRE, ET VITAM IMPENDERE VERO.[27]

MR. SARCASTIC.

I tried that in my youth, when I was troubled with the *passion for reforming the world;*[28] of which I have been long cured, by the conviction of the inefficacy of moral theory with respect to producing a practical change in the mass of mankind. Custom is the pillar round which opinion twines, and interest is the tie that binds it. It is not by reason that practical change can be effected, but by making a puncture to the quick in the feelings of personal hope and personal fear. The Reformation in England is one of the supposed triumphs

---

˙ See Forsyth's Principles of Moral Science.

of reason. But if the passions of Henry the Eighth had not been interested in that measure, he would as soon have built mosques as pulled down abbies: and you will observe, that, in all cases, reformation never goes as far as reason requires, but just as far as suits the personal interest of those who conduct it. Place Temperance and Bacchus side by side, in an assembly of jolly fellows, and endow the first with the most powerful eloquence that mere reason can give, with the absolute moral force of mathematical demonstration, Bacchus need not take the trouble of refuting one of her arguments; he will only have to say, "Come, my boys; here's *Damn Temperance* in a bumper," and you may rely on the toast being drank with an unanimous three times three.

(At the sound of the word bumper, *with which Captain Hawltaught had made him very familiar, Sir Oran Haut-ton looked round for his glass, but, finding it vanished, comforted himself with a dish of tea from the fair hand of Miss Danaretta, which, as his friend Mr. Forester had interdicted him from the use of sugar, he sweetened as well as he could with a copious infusion of cream.)*

SIR TELEGRAPH PAXARETT.

As an Opposition orator in the Honourable House will bring forward a long detail of un-answerable arguments, without even expecting that they will have the slightest influence on the vote of the majority.

MR. SARCASTIC.

A reform of that honourable body, if ever it should take place, will be one of the *"triumphs of reason."* But reason will have little to do with it. All that reason can say on the subject, has been said for years, by men of all parties—while they were *out:* but the moment they were *in,* the moment their own

---

* "Il buvoit du vin, mais le laissoit volontiers pour du lait, du thé, ou d'autres liqueurs douces."—BUFFON *of the Oran Outang, whom he saw himself in Paris.*[29]

interest came in contact with their own reason, the victory of interest was never for a moment doubtful. While the great fountain of interest, rising in the caverns of borough patronage and ministerial influence, flowed through the whole body of the kingdom by the channels of paper-money,[30] and loans, and contracts, and jobs, and places either found or made for the useful dealers in secret services,[31] so long the predominant interests of corruption overpowered the true and permanent interests of the country: but as those channels become dry, and they are becoming so with fearful rapidity, the crew of every boat that is left aground are convinced not by reason—that they had long heard and despised—but by the unexpected pressure of personal suffering, that they had been going on in the wrong way. Thus the re-action of interest takes place; and when the concentrated interests of thousands, combined by the same pressure of personal suffering, shall have created an independent power, greater than the power of the interest of corruption, then, and not till then, the latter will give way, and this will be called the triumph of reason, though, in truth, like all the changes in human society, that have ever taken place from the birth-day of the world, it will be only the triumph of one mode of interest over another: but as the triumph in this case will be of the interest of the many, over that of the few, it is certainly a consummation devoutly to be wished.[32]

MR. FORESTER.

If I should admit that "the hope of personal advantage, and the dread of personal punishment,"[33] are the only springs that set the mass of mankind in action, the inefficacy of reason, and the inutility of moral theory, will by no means follow from the admission. The progress of truth is slow, but its ultimate triumph is secure; though its immediate effects may be rendered almost imperceptible, by the power of habit and interest. If the philosopher cannot reform his own times, he may lay the foundation of amendment in those that follow. Give currency to reason, improve the moral code of society, and the theory of one generation will be the practice of the next. After a certain period of life, and that no very advanced one, men in general become perfectly unpersuadable to all practical purposes. Few philosophers, therefore, I believe, expect to produce much change in the habits of their contemporaries, as Plato proposed[34] to banish from his republic all above the age of ten, and give a good education to the rest.

MR. SARCASTIC.

Or, as Heraclitus the Ephesian[35] proposed to his countrymen, that all above the age of fourteen should hang themselves, before he would consent to give laws to the remainder.

CHAPTER XXII.

THE BOROUGH OF ONEVOTE.

THE day of election arrived. Mr. Sarcastic's rumoured preparations, and the excellence of the ale which he had broached in the city of Novote, had given a degree of *éclat*[1] to the election for the borough of Onevote, which it had never before possessed; the representatives usually sliding into their nomination with the same silence and decorum with which a solitary spinster slides into her pew at Wednesday or Friday's prayers in a country church. The resemblance holds good also in this respect, that, as the curate addresses the solitary maiden with the appellation of *dearly beloved brethren*,[2] so the representatives always pluralized their solitary elector, by conferring on him the appellation of *a respectable body of constituents*.[3] Mr. Sarcastic, however, being determined to amuse himself at the expense of this most "venerable *feature*" in our old constitution, as Lord C. calls a rotten borough,[4] had brought Mr. Christopher Corporate into his views, by the adhibition[5] of *persuasion in a tangible shape*. It was generally known in Novote, that something would be going forward at Onevote, though nobody could tell precisely what, except that a long train of brewer's drays had left the city for the borough, in grand procession, on the preceding day, under the escort of a sworn band of special constables, who were to keep guard over the ale all night. This detachment was soon followed by another, under a similar escort, and with similar injunctions: and it was understood that this second expedition of *frothy rhetoric*[6] was sent forth under the auspices of Sir Oran Haut-ton, Baronet, the brother candidate of Simon Sarcastic, Esquire, for the representation of the ancient and honourable borough.

The borough of Onevote stood in the middle of a heath, and consisted of a solitary farm, of which the land was so poor and untractable, that it would not have been worth the while of any human being to cultivate it, had not the Duke of Rottenburgh found it very well worth his to pay his tenant for living there, to keep the honourable borough in existence.[7]

Mr. Sarcastic left the city of Novote some hours before his new acquaintance, to superintend his preparations, followed by crowds of persons of all descriptions, pedestrians and equestrians;[8] old ladies in chariots,[9] and young ladies on donkies; the farmer on his hunter,[10] and the tailor on his hack;[11] the grocer and his family six in a chaise;[12] the dancing-master in his tilbury;[13] the banker in his tandem;[14] mantua-makers[15] and servant-maids twenty-four in the waggon, fitted up for the occasion with a canopy of evergreens; pastry-cooks, men-milliners,[16] and journeymen tailors, by the stage, running for that day only, six inside and fourteen out;[17] the sallow artizan emerging from the cellar or the furnace, to freshen himself with the pure breezes of Onevote Heath; the bumpkin in his laced boots and Sunday coat, trudging through the dust with his cherry-cheeked lass on his elbow;[18] the gentleman coachman on his box,[19] with his painted charmer by his side; the lean curate on his half-starved Rosinante;[20] the plump bishop setting an example of Christian humility in his carriage and six;[21] the doctor on his white horse, like Death in the Revelations;[22] and the lawyer on his black one, like the devil in the Wild Huntsmen.[23]

Almost in the rear of this motley cavalcade went the barouche of Sir Telegraph Paxarett, and rolled up to the scene of action amidst the shouts of the multitude.

The heath had very much the appearance of a race ground; with booths and stalls, the voices of pie-men and apple-women, the grinding of barrel organs,[24] the scraping of fiddles, the squeaking of ballad-singers, the chirping of corkscrews, the vociferations of ale-drinkers, the cries of the "last dying speeches of desperate malefactors," and of "The History and Antiquities of the honourable Borough of Onevote, a full and circumstantial account, all in half a sheet, for the price of one halfpenny!"

The hustings[25] were erected in proper form, and immediately opposite to them was an enormous marquee with a small opening in front, in which was seated the important person of Mr. Christopher Corporate, with a tankard of ale and a pipe. The ladies remained in the barouche under the care of Sir Telegraph and Mr. Hippy. Mr. Forester, Mr. Fax, and Sir Oran Haut-ton, joined Mr. Sarcastic on the hustings.

Mr. Sarcastic stepped forward amidst the shouts of the assembled crowd, and addressed Mr. Christopher Corporate:

"Free, fat, and dependent[26] burgess of this ancient and honourable borough! I stand forward an unworthy candidate, to be the representative of so important a personage, who comprises in himself a three hundredth part of the whole elective capacity of this extensive empire.[27] For if the whole population be estimated at eleven millions,[28] with what awe and veneration must I look on one, who is, as it were, the abstract and quintessence of thirty-three thousand six hundred and sixty-six people! The voice of Stentor[29] was like the voice of fifty, and the voice of Harry Gill[*][30] was like the voice of three; but what are these to the voice of Mr. Christopher Corporate, which gives utterance in one breath to the concentrated power of thirty-three thousand six hundred and sixty-six voices? Of such an one it may indeed be said, that *he is himself an host*, and that *none but himself can be his parallel*.[31]

"Most potent, grave, and reverend signor![32] it is usual on these occasions to make a great vapouring[33] about honour and conscience: but as those words are now generally acknowledged to be utterly destitute of meaning, I have too much

---

[*] See Mr. Wordsworth's Lyrical Ballads.

respect for your understanding to say any thing about them. *The monied interest,*[34] Mr. Corporate, for which you are as illustrious *as the sun at noon-day,*[35] is the great point of connexion and sympathy between us: and no circumstances can throw a *wet blanket* on the ardour of our reciprocal esteem, while the *fundamental feature* of our mutual interests presents itself to us in so *tangible a shape.*[36] How high a value I set upon your voice, you may judge by the price I have paid for half of it: which, indeed, deeply lodged as my feelings are in my pocket, I yet see no reason to regret, since you will thus confer on mine, a transmutable and marketable value,[37] which I trust with proper management will leave me no loser by the bargain."

"Huzza!" said Mr. Corporate.

"People of the city of Novote!" proceeded Mr. Sarcastic, "some of you, I am informed, consider yourselves aggrieved, that, while your large and populous city has no share whatever in the formation of the Honourable House, the *plural unity*[38] of Mr. Christopher Corporate should be invested with the privilege of double representation. But, gentlemen, representation is of two kinds, actual, and virtual: an important distinction, and of great political consequence.

"The Honourable Baronet and myself being the actual representatives of the fat burgess of Onevote, shall be the virtual representatives of the worthy citizens of Novote; and you may rely on it, gentlemen, *(with his hand on his heart,)* we shall always be deeply attentive to your interests, when they happen, as no doubt they sometimes will, to be perfectly compatible with our own.

"A member of Parliament, gentlemen, to speak to you in your own phrase, is a sort of staple commodity, manufactured for home consumption. Much has been said of the

---

* The figures of speech marked in Italics are familiar to the admirers of parliamentary rhetoric.

improvement of machinery in the present age, by which one man may do the work of a dozen. If this be admirable, and admirable it is acknowledged to be by all the civilized world, how much more admirable is the improvement of political machinery, by which one man does the work of thirty thousand! I am sure, I need not say another word to a great manufacturing population like the inhabitants of the city of Novote, to convince them of the beauty and utility of this most luminous arrangement.

"The duty of a representative of the people, whether actual or virtual, is simply *to tax.* Now this important branch of public business is much more easily and expeditiously transacted by the means of virtual, than it possibly could be by that of actual representation. For when the minister draws up his scheme of ways and means, he will do it with much more celerity and confidence, when he knows that the propitious countenance of virtual representation will never cease to smile upon him as long as he continues in place, than if he had to encounter the doubtful aspect of actual representation, which might, perhaps, look black on some of his favourite projects, thereby greatly impeding the distribution of secret service money[39] at home, and placing foreign legitimacy[40] in a very awkward predicament. The carriage of the state would then be like a chariot in a forest, turning to the left for a troublesome thorn, and to the right for a sturdy oak; whereas it now rolls forward like the car of Jaggernaut[41] over the plain, crushing whatever offers to impede its way.

"The constitution says that no man shall be taxed but by his own consent:[42] a very plausible theory, gentlemen, but not reducible to practice. Who will apply a lancet[43] to his own arm, and bleed himself? Very few, you acknowledge. Who then, *à fortiori*, would apply a lancet to his own pocket, and draw off what is dearer to him than his blood—his money? Fewer still of course: I humbly opine, none.—What then remains but to appoint a royal college of state surgeons, who may operate on the patient according to their views of his case? Taxation is political phlebotomy: the Honourable House is, figuratively speaking, a royal college of state surgeons. A good surgeon must have firm nerves and a steady hand; and, perhaps, the less feeling the better. Now, it is manifest, that, as all feeling is founded on sympathy,[44] the fewer constituents a representative has, the less must be his sympathy with the public, and the less, of course, as is desirable, his feeling for his patient—the people:—who, therefore, with so much *sang-froid*,[45] can phlebotomize the nation, as the representative of half an elector?

"Gentlemen, as long as a *full Gazette*[46] is pleasant to the *quidnunc*;[47] as long as an empty purse is delightful to the spendthrift; as long as the cry of *Question* is a satisfactory *answer* to an argument,[48] and to outvote reason, is to refute it; as long as the way to pay old debts is to incur new ones of five times the amount; as long as the grand recipes of political health and longevity are *bleeding* and *hot water*—so long must you rejoice in the privileges of Mr. Christopher Corporate, so long must you acknowledge, from the very bottom of your pockets, the benefits and blessings of *virtual representation*."

This harangue was received with great applause, acclamations rent the air, and ale flowed in torrents. Mr. Forester declined speaking, and the party on the hustings proceeded to business. Sir Oran Haut-ton, Baronet, and Simon Sarcastic, Esquire, were nominated in form. Mr. Christopher Corporate held up both his hands, with his tankard in one, and his pipe in the other: and neither poll nor scrutiny being demanded,[49] the two candidates were pronounced duly elected, as representatives of the ancient and honourable borough of Onevote.

The shouts were renewed: the ale flowed rapidly: the pipe and tankard of Mr. Corporate were replenished. Sir Oran

Haut-ton, Baronet, M. P. bowed gracefully to the people with his hand on his heart.

A cry was now raised of "Chair[50] 'em! chair 'em!" when Mr. Sarcastic again stepped forward.

"Gentlemen!" said he, "a slight difficulty opposes itself to the honour you would confer on us. The members should, according to form, be chaired by their electors: and how can one elector, great man as he is, chair two representatives? But to obviate this dilemma as well as circumstances admit, I move that the 'large body corporate of one'[51] whom the Honourable Baronet and myself have the honour to represent, do resolve himself into a committee."[52]

He had no sooner spoken, than the marquee opened, and a number of bulky personages, all in dress, aspect, size, and figure, very exact resemblances of Mr. Christopher Corporate, each with his pipe and his tankard, emerged into daylight, who encircling their venerable prototype, lifted their tankards high in air, and pronounced with Stentorian symphony, "HAIL, PLURAL UNIT!" Then, after a simultaneous draught, throwing away their pipes and tankards, for which the mob immediately scrambled, they raised on high two magnificent chairs, and prepared to carry into effect the last ceremony of the election. The party on the hustings descended. Mr. Sarcastic stepped into his chair; and his part of the procession, headed by Mr. Christopher Corporate, and surrounded by a multiform and many-coloured crowd, moved slowly off towards the city of Novote, amidst the undistinguishable clamour of multitudinous voices.

Sir Oran Haut-ton watched the progress of his precursor, as his chair rolled and swayed over the sea of heads, like a boat with one mast on a stormy ocean; and the more he watched the agitation of its movements, the more his countenance gave indications of strong dislike to the process: so that when his seat in the second chair was offered to him, he with a very polite bow declined the honour. The party that was to carry him, thinking that his repugnance arose entirely from diffidence, proceeded with gentle force to overcome his scruples, when not precisely penetrating their motives, and indignant at this attempt to violate the freedom of the natural man, he seized a stick from a sturdy farmer at his elbow, and began to lay about him with great vigour and effect. Those who escaped being knocked down by the first sweep of his weapon, ran away with all their might, but were soon checked by the pressure of the crowd, who hearing the noise of conflict, and impatient to ascertain the cause, bore down from all points upon a common centre, and formed a circumferential pressure that effectually prohibited the egress of those within; and they in their turn, in their eagerness to escape from Sir Oran (who, like Artegall's Iron Man, or like Ajax among the Trojans, or like Rhodomont in Paris, or like Orlando among the soldiers of Agramant,[53] kept clearing for himself an ample space, in the midst of the encircling crowd), waged desperate conflict with those without; so that from the equal and opposite action of the centripetal and centrifugal forces, resulted a stationary combat, raging between the circumferences of two concentric circles, with barbaric dissonance of deadly feud, and infinite variety of oath and execration, till Sir Oran, charging desperately along one of the radii, fought a free passage through all opposition; and rushing to the barouche of Sir Telegraph Paxarett, sprang to his old station on the box, from whence he shook his sapling at the foe, with looks of mortal defiance. Mr. Forester, who had been forcibly parted from him at the commencement of the strife, and had been all anxiety on his account, mounted with great alacrity to his station on the roof: the rest of the party was already seated: the Honourable Mrs. Pinmoney, half-fainting with terror, earnestly entreated Sir Telegraph to fly: Sir Telegraph cracked his whip: the horses sprang forward like racers: the wheels went round like the wheels of a firework. The tumult of battle lessening as they receded, came wafted to them on the wings of the wind: for the flame of discord having been once kindled, was not extinguished by the departure of its first flambeau—Sir Oran; but war raged wide and far, here in the thickest mass of central fight, there in the light skirmishing of flying detachments. The hustings were demolished, and the beams and planks turned into offensive weapons: the booths were torn to pieces, and the canvass converted into flags floating over the heads of magnanimous heroes that rushed to revenge they knew not what, in deadly battle with they knew not whom. The stalls and barrows were upset; and the pears, apples, oranges, mutton-pies, and masses of gingerbread, flew like missiles of fate in all directions. The *sanctum sanctorum*[54] of the ale was broken into, and the guardians of the Hesperian liquor[55] were put to ignominious rout. Hats and wigs[56] were hurled into the air, never to return to the heads from which they had suffered violent divorce. The collision of sticks, the ringing of empty ale-casks, the shrieks of women, and the vociferations of combatants, mingled in one deepening and indescribable tumult: till at length, every thing else being levelled with the heath, they turned the mingled torrent of their wrath on the cottage of Mr. Corporate, to which they triumphantly set fire, and danced round the blaze, like a rabble of village boys round the effigy of the immortal Guy.[57] In a few minutes the ancient and honourable borough of Onevote was reduced to ashes: but we have the satisfaction to state that it was rebuilt a few days afterwards, at the joint expense of its two representatives, and His Grace the Duke of Rottenburgh.

CHAPTER XXIII.

THE COUNCIL OF WAR.

THE compassionate reader will perhaps sympathize in our anxiety, to take one peep at Lord Anophel Achthar and the Reverend Mr. Grovelgrub, whom we left[1] perched on the summit of the rock, where Sir Oran had placed them, looking at each other as ruefully as Hudibras and Ralpho in their "wooden bastile,"[2] and falling by degrees into as knotty an argument, the *quæritur*[3] of which was, how to descend from their elevation—an exploit which to them seemed replete with danger and difficulty. Lord Anophel, having, for the first time in his life, been made acquainted with the salutary effects of manual discipline, sate boiling with wrath and revenge; while the Reverend Mr. Grovelgrub, who in his youthful days had been beaten black and blue in the capacity of *fag*[4] (a practice which reflects so much honour on our public seminaries), bore the infliction with more humility.

LORD ANOPHEL ACHTHAR, *(rubbing his shoulder.)*

This is all your doing, Grovelgrub—all your fault, curse me!

THE REVEREND MR. GROVELGRUB.

Oh, my Lord! my intention was good, though the catastrophe is ill. The race is not always to the swift, nor the battle to the strong.[5]

LORD ANOPHEL ACHTHAR.

But the battle was to the strong in this instance, Grovelgrub, curse me! though, from the speed with which you began to run off on the first alarm, it was no fault of yours that the race was not to the swift.

THE REVEREND MR. GROVELGRUB.

I must do your Lordship the justice to say, that you too started with a degree of celerity highly creditable to your capacity of natural locomotion; and if that ugly monster, the dumb Baronet, had not knocked us both down in the incipiency[6] of our progression——

LORD ANOPHEL ACHTHAR.

We should have escaped as our two rascals did, who shall bitterly rue their dereliction. But as to the dumb Baronet, who has treated me with gross impertinence on various occasions, I shall certainly call him out, to give me the satisfaction of a gentleman.

THE REVEREND MR. GROVELGRUB.

Oh, my Lord,

> Though with pistols 't is the fashion,
> To satisfy your passion;
> Yet where's the satisfaction,
> If you perish in the action?[7]

LORD ANOPHEL ACHTHAR.

One of us must perish, Grovelgrub, 'pon honour. Death or revenge! We're blown, Grovelgrub. He took off our masks; and though he can't speak, he can write, no doubt, and read, too, as I shall try with a challenge.

THE REVEREND MR. GROVELGRUB.

Can't speak, my Lord, is by no means clear. Won't speak, perhaps: none are so dumb as those who won't speak.[8] Don't you think, my Lord, there was a sort of melancholy about him—a kind of sullenness? Crossed in love I suspect. People crossed in love, Saint Chrysostom says, lose their voice.[9]

LORD ANOPHEL ACHTHAR.

Then I wish you were crossed in love, Grovelgrub, with all my heart.

THE REVEREND MR. GROVELGRUB.

Nay, my Lord, what so sweet in calamity as the voice of the spiritual comforter? All shall be well yet, my Lord. I have an infallible project hatching here: Miss Melincourt shall be ensconced in Alga Castle,[10] and then the day is our own.

LORD ANOPHEL ACHTHAR.

Grovelgrub, you know the old receipt for stewing a carp: "First, catch your carp."[11]

THE REVEREND MR. GROVELGRUB.

Your Lordship is pleased to be facetious: but if the carp be not caught, let me be devilled like a biscuit after the second bottle, or a turkey's leg at a twelfth night supper.[12] The carp shall be caught.

LORD ANOPHEL ACHTHAR.

Well, Grovelgrub, only take notice that I'll not come again within ten miles of dummy.

THE REVEREND MR. GROVELGRUB.

You may rely upon it, my Lord, I shall always know my distance from the Honourable Baronet. But my plot is a good plot, and cannot fail of success.

LORD ANOPHEL ACHTHAR.

You are a very skilful contriver, to be sure: this is your contrivance, our perch on the top of this rock. Now contrive, if you can, some way of getting to the bottom of it.

THE REVEREND MR. GROVELGRUB.

My Lord, there is a passage in Æschylus, very applicable to our situation,[13] where the chorus wishes to be in precisely such a place.

LORD ANOPHEL ACHTHAR.

Then I wish the chorus were here instead of us, Grovelgrub, with all my soul.

THE REVEREND MR. GROVELGRUB.

It is a very fine passage, my Lord, and worth your attention: the rock is described as

λισσας αιγιλιψ απροσδεικτος
οιοφρων ερημας γυπιας πετρα,
βαθυ πτωμα μαρτυρουσα μοι.*

That is, my Lord, a precipitous rock, inaccessible to the goat—not to be pointed at (from having, as I take it, its head in the clouds), where there is the loneliness of mind, and the solitude of desolation, where the vulture has its nest, and the precipice testifies a deep and headlong fall.

LORD ANOPHEL ACHTHAR.

I'll tell you what, Grovelgrub; if ever I catch you quoting Æschylus again, I'll cashier you from your tutorship—that's positive.

THE REVEREND MR. GROVELGRUB.

I am dumb, my Lord.

LORD ANOPHEL ACHTHAR.

Think, I tell you, of some way of getting down.

THE REVEREND MR. GROVELGRUB.

Nothing more easy, my Lord.

LORD ANOPHEL ACHTHAR.

Plummet fashion, I suppose?

THE REVEREND MR. GROVELGRUB.

Why, as your Lordship seems to hint, that certainly is the most expeditious method; but not, I think, in all points of view, the most advisable. On this side of the rock is a *dume-tum*.[14] we can descend, I think, by the help of the roots and shoots. O dear! I shall be like Virgil's goat: I shall be seen from

---

* Supplices. 807. Ed. Schutz.

far to hang from the bushy rock, *Dumosâ pendere procul de rupe videbor!*[15]

LORD ANOPHEL ACHTHAR.

Confound your Greek and Latin! you know there is nothing I hate so much; and I thought you did so too, or you have *finished* your *education* to no purpose at college.

THE REVEREND MR. GROVELGRUB.

I do, my Lord: I hate them mortally, more than any thing except philosophy and the dumb Baronet.

Lord Anophel Achthar proceeded to examine the side of the rock to which the Reverend Mr. Grovelgrub had called his attention; and as it seemed the most practicable mode of descent, it was resolved to submit to necessity, and make a valorous effort to regain the valley; Lord Anophel, however, insisting on the Reverend Mr. Grovelgrub leading the way. The Reverend gentleman seized with one hand the stem of a hazel, with the other the branch of an ash; set one foot on the root of an oak, and deliberately lowered the other in search of a resting-place; which having found on a projecting point of stone, he cautiously disengaged one hand and the upper foot, for which in turn he sought and found a firm *appui*;[16] and thus by little and little he vanished among the boughs from the sight of Lord Anophel, who proceeded with great circumspection to follow his example.

Lord Anophel had descended about one third of the elevation, comforting his ear with the rustling of the boughs below, that announced the safe progress of his reverend precursor: when suddenly, as he was shifting his right hand, a treacherous twig in his left gave way, and he fell with fearful lapse from bush to bush, till, striking violently on a bough to which the unfortunate divine was appended, it broke beneath the shock, and down they went, crashing through the bushes together. Lord Anophel was soon wedged into the middle of a large holly, from which he heard the intermitted sound of the boughs as they broke, and were broken by, the fall of his companion: till at length they ceased, and fearful silence succeeded. He then extricated himself from the holly as well as he could, at the expense of a scratched face, and lowered himself down without further accident. On reaching the bottom, he had the pleasure to find the reverend gentleman in safety, sitting on a fragment of stone, and rubbing his shin. "Come, Grovelgrub," said Lord Anophel, "let us make the best of our way to the nearest inn."—"And pour oil and wine into our wounds," pursued the reverend gentleman, "and over our Madeira and walnuts lay a more hopeful scheme for our next campaign."

CHAPTER XXIV.

THE BAROUCHE.

THE morning after the election[1] Sir Oran Haut-ton and his party took leave of Mr. Sarcastic, Mr. Forester having previously obtained from him a promise to be present at the Antisaccharine fête. The barouche left the city of Novote, decorated with ribands: Sir Oran Haut-ton was loudly cheered by the populace, and not least by those whom he had most severely beaten; the secret of which was, that a double allowance of ale had been distributed over-night, to wash away the effects of his indiscretion: it having been ascertained by political economists, that a practical appeal either to the palm or the palate, will induce the friends of *things as they are*[2] to submit to any thing.

Autumn was now touching on the confines of winter, but the day was mild and sunny. Sir Telegraph asked Mr. Forester, if he did not think the mode of locomotion very agreeable?

MR. FORESTER.

That I never denied: all I question is, the right of any individual to indulge himself in it.

SIR TELEGRAPH PAXARETT.

Surely a man has a right to do what he pleases with his own money.

MR. FORESTER.

A legal right, certainly, not a moral one. The possession of power does not justify its abuse. The quantity of money in a nation, the quantity of food, and the number of animals that consume that food, maintain a triangular harmony, of which, in all the fluctuations of time and circumstance, the proportions are always the same. You must consider, therefore, that for every horse you keep for pleasure, you pass sentence of non-existence on two human beings.

SIR TELEGRAPH PAXARETT.

Really, Forester, you are a very singular fellow. I should not much mind what you say, if you had not such a strange habit of practising what you preach; a thing quite unprecedented, and, egad, preposterous. I cannot think where you got it: I am sure you did not learn it at college.

MR. FAX.

In a political light, every object of perception may be resolved into one of these three heads: the food consumed—the consumers—and money. In this point of view all convertible property that does not eat and drink, is money. Diamonds are money. When a man changes a bank-note for a diamond, he merely changes one sort of money for another, differing only in the facility of circulation and the stability of value. None of the produce of the earth is wasted by the permutation.

MR. FORESTER.

The most pernicious species of luxury, therefore, is that which applies the fruits of the earth to any other purposes than those of human subsistence. All luxury is indeed pernicious, because its infallible tendency is to enervate the few, and enslave the many: but luxury, which, in addition to this evil tendency, destroys the fruits of the earth in the wantonness of idle ostentation, and thereby prevents the existence of so many human beings, as the quantity of food so destroyed would maintain, is marked by criminality of a much deeper die.

MR. FAX.

At the same time you must consider, that, in respect of population, the great desideratum is not number, but quality. If the whole surface of this country were divided into gardens, and in every garden were a cottage, and in every cottage a family living entirely on potatoes, the number of its human inhabitants would be much greater than at present: but where would be the spirit of commercial enterprise, the researches of science, the exalted pursuits of philosophical leisure, the communication with distant lands, and all that variety of human life and intercourse, which is now so beautiful and so interesting? Above all, where would be the refuge of such a population in times of the slightest defalcation?[3] Now, the waste of plenty is the resource of scarcity. The canal that does not overflow in the season of rain, will not be navigable in the season of drought. The rich have been often ready, in days of emergency, to lay their superfluities aside; but when the fruits of the earth are applied, in plentiful or even ordinary seasons, to the utmost possibility of human subsistence, the days of deficiency in their produce, must be days of inevitable famine.

MR. FORESTER.

When then will you say of those, who, in times of actual famine, persevere in their old course, in the wanton waste of luxury?

MR. FAX.

Truly I have nothing to say for them, but that they know not what they do.[4]

MR. FORESTER.

If, in any form of human society, any one human being dies of hunger, while another wastes or consumes in the wantonness of vanity, as much as would have preserved his existence, I hold that second man guilty of the death of the first.

SIR TELEGRAPH PAXARETT.

Surely, Forester, you are not serious?

MR. FORESTER.

Indeed I am. What would you think of a family of four persons, two of whom should not be contented with consuming their own share of diurnal provision, but, having adventitiously the pre-eminence of physical power, should either throw the share of the two others into the fire, or stew it down into a condiment for their own?

SIR TELEGRAPH PAXARETT.

I should think it very abominable, certainly.

MR. FORESTER.

Yet what is human society, but one great family? What is moral duty, but that precise line of conduct which tends to promote the greatest degree of general happiness? And is not this duty most flagrantly violated, when one man appropriates to himself the subsistence of twelve; while, perhaps, in his immediate neighbourhood, eleven of his fellow-beings are dying with hunger? I have seen such a man walk with a demure face into church, as regularly as if the Sunday bell had been a portion of his corporeal mechanism, to hear a bloated and beneficed sensualist hold forth on the text of *Do as ye would be done by*,[5] or, *Inasmuch as ye have done it unto the least of these my brethren, ye have done it unto me*.[6] whereas, if he had wished his theory to coincide with his practice, he would have chosen for his text, *Behold a man gluttonous and a wine-bibber, a friend of publicans and sinners*:*[7] and when the duty of words was over, the auditor and his ghostly adviser, issuing forth together, have committed poor Lazarus[8] to the care of Providence, and proceeded to feast in the lordly mansion, like Dives that lived in purple.†[9]

---

* Matthew, xi. 19.

† "He that will mould a modern bishop into a primitive, must yield him to be elected by the popular voice, undiocesed, unrevenued, unlorded, and leave him nothing but brotherly equality, matchless temperance, frequent fasting, incessant prayer and preaching, continual watchings and labours in his ministry, which, what a rich booty it would be, what a plump endowment to the many-bene-fice-gaping mouth of a prelate, what a relish it would give to his canary-sucking and swan-eating palate, let old bishop Mountain judge for me.—They beseech us, that we would think them fit to be our justices of peace, our lords, our highest

SIR TELEGRAPH PAXARETT.

Well, Forester, there I escape your shaft; for I have "forgotten what the inside of a church is made of"[10] since they made me go to chapel twice a day at college. But go on, and don't spare *me*.

MR. FAX.

Let us suppose that ten thousand quarters of wheat will maintain ten thousand persons during any given portion of time: if the ten thousand quarters be reduced to five, or if the ten thousand persons be increased to twenty, the consequence will be immediate and general distress: yet if the proportions be equally distributed, as in a ship on short allowance, the general perception of necessity and justice will preserve general patience and mutual good-will: but let the first supposition remain unaltered, let there be ten thousand quarters of wheat, which shall be full allowance for ten thousand people; then, if four thousand persons take to themselves the portion of eight thousand, and leave to the remaining six thousand the portion of two (and this I fear is even an inadequate picture of the common practice of the world); these latter will be in a much worse condition on the last, than on the first supposition: while the habit of selfish prodigality deadening all good feelings and extinguishing all sympathy on the one hand, and the habit of debasement and suffering combining with the inevitable sense of oppression and injustice on the other, will produce an action and re-action of open, unblushing, cold-hearted pride, and servile, inefficient, ill-disguised resentment, which no philanthropist can contemplate without dismay.

officers of state, though they come furnished with no more knowledge than they learnt between the cook and the manciple, or more profoundly at the college audit, or the regent house, or to come to their deepest insight, at their patron's table."—MILTON: *Of Reformation in England.*

MR. FORESTER.

What then will be the case if the same disproportionate division continues by regular gradations through the remaining six thousand, till the lowest thousand receive such a fractional pittance as will scarcely keep life together? If any of these perish with hunger, what are they but the victims of the first four thousand, who appropriated more to themselves than either nature required or justice allowed? This, whatever the temporizers with the world may say of it, I have no hesitation in pronouncing to be wickedness of the most atrocious kind: and this I make no doubt was the sense of the founder of the Christian religion when he said, *It is easier for a camel to pass through the eye of a needle, than for a rich man to enter the kingdom of heaven.*[11]

MR. FAX.

You must beware of the chimæra of an agrarian law,[12] the revolutionary doctrine of an equality of possession: which can never be possible in practice, till the whole constitution of human nature be changed.

MR. FORESTER.

I am no revolutionist. I am no advocate for violent and arbitrary changes in the state of society. I care not in what proportions property is divided (though I think there are certain limits which it ought never to pass, and approve the wisdom of the American laws[13] in restricting the fortune of a private citizen to twenty thousand a year), provided the rich can be made to know that they are but the stewards of the poor, that they are not to be the monopolizers of solitary spoil, but the distributors of general possession; that they are responsible for that distribution to every principle of general justice, to every tie of moral obligation, to every feeling of human sympathy: that they are bound to cultivate simple habits in themselves, and to encourage most such arts of industry and peace, as are most compatible with the health and liberty of others.

MR. FAX.

On this principle, then, any species of luxury in the artificial adornment of persons and dwellings, which condemns the artificer to a life of pain and sickness in the alternations of the furnace and the cellar, is more baleful and more criminal, than even that which consuming in idle prodigality the fruits of the earth, destroys altogether in the proportion of its waste, so much of the possibility of human existence: since it is better not to be, than to be in misery.

SIR TELEGRAPH PAXARETT.

That is some consolation for me, as it shows me that there are others worse than myself: for I really thought you were going, between you, to prove me one of the greatest rogues in England. But seriously, Forester, you think the keeping of pleasure-horses, for the reasons you have given, a selfish and criminal species of luxury?

MR. FORESTER.

I am so far persuaded of it, that I keep none myself.[14]

SIR TELEGRAPH PAXARETT.

But are not these four very beautiful creatures? Would you wish not to see them in existence, living, as they do, a very happy and easy kind of life?

MR. FORESTER.

That I am disposed to question, when I compare the wild horse in his native deserts, in the full enjoyment of health, and liberty, and all the energies of his nature, with those docked, cropped, curtailed, mutilated animals, pent more than half their lives in the close confinement of a stable, never let out

* See Vol. I. page 156.

but to run in trammels,[15] subject, like their tyrant man, to an infinite variety of diseases, the produce of civilization and unnatural life, and tortured every now and then by some villain of a farrier, who has no more feeling for them than a West Indian planter has for his slaves; and when you consider, too, the fate of the most cherished of the species, racers and hunters, instruments and often victims of sports equally foolish and cruel, you will acknowledge that the life of the civilized horse is not an enviable destiny.

MR. FAX.

Horses are noble and useful animals; but as they must necessarily exist in great numbers for almost every purpose of human intercourse and business, it is desirable that none should be kept for purposes of mere idleness and ostentation. A pleasure-horse is a sort of four-footed sinecurist.

SIR TELEGRAPH PAXARETT.

Not quite so mischievous as a two-footed one.

MR. FORESTER.

Perhaps not: but the latter has always a large retinue of the former, and therefore the evil is doubled.

SIR TELEGRAPH PAXARETT.

Upon my word, Forester, you will almost talk me out of my barouche, and then what will become of me? What shall I do to kill time?

MR. FORESTER.

Read ancient books, the only source of permanent happiness left in this degenerate world.

SIR TELEGRAPH PAXARETT.

Read ancient books! That may be very good advice to some people: but you forget that I have been at college, and *finished* my *education*. By the by, I have one inside, a portable advocate for my proceedings, no less a personage than old Pindar.[16]

MR. FORESTER.

Pindar has written very fine odes on driving, as Anacreon[17] has done on drinking; but the first can no more be adduced to prove the morality of the whip, than the second to demonstrate the virtue of intemperance. Besides, as to the mental tendency and emulative associations of the pursuit itself, no comparison can be instituted between the charioteers of the Olympic games, and those of our turnpike roads; for the former were the emulators of heroes and demigods, and the latter of grooms and mail-coachmen.

SIR TELEGRAPH PAXARETT.

Well, Forester, as I recall to mind the various subjects against which I have heard you declaim, I will make you a promise. When ecclesiastical dignitaries imitate the temperance and humility of the founder of that religion by which they feed and flourish: when the man in place acts on the principles which he professed while he was out: when borough-electors will not sell their suffrage, nor their representatives their votes: when poets are not to be hired for the maintenance of any opinion: when learned divines can afford to have a conscience: when universities are not a hundred years in knowledge behind all the rest of the world: when young ladies speak as they think, and when those who shudder at a tale of the horrors of slavery will deprive their own palates of a sweet taste, for the purpose of contributing all in their power to its extinction:—why then, Forester, I will lay down my barouche.

CHAPTER XXV.

THE WALK.

They were to pass, in their return, through an estate belonging to Mr. Forester, for the purpose of taking up his aunt Miss Evergreen, who was to accompany them to Redrose Abbey. On arriving at an inn on the nearest point of the great road, Mr. Forester told Sir Telegraph, that, from the arrangements he had made, it was impossible for any carriage to enter his estate, as he had taken every precaution for preserving the simplicity of his tenants from the contagious exhibitions and examples of luxury. "This road," said he, "is only accessible to pedestrians and equestrians: I have no wish to exclude the visits of laudable curiosity, but there is nothing I so much dread and deprecate as the intrusion of those heartless fops, who take their fashionable autumnal tour, to gape at rocks and waterfalls, for which they have neither eyes nor ears, and to pervert the feelings and habits of the once simple dwellers of the mountains.*[1] Nature seems to have raised her mountain-

---

* "Much have those travellers to answer for, whose casual intercourse with this innocent and simple people tends to corrupt them; disseminating among them ideas of extravagance and dissipation—giving them a taste for pleasures and gratifications of which they had no ideas—inspiring them with discontent at home—and tainting their rough industrious manners with idleness and a thirst after dishonest means.

"If travellers would frequent this country, with a view to examine its grandeur and beauty, or to explore its varied and curious regions with the eye of philosophy — if, in their passage through it, they could be content with such fare as the country produces, or at least reconcile themselves to it, by manly exercise and fatigue (for there is a time when the stomach and the plainest food will be found in perfect harmony)—if they could thus, instead of corrupting the manners of an innocent people, learn to amend their own, by seeing in how narrow a compass the wants of human life may be compressed—a journey through these wild scenes might be attended, perhaps, with more improvement than a journey to Rome or Paris. Where manners are polished into vicious refinement, simplifying is the best mode of improving; and the example of innocence is a more instructive lesson than any that can be taught by artists and literati.

barriers for the purpose of rescuing a few favoured mortals from the vortex of that torrent of physical and moral degeneracy, which seems to threaten nothing less than the extermination of the human species˙: but in vain, while the annual opening of its sluices lets out a side stream of the worst specimens of what is called refined society, to inundate the mountain valleys with the corruptions of metropolitan folly. Thus innocence, and health, and simplicity of life and manners, are banished from their last retirement, and no where more lamentably so than in the romantic scenery of the northern lakes, where every wonder of nature is made an article of trade, where the cataracts are locked up, and the echoes are sold: so that even the rustic character of that ill-fated region is condemned to participate in the moral stigma which must dwell indelibly on its poetical name."

The party alighted, and a consultation being held, it was resolved to walk to the village in a body, the Honourable Mrs. Pinmoney lifting up her hands and eyes in profound astonishment at Mr. Forester's old-fashioned notions.

"But these parts are too often the resort of gay company, who are under no impressions of this kind—who have no ideas but of extending the sphere of their amusements, or of varying a life of dissipation. The grandeur of the country is not taken into the question, or at least it is no otherwise considered than as affording some new mode of pleasurable enjoyment. Thus, even the diversions of Newmarket are introduced—diversions, one would imagine, more foreign to the nature of this country than any other. A number of horses are carried into the middle of the lake in a flat boat: a plug is drawn from the bottom: the boat sinks, and the horses are left floating on the surface. In different directions they make to land, and the horse which arrives soonest secures the prize."—GILPIN's *Picturesque Observations on Cumberland and Westmoreland*, vol. ii. p. 67.

˙ "The necessary consequence of men living in so unnatural a way with respect to houses, clothes, and diet, and continuing to live so for many generations, each generation adding to the vices, diseases, and weaknesses produced by the unnatural life of the preceding, is, that they must gradually decline in strength, health, and longevity, till at length the race dies out. To deny this would be to deny that the life allotted by nature to man is the best life for the preservation of his health and strength; for, if it be so, I think it is demonstration that the constant deviation from it, going on for many centuries, must end in the extinction of the race."—*Ancient Metaphysics*, vol. v. p. 237.

They followed a narrow winding path, through rocky and sylvan hills. They walked in straggling parties of ones, twos, and threes. Mr. Forester and Anthelia went first. Sir Oran Haut-ton followed alone, playing a pensive tune on his flute. Sir Telegraph Paxarett walked between his aunt and cousin, the Honourable Mrs. Pinmoney and Miss Danaretta. Mr. Hippy, in a melancholy vein, brought up the rear with Mr. Fax. A very beautiful child which had sat on the old gentleman's knee, at the inn where they breakfasted, had thrown him, not for the first time on a similar occasion, into a fit of dismal repentance, that he had not one of his own: he stalked along accordingly, with a most ruefully lengthened aspect, uttering every now and then a deep-drawn sigh. Mr. Fax in philosophic sympathy determined to console him, by pointing out to him the true nature and tendency of the principle of population, and the enormous evils resulting from the multiplication of the human species: observing, that the only true criterion of the happiness of a nation was to be found in the number of its old maids and bachelors, whom he venerated as the sources and symbols of prosperity and peace. Poor Mr. Hippy walked on sighing and groaning, deaf as the adder to the voice of the charmer:[2] for, in spite of all the eloquence of the antipopulationist, the image of the beautiful child which he had danced on his knee, continued to haunt his imagination, and threatened him with the blue devils for the rest of the day.

"I see," said Sir Telegraph to Mrs. Pinmoney, "my hopes are at an end. Forester is the happy man, though I am by no means sure that he knows it himself."

"Impossible," said Mrs. Pinmoney: "Anthelia may be amused a little while with his rhapsodies, but nothing more, believe me. The man is out of his mind. Do you know, I heard him say the other day, 'that not a shilling of his property was his own, that it was a portion of the general possession of human society, of which the distribution had devolved upon him; and that for the mode of that distribution he was most rigidly responsible to the principles of immutable justice. If such a mode of talking——"

"And acting too," said Sir Telegraph; "for I assure you he quadrates[3] his practice as nearly as he can to his theory."

"Monstrous!" said Mrs. Pinmoney: "what would our reverend friend, poor dear Doctor Bosky, say to him? But if such a way of talking and acting be the way to win a young heiress, I shall think the whole world is turned topsy-turvy."

"Your remark would be just," said Sir Telegraph, "were that young heiress any other than Anthelia Melincourt."

"Well," said Mrs. Pinmoney, "there are maidens in Scotland more lovely by far——"

"That I deny," said Sir Telegraph.

"Who will gladly be bride to the young Lochinvar,"[4] proceeded Mrs. Pinmoney.

"That will not do," said Sir Telegraph: "I shall resign with the best grace I can muster to a more favoured candidate, but I shall never think of another choice."

"Twelve months hence," said Mrs. Pinmoney, "you will tell another tale. In the mean time you will not die of despair as long as there is a good turnpike road and a pipe of Madeira in England."

"You will find," said Mr. Forester to Anthelia, "in the little valley we are about to enter, a few specimens of that simple and natural life which approaches as nearly as the present state of things will admit, to my ideas of the habits and manners of the primæval agriculturists, or the fathers of the Roman republic. You will think perhaps of Fabricius under his oak,[5] of Curius in his cottage,[6] of Regulus,[7] when he solicited recall from the command of an army, because the man whom he had intrusted, in his absence, with the cultivation of his field and garden, had run away with his spade and rake, by which his wife and children were left without support; and when the senate decreed that the implements should be replaced, and a man provided at the public expense to maintain the consul's family, by cultivating his fields in his absence. Then poverty was as honourable, as it is now disgraceful: then the same public respect was given to him who could most simplify his habits and manners, that is now paid exclusively to those who can make the most shameless parade of wanton and selfish prodigality. Those days are past for ever: but it is something in the present time to resuscitate their memory, to call up even the shadow of the reflection of republican Rome—*Rome, the seat of glory and of virtue, if ever they had one on earth.* ”*8

"You excite my curiosity very highly," said Anthelia; "for, from the time when I read

> "——in those dear books that first
> Woke in my heart the love of poesy,
> How with the villagers Erminia dwelt,
> And Calidore, for a fair shepherdess,
> Forgot his quest to learn the shepherd's lore;"9

how much have I regretted never to discover in the actual inhabitants of the country, the realization of the pictures of Spenser and Tasso!"

"The palaces," said Mr. Forester, "that every where rise around them to shame the meanness of their humble dwellings, the great roads that every where intersect their valleys, and bring them continually in contact with the overflowing corruption of cities, the devastating monopoly of large farms, that has almost swept the race of cottagers from the face of the earth, sending the parents to the workhouse or the army, and

---

* "Rome, le siège de la gloire et de la vertu, si jamais elles en eurent un sur la terre." —ROUSSEAU.

the children to perish like untimely blossoms in the blighting imprisonment of manufactories, have combined to diminish the numbers and deteriorate the character of the inhabitants of the country: but whatever be the increasing ravages of the Triad of Mammon, avarice, luxury, and disease, they will always be the last involved in the vortex of progressive degeneracy, realizing the beautiful fiction of ancient poetry, that, when primæval Justice departed from the earth, her last steps were among the cultivators of the fields."*

* ——extrema per illos
Justitia, excedens terris, vestigia fecit.—Virg.[10]

CHAPTER XXVI.

THE COTTAGERS.

THE valley expanded into a spacious amphitheatre, with a beautiful stream winding among pastoral meadows, which, as well as the surrounding hills, were studded with cottages, each with its own trees, its little garden, and its farm. Sir Telegraph was astonished to find so many human dwellings in a space that, on the modern tactics of rural œconomy, appeared only sufficient for three or four *moderate* farms; and Mr. Fax looked perfectly aghast to perceive the principle of population in such a fearful state of activity. Mrs. and Miss Pinmoney expressed their surprise at not seeing a single lordly mansion asserting its regal pre-eminence over the dwellings of its miserable vassals; while the voices of the children at play served only to condense the vapours that offuscated the imagination of poor Mr. Hippy. Anthelia, as their path wound among the cottages, was more and more delighted with the neatness and comfort of the dwellings, the exquisite order of the gardens, the ingenuous air of happiness and liberty that characterized the simple inhabitants, and the health and beauty of the little rosy children that were sporting in the fields. Mr. Forester had been recognised from a distance. The cottagers ran out in all directions to welcome him: the valley and the hills seemed starting into life, as men, women, and children poured down, as with one impulse, on the path of his approach, while some hastened to the residence of Miss Evergreen, ambitious of being the first to announce to her the arrival of her nephew. Miss Evergreen came forward to meet the party, surrounded by a rustic crowd of both sexes and of every age, from the old man leaning on his stick, to the little child that could just run alone, but had already learned to attach something magical to the sound of the name of Forester.

The first idea they entertained at the sight of his party was, that he was married, and had brought his bride to visit his little colony; and Anthelia was somewhat disconcerted by the benedictions that were poured upon her under this impression of the warm-hearted rustics.

They entered Miss Evergreen's cottage, which was small, but in a style of beautiful simplicity. Anthelia was much pleased with her countenance and manners; for Miss Evergreen was an amiable and intelligent woman, and was single, not from having wanted lovers, but from being of that order of minds which can love but once.

Mr. Fax took occasion, during a temporary absence of Miss Evergreen from the apartment in which they were taking refreshment, to say, he was happy to have seen so amiable a specimen of that injured and calumniated class of human beings commonly called old maids, who were often so from possessing in too high a degree the qualities most conducive to domestic happiness; for it might naturally be imagined, that the least refined and delicate minds would be the soonest satisfied in the choice of a partner, and the most ready to repair the loss of a first love by the substitution of a second. This might have led to a discussion, but Miss Evergreen's re-entrance prevented it. They now strolled out among the cottages in detached parties and in different directions. Mr. Fax attached himself to Mr. Hippy and Miss Evergreen. Anthelia and Mr. Forester went their own way. She was above the little affectation of feeling her *dignity* offended, as our female novel-writers express it, by the notions which the peasants had formed respecting her. "You see," said Mr. Forester, "I have endeavoured as much as possible to recall the images of better times, when the country was well peopled, from the farms being small, and cultivated chiefly by cottagers who lived in what was in Scotland called a *cottar town.*[*][1] Now you may go over vast tracts of country without seeing any thing like an *old English cottage,* to say nothing of the fearful difference which has been caused in the interior of the few that remain by the pressure of exorbitant taxation, of which the real, though not the nominal burden always falls most heavily on the labouring classes, backed by that *canker at the heart of national prosperity,* the imaginary riches of paper-credit,[2] of which the means are delusion, the progress monopoly, and the ultimate effect the extinction of the best portion of national population, a healthy and industrious peasantry. Large farms bring more rent to the landlord, and, therefore, landlords in general make no scruple to increase their rents by depopulating their estates,[†][3] though Anthelia Melincourt will not comprehend the mental principle in which such feelings originate."

"Is it possible," said Anthelia, "that you, so young as you are, can have created such a scene as this?"

"My father," said Mr. Forester, "began what I merely perpetuate. He estimated his riches, not by the amount of rent his estate produced, but the number of simple and happy beings it maintained. He divided it into little farms of such a size as were sufficient, even in indifferent seasons, to produce rather more than the necessities of their cultivators required. So that all these cottagers are rich according to the definition of Socrates;[‡][4] for they have at all times a little more than they actually need, a subsidium[5] for age, or sickness, or any accidental necessity."

They entered several of the cottages, and found in them all the same traces of comfort and content, and the same

---

[*] Ancient Metaphysics, vol. v. book iv. chap. 8.
[†] Ancient Metaphysics, vol. v. book iv. chap. 8.
[‡] See Xenophon's Memorabilia.

images of the better days of England: the clean-tiled floor, the polished beechen table, the tea-cups on the chimney, the dresser with its glittering dishes, the old woman with her spinning-wheel by the fire, and the old man with his little grandson in the garden, giving him his first lessons in the use of the spade, the goodwife busy in her domestic arrangements, and the pot boiling on the fire for the return of her husband from his labour in the field.

"Is it not astonishing," said Mr. Forester, "that there should be any who think, as I know many do, the number of cottagers on their land a grievance, and desire to be quit of them,[*][6] and have no feeling of remorse in allotting to one solitary family as much extent of cultivated land as was ploughed by the whole Roman people in the days of Cincinnatus?[†][7] The three great points of every political system are the health, the morals, and the number of the people. Without health and morals, the people cannot be happy; but without numbers they cannot be a great and powerful nation, nor even exist for any considerable time.[‡][8] And by numbers I do not mean the inhabitants of the cities, the sordid and sickly victims of commerce, and the effeminate and enervated slaves of luxury; but in estimating the power and the riches of a country I take my only criterion from its agricultural population."

---

[*] Ancient Metaphysics, vol. v. book iv. chap. 8.
[†] Si tantum culti solus possederis agri,
    Quantum sub Tatio populus Romanus arabat.—Juv.
[‡] Ancient Metaphysics, vol. v. book iv. chap. 8.

CHAPTER XXVII.

THE ANTI-SACCHARINE FETE.

MISS Evergreen accompanied them in their return, to preside at the Anti-saccharine fête. Mr. Hippy was turned out to make room for her in the barouche, and took his seat on the roof with Messieurs Forester and Fax. Anthelia no longer deemed it necessary to keep a guard over her heart; the bud of mutual affection between herself and Mr. Forester, both being, as they were, perfectly free and perfectly ingenuous, was rapidly expanding into the full bloom of happiness: they dreamed not that evil was near to check, if not to wither it.

The whole party was prevailed on by Miss Evergreen to be her guests at Redrose Abbey till after the Anti-saccharine fête, which very shortly took place, and was attended by the principal members of the Anti-saccharine Society, and by an illustrious assemblage from near and from far: amongst the rest by our old acquaintance, Mr. Derrydown, Mr. O'Scarum, Major O'Dogskin, Mr. Sarcastic, the Reverend Mr. Portpipe, and Mr. Feathernest the poet, who brought with him his friend Mr. Vamp the reviewer. Lord Anophel Achthar and the Reverend Mr. Grovelgrub deemed it not expedient to join the party, but ensconced themselves in Alga Castle, studying *michin malicho,* which means mischief.[1]

The Anti-saccharine fête commenced with a splendid dinner, as Mr. Forester thought to make luxury on this occasion subservient to morality, by showing what culinary art could effect without the intervention of West Indian produce; and the preparers of the feast, under the superintendence of Miss Evergreen, had succeeded so well, that the company testified very general satisfaction, except that a worthy Alderman and Baronet[2] from London (who had been studying the

picturesque at Low-wood Inn, and had given several manifestations of exquisite taste that had completely won the
hearts of Mr. O'Scarum and Major O'Dogskin) having just
helped himself to a slice of venison, fell back aghast against
the back of his chair, and dropped the knife and fork from
his nerveless hands, on finding that currant-jelly was prohibited: but being recovered by an application of the Honourable
Mrs. Pinmoney's vinaigrette, he proceeded to revenge himself
on a very fine pheasant, which he washed down with floods
of Madeira, being never at a loss for some one to take wine
with him, as he had the good fortune to sit opposite to the
Reverend Mr. Portpipe, who was *toujours prêt*[3] on the occasion, and a *coup-d'œil*[4] between them arranged the whole preliminary of the compotatory[5] ceremonial.

After dinner Mr. Forester addressed the company. They had
seen, he said, that culinary luxury could be carried to a great
degree of refinement without the intervention of West Indian
produce: and though he himself deprecated luxury altogether,
yet he would wave[6] that point for the present, and concede a
certain degree of it to those who fancied they could not do
without it, if they would only in return make so very slight a
concession to philanthropy, to justice, to liberty, to every feeling
of human sympathy, as to abstain from an indulgence which
was obtained by the most atrocious violation of them all, an
indulgence of which the foundations were tyranny, robbery,
and murder, and every form of evil, anguish, and oppression,
at which humanity shudders; all which were comprehended
in the single name of SLAVERY. "Sugar," said he, "is œconomically superfluous, nay, worse than superfluous: in the middling
classes of life it is a formidable addition to the expenses of a
large family, and for no benefit, for no addition to the stock of
domestic comfort, which is often sacrificed in more essential
points to this frivolous and wanton indulgence. It is physically

pernicious, as its destruction of the teeth, and its effects on the health of children much pampered with sweetmeats, sufficiently demonstrate. It is morally atrocious, from being the primary cause of the most complicated corporeal suffering and the most abject mental degradation that ever outraged the form, and polluted the spirit of man. It is politically abominable, for covering with every variety of wretchedness some of the fairest portions of the earth, which, if the inhabitants of free countries could be persuaded *to abstain from sugar, till it were sent to them by freemen,* might soon become the abodes of happiness and liberty. Slaves cannot breathe in the air of England: 'They touch our country, and their fetters fall.'[7] Who is there among you that is not proud of this distinction?— Yet this is not enough: the produce of the labour of slavery should be banished from our shores. Not any thing—not an atom of any thing, should enter an Englishman's dwelling, on which the Genius of Liberty had not set his seal. What would become of slavery if there were no consumers of its produce? Yet I have seen a party of pretended philanthropists sitting round a tea-table, and while they dropped the sugar into their cups, repeat some tale of the sufferings of a slave, and execrate the colonial planters, who are but their caterers and stewards— the obsequious ministers of their unfeeling sensuality! O my fair countrywomen! you who have such tender hearts, such affectionate spirits, such amiable and delicate feelings, do you consider the mass of mischief and cruelty to which you contribute, nay, of which you are among the primary causes, when you indulge yourselves in so paltry, so contemptible a gratification as results from the use of sugar? while to abstain from it entirely, is a privation so trivial, that it is most wonderful to think that Justice and Charity should have such a boon to beg from Beauty in the name of the blood and the tears of human beings. Be not deterred by the idea that you will have few companions by the better way: so much the rather should it be strictly followed by amiable and benevolent minds.* Secure to yourselves at least the delightful consciousness of reflecting that you are in no way whatever accomplices in the cruelty and crime of slavery, and accomplices in it you certainly are, nay, its very original springs, as long as you are receivers and consumers of its iniquitous acquisitions."

"I will answer you, Mr. Forester," said Mr. Sarcastic, "for myself and the rest of the company. You shock our feelings excessively by calling us the primary causes of slavery; and there are very few among us who have not shuddered at the tales of West Indian cruelty. I assure you we are very liberal of theoretical sympathy; but as to practical abstinence from the use of sugar, do you consider what it is you require? Do you consider how very agreeable to us is the sensation of sweetness in our palates? Do you suppose we would give up that sensation because human creatures of the same flesh and blood as ourselves are oppressed and enslaved, and flogged and tortured, to procure it for us? Do you consider that Custom† is

---

* "Pochi compagni avrai per l'altra via:
Tanto ti prego più, gentile spirto,
Non lasciar la magnanima tua impresa."
                                    PETRARCA.[8]

† "If it were seriously asked (and it would be no untimely question), who of all teachers and masters that have ever taught hath drawn the most disciples after him, both in religion and in manners, it might be not untruly answered, Custom. Though Virtue be commended for the most persuasive in her theory, and Conscience in the plain demonstration of the spirit finds most evincing; yet, whether it be the secret of divine will, or the original blindness we are born in, so it happens for the most part, that Custom still is silently received for the best instructor. Except it be because her method is so glib and easy, in some manner like to that vision of Ezekiel, rolling up her sudden book of implicit knowledge, for him that will to take and swallow down at pleasure; which proving but of bad nourishment in the concoction, as it was heedless in the devouring, puffs up unhealthily a certain big face of pretended learning, mistaken among credulous men for the wholesome habit of soundness and good constitution, but is, indeed, no other than that swoln visage of counterfeit knowledge and literature which not only in private mars our education, but also in public is the common climber into every chair where either religion is preached or law reported, filling each estate of life and profession with abject and servile principles, depressing the high and heaven-born spirit of man, far beneath the condition wherein either God created him, or sin hath sunk him. To pursue the allegory, Custom being

the great lord and master of our conduct?[9] And do you suppose that any feelings of pity, and sympathy, and charity, and benevolence, and justice, will overcome the power of Custom, more especially where any pleasure of sense is attached to his dominion? In appealing to our pockets, indeed, you touched us to the quick: you aimed your eloquence at our weak side— you hit us in the vulnerable point; but if it should appear that in this particular we really might save our money, yet being expended in a matter of personal and sensual gratification, it is not to be supposed so completely lost and wasted as it would be if it were given either to a friend or a stranger in distress. I will admit, however, that you have touched our feelings a little, but this disagreeable impression will soon wear off: with some of us it will last as long as pity for a starving beggar, and with others as long as grief for the death of a friend; and I find, on a very accurate average calculation, that the duration of the former may be considered to be at least three minutes, and that of the latter at most ten days."

"Mr. Sarcastic," said Anthelia, "you do not render justice to the feelings of the company; nor is human nature so selfish

---

but a mere face, as Echo is a mere voice, rests not in her unaccomplishment, until by secret inclination she accorporate herself with Error, who being a blind and serpentine body, without a head, willingly accepts what he wants, and supplies what her incompleteness went seeking: hence it is that Error supports Custom, Custom countenances Error, and these two, between them, would persecute and chase away all truth and solid wisdom out of human life, were it not that God, rather than man, once in many ages calls together the prudent aud religious counsels of men deputed to repress the encroachments, and to work off the inveterate blots and obscurities wrought upon our minds by the subtle insinuating of Error and Custom, who, with the numerous and vulgar train of their followers, make it their chief design to envy and cry down the industry of free reasoning, under the terms of humour and innovation, as if the womb of teeming Truth were to be closed up, if she presume to bring forth aught that sorts not with their unchewed notions and suppositions; against which notorious injury and abuse of man's free soul, to testify and oppose the utmost that study and true labour can attain, heretofore the incitement of men reputed grave hath led me among others, and now the duty and the right of an instructed Christian calls me through the chance of good or evil report TO BE THE SOLE ADVOCATE OF A DISCOUNTENANCED TRUTH." —MILTON: *The Doctrine and Discipline of Divorce.*

and perverted as you seem to consider it. Though there are undoubtedly many who sacrifice the general happiness of human kind to their own selfish gratification, yet even these, I am willing to believe, err not in cruelty but in ignorance, from not seeing the consequences of their own actions; but it is not by persuading them that all the world is as bad as themselves, that you will give them clearer views and better feelings. Many are the modes of evil—many the scenes of human suffering; but if the general condition of man is ever to be ameliorated, it can only be through the medium of BELIEF IN HUMAN VIRTUE."

"Well, Forester," said Sir Telegraph, "if you wish to increase the numbers of the Anti-saccharine Society, set me down for one."

"Remember," said Mr. Forester, "by enrolling your name among us you pledge yourself to perpetual abstinence from West Indian produce."

"I am aware of it," said Sir Telegraph, "and you shall find me zealous in the cause."

The fat Alderman cried out about the ruin of commerce, and Mr. Vamp was very hot on the subject of the revenue. The question was warmly canvassed, and many of the party who had not been quite persuaded by what Mr. Forester had said in behalf of the Anti-saccharine system, were perfectly convinced in its favour when they had heard what Mr. Vamp and the fat Alderman had to say against it; and the consequence was, that, in spite of Mr. Sarcastic's opinion of the general selfishness of mankind, the numbers of the Anti-saccharine Society were very considerably augmented.

"You see," said Mr. Fax to Mr. Sarcastic, "the efficacy of associated sympathies. It is but to give an impulse of co-operation to any good and generous feeling, and its progressive accumulation, like that of an Alpine avalanche, though but a snowball at the summit, becomes a mountain in the valley."

CHAPTER XXVIII.

THE CHESS DANCE.

THE dinner was followed by a ball, for the opening of which Sir Telegraph Paxarett, who officiated as master of the ceremonies, had devised a fanciful scheme,[1] and had procured for the purpose a number of appropriate masquerade dresses. An extensive area in the middle of the ball-room was chalked out into sixty-four squares of alternate white and red, in lines of eight squares each. Sir Telegraph, while the rest of the company was sipping, not without many wry faces, their anti-saccharine tea, called out into another apartment the gentlemen whom he had fixed on to perform in his little ballet; and Miss Evergreen at the same time withdrew with the intended female performers. Sir Telegraph now invested Mr. Hippy with the dignity of White King, Major O'Dogskin with that of Black King, and the Reverend Mr. Portpipe with that of White Bishop, which the latter hailed as a favourable omen, not precisely comprehending what was going forward. As the reverend gentleman was the only one of his cloth in the company, Sir Telegraph was under the necessity of appointing three lay Bishops, whom he fixed on in the persons of two country squires, Mr. Hermitage and Mr. Heeltap,[2] and of the fat Alderman already mentioned, Sir Gregory Greenmould.[3] Sir Telegraph himself, Mr. O'Scarum, Mr. Derrydown, and Mr. Sarcastic, were the Knights: and the Rooks were Mr. Feathernest the poet; Mr. Paperstamp,[4] another variety of the same genus, chiefly remarkable for an affected infantine lisp in his speech, and for always wearing waistcoats of duffil grey; Mr. Vamp the Reviewer; and Mr. Killthedead,[5] from Frogmarsh Hall, a great compounder of narcotics, under the denomination of

BATTLES, for he never heard of a deadly field, especially if dotage and superstition, to which he was very partial, gained the advantage over generosity and talent, both of which he abhorred, but immediately seizing his goosequill and foolscap,

> He fought the BATTLE o'er again,
> And thrice he slew the slain.[6]

Mr. Feathernest was a little nettled on being told that he was to be the *King's Rook*,[7] but smoothed his wrinkled brow on being assured that no *mauvaise plaisanterie*[8] was intended.

The Kings were accordingly crowned, and attired in regal robes. The Reverend Mr. Portpipe and his three brother Bishops were arrayed in full canonicals.[9] The Knights were equipped in their white and black armour, with sword, and dazzling helm, and nodding crest.[10] The Rooks were enveloped in a sort of mural robe,[11] with a headpiece formed on the model of that which occurs in the ancient figures of Cybele; and thus attired, they bore a very striking resemblance to the walking wall in Pyramus and Thisbe.[12]

The Kings now led the way to the ball-room, and the two beautiful Queens, Miss Danaretta Contantina Pinmoney, and Miss Celandina Paperstamp,[13] each with eight beautiful Nymphs, arrayed for the mimic field in light Amazonian dresses, white and black, did such instant execution among the hearts of the young gentlemen present, that they might be said to have "fought and conquered ere a sword was drawn."[14]

They now proceeded to their stations on their respective squares; but before we describe their manœuvres, we will recapitulate the

TRIPUDII PERSONÆ.[15]

WHITE.

King . . .	Mr. Hippy.
Queen . . .	Miss Danaretta Contantina Pinmoney.
King's Bishop	The Reverend Mr. Portpipe.
Queen's Bishop	Sir Gregory Greenmould.
King's Knight	Mr. O'Scarum.
Queen's Knight	Sir Telegraph Paxarett.
King's Rook .	Mr. Feathernest.
Queen's Rook .	Mr. Paperstamp.
Eight Nymphs.	

BLACK.

King	Major O'Dogskin.
Queen . . .	Miss Celandina Paperstamp.
King's Bishop .	Squire Hermitage.
Queen's Bishop	Squire Heeltap.
King's Knight	Mr. Sarcastic.
Queen's Knight	Mr. Derrydown.
King's Rook .	Mr. Killthedead.
Queen's Rook .	Mr. Vamp.
Eight Nymphs.	

Mr. Hippy took his station on a black square, near the centre of one of the extreme lines, and Major O'Dogskin on an opposite white square of the parallel extreme. The Queens, who were to command in chief, stood on the left of the Kings: the Bishops were posted to the right and left of their respective Sovereigns; the Knights next to the Bishops; the corners were occupied by the Rooks. The two lines in front of these principal personages were occupied by the Nymphs;—a space of four lines of eight squares each being left between the opposite parties for the field of action.

The array was now complete, with the exception of the Reverend Mr. Portpipe, who being called by Miss Danaretta to take his place at the right hand of Mr. Hippy, and perceiving that he should be necessitated, in his character of Bishop, to take a very active part in the diversion, began to exclaim with great vehemence, NOLO EPISCOPARI![16] which is probably the only occasion on which these words were ever used with sincerity. But Mr. O'Scarum, in his capacity of White Knight, pounced on the reluctant divine, and placing him between himself and Mr. Hippy, stood by him with his sword drawn, as if to prevent his escape; then clapping a sword into the hand of the reverend gentleman, exhorted him to conduct himself in a manner becoming an efficient member of the true church militant.[17]

Lots were then cast for the privilege of attack; and the chance falling on Miss Danaretta, the music struck up the tune of *The Triumph*,[18] and the whole of the white party began dancing, with their faces towards the King, performing at the same time various manœuvres of the sword exercise, with appropriate pantomimic gestures, expressive of their entire devotion to His Majesty's service, and their desire to be immediately sent forward on active duty. In vain did the Reverend Mr. Portpipe remonstrate with Mr. O'Scarum that his dancing days were over: the inexorable Knight compelled him to caper and flourish his sword, "till the toil-drops fell from his brows like rain."[19] Sir Gregory Greenmould did his best on the occasion, and danced like an elephant in black drapery; but Miss Danaretta and her eight lovely Nymphs rescued the exertions of the male performers from too critical observation. King Hippy received the proffered service of his army with truly royal condescension. Miss Danaretta waved her sword with inimitable grace, and made a sign to the damsel in front of the King to advance two squares.[20] The same manœuvres now took place on the black side; and Miss Celandina sent forward the Nymph in front of Major O'Dogskin to obstruct the further progress of the white damsel. The dancing now recommenced on the white side, and Miss Danaretta ordered out the Reverend Mr. Portpipe to occupy the fourth square in front of Squire Heeltap. The reverend gentleman rolled forward with great alacrity, in the secret hope that he should very soon be taken prisoner, and put *hors de combat*[21] for the rest of the evening. Squire Hermitage was detached by Miss Celandina on a similar service; and these two episcopal heroes being thus brought together in the centre of the field, entered, like Glaucus and Diomede, into a friendly parle,[22] in the course of which the words Claret and Burgundy were repeatedly overheard. The music frequently varied, as in a pantomime, according to circumstances: the manœuvres were always directed by the waving of the sword of the Queen, and were always preceded by the dancing of the whole party, in the manner we have mentioned, which continued *ad libitum*,[23] till she had decided on her movement. The Nymph in front of Sir Gregory Greenmould advanced one square. Mr. Sarcastic stepped forward to the third square of Squire Hermitage. Miss Danaretta's Nymph advanced two squares, and being immediately taken prisoner by the Nymph of Major O'Dogskin, conceded her place with a graceful bow, and retired from the field. The Nymph in front of Sir Gregory Greenmould avenged the fate of her companion; and Mr. Hippy's Nymph withdrew in a similar manner. Squire Hermitage was compelled to cut short his conversation with Mr. Portpipe, and retire to the third square in front of Mr. Derrydown. Sir Telegraph skipped into the place which Sir Gregory Greenmould's Nymph had last forsaken. Mr. Killthedead danced into the deserted quarters of Squire Hermitage, and Major O'Dogskin swept round him with a minuet[24] step into those of Mr. Sarcastic. To carry on the detail would require more time than we can spare, and, perhaps, more patience than our readers possess. The Reverend Mr. Portpipe saw his party fall around him, one by one, and survived against his will to the close of the contest. Miss Danaretta and Miss Celandina moved like light over the squares, and Fortune alternately smiled and frowned on their respective banners, till the heavy mural artillery of Mr. Vamp being brought to bear on Mr. Paperstamp, who fancied himself a tower of strength, the latter was overthrown and carried off the field. Mr. Feathernest avenged his fate on the embattled front of Mr. Killthedead, and fell himself beneath the sword of Mr. Sarcastic. Squire Heeltap was taken off by the Reverend Mr. Portpipe, who begged his courteous prisoner to walk to the sideboard and bring him a glass of Madeira; for Homer, he said, was very orthodox in his opinion that wine was a great refresher in the toils of war.*[25] The changeful scene concluded by Miss Danaretta, with the aid of Sir Telegraph and the Reverend Mr. Portpipe, hemming Major O'Dogskin into a corner, where he was reduced to an incapacity of locomotion;[26] on which the Major bowed, and made the best of his way to the sideboard, followed by the reverend gentleman, who, after joining the Major in a pacific libation, threw himself into an arm-chair, and slept very comfortably till the annunciation of supper.

Waltzes,[27] quadrilles,[28] and country dances followed in succession, and, with the exception of the interval of supper, in which Miss Evergreen developed all the treasures of anti-saccharine taste, were kept up with great spirit till the rising of the sun.

Anthelia, who of course did not join in the former, expressed to Mr. Forester her astonishment to see waltzing in Redrose Abbey. "I did not dream of such a thing," said Mr. Forester; "but I left the whole arrangement of the ball to Sir Telegraph, and I suppose, he deemed it incumbent on him to consult *the general taste of the young ladies.* Even I, young

---

* *Iλ. Z.* 261.

as I am, can remember the time when there was no point of resemblance between an English girl in a private ball-room, and a French *figurante*[29] in a theatrical *ballet:* but waltzing and Parisian drapery have levelled the distinction, and the only criterion of the difference is the place of the exhibition. Thus every succeeding year witnesses some new inroad on the simple manners of our ancestors; some importation of continental vice and folly; some unnatural fretwork of tinsel and frippery on the old Doric column[30] of the domestic virtues of England. An Englishman in stays,[31] and an Englishwoman waltzing in treble-flounced short petticoats,[32] are anomalies so monstrous, that till they actually existed, they never entered the most ominous visions of the speculators on progressive degeneracy. What would our Alfred, what would our third Edward, what would our Milton, and Hampden, and Sidney, what would the barons of Runnymead[33] have thought, if the voice of prophecy had denounced to them a period, when, the perfection of accomplishment in the daughters of England would be found in the dress, manner, and action of the dancing girls of Paris?"

The supper, of course, did not pass off without songs; and among them Anthelia sang the following, which recalled to Mr. Forester their conversation on the sea-shore.

THE MORNING OF LOVE.[34]

O! the spring-time of life is the season of blooming,
And the morning of love is the season of joy;
Ere noontide and summer, with radiance consuming,
Look down on their beauty, to parch and destroy.
O! faint are the blossoms life's pathway adorning,
When the first magic glory of hope is withdrawn;
For the flowers of the spring, and the light of the morning,
Have no summer budding, and no second dawn.

Through meadows all sunshine, and verdure, and flowers,
The stream of the valley in purity flies;
But mixed with the tides, where some proud city lowers,
O! where is the sweetness that dwelt on its rise?
The rose withers fast on the breast it first graces;
Its beauty is fled ere the day be half done:—
And life is that stream which its progress defaces,
And love is that flower which can bloom but for one.

THE END OF VOL. II.

CHAPTER XXIX.

THE DISAPPEARANCE.

THE morning after the fête Anthelia and her party returned to Melincourt. Before they departed she conversed a few minutes alone with Mr. Forester in his library. What was said on this occasion we cannot precisely report; but it seemed to be generally suspected that Mr. Hippy's authority would soon be at an end, and that the services of the Reverend Mr. Portpipe would be required in the old chapel of Melincourt Castle, which, we are sorry to say, had fallen for some years past very much into disuse, being never opened but on occasions of birth, marriage, and death in the family; and these occasions, as our readers are aware, had not of late been very numerous.

The course of mutual love between Anthelia and Mr. Forester was as smooth[1] as the gliding of a skiff down a stream, through the flowery meadows of June: and if matters were not quite definitively settled between them, yet, as Mr. Forester was shortly to be a visitor at the Castle, there was a very apparent probability that their intercourse would terminate in that grand climax and finale of all romantic adventure—marriage.

After the departure of the ladies, Mr. Forester observed with concern, that his friend Sir Oran's natural melancholy was visibly increased, and Mr. Fax was of opinion that he was smitten with the tender passion: but whether for Miss Melincourt, Mrs. Pinmoney, or Miss Danaretta, it was not so easy to determine. But Sir Oran grew more and more fond of solitude, and passed the greater part of the day in the woods, though it was now the reign of the gloomy November, which, however, accorded with the moody temper of his spirit; and he often went without his breakfast, though he always came home to dinner. His perpetual companion was his flute, with which he made sad response to the wintry wind.

Mr. Forester and Mr. Fax were one morning consulting on the means to be adopted for diverting Sir Oran's melancholy, when Sir Telegraph Paxarett drove up furiously to the door—sprang from the box—and rushed into the apartment with the intelligence that Anthelia had disappeared. No one had seen her since the hour of breakfast on the preceding day. Mr. Hippy, Mr. Derrydown, Mr. O'Scarum, and Major O'Dogskin, were scouring the country in all directions in search of her.

Mr. Forester determined not to rest night or day till he had discovered Anthelia. Sir Telegraph drove him, with Mr. Fax and Sir Oran, to the nearest inn, where leaving Sir Telegraph to pursue another track, they took a chaise and four, and posted over the country in all directions, day after day, without finding any clue to her retreat. Mr. Forester had no doubt that this adventure was connected with that which we have detailed in the eighteenth Chapter;[2] but his ignorance of the actors on that occasion[3] prevented his deriving any light from the coincidence. At length, having investigated in vain all the main and cross roads for fifty miles round Melincourt, Mr. Fax was of opinion that she could not have passed so far along any of them, being conveyed, as no doubt she was, against her will, without leaving some trace of her course, which their indefatigable inquiries must have discovered. He therefore advised that they should discontinue their system of posting, and take a thorough pedestrian perlustration[4] of all the most bye and unfrequented paths of the whole mountain-district, in some secluded part of which he had a strong presentiment she would be found. This plan was adopted; but the season was unfavourable to its expeditious accomplishment; and they could sometimes make but little progress in a day, being often compelled to turn aside from the wilder tracks, in search of a town or village, for the purposes of refreshment or rest:—there being this remarkable difference between the lovers of the days of chivalry, and those of modern times, that the former could pass a week or two in a desert or a forest, without meat, drink, or shelter—a very useful art for all travellers, whether lovers or not, which these degenerate days have unfortunately lost.

They arrived in the evening of the first day of their pedestrianism at a little inn among the mountains. They were informed they could have no beds; and that the only parlour was occupied by two gentlemen, who meant to sit up all night, and would, perhaps, have no objection to their joining the party. A message being sent in, an affirmative answer was very politely returned: and on entering the apartment, they discovered Mr. O'Scarum and Major O'Dogskin engaged in a deep discussion over a large jug of wine.

"Troth, now," said Mr. O'Scarum, "and this is a merry meeting, sure enough, though it's on a dismal occasion, for it's Miss Melincourt you're looking for, as we are too, though you have most cause, Mr. Forester; for I understand you are to be the happy man. Troth, and I did not know so much when I came to your fête, or, perhaps, I should have been for arguing the point of a prior claim (as far as my own consent was concerned), over a bit of neat turf,⁵ twelve yards long; but Major O'Dogskin tells me, that by getting muzzy,⁶ and so I did, sure enough, on your old Madeira, and rare stuff it is, by my conscience, when Miss Melincourt was in your house, I have sanctioned the matter, and there's an end of it: but, by my soul, I did not mean to have been cut out quietly: and the Major says, too, you're too good a fellow to be kilt, and that's true enough: so I'll keep my ammunition for other friends; and here's to you and Miss Melincourt, and a happy meeting to you both, and the devil take him that parts you, says Harum O'Scarum."—"And so says Dermot O'Dogskin," said the Major. "And my friend O'Scarum and myself will ride about till we get news of her, for we don't mind a little hardship.—You shall be wanting some dinner, joys, and there's nothing but fat bacon and potatoes; but we have made a shift with it, and then here is the very creature itself, old sherry, my jewels! troth, and how did we come home by it, think you? I know what it is to pass a night in a little inn in the hills, and you don't find Major O'Dogskin turning out of the main road, without giving his man a couple of kegs of wine just to balance the back of his saddle. Sherry's a good traveller, and will stand a little shaking; and what would one do without it in such a place as this, where it is water in the desert, and manna in the wilderness?"[7]

Mr. Forester thanked them very warmly for their good wishes and active exertions. The humble dinner of himself and his party was soon dispatched; after which, the Major placed the two little kegs on the table, and said, "They were both filled to-day; so, you see, there is no lack of the good creature to keep us all alive till morning, and then we shall part again in search of Miss Melincourt, the jewel! for there is not such another on the face of the earth. Och!"[8] continued the Major, as he poured the wine from one of the kegs into a brown jug; for the house could not afford them a decanter, and some little ale tumblers supplied the place of wine-glasses; "Och! the ould jug, that never held any thing better than sour ale: how proud he must feel of being filled to the brim with sparkling sherry, for the first and last time in the course of his life!"

CHAPTER XXX.

THE PAPER-MILL.

Taking leave of Mr. O'Scarum and Major O'Dogskin, they continued their wanderings as choice or chance directed: sometimes penetrating into the most sequestered valleys; sometimes returning into the principal roads, and investigating the most populous districts. Passing through the town of Gullgudgeon,[1] they found an immense crowd assembled in a state of extreme confusion, exhibiting every symptom of hurry, anxiety, astonishment, and dismay. They stopped to inquire the cause of the tumult, and found it to proceed from the sudden explosion of a paper-mill, in other words, the stoppage of the country-bank of Messieurs Smokeshadow, Airbubble, Hopthetwig, and Company.[2] Farmers, bumpkins, artisans, mechanics, tradesmen of all descriptions, the innkeeper, the lawyer, the doctor, and the parson; soldiers from the adjoining barracks, and fishermen from the neighbouring coast, with their shrill-voiced and masculine wives, rolled in one mass, like a stormy wave, around a little shop, of which the shutters were closed, with the word BANK in golden letters over the door, and a large board on the central shutter, notifying that "Messieurs Smokeshadow, Airbubble, Hopthetwig, and Company, had found themselves under the disagreeable necessity of suspending their payments;" in plain English, had found it expedient to fly by night, leaving all the machinery of their mill, and all the treasures of their mine, that is to say, several reams of paper, half a dozen account-books, a desk, a joint-stool, an ink-stand, a bunch of quills, and a copper-plate, to satisfy the claims of the distracted multitude, who were shoaling in[3] from all quarters with *promises to pay*,[4] of the said Smokeshadow, Airbubble,

Hopthetwig, and Company, to the amount of a hundred thousand pounds.

Mr. Fax addressed himself for an explanation of particulars to a plump and portly divine, who was standing at a little distance from the rest of the crowd, and whose countenance exhibited no symptoms of the rage, grief, and despair, which were depicted in the physiognomies of his dearly-beloved brethren of the town of Gullgudgeon. "You seem, Sir," said Mr. Fax, "to bear the general calamity with Christian resignation."—"I do, Sir," said the reverend gentleman, "and for a very orthodox reason—I have none of their notes—not I. I was obliged to take them now and then against my will, but I always sent them off to town, and got cash[5] for them directly."

"You mean to say," said Mr. Forester, "you got a Threadneedle Street note for them."

"To be sure, Sir," said the divine, "and that is the same thing as cash. There is a Jacobin rascal[6] in this town, who says it is a bad sign when the children die before the parent, and that a day of reckoning[7] must come sooner or later for the old lady as well as for her daughters; but myself and my brother magistrates have taken measures for him, and shall soon make the town of Gullgudgeon too hot to hold him, as sure as my name is Peppertoast."[8]

"You seriously think, Sir," said Mr. Fax, "that his opinion is false?"

"Sir," said the reverend gentleman, somewhat nettled, "I do not know what right any one can have to ask a man of my cloth what he seriously thinks, when all that the world has to do with is what he seriously says."

"Then you seriously say it, Sir?" said Mr. Fax.

"I do, Sir," said the divine; "and for this very orthodox reason, that the system of paper-money is inseparably interwoven with the present order of things, and the present order of things I have made up my mind to stick by precisely as long as it lasts."

"*And no longer?*" said Mr. Fax.

"I am no fool, Sir," said the divine.

"But, Sir," said Mr. Fax, "as you seem to have perceived the instability of what was called (like *lucus à non lucendo*),⁹ the *firm* of Smokeshadow, Airbubble, Hopthetwig, and Company, why did you not warn your flock of the impending danger?"

"Sir," said the reverend gentleman, "I dined every week with one of the partners."

Mr. Forester took notice of an elderly woman, who was sitting with a small handful of dirty paper, weeping bitterly on the step of a door. "Forgive my intrusion," said he; "I need not ask you why you weep: the cause is in your hand."—"Ah, Sir!" said the poor woman, who could scarcely speak for sobbing, "all the savings of twenty years taken from me in a moment: and my poor boy, when he comes home from sea——" She could say no more: grief choked her utterance.

"Good God!" said Mr. Fax, "did you lay by your savings in country paper?"

"O Sir!" said the poor woman, "how was I to know that one piece of paper was not as good as another? And every body said that the firm of Smokeshadow, Airbubble, Hopthetwig, and Company, was as good as the Bank of England." She then unfolded one of the *promises to pay*, and fell to weeping more bitterly than ever. Mr. Forester comforted her as well as he could; but he found the purchasing of one or two of her notes much more efficacious than all the lessons of his philosophy.

"This is all your fault," said a fisherman to his wife: "you would be hoarding and hoarding, and stinting me of my drop of comfort when I came in after a hard day's work, tossed, and beaten, and wet through with salt-water, and there's what we've got by it."

"It was all your fault," retorted the wife: "when we had scraped together twenty as pretty golden guineas[10] as ever laid in a chest, you would sell 'em, so you would, for twenty-seven pounds of Mr. Smokeshadow's paper; *and now you see the difference.*"

"Here is an illustration," said Mr. Fax to Mr. Forester, "of the old maxim of *experience teaching wisdom*, or, as Homer expresses it, *Ρεχθεν δε τε νηπιος εγνω.*"[11]

"*We ought now to be convinced, if not before,*" said Mr. Forester, "*that what Plato has said is strictly true, that there will be no end of human misery till governors become philosophers, or philosophers governors;* and that all the evils which this country suffers, and, I fear, will suffer, to a much greater extent, from the bursting of this fatal bubble of paper-money—this chimerical symbol of imaginary riches—*are owing to the want of philosophy and true political wisdom in our rulers, by which they might have seen things in their causes, not felt them only in their effects, as every the most vulgar man does; and by which foresight, all the mischiefs that are befalling us might have been prevented.*"*[12]

"Very hard," said an old soldier, "very, very hard:—a poor five pounds, laid up for a rainy day—hardly got, and closely kept—very, very hard."

"Poor man!" said Mr. Forester, who was interested in the soldier's physiognomy, "let me repair your loss. Here is better paper for you; but get gold and silver for it as soon as you can."

"God bless your Honour," said the soldier, "and send as much power as good will to all such generous souls. Many is the worthy heart that this day's work will break, and here is more damage than one man can mend. God bless your Honour."

---

* The words in italics are Lord Monboddo's: Ancient Metaphysics, vol. iii. preface, p. 79.

A respectable-looking female approached the crowd, and addressing herself to Mr. Fax, who seemed most at leisure to attend to her, asked him what chance there seemed to be for the creditors of Messieurs Smokeshadow, Airbubble, Hopthetwig, and Company. "By what I can gather from the people around me," said Mr. Fax, "none whatever." The lady was in great distress at this intelligence, and said they were her bankers, and it was the second misfortune of the kind that had happened to her. Mr. Fax expressed his astonishment that she should have been twice the victim of the system of paper-coinage, which seemed to contradict the old adage about a burnt child; and said it was for his part astonishing to him how any human being could be so deluded after the perils of the system had been so clearly pointed out, and, amongst other things, in a pamphlet of his own on the Insubstantiality of Smoke. "Indeed," she said, "she had something better to do than to trouble herself about politics, and wondered he should insult her in her distress by talking of such stuff to her."

"Was ever such infatuation?" said Mr. Fax, as the lady turned away. "This is one of those persons who choose to walk blindfold on the edge of a precipice, because it is too much trouble to see,[13] and quarrel with their best friends for requesting them to make use of their eyes. There are many such, who think they have no business with politics: but they find to their cost that politics will have business with them."

"A curse light on all kite-flyers!" vociferated a sturdy farmer. "Od rabbit me! here be a bundle o' trash, measters! not worth a voive-and-zixpenny dollar[14] all together. This comes o'peaper-mills. 'I promise to pay,' ecod! O the good old days o' goulden guineas, when I used to ride whoame vrom market wi'a great heavy bag in my pocket; and when I wapped it down on the old oak teable, it used to make zuch a zound as did one's heart good to hear it. No *promise to pay* then. Now a man may eat his whole vortin in a zandwich, or zet vire to it in a vardin rushlight. Promise to pay!—the lying rascals, they never meant to pay: they knew all the while they had no effects to pay: but zuch a pretty, zmooth-spoken, palavering zet o' fellers! why, Lord bless you! they'd ha' made you believe black was white! and though you could never get any thing of 'em but one o' their own dirty bits o'peaper in change vor another, they made it out as clear as daylight, that they were as rich as zo many Jews. Ecod! and we were all vools enough to believe 'em, and now mark the end o't."

"Yes, father," said a young fop at his elbow, "all blown, curse me!"

"Ees," said the farmer, "and thee beest blown, and thee mun zell thy hunter, and turn to the plough-tail; and thy zisters mun churn butter, and milk the cows, instead o' jingling penny-vorties, and dancing at race-balls wi' squires. We mun be old English varmers again, and none o'your voine high-flying promise to pay gentlevolks. There they be—spell 'em: *I promise to pay to Mr. Gregory Gas, or bearer, on demand, the zum o' voive pounds. Gullgudgeon Bank, April the virst. Vor Zmokeshadow, Airbubble, Zelf, and Company, Henry Hopthetwig. Entered, William Walkoff.* And there be their coat o' arms: two black-smiths blowing a vorge, wi' the chimney vor a crest, and a wreath o' smoke coming out o' t; and the motto, 'YOU CAN'T CATCH A BOWL-FULL.' Od rabbit me! here be a whole handvul of 'em, and I'll zell 'em all vor a voive-and-zixpenny dollar."

The "Jacobin rascal," of whom the reverend gentleman had spoken, happened to be at the farmer's elbow. "I told you how it would be," said he, "Master Sheepshead, many years ago; and I remember you wanted to put me in the stocks for my trouble."

"Why I believe I did, Measter Lookout," said the farmer, with a very penitent face; "but if you'll call on me zome day we'll drown old grudges in a jug o' ale, and light our poipes wi' the promises o' Measter Hopthetwig and his gang."

"Not with all of them, I entreat you," said Mr. Lookout. "I hope you will have one of them framed and glazed, and suspended over your chimney, as a warning to your children, and your children's children for ever, against '*the blessed comforts of paper-money*.'"

"Why, Lord love you, Measter Lookout," said the farmer, "we shall ha' nothing but peaper-money still, you zee, only vrom another mill like."

"As to that, Master Sheepshead," replied Mr. Lookout, "I will only say to you in your own phrase, MARK THE END O'T."

"Do you hear him?" said the Reverend Mr. Peppertoast; "do you hear the Jacobin rascal? Do you hear the libellous, seditious, factious, levelling, revolutionary, republican, democratical, atheistical villain?"

CHAPTER XXXI.

CIMMERIAN LODGE.

AFTER a walk of some miles from the town of Gullgudgeon, where no information was to be obtained of Anthelia, their path wound along the shores of a lonely lake, embosomed in dark pine-groves and precipitous rocks. As they passed near a small creek, they observed a gentleman just stepping into a boat, who paused and looked up at the sound of their approximation; and Mr. Fax immediately recognised the poeticopolitical,[1] rhapsodicoprosaical,[2] deisidæmoniacoparadoxographical,[3] pseudolatreiological,[4] transcendental[5] meteorosophist,[6] Moley Mystic,[7] Esquire, of Cimmerian Lodge.[8] This gentleman's Christian name, according to his own account, was improperly spelt with an *e*, and was in truth nothing more nor less than

> "That Moly,
> Which Hermes erst to wise Ulysses gave;"[9]

and which was, in the mind of Homer, a *pure anticipated cognition* of the system of Kantian metaphysics,[10] or grand transcendental science of the *luminous obscure*;[11] for it had a *dark root,** which was mystery; and *a white flower*, which was abstract truth: *it was called Moly by the gods*,[12] who then kept it to themselves; and was *difficult to be dug up by mortal men*, having, in fact, lain *perdu* in subterranean darkness till the immortal Kant dug for it *under the stone of doubt*, and produced it to the astonished world as the *root of human science*.[13] Other persons, however, derived his first name differently;

---

* Ρίζῃ μεν μελαν εστι, γαλακτι δε εικελον ανθος,
ΜΩΛΥ δε μιν καλεουσι θεοι, χαλεπον δε τ' ορυσσειν
Θνητοις ανθρωποισι.

and maintained that the *e* in it showed it very clearly to be a corruption of *Mole-eye*, it being the opinion of some naturalists that the *mole* has *eyes*,[14] which it can withdraw or project at pleasure, implying a faculty of wilful blindness, most happily characteristic of a transcendental metaphysician; since, according to the old proverb, *None are so blind as those who won't see.*[15] But be that as it may, Moley Mystic was his name, and Cimmerian Lodge was his dwelling.

Mr. Mystic invited Mr. Fax and his friends to step with him into the boat, and cross over his lake, which he called the *Ocean of Deceitful Form*, to the *Island of Pure Intelligence*,[16] on which Cimmerian Lodge was situated: promising to give them a great treat in looking over his grounds, which he had laid out according to the *topography of the human mind*;[17] and to enlighten them, through the medium of "darkness visible,"[18] with an opticothaumaturgical[19] process of transcendentalising a *cylindrical mirror*,[20] which should teach them the difference between *objective* and *subjective reality.*[21] Mr. Forester was unwilling to remit his search, even for a few hours: but Mr. Fax observing that great part of the day was gone, and that Cimmerian Lodge was very remote from the human world; so that if they did not avail themselves of Mr. Mystic's hospitality, they should probably be reduced to the necessity of passing the night among the rocks, *sub Jove frigido*,[23] which he did not think very inviting, Mr. Forester complied; and with Mr. Fax and Sir Oran Haut-ton, stepped into the boat. The reader who is deficient in *taste for the bombast*, and is no *admirer of the*

---

* The reader who is desirous of elucidating the mysteries of the words and phrases marked in italics in this chapter, may consult the German works of Professor Kant, or Professor Born's Latin translation of them, or M. Villars's *Philosophie de Kant, ou Principes fondamentaux de la Philosophie Transcendentale*; or the first article of the second number of the Edinburgh Review, or the article *Kant*, in the Encyclopædia Londinensis, or Sir William Drummond's *Academical Questions*, Book II. chap. ix.[22]

obscure, may as well wait on the shore till they return.²⁴
But we must not enter the regions of mystery without an
Orphic invocation.²⁵

ΎΠΝΕ αναξ, καλεω σε μολειν κεχαρηοτα ΜΥΣΤΑΙΣ·
Και σε, μακαρ, λιτομαι, τανυσιπτερε, ουλε ΟΝΕΙΡΕ·
Και ΝΕΦΕΛΑΣ καλεω, δροσοειμονας, ηεροπλαγκτους·
ΝΥΚΤΑ τε πρεσβιστην, πολυηρατον ΟΡΓΙΟΦΑΝΤΑΙΣ,
ΝΥΚΤΕΡΙΟΥΣ τε ΘΕΟΥΣ, ύπο κευθεσιν οικι' εχοντας,
Αντρῳ εν ηεροεντι, παρα ΣΤΥΓΟΣ ίερον ύδωρ·
ΠΡΩΤΕΪ συν πολυβουλῳ, όν ΟΛΒΟΔΟΤΗΝ * καλεουσιν.

O sovereign Sleep! in whose papaverous glen
Dwell the dark Muses of Cimmerian men!
O Power of Dreams! whose dusky pinions shed
Primæval chaos on the slumberer's head!
Ye misty Clouds! amid whose folds sublime
Blind Faith invokes the Ghost of Feudal Time!
And thou, thick Night! beneath whose mantle rove
The Phantom Powers of Subterranean Jove!
Arise, propitious to the mystic strain,
From Lethe's flood, and Zeal's Tartarian fane;
Where Freedom's Shade, 'mid Stygian vapours damp,
Sits, cold and pale, by Truth's extinguished lamp;
While Cowls and Crowns portentous orgies hold,
And tuneful Proteus seals his eyes with gold!

They had scarcely left the shore when they were involved
in a fog of unprecedented density, so that they could not see
one another; but they heard the dash of Mr. Mystic's oars, and
were consoled by his assurances that he could not miss his
way in a state of the atmosphere so very consentaneous to²⁸
his peculiar mode of vision; for that, though, in navigating his
little skiff on the *Ocean of Deceitful Form*, he had very often

---

* Πρωτευς Ολβοδοτης, *Proteus the giver of riches*,²⁶ certainly deserves a place
among the *Lares* of every poetical and political turncoat.²⁷

wandered wide and far from the *Island of Pure Intelligence*, yet this had always happened when he went with his eyes open, in broad daylight; but that he had soon found the means of obviating this little inconvenience, by always keeping his eyes close shut whenever the sun had the impertinence to shine upon him.

He immediately added, that he would take the opportunity of making a remark perfectly in point: "that Experience was a Cyclops, with his eye in the back of his head;"[29] and when Mr. Fax remarked, that he did not see the connexion, Mr. Mystic said he was very glad to hear it; for he should be sorry if any one but himself could see the connexion of his ideas, as he arranged his thoughts *on a new principle.*[30]

They went steadily on through the dense and heavy air, over waters that slumbered like the Stygian pool;[31] a chorus of frogs, that seemed as much delighted with their own melody, as if they had been an oligarchy of poetical critics, regaling them all the way with the Aristophanic symphony of Brek-ek-ek-ex! ko-ax! ko-ax!*[32] till the boat fixed its keel in the *Island of Pure Intelligence;* and Mr. Mystic landed his party, as Charon did Æneas and the Sibyl,[33] in a bed of weeds and mud†: after floundering in which for some time, from losing their guide in the fog, they were cheered by the sound of his voice from above, and scrambling up the bank, found themselves on a hard and barren rock; and, still following the sound of Mr. Mystic's voice, arrived at Cimmerian Lodge.

The fog had penetrated into all the apartments: there was fog in the hall, fog in the parlour, fog on the staircases, fog in the bedrooms;

---

* See the Βατραχοι of Aristophanes.
† Informi limo glaucâque exponit in ulvâ.

> "The fog was here, the fog was there,
> The fog was all around."[34]

It was a little rarefied in the kitchen, by virtue of the enormous fire; so far, at least, that the red face of the cook shone through it, as they passed the kitchen-door, like the disk of the rising moon through the vapours of an autumnal river: but to make amends for this, it was condensed almost into solidity in the library, where the voice of their invisible guide bade them welcome to the *adytum*[35] of the LUMINOUS OBSCURE.[36]

Mr. Mystic now produced what he called his *synthetical torch*,[37] and requested them to follow him, and look over his grounds. Mr. Fax said it was perfectly useless to attempt it in such a state of the atmosphere; but Mr. Mystic protested it was the only state of the atmosphere in which they could be seen to advantage: as daylight and sunshine utterly destroyed their beauty.

They followed the "darkness visible" of the *synthetical torch*, which, according to Mr. Mystic, *shed around it the rays of transcendental illumination;*[38] and he continued to march before them, walking, and talking, and pointing out innumerable images of singularly nubilous[39] beauty, though Mr. Forester and Mr. Fax both declared they could see nothing but the fog and "*la pale lueur du magique flambeau.*"[40] till Mr. Mystic observing that they were now in a *Spontaneity free from Time and Space*,[41] and at the point of *Absolute Limitation*,[42] Mr. Fax said he was very glad to hear it; for in that case they could go no further. Mr. Mystic observed that they must go further; for they were entangled in a maze, from which they would never be able to extricate themselves without his assistance; and he must take the liberty to tell them, that *the categories of modality were connected into the idea of absolute necessity.*[43] As this was spoken in a high tone, they took it to be meant for a reprimand; which carried the more weight as it was the less understood. At length, after floundering on another half hour, the fog still thicker and thicker, and the torch still dimmer and dimmer, they found themselves once more in Cimmerian Lodge.

Mr. Mystic asked them how they liked his grounds, and they both repeated they had seen nothing of them: on which he flew into a rage,[44] and called them *empirical psychologists*,[45] and *slaves of definition, induction, and analysis*,[46] which he intended for terms of abuse, but which were not taken for such by the persons to whom he addressed them.

Recovering his temper, he observed that it was nearly the hour of dinner; and as they did not think it worth while to be angry with him, they contented themselves with requesting that they might dine in the kitchen, which seemed to be the only spot on the *Island of Pure Intelligence* in which there was a glimmer of light.

Mr. Mystic remarked that he thought this very bad taste, but that he should have no objection if the cook would consent; who, he observed, had paramount dominion over that important division of the *Island of Pure Intelligence*. The cook, with a little murmuring, consented for once to evacuate her citadel as soon as the dinner was on table; entering, however, a protest, that this infringement on her privileges should not be pleaded as a precedent.

Mr. Fax was afraid that Mr. Mystic would treat them as Lord Peter treated his brothers:[47] that he would put nothing on the table, and regale them with a dissertation on the *pure idea of absolute substance*;[48] but in this he was agreeably disappointed; for the *anticipated cognition* of a good dinner very soon smoked before them, in the *relation of determinate co-existence*;[49] and the *objective phænomenon*[50] of some super-excellent Madeira quickly put the whole party in perfect good-humour. It appeared, indeed, to have a diffusive quality of occult and mysterious virtue; for, with every glass they drank, the fog grew thin, till by the time they had taken off four bottles among them, it had totally disappeared.

Mr. Mystic now prevailed on them to follow him to the library, where they found a blazing fire and a four-branched gas lamp,[51] shedding a much brighter radiance than that of the *synthetical torch.* He said he had been obliged to light this lamp, as it seemed they could not see by the usual illumination of Cimmerian Lodge. The brilliancy of the gas lights he much disapproved; but he thought it would be very unbecoming in a transcendental philosopher to employ any other material for a purpose to which *smoke* was applicable. Mr. Fax said, he should have thought, on the contrary, that *ex fumo dare lucem*[52] would have been, of all things, the most repugnant to his principles; and Mr. Mystic replied, that it had not struck him so before, but that Mr. Fax's view of the subject "was exquisitely dusky and fuliginous:"[53] this being his usual mode of expressing approbation, instead of the common phraseology of *bright thoughts* and *luminous ideas,* which were equally abhorrent to him both in theory and practice. However, he said, there the light was, for their benefit, and not for his: and as other men's light was his darkness, he should put on a pair of spectacles of smoked glass,[54] which no one could see through but himself. Having put on his spectacles, he undrew a black curtain, discovered a *cylindrical mirror,* and placed a sphere before it with great solemnity. "This sphere," said he, "is an oblong spheroid[55] in the perception of the cylindrical mirror: as long as the mirror thought that the object of his perception was a real external oblong spheroid, he was a mere *empirical philosopher;* but he has grown wiser since he has been in my library; and by reflecting very deeply on the degree in which the manner of his construction might influence the forms of his perception, has taken a very opaque and tenebricose[56] view of how much of the spheroidical[57] perception belongs to the *object,* which is the sphere, and how much to the *subject,* which is himself, in his quality of *cylindrical mirror.* He has thus discovered the difference between *objective* and *subjective reality:* and this point of view is *transcendentalism.*"[58]

"A very dusky and fuliginous speculation, indeed," said Mr. Fax, complimenting Mr. Mystic in his own phrase.

Tea and coffee were brought in. "I divide my day," said Mr. Mystic, "*on a new principle:*[59] I am always poetical at breakfast, moral at luncheon, metaphysical at dinner, and political at tea. Now you shall know my opinion of the hopes of the world.— General discontent shall be the basis of public resignation!* The materials of political gloom will build the steadfast frame of hope.[†][60] The main point is to get rid of analytical reason, which is experimental and practical, and live only by faith‡, which is synthetical and oracular.[61] The contradictory interests of ten millions may neutralize each other.[§][62] But the spirit of Antichrist is abroad.[¶][63]—the people read!—nay, they think!! The people read and think!!! The public, the public in general, the swinish multitude, the many-headed monster, actually reads and thinks!!!!"[64] Horrible in thought, but in fact most horrible! Science classifies flowers. Can it make them bloom where it has placed them in its classification?[††][66] No. Therefore flowers ought not to be classified. This is transcendental logic. Ha! in that cylindrical mirror I see three shadowy forms:— dimly I see them through the smoked glass of my spectacles. Who art thou?—MYSTERY!—I hail thee! Who art thou?—

---

* Coleridge's Lay Sermon, p. 10.
† Ibid.
‡ Ibid. p. 21.
§ Ibid. p. 25.
¶ Ibid. p. 27.
" Ibid. p. 45, 46 (where the reader may find in a note the two worst jokes that ever were cracked).[65]
†† Coleridge's Lay Sermon, p. xvii.

JARGON!—I love thee! Who art thou?—SUPERSTITION!—I
worship thee! Hail, transcendental TRIAD!"

Mr. Fax cut short the thread of his eloquence by saying he
would trouble him for the cream-jug.

Mr. Mystic began again, and talked for three hours without intermission,[67] except that he paused a moment on the
entrance of sandwiches and Madeira. His visitors sipped his
wine in silence till he had fairly talked himself hoarse. Neither
Mr. Fax nor Mr. Forester replied to his paradoxes; for to what
end, they thought, should they attempt to answer what few
would hear, and none would understand?

It was now time to retire, and Mr. Mystic showed his
guests to the doors of their respective apartments, in each of
which a gas-light was burning, and ascended another flight
of stairs to his own dormitory, with a little twinkling taper
in his hand. Mr. Forester and Mr. Fax stayed a few minutes
on the landing-place, to have a word of consultation before
they parted for the night. Mr. Mystic gained the door of his
apartment—turned the handle of the lock—and had just
advanced one step—when the whole interior of the chamber
became suddenly sheeted with fire: a tremendous explosion
followed; and he was precipitated to the foot of the stairs
in *the smallest conceivable fraction of the infinite divisibility of
time.*[68]

Mr. Forester picked him up, and found him not much hurt;
only a little singed, and very much frightened. But the whole
interior of the apartment continued to blaze. Mr. Forester and
Sir Oran Haut-ton ran for water: Mr. Fax rang the nearest
bell: Mr. Mystic vociferated "Fire!" with singular energy: the
servants ran about half-undressed: pails, buckets, and pitch-
ers, were in active requisition; till Sir Oran Haut-ton ascending the stairs with the great rain-water tub, containing one

hundred and eight gallons of water,* threw the whole contents on the flames with one sweep of his powerful arm.

The fire being extinguished, it remained to ascertain its cause. It appeared that the gas-tube in Mr. Mystic's chamber had been left unstopped,[70] and the gas evolving without combustion (the apartment being perfectly air-tight),[71] had condensed into a mass, which, on the approach of Mr. Mystic's taper, instantly ignited, blowing the transcendentalist down stairs, and setting fire to his curtains and furniture.

Mr. Mystic, as soon as he recovered from his panic, began to bewail the catastrophe: not so much, he said, for itself, as because such an event in Cimmerian Lodge was an infallible omen of evil[72]—a type and symbol of an approaching period of public light—when the smoke of metaphysical mystery, and the vapours of ancient superstition, which he had done all that in him lay to consolidate in the spirit of man, would explode at the touch of analytical reason, leaving nothing but the plain common-sense matter-of-fact of moral and political truth—a day that he earnestly hoped he might never live to see.

"Certainly," said Mr. Forester, "it is a very bad omen for all who make it their study to darken the human understanding, when one of the pillars of their party is *blown up by his own smoke;*[73] but the symbol, as you call it, may operate as a warning to the apostles of superstitious chimæra and political fraud, that it is very possible *for smoke to be too thick;*[74] and that, in condensing in the human mind the vapours of ignorance and delusion, they are only compressing a body of inflammable gas, of which the explosion will be fatal in precise proportion to its density.

---

* "Some travellers speak of his strength as wonderful; greater, they say, than that of ten men such as we."—*Ancient Metaphysics*, vol. iii. p. 105.[69]

CHAPTER XXXII.

THE DESERTED MANSION.

THEY rose, as usual, before daylight, that they might pursue their perlustration; and, on descending, found Mr. Mystic awaiting them at a table covered with a sumptuous apparatus of tea and coffee, a pyramid of hot rolls, and a variety of cold provision. Cimmerian Lodge, he said, was famous for its breed of tame geese, and he could recommend the cold one on the table as one of his own training. The breakfast being dispatched, he rowed them over the *Ocean of Deceitful Form* before the sun rose to disturb his navigation.

After walking some miles, a ruined mansion at the end of an ancient avenue of elms attracted their attention. As they made a point of leaving no place unexamined, they walked up to it. There was an air of melancholy grandeur in its loneliness and desolation which interested them to know its history. The briers that choked the court, the weeds that grew from the fissures of the walls and on the ledges of the windows, the fractured glass, the half-fallen door, the silent and motionless clock, the steps worn by the tread of other years, the total silence of the scene of ancient hospitality, broken only by the voices of the rooks whose nests were in the elms, all carried back the mind to the years that were gone. There was a sun-dial in the centre of the court: the sun shone on the brazen plate, and the shadow of the index[1] fell on the line of noon. "Nothing impresses me more," said Mr. Forester, "in a ruin of this kind, than the contrast between the sun-dial and the clock, which I have frequently observed. This contrast I once made the basis of a little poem, which the similarity of circumstances induces me to repeat to you, though you are no votary of the spirit of rhyme."

THE SUN-DIAL.

The ivy o'er the mouldering wall
Spreads like a tree, the growth of years:
The wild wind through the doorless hall
A melancholy music rears,
A solitary voice, that sighs
O'er man's forgotten pageantries.

Above the central gate, the clock,
Through clustering ivy dimly seen,
Seems, like the ghost of Time, to mock
The wrecks of power that once has been.
The hands are rusted on its face;
Even where they ceased, in years gone by,
To keep the flying moments pace;
Fixing, in Fancy's thoughtful eye,
A point of ages passed away,
A speck of time, that owns no tie
With aught that lives and breathes to-day.

But 'mid the rank and towering grass,
Where breezes wave, in mournful sport,
The weeds that choke the ruined court,
The careless hours that circling pass,
Still trace upon the dialled[2] brass
The shade of their unvarying way:
And evermore, with every ray
That breaks the clouds and gilds the air,
Time's stealthy steps are imaged there:
Even as the long-revolving years
In self-reflecting circles flow,
From the first bud the hedge-row bears,
To wintry Nature's robe of snow.
The changeful forms of mortal things
Decay and pass; and art and power
Oppose in vain the doom that flings
Oblivion on their closing hour:
While still, to every woodland vale,

New blooms, new fruits, the seasons bring,
For other eyes and lips to hail
With looks and sounds of welcoming:
As where some stream light-eddying roves
By sunny meads and shadowy groves,
Wave following wave departs for ever,
But still flows on the eternal river.

An old man approached them, in whom they observed that look of healthy and cheerful antiquity which showed that time only, and neither pain nor sickness, had traced wrinkles on his cheek. Mr. Forester made inquiries of him on the object he had most at heart; but the old man could give no gleam of light to guide his steps. Mr. Fax then asked some questions concerning the mansion before them.

"Ah, Zur!" said the old man, "this be the zeat o' Squire Openhand: but he doant live here now: the house be growed too large vor 'n, as one may zay. I remember un playing about here on the grass-plot, when he was half as high as the zundial poast, as if it was but yesterday. The days that I ha' zeed here! Rare doings there used to be wi' the house vull o' gentlevolks zometimes to be zure: but what he loiked best was, to zee a merry-making of all his tenants, round the great oak that stands there in the large vield by himzelf. He used to zay if there was any thing he could not abide, it was the zight of a zorrowful feace; and he was always prying about to voind one: and if he did voind one, Lord bless you! it was not a zorrowful feace long, if it was any thing that he could mend. Zo he lived to the length of his line, as the zaying is; and when times grew worse, it was a hard matter to draw in: howzomdever he did; and when the tax-gatherers[3] came every year vor more and more, and the peaper-money vlew about, buying up every thing in the neighbourhood; and every vifty pounds he got in peaper was n't worth, as he toald me, vorty pounds o' real money,[4] why there was every year fewer horses in his steable, and less wine on his board: and every now and then came a queer zort o' chap dropped out o' the sky like,—a vundholder[5] he called un,—and bought a bit o'ground vor a handvul o' peaper, and built a cottage-horny,[6] as they call it—there be one there, on the hill zide—and had nothing to do wi' the country-people, nor the country-people wi' he: nothing in the world to do, as we could zee, but to eat and drink, and make little bits o' shrubberies, o' quashies, and brutuses, and zelies, and cubies, and filligrees, and ruddydunderums, instead o'the oak plantations, the old landlords used to plant; and the Squire could never abide the zight o' one o' they gimcrack[7] boxes; and all the while he was nailing up a window or two every year, and his horses were going one way, and his dogs another, and his old zervants were zent away one by one, wi' heavy hearts, poor zouls, and at last it came that he could not get half his rents, and zome o'his tenants went to the workhouse, and others ran away, because o' the poor-rates, and every thing went to zixes and zevens,[8] and I used to meet the Squire in his walks, and think to myzelf it was very hard that he who could not bear to zee a zorrowful feace, should have zuch a zorrowful one of his own; and he used to zay to me whenever I met un: 'All this comes o' peaper-money, Measter Hawthorn.' Zo the upshot was, he could not afford any longer to live in his own great house, where his vorevathers had lived out o' memory o' man, and went to zome outlandish place wi' his vamily to live, as he said, in much zuch a box as that gimcrack thing on the hill."

"You have told us a very melancholy story," said Mr. Forester; "but at present, I fear, a very common one, and one of which, if the present system continue, every succeeding year will multiply examples."

"Ah, Zur!" said the old man, "there was them as vorezeed it long ago, and voretold it too, up in the great house in Lunnun,[9] where they zettles the affairs o' the nation: a pretty way o' zettling it be, to my thinking, to vill the country wi' tax-gatherers and vundholders, and peaper-money men, that turns all the old vamilies out o' the country, and zends their tenants to the workhouse: but there was them as vorezeed and voretold it too, but nobody minded 'em then: they begins to mind 'em now."

"But how do you manage in these times?" said Mr. Forester.

"I lives, Measter," said the old man, "and pretty well too, vor myzelf. I had a little vreehold varm¹⁰ o' my own, that has been in my vamily zeven hundred year, and we woant part wi' it, I promise you, vor all the tax-collectors and vundholders in England. But my zon was never none o' your gentleman varmers, none o' your reacing and hunting bucks, that it's a sheame vor a honest varmer to be: he always zet his shoulders to the wheel—always a-vield by peep o'day: zo now I be old, I've given up the varm to him; and that I would n't ha' done to the best man in all the county bezide: but he's my zon, and I loves un. Zo I walks about the vields all day, and zits all the evening in the chimney-corner wi' an old neighbour or zo, and a jug o' ale, and talks over old times, when the Openhands, and zuch as they, could afford to live in the homes o' their vorevathers. It be a bad state o' things, my measters, and must come to a bad end, zooner or later; but it'll last my time."

"You are not in the last stage of a consumption, are you, honest friend?" said Mr. Fax.

"Lord love you, no, Measter," said the old farmer, rather frightened; "do I look zo?"

"No," said Mr. Fax; "but you talked so."

"Ah! thee beest a wag, I zee," said the farmer. "Things be in a conzumption zure enough, but they'll last my time vor all that; and if they doant, it's no vault o' mine; and I'se no money in the vunds, nor no zinecure pleace, zo I eats my beef-steak and drinks my ale, and lets the world slide."

CHAPTER XXXIII.

THE PHANTASM.

THE course of their perambulations brought them into the vicinity of Melincourt, and they stopped at the Castle to inquire if any intelligence had been obtained of Anthelia. The gate was opened to them by old Peter Gray, who informed them that himself and the female domestics were at that time the only inmates of the Castle, as the other male domestics had gone off at the same time with Mr. Hippy in search of their young mistress; and the Honourable Mrs. Pinmoney and Miss Danaretta were gone to London, because of the opera being open.[1]

Mr. Forester inquired into the manner of Anthelia's disappearance. Old Peter informed him that she had gone into her library as usual after breakfast, and when the hour of dinner arrived she was missing. The central window was open, as well as the little postern door of the shrubbery, that led into the dingle, the whole vicinity of which they had examined, and had found the recent print of horses' feet on a narrow green road that skirted the other side of the glen: these traces they had followed till they had totally lost them, in a place where the road became hard and rocky, and divided into several branches: the pursuers had then separated into parties of two and three, and each party had followed a different branch of the road, but they had found no clue to guide them, and had hitherto been unsuccessful. He should not himself, he said, have remained inactive, but Mr. Hippy had insisted on his staying to take care of the Castle. He then observed, that, as it was growing late, he should humbly advise their continuing where they were till morning. To this they assented, and he led the way to the library.

Every thing in the library remained precisely in the place in which Anthelia left it. Her chair was near the table, and the materials of drawing were before it. The gloom of the winter evening, which was now closing in, was deepened through the stained glass of the windows. The moment the door was thrown open, Mr. Forester started, and threw himself forward into the apartment towards Anthelia's chair; but before he reached it, he stopped, placed his hand before his eyes, and turning round, leaned for support on the arm of Mr. Fax. He recovered himself in a few minutes, and sate down by the table. Peter Gray, after kindling the fire, and lighting the Argand lamp,[2] that hung from the centre of the apartment, went to give directions on the subject of dinner.

Mr. Forester observed, from the appearance of the drawing materials, that they had been hastily left, and he saw that the last subject on which Anthelia had been employed was a sketch of Redrose Abbey. He sate with his head leaning on his hand, and his eyes fixed on the drawing in perfect silence. Mr. Fax thought it best not to disturb his meditations, and took up a volume that was lying open on the table, the last that Anthelia had been reading. It was a posthumous work of the virtuous and unfortunate Condorcet,[3] in which that most amiable and sublime enthusiast, contemplating human nature in the light of his own exalted spirit, had delineated a beautiful vision of the future destinies of mankind.*

Sir Oran Haut-ton kept his eyes fixed on the door with looks of anxious impatience, and showed manifest and increasing disappointment at every re-entrance of old Peter, who at length summoned them to dinner.

Mr. Fax was not surprised that Mr. Forester had no appetite, but that Sir Oran had lost his, appeared to him extremely curious. The latter grew more and more uneasy, rose from

---

* *Esquisse d'un Tableau historique des Progrès de l'Esprit humain.*

table, took a candle in his hand,[4] and wandered from room to room, searching every closet and corner in the Castle, to the infinite amazement of old Peter Gray, who followed him every where, and became convinced that the poor gentleman was crazed for love of his young mistress, who, he made no doubt, was the object of his search; and the conviction was strengthened by the perfect inattention of Sir Oran to all his assurances that his dear young lady was not in any of those places which he searched so scrupulously. Sir Oran at length having left no corner of the habitable part of the Castle unexamined, returned to the dining-room, and throwing himself into a chair began to shed tears in great abundance.[*][5]

Mr. Fax made his two disconsolate friends drink several glasses of Madeira, by way of raising their spirits, and then asked Mr. Forester what it was that had so affected him on their first entering the library.

MR. FORESTER.

It was the form of Anthelia, in the place where I first saw her, in that chair by the table. The vision was momentary, but, while it lasted, had all the distinctness of reality.

MR. FAX.

This is no uncommon effect of the association of ideas when external objects present themselves to us, after an interval of absence,[6] in their remembered arrangement, with only one form wanting, and that the dearest among them, to perfect the resemblance between the present sensation and the recollected idea. A vivid imagination, more especially when the nerves are weakened by anxiety and fatigue, will, under such circumstances, complete the imperfect scene, by replacing for a moment the one deficient form among those accustomed objects which had long formed its accompaniments in the

[*] See vol. i. p. 73, note.

contemplation of memory. This single mental principle will explain the greater number of *credible* tales of apparitions,[7] and at the same time give a very satisfactory reason why a particular spirit is usually found haunting a particular place.

MR. FORESTER.

Thus Petrarch's beautiful pictures of the Spirit of Laura on the banks of the Sorga,[8] are assuredly something more than the mere fancies of the closet, and must have originated in that system of mental connexion, which, under peculiar circumstances, gives ideas the force of sensations. Anxiety and fatigue are certainly great promoters of the state of mind most favourable to such impressions.

MR. FAX.

It was under the influence of such excitements that Brutus saw the spirit of Cæsar;[9] and in similar states of feeling, the phantoms of poetry are usually supposed to be visible: the ghost of Banquo, for example, and that of Patroclus.[10] But this only holds true of the poets who paint from nature; for their artificial imitators, when they wish to call a spirit from the vasty deep,[11] are not always so attentive to the mental circumstances of the persons to whom they present it. In the early periods of society, when apparitions form a portion of the general creed; when the life of man is wandering, precarious, and turbulent; when the uncultured wildness of the heath and the forest harmonizes with the chimæras of superstition, and when there is not, as in later times, a rooted principle of reason and knowledge, to weaken such perceptions in their origin, and destroy the seeming reality of their subsequent recollection, impressions of this nature will be more frequent, and will be as much invested with the character of external existence, as the scenes to which they are attached by the connecting power of the mind. They will always be found with their own appropriate character of time, and place, and circumstance.

The ghost of the warrior will be seen on the eve of battle by him who keeps his lonely watch near the blaze of the nightly fire, and the spirit of the huntress maid will appear to her lover when he pauses on the sunny heath, or rests in the moonlight cave.

CHAPTER XXXIV.

THE CHURCHYARD.

THE next morning Mr. Forester determined on following the mountain-road on the other side of the dingle, of which Peter Gray had spoken: but wishing first to make some inquiries of the Reverend Mr. Portpipe, they walked to his vicarage, which was in a village at some distance. Just as they reached it the reverend gentleman emerged in haste, and seeing Mr. Forester and his friends, said he was very sorry that he could not attend to them just then, as he had a great press of business to dispose of, namely, a christening, a marriage, and a funeral, but he would knock them off[1] as fast as he could, after which he should be perfectly at their service, hoped they would wait in the vicarage till his return, and observed he had good ale and a few bottles of London Particular.[2] He then left them to dispatch his affairs in the church.

They preferred waiting in the churchyard. "A christening, a marriage, and a funeral!" said Mr. Forester. "With what indifference he runs through the whole drama of human life, raises the curtain on its commencement, superintends the most important and eventful action of its progress, and drops the curtain on its close !"

MR. FAX.

Custom has rendered them all alike indifferent to him.[3] In every human pursuit and profession the routine of ordinary business renders the mind indifferent to all the forms and objects of which that routine is composed. The sexton "sings at grave-making;"[4] the undertaker walks with a solemn face before the coffin, because a solemn face is part of his trade: but his heart is as light as if there were no funeral at his heels: he is quietly conning over the items of his bill, or thinking of

the party in which he is to pass his evening; and the reverend gentleman who concludes the process, and consigns to its
last receptacle the shell of extinguished intelligence, has his
thoughts on the wing to the sports of the field, or the jovial
board of the Squire.

MR. FORESTER.

Your observation is just. It is this hardening power of
custom that gives steadiness to the hand of the surgeon,
firmness to the voice of the criminal judge, coolness to the
soldier "in the imminent deadly breach,"[5] self-possession to
the sailor in the rage of the equinoctial storm. It is under
this influence that the lawyer deals out writs and executions[6]
as carelessly as he deals out cards at his evening whist; that
the gaoler turns the key with the same stern indifference
on unfortunate innocence as on hardened villany; that the
venal senator votes away by piecemeal the liberties of his
country; and that the statesman sketches over the bottle
his series of deliberate schemes for the extinction of human
freedom, the enchaining of human reason, and the waste of
human life.

MR. FAX.

Contemplate any of these men only in the sphere of
their routine, and you will think them utterly destitute of
all human sympathy. Make them change places with each
other, and you will see symptoms of natural feelings. Custom
cannot kill the better feelings of human nature: it merely lays
them asleep.

MR. FORESTER.

You must acknowledge then, at least, that their sleep is very
sound.

MR. FAX.

In most cases certainly as sound as that of Epimenides, or
of the seven sleepers of Ephesus.[7] But these did wake at last,

and, therefore, according to Aristotle, they had always the capacity of waking.

MR. FORESTER.

You must allow me to wait for a similar proof, before I admit such a capacity in respect to the feelings of some of the characters we have mentioned. Yet I am no sceptic in human virtue.

MR. FAX.

You have no reason to be, with so much evidence before your eyes, of the excellence of the past generation, and I do not suppose the present is much worse than its predecessors. Read the epitaphs around you, and see what models and mirrors of all the social virtues have left the examples of their shining light to guide the steps of their posterity.

MR. FORESTER.

I observe the usual profusion of dutiful sons, affectionate husbands, faithful friends, kind neighbours, and honest men. These are the luxuriant harvest of every churchyard. But is it not strange, that even the fertility of fiction should be so circumscribed in the variety of monumental panegyric? Yet a few words comprehend the summary of all the moral duties of ordinary life. Their degrees and diversities are like the shades of colour, that shun for the most part the power of language: at all events, the nice distinctions and combinations that give individuality to historical character, scarcely come within the limits of sepulchral inscription, which merely serves to testify the regret of the survivors for one whose society was dear, and whose faults are forgotten. For there is a feeling in the human mind, that, in looking back on former scenes of intercourse with those who are past for ever beyond the limits of injury and resentment, gradually destroys all the bitterness and heightens all the pleasures of the remembrance; as, when we revert in fancy to the days of our childhood, we scarcely find a vestige of their tears, pains, and disappointments, and perceive only their fields, their flowers, and their sunshine, and the smiles of our little associates.

MR. FAX.

The history of common life seems as circumscribed as its moral attributes: for the most extensive information I can collect from these gravestones is, that the parties married, lived in trouble, and died of a conflict between a disease and a physician. I observe a last request, which I suppose was very speedily complied with: that of a tender husband to his loving wife not to weep for him long. If it be as you say, that the faults of the dead are soon forgotten, yet the memory of their virtues is not much longer lived;[8] and I have often thought that these words of Rabelais would furnish an appropriate inscription for ninety-nine gravestones out of every hundred: *Sa mémoire expira avecques le son des cloches qui carillonarent à son enterrement.*[9]

CHAPTER XXXV.

THE RUSTIC WEDDING.

THE bride and bridegroom, with half a dozen of their friends, now entered the churchyard. The bride, a strong, healthy-looking country girl, was clinging to the arm of her lover, not with the light and scarcely perceptible touch, with which Miss Simper[1] complies with the request of Mr. Giggle, "that she will do him the honour to take his arm," but with a cordial and unsophisticated pressure that would have made such an arm as Mr. Giggle's black and blue. The bridegroom, with a pair of chubby cheeks, which in colour precisely rivalled his new scarlet waistcoat, and his mouth expanded into a broad grin, that exhibited the total range of his teeth, advanced in a sort of step that was half a walk and half a dance, as if the preconceived notion of the requisite solemnity of demeanour were struggling with the natural impulses of the overflowing joy of his heart.

Mr. Fax looked with great commiseration on this bridal pair, and determined to ascertain if they had a clear notion of the evils that awaited them in consequence of the rash step they were about to take. He therefore accosted them with an observation that the Reverend Mr. Portpipe was not at leisure, but would be in a few minutes. "In the mean time," said he, "I stand here as the representative of general reason, to ask if you have duly weighed the consequences of your present proceeding?"

THE BRIDEGROOM.

General Reason! I be's no soger man, and bea'n't countable to no General what-zomecomedever. We bea'n't under martial law, be we? Voine toimes indeed if General Reason be to interpole between a poor man and his sweetheart.

MR. FAX.

That is precisely the case which calls most loudly for such an interposition.

THE BRIDEGROOM.

If General Reason waits till I or Zukey calls loudly vor'n, he'll wait long enough. Woa'n't he, Zukey?

THE BRIDE.

Ees, zure, Robin.

MR. FAX.

General reason, my friend, I assure you, has nothing to do with martial law, nor with any other mode of arbitrary power, but with authority that has truth for its fountain, benevolence for its end, and the whole universe for its sphere of action.

THE BRIDEGROOM. *(Scratching his head.)*

There be a mort o'voine words, but I zuppose you means to zay as how this General Reason be a Methody preacher;[2] but I be's true earthy-ducks church, and zo be Zukey: bea'n't you, Zukey?

THE BRIDE.

Ees, zure, Robin.

THE BRIDEGROOM.

And we has nothing to do wi' General Reason neither on us. Has we, Zukey?

THE BRIDE.

No, zure, Robin.

MR. FAX.

Well, my friend, be that as it may, you are going to be married?

THE BRIDEGROOM.

Why, I thinks zo, Zur, wi' General Reason's leave. Be'an't we, Zukey?

THE BRIDE.

Ees, zure, Robin.

MR. FAX.

And are you fully aware, my honest friend, what marriage is?

THE BRIDEGROOM.

Vor zartin I be: Zukey and I ha' got it by heart out o' t' Book o' Common Prayer.[3] Ha'n't we, Zukey? *(This time Susan did not think proper to answer.)* It be ordained that zuch parsons as hav'n't the gift of——*(Susan gave him such a sudden and violent pinch on the arm, that his speech ended in a roar.)* Od rabbit me! that wur a twinger! I'll have my revenge, howzomecomedever. *(And he imprinted a very emphatical kiss on the lips of his blushing bride, that greatly scandalized Mr. Fax.)*

MR. FAX.

Do you know, that in all likelihood, in the course of six years, you will have as many children?

THE BRIDEGROOM.

The more the merrier, Zur. Be'an't it, Zukey? *(Susan was mute again.)*

MR. FAX.

I hope it may prove so, my friend; but I fear you will find the more the sadder. What are your occupations?

THE BRIDEGROOM.

Anan,[4] Zur?

MR. FAX.

What do you do to get your living?

THE BRIDEGROOM.

Works vor varmer Brownstout: sows and reaps, threshes, and goes to market wi' corn and cattle, turns to plough-tail when hap chances, cleans and feeds horses, hedges and ditches, fells timber, gathers in t' orchard, brews ale, and drinks it, and gets vourteen shill'ns a week vor my trouble. And Zukey here ha' laid up a mint o'money: she wur dairy-maid at varmer Cheesecurd's, and ha' gotten vour pounds zeventeen shill'ns and ninepence, in t' old chest wi' three vlat locks and a pad-lock. Ha'n't you, Zukey?

THE BRIDE.

Ees, zure, Robin.

MR. FAX.

It does not appear to me, my worthy friend, that your four-teen shillings a week, even with Mistress Susan's consolidated fund of four pounds seventeen shillings and ninepence, will be all together adequate to the maintenance of such a family as you seem likely to have.

THE BRIDEGROOM.

Why, Zur, in t' virst pleace I doan't know what be Zukey's intentions in that respect——Od rabbit it, Zukey! doan't pinch zo——and in t' next pleace, wi' all due submission to you and General Reason the Methody preacher, I takes it be our look-out,[5] and none o' nobody's else.

MR. FAX.

But it is somebody's else, for this reason: that if you cannot maintain your own children, the parish must do it for you.[6]

THE BRIDEGROOM.

Vor zartin—in a zort o' way; and bad enough at best. But I wants no more to do wi' t' parish than parish wi' me.

MR. FAX.

I dare say you do not, at present. But, my good friend, when the cares of a family come upon you, your independence of spirit will give way to necessity; and if, by any accident, you are thrown out of work, as in the present times many honest fellows are, what will you do then?

THE BRIDEGROOM.

Do the best I can, Measter, as I always does, and nobody can't do no better.

MR. FAX.

Do you suppose, then, you are doing the best you can now, in marrying, with such a doubtful prospect before you? How will you bring up your children?

THE BRIDEGROOM.

Why, in the vear o' the Lord, to be zure.

MR. FAX.

Of course: but how will you bring them up to get their living?

THE BRIDEGROOM.

That's as thereafter may happen. They woan't starve, I'se warrant 'em, if they teakes after their veyther. But I zees now who General Reason be. He be one o' your zinecure vund-holder peaper-money taxing men, as is n't zatisfied wi' takin' t' bread out o' t' poor man's mouth, and zending his chillern to army and navy, and vactories, and zuch-like, but wants to take away his wife into t' bargain.

MR. FAX.

There, my honest friend, you have fallen into a radical mistake, which I shall try to elucidate for your benefit. It is owing to poor people having more children than they can maintain, that those children are obliged to go to the army and navy, and consequently that statesmen and conquerors find so many ready instruments for the oppression and destruction of the human species: it follows, therefore, that if people would not marry till they could be certain of maintaining all their children comfortably at home——

THE BRIDEGROOM.

Lord love you, that be all mighty voine rigmarol; but the short and the long be this: I can't live without Zukey, nor Zukey without I, can you, Zukey?

THE BRIDE.

No, zure, Robin.

THE BRIDEGROOM.

Now there be a plain downright honest-hearted old English girl: none o' your quality madams, as zays one thing and means another; and zo you may tell General Reason he may teake away chair and teable, salt-box and trencher,[7] bed and bedding, pig and pig-sty, but neither he nor all his peaper-men together, shall take away his own Zukey vrom Robin Ruddyface; if they shall I'm dom'd.

"What profane wretch," said the Reverend Mr. Portpipe, emerging from the church, "what profane wretch is swearing in the very gate of the temple?" and seeing by the bridegroom's confusion that he was the culprit, he reprimanded him severely, and declared he would not marry him that day. The very thought of such a disappointment was too much for poor Robin to bear, and, after one or two ineffectual efforts to speak, he distorted his face into a most rueful expression, and struck up such a roar of crying as completely electrified the Reverend Mr. Portpipe, whose wrath, nevertheless, was not to be mollified by Robin's grief and contrition, but yielded at length to the intercessions of Mr. Forester. Robin's face cleared up in an instant, and the natural broad grin of his ruddy countenance shone forth through his tears like the sun through a shower. "You are such an honest and warm-hearted fellow," said Mr. Forester, putting a bank-note into Robin's hand, "that you must not refuse me the pleasure of making this little addition to Mistress Susan's consolidated fund."—"Od rabbit me!"

said the bridegroom, overcome with joy and surprise, "I doan't know who thee beest, but thee bees'n't General Reason, that's vor zartin."

The rustic party then followed the Reverend Mr. Portpipe into the church. Robin, when he reached the porch, looked round over his shoulder to Mr. Fax, and said with a very arch look, "My dutiful sarvice to General Reason." And looking round a second time before he entered the door, added: "and Zukey's too."

CHAPTER XXXVI.

THE VICARAGE.

When the Reverend Mr. Portpipe had dispatched his "press of business,"[1] he set before his guests in the old oak parlour of his vicarage a cold turkey and ham, a capacious jug of "incomparable ale," and a bottle of his London Particular; all which, on trial, were approved to be excellent, and a second bottle of the latter was very soon required, and produced with great alacrity. The reverend gentleman expressed much anxiety in relation to the mysterious circumstance of the disappearance of Anthelia, on whom he pronounced a very warm eulogium, saying she was the flower of the mountains, the type of ideal beauty, the daughter of music, the rosebud of sweetness, and the handmaid of charity. He professed himself unable to throw the least light on the transaction, but supposed she had been spirited away for some nefarious purpose. He said that the mountain road had been explored without success in all its ramifications,[2] not only by Mr. Hippy and the visitors and domestics of Melincourt, but by all the peasants and mountaineers of the vicinity— that it led through a most desolate and inhospitable tract of country, and he would advise them, if they persisted in their intention of following it themselves, to partake of his poor hospitality till morning, and set forward with the first dawn of daylight. Mr. Fax seconded this proposal, and Mr. Forester complied.

They spent the evening in the old oak parlour, and conversed on various subjects, during which a knotty point opposing itself to the solution of an historical question, Mr. Forester expressed a wish to be allowed access to the reverend gentleman's library. The reverend gentleman hummed awhile with great gravity and deliberation: then slowly rising from his large arm-chair, he walked across the room to the further corner, where throwing open the door of a little closet, he said with extreme complacency, "There is my library: Homer, Virgil, and Horace, for old acquaintance sake, and the credit of my cloth: Tillotson, Atterbury, and Jeremy Taylor,[3] for materials of exhortation and ingredients of sound doctrine: and for my own private amusement, in an occasional half hour between my dinner and my nap, a translation of Rabelais and the Tale of a Tub."[4]

MR. FAX.

A well-chosen collection.

THE REVEREND MR. PORTPIPE.

Multum in parvo.[5] But there is something that may amuse you: a little drawer of mineral specimens that have been picked up in this vicinity, and a fossil or two. Among the latter is a curious bone that was found in a hill just by, invested with stalactite.[6]

MR. FORESTER.

The bone of a human thumb, unquestionably.

THE REVEREND MR. PORTPIPE.

Very probably.

MR. FORESTER.

Which, by its comparative proportion, must have belonged to an individual about eleven feet six or seven inches in height: there are no such men now.

MR. FAX.

Except, perhaps, among the Patagonians,[7] whose existence is, however, disputed.

MR. FORESTER.

It is disputed on no tenable ground, but that of the narrow and bigoted vanity of civilized men, who, pent in the unhealthy limits of towns and cities, where they dwindle from generation to generation in a fearful rapidity of declension towards the abyss of the infinitely little, in which they will finally vanish from the system of nature, will not admit that there ever were, or are, or can be better, stronger, and healthier men than themselves. The Patagonians are a vagrant nation, without house or home, and are, therefore, only occasionally seen on the coast: but because some voyagers have not seen them, I know not why we should impeach the evidence of those who have. The testimony of a man of honour, like Mr. Byron,[8] would alone have been sufficient: but all his officers and men gave the same account. And there are other testimonies; that, for instance, of M. de Guyot, who brought from the coast of Patagonia a skeleton of one of these great men, which measured between twelve and thirteen feet. This skeleton he was bringing to Europe, but happening to be caught in a great storm, and having on board a Spanish Bishop (the Archbishop of Lima), who was of opinion that the storm was caused by the bones of this Pagan which they had on board; and having persuaded the crew that this was the case, the captain was obliged to throw the skeleton overboard. The Bishop died soon after, and was thrown overboard in his turn. I could have wished that he had been thrown overboard sooner, and then the bones of the Patagonian would have arrived in Europe."[9]

THE REVEREND MR. PORTPIPE.

Your wish is orthodox, inasmuch as the Bishop was himself a Pagan, and moreover an Inquisitor. And your doctrine of large men is also orthodox, for the sons of Anak and the family of Goliah[10] did once exist, though now their race is extinct.

MR. FORESTER.

The multiplication of diseases, the diminution of strength, and the contraction of the term of existence, keep pace with

---

* Ancient Metaphysics, vol. iii. p. 139.

the diminution of the stature of men. The mortality of a manufacturing town, compared with that of a mountain-village, is more than three to one, which clearly shows the evil effects of the departure from natural life, and of the coacervation of multitudes within the narrow precincts of cities, where the breath of so many animals, and the exhalations from the dead, the dying, and corrupted things of all kinds, make the air little better than a slow poison, and so offensive as to be perceptible to the sense of those who are not accustomed to it; for the wandering Arabs will smell a town at the distance of several leagues. And in this country the cottagers who are driven by the avarice of landlords and great tenants to seek a subsistence in towns, are very soon destroyed by the change.[*11] And this hiving of human beings is not the only evil effect of commerce, which tends also to keep up a constant circulation of the elements of destruction, and to make the vices and diseases of one country the vices and diseases of all.[†12] Thus, with every extension of our intercourse with distant lands, we bring home some new seed of death; and how many we leave as vestiges of our visitation, let the South Sea Islanders testify. Consider, too, the frightful consequences of the consumption of spiritous liquors: a practice so destructive, that if all the devils were again to be assembled in Pandemonium, to contrive the ruin of the human species, nothing so mischievous could be devised by them;[‡13] but which it is considered politic to encourage, according to our method of raising money on the vices of the people.[§14] When these and many other causes of destruction are considered, it would be wonderful indeed, if every new generation were not, as all experience proves that

* Ancient Metaphysics, vol. iii. p. 193.
† Ancient Metaphysics, vol. iii. p. 191.
‡ Ibid. p. 181.
§ Ibid. p. 182.

it is, smaller, weaker, more diseased, and more miserable than the preceding.

MR. FAX.

Do you find, in the progress of science and the rapid diffusion of intellectual light, no counterpoise to this mass of physical calamity, even admitting it to exist in the extent you suppose?

MR. FORESTER.

Without such a counterpoise the condition of human nature would be desperate indeed. The intellectual, as I have often observed to you, are nourished at the expense of the animal faculties.

MR. FAX.

You cannot, then, conceive the existence of *mens sana in corpore sano?*[15]

MR. FORESTER.

Scarcely in the present state of human degeneracy: at best in a very limited sense.

MR. FAX.

Nevertheless you do, nay, you must, acknowledge that the intellectual, which is the better part of human nature, is in a progress of rapid improvement, continually enlarging its views and multiplying its acquisitions.

MR. FORESTER.

The collective stock of knowledge which is the common property of scientific men necessarily increases, and will increase from the circumstance of admitting the co-operation of numbers: but collective knowledge is as distinct from individual mental power as it is confessedly unconnected with wisdom and moral virtue, and independent of political liberty. A man of modern times, with machines of complicated powers, will lift a heavier mass than that which Hector hurled from his unassisted arm against the Grecian gates;[16] but take away his mechanism, and what comparison is there between him and Hector? In the same way a modern man of science *knows* more than Pythagoras knew: but consider them with relation only to *mental power*, and what comparison remains between them? No more than between a modern poet and Homer—a comparison which the most strenuous partisan of modern improvement will scarcely venture to institute.

MR. FAX.

I will venture to oppose Shakespeare to him nevertheless.

MR. FORESTER.

That is, however, going back two centuries, to a state of society very peculiar, and very fertile in genius. Shakespeare is the great phænomenon of the modern world, but his men and women are beings like ourselves; whereas those of Homer are of a nobler and mightier race; and his poetry is worthy of his characters: it is the language of the gods.

Mr. Forester rose, and approached the little closet, with the avowed intention of taking down Homer. "Take care how you touch him," said the Reverend Mr. Portpipe: "he is in a very dusty condition, for he has not been disturbed these thirty years."

CHAPTER XXXVII.

THE MOUNTAINS.

THEY followed the mountain-road till they arrived at the spot where it divided into several branches, one of which they selected on some principle of preference, which we are not sagacious enough to penetrate. They now proceeded by a gradual ascent of several miles along a rugged passage of the hills, where the now flowerless heath was the only vestige of vegetation; and the sound of the little streams that every where gleamed beside their way, the only manifestation of the life and motion of nature.

"It is a subject worthy of consideration," said Mr. Fax, "how far scenes like these are connected with the genius of liberty: how far the dweller of the mountains, who is certainly surrounded by more sublime excitements, has more loftiness of thought, and more freedom of spirit, than the cultivator of the plains?"

MR. FORESTER.

A modern poet[1] has observed, that the voices of the sea and of the mountains, are the two voices of liberty: the words mountain-liberty have, indeed, become so intimately associated, that I never yet found any one who even thought of questioning their necessary and natural connexion.

MR. FAX.

And yet I question it much; and in the present state of human society I hold the universal inculcation of such a sentiment in poetry and romance, to be not only a most gross delusion, but an error replete with the most pernicious practical consequences. For I have often seen a young man of high and aspiring genius, full of noble enthusiasm for the diffusion of truth and the general happiness of mankind, withdrawn from all intercourse with polished and intellectual society, by the distempered idea, that he would no where find fit aliment for his high cogitations, but among heaths, and rocks, and torrents.

MR. FORESTER.

In a state of society so corrupted as that in which we live, the best instructors and companions are ancient books; and these are best studied in those congenial solitudes, where the energies of nature are most pure and uncontrolled, and the aspect of external things recalls in some measure the departed glory of the world.

MR. FAX.

Holding, as I do, that no branch of knowledge is valuable, but such as in its ultimate results has a plain and practical tendency to the general diffusion of moral and political truth, you must allow me to doubt the efficacy of solitary intercourse with stocks and stones, however rugged and fantastic in their shapes, towards the production of this effect.

MR. FORESTER.

It is matter of historical testimony that occasional retirement into the recesses of nature has produced the most salutary effects of the very kind you require, in the instance of some of the most illustrious minds that have adorned the name of man.

MR. FAX.

That the health and purity of the country, its verdure and its sunshine, have the most beneficial influence on the mental and corporeal faculties, I am very far from being inclined to deny: but this is a different consideration from that of the connexion between the scenery of the mountains and the genius of liberty.[2] Look into the records of the world. What have the mountains done for freedom and mankind? When have the mountains, to speak in the cant of the new school of poetry,[3] "sent forth a voice of power"[4] to awe the oppressors of the world? Mountaineers are for the most part a stupid and ignorant race; and where there are stupidity and ignorance, there will be superstition; and where there is superstition, there will be slavery.

MR. FORESTER.

To a certain extent I cannot but agree with you. The names of Hampden and Milton[5] are associated with the level plains and flat pastures of Buckinghamshire; but I cannot now remember what names of true greatness and unshaken devotion to general liberty, are associated with these heathy rocks and cloud-capped mountains of Cumberland. We have seen a little horde of poets,[6] who brought hither from the vales of the south, the harps which they had consecrated to Truth and Liberty, to acquire new energy in the mountain-winds: and now those harps are attuned to the praise of luxurious power, to the strains of courtly sycophancy, and to the hymns of exploded superstition. But let not the innocent mountains bear the burden of their transgressions.

MR. FAX.

All I mean to say is, that there is nothing in the nature of mountain-scenery either to make men free, or to keep them so. The only source of freedom is intellectual light. The ignorant are always slaves, though they dwell among the Andes. The wise are always free, though they cultivate a savannah. Who is so stupid and so servile as a Swiss, whom you find, like a piece of living furniture, the human latch of every great man's door?[7]

MR. FORESTER.

Let us look back to former days, to the mountains of the North:

"Wild the Runic faith,
And wild the realms where Scandinavian chiefs
And Scalds arose, and hence the Scald's strong verse
Partook the savage wildness. And methinks,
Amid such scenes as these the poet's soul
Might best attain full growth."[8]

MR. FAX.

As to the "Scald's strong verse," I must say I have never seen any specimens of it, that I did not think mere trash. It is little more than a rhapsody of rejoicing in carnage, a ringing of changes on the biting sword and the flowing of blood and the feast of the raven and the vulture, and fulsome flattery of the chieftain, of whom the said Scald was the abject slave, vassal, parasite, and laureat, interspersed with continual hints that he ought to be well paid for his lying panegyrics.[9]

MR. FORESTER.

There is some justice in your observations: nevertheless, I must still contend that those who seek the mountains in a proper frame of feeling, will find in them images of energy and liberty, harmonizing most aptly with the loftiness of an unprejudiced mind, and nerving the arm of resistance to every variety of oppression and imposture, that winds the chains of power round the free-born spirit of man.

CHAPTER XXXVIII.

THE FRACAS.

AFTER a long ramble among heath and rock, and over moss and moor, they began to fear the probability of being benighted[1] among those desolate wilds, when fortunately they found that their track crossed one of the principal roads, which they followed for a short time, and entered a small town, where they stopped for the night at an inn. They were shown up stairs into an apartment separated from another only by a moveable partition, which allowed the two rooms to be occasionally laid into one. They were just sitting down to dinner when they heard the voices of some newly-arrived company in the adjoining apartment, and distinguished the tones of a female voice indicative of alarm and anxiety, and the masculine accents of one who seemed to be alternately comforting the afflicted fair one, and swearing at the obsequious waiter, with reiterated orders, as it appeared, for another chaise immediately. Mr. Fax was not long in divining that the new-comers were two runaway lovers in momentary apprehension of being overtaken; and this conjecture was confirmed, when, after a furious rattle of wheels in the yard, the door of the next apartment was burst open, and a violent scream from the lady was followed by a gruff shout of—"So, ho, Miss, here you are. Gretna,[2] eh? Your journey's marred for this time; and if you get off again, say you have my consent—that's all." Low soft tones of supplication ensued, but in undistinguishable words, and continued to be repeated in the intervals of the following harangue: "Love indeed! don't tell me. Are'n't you my daughter? Answer me that. And have'n't I a right over you till you are twenty-one? You may marry then; but not a rap of the ready:[3] my money's my own all my life. Have'n't I chosen you a proper husband—a nice rich young fellow not above forty-five?—Sixty, you minx! no such thing. Rolling in riches: member for Threevotes: two places, three pensions, and a sinecure: famous borough interest to make all your children generals and archbishops. And here a miserable vagabond with only five hundred a year[4] in landed property.—Pish! love indeed!—own age—congenial minds—pshaw! all a farce. Money—money—money—that's the matter—money is the first thing—money is the second thing—money is the third thing—money is the only thing—money is every thing and all things."—"Vagabond, Sir," said a third voice: "I am a gentleman, and have money sufficient to maintain your daughter in comfort."—"Comfort!" said the gruff voice again; "comfort with five hundred a year, ha! ha! ha! eh! Sir Bonus?"—"Hooh! hooh! hooh! very droll indeed," said a fourth voice, in a sound that seemed a mixture of a cough and a laugh. "Very well, Sir," said the third voice; "I shall not part with my treasure quietly, I assure you."—"Rebellion! flat rebellion against parental authority," exclaimed the second. "But I'm too much for you, youngster. Where are all my varlets and rascals?"

A violent trampling of feet and various sounds of tumult ensued, as if the old gentleman and his party were tearing the lovers asunder by main force; and at length an agonizing scream from the young lady seemed to announce that their purpose was accomplished. Mr. Forester started up with a view of doing all in his power to assist the injured damsel; and Sir Oran Haut-ton, who, as the reader has seen, had very strong feelings of natural justice, and a most chivalrous sympathy with females in distress, rushed with a desperate impulse against the partition, and hurled a great portion of it, with a violent crash, into the adjoining apartment. This unexpected event had the effect of fixing the whole group within for a few moments in motionless surprise in their respective places.

The fat and portly father, who was no other than our old acquaintance Sir Gregory Greenmould, and the old valetudinarian he had chosen for his daughter, Sir Bonus Mac Scrip,[5] were directing the efforts of their myrmidons[6] to separate the youthful pair. The young lady was clinging to her lover with the tenacity of the tendrils of a vine: the young gentleman's right arm was at liberty, and he was keeping the assailants at bay with the poker, which he had seized on the first irruption[7] of the foe, and which had left vestiges of its impression, to speak in ancient phraseology, in various green wounds and bloody coxcombs.[8]

As Sir Oran was not habituated to allow any very long process of syllogistic reasoning to interfere between his conception and execution of the dictates of natural justice, he commenced operations by throwing the assailants one by one down stairs, who, as fast as they could rise from the ground, ran or limped away into sundry holes and coverts.[9] Sir Bonus Mac Scrip retreated through the breach, and concealed himself under the dining-table in Mr. Forester's apartment. Mr. Forester succeeded in preventing Sir Gregory from being thrown after his myrmidons: but Sir Oran kept the fat Baronet a close prisoner in the corner of the room, while the lovers slipped away into the inn-yard, where the chaise they had ordered was in readiness; and the cracking of whips, the trampling of horses, and the rattling of wheels, announced the final discomfiture of the schemes of Sir Gregory Greenmould, and the hopes of Sir Bonus Mac Scrip.

CHAPTER XXXIX.

MAINCHANCE VILLA.[1]

THE next day they resumed their perquisitions,[2] still without any clue to guide them in their search. They had hitherto had the advantage of those halcyon days, which often make the middle of winter[3] a season of serenity and sunshine; but, on this day towards the evening, the sky grew black with clouds, the snow fell rapidly in massy flakes, and the mountains and valleys were covered with one uniform veil of whiteness. All vestiges of road and paths were obliterated. They were winding round the side of a mountain, and their situation began to wear a very unpromising aspect, when, on a sudden turn of the road, the trees and chimneys of a villa burst upon their view in the valley below. To this they bent their way, and on ringing at the gate-bell, and making the requisite inquiries, they found it to be Mainchance Villa, the new residence of Peter Paypaul[4] Paperstamp, Esquire, whom we introduced to our readers in the twenty-eighth Chapter.[5] They sent in their names, and received a polite invitation to walk in. They were shown into a parlour, where they found their old acquaintance Mr. Derrydown tête-à-tête at the piano with Miss Celandina, with whom he was singing a duet. Miss Celandina said, "her papa was just then engaged, but would soon have the pleasure of waiting on them: in the mean time Mr. Derrydown would do the honours of the house." Miss Celandina left the room; and they learned in conversation with Mr. Derrydown, that the latter, finding his case hopeless with Anthelia, had discovered some good reasons in an old ballad for placing his affections where they would be more welcome;[6] he had therefore thrown himself at the feet of Miss Celandina Paperstamp; the young lady's father, having inquired into Mr. Derrydown's fortune, had concluded, from the answer he received, that it would be a very *good match*[7] for his daughter; and the day was already definitively arranged, on which Miss Celandina Paperstamp was to be metamorphosed into Mrs. Derrydown.

Mr. Derrydown informed them, that they would not see Mr. Paperstamp till dinner, as he was closeted in close conference with Mr. Feathernest, Mr. Vamp, Mr. Killthedead, and Mr. Anyside Antijack,[8] a very important personage just arrived from abroad on the occasion of a letter from Mr. Mystic[9] of Cimmerian Lodge, denouncing an approaching period of public light, which had filled Messieurs Paperstamp, Feathernest, Vamp, Killthedead, and Antijack, with the deepest dismay; and they were now holding a consultation on the best means to be adopted for totally and finally extinguishing the light of the human understanding. "I am excluded from the council," proceeded Mr. Derrydown, "and it is their intention to keep me altogether in the dark on the subject; but I shall wait very patiently for the operation of the second bottle, when the wit will be out of the brain, and the cat will be out of the bag."

"Is that picture a family piece?" said Mr. Fax.

"I hardly know," said Mr. Derrydown, "whether there is any relationship between Mr. Paperstamp and the persons there represented; but there is at least a very intimate connexion. The old woman in the scarlet cloak is the illustrious Mother Goose—the two children playing at see-saw, are Margery Daw,[10] and Tommy with his Banbury cake[11]—the little boy and girl, the one with a broken pitcher, and the other with a broken head, are little Jack and Jill:[12] the house, at the door of which the whole party is grouped, is the famous house that Jack built;[13] you see the clock through the window, and the mouse running up it, as in that sublime strain of immortal genius, entitled Dickery Dock:[14] and the boy in the corner is little Jack Horner[15] eating his Christmas pie. The latter is one of the most splendid examples on record of the admirable practical doctrine of "taking care of number one,"[16] and he is therefore in double favour with Mr. Paperstamp, for his excellence as a pattern of moral and political wisdom, and for the beauty of the poetry in which his great achievement of extracting a plum from the Christmas pie is celebrated. Mr. Paperstamp, Mr. Feathernest, Mr. Vamp, Mr. Killthedead, and Mr. Anyside Antijack, are unanimously agreed that the Christmas pie in question is a type and symbol of the public purse; and as that is a pie in which every one of them has a finger, they look with great envy and admiration on little Jack Horner, who extracted a *plum* from it, and who I believe haunts their dreams with his pie and his plum, saying, "Go, and do thou likewise!"[17]

The secret council broke up, and Mr. Paperstamp entering with his four compeers, bade the new-comers welcome to Mainchance Villa, and introduced to them Mr. Anyside Antijack. Mr. Paperstamp did not much like Mr. Forester's modes of thinking; indeed he disliked them the more, from their having once been his own; but a man of large landed property was well worth a little civility, as there was no knowing what turn affairs might take, what party might come into place, and who might have the cutting up of the Christmas pie.

They now adjourned to dinner, during which, as usual, little was said, and much was done. When the wine began to circulate, Mr. Feathernest held forth for some time in praise of himself; and by the assistance of a little smattering in Mr. Mystic's synthetical logic,[18] proved himself to be a model of taste, genius, consistency, and public virtue. This was too good an example to be thrown away; and Mr. Paperstamp followed it up with a very lofty encomium on his own virtues and talents, declaring that he did not believe so great a genius, or so amiable a man, as himself, Peter Paypaul Paperstamp, Esquire, of Mainchance Villa, had appeared in the world since the days of Jack the Giant-killer, whose *coat of darkness*[19] he hoped would become the costume of all the rising generation, whenever adequate provision should be made for the whole people to be taught and trained.

Mr. Vamp, Mr. Killthedead, and Mr. Anyside Antijack, were all very loud in their encomiums of the wine, which Mr. Paperstamp observed had been tasted for him by his friend Mr. Feathernest, who was a great connoisseur in "Sherris sack."[20]

Mr. Derrydown was very intent on keeping the bottle in motion, in the hope of bringing the members of the criticopoetical[21] council into that state of blind self-love, when the great vacuum of the head, in which brain was, like Mr. Harris's indefinite article, *supplied by negation,*[22] would be inflated with œnogen[23] gas, or, in other words, with the fumes of wine, the effect of which, according to psychological chemistry, is, after filling up every chink and crevice of the cranial void, to evolve through the labial valve,[24] bringing with it all the secrets both of memory and anticipation, which had been carefully laid up in the said chinks and crevices. This state at length arrived; and Mr. Derrydown, to quicken its operation, contrived to pick a quarrel with Mr. Vamp, who being naturally very testy and waspish, poured out upon him a torrent of invectives, to the infinite amusement of Mr. Derrydown, who, however, affecting to be angry, said to him in a tragical tone,

> "Thus in dregs of folly sunk,
> Art thou, miscreant, mad or drunk?
> Cups intemperate always teach
> Virulent abusive speech.'"[25]

---

* Cottle's Edda, or, as the author calls it, *Translation* of the Edda, which is a misnomer.

This produced a general cry of Chair! chair! Mr. Paperstamp called Mr. Derrydown to order. The latter apologized with as much gravity as he could assume, and said, to make amends for his warmth, he would give them a toast, and pronounced accordingly: "Your scheme for extinguishing the light of the human understanding: may it meet the success it merits!"

MR. ANYSIDE ANTIJACK.

Nothing can be in a more hopeful train. We must set the alarmists at work, as in the days of the Antijacobin war: when, to be sure, we had one or two honest men among our opposers* [26]—*(Mr. Feathernest and Mr. Paperstamp smiled and bowed)*—though they were for the most part ill read in history, and ignorant of human nature.† [27]

MR. FEATHERNEST AND MR. PAPERSTAMP.

How, Sir?

MR. ANYSIDE ANTIJACK.

For the most part, observe me. Of course, I do not include my quondam antagonists, and now very dear friends, Mr. Paperstamp and Mr. Feathernest, who have altered their minds, as the sublime Burke altered his mind,‡ from the most disinterested motives. [28]

MR. FORESTER.

Yet there are some persons, and those not the lowest in the scale of moral philosophy, who have called the sublime Burke a pensioned apostate. [29]

MR. VAMP.

Moral philosophy! Every man who talks of moral philosophy is a thief and a rascal, and will never make any scruple

---

* Quarterly Review, No. XXXI. p. 237.
† Ibid.
‡ Quarterly Review, No. XXXI. p. 252.

of seducing his neighbour's wife, or stealing his neighbour's property.[*][30]

MR. FORESTER.

You can prove that assertion, of course?

MR. VAMP.

Prove it! The editor of the Legitimate Review required to prove an assertion!

MR. ANYSIDE ANTIJACK.

The church is in danger![31]

MR. FORESTER.

I confess I do not see how the church is endangered by a simple request to prove the asserted necessary connexion between the profession of moral philosophy and the practice of robbery.

MR. ANYSIDE ANTIJACK.

For your satisfaction, Sir, and from my disposition to oblige you, as you are a gentleman of family and fortune, I will prove it. Every moral philosopher discards the creed and command-ments:[†][32] the sixth commandment says, Thou shalt not steal; therefore, every moral philosopher is a thief.

MR. FEATHERNEST, MR. KILLTHEDEAD, AND MR. PAPERSTAMP.

Nothing can be more logical. The church is in danger! The church is in danger!

MR. VAMP.

Keep up that. It is an infallible tocsin[33] for rallying all the old women in the country about us, when every thing else fails.

---

[*] Quarterly Review, No. XXXI. p. 227.
[†] Quarterly Review, No. XXXI. p. 227.

MR. VAMP, MR. FEATHERNEST, MR. PAPERSTAMP,
MR. KILLTHEDEAD, AND MR. ANYSIDE ANTIJACK.

The church is in danger! the church is in danger!

MR. FORESTER.

I am very well aware that the time has been when the voice of reason could be drowned by clamour, and by rallying round the banners of corruption and delusion a mass of blind and bigoted prejudices, that had no real connexion with the political question which it was the object to cry down: but I see with pleasure that those days are gone. The people read and think;[34] their eyes are opened; they know that all their grievances arise from the pressure of taxation far beyond their means, from the fictitious circulation of paper-money, and from the corrupt and venal state of popular representation. These facts lie in a very small compass; and till you can reason them out of this knowledge, you may vociferate "The church is in danger" for ever, without a single unpaid voice to join in the outcry.

MR. FEATHERNEST.

My friend Mr. Mystic holds that it is a very bad thing for the people to read:[35] so it certainly is. Oh for the happy ignorance of former ages! when the people were dolts, and knew themselves to be so.[*][36] An ignorant man judging from instinct, judges much better than a man who reads, and is consequently misinformed.[†][37]

MR. VAMP.

Unless he reads the Legitimate Review.

MR. PAPERSTAMP.

Darkness! darkness! Jack the Giant-killer's coat of darkness! That is your only wear.

---

[*] Quarterly Review, No. XXXI. p. 226.
[†] Ibid.

MR. ANYSIDE ANTIJACK.

There was a time when we could lead the people any way, and make them join with all their lungs in the yell of war: then they were people of sound judgment, and of honest and honourable feelings:[*][38] but when they pretend to feel the pressure of personal suffering, and to read and think about its causes and remedies—such impudence is intolerable.

MR. FAX.

Are they not the same people still? If they were capable of judging then, are they not capable of judging now?

MR. ANYSIDE ANTIJACK.

By no means: they are only capable of judging when they see with our eyes; then they see straight forward; when they pretend to use their own, they squint.[†][39] They saw with our eyes in the beginning of the Antijacobin war. They would have determined on that war, if it had been decided by universal suffrage.[‡][40]

MR. FAX.

Why was not the experiment tried?

MR. ANYSIDE ANTIJACK.

It was not convenient. But they were in a most amiable ferment of intolerant loyalty.[§][41]

MR. FORESTER.

Of which the proof is to be found in the immortal Gagging Bills,[42] by which that intolerant loyalty was coerced.

MR. ANYSIDE ANTIJACK.

The Gagging Bills? Hem! ha! What shall we say to that?— *(To Mr. Vamp.)*

---

[*] Quarterly Review, No. XXXI. p. 236.
[†] Quarterly Review, No. XXXI. p. 226.
[‡] Ibid. p. 228.
[§] Ibid.

MR. VAMP.

Say? The church is in danger!

MR. FEATHERNEST, MR. PAPERSTAMP,
MR. KILLTHEDEAD, AND MR. ANYSIDE ANTIJACK.

The church is in danger! the church is in danger!

MR. FORESTER.

Why was a war undertaken to prevent revolution, if all the people of this country were so well fortified in loyalty? Did they go to war for the purpose of forcibly preventing themselves from following a bad example against their own will? For this is what your argument seems to imply.

MR. FAX.

That the people were in a certain degree of ferment, is true: but it required a great deal of management and delusion to turn that ferment into the channel of foreign war.

MR. ANYSIDE ANTIJACK.

Well, Sir, and there was no other way to avoid domestic reform, which every man who desires is a ruffian, a scoundrel, and an incendiary,[*43] as much so as those two rascals Rousseau and Voltaire, who were the trumpeters of Hebert and Marat.[†44] Reform, Sir, is not to be thought of; we have been at war twenty-five years to prevent it; and to have it after all, would be very hard. We have got the national debt instead of it: in my opinion a very pretty substitute.

MR. DERRYDOWN *sings.*

And I'll hang on thy neck, my love, my love,
And I'll hang on thy neck for aye!
And closer and closer I'll press thee, my love,
Until my *dying day.*[45]

---

[*] Quarterly Review, No. XXXI. p. 273, *et passim.*
[†] Ibid. p. 258.

MR. ANYSIDE ANTIJACK.

I am happy to reflect that the silly question of reform will have very few supporters in the Honourable House: but few as they are, the number would be lessened, if all who come into Parliament by means which that question attempts to stigmatize, would abstain from voting upon it. Undoubtedly such practices are scandalous, as being legally, and therefore morally wrong: but it is false that any evil to the legislature arises from them.* [46]

MR. FORESTER.

Perhaps not, Sir; but very great evil arises through them from the legislature to the people. Your admission, that they are legally, and *therefore* morally wrong, implies a very curious method of deriving morality from law; but I suspect there is much immorality that is perfectly legal, and much legality that is supremely immoral. But these practices, you admit, are both legally and morally wrong; yet you call it a silly question to propose their cessation; and you assert, that all who wish to abolish them, all who wish to abolish illegal and immoral practices, are ruffians, scoundrels, and incendiaries.

MR. KILLTHEDEAD.

Yes, and madmen moreover, and villains.† [47] We are all upon gunpowder! The insane and the desperate are scattering

---

* Quarterly Review, No. XXXI. p. 258.
† Quarterly Review, No. XXXI. p. 249. It is curious, that in the fourth article of the same number, [48] from which I have borrowed so many exquisite passages, the reviewers are very angry that certain "scandalous and immoral practices" in the island of Wahoo are not reformed: but certainly, according to the logic of these reviewers, the government of Wahoo is entitled to look upon *them* in the light of "ruffians, scoundrels, incendiaries, firebrands, madmen, and villains;" since all these hard names belong of primary right to those who propose the reformation of "scandalous and immoral practices!" The people of Wahoo, it appears, are very much addicted to drunkenness and debauchery; and the reviewers, in the plenitude of their wisdom, recommend that a few clergymen should be sent out to them, by way of mending their morals. It does not appear, whether King

firebrands!'[50] We shall all be blown up in a body: sinecures, rotten boroughs, secret-service-men, and the whole *honourable band of gentlemen pensioners*, will all be blown up in a body! *A stand! a stand! it is time to make a stand against popular encroachment!*

MR. VAMP, MR. FEATHERNEST, AND
MR. PAPERSTAMP.

The church is in danger!

MR. ANYSIDE ANTIJACK.

Here is the great blunderbuss that is to blow the whole nation to atoms! the *Spencean* blunderbuss![51]—*(Saying these*

Tamaahmaah is a king by *divine right*; but we must take it for granted that he is not; as otherwise, the Quarterly Reviewers would either not admit that there were any "scandalous and immoral practices" under his government, or, if they did admit them, they would not be such "incendiaries, madmen, and villains," as to advocate their reformation. There are some circumstances, however, which are conclusive against the *legitimacy* of King Tamaahmaah, which are these: that he is a man of great "feeling, energy, and steadiness of conduct;" that he "goes about among his people to learn their wants;" and that he has "prevented the recurrence of those horrid murders" which disgraced the reigns of his predecessors: from which it is obvious that he has neither put to death brave and generous men, who surrendered themselves under the faith of treaties, nor re-established a fallen Inquisition, nor sent those to whom he owed his crown, to the dungeon and the galleys.

In the tenth article of the same number,[49] the reviewers pour forth the bitterness of their gall against Mr. Warden of the Northumberland, who has detected them in promulgating much gross and foolish falsehood concerning the captive Napoleon. They labour most assiduously to *impeach his veracity* and to *discredit his judgment*. On the first point, it is sufficient evidence of the truth of his statements, that the Quarterly Reviewers contradict them: but, on the second, they accuse him, among other misdemeanors, of having called their Review "*a respectable work!*" which certainly *discredits his judgment* completely.

˙ Quarterly Review, No. XXXI. p. 249.—The reader will be reminded of *Croaker* in the fourth act of the *Good-natured Man:* "Blood and gunpowder in every line of it. Blown up! murderous dogs! all blown up! *(Reads.)* 'Our pockets are low, and money we must have.' Ay, there's the reason: they'll blow us up *because they have got low pockets.* . . . . . Perhaps this moment I'm treading on lighted matches, blazing brimstone, and barrels of gunpowder. They are preparing to blow me up into the clouds. Murder! . . . . . Here, John, Nicodemus, search the house. Look into the cellars, to see if there be any combustibles below, and above in the apartments, that no matches be thrown in at the windows. *Let all the fires be put out,* and let the *engine* be drawn out in the yard, to *play upon the house* in case of necessity."—*Croaker* was a deep politician. The *engine* to *play* upon the *house:* mark that!

words, he produced a pop-gun[52] *from his pocket,* *and shot off a paper pellet*[59] *in the ear of Mr. Paperstamp,*

> *"Who in a kind of study sate*
> *Denominated brown;"*[60]

which made the latter spring up in sudden fright, to the irreme-diable perdition of a decanter of "Sherris sack," over which Mr. Feathernest lamented bitterly.)

MR. FORESTER.

I do not see what connexion the Spencean theory, the impracticable chimæra of an obscure herd of fanatics, has with the great national question of parliamentary reform.

MR. ANYSIDE ANTIJACK.

Sir, you may laugh at this popgun, but you will find it the mallet of Thor.[†61] The Spenceans are far more respectable than the parliamentary reformers, and have a more distinct and intelligible system!!![‡62]

---

* This illustration of the old fable of the mouse and the mountain,[53] falls short of an exhibition in the Honourable House, on the 29th of January 1817; when Mr. Canning, amidst a tremendous denunciation of the parliamentary reform-ers, and a rhetorical chaos of storms, whirlwinds, rising suns, and twilight assas-sins, produced in proof of his charges—*Spence's Plan!*[54] which was received with an *éclat* of laughter on one side, and shrugs of surprise, disappointment, and dis-approbation, on the other. I can find but one parallel for the Right Honourable Gentleman's dismay:

> So having said, awhile he stood, expecting
> Their universal shout and high applause
> To fill his ear; when contrary he hears
> On all sides, from innumerable tongues,
> A dismal universal hiss, the sound
> Of public scorn. *Paradise Lost*, X. 504.[55]

This Spencean chimæra, which is the very foolishness of folly,[56] and which was till lately invisible to the naked eye of the political entomologist, has since been subjected to a *lens* of *extraordinary power*, under which, like an insect in a micro-scope, it has appeared a formidable and complicated monster, all bristles, scales, and claws, with a "husk about it like a chestnut:"[57] *Horridus, in jaculis, et pelle Libystidis ursæ!*[58]

† Quarterly Review, No. XXXI. p. 271.
‡ Ibid.

MR. VAMP.

Bravo! bravo! bravo! There is not another man in our corps with brass enough to make such an assertion, but Mr. Anyside Antijack.—*(Reiterated shouts of Bravo! from Mr. Vamp, Mr. Feathernest, Mr. Paperstamp, and Mr. Killthedead.)*

MR. KILLTHEDEAD.

Make out that, and our job is done.

MR. ANYSIDE ANTIJACK.

Make it out! Nonsense! I shall take it for granted: I shall set up the Spencean plan as a more sensible plan than that of the parliamentary reformers: then knock down the former, and argue against the latter, *à fortiori.*—*(The shouts of Bravo! here became perfectly deafening, the criticopoetical corps being by this time much more than half-seas-over.)*[63]

MR. KILLTHEDEAD.

The members for rotten boroughs are the most independent members in the Honourable House, and the representatives of most constituents least so.[*][64]

MR. FAX.

How will you prove that?

MR. KILLTHEDEAD.

By calling the former gentlemen, and the latter, mob-representatives.[†][65]

MR. VAMP.

Nothing can be more logical.

MR. FAX.

Do you call that logic?

MR. VAMP.

Excellent logic. At least it will pass for such with our readers.

---

[*] Quarterly Review, No. XXXI. p. 258.
[†] Ibid.

MR. ANYSIDE ANTIJACK.

We, and those who think with us, are the only wise and good men.[66]

MR. FORESTER.

May I take the liberty to inquire, what you mean by a wise and a good man?

MR. ANYSIDE ANTIJACK.

A wise man is he who looks after the one thing needful; and a good man[67] is he who has it. The acme of wisdom and goodness in conjunction, consists in appropriating as much as possible of the public money; and saying to those from whose pockets it is taken, "I am perfectly satisfied with things as they are.[68] Let *well* alone!"

MR. PAPERSTAMP.

We shall make out a very good case; but you must not forget to call the present public distress an awful dispensation:[†69] a little pious cant goes a great way towards turning the thoughts of men from the dangerous and jacobinical propensity of looking into moral and political causes, for moral and political effects.

MR. FAX.

But the moral and political causes are now too obvious, and too universally known, to be obscured by any such means. All the arts and eloquence of corruption may be overthrown by the enumeration of these simple words: boroughs, taxes, and paper-money.

MR. ANYSIDE ANTIJACK.

Paper-money! What, is the ghost of bullion abroad?[‡70]

---

[*] Quarterly Review, No. XXXI. p. 273.
[†] Quarterly Review, No. XXXI. p. 276.
[‡] Ibid. p. 260.

MR. FORESTER.

Yes! and till you can make the buried substance burst the paper cerements of its sepulchre, its ghost will continue to walk like the ghost of Cæsar, saying to the desolated nation: "I am thy evil spirit!"[71]

MR. ANYSIDE ANTIJACK.

I must say, I am very sorry to find a gentleman like you, taking the part of the swinish multitude,[72] who are only fit for beasts of burden, to raise subsistence for their betters, pay taxes for placemen, and recruit the army and navy for the benefit of legitimacy, divine right, the Jesuits, the Pope, the Inquisition, and the Virgin Mary's petticoat.[73]

MR. PAPERSTAMP.

Hear! hear! hear! Hear the voice which the stream of Tendency[74] is uttering for elevation of our thought!

MR. FORESTER.

It was once said by a poet,[75] whose fallen state none can more bitterly lament than I do:

> We shall exult if they who rule the land
> Be men who hold its many blessings dear,
> Wise, upright, valiant; not a venal band,
> Who are to judge of danger which they fear,
> And honour which they do not understand.

MR. FEATHERNEST.

Poets, Sir, are not amenable to censure, however frequently their political opinions may exhibit marks of inconsistency.[*][76] The Muse, as a French author says, is a mere *étourdie*, a *folâtre*[77] who may play at her option on heath or on turf, and transfer her song at pleasure, from Hampden to Ferdinand, and from Washington to Louis.[78]

---

[*] Quarterly Review, No. XXXI. p. 192.

MR. FORESTER.

If a poet be contented to consider himself in the light of a merry-andrew,[79] be it so. But if he assume the garb of moral austerity, and pour forth against corruption and oppression the language of moral indignation, there would at least be some decency, if, when he changes sides, he would let the world see that conversion and promotion have not gone hand in hand.

MR. FEATHERNEST.

What decency might be in that, I know not: but of this I am very certain, that there would be no wisdom in it.

MR. ANYSIDE ANTIJACK.

No! no! there would be no wisdom in it.

MR. FEATHERNEST.

Sir, I am a wise and a good man: mark that, Sir; ay, and an honourable man.

MR. VAMP.

"So are we all, all honourable men!"[80]

MR. ANYSIDE ANTIJACK.

And we will stick by one another with heart and hand——

MR. KILLTHEDEAD.

To make a stand against popular encroachment——

MR. FEATHERNEST.

To bring back the glorious ignorance of the feudal ages——

MR. PAPERSTAMP.

To rebuild the mystic temples of venerable superstition——

MR. VAMP.

To extinguish, totally and finally, the light of the human understanding——

MR. ANYSIDE ANTIJACK.

And to get all we can for our trouble!

MR. FEATHERNEST.

So we will all say.

MR. PAPERSTAMP.

And so we will all sing.

QUINTETTO.

MR. FEATHERNEST, MR. VAMP, MR. KILLTHEDEAD,
MR. PAPERSTAMP, AND MR. ANYSIDE ANTIJACK.
To the tune of *"Turning, turning, turning, as
the wheel goes round."*[81]

RECITATIVE. MR. PAPERSTAMP.
Jack Horner's CHRISTMAS PIE my learned nurse
Interpreted to mean the *public purse.*
From thence a *plum* he drew. O happy Horner!
Who would not be ensconced in thy snug corner?

THE FIVE.
While round the public board all eagerly we linger,
For what we can get we will try, try, try:
And we'll all have a finger, a finger, a finger,
We'll all have a finger in the CHRISTMAS PIE.

MR. FEATHERNEST.
By my own poetic laws, I'm a dealer in applause
For those who don't deserve it, but will buy, buy, buy:
So round the court I linger, and thus I get a finger,
A finger, finger, finger in the CHRISTMAS PIE.

THE FIVE.
And we'll all have a finger, a finger, a finger,
We'll all have a finger in the CHRISTMAS PIE.

MR. VAMP.
My share of pie to win, I will dash through thick and thin,
And philosophy and liberty shall fly, fly, fly:
And truth and taste shall know, that their everlasting foe
Has a finger, finger, finger in the CHRISTMAS PIE.

THE FIVE.

And we'll all have a finger, a finger, a finger,
We'll all have a finger in the CHRISTMAS pie.

MR. KILLTHEDEAD.

I'll make my verses rattle with the din of war and battle,
For war doth increase sa-la-ry, ry, ry:[82]
And I'll shake the public ears with the triumph of Algiers,
And thus I'll get a finger in the CHRISTMAS pie.

THE FIVE.

And we'll all have a finger, a finger, a finger,
We'll all have a finger in the CHRISTMAS pie.

MR. PAPERSTAMP.

And while you thrive by ranting, I'll try my luck at canting,[83]
And scribble verse and prose all so dry, dry, dry:
And Mystic's patent smoke[84] public intellect shall choke,
And we'll all have a finger in the CHRISTMAS pie.

THE FIVE.

We'll all have a finger, a finger, a finger,
We'll all have a finger in the CHRISTMAS pie.

MR. ANYSIDE ANTIJACK.

My tailor is so clever, that my coat will turn for ever,
And take any colour you can dye, dye, dye:
For all my earthly wishes are among the loaves and fishes,[85]
And to have my little finger in the CHRISTMAS pie.

THE FIVE.

And we'll all have a finger, a finger, a finger,
We'll all have a finger in the CHRISTMAS pie.[86]

CHAPTER XL.

THE HOPES OF THE WORLD.

THE mountain-roads being now buried in snow, they were compelled,[1] on leaving Mainchance Villa, to follow the most broad and beaten track, and they entered on a turnpike road which led in the direction of the sea.

"I no longer wonder," said Mr. Fax, "that men in general are so much disposed, as I have found them, to look with supreme contempt on the literary character, seeing the abject servility and venality by which it is so commonly debased."*

MR. FORESTER.

What then becomes of the hopes of the world, which you have admitted to consist entirely in the progress of mind, allowing, as you must allow, the incontrovertible fact of the physical deterioration of the human race?

MR. FAX.

When I speak of the mind, I do not allude either to poetry or to periodical criticism, nor in any great degree to physical

---

* "To scatter praise or blame without regard to justice, is to destroy the distinction of good and evil. Many have no other test of actions than general opinion; and all are so far influenced by a sense of reputation, that they are often restrained by fear of reproach, and excited by hope of honour, when other principles have lost their power; nor can any species of prostitution promote general depravity more, than that which destroys the force of praise by showing that it may be acquired without deserving it, and which, by setting free the active and ambitious from the dread of infamy, lets loose the rapacity of power, and weakens the only authority by which greatness is controlled. What credit can he expect who professes himself the hireling of vanity however profligate, and without shame or scruple celebrates the worthless, dignifies the mean, and gives to the corrupt, licentious, and oppressive, the ornaments which ought only to add grace to truth, and loveliness to innocence? EVERY OTHER KIND OF ADULTERATION, HOWEVER SHAMEFUL, HOWEVER MISCHIEVOUS, IS LESS DETESTABLE THAN THE CRIME OF COUNTERFEITING CHARACTERS, AND FIXING THE STAMP OF LITERARY SANCTION UPON THE DROSS AND REFUSE OF THE WORLD." —*Rambler*, No. 136.[2]

science; but I rest my hopes on the very same basis with Mr. Mystic's fear—the general diffusion of moral and political truth.

MR. FORESTER.

For poetry, its best days are gone. Homer, Shakespeare, and Milton, will return no more.

MR. FAX.

Lucretius[3] we yet may hope for.

MR. FORESTER.

Not till superstition and prejudice have been shorn of a much larger portion of their power. If Lucretius should arise among us in the present day, exile or imprisonment would be his infallible portion. We have yet many steps to make, before we shall arrive at the liberality and toleration of Tiberius!*[4] And as to physical science, though it does in some measure weaken the dominion of mental error, yet I fear, where it proves itself, in one instance, the friend of human liberty, it will be found in ninety-nine, the slave of corruption and luxury.

MR. FAX.

In many cases, science is both morally and politically neutral, and its speculations have no connexion whatever with the business of life.

MR. FORESTER.

It is true; and such speculations are often called sublime: though the sublimity of uselessness passes my comprehension. But the neutrality is only apparent: for it has in these cases the real practical effect, and a most pernicious one it is, of withdrawing some of the highest and most valuable minds from the only path of real utility, which I agree with you to be

---

* Deorum injurias diis curæ. *Tiberius apud Tacit. Ann. I.* 73.

that of moral and political knowledge, to pursuits of no more real importance than that of keeping a dozen eggs at a time dancing one after another in the air.

MR. FAX.

If it be admitted on the one hand, that the progress of luxury has kept pace with that of physical science, it must be acknowledged on the other, that superstition has decayed in at least an equal proportion; and I think it cannot be denied that the world is a gainer by the exchange.

MR. FORESTER.

The decay of superstition is immeasurably beneficial: but the growth of luxury is not therefore the less pernicious. It is lamentable to reflect that *there is most indigence in the richest countries;*[5] and that the increase of superfluous enjoyment in

---

* "Besides all these evils of modern times which I have mentioned, there is in some countries of Europe, and particularly in England, another evil peculiar to civilized countries, but quite unknown in barbarous nations. The evil I mean is *indigence,* and the reader will be surprised when I tell him that it is *greatest in the richest countries;* and, therefore, in England, which I believe is the richest country in Europe, there is more indigence than in any other; for the number of people that are there maintained on public or private charity, and who may therefore be called *beggars,* is prodigious. What proportion they may bear to the whole people, I have never heard computed: but I am sure it must be very great. And I am afraid in those countries they call rich, indigence is not confined to the lower sort of people, but extends even to the better sort: for such is the effect of wealth in a nation, that (however paradoxical it may appear) it does at last make all men poor and indigent; the lower sort through idleness and debauchery, the better sort through luxury, vanity, and extravagant expense. Now I would desire to know from the greatest admirers of modern times, who maintain that the human race is not degenerated but rather improved, whether they know any other source of human misery, besides vice, disease, and indigence, and whether these three are not in the greatest abundance in the rich and flourishing country of England? I would further ask these gentlemen, whether in the cities of the ancient world there were poor's houses, hospitals, infirmaries, and those other receptacles of indigence and disease, which we see in the modern cities? And whether in the streets of ancient Athens and Rome there were so many objects of disease, deformity, and misery to be seen, as in our streets, besides those which are concealed from public view in the houses above mentioned. In later times, indeed, in those cities, when the corruption of manners was almost as great as among us, some such things might have been seen, as we are sure they were to be seen in Constantinople, under the later Greek Emperors."—*Ancient Metaphysics,* vol. iii. p. 194.

the few, is counterbalanced by the proportionate diminution of comfort in the many. Splendid equipages and sumptuous dwellings are far from being symbols of general prosperity. The palace of luxurious indolence is much rather the symbol of a thousand hovels, by the labours and privations of whose wretched inhabitants that baleful splendour is maintained. Civilization, vice, and folly grow old together. Corruption begins among the higher orders, and from them descends to the people; so that in every nation the ancient nobility is the first to exhibit symptoms of corporeal and mental degeneracy, and to show themselves unfit both for council and war. If you recapitulate the few titled names that will adorn the history of the present times, you will find that almost all of them are new creations.[6] The corporeal decay of mankind I hold to be undeniable: the increase of general knowledge I allow: but reason is of slow growth; and if men in general only become more corrupt as they become more learned, the progress of literature will oppose no adequate counterpoise to that of avarice, luxury, and disease.

MR. FAX.

Certainly, the progress of reason is slow, but the ground which it has once gained it never abandons. The interest of rulers, and the prejudices of the people, are equally hostile to every thing that comes in the shape of innovation; but all that now wears the strongest sanction of antiquity was once received with reluctance under the semblance of novelty: and that reason, which in the present day can scarcely obtain a footing from the want of precedents, will grow with the growth of years, and become a precedent in its turn.[*]

---

[*] "Omnia, quæ nunc vetustissima creduntur, nova fuêre. Inveterascet hoc quoque: et, quod hodie exemplis tuemur, inter exempla erit."—TACITUS, *Ann. XI.* 24.[7]

MR. FORESTER.

Reason may be diffused in society, but it is only in minds which *have courage enough to despise prejudice, and virtue enough to love truth only for itself,*[8] that its seeds will germinate into wholesome and vigorous life. The love of truth is the most noble quality of human intellect, the most delightful in the interchange of private confidence, the most important in the direction of those speculations which have public happiness for their aim. Yet of all qualities this is the most rare: it is the Phœnix of the intellectual world. In private intercourse, how very very few are they whose assertions carry conviction! How much petty deception, paltry equivocation, hollow profession, smiling malevolence, and polished hypocrisy, combine to make a desert and a solitude of what is called society! How much empty pretence, and simulated patriotism, and shameless venality, and unblushing dereliction of principle, and clamorous recrimination, and daring imposture, and secret cabal, and mutual undermining of "Honourable Friends,"[9] render utterly loathsome and disgusting the theatre of public life! How much timid deference to vulgar prejudice, how much misrepresentation of the motives of conscientious opponents, how many appeals to unreflecting passion, how much assumption of groundless hypotheses, how many attempts to darken the clearest light and entangle the simplest clue, render not only nugatory but pernicious the speculations of moral and political reason! pernicious, inasmuch as it is better for the benighted traveller to remain stationary in darkness, than to follow an *ignis fatuus*[10] through the fen! Falsehood is the great vice of the age: falsehood of heart, falsehood of mind, falsehood of every form and mode of intellect and intercourse: so that it is hardly possible *to find a man of worth and goodness of whom to make a friend: but he who does find such an one will have*

---

* Drummond's Academical Questions—Preface, p. 4.

more enjoyment of friendship, than in a better age; for he will be doubly fond of him, and will love him as Hamlet does Horatio, and with him retiring, and getting as it were under the shelter of a wall, will let the storm of life blow over him.[*11]

MR. FAX.

But that retirement must be consecrated to philosophical labour, or, however delightful to the individuals, it will be treason to the public cause. Be the world as bad as it may, it would necessarily be much worse if the votaries of truth and the children of virtue were all to withdraw from its vortex, and leave it to itself. If reason be progressive, however slowly, the wise and good have sufficient encouragement to persevere; and even if the doctrine of deterioration be true, it is no less their duty to contribute all in their power to retard its progress, by investigating its causes and remedies.

MR. FORESTER.

Undoubtedly. But the progress of theoretical knowledge has a most fearful counterpoise in the accelerated depravation of practical morality. The frantic love of money, which seems to govern our contemporaries to a degree unprecedented in the history of man, paralyses the energy of independence, darkens the light of reason, and blights the blossoms of love.

MR. FAX.

The *amor sceleratus habendi*[12] is not peculiar either to our times or to civilized life. *Money you must have, no matter from whence,* is a sentence, if we may believe Euripides, as old as the heroic age:[13] and *the monk Rubruquis says of the Tartars, that, as parents keep all their daughters till they can sell them, their maids are sometimes very stale before they are married.*[†14]

---

[*] Ancient Metaphysics, vol. iii. p. 280.
[†] Malthus on Population, book i. chap. vii.

MR. FORESTER.

In that respect, then, I must acknowledge the Tartars and we are much on a par. It is a collateral question well worth considering, how far the security of property, which contributes so much to the diffusion of knowledge, and the permanence of happiness, is favourable to the growth of individual virtue?

MR. FAX.

Security of property tranquillizes the minds of men, and fits them to shine rather in speculation than in action. In turbulent and insecure states of society, when the fluctuations of power, or the incursions of predatory neighbours, hang like the sword of Damocles[15] over the most flourishing possessions, friends are more dear to each other, mutual services and sacrifices are more useful and more necessary, the energies of heart and hand are continually called forth, and shining examples of the self-oblivious virtues are produced in the same proportion as mental speculation is unknown or disregarded: but our admiration of these virtues must be tempered by the remark, that they arise more from impulsive feeling than from reflective principle; and that, where life and fortune hold by such a precarious tenure, the first may be risked, and the second abandoned, with much less effort than would be required for inferior sacrifices in more secure and tranquil times.

MR. FORESTER.

Alas, my friend! I would willingly see such virtues as do honour to human nature, without being very solicitous as to the comparative quantities of impulse and reflection in which they originate. If the security of property and the diffusion of general knowledge were attended with a corresponding increase of benevolence and *individual mental power*, no philanthropist could look with despondency on the prospects of the world: but I can discover no symptoms of either the one or the other.

Insatiable accumulators, overgrown capitalists, fatteners on public spoil, I cannot but consider as excrescences on the body politic, typical of disease and prophetic of decay: yet it is to these and such as these, that the poet tunes his harp, and the man of science consecrates his labours: it is for them that an enormous portion of the population is condemned to unhealthy manufactories, not less deadly but more lingering than the pestilence: it is for them that the world rings with lamentations, if the most trivial accident, the most transient sickness, the most frivolous disappointment befal them: but when the prisons swarm, when the workhouses overflow, when whole parishes declare themselves bankrupt, when thousands perish by famine in the wintry streets, where then is the poet, where is the man of science, where is the *elegant* philosopher?[16] The poet is singing hymns to the great ones of the world, the man of science is making discoveries for the adornment of their dwellings or the enhancement of their culinary luxuries, and the *elegant* philosopher is much too refined a personage to allow such vulgar subjects as the sufferings of the poor to interfere with his sublime speculations. *They are married, and cannot come!*[17]

MR. FAX.

Εψαυσας αλγεινοτατας εμοι μεριμνας! [18] Those *elegant* philosophers are among the most fatal enemies to the advancement of moral and political knowledge: laborious triflers, profound investigators of nothing, everlasting talkers about taste and beauty, who see in the starving beggar only the picturesqueness of his rags, and in the ruined cottage only the harmonizing tints of moss, mildew, and stonecrop.[19]

MR. FORESTER.

We talk of public feeling and national sympathy. Our dictionaries may define those words, and our lips may echo

---

* Sophocles, Antigone, 850. (Ed. Erfurdt.)

them: but we must look for the realities among less enlightened nations. The Canadian savages cannot imagine the possibility of any individual in a community having a full meal, while another has but half an one:[20] still less could they imagine that one should have too much, while another had nothing. Theirs is that bond of brotherhood which nature weaves and civilization breaks, and from which, the older nations grow, the farther they recede.

MR. FAX.

It cannot be otherwise. The state you have described, is adapted only to a small community, and to the infancy of human society. I shall make a very liberal concession to your views, if I admit it to be possible that the middle stage of the progress of man, is worse than either the point from which he started, or that at which he will arrive. But it is my decided opinion that we have passed that middle stage, and that every evil incident to the present condition of human society will be removed by the diffusion of moral and political knowledge, and the general increase of moral and political liberty. I contemplate with great satisfaction the rapid decay of many hoary absurdities, which a few transcendental hierophants of the venerable and the mysterious are labouring in vain to revive. I look with well-grounded confidence to a period when there will be neither slaves among the northern, nor monks among the southern Americans. The sun of freedom has risen over that great continent, with the certain promise of a glorious day. I form the best hopes for my own country, in the mental

---

* "It is notorious, that towards one another the Indians are liberal in the extreme, and for ever ready to supply the deficiencies of their neighbours with any superfluities of their own. They have no idea of amassing wealth for themselves individually; and they wonder that persons can be found in any society so destitute of every generous sentiment, as to enrich themselves at the expense of others, and to live in ease and affluence regardless of the misery and wretchedness of members of the same community to which they themselves belong." —WELD's *Travels in Canada; Letter XXXV.*

improvement of the people, whenever she shall breathe from the pressure of that preposterous system of finance which sooner or later must fall by its own weight.

MR. FORESTER.

I apply to our system of finance, a fiction of the northern mythology.[21] The ash of Yggdrasil overshadows the world: Ratatosk, the squirrel, sports in the branches: Nidhogger, the serpent, gnaws at the root.* The ash of Yggdrasil is the tree of national prosperity: Ratatosk the squirrel is the careless and unreflecting fundholder: Nidhogger the serpent is POLITICAL CORRUPTION, which will in time consume the root, and spread the branches on the dust. What will then become of the squirrel?

MR. FAX.

Ratatosk must look to himself: Nidhogger must be killed: and the ash of Yggdrasil will rise like a vegetable Phœnix to flourish again for ages.

Thus conversing, they arrived on the sea-shore, where we shall leave them to pursue their way, while we investigate the fate of Anthelia.

* See the Edda and the Northern Antiquities.

CHAPTER XLI.

ALGA CASTLE.

ANTHELIA had not ventured to resume her solitary rambles after her return from Onevote; more especially as she anticipated the period when she should revisit her favourite haunts in the society of one congenial companion, whose presence would heighten the magic of their interest, and restore to them that feeling of security which her late adventure had destroyed. But as she was sitting in her library on the morning of her disappearance, she suddenly heard a faint and mournful cry like the voice of a child in distress. She rose, opened the window, and listened. She heard the sounds more distinctly. They seemed to ascend from that part of the dingle immediately beneath the shrubbery that fringed her windows. It was certainly the cry of a child. She immediately ran through the shrubbery and descended the rocky steps[1] into the dingle, where she found a little boy tied to the stem of a tree, crying and sobbing as if his heart would break. Anthelia easily set him at liberty, and his grief passed away like an April shower. She asked who had had the barbarity to treat him in such a manner. He said he could not tell—four strange men on horseback had taken him up on the common where his father lived, and brought him there and tied him to the tree, he could not tell why. Anthelia took his hand, and was leading him from the dingle, intending to send him home by Peter Gray, when the men who had made the little child their unconscious decoy, broke from their ambush, seized Anthelia, and taking effectual precautions to stifle her cries, placed her on one of their horses, and travelled with great rapidity along narrow and unfrequented ways, till they arrived at a solitary castle on the sea-shore, where they conveyed her to a splendid suite of apartments, and left her in solitude, locking, as they retired, the door of the outer room.

She was utterly unable to comprehend the motive of so extraordinary a proceeding, or to form any conjecture as to its probable result. An old woman of a very unmeaning physiognomy shortly after entered, to tender her services; but to all Anthelia's questions, she only replied with a shake of her head, and a smile which she meant to be very consolatory.

The old woman retired, and shortly after re-appeared with an elegant dinner, which Anthelia dismissed untouched. "There is no harm intended you, my sweet lady," said the old woman: "so pray don't starve yourself." Anthelia assured her she had no such intention, but had no appetite at that time; but she drank a glass of wine at the old woman's earnest entreaty.

In the evening the mystery was elucidated by a visit from Lord Anophel Achthar; who falling on his knees before her, entreated her to allow the violence of his passion to plead his pardon for a proceeding which nothing but the imminent peril of seeing her in the arms of a rival could have induced him to adopt. Anthelia replied, that if his object were to obtain her affections, he had taken the most effectual method to frustrate his own views; that if he thought by constraint and cruelty to obtain her hand without her affections, he might be assured that he would never succeed. Her heart, however, she candidly told him, was no longer in her power to dispose of; and she hoped, after this frank avowal, he would see the folly, if not the wickedness, of protracting his persecution.

He now, still on his knees, broke out into a rhapsody about love, and hope, and death, and despair, in which he developed the whole treasury of his exuberant and overflowing folly. He then expatiated on his expectations, and pointed out all the advantages of wealth and consequence attached to the title of Marchioness of Agaric, and concluded by saying, that she must be aware so important and decisive a measure had not been taken without the most grave and profound deliberation, and that he never could suffer her to make her exit from Alga Castle in any other character than that of Lady Achthar. He then left her to meditate on his heroic resolution.

The next day he repeated his visit—resumed his supplications—reiterated his determination to persevere—and received from Anthelia the same reply. She endeavoured to reason with him on the injustice and absurdity of his proceedings; but he told her the Reverend Mr. Grovelgrub and Mr. Feathernest the poet had taught him that all reasonings pretending to point out absurdity and injustice were manifestly Jacobinical, which he, as one of the pillars of the state, was bound not to listen to.

He renewed his visits every day for a week, becoming, with every new visit, less humble and more menacing, and consequently more disagreeable to Anthelia, as the Reverend Mr. Grovelgrub, by whose instructions he acted, secretly foresaw and designed. The latter now undertook to plead his Lordship's cause, and set in a clear point of view to Anthelia the inflexibility of his Lordship's resolutions, which, properly expounded, could not fail to have due weight against the alternatives of protracted solitude and hopeless resistance.

The reverend gentleman, however, had other views than those he held out to Lord Anophel, and presented himself to Anthelia with an aspect of great commiseration. He said he was an unwilling witness of his Lordship's unjust proceedings, which he had done all in his power to prevent, and which had been carried into effect against his will. It was his firm intention to set her at liberty as soon as he could devise the means of doing so; but all the outlets of Alga Castle were so guarded, that he had not yet been able to devise any feasible scheme for her escape: but it should be his sole study night and day to effect it.

Anthelia thanked him for his sympathy, and asked why he could not give notice to her friends of her situation; which would accomplish the purpose at once. He replied, that Lord Anophel already mistrusted him, and that if any thing of the kind were done, how ever secretly he might proceed, the suspicion would certainly fall upon him, and that he should then be a ruined man, as all his worldly hopes rested on the Marquis of Agaric. Anthelia offered to make him the utmost compensation for the loss of the Marquis of Agaric's favour; but he said that was impossible, unless she could make him a bishop, as the Marquis of Agaric would do. His plan, he said, must be to effect her liberation, without seeming to be himself in any way whatever concerned in it; and though he would willingly lose every thing for her sake, yet he trusted she would not think ill of him for wishing to wait a few days, that he might try to devise the means of serving her without ruining himself.

He continued his daily visits of sympathy, sometimes amusing her with a hopeful scheme, at others detailing with a rueful face the formidable nature of some unexpected obstacle, hinting continually at his readiness to sacrifice every thing for her sake, lamenting the necessity of delay, and assuring her that in the mean while no evil should happen to her. He flattered himself that Anthelia, wearied out with the irksomeness of confinement and the continual alternations of hope and disappointment, and contrasting the respectful tenderness of his manner with the disagreeable system of behaviour to which he had fashioned Lord Anophel, would at length come to a determination of removing all his difficulties by offering him her hand and fortune as a compensation for his anticipated bishopric. It was not, however, very long before Anthelia penetrated his design; but as she did not deem it prudent to come to a rupture with him at that time, she continued to listen to his daily details of plans and impediments, and allowed him to take to himself all the merit he seemed to assume for supplying her with music and books; though he expressed himself very much shocked at her asking him for Gibbon and Rousseau, whose works, he said, ought to be burned *in foro* by the hands of *Carnifex*.[2]

The windows of her apartment were at an immense elevation from the beach, as that part of the castle-wall formed a continued line with the black and precipitous side of the rock on which it stood. During the greater portion of the hours of daylight she sate near the window with her harp, gazing on the changeful aspects of the wintry sea, now slumbering like a summer lake in the sunshine of a halcyon day—now raging beneath the sway of the tempest, while the dancing snow-flakes seemed to accumulate on the foam of the billows, and the spray was hurled back like snow-dust from the rocks. The feelings these scenes suggested she developed in the following stanzas, to which she adapted a wild and impassioned air, and they became the favourite song of her captivity.

THE MAGIC BARK.

1.

O Freedom! power of life and light!
Sole nurse of truth and glory!
Bright dweller on the rocky cliff!
Lone wanderer on the sea!
Where'er the sunbeam slumbers bright
On snow-clad mountains hoary;
Wherever flies the veering skiff,
O'er waves that breathe of thee!
Be thou the guide of all my thought—
The source of all my being—
The genius of my waking mind—
The spirit of my dreams!
To me thy magic spell be taught,
The captive spirit freeing,

To wander with the ocean-wind
Where'er thy beacon beams.

II.

O! sweet it were, in magic bark,
On one loved breast reclining,
To sail around the varied world,
To every blooming shore;
And oft the gathering storm to mark
Its lurid folds combining;
And safely ride, with sails unfurled,
Amid the tempest's roar;
And see the mighty breakers rave
On cliff, and sand, and shingle,
And hear, with long re-echoing shock,
The caverned steeps reply;
And while the storm-cloud and the wave
In darkness seemed to mingle,
To skim beside the surf-swept rock,
And glide uninjured by.

III.

And when the summer seas were calm,
And summer skies were smiling,
And evening came, with clouds of gold,
To gild the western wave;
And gentle airs and dews of balm,
The pensive mind beguiling,
Should call the Ocean Swain to fold
His sea-flocks in the cave,
Unearthly music's tenderest spell,
With gentlest breezes blending
And waters softly rippling near
The prow's light course along,
Should flow from Triton's winding shell,
Through ocean's depths ascending
From where it charmed the Nereid's ear,
Her coral bowers among.

IV.

How sweet, where eastern Nature smiles,
With swift and mazy motion
Before the odour-breathing breeze
Of dewy morn to glide;
Or, 'mid the thousand emerald isles
That gem the southern ocean,
Where fruits and flowers, from loveliest trees,
O'erhang the slumbering tide:
Or up some western stream to sail,
To where its myriad fountains
Roll down their everlasting rills
From many a cloud-capped height,
Till mingling in some nameless vale,
'Mid forest-cinctured mountains,
The river-cataract shakes the hills
With vast and volumed might.

V.

The poison-trees their leaves should shed,
The yellow snake should perish,
The beasts of blood should crouch and cower,
Where'er that vessel past:
All plagues of fens and vapours bred,
That tropic fervors cherish,
Should fly before its healing power,
Like mists before the blast.
Where'er its keel the strand imprest,
The young fruit's ripening cluster,
The bird's free song, its touch should greet,
The opening flower's perfume;
The streams along the green earth's breast
Should roll in purer lustre,
And love should heighten every sweet,
And brighten every bloom.

VI.

And, Freedom! thy meridian blaze
Should chase the clouds that lower,
Wherever mental twilight dim
Obscures Truth's vestal flame,
Wherever Fraud and Slavery raise
The throne of blood-stained Power,
Wherever Fear and Ignorance hymn
Some fabled dæmon's name!
The bard, where torrents thunder down
Beside thy burning altar,
Should kindle, as in days of old,
The mind's ethereal fire;
Ere yet beneath a tyrant's frown
The Muse's voice could falter,
Or Flattery strung with chords of gold
The minstrel's venal lyre.

CHAPTER XLII.

CONCLUSION.

LORD Anophel one morning paid Anthelia his usual visit. "You must be aware, Miss Melincourt," said he, "that if your friends could have found you out, they would have done it before this; but they have searched the whole country far and near, and have now gone home in despair."

ANTHELIA.

That, my Lord, I cannot believe; for there is one, at least,[1] who I am confident will never be weary of seeking me, and who, I am equally confident, will not always seek in vain.

LORD ANOPHEL ACHTHAR.

If you mean the young lunatic of Redrose Abbey, or his friend the dumb Baronet, they are both gone to London to attend the opening of the Honourable House;[2] and if you doubt my word, I will show you their names in the Morning Post, among the Fashionable Arrivals at Wildman's Hotel.

ANTHELIA.

Your Lordship's word is quite as good as the authority you have quoted.[3]

LORD ANOPHEL ACHTHAR.

Well, then, Miss Melincourt, I presume you perceive that you are completely in my power, and that I have gone too far to recede. If, indeed, I had supposed myself an object of such very great repugnance to you, which I must say *(looking at himself in a glass)* is quite unaccountable, I might not, perhaps, have laid this little scheme, which I thought would be only settling the affair in a compendious way; for, that any woman in England would consider it a very great hardship to be Lady Achthar, and hereafter Marchioness of Agaric, and would feel any very mortal resentment for means that tended to make her so, was an idea, egad, that never entered my head. However, as I have already observed, you are completely in my power: both our characters are compromised, and there is only one way to mend the matter, which is, to call in Grovelgrub, and make him strike up "Dearly beloved."[4]

ANTHELIA.

As to your character, Lord Anophel, that must be your concern. Mine is in my own keeping; for, having practised all my life a system of uniform sincerity,[5] which gives me a right to be believed by all who know me, and more especially by all who love me, I am perfectly indifferent to private malice or public misrepresentation.

LORD ANOPHEL ACHTHAR.

There is such a thing, Miss Melincourt, as tiring out a man's patience; and 'pon honour, if gentle means don't succeed with you, I must have recourse to rough ones, 'pon honour.

ANTHELIA.

My Lord!

LORD ANOPHEL ACHTHAR.

I am serious, curse me. You will be glad enough to hush all up then, and we'll go to court together in due form.

ANTHELIA.

What you mean by hushing up, Lord Anophel, I know not: but of this be assured, that under no circumstances will I ever be your wife; and that whatever happens to me in any time or place, shall be known to all who are interested in my welfare. I know too well the difference between the true modesty of a pure and simple mind, and the false affected quality which goes by that name in the world, to be intimidated by threats which can only be dictated by a supposition that your wickedness would be my disgrace, and that false shame would induce me to conceal what both truth and justice would command me to make known.

Lord Anophel stood aghast for a few minutes, at the declaration of such unfashionable sentiments. At length saying, "Ay, preaching is one thing, and practice another, as Grovelgrub can testify;" he seized her hand with violence, and threw his arm round her waist. Anthelia screamed, and at that very moment a violent noise of ascending steps was heard on the stairs; the door was burst open, and Sir Oran Haut-ton appeared in the aperture, with the Reverend Mr. Grovelgrub in custody, whom he dragged into the apartment, followed by Mr. Forester and Mr. Fax. Mr. Forester flew to Anthelia, who threw herself into his arms, hid her face in his bosom, and burst into tears: which when Sir Oran saw, his wrath grew boundless, and quitting his hold of the Reverend Mr. Grovelgrub (who immediately ran down stairs, and out of the castle, as fast as a pair of short thick legs could carry him), seized on Lord Anophel Achthar, and was preparing to administer natural justice by throwing him out at the window; but Mr. Fax interposed, and calling Mr. Forester's attention, which was totally engaged with Anthelia, they succeeded in rescuing the terrified sprig of nobility; who immediately leaving the enemy in free possession, flew down stairs after his reverend tutor; whom, on issuing from the castle, he discovered at an immense distance on the sands, still running with all his might. Lord Anophel gave him chase, and after a long time came within hail of him, and shouted to him to stop. But this only served to quicken the reverend gentleman's speed; who, hearing the voice of pursuit, and too much terrified to look back, concluded that the dumb Baronet had found his voice, and was then in the very act of gaining on his flight. Therefore, the more Lord Anophel shouted "Stop!" the more nimbly the reverend gentleman sped along the sands, running and roaring all the way, like Falstaff on Gads-hill;[6] his Lordship still exerting all his powers of speed in the rear, and gaining on his flying Mentor[7] by very imperceptible gradations: where we shall leave them to run *ad libitum*,[8] while we account for the sudden appearance of Mr. Forester and his friends.

We left them walking along the shore of the sea, which they followed, till they arrived in the vicinity of Alga Castle, from which the Reverend Mr. Grovelgrub emerged in evil hour, to take a meditative walk on the sands. The keen sight of the natural man descried him from far. Sir Oran darted on his prey; and though it is supposed that he could not have overtaken the swift-footed Achilles,[*][9] he had very little difficulty in overtaking the Reverend Mr. Grovelgrub, who had begun to run for his life as soon as he was aware of the foe. Sir Oran shook his stick over his head, and the reverend gentleman dropping on his knees, put his hands together, and entreated for mercy, saying "he would confess all."[10] Mr. Forester and Mr. Fax came up in time to hear the proposal: the former restrained the rage of Sir Oran, who, however, still held his prisoner fast by the arm; and the reluctant divine, with many a heavy groan, conducted his unwelcome company to the door of Anthelia's apartments.

"O Forester!" said Anthelia, "you have realized all my wishes. I have found you the friend of the poor, the enthusiast of truth, the disinterested cultivator of the rural virtues, the active promoter of the cause of human liberty. It only remained that you should emancipate a captive damsel, who, however,

---

[*] "The civilized man will submit to the greatest pain and labour, in order to excel in any exercise which is honourable; and this induces me to believe that such a man as Achilles might have beat in running even an oran outang, or the savage of the Pyrenees, whom nobody could lay hold of, though that be the exercise in which savages excel the most, and though I am persuaded that the oran outang of Angola is naturally stronger and swifter of foot than Achilles was, or than even the heroes of the preceding age, such as Hercules, and such as Theseus, Pirithous, and others mentioned by Nestor."—*Ancient Metaphysics*, vol. iii. p. 76.

will but change the mode of her durance,[11] and become your captive for life."

———

It was not long after this event, before the Reverend Mr. Portpipe, and the old chapel of Melincourt Castle, were put in requisition, to make a mystical unit[12] of Anthelia and Mr. Forester. The day was celebrated with great festivity throughout their respective estates, and the Reverend Mr. Portpipe was *voti compos:*[13] that is to say, he had taken a resolution on the day of Anthelia's christening, that he would on the day of her marriage drink one bottle more than he had ever taken at one sitting on any other occasion; which resolution he had now the satisfaction of carrying into effect.

Sir Oran Haut-ton continued to reside with Mr. Forester and Anthelia. They discovered in the progress of time, that he had formed for the latter the same kind of reverential attachment, as the Satyr in Fletcher forms for the Holy Shepherdess:* [14] and Anthelia might have said to him in the words of Clorin:

---

* See Fletcher's FAITHFUL SHEPHERDESS. The following extracts from the Satyr's speeches to Clorin will explain the allusion in the text.

> But behold a fairer sight!
> By that heavenly form of thine,
> Brightest fair! thou art divine!
> Sprung from great immortal race
> Of the gods; for in thy face
> Shines more awful majesty,
> Than dull weak mortality
> Dare with misty eyes behold,
> And live! Therefore on this mould
> Lowly do I bend my knee,
> In worship of thy deity.
> > *Act I. Scene I.*

> Brightest! if there be remaining
> Any service, without feigning
> I will do it: were I set
> To catch the nimble wind, or get

"—They wrong thee that do call thee rude:
Though thou be'st outward rough and tawny-hued,
Thy manners are as gentle and as fair,
As his who boasts himself born only heir
To all humanity."[15]

His greatest happiness was in listening to the music of her harp and voice: in the absence of which he solaced himself, as usual, with his flute and French horn. He became likewise a proficient in drawing; but what progress he made in the art of speech, we have not been able to ascertain.

Mr. Fax was a frequent visitor at Melincourt, and there was always a cover at the table for the Reverend Mr. Portpipe.

Shadows gliding on the green,
Or to steal from the great queen
Of the fairies all her beauty,
I would do it, so much duty
Do I owe those precious eyes.
Act IV. Scene II.

Thou divinest, fairest, brightest,
Thou most powerful maid, and whitest,
Thou most virtuous and most blessed,
Eyes of stars, and golden tressed
Like Apollo! Tell me, sweetest,
What new service now is meetest
For the Satyr? Shall I stray
In the middle air, and stay
The sailing rack? or nimbly take
Hold by the moon, and gently make
Suit to the pale queen of night
For a beam to give thee light?
Shall I dive into the sea,
And bring thee coral, making way
Through the rising waves that fall
In snowy fleeces? Dearest, shall
I catch thee wanton fawns, or flies
Whose woven wings the summer dyes
Of many colours? Get thee fruit?
Or steal from heaven old Orpheus' lute?
All these I'll venture for, and more,
To do her service all these woods adore.
Act V. Scene V.

Mr. Hippy felt half inclined to make proposals to Miss Evergreen; but understanding from Mr. Forester, that, from the death of her lover in early youth, that lady had irrevocably determined on a single life,[*][16] he comforted himself with passing half his time at Melincourt Castle, and dancing the little Foresters on his knee, whom he taught to call him "grandpapa Hippy," and seemed extremely proud of the imaginary relationship.

Mr. Forester disposed of Redrose Abbey to Sir Telegraph Paxarett, who, after wearing the willow[17] twelve months, married, left off driving, and became a very respectable specimen of an English country gentleman.

We must not conclude without informing those among our tender-hearted readers, who would be much grieved if Miss Danaretta Contantina Pinmoney should have been disappointed in her principal object of making a *good match*,[18] that she had at length the satisfaction, through the skilful management of her mother, of making the happiest of men of Lord Anophel Achthar.[19]

THE END.

---

[*] "There are very few women who might not have married in some way or other. The old maid, who has either never formed an attachment, or has been disappointed in the object of it, has, under the circumstances in which she has been placed, conducted herself with the most perfect propriety; and has acted a much more virtuous and honourable part in society, than those women who marry without a proper degree of love, or at least of esteem, for their husbands; a species of immorality which is not reprobated as it deserves."—MALTHUS *on Population*, book iv. chap. viii.

APPENDIX

Peacock's Preface of 1856

A holograph manuscript of the preface to the 1856 Chapman and Hall edition of *Melincourt* is owned by the Historical Society of Pennsylvania, Philadelphia, in the Ferdinand J. Dreer Autograph Collection, Box 215, Folder 28. The five leaves, which measure 18.6 cm x 11.5 cm, appear to have been part of a notebook. TLP has written only on the rectos. The handwriting is very clear and neat. The only difference between the final readings in this manuscript and the readings in *1856* is that the latter prints some words in capital letters (either large or small capitals). Despite a few corrections and revisions, the manuscript could easily serve as printer's copy, and the only evidence that it did not is the absence of inky fingermarks. Manuscripts that printers used have such fingermarks; see Donald H. Reiman, review of Lord Byron, *The Complete Poetical Works*, ed. Jerome J. McGann, vols. 6–7 (Oxford: Oxford University Press, 1991–3), *Nineteenth-Century Literature*, 50 (September 1995), 259–71 (p. 262).

PREFACE.

"MELINCOURT" was first[1] published thirty-nine[2] years ago. Many changes have since occurred, social, mechanical, and political. The boroughs of Onevote and Threevotes have been extinguished: but there remain boroughs of Fewvotes, in which Sir Oran Hautton might still find a free and enlightened constituency.[3] Beards

---

[1] **first:** In the Historical Society of Pennsylvania MS, 'first published' follows deleted 'wr'.

[2] **thirty-nine:** In the MS, 'thirty' is written above deleted 'twenty'.

[3] **The boroughs ... constituency:** The Reform Bill of 1832 removed the most egregious rotten boroughs (see Introduction), but the franchise was still small. In his preface to the 1837 Standard Novels edition of *Headlong Hall* and three other novels, TLP observes that *CC* involves a rotten borough, and he comments that 'the rotten boroughs of 1830 have ceased to exist, though there are some very pretty pocket properties, which are their worthy successors' (*CC*, p. 162).

disfigure the face, and tobacco poisons the air, in a degree not then imagined.[4] A boy,[5] with a cigar in his mouth,[6] was a phenomenon yet unborn. Multitudinous bubbles have been blown and have burst:[7] sometimes prostrating dupes and imposters together; sometimes leaving a colossal jobber[8] upright in his triumphal chariot, which has crushed[9] as many victims[10] as the car of Juggernaut.[11] Political mountebanks have founded profitable investments on public gullibility. British colonists have been compelled to emancipate their slaves; and foreign slave labour, under the pretext of free trade, has been brought to bear against[12] them by the friends of liberty.[13] The Court is more moral: therefore, the public is more moral; more decorous, at least, in external semblance, wherever the homage,[14] which Hypocrisy pays to Virtue,[15] can yield any profit to the professor; but always ready for the same reaction, with which the profligacy

---

[4] **Beards . . . imagined:** On facial hair in 1817, see *Mel*, ch. 2, n. 31, and ch. 4, n. 18. In the MS, 'imagined' follows deleted 'dream'.

[5] **boy:** In the MS, 'boy' follows deleted 'cigar'.

[6] **mouth:** TLP wrote 'mouth' at the bottom-right corner of f. 1r of the MS as a catchword, 'mouth' being the first word on f. 2r.

[7] **bubbles have been blown and have burst:** The eighteenth-century 'bubble' metaphor figures in the novel in the name 'Airbubble', and in Forester's prediction of 'the bursting of this fatal bubble of paper-money' (ch. 30).

[8] **jobber:** 'A wholesale dealer or principal on a stock exchange (esp. the London Stock Exchange) who buys and sells stocks for his or her own account' (*OED* 'jobber', *n.²*, 1).

[9] **crushed:** In the MS, 'crushed' is written above deleted 'rolled over'.

[10] **victims:** In the MS, 'victims' follows deleted 'chariot'.

[11] **Juggernaut:** See ch. 22, n. 41.

[12] **against:** TLP wrote 'against' at the bottom-right corner of f. 2r of the MS as if it were a catchword, yet on the next page he did not repeat 'against', but continued with the next word, 'them'.

[13] **British colonists . . . friends of liberty:** Although slavery had been banned in British colonies by an 1833 statute, trade with slave-holding states in the United States flourished.

[14] **homage:** In the MS, 'homage' follows deleted 'sort of'. TLP either ruled out 'sort of' promptly after writing it, and continued by writing 'homage', or he wrote 'sort of homage' and later rejected the first two words.

[15] **which Hypocrisy pays to Virtue:** David Garnett suspected 'a slip of the pen': 'Hypocrisy does not pay homage to Virtue, but is itself the homage paid to Virtue by Vice' (Garnett, *Novels*, 1.101).

of the Restoration rolled, like a spring-tide, over the puritanism of the Commonwealth. The progress of intellect,[16] with all deference to those who believe in it,[17] is not quite so obvious as the progress of mechanics. The[18] "reading public"[19] has increased its capacity of swallow, in[20] a proportion far exceeding that of its[21] digestion. Thirty-nine years ago, steam-boats were just coming into action, and the railway locomotive was not even thought of. Now everybody goes everywhere: going for the sake of going, and rejoicing in the rapidity with which they accomplish nothing. *On va, mais on ne voyage pas.*[22] Strenuous idleness drives us on the wings of steam in boats and trains, seeking the art of enjoying[23] life, which, after all, is in the regulation of the mind, and not in the whisking about of the body.*[24] Of the disputants whose[25] opinions and public characters

---

[16] **The progress of intellect:** On the 'march of intellect', see *CC*, ch. 1, n. 31. On the 'march of mind', see *CC*, ch. 1, n. 53. Henry Chorley, commenting on this preface in *The Athenæum*, wondered why 'those who were in their morning and noon most eager to promote progress become towards their afternoon or evening the most earnest in denying that progress has been made'; *The Athenæum* (19 Apr. 1856), p. 486.

[17] **it:** In the MS, TLP wrote 'The progress of intellect is not quite so obvious', with a line break after 'is', and later wrote 'with' over the original 'is', obscuring it, and inserted 'all deference to those who believe in it, is' between the lines.

[18] **The:** In the MS, 'The' follows deleted 'Thirty'. Presumably 'Thirty' was the result of an eye-skip; 'Thirty-nine' is the first word of the next sentence.

[19] **reading public:** See ch. 31, n. 64.

[20] **in:** In the MS, 'in a proportion' (on f. 4r) follows deleted 'more' (at the end of the last line on f. 3r). There is no catchword at the bottom of f. 3r.

[21] **that of its:** In the MS, these three words are interlined above deleted 'its powers of'.

[22] *On va, mais on ne voyage pas:* 'We go, but we do not travel' (French).

[23] **enjoying:** In the MS, 'enjoying life' follows deleted 'enjoymen'.

[24] **whisking about of the body:** TLP's footnote refers to Horace, *Epistle* 1.27–30, where the poet writes that 'We are but ciphers, born to consume earth's fruits, Penelope's good-for-naught suitors, young courtiers of Alcinous, unduly busy in keeping their skins sleek'; *Satires, Epistles, and Ars Poetica*, trans. H. Rushton Fairclough (Cambridge: Harvard University Press and London: William Heineman, 1961), p. 265.

[25] **whose:** In the MS, TLP used 'whose' as a catchword at the bottom of f. 4r, and 'whose' is indeed the first word on f. 5r.

(for I never trespassed on private life)[26] were shadowed in some of the persons of the[27] story, almost all have passed from the diurnal scene. Many of the questions, discussed in the dialogues, have more of general than of temporary application, and have still their advocates on both sides: and new questions have arisen, which furnish abundant argument for similar conversations, and of which I may yet, perhaps, avail myself on some future occasion.

THE AUTHOR OF "HEADLONG HALL."

March, 1856.

* Hor. Epist. I. ii. 27–30.

---

[26] **private life:** In his 1837 preface, TLP boasted that he had 'never intruded on the personality of others, nor taken any liberties but with public conduct and public opinions' (*CC*, p. 161). In 1839 Spedding objected that there were 'a few cases, in which, not content with public conduct and opinions, [TLP] undertakes, not very happily, to interpret motives and exhibit personal qualities'; [Spedding], review, *Edinburgh Review*, 68 (1839), 443.

[27] **the:** In the MS, 'the' is interlined with a caret.

NOTE ON THE TEXT

The text is based on the first edition of *Melincourt*, printed by Samuel Gosnell and published in 1817 by Thomas Hookham and Baldwin, Cradock and Joy. *1817* is the only textual authority (not even a fragment of manuscript survives). It presents few textual issues, although if 'South America' in Chapter 6 is a compositor's error for 'Sumatra', as Nicholas A. Joukovsky has suggested, then the proofreading was not always adequate.[1] I depart from the readings of the base text only when those readings cannot be accounted for except as printing errors (the list of 'Emendations and Variants' (pp. 314–37) records these departures). Inconsistencies are retained, so that 'Dr Bosky' (Chapter 2) reappears as 'Doctor Bosky' (Chapter 25). All of Peacock's quotations from published sources are reproduced as they appear in *1817*, except, again, for obvious printing errors. Ambiguous hyphenations at the ends of lines have been disambiguated, when possible, by referring to other occurrences of the word in the novel (see 'Ambiguous Line-End Hyphenations', pp. 338–9). *1817* often inserts spaces before or after punctuation when the conventions of the twenty-first century do not demand a space, but in general I have not reproduced this spacing (and the list of 'Emendations and Variants' ignores such variations). In forms where 'will', 'is', 'am', 'are' or 'have' are conventionally contracted, any spaces have been removed ('I 'll' becomes 'I'll', 'I 'm' becomes 'I'm', 'that 's' becomes 'that's', 'I 've' becomes 'I've', and so on), although ''t is', 'is n't', 'was n't', and 'would n't' have been left

---

[1] Joukovsky, 'Peacock's Sir Oran Haut-ton', p. 173, n. 1.

as they were. Peacock's footnotes appear at the bottom of the page, as they do in *1817*. Footnotes are indicated in *1817* with asterisks (for the first note on a page), daggers (for the second) and similar marks; this edition, where the pagination necessarily is different, starts the sequence of symbols anew on each page. Whereas *1817* places asterisks and other symbols for footnotes before commas, periods and other requisite punctuation, this edition places such symbols after the punctuation. *1817* uses the abbreviation 'Ibid' whenever a footnote referred to the same text as a previous footnote on that page; these footnotes are printed here as they appear in *1817*. Superscript numbers in the text or in TLP's footnotes indicate editorial explanatory notes (each explanatory note that glosses one of TLP's footnotes is marked '[Footnote]').

In general, the printers of the 1856 Chapman and Hall edition, Bradbury and Evans, followed *1817*, although at times they made the text conform to their own style. Punctuation often is amended, and '-ize' and '-izing' become '-ise' and '-ising', while forms like 'I 'll' became 'I'll'. *1856* corrects obvious errors, so that 'considesed' (Chapter 10; *1817*, 1.145) becomes 'considered' (*1856*, 71). Some eccentric spellings are abandoned, so that 'œconomically' (Chapter 27; *1817*, 2.189) is 'economically' (*1856*, 201), but some eccentricities remain: '*Love's Labour Lost*' is printed this way in both editions. *1856* updated TLP's footnotes that in *1817* referred to page numbers in that three-volume edition: 'See Vol. I. page 156' (*1817*, 2.158) became 'See p. 78' (*1856*, 185), and 'See vol. i. p. 73, note' (*1817*, 3.63) became 'See p. 36, note' (*1856*, 246). Like *1817*, *1856* uses 'Ibid.' whenever a footnote refers to the same text as a previous footnote on that page. The list of 'Emendations and Variants' records these *1856* readings, even though they are simply dictated by the format of the later edition. *1856* omits the epigraphs from Horace and Rousseau that appear at the beginning of each volume of the first edition, and there is no table of contents. The most noticeable change from *1817* lies in how speech is represented when TLP switches to stage dialogue. *1817* reads:

ANTHELIA.
I am sorry for it. (*1817*, 1.25)

The same passage appears thus in the Chapman and Hall edition:
Anthelia.—I am sorry for it. (*1856*, 13)

Bradbury and Evans probably chose on their own initiative to put the speech tags on the same line as the speech itself. One advantage of this arrangement was that it saved space, which was desirable when fitting a 78,000-word novel into a single volume. (In contrast, Bentley's 1837 Standard Novels edition of four TLP works prints the dialogue much as Hookham's editions print it.) Ultimately, it is remarkable how little *1856* departs from the first edition; the two texts conform even when one might not expect conformity. For example, *1856* reproduces all but one of the twenty-three double em-dashes in *1817* (e.g. "solitary——" (*1817*, 1.21) appears as "solitary——" (*1856*, 11). The phrase 'one more less' that appears in *1817* (1.61) was reproduced in *1856* (30), even though the Halliford editors saw fit to correct it to 'one more or less' (Halliford, 2.48), which is the reading in this edition.

EMENDATIONS AND VARIANTS

The word or phrase as emended appears first, before the bracket. The emendation is located, its source identified and the rejected reading of the copytext follows. Two symbols indicate changes in punctuation. The swung dash (~) stands for the word previously cited when the variant is not in that word but in associated punctuation. The caret (^) stands for the absence of punctuation at a given point. A dropped letter or number or punctuation mark is indicated by square brackets [ ].

The following list records all substantive or semi-substantive variants between the only two authorized lifetime editions of *Melincourt*: the first edition copytext (here '1817') and the reprint *Melincourt, or Sir Oran Haut-ton*, in Chapman and Hall's 'Select Library of Fiction' ('1856'). It also records all emendations of the 1817 copytext, whether based on the 1856 edition or on the editor's judgment. In the case of variants, the reading that precedes the bracket is that of the 1817 copytext, while the reading that follows the bracket is the variant of the 1856 edition, labelled as such. If the text has been emended by reference to 1856, the date of that edition immediately follows the bracket. Otherwise the rejected readings of both editions follow the bracket, and the emendation can be ascribed to the editor.

All variants in substantives, spelling or capitalization are included. Variants in punctuation are recorded, except for most variations in spacing between a word and a punctuation mark. Some other variants are not recorded: the practice in 1817 is not to indent the first line of the first paragraph of each chapter, whereas 1856 indents these lines; chapters in 1817 begin with an extra-large capital letter, but this practice is not followed in 1856. This list ignores discrepancies between 1817 and 1856 that result from Bradbury and

Evans's different mode of handling speech tags. It also ignores differences in the italicization of punctuation marks, in the number and arrangement of periods in ellipses, in the centring of footnotes, in the indentation of quotations, and in the extra space before and after each section of dramatic dialogue.

CHAPTER 1

page 5, line 1	CHAPTER] 1856; CHAP. 1817
page 8, line 5	tenour] tenor 1856
page 8, line 12	developement] development 1856
page 9, line 32	realize] realise 1856

CHAPTER 2

page 11, line 1	CHAPTER] 1856; CHAP. 1817
page 11, line 8	Honourable] honourable 1856
page 14, line 14	apologize] apologise 1856
page 15, line 3	life:] ~; 1856
page 15, line 18	feelings,] 1856; feelings[ ] 1817
page 16, line 12	sympathized] sympathised 1856
page 17, line 21	feeble—to] ~, ~ 1856
page 17, line 26	mountain-caverns] ~ ^ ~ 1856
page 18, line 10	who] ~, 1856
page 18, line 10	by] ~, 1856

CHAPTER 3

page 19, line 1	CHAPTER] 1856; CHAP. 1817
page 19, line 14	relation, a] ~ — ~ 1856
page 19, line 17	Hippy: Humphrey] ~ — ~ 1856
page 19, line 27	and] ~, 1856
page 19, line 27	believe] ~, 1856
page 20, line 8	gib cat] gib-cat 1856
page 20, line 9	case,] ~ ^ 1856

CHAPTER 4

CHAPTER 5

page 33, line 19	more or] Halliford more 1818, 1856
page 35, line 18	organize] organise 1856

CHAPTER 6

page 36, line 1	CHAPTER] 1856; CHAP. 1817
page 36, line 4	Sɪʀ] Sir 1856
page 36, line 11	civilized] civilised 1856
page 36, footnote, paragraph 4, line 8	thing,] ~ ^ 1856
page 36, footnote, paragraph 4, line 8	least,] ~ ^ 1856
page 37, top footnote, line 2	then,] ~ ^ 1856
page 37, footnote *, line 2	hémisphere] hémisphère 1856
page 37, line 6	fac simile] fac-simile 1856
page 37, line 12	civilization] civilisation‸ 1856
page 38, footnote *, line 4	says] ~, 1856
page 38, footnote *, line 6	species] 1856; specieses 1817
page 38, footnote *, line 8	any thing] anything 1856
page 38, footnote †, line 5	oran outang] ouran outang 1856
page 39, footnote, line 5	measure,] ~ ^ 1856
page 39, footnote, line 6	always] alway[ ] 1817, 1856
page 39, line 21	speech] 1856; ~* 1817
page 39, line 23	sympathize] sympathise 1856
page 40, footnote *, line 4	portames] portâmes 1856
page 40, footnote *, line 4	quaud] quand 1856
page 41, line 6	say,] ~ ^ 1856
page 41, line 10	familiarized] familiarised 1856
page 41, line 11	me,] ~ ^ 1856
page 42, line 10	by and by] by-and-by 1856
page 42, line 26	civilized] civilised 1856
page 42, line 33	man:] ~; 1856
page 43, line 5	by] bye 1856
page 43, footnote †, line 11	descendere] déscendere 1856

page 43, footnote †, para 2,
line 3   où infirmer] ou infirmer 1856
page 43, footnote †, para 2,
line 3   relations] rélations 1856
page 44, footnote *, para 2,
line 10   reculés] réculés 1856
page 45, line 17   Κοσμοκρατωρ] κοσμοκρατωρ 1856
page 46, line 11   Civilized] Civilised 1856
page 46, line 12   civilized] civilised 1856
page 46, line 19   civilized] civilised 1856
page 46, line 24   civilized] civilised 1856
page 47, line 2   *prisoners,*] ~ ^ 1856
page 47, line 7   *civilized*] *civilised* 1856
page 47, line 11   *tamed,*] ~ ^ 1856
page 48, top footnote, line 2   collection] ~, 1856
page 48, line 12   *civilized*] *civilised* 1856
page 48, footnote ‡, line 9   hémisphere] hémisphère 1856
page 49, footnote, line 1   croire;] ~: 1856

CHAPTER 7

page 50, line 1   CHAPTER] 1856; CHAP. 1817
page 50, line 12   developements] developments 1856
page 50, line 26   good will] good-will 1856
page 53, line 9   "When] ^ ~ 1856
page 53, line 9   ghost."] ~.^ 1856
page 53, line 19   developements] developments 1856
page 54, line 2   infirmity,] ~ ^ 1856
page 54, line 18   improvement,] ~ ^ 1856

CHAPTER 8

page 55, line 1   CHAPTER] 1856; CHAP. 1817
page 55, line 3   Telegraph] TELEGRAPH 1856
page 55, line 17   the] "~ 1817, 1856

page 55, line 24	"to] '~ 1856
page 55, line 25	Europe"] ~' 1856
page 55, line 25	"Whatever] '~ 1817, 1856
page 55, line 26	right."] ~.'" 1817, 1856
page 56, line 33	Feathernest,] ~ ^ 1856
page 57, line 12	day] ~, 1856
page 57, line 19	ballads,] ~ ^ 1856
page 57, line 26	gift:"] ~;" 1856
page 58, line 2	Danaretta:] ~; 1856
page 58, line 6	mind,] ~ ^ 1856
page 58, line 24	reply,] ~ ^ 1856
page 59, line 6	soliloquized] soliloquised 1856
page 59, line 12	soliloquized] soliloquised 1856
page 59, line 13	Derrydown:] ~; 1856
page 59, line 19	Arthur] 1856; Ar thur 1817

CHAPTER 9

page 60, line 1	CHAPTER] 1856; CHAP. 1817
page 62 line 6	developement] development 1856
page 62 line 9	harmonized] harmonised 1856
page 63 line 12	asked] ask'd 1856
page 64, line 1	"Young] ^ ~ 1856
page 64 line 1	asked] ask'd 1856
page 64, line 1	bride;"] ~;^ 1856
page 64 line 13	"But] ^ ~ 1856
page 64 line 13	beside."] ~.^ 1856
page 64, line 31	ha' n't] ha'nt 1856
page 65 line 03	"Will] ^ ~ 1856
page 65, line 4	kitchen?"] ~? ^ 1856
page 65, line 26	"God] ^ ~ 1856
page 65, line 27	all."] ~. ^ 1856
page 65, line 30	Old] old 1856
page 67, line 8	weed-flowered] weed-flower'd 1856
page 67, line 13	Scattered] Scatter'd 1856

page 67, line 17	Mouldered] Moulder'd 1856
page 67, line 19	thrall] ~; 1856
page 67, line 20	perished] perish'd 1856
page 67, line 22	cherished] cherish'd 1856
page 67, line 27	tipped] tipp'd 1856
page 67, line 31	stone——] ~ — 1856

CHAPTER 10

page 68, line 1	CHAPTER] 1856; CHAP. 1817
page 69, line 12	which] whence 1856
page 70, line 18	years] ~, 1856
page 71, line 10	considered] 1856; considesed
page 71, line 21	after,] ~ ₍ 1856
page 71, footnote †, paragraph 2, line 2	51.;] ~; 1856
page 72, footnote, line 2	c.] chap. 1856
page 72, line 13	stranger,] ~ ₍ 1856
page 72, line 14	apprehension,] ~ ₍ 1856
page 72, line 15	fashion,] ~ ₍ 1856
page 72, line 15	characterized] characterised 1856
page 73, line 3	head,] ~ ₍ 1856
page 73, line 9	it,] ~ ₍ 1856
page 73, line 12	talking,] ~ ₍ 1856
page 73, line 15	great coat] ~ - ~ 1856
page 73, line 25	part,] ~ ₍ 1856
page 74, line 1	Hercules, quite] ~ — ~ 1856
page 74, lines 3–4	mushrooms:] ~; 1856

CHAPTER 11

page 75, line 1	CHAPTER] 1856; CHAP. 1817
page 75, line 3	Oran Haut-ton] ORAN HAUT-TON 1856
page 75, line 6	Anthelia,] ~ ₍ 1856

page 75, line 10	strength,] ~ ‸ 1856
page 75, line 27	he] ~, 1856
page 75, line 27	Haut-ton] ~, 1856
page 76, line 1	pieces] ~, 1856
page 76, line 15	him,] ~ ‸ 1856
page 76, line 16	be,] ~ ‸ 1856
page 77, line 27	Voltaire?] ~?— 1856
page 77, line 28	"Le] ~ 1856
page 77, line 30	mérite."] ~. ‸ 1856
page 78, line 27	beauty] ~, 1856
page 79, line 18	penny cha[ ]/rity] penny charity 1856
page 80, line 15	comprise] ~, 1856
page 80, lines 16–17	opinions,] ~ ‸ 1856
page 80, line 18	rare] ~, 1856
page 81, line 4	multitude,] ~ ‸ 1856
page 81, line 20	qualities,] ~ ‸ 1856
page 81, line 24	coexistent] co-existent 1856

CHAPTER 12

page 83, line 1	CHAPTER] 1856; CHAP. 1817
page 83, line 10	generation,] ~ ‸ 1856
page 83, line 14	wind-and-water-tight] wind and water tight 1856
page 83, line 19	connexion] connection 1856
page 83, line 27	roll,] ~ ‸ 1856
page 84, line 4	*together,*] ~ ‸ 1856
page 84, line 30	connexion] connection 1856
page 85, line 14	equalize] equalise 1856
page 86, line 2	Calamity] calamity 1856
page 86, line 9	poverty,] ~ ‸ 1856
page 86, line 15	yea,] ~ ‸ 1856
page 86, line 21	poverty,] ~ ‸ 1856
page 87, line 11	succeeded,] ~ ‸ 1856

CHAPTER 13

page 88, line 1	CHAPTER] 1856; CHAP. 1817
page 89, line 1	"The] ˄The 1856
page 89, line 3	more."] more. ˄ 1856
page 89, line 15	foundations] foundation 1856
page 89, line 30	phænomenon] phenomenon 1856
page 90, line 31	scissars] scissors 1856
page 91, line 14	away] 1818, 1856; away with Halliford
page 91, line 20	*noon-day*] *noonday* 1856
page 91, line 32	*shape*] ~, 1856
page 93, line 1	every where] everywhere 1856
page 95, line 22	embarrassed:] ~; 1856
page 96, line 12	ocean,] ~ ˄ 1856
page 96, line 14	visitor:] ~; 1856
page 98, line 4	organize] organise 1856

CHAPTER 14

page 100, line 1	CHAPTER] 1856; CHAP. 1817
page 100, line 4	CANNOT] cannot 1856
page 100, line 22	therefore,] ~ ˄ 1856
page 102, line 27	again;] ~, 1856
page 103, line 6–7	tranquillized] tranquillised 1856
page 103, footnote †, line 17	*Ibid.*] *Origin and Progress of Language*, book ii. chap. 4. 1856
page 104, line 3	civilized] civilised 1856
page 104, line 30	and, therefore,] ~ ˄ ~ ˄ 1856
page 105, line 5	process] ~, 1856
page 105, line 6	dress,] ~ ˄ 1856
page 106, line 1	in,] ~ ˄ 1856
page 106, line 2	We] we 1856
page 106, line 5	solicitation,] ~ ˄ 1856
page 106, line 10	cried,] ~ ˄ 1856

page 106, line 10   kicked,] ~ ₍ 1856

page 106, line 15   testified,] ~ ₍ 1856

page 106, line 33   boy] ~, 1856

CHAPTER 15

page 108, line 1   CHAPTER] 1856; CHAP. 1817

page 108, line 3   Forester] Forester 1856

page 108, line 26   *die,*] ~ ₍ 1856

page 108, line 27   *love.*"] ~.₍ 1856

page 112, line 30   Calypso] ~, 1856

page 113, line 29   bye] by 1856

page 115, footnote, line 2   Buffon,] ~. 1856

CHAPTER 16

page 116, line 1   CHAPTER] 1856; CHAP. 1817

page 116, line 20   "Of] ₍ ~ 1856

page 116, line 25   crystals!"] ~!₍ 1856

page 116, footnote   Sea Voyage.] "Sea Voyage." 1856

page 117, line 23   adhibition] 1856; adhihition 1817

page 118, line 21   *Looking*] *looking* 1856

page 118, line 21   *glass,*] ~ ₍ 1856

page 119, line 28   unstigmatized] unstigmatised 1856

page 120, line 21   "This] ₍This 1856

page 120, line 21   well-furnished] well-furnish'd 1856

page 120, line 24   get."] get. ₍ 1856

page 121, line 2   Baronet] baronet 1856

page 121, line 24   most] 1856; [ ]ost 1817

page 122, line 17   "What] ₍ ~ 1856

page 122, line 20   more."] ~.₍ 1856

page 123, line 1   GLEE] Glee 1856

page 123, line 32   civilization] civilisation 1856

page 124, line 4   civilized] civilised 1856

page 124, line 11   civilized] civilised 1856

page 124, lines 20–21   artizan] artisan 1856

page 125, footnote *, line 1   Ancient Metaphysics] "~ ~" 1856
page 125, footnote *, line 2   Discourse] "~ 1856
page 125, footnote *, line 2   Inequality] ~" 1856
page 125, footnote *, line 2   Arts and Sciences.] "~ ~ ~." 1856
page 125, footnote †, line 1   "Nam] ˌ~ 1856
page 125, footnote †, lines 3–4   &c."/ Juv.] &c.—Juv. 1856

CHAPTER 17

page 128, line 1   CHAPTER] 1856; CHAP. 1817
page 128, line 5   stigmatizing] stigmatising 1856
page 128, lines 19–20   luxuries] luxury 1856
page 128, line 28   'T is] 'Tis 1856
page 129, line 24   harmonized] harmonised 1856
page 129, line 27   following] ~. 1856
page 129, lines 28–30   BALLAD TERZETTO. [*new line*] THE LADY, THE KNIGHT, AND THE FRIAR.] BALLAD TERZETTO.— THE LADY, THE KNIGHT, AND THE FRIAR. 1856
page 130, line 11   't is] 'tis 1856
page 130, line 15   propitious;] ~: 1856
page 131, line 15   pencil] ~, 1856
page 132, line 13   "To prove] ˌTo prove 1856
page 132, line 14   knocks,"] knocks, ˌ 1856

CHAPTER 18

page 134, line 1   CHAPTER] 1856; CHAP. 1818
page 135, line 1   cause,] ~ˌ 1856
page 135, line 28   Anthelia,] ~ˌ 1856
page 136, line 21   listen:] ~; 1856
page 136, line 31   chaise and four] chaise-and-four 1856
page 137, line 24   them from   Oran] them from Sir Oran 1856

CHAPTER 19

page 139, line 1	CHAPTER] 1856; CHAP. 1817
page 139, line 10	inclination] ~, 1856
page 139, line 14	Honourable] honourable 1856
page 140, footnote †, line 3	any thing] anything 1856
page 140, footnote †, line 5	Τειχοσκοπια,] ~ ^ 1856
page 142, footnote, paragraph 2, line 2	observation,] ~ ˄ 1856
page 143, line 5	whip] ~, 1856
page 143, line 21	"the poet's] ˄the poet's 1856
page 143, line 22	rest,"] rest, ˄ 1856
page 144, line 23	over-head] overhead 1856
page 144, line 24	network] net-work 1856
page 145, line 2	still,] ~ ˄ 1856
page 146, line 1	fob,] ~ ˄ 1856
page 146, line 8	expect,] ~ ˄ 1856
page 146. line 19	and,] ~ ˄ 1856
page 146. footnote, line 2	κτλ.] κ.τ.λ. 1856

CHAPTER 20

page 147, line 1	CHAPTER] 1856; CHAP. 1817
page 149, line 14	so,] ~ ˄ 1856
page 149, line 17	be,] ~ ˄1856
page 149, line 24	other,] ~ ˄ 1856
page 150, line 8	you,] ~ ˄ 1856
page 150, line 8	course,] ~ ˄ 1856

CHAPTER 21

page 151, line 1	CHAPTER] 1856; CHAP. 1817
page 151, line 9	Onevote;] ~: 1856
page 151, line 14	signalized] signalised 1856
page 151, line 22	Esquire,] Esq., 1856
page 153, line 25	stigmatized] stigmatised 1856
page 155, footnote	Hudibras:] ~, 1856

page 156, line 2	His] his 1856
page 156, line 7	present] ~, 1856
page 157, line 3	observe,] ~ ₍ₐ₎ 1856
page 157, line 11	boys;] ~, 1856
page 157, lines 29–30	subject,] ~ ₍ₐ₎ 1856
page 158, line 5	by the] in 1856
page 158, line 11	convinced] ~, 1856
page 158, line 19	reason,] ~; 1856
page 158, line 20	society,] ~ ₍ₐ₎ 1856
page 158, line 23	many,] ~ ₍ₐ₎ 1856

CHAPTER 22

page 160, line 1	CHAPTER] 1856; CHAP. 1817
page 160, line 13	pluralized] pluralised 1856
page 161, lines 16–17	artizan] artisan 1856
page 163, line 11	with] by 1856
page 164, line 3	civilized] civilised 1856
page 164, line 33	still] ~, 1856
page 165, line 9	course,] ~ ₍ₐ₎ 1856
page 165, line 10	*sang-froid*] *sang froid* 1856
page 165, line 11	phlebotomize] phlebotomise 1856
page 165, line 16	reason,] ~ ₍ₐ₎ 1856
page 165, line 21	acknowledge,] ~ ₍ₐ₎ 1856
page 165, line 31	elected,] ~ ₍ₐ₎ 1856
page 166, line 1	M. P.] M. P., 1856
page 166, line 5	Gentlemen!] ~, 1856
page 166, line 7	electors:] ~; 1856
page 167, line 13	they] ~, 1856
page 167, line 14	who,] ~ ₍ₐ₎ 1856
page 167, line 17	space,] ~ ₍ₐ₎ 1856
page 167, line 33	whip:] ~, 1856
page 167, line 34	racers:] ~, 1856
page 168, line 24	blaze,] ~ ₍ₐ₎ 1856

CHAPTER 23

page 169, line 1	CHAPTER] 1856; CHAP. 1817
page 169, line 3	sympathize] sympathise 1856
page 170, line 15	't is] 'tis 1856
page 170, line 15	fashion,] ~ ∧ 1856
page 170, line 22	read,] ~ ∧ 1856
page 171, line 12	twelfth night] twelfth-night 1856
page 173, line 8	any thing] anything 1856
page 173, line 16	Reverend] reverend 1856

CHAPTER 24

page 175, line 1	CHAPTER] 1856; CHAP. 1817
page 175, lines 5–6	Anti-saccharine] anti-saccharine 1856
page 177, line 14	produce,] ~ ∧ 1856
page 177, line 26	vanity,] ~ ∧ 1856
page 178, line 8	society,] ~ ∧ 1856
page 179, line 3	of] ~, 1856
page 179, line 14	good-/will] goodwill 1856
page 179, line 21	last,] ~ ∧ 1856
page 180, line 9	temporizers] temporisers 1856
page 180, line 13	*needle,*] ~ ∧ 1856
page 180, line 28	monopolizers] monopolisers 1856
page 181, line 7	criminal,] ~ ∧ 1856
page 181, footnote	See Vol. I. page 156.] See p. 78 1856
page 182, line 8	civilized] civilised 1856
page 182, line 31	by] bye 1856

CHAPTER 25

page 184, line 1	CHAPTER] 1856; CHAP. 1817
page 184, footnote, paragraph 2, line 1	country,] ~ ∧ 1856

page 185, footnote *, line 5	longevity,] ~ ₐ 1856
page 187, line 2	him;] ~ ₐ 1856
page 187, line 4	talking——"] 1856; ~ —— 1817
page 187, line 7	Pinmoney:] ~, 1856
page 188, line 14	Anthelia;] ~, 1856
page 188, line 16	——in] —— ~ 1856
page 188, line 20	quest] guest 1817, 1856
page 188, line 22	realization] realisation 1856
page 188, line 24	every where] everywhere 1856
page 188, line 26	every where] everywhere 1856
page 189, line 7	realizing] realising 1856

CHAPTER 26

page 190, line 1	CHAPTER] 1856; CHAP. 1817
page 190, line 8	œconomy] economy 1856
page 190, line 20	characterized] characterised 1856
page 190, line 31	stick,] ~ ₐ 1856
page 192, line 3	any thing] anything 1856
page 192, footnote †	Ancient Metaphysics, vol. v. book iv. chap. 8] Ibid. 1856

CHAPTER 27

page 194, line 1	CHAPTER] 1856; CHAP. 1817
page 194, line 2	FETE] FÊTE 1856
page 194, line 3	Evergreen] EVERGREEN 1856
page 195, line 28	SLAVERY] SLAVERY 1856
page 195, lines 28–29	œconomically] economically 1856
page 196, line 12	country,] ~ ₐ 1856
page 196, line 15	thing—not] thing, not 1856
page 197, footnote *, lines 3–4	impresa."/ PETRARCA.] impresa."—PETRARCA. 1856

CHAPTER 28

page 200, line 1	CHAPTER] 1856; CHAP. 1817
page 200, line 30	Reviewer] reviewer 1856
page 201, line 21	ball-room] ~ ^ ~ *1856*
page 202, line 3	King] *King* 1856
page 202, line 3	Mr. Hippy.] Mr. Hippy. 1856
page 202, line 4	Queen] *Queen* 1856
page 202, line 4	Miss Danaretta Contantina Pinmoney.] Miss Danaretta Contantina Pinmoney. 1856
page 202, line 5	King's Bishop] *King's Bishop* 1856
page 202, line 5	The Reverend Mr. Portpipe.] The Reverend Mr. Portpipe. 1856
page 202, line 6	Queen's Bishop] *Queen's Bishop* 1856
page 202, line 6	Sir Gregory Greenmould.] Sir Gregory Greenmould. 1856
page 202, line 7	King's Knight] *King's Knight* 1856
page 202, line 7	Mr. O'Scarum.] Mr. O'Scarum. 1856
page 202, line 8	Queen's Knight] *Queen's Knight* 1856
page 202, line 8	Sir Telegraph Paxarett.] Sir Telegraph Paxarett. 1856
page 202, line 9	King's Rook] *King's Rook* 1856
page 202, line 9	Mr. Feathernest.] Mr. Feathernest. 1856
page 202, line 10	Queen's Rook] *Queen's Rook* 1856
page 202, line 10	Mr. Paperstamp.] Mr. Paperstamp. 1856
page 202, line 11	Eight Nymphs.] *Eight Nymphs.* 1856
page 202, line 13	King] *King* 1856
page 202, line 13	Major O'Dogskin.] Major O'Dogskin. 1856

page 202, line 14	Queen] *Queen* 1856
page 202, line 14	Miss Celandina Paperstamp.] Miss Celindina Paperstamp. 1856
page 202, line 15	King's Bishop] *King's Bishop* 1856
page 202, line 15	Squire Hermitage.] Squire Hermitage. 1856
page 202, line 16	Queen's Bishop] *Queen's Bishop* 1856
page 202, line 16	Squire Heeltap.] Squire Heeltap. 1856
page 202, line 17	King's Knight] *King's Knight* 1856
page 202, line 17	Mr. Sarcastic.] Mr. Sarcastic. 1856
page 202, line 18	Queen's Knight] *Queen's Knight* 1856
page 202, line 18	Mr. Derrydown.] Mr. Derrydown. 1856
page 202, line 19	King's Rook] *King's Rook* 1856
page 202, line 19	Mr. Killthedead.] Mr. Killthedead. 1856
page 202, line 20	Queen's Rook] *Queen's Rook* 1856
page 202, line 20	Mr. Vamp.] Mr. Vamp. 1856
page 202, line 21	Eight Nymphs.] *Eight Nymphs.* 1856
page 205, line 17	locomotion;] ~: 1856
page 205, line 17	bowed,] ~ ₐ 1856
page 207, line 3	mixed] mix'd 1856

CHAPTER 29

page 208, line 1	CHAPTER] 1856; CHAP. 1817
page 209, line 9	O'Dogskin,] ~ ₐ 1856
page 209, line 15	day,] ~ ₐ 1856
page 210, line 5	drink,] ~ ₐ 1856

page 211, line 15	dispatched] despatched 1856
page 211, line 16	table,] ~ ₍ 1817
page 211, line 23	wine-glasses;] wine-glasses. 1856

CHAPTER 30

page 212, line 1	CHAPTER] 1856; CHAP. 1817
page 212, line 23	Company,] ~ ₍ 1856
page 213, line 13	directly."] 1856; ~.₍ 1817
page 214, line 12	woman,] ~ ₍ 1856
page 214, line 23	every body] everybody 1856
page 215, line 1	wife:] ~; 1856
page 215, line 26	soon as] soon as soon as 1856
page 216, line 14	and,] ~ ₍ 1856
page 217, line 17	promise to pay] ~ - ~ - ~ 1856
page 217, line 21	o'arms:] o' arms: 1856
page 217, line 23	o' t;] o't 1856

CHAPTER 31

page 219, line 1	CHAPTER] 1856; CHAP. 1817
page 219, line 1	XXXI.] XXXI 1856
page 219, line 16	"That] ₍ ~ 1856
page 219, line 17	gave;"] ~;₍ 1856
page 220, footnote, line 2	chapter,] ~ ₍ 1856
page 222, line 10	connexion] connection 1856
page 222, line 12	connexion] connection 1856
page 222, line 30	bedrooms] bed-/rooms 1817, bed-rooms 1856
page 223, line 1	"The] ₍ ~ 1856
page 223, line 2	around."] ~.₍ 1856
page 224, line 2	half hour] ~ - ~ 1856
page 226, footnote §	Ibid. p. 25.] Coleridge's Lay Sermon, p. 25. 1856
page 226, footnote **	p.] pp. 1856

page 226, footnote ††   Coleridge's Lay Sermon, p. xvii.]
                                     Ibid. p. xvii. 1856

page 227, between lines 2 and 3 *extra vertical space after* "TRIAD!"]
                                     no space 1856

CHAPTER 32

page 229, line 1	CHAPTER] 1856; CHAP. 1817
page 230, line 14	pace;] ~: 1856
page 230, line 35	hour:] ~; 1856
page 231, line 12	heart;] ~: 1856
page 231, line 16	now:] ~; 1856
page 231, line 22	to] too 1856
page 231, line 31	vlew] flew 1856
page 231, line 31–32	every thing] everything 1856
page 231, line 33	was n't] wasn't 1856
page 232, line 2	like,—a] ~ ‸ — ~ 1856
page 232, line 3	un,—and] un ‸ —and 1856
page 232, line 3	o'ground] o' ground 1856
page 232, line 5	there,] ~ ‸ 1856
page 232, line 15	zouls] souls 1856
page 232, line 17	every thing] everything 1856
page 233, line 4	there] their 1856
page 233, lines 13–14	sheame vor] shame for 1856
page 233, line 15	always] alway 1856
page 233, line 17	zon] son 1856
page 233, line 29	"Ah!] ~! 1856
page 233, line 31	vault] fault 1856
page 233, line 32	zinecure] sinecure 1856

CHAPTER 33

page 234, line 1	CHAPTER] 1856; CHAP. 1817
page 234, line 16	postern door] postern-door 1856
page 234, line 31	Every thing] Everything 1856

page 236, line 4   every where] everywhere 1856

page 236, footnote   See vol. i. p. 73, note.] See p. 36, note. 1856

page 236, line 23   us,] ~ ˄ 1856

page 237, line 9   connexion] connection 1856

page 237, line 25   harmonizes] harmonises 1856

page 237, line 25   superstition,] ~; 1856

CHAPTER 34

page 239, line 1   CHAPTER] 1856; CHAP. 1817

page 239, line 7   it] ~, 1856

page 239, line 11   of,] ~; 1856

page 239, line 11   funeral,] ~; 1856

page 239, line 29   trade:] ~; 1856

page 241, line 4   proof,] ~ ˄ 1856

page 241, line 10   eyes,] ~ ˄ 1856

page 241, line 19   strange,] ~ ˄ 1856

page 242, line 10   with: that] ~ — ~ 1856

page 242, line 15   gravestones] grave-stones 1856

page 242, line 15   hundred:] hundred:— 1856

CHAPTER 35

page 243, line 1   CHAPTER] 1856; CHAP. 1817

page 243, line 6   touch,] ~ ˄ 1856

page 243, line 13   grin,] grin ˄ 1856

page 243, line 30   toimes] times 1856

page 244, line 17   bea'n't] be'an't 1856

page 245, line 15   *scandalized*] *scandalised* 1856

page 245, line 30   sows] zows 1856

page 247, line 19   chillern] chilern 1856

page 247, line 20   zuch-like] such-like 1856

page 248, line 9   girl:] ~; 1856

page 248, line 14   dom'd] doom'd 1856

CHAPTER 36

CHAPTER 37

CHAPTER 38

CHAPTER 39

page 264, line 26	see-saw,] ~ - ~ ̞ 1856
page 264, line 27	Daw,] ~ ̞ 1856
page 264, line 27	cake—the] ~; ~1856
page 265, line 12	who] ~, 1856
page 265, line 12	believe] ~, 1856
page 266, line 20	anticipation,] ~ ̞ 1856
page 267, line 2	apologized] apologised 1856
page 267, footnote *	XXXI.] xxxi. 1856
page 267, line 18	course,] ~ ̞ 1856
page 267, footnote ‡	XXXI.] xxxi. 1856
page 268, footnote *	Quarterly Review, No. XXXI. p. 227.] Ibid. p. 227. 1856
page 268, line 12	connexion] connection 1856
page 268, footnote †	Quarterly Review, No. XXXI. p. 227.] Ibid. 1856
page 268, line 27	us,] ~ ̞ 1856
page 269, line 8	connexion] connection 1856
page 269, line 10	think;] ~: 1856
page 269, footnote *	XXXI.] xxxi. 1856
page 270, footnote *	XXXI.] xxxi. 1856
page 270, footnote †	Quarterly Review, No. XXXI. p. 226.] Ibid. p. 226. 1856
page 271, footnote *	XXXI.] xxxi. 1856
page 271, line 25	*sings.*] sings— 1856
page 272, line 6	stigmatize] stigmatise 1856
page 272, footnote *	Quarterly Review, No. XXXI. p. 258.] Ibid. 1856
page 272, footnote †	XXXI.] xxxi. 1856
page 273, top footnote, paragraph 1, line 6	these:] ~; 1856
page 273, top footnote, paragraph 1, line 12	crown,] ~ ̞ 1856
page 273, top footnote, paragraph 2, line 6	but,] ~ ̞ 1856

page 273, footnote *, line 1	XXXI.] xxxi. 1856
page 274, line 1	*words,*] ~ ₐ 1856
page 274, footnote *, line 14	X.] x. 1856
page 274, line 3	"*Who*] ₐ~ 1856
page 274, line 4	*brown;"*] ~; ₐ 1856
page 274, line 9	connexion] connection 1856
page 274, footnote †	XXXI.] xxxi. 1856
page 275, footnote *	XXXI.] xxxi. 1856
page 275, line 22	latter,] ~ ₐ 1856
page 276, footnote *	Quarterly Review, No. XXXI. p. 273] Ibid. p. 273. 1856
page 276, footnote †	Quarterly Review, No. XXXI. p. 276.] Ibid. p. 276. 1856
page 276, footnote ‡	Ibid. p. 260.] Quarterly Review, No. xxxi. p. 260. 1856
page 277, line 7	you,] ~ ₐ 1856
page 277, footnote	XXXI.] xxxi. 1856

CHAPTER 40

page 281, line 1	CHAPTER] 1856; CHAP. 1817
page 281, line 5	turnpike road] turnpike-road 1856
page 282, footnote	curæ. *Tiberius*] ~ .— ~ 1856
page 282, line 22	connexion] connection 1856
page 283, footnote, line 3	civilized] civilised 1856
page 283, footnote, line 21	disease,] ~ ₐ 1856
page 284, line 7	Civilization] Civilisation 1856
page 284, line 24	every thing] everything 1856
page 285, line 15	simulated] stimulated 1856
page 285, line 23	hypotheses] hypothesis 1856
page 286, line 1	*friendship,*] ~ ₐ 1856
page 286, line 3	*retiring,*] ~ ₐ 1856
page 286, line 26	civilized] civilised 1856

page 287, line 9	tranquillizes] tranquillises 1856
page 288, line 20	*married,*] ~ ˄ 1856
page 288, line 24	knowledge:] ~; 1856
page 288, line 28	harmonizing] harmonising 1856
page 288, line 28	mildew,] ~ ˄ 1856
page 289, footnote, line 8	WELD'S] WELD'S 1856
page 289, line 7	civilization] civilisation 1856

CHAPTER 41

page 291, line 1	CHAPTER] 1856; CHAP. 1817
page 291, line 6	companion,] ~ ˄ 1856
page 291, line 10	cry] ~, 1856
page 292, line 10	woman:] ~; 1856
page 292, line 15	who] ~, 1856
page 292, line 26	wickedness,] ~ ˄ 1856
page 294, line 4	any thing] anything 1856
page 294, line 14	every thing] everything 1856
page 294, line 21	every thing] everything 1856
page 294, line 23	mean while] meanwhile 1856
page 297, line 27	imprest,] ~ ˄ 1856

CHAPTER 42

page 299, line 1	CHAPTER] 1856; CHAP. 1817
page 299, line 3	Anophel] ANOPHEL 1856
page 302, footnote, line 1	civilized] civilised 1856
page 302, line 23	realized] realised 1856
page 303, line 3	*device*] *no device* 1856
page 303, footnote, line 14	*Act I.*] *Act I.*, 1856
page 304, footnote, line 6	*IV.*] *IV.*, 1856
page 304, footnote, line 18	light?] ~! 1856
page 304, footnote, line 29	*Act V.*] *Act V.*, 1856
page 304, line 1	"—They] ˄˄ ~ 1856
page 304, line 5	humanity."] ~.˄ 1856

AMBIGUOUS LINE-END HYPHENATIONS

The hyphenated word in the copytext appears on the left; the word as it is printed in this edition appears on the right.

page 5, line 29	castle-/rock]	castle-rock
page 20 line 6	blue-/devilled]	blue-devilled
page 39, line 4	prize-/money]	prize-money
page 52, line 32	over-/shadowed]	overshadowed
page 59, line 30	coach-/men]	coachmen
page 65, line 6	Here-/upon]	Hereupon
page 70, line 4	water-/spout]	water-spout
page 71, footnote †, paragraph 3, line 1	palm-/tree]	palm-tree
page 84, line 24	work-/house]	workhouse
page 91, line 20	*noon-/day*]	*noon-day*
page 104, line 12	fir-/tree]	fir-tree
page 107, line 4	co-/operated]	co-operated
page 136, line 2	country-/man]	country-man
page 136, line 10	sun-/beams]	sunbeams
page 152, line 1	semi-/circle]	semicircle
page 165, line 10	*sang-/froid*]	*sang-froid*
page 168, line 19	ale-/casks]	ale-casks
page 178, lines 21–22	*wine-/bibber*]	*wine-bibber*
page 179, line 14	good-/will]	good-will
page 183, line 8	turn-/pike]	turnpike
page 186, line 9	break-/fasted]	breakfasted
page 201, line 21	ball-/room]	ball-room
page 205, line 18	side-/board]	sideboard

page 211, line 23	wine-/glasses]	wine-glasses
page 217, line 15	race-/balls]	race-balls
page 224, line 34	good-/humour]	good-humour
page 227, line 14	gas-/light]	gas-light
page 228, line 4	gas-/tube]	gas-tube
page 228, line 6	air-/tight]	air-tight
page 232, line 3	hand-/vul]	handvul
page 232, line 16	work-/house]	workhouse
page 233, line 2	vund-/holders]	vundholders
page 239, line 17	church-/yard]	churchyard
page 242, line 2	sun-/shine]	sunshine
page 246, line 13	nine-/pence]	ninepence
page 248, line 8	honest-/hearted]	honest-hearted
page 248, line 12	pig-/sty]	pig-sty
page 260, line 19	run-/away]	runaway
page 266, line 16	œno-/gen]	œnogen
page 270, line 15	Anti-/jacobin]	Antijacobin
page 279, line 31	ever-/lasting]	everlasting
page 286, line 18	counter-/poise]	counterpoise
page 288, line 28	stone-/crop]	stonecrop
page 290, line 18	sea-/shore]	sea-shore
page 302, line 1	Gads-/hill]	Gads-hill

EXPLANATORY NOTES

Notes on TLP's quotations from printed books record variants in substantives but usually disregard variants in punctuation, spelling or capitalization.

Place of publication, unless otherwise stated, is London.

TITLE PAGE AND PRELIMS

VOCEM COMŒDIA TOLLIT: Horace in his *Ars Poetica* states that comedy or tragedy each requires its own style, but 'interdum tamen et vocem comœdia tollit' (line 93); 'sometimes even comedy assumes a [tragic] voice'. TLP implies that *Mel*, while primarily comic, adopts the tragic style when fitting, or that individual characters in this comic novel must speak in the style suited to tragic subjects.

'Nous nous . . . ROUSSEAU': From Jean-Jacques Rousseau's *Émile, ou de L'Éducation* (1762), book 5; see *Œuvres complètes*, ed. Bernard Gagnebin, Marcel Raymond et al., 5 vols. (Paris: Gallimard, 1959–95), vol. 4, p. 473. The epigraph has been translated as 'We make a jest of knights errant! . . . When these romantick principles first became ridiculous, the ridicule was not so much the result of reason as of depravity' (J. J. Rousseau, *Emilius and Sophia; or, A New System of Education*, 4 vols. (T. Becket and R. Baldwin, 1783), vol. 3, p. 245); and 'We make fun of the Paladins. . . . When these romantic maxims began to become ridiculous, the change was less the work of reason than of bad morals' (*Emile, or On Education: Includes Emile and Sophie, or the Solitaries*, trans. and ed. Christopher Kelly and Allan Bloom (Hanover, NH: UP of New England, 2009), vol. 13 of *The Collected Writings of Rousseau*, ed. Roger D. Masters and Christopher

Kelly, (1990–2009), p. 571. In *CC*, Mr Chainmail says that, in the nineteenth century, 'We can no more feel the high impassioned love of the ages, which some people have the impudence to call dark, than we can wield King Richard's battleaxe' (ch. 12).

CHAPTER I

1 **Anthelia**: Her name comes from the Greek *anthelion*, meaning 'opposite to the sun' or 'against the sun'. TLP's meaning seems to be that Anthelia can compete with the sun.

2 **Westmoreland**: The decision to set *Mel* in Westmorland and Cumberland appears to have been motivated by two considerations. First, the picturesque scenery of the Lake District, described in William Gilpin, *Observations, Relative Chiefly to Picturesque Beauty, Made in the Year 1772, On Several Parts of England; Particularly the Mountains, and Lakes of Cumberland, and Westmoreland*, 2 vols. (R. Blamire, 1786), which TLP quotes in ch. 25 (he owned a copy of the first edition of Gilpin's book at the time of his death (*Sale Catalogue* 201)). Second, the association of the Lake District with Robert Southey, poet laureate from 1813 until his death, William Wordsworth, and Samuel Taylor Coleridge. Fax later refers to 'the cant of the new school of poetry' and to the 'little horde of poets' who retreated to the Lakes (ch. 37). In 'The Four Ages of Poetry', TLP referred to 'the Lake Poets' as an 'egregious confraternity of rhymesters' who 'wrote verses on a new principle; saw rocks and rivers in a new light; and remaining studiously ignorant of history, society, and human nature, cultivated the phantasy only at the expence of the memory and the reason; and contrived, though they had retreated from the world for the express purpose of seeing nature as she was, to see her only as she was not, converting the land they lived in into a sort of fairy-land, which they peopled with mysticisms and chimæras' (*NA*, Appendix C, pp. 149–50). In the fragmentary *Calidore*, written just after *Mel*, the news that a

'philosopher' whom Calidore selects will receive a pension large enough to 'keep in pay two whole gangs of Legitimate Reviewers' has the effect that 'all the seats of the Carlisle [mail-coaches] were engaged every night for a week in bringing up shoals of embryo laureats and poetical philosophers from Cumberland' (Halliford, 8.340).

3   **both Irishmen and clergymen**: Two stereotypical groups of men in search of rich wives.

4   **disinterested passion**: The first of eleven appearances in *Mel* of 'disinterested', i.e. 'Not influenced by interest; impartial, unbiased, unprejudiced; now always, Unbiased by personal interest; free from self-seeking' (*OED* 2). This adjective is essential to TLP's celebration of impartial judgment. Chivalry, one of *Mel*'s keywords, is defined in terms of 'disinterested benevolence' (chs. 2, 8).

5   **this calculating age**: A catch-phrase. Charles James Fox said in the House of Commons that 'In this calculating age, we ascertain to a scruple what an object is really worth' (*Speech of the Right Honourable Charles James Fox, on Mr. Whitbread's Motions on the Russian Armament, Thursday, March 1, 1792* [J. Debrett, 1792], p. 24).

6   **Melincourt Castle**: Anthelia's country seat is a real medieval castle, unlike Crotchet Castle, which merely lies near a Roman *castellum* (*CC*, ch. 1). The only 'Melincourt' certainly known to TLP was Melincourt Falls, in the Neath Valley in Wales; he visited Wales with Percy Shelley in 1813. There is a Captain Melincourt in Charlotte Smith's novel *Marchmont*, 4 vols. (Sampson Low, 1796); see vol. 4, pp. 107–21.

7   **a narrow ledge**: In ch. 10, TLP reveals that a person can leave the castle precincts by a route other than this ledge: amid the shrubbery by Anthelia's apartment, 'a little postern door' leads to 'a flight of rugged steps' that leads 'into the gloomy glen of the torrent that dashed round the base of the castle rock' (ch. 10).

8 **the picturesque tourist**: The allusion is to travellers sketching the wonders of the Lake District and exhibiting their works in London. One such traveller is interrupted by Sir Oran in ch. 14. For a satirical account of such tourism, see [William Combe], *The Tour of Doctor Syntax in Search of the Picturesque: A Poem*, ill. Thomas Rowlandson (Rudolph Ackermann, [1812]). In ch. 40, Fax criticizes 'everlasting talkers about taste and beauty, who see in the starving beggar only the picturesqueness of his rags, and in the ruined cottage only the harmonizing hints of moss, mildew, and stone-crop'. Disputes over picturesque landscape gardening are central to *HH*; the wild scenery near Melincourt Castle seems calculated to offend the aesthetic standards of that novel's Mr Milestone (ch. 6). TLP's Calidore visits 'a very good inn for the accommodation of picturesque tourists' (Halliford, 8.304).

9 **October**: 'A kind of strong ale traditionally brewed in October' (*OED*, sense 2).

10 **the Reverend Mr. Portpipe**: One of TLP's many heavy-drinking clergymen of the Church of England. A pipe is 'a liquid (or solid) measure, esp. of wine, equal to the capacity of a pipe. Typically equal to two hogsheads or 63 wine gallons (105 imperial gallons, approx. 477 litres), but varying with the substance or the kind of wine' (*OED*). A pipe in this sense is 'Sometimes identified with a Butt', meaning 'A cask for wine or ale, of capacity varying from 108 to 140 gallons', and 'Afterwards also as a measure of capacity = 2 hogsheads, i.e. usually . . . in wine measure 126 gallons; but these standards were not always precisely adhered to'. The name of Roderick Sackbut in *NA* refers to the butt of wine that the poet laureate received as his compensation (sack being fortified white wine from Spain or the Canary Islands). Mr Feathernest in *Mel*, who, like Sackbut, is meant to remind the reader of Robert Southey, says that his loyalties have shifted because of the 'pipe of wine' he receives each year (ch. 16).

11 **Madeira**: A fortified wine from the island of that name,
favoured by the male characters in *Mel*. In ch. 4, Sir Telegraph
needs his 'regular diurnal allowance of fish, fowl, and Madeira';
Mrs Pinmoney says that Sir Telegraph 'will not die of despair
as long as there is a good turnpike road and a pipe of Madeira
in England' (ch. 25). Forester serves madeira (ch. 6), as does
Mr Mystic (ch. 31); Forester and his friends drink Anthelia's
madeira (ch. 33). Mr Sarcastic imagines 'rivers of Madeira' (ch.
21), and Lord Anophel and Grovelgrub will talk over 'Madeira
and walnuts' (ch. 23). In *NA*, Mr Larynx is apt to 'drink Madeira
with Scythrop' (ch. 1); Scythrop at the end of the 1837 version
of *NA* asks for madeira. Dr Folliott in *CC* favours madeira, even
though 'The current of opinion sets in favor of Hock' (ch. 4). For
TLP and madeira, see *Letters*, 2.362. TLP's friend Percy Shelley
wrote in *A Vindication of Natural Diet* (1813) that someone
following such a diet will 'require . . . no wines from Portugal,
Spain, France, or Madeira', and indeed require 'none of those
multitudinous articles of luxury, for which every corner of the
globe is rifled, and which are the causes of so much individual rivalship, such calamitous and sanguinary national disputes'
(*PBS Prose*, 85).

12 **blue devils . . . black, white, and grey**: 'Blue devils' is slang for
melancholy, an affliction supposedly caused by such supernat-
ural beings, and here the narrator juxtaposes these figurative
demons with the literal ones commanded by Hecate in *Macbeth*:
'Black Spirits and white, / Red Spirits and grey' (act 4, scene
1, textual notes, *Riverside Shakespeare: The Complete Works*, ed.
G. Blakemore Evans et al., 2nd ed. (Boston: Houghton Mifflin,
1997), p. 1389). In *NA*, Flosky says that, in modern literature,
blue devils are 'the staple commodity; but, as they will not always
be commanded, the black, red, and grey, may be admitted as
substitutes' (ch. 6).

13 **the heretical notion . . . rational beings**: Mary Wollstonecraft
wrote, 'My own sex, I hope, will excuse me, if I treat them

like rational creatures, instead of flattering their *fascinating* graces, and viewing them as if they were in a state of perpetual childhood, unable to stand alone'; *A Vindication of the Rights of Woman: with Strictures on Political and Moral Subjects* (J. Johnson, 1792), p. 6.

14 **The majestic forms and wild energies of Nature**: One of the earliest references in *Mel* to Wordsworthian worship of Nature.

15 **the muses of Italy**: Later we learn that Anthelia reads Torquato Tasso (chs. 15, 17). In *CC*, Susanna Touchandgo has read 'the four great poets of Italy' (ch. 14), presumably Dante, Petrarch, Tasso and Ariosto. In *NA*, Mr Listless comments that Dante 'is growing fashionable' (ch. 6).

16 **St. Paul's precept of being all things to all men**: St Paul wrote that 'I am made all things to all men, that I might by all means save some' (1 Corinthians, ch. 9, v. 22).

17 **Tros Tyriusque mihi nullo discrimine agetur**: In Virgil's *Aeneid*, book 1, line 574, Dido says that she 'will not differentiate between Trojan and Tyrian'.

18 **Acheron**: The river in Hades over which Charon ferried the dead.

19 **'and all she thought of all she saw'**: Not traced.

20 **the tablet of her memory**: Shakespeare's Hamlet says, that 'from the table of my memory / I'll wipe away all trivial fond records' (act 1, scene 5, lines 98–9). In TLP's *Cal*, 'some prudent counsels had been carefully engraven on the tablets of [Calidore's] memory' (Halliford, 8.306–7).

CHAPTER 2

1 **Fashionable Arrivals**: The 'Fashionable Arrivals' section of *The Morning Post* reported on the movements of the social elite. On 31 Jan. 1814, for example, the newspaper announced the arrival of 'The Duke and Duchess of Somerset and Family, at their house, in Park-lane, from their seat in Devonshire'; *The*

Morning Post (31 Jan. 1814), 3. In *Cal*, the news 'that a stranger of great consequence was arrived from Terra Incognita' is 'significantly told in dashes by the *Morning Post*. (*The Morning Post* resorted to dashes when the topic was delicate: 'On Tuesday last a duel took place near Cork, between W——R C——R, Esq. and W——K C——N, Esq. and after exchanging shots, fortunately without injury to either party, the business was amicably adjusted' (16 Apr. 1816), 3.) In canto 13 of Lord Byron's *Don Juan* (1823), *The Morning Post* announces the 'Departure for his country seat today / Lord H. Amundeville and Lady A.', and that their guests will include not only British nobles such as 'The Duke of D—' but also 'a foreigner of high condition' – that is, Juan (canto 13, stanza 51, lines 7–8; stanza 52, lines 5, 7). Quotations from *Don Juan* use the text in Byron, *The Complete Poetical Works*, ed. Jerome J. McGann, 7 vols. (Oxford: Oxford University Press, 1980–93), vol. 5 (1986). In ch. 42 of *Mel*, Lord Anophel Achtar appears foolish when he treats *The Morning Post* as trustworthy.

2 **elegant post-chariot**: A 'chariot' was 'a light-wheeled carriage with only back seats, and differing from the post-chaise in having a coach box' (*OED* 1.d.). A 'chariot', 'A four-wheeled coupé or cut-down coach, usually seating two passengers facing forward' was 'Usually drawn by two horses harnessed in pole gear'; D. J. M. Smith, *A Dictionary of Horse-Drawn Vehicles* (J. A. Allen, 1988), p. 43. According to Smith's *Dictionary*, a 'post-chariot' was a 'Privately owned chariot that could be converted into a Post Chaise' (p. 134). A 'post-chaise' was 'A horse-drawn, usually four-wheeled carriage (in Britain usually having a closed body, the driver or postillion riding on one of the horses) used for carrying mail and passengers' (*OED*). (A postillion is 'A person who rides the (leading) nearside (left-hand side) horse drawing a coach or carriage, esp. when one pair only is used and there is no coachman'; *OED*.) According to Smith, the post-chaise was a 'Type of four-wheeled travelling carriage or chariot used

for public hire, operating between inns and post houses where fresh horses and drivers could also be engaged'; it was 'Often a cut-down and discarded travelling carriage, the box seat was removed and driven either to pairs in pole gear or four-in-hand teams guided by postillions' (*Dictionary of Horse-Drawn Vehicles*, p. 134) – the phrase 'four-in-hand' meant 'A vehicle with four horses driven by one person' (*OED*, first example 1793). In *NA*, Mr Glowry has a 'travelling chariot' (ch. 14). When TLP was writing *Mel*, Percy Shelley owned a carriage that was either a post-chaise or a chariot; see Kenneth Neill Cameron, 'Shelley's Chariot', *Shelley and His Circle*, 3.160–2. TLP pays attention to vehicles: in *HH*, 'every chariot, coach, barouche and barouchette, landau and laudaulet, chaise, curricle, buggy, whiskey, and tilbury' in Caernarvon, Meirionnydd or Anglesea is on its way to the Headlongs' Christmas ball (ch. 11), and ch. 22 of *Mel* provides a catalogue of the modes of transport used by the citizens of Novote.

3　**the Honourable Mrs. Pinmoney**: 'Pin money' was the allowance a woman's marriage settlement provided for her personal expenses; the *OED* defines 'pin money' as 'A (usually annual) sum allotted to a woman for clothing and other personal expenses; *esp.* such an allowance provided for a wife's private expenditure'. In *Cal*, rumour has it that the woman Calidore marries will 'receive a most splendid allowance of pin-money' upon reaching his home, Terra Incognita (Halliford, 8.340). Catherine Gore entitled one of her novels *Pin Money* (1831). Pin money differs from a woman's jointure, which involves her ownership of property; see William Blackstone, *Commentaries on the Laws of England, in Four Books*, 14th ed., 4 vols. (T. Cadell and W. Davies, 1803), vol. 2, pp. 136–8. The prefix 'the honourable' was reserved for two groups of women, maids of honour and the daughters of viscounts and barons. Although Lord Byron addressed his mother as 'the Honourable Mrs. Byron', she was 'without any right to the distinction', as Thomas Moore observed; *Letters and Journals* *of Lord Byron: with Notices of His Life*, 2 vols. (John Murray, 1830–1), vol. 1, p. 150n. Mrs Pinmoney's late husband is merely 'Mr Pinmoney', and if his widow is 'the Honourable' because her father was a viscount or a baron, the reader perhaps should conclude that she married beneath her rank for money.

4 **Miss Danaretta Contantina**: TLP's footnote suggests that her names are 'female diminutives of the Italian words *danaro contante*, signifying *ready money* ...'. An additional irony here is that 'ready money' usually meant cash, and the Bank of England had suspended cash payments (see ch. 21, n. 30).

5 **Strephons**: In pastoral literature, 'Strephon' was a conventional name for a man or boy who is in love. In *NA*, Scythrop is an 'irritable Strephon' (ch. 9); Nicholas A. Joukovsky relates the word particularly to Sir Philip Sidney's *Arcadia* (1590), book 1, ch.1 (*NA*, p. 243).

6 *commodity*: In *HH* the novels of Miss Philomela Poppyseed have taught 'the young ladies of the age ... to consider themselves as a sort of commodity' (*HH*, ch. 6). However, by italicizing 'commodity' in *Mel*, TLP invites the reader to look for a secondary meaning, and there is one to be found: according to Francis Grose's *A Classical Dictionary of the Vulgar Tongue* (S. Hooper, 1785; not paginated), a woman's 'commodity' meant her 'private parts'.

7 **our good friend Hookham's Library**: The lending library owned by Thomas Hookham, Thomas Hookham Junior (the publisher of *Mel*) and E. T. Hookham contained 'Near One Hundred Thousand Volumes in English, French, and Italian ... Including all the Books That Have Been Lately Published in Almost Every Branch of Literature' (from the full title of *A New Catalogue of Hookham's Original Circulating Library* [printed Samuel Gosnell; The Library, (1812)]). The three men's partnership in the library was dissolved nine months after *Mel* appeared (*Times* (3 Nov. 1817)). TLP is not the only author in the period to refer to his publisher in this fashion. In *Prospectus and Specimen of an Intended National Work. By William and Robert Whistlecraft, of Stow-Market,*

in Suffolk, Harness and Collar-Makers. Intended to Comprise the Most Interesting Particulars Relating to King Arthur and His Round Table: Cantos III and IV (John Murray, 1818), John Hookham Frere says that he decided to write two more cantos because of 'a proposal . . . from Mr. Murray', who 'offer[ed] handsomely—the money down' (p. [1]).

8 *Corydon sospiroso*: Italian, a sighing Corydon; 'Corydon' is a conventional term in pastoral literature for a lover (see, for example, Virgil, eclogue 2).

9 **the old lady in Threadneedle Street**: A common term for the Bank of England, which was located in that street in the City of London. When James Watson was tried for treason in June 1817 for his role in the events at Spa Fields (see Introduction), John Castle testified that the insurrectionists were to meet 'At the Old Lady, which was the cant name for the Bank'; T. B. Howell, ed., *A Complete Collection of State Trials*, 34 vols. (Longman, 1809–28), vol. 32, p. 231. Later in *Mel*, Mr Lookout warns that 'a day of reckoning must come sooner or later for the old lady as well as for her daughters' (see ch. 30).

10 **a *good man***: In *The Examiner* (19 Jan. 1817), Leigh Hunt criticized the corruption of language that makes words reflect 'interested standards of vice and virtue' that are 'not measurable to the common good'. In the City of London, he observed, the phrase 'a good man' denotes 'not one who uses his money well, but one who has money to use, and who never puts you to inconvenience in your dealings with him'. Similarly, in the West End, a 'loyal man' 'is not a man who holds by the laws, but who can hold by them or let them go just as it suits the King and his Ministers'. Hunt deplored how 'the interests of the few substituted for those of the many; till by degrees the social virtues are displaced by absolute selfish vices' (*The Examiner* (19 Jan. 1817), 33).

11 **the *Alley***: Exchange Alley, in the City, where the buying and selling of securities originally was centered. Some of the writers in 'our good friend Hookham's Library' would deem such

'certificates' of wealth to be adequate. In *HH*, Panoscope, who is 'heir-apparent to an estate of ten thousand a-year', fails to recognize how much his wealth will matter to 'his female acquaintance, whose morals had been formed by the novels of such writers as Miss Philomela Poppyseed' (ch. 6). The 'fundamental principle' of Poppyseed's work-in-progress is 'that a thousand a-year is an indispensable ingredient in the passion of love, and that no man, who is not so far gifted *by nature*, can reasonably presume to feel that passion himself, or be correctly the object of it with a well-educated female' (ch. 6). See also TLP's footnote in *NA* regarding the 'vocabulary' to be found in 'any Novel by any literary lady' (ch. 4).

12 **postboys**: A 'post boy' is 'The postil[l]ion of a stagecoach, post-chaise, or hired carriage' (*OED*). In this instance, the postboys determine where Mrs Pinmoney's post-chariot goes.

13 **Banditti**: Italian plural, 'bandits', although 'banditti' was often used to refer specifically to the romanticized thieves depicted either in Italian painting or in gothic fiction which was set in the Mediterranean countries, e.g. Regina Maria Roche, *The Discarded Son; or, Haunt of the Banditti. A Tale*, 5 vols. (Lane, Newman, and Co., 1807); Catherine Smith, *The Castle of Arragon; or The Banditti of the Forest. A Romance*, 4 vols. (Henry Colburn, 1809–10); Eleanor Sleath, *Pyrenean Banditti: A Romance*, 3 vols. (A. K. Newman, 1811); and P[eter] M[iddleton] Darling, *The Forest of Valancourt, or the Haunt of the Banditti; A Romance* (Edinburgh: for the author, 1813).

14 **Dr. Bosky**: 'Bosky' was a slang adjective, meaning 'Somewhat the worse for drink, tipsy' (*OED*). Dr Bosky is another of TLP's clergy devoted to drink (cf. Mr Portpipe) and to defending their privileges.

15 **a style of modern Gothic**: The court has been renovated in imitation of gothic architecture, perhaps by Anthelia's father.

16 **called the enlightened age ... discover**: This observation is typical of TLP's view of the relation between the Middle Ages and

the early nineteenth century: though the past does not deserve to be romanticized, his own age should not commend itself. Cf. the middle chapters (9 and 10) of *CC*. In *NA*, Mr Toobad believes that the Evil Principle rules in 'this precise period of time, commonly called the enlightened age' (ch. 1). See also the account of Taliesin's education, and TLP's contrast between the wisdom of the sixth century and that of the present, in *ME*, ch. 6.

17 **the furniture Grecian**: Furniture in a 'Grecian' style became popular in this period. See David Watkin, *Thomas Hope 1769–1831 and the Neo-Classical Idea* (John Murray, 1968). If Anthelia's apartment is gothic because her father decided that the new court must imitate the gothic style of the older sections of the castle, her furniture is Greek because she admires Greece.

18 **the decision . . . of picturesque and antiquarian disputants**: The debates between advocates of the picturesque (see ch. 1, n. 2 and n. 8) and advocates of antiquity.

19 **attitudes**: 'A posture of the body proper to, or implying, some action or mental state assumed by human beings or animals. *to strike an attitude*: to assume it theatrically, and not as the unstudied expression of action or passion' (*OED* 'attitude', n, 2.a.). In *NA*, Scythrop assumes 'what the French call an imposing attitude' (ch. 3).

20 **the tea would have satisfied Johnson, and the coffee enchanted Voltaire**: For Samuel Johnson's love of tea, see his review of Jonas Hanway, *A Journal of Eight Days Journey*, 2nd ed. (1757), in *Johnson on Demand: Reviews, Prefaces, and Ghost-Writings*, ed. O. M. Brack, Jr, and Robert DeMaria, Jr (New Haven, CT and London: Yale University Press, 2018), vol. 20 of *The Yale Edition of the Works of Samuel Johnson*, ed. John H. Middendorf et al., 23 vols. (New Haven, CT and London: Yale University Press, 1958–2018), pp. 359–71; and James Boswell, *Boswell's Life of Johnson: Together with Boswell's Journal of a Tour to the Hebrides and Johnson's Diary of a Journey into North Wales*, ed. George

Birkbeck Hill, rev. L. F. Powell, 6 vols. (1934; Oxford: Clarendon Press, 1971), vol. 1, pp. 313–14. Voltaire was fond of coffee, and wrote in a 1772 letter that 'I keep faithful to my coffee, which I have taken these seventy years'; *Correspondence. Letters Between Frederic II. and M. de Voltaire*, trans. Thomas Holcroft, 3 vols. (G. G. J. and J. Robinson, 1789), vol. 3, p. 237.

21 **solitary——**: The first of *1817*'s double em-dashes, which are used repeatedly to indicate interruptions in speech. This longer dash, like most of those in *1817*, is retained in *1856*.

22 **THE HONOURABLE MRS. PINMONEY.**: Here TLP switches to stage dialogue for the first time in *Mel*. See Introduction on the patterns in his use of stage dialogue.

23 **blue devils**: See ch. 1, n. 12.

24 **a *preux chevalier***: By referring to a gallant knight, Miss Danaretta again voices her enthusiasm for romance conventions.

25 **driving the mail**: Travelling by mail coach had only recently become a viable mode of fast transportation. See Southey, *Letters from England* (1807), and De Quincey, 'The English Mail-Coach' (1849).

26 **acting Hamlet**: Primarily an allusion to Robert 'Romeo' Coates, the wealthy amateur actor who took on major Shakespeare roles at the principal London theatres between 1811 and 1816. In 'An Essay on Fashionable Literature' (written July–Aug. 1818), TLP wrote that Coates 'attracted some three or four audiences by the mere force of excessive absurdity' (*NA*, p. 109). In TLP's 'The Dilettanti' Sir Harry Flourish takes the role of the Prince of Denmark, and O'Prompt calls Sir Harry 'Mr. Dilettante Hamlet' (Halliford, 7.369).

27 **philosophical lectures**: The most obvious reference here would be to Coleridge, although his public lectures on literature did not begin to focus on issues of philosophy until 1818.

28 **the marvellous . . . the grim**: For 'the marvellous', see Joanna Southcott, *The Book of Wonders, Marvellous and True* (W. Tozer, 1813). The reference to 'the simple' is in part an allusion to

Amelia Alderson Opie, *Simple Tales*, 4 vols. (Longman, 1806). In *NA*, Flosky excels in the 'the grim and the tearful' (see ch. 1).

29 **banditti**: See ch. 2, n. 13.

30 **ghosts**: In *NA* Flosky says that the 'part of the *reading public* which shuns the solid food of reason for the light diet of fiction' has 'lived upon ghosts, goblins, and skeletons' (ch. 6).

31 **German whiskers**: The facial hair common among German men, and many other things German, became fashionable in the early Regency. The great satire upon this love of things German is Lord Byron's *Waltz: An Apostrophic Hymn*, published early in 1813. The Prince Regent was among those men who sported giant sideburns. See Introduction, pp. cxlviii–cxlix.

32 **enjoying the country in November, and wintering in London till the end of the dog-days**: Cf. the schedule of Sir Henry Melincourt, who spends the winter in London but is back at Melincourt Castle for the dog days of summer (ch. 1).

33 **making shoes**: Reference not traced.

34 **picturesque tours**: See ch. 1, n. 8.

35 **essays on taste**: See, for example, Richard Payne Knight (1751–1824), *An Analytical Inquiry into the Principles of Taste* (1805), a work of importance to *HH*.

36 **the very pink**: 'The most excellent example of something; the embodiment or model of a particular quality' (*OED* 'pink' n.⁵, A.II.3a).

37 **a gentleman's character**: Mrs Pinmoney understands 'character' to mean not personal attributes (*OED* 9.a. and 9.b.), which is how Anthelia uses the word, but reputation (*OED* 13.a.).

38 **equippage**: 'A carriage and horses, with the attendant servants; in later use sometimes applied to a carriage alone' (*OED* 12).

39 **a town and country house**: While families of the landed elite generally possessed a house in the metropolis and a house in the country, Anthelia and Forester both do without the town house.

40 **routs**: 'A fashionable gathering; a large evening party or soirée of a type fashionable in the 18th and early 19th centuries' (*OED*

'rout' 8, first example 1741). Mrs Pinmoney distinguishes 'routs', or evening parties, from 'dinners'.

41 **a good settlement**: A marriage settlement was the contract by which the disposition of property was agreed upon. See Edward Burtenshaw Sugden, *A Series of Letters to a Man of Property, on the Sale, Purchase, Lease, Settlement, and Devise of Estates* (J. Harding, 1809), pp. 80–2.

42 **The age of chivalry is gone**: Any reader in 1817 would identify this phrase as originating in Edmund Burke's tribute to Marie Antoinette in *Reflections on the Revolution in France* (1790): 'I thought ten thousand swords must have leaped from their scabbards to avenge even a look that threatened her with insult.—But the age of chivalry is gone.—That of sophisters, oeconomists, and calculators, has succeeded; and the glory of Europe is extinguished for ever'; *The Writings and Speeches of Edmund Burke*, vol. 8, pp. 126–7.

43 **its spirit survives**: A common sentiment in the period. In 1798 Joseph Phillimore wrote that 'the institutions, by which [chivalry] was propagated, cherished, and kept alive, [fell] to the ground—while the spirit still survives', and 'a strict adherence to the principles of chivalry, confined within their proper bounds, stamps the character of a gentleman'. In *A View of the State of Europe During the Middle Ages* (1818), Henry Hallam wrote that 'The spirit of chivalry left behind it a more valuable successor' when 'The character of knight gradually subsided in that of gentleman', and in 1825 Charles Mills wrote that the 'spirit, though not the form, of the chivalric times has survived to ours, and forms one of our graces and distinctions'; Joseph Phillimore, 'Chivalry' (1798), in *The Oxford English Prize Essays* (Oxford: D. A. Talboys, 1830), vol. 2, pp. 137–8; Henry Hallam, *View of the State of Europe During the Middle Ages*, 4 vols. (Philadelphia: Thomas Dobson, 1821), vol. 4, p. 364; Charles Mills, *The History of Chivalry or Knighthood and Its Times* (1825; 2nd ed., 2 vols., Longman, 1826), vol. 2, pp. 360–1.

44 **Disinterested benevolence**: Twice in *Mel* chivalry is characterized in terms of 'disinterested benevolence' (chs. 2, 8), a phrase
that points to the 'system of disinterested benevolence' William
Godwin advocated; see *An Enquiry Concerning Political Justice*,
vol. 1, p. 359. TLP received a copy of *Political Justice* from E.
T. Hookham in 1809 (*Letters*, 1.136). Though no admirer of
'chivalry', Godwin did write in 1803 that 'out of [chivalry and
romance] have sprung the principle of modern honour in the
best sense of that term, the generosity of disinterested adventure, and the more persevering and successful cultivation of the
private affections'; *Life of Geoffrey Chaucer, the Early English
Poet: Including Memoirs of His Near Friend and Kinsman, John of
Gaunt, Duke of Lancaster: with Sketches of the Manners, Opinions,
Arts and Literature of England in the Fourteenth Century*, 2 vols.
(Richard Phillips, 1803), vol. 1, p. 361.

45 **the 'little tyrant of a little corporation'**: TLP's footnote attributes this phrase to 'Junius', meaning the letters on contemporary
politics that appeared in the *Public Advertiser* between 1769 and
1772, composed by the anonymous writer who called himself
'Junius'. See Letter XIX, 19 Sept. 1769, 'To his grace the D— of
——' (the Duke of Bedford): an 'independent virtuous Duke
of Bedford', unlike the actual duke, 'would not have thought it
consistent with his rank in the state, or even with his personal
importance, to be the little tyrant of a little corporation'; John
Cannon, ed., *The Letters of Junius* (Oxford: Clarendon Press,
1978), pp. 117, 119. Anthelia's quotation of this phrase is per-
tinent to TLP's concern with rotten boroughs. At about the time
when TLP wrote *Mel*, John Taylor put forward the claim which
eventually prevailed, that Junius was actually Sir Philip Francis
(1740–1818); see *The Identity of Junius with A Distinguished
Living Character Established* (Taylor and Hessey, 1816). In the
Quarterly Review Robert Southey was moved to call Junius not
only 'the most influential' but also 'the most pernicious English
writer of his age' – 'the founder of that school of writers, who,

setting truth at defiance, impose the most audacious misrepresentations upon a credulous public, and seasoning sophistry with slander, carry into literary and political disquisition a spirit of personal malevolence'; 'The Rise and Progress of Popular Disaffection', *Quarterly Review*, vol. 16, no. 32 (Jan. 1817), 511–12 (530–1).

46 **liberal**: 'Free from bias, prejudice, or bigotry; open-minded, tolerant; governing or governed by relaxed principles or rules' (*OED* 4.a.; first example 1772). In this period the term 'liberal' began to take on its now-familiar political connotations. See Jonathan David Gross, *Byron: The Erotic Liberal* (Lanham, MD: Rowman & Littlefield, 2001).

47 **Telegraph**: An 'English two-wheeled chaise of the late 1790's and early 1800's', the telegraph was 'A compromise between the dogcart and the whisky' (Smith, *Dictionary of Horse-Drawn Vehicles*, p. 160). The telegraph would be smaller than the barouche that Sir Telegraph drives, though it evidently was favoured by some elite men. The *OED*, which notes simply that 'telegraph' was 'A fancy name for some kind of carriage' (*OED* 6), cites Sarah Green's novel *The Reformist!!! A Serio-Comic Political Novel!* (A. K. Newman, 1810), in which the narrator refers to 'the whimsical vehicle which conveys the man of high *ton*, be it either dog-cart, telegraph, or *barouchette*' (vol. 2, p. 130).

48 **Paxarett**: Paxarete is a mixture of wine and grape juice. In TLP's *The Three Doctors* (written in 1813), Sir Peter Paxarett 'thought of nothing but liquor and pipes' (Halliford, 7.386).

49 **driving**: The fad for gentlemen driving themselves is noted in *HH*, when Lord Littlebrain is 'driving four-in-hand' (ch. 6). As noted earlier, 'four-in-hand' meant 'A vehicle with four horses driven by one person' (*OED*); in *Vanity Fair* (1847–8), Thackeray mentions 'four-in-hand driving' as a hobby of the Regency aristocracy (ch. 10). Edward Noel Long wrote to Lord Byron on 18 Mar. 1807 that the latter's reputation among fashionable young men at Cambridge would improve 'the more you resemble a

Stage Coachman' (John Murray Archive, National Library of Scotland). Sarah Green's novel *The Reformist!!!* informs us that 'gaping natives', when they see 'the man of high *ton*' driving himself, 'often take him, at first sight, for a coachman' (vol. 2, p. 130). TLP reveals that Sir Telegraph's driver rides inside the barouche if there are no passengers, ch. 4; the driver is left behind at the time of the excursion to Onevote, ch. 19.

50 **barouche**: Sir Telegraph owns and drives a large, expensive carriage. The word 'barouche', from German, had made its way into English by 1801, according to the *OED* (the earliest appearance with TLP's spelling dates from 1805). It came to mean 'A four-wheeled carriage with a half-head behind which can be raised or let down at pleasure, having a seat in front for the driver, and seats inside for two couples to sit facing each other' (*OED*). Smith's *Dictionary of Horse-Drawn Vehicles* explains that 'Passengers normally faced in the direction of travel, although some vehicles had folding seats, on which others might be seated vis-à-vis.' The barouche was 'Essentially a town vehicle for summer driving, although some eventually had a protective screen able to close against the raised hood.' Although a barouche was 'Usually drawn by two horses in pole gear' (p. 12), Sir Telegraph's is a 'four-in-hand barouche' (ch. 3), and indeed Mr Fax later notices that it is pulled by 'four horses' (ch. 7). Ten years before *Mel*, there appeared Charles Sedley's *The Barouche Driver and His Wife: A Tale for the Haut Ton. Containing a Curious Biography of Living Characters, with Notes Explanatory*, 3rd ed., 2 vols., (J. F. Hughes, 1807); for the barouche of Sedley's protagonist, see vol. 1, pp. 88–90. In Jane Austen's novels, owning a barouche is a sign of affluence. In *Sense and Sensibility* (1811), Mr Palmer owns a barouche, while Edward Ferrars has 'no turn for great men or barouches'; Lady Catherine de Bourgh in *Pride and Prejudice* (1813) and Henry Crawford in *Mansfield Park* (1814) own barouches; and in *Emma* (1815), Mrs Elton boasts that her brother and his wife have a 'barouche-landau', a barouche-landau being a 'Sporting

barouche with a higher than average box seat' (Smith, *Dictionary of Horse-Drawn Vehicles*, p. 12). The Cambridge Edition of the Works of Jane Austen, ed. Janet Todd et al., 9 vols. (Cambridge: Cambridge University Press, 2005–8), *Sense and Sensibility*, vol. 1, ch. 3, p. 18; *Pride and Prejudice*, vol. 2, ch. 14, p. 234; *Mansfield Park*, vol. 1, ch. 6, p. 69; vol. 1, ch. 8, p. 90; *Emma*, vol. 1, ch. 14, p. 295. Percy Shelley's vehicle, which was either a post-chaise or chariot, would have been smaller, holding two passengers inside; see Cameron, 'Shelley's Chariot', 160–2.

CHAPTER 3

1 **Hypocon House**: 'Hypocon' is an abbreviation of 'hypochondria'. The sole example in the *OED* dates from 1704.

2 **the scale of moral utility**: The narrator slights Sir Telegraph in a manner that the rest of the novel suggests he does not deserve.

3 **a lord seneschal**: The medieval term for the equivalent of a steward.

4 **Hippy**: 'Hippy', like the name of Hypocon House, suggests hypochondria. The name 'Hippy' appears in TLP's farce *The Three Doctors* (Halliford, 7.385ff), as does 'Paxarett' (see ch. 2, n. 48).

5 **little Lucy**: Peter Gray is related to the title character in Wordsworth's poem 'Lucy Gray', first published in the 2nd ed. (1800) of *Lyrical Ballads*. In 'The Four Ages of Poetry', TLP wrote that Wordsworth 'cannot describe a scene under his own eyes without putting into it the shadow of a Danish boy or the living ghost of Lucy Gray, or some similar phantastical parturition of the moods of his own mind' (*NA*, p. 150). TLP's asterisk at 'little Lucy' and the asterisk at 'little Alice' refer to a single footnote, which advises the reader to seek information on Lucy and Alice in Wordsworth's *Lyrical Ballads*.

6 **a distant relation . . . 'belonged to Durham'**: TLP implies that his readers are all-too-familiar with Wordsworth's poetry, but

the footnote directs the reader to the wrong place: 'Alice Fell; or, Poverty' first appeared in *Poems in Two Volumes* (1807), not in *Lyrical Ballads*. In TLP's *Sir Proteus*, one of the three 'wise men' that Sir Proteus appears to have become 'chattered, chattered still, / With meaning none at all, / Of Jack and Jill, and Harry Gill, / And Alice Fell so small' (Halliford, 6.290); TLP alludes not only to 'Alice Fell' but also to 'Goody Blake, and Harry Gill, A True Story', first published in *Lyrical Ballads, with a Few Other Poems* (1798).

7 **blue-devilled**: On 'blue devils', see ch. 1, n. 12. The earliest example of 'blue-devilled' in the *OED* occurs in T. S. Surr's *The Mask of Fashion* (1807).

8 **vapourish**: The adjective 'vapourish', meaning a person afflicted with 'the vapours' (hypochondria and depression), was common in the eighteenth century.

9 **melancholy as a gib cat**: Shakespeare's Falstaff says that he is 'as melancholy as a gib cat or a lugg'd bear' (*1 Henry IV*, act 1, scene 2, lines 73–4). The term 'gib cat' could mean a tom cat, but George Steevens glossed Falstaff's comment by observing that 'a *gib'd cat* is a cat who has been qualified for the seraglio; for all animals so mutilated, become drowsy and melancholy' (Johnson–Steevens, 2.200–1). In a letter to T. J. Hogg, 20 Mar. 1818, TLP juxtaposes this Shakespearean phrase with one from Wordsworth: TLP had been in Marlow 'since Monday, as lonely as a cloud, and as melancholy as a gib cat' (*Letters*, 1.118). *1 Henry IV*'s Falstaff is quoted four times in *Mel*, by four different characters: Forester (ch. 7); Feathernest (ch. 16); Sarcastic (ch. 21); and Sir Telegraph (ch. 24). In the final chapter the narrator says that Grovelgrub is 'running and roaring all the way, like Falstaff on Gadshill'.

10 **chariot**: 'Applied in the 18th c. to a light-wheeled carriage with only back seats, and differing from the post-chaise in having a coach box' (*OED* 'chariot', 1.d.). According to William Felton's *A Treatise on Carriages* (1794), the bodies of the chariot and the

post-chaise are the same, and they are called by different names according to 'The occasion for their use': 'by the addition of a coach-box to the *carriage* part, they are called Chariots; the post-chaise being intended for road-work, and the chariot for town use'; *A Treatise on Carriages: Comprehending Coaches, Chariots, Phaetons, Curricles, Whiskeys, &c. Together with Their Proper Harness*, 2 vols. (for the author, 1794), vol. 1, p. 26. (However, Falconer in *GG* owns 'a comfortable travelling-chariot, without a box to intercept his view'; ch. 22.) Hippy's chariot is humbler than Sir Telegraph's barouche, though it also requires four horses. At least two men, postillions, ride the horses.

11 **four high-mettled posters**: Although Mr Hippy owns a chariot, he does not keep horses. A 'poster' is a post-horse (*OED* 3, citing this line from *Mel*); a 'post-horse' is 'A horse kept at a post-house or inn for the use of post-riders, or for hire by travellers' (*OED*). In *GG* Falconer uses 'post-horses after the fashion of the olden time' (ch. 22).

12 **old Harry vaulted into the dicky, the postillions cracked their whips**: If a chariot by definition has a coach box (see above, ch. 3, n. 10), it is unclear why this coach is steered by postillions, who ride the horses, rather than by a driver who sits on the coach box. A 'dicky' was 'The seat in a carriage on which the driver sits' or 'A seat at the back of a carriage for servants, etc., or of a mail-coach for the guard' (*OED*). Given that the postillions crack their whips, the dicky Harry occupies must be of the latter kind.

13 **'Over the hills and the plains, / Over the rivers and rocks'**: In Robert Southey, *Thalaba the Destroyer*, 2nd ed., 2 vols. (Longman, 1809), vol. 2, p. 96, the 'magic car' travels 'Over the hills and the plains, / Over the rivers and rocks, / Over the sands of the shore'.

14 **galloway**: 'One of a small but strong breed of horses peculiar to Galloway; hence a small-sized horse, esp. for riding' (*OED*, first example 1598).

15 **the usual poetical style of a Cumberland peasant**: Another allusion to Wordsworth, in whose poetry Cumberland peasants sometimes philosophize.

16 **four-in-hand barouche**: See ch. 2, n. 50. Again, the point is that Sir Telegraph is his own driver.

CHAPTER 4

1 **Houhynnhmns**: The Houhynnhmns are the rational horses in part 4 of Lemuel Gulliver [Jonathan Swift], *Travels into Several Remote Nations of the World* (1726). TLP refers to Swift's horses a few pages before the reader of *Mel* meets a rational oran outang.

2 **Sylvan Forester**: Both names connote wooded land; both would also befit a 'wild man of the woods' such as Forester's companion Sir Oran (ch. 6). 'Sylvan' is the name of the oran outang in Walter Scott's *Count Robert of Paris* (1831).

3 **But what . . . in Westmoreland**: Shakespeare's Hamlet asks Horatio, 'But what, in faith, make you from Wittenberg?' (act 1, scene 2, line 168).

4 **the abbey of Rednose**: The name 'Rednose Abbey' is another of TLP's allusions to clerical drinking, like Rubygill Abbey in *MM*. See also TLP's unfinished 'Boozabowt Abbey' (Halliford, 8.397–402); it was begun no earlier than 1859 (see Halliford, 8.539). Forester implies that 'the reverend Fellows of our old college' have similar drinking habits.

5 **the nature and progress of man**: This phrase might lead a reader to think of James Burnett, Lord Monboddo, whose *Of the Origin and Progress of Language* (1773–92) is central to *Mel*, although neither Monboddo nor any of his writings has been mentioned by name up to this point.

6 **an original character**: This phrase echoes 'original men' in the previous paragraph.

7 **one of his grooms . . . the coachman**: Only now does the reader learn that anyone accompanies Sir Telegraph. The coachman

has an easy job, being called upon only when Sir Telegraph does not wish to drive himself.

8 **the human species is gradually decreasing in size and strength**: The context is Monboddo's writings, particularly *Antient Metaphysics*, vol. 3 (1784), ch. 5, which TLP cites in footnotes to a later scene at Redrose Abbey (ch. 19). In *HH* Escot buys 'a skull of very extraordinary magnitude' that a sexton claims is the skull of Cadwallader (ch. 9); Escot argues that this man must have been at least 9 feet tall (ch. 10).

9 **skull polished and set in silver . . . wine out of it**: In *HH* Escot says he will have Cadwallader's skull 'bound with a silver rim, and filled with mantling wine, with this inscription: NUNC TANDEM: signifying that that pernicious liquor has at length found its proper receptacle: for, when the wine is in, the brain is out' (ch. 9). Mr Glowry makes his ancestor's skull into a punchbowl in *NA*, ch. 1. Byron's 'Lines inscribed upon a Cup formed from a Skull' was first printed in the seventh edition (1814) of *Childe Harold's Pilgrimage*. On this cup, see Lovell, ed., *Medwin's Conversations of Lord Byron*, pp. 64–5.

10 **one bottle of Madeira and another of claret**: Whereas the Rev. Mr Portpipe and Mr Hippy drink only Madeira, Sir Telegraph prefers to supplement it with another kind of wine.

11 **beeves**: oxen.

12 **white jean trowsers, with very thin silk stockings and pumps**: Sir Telegraph's clothes may be inconvenient when he is driving a barouche, just as they are inconvenient when dealing with furze and bramble. In contrast, in Sarah Green's *The Reformist!!!*, onlookers are surprised by 'the high consequence of the driver, who appears little better in dress, than John the ploughman who gazes after him' (vol. 2, pp. 130–1).

13 **'Forced . . . bramble;'**: This 'old song' also appears in TLP's *The Three Doctors* (Halliford, 7.388).

14 **'sensible to feeling as to sight'**: 'Art thou not, fatal vision, sensible / To feeling as to sight?' (*Macbeth*, act 2, scene 1, lines

36–7). The Honourable Mr Listless quotes this in *NA*, ch. 12 (he replaces 'sensible' with 'palpable', a word that Macbeth used a few lines later).

15 **green coat and nankins**: 'In *sing.* and (usu.) *pl.* Trousers made of nankeen' with nankeen being 'A kind of pale yellowish cloth, originally made at Nanking from a yellow variety of cotton, but subsequently manufactured from ordinary cotton which is then dyed' (*OED* 'nankeen', A. I. 1). Nankins were most suited for summer wear: according to TLP's journal, a drop in the temperature on 11 Sept. 1818 meant that he 'Left off nankins' and 'took to cloth trousers & flannel waistcoats' (*Letters*, 1.140). It is autumn when Sir Telegraph arrives at Redrose Abbey, and perhaps Sir Oran's enthusiasm for fashionable dress leads him to persist with nankins later than most men would in northern England.

16 **Sir Oran Haut-ton**: The noun 'haut ton' meant 'High fashion; *ellipt.*, people of high fashion' (*OED*); the earliest occurrence noted in the *OED* is from the *Sporting Magazine*, 17 (1801): 22, 'People of the *Haut Ton* are about to return to town'.

17 **too polite to laugh**: Later, Forester says that because Sir Oran's physical appearance provokes laughter, he chose 'to introduce him only into the best society, where politeness would act as a preventive to the propensity to laugh' (ch. 6).

18 **enormous whiskers**: As Mrs Pinmoney indicated earlier (see ch. 2, n. 31), facial hair became popular in the Regency.

19 **a vast cravat**: In the first decade of the nineteenth century, one principal kind of men's neckcloth was the cravat, 'A large square of lawn, muslin, or silk, folded cornerwise into a band and wrapped round the neck with the ends tied in a knot or bow in front'; C. Willett Cunnington and Phillis Cunnington, *Handbook of English Costume in the Nineteenth Century*, 3rd ed. (Faber, 1970), p. 67. In the second decade, that of *Mel*, 'The shirt collar was rising higher so that neckcloths were larger and heavily starched or supported with wide stiffeners', and the

cravat 'was now more scarf-like and arranged in a multitude of different ways, each with its name' (p. 87).

20 **thought Sir Telegraph**: This is one of the few occasions in *Mel* when the narrator describes a character's thoughts directly.

21 **great proficiency in the dissection of game**: Monboddo wrote that one reason oran outangs remained healthy was that they eat nothing but vegetables (*AM*, 3.175). In *A Vindication of Natural Diet* (1813) and *Queen Mab* (1813), Percy Shelley compared human with oran outang anatomy in order to argue that human beings are, like these apes, naturally vegetarians; *The Prose Works of Percy Bysshe Shelley*, ed. E. B. Murray, vol. 1 (Oxford: Clarendon Press, 1993), p. 80; Donald H. Reiman and Neil Fraistat, ed., *The Complete Poetry of Percy Bysshe Shelley*, vol. 2 (Baltimore: Johns Hopkins University Press, 2004), p. 300. However, Sir Oran evidently eats meat along with all the other denizens of corrupt civilization. His 'great proficiency in the dissection of game' is a rare instance of TLP failing to provide a source for Sir Oran's actions in Monboddo or a like writer.

22 **the *Placari genius* . . . of Horace**: In his *Ars Poetica* (line 210) Horace records that drinking was permissible on festal days, and in *Odes* book 4, ode 12, line 28, Horace, inviting Virgil to visit, says that it is pleasant on appropriate occasions to act foolishly.

23 ***Beviamo tutti tre***: Literally, 'Let us drink, all three of us.' A drinking song (or 'catch') of this title, composed by Felice Giardini, became popular in the 1760s.

24 **harlequin**: the clown character in the *commedia dell'arte* and in the pantomimes of TLP's day. See *CC*, ch. 1, n. 63.

25 **videlicet**: This Latin term, meaning 'to wit', 'namely' or 'that is to say', appears five times in *Mel* (used twice by the narrator, twice by Sir Telegraph, and once by the lawyer Richard Ratstail). The frequency with which it appears reflects TLP's tendency toward Latinisms. See also *HH*, ch. 10; *NA*, ch. 1; *CC*, ch. 1.

CHAPTER 5

1   **heeltap**: 'The liquor left at the bottom of a glass after drinking; also, the fag-end of a bottle' (*OED* 'heel-tap' n, 2.a.). The first occurrence noted by the *OED* is from 1780; it also appears in Shelley's *Oedipus Tyrannus; or Swellfoot the Tyrant* (wr. 1820/21), act 2, scene 2, line 35. A Mr Heeltap makes an appearance in *Mel*, ch. 28.

2   **titubant**: The first occurrence of this word (meaning 'unsteady') that is recorded in the *OED*.

3   **say with Pilate...*to it?***: 'When Pilate saw that he could prevail nothing, but that rather a tumult was made, he took water, and washed his hands before the multitude, saying, I am innocent of the blood of this just person: see ye to it' (Matthew, ch. 27, v. 24).

4   ***quiz***: 'Quiz' here means 'An odd or eccentric person; a person whose appearance is peculiar or ridiculous' (*OED*).

5   **coacervation**: 'The action of heaping together, or fact of being heaped together; accumulation' (*OED*).

6   **Hercules and Alpheus**: Hercules diverted the river Alpheus in order to clean decades of filth from the Augean stables.

7   **'We are bad ourselves, because we despair of the goodness of others'**: In *The Friend*, No. 5 (14 Sept. 1809), Coleridge reflects on the general reluctance to acknowledge that education can instil virtue: 'What an awful Duty, what a Nurse of all other, the fairest Virtues, does not hope become! We are bad ourselves, because we despair of the goodness of others'; *The Friend*, 2 vols., ed. Barbara Rooke (Princeton: Princeton University Press, 1969), vol. 2, p. 70. It is ironic that Forester quotes Coleridge as an authority even though Coleridge is often one of TLP's targets in *Mel*; it is doubly ironic that Forester quotes Coleridge's endorsement of popular education even though the Coleridge of *The Statesman's Manual* (figured in *Mel* as Mr Mystic) objected that the 'reading public' was so broad and so influential (*LS*, 36–8).

8   **Wesleyites ... Anythingarians**: Sir Telegraph refers to followers of an assortment of seventeenth- and eighteenth-century

English sectaries: John Wesley and his Methodist associate George Whitefield; the Calvinist William Huntington; and the Unitarian Lodowicke Muggleton. The only occurrence of 'Wesleyite' for 'Wesleyan' recorded in the *OED* dates from 1807 (the noun 'Wesleyan' was used as early as 1791). The Moravians became active in England in the early eighteenth century, the Unitarians in the later.

9 **types, symbols, and mysteries**: These terms of Christian exegesis recur frequently in TLP's writings. Mr Mystic says that the explosion at Cimmerian Lodge is 'a type and symbol of an approaching period of public light' (ch. 31); Jack Horner's Christmas pie is viewed by Mr Paperstamp and his allies as 'a type and symbol of the public purse' (ch. 39).

10 *à fortiori*: 'With stronger reason, still more conclusively' (*OED*); cf. *NA*, ch. 7.

11 **tabernacle**: A meeting house of Dissenters (*OED* 6.b.; earliest example 1768).

12 **Sandemonian chapel**: Sandemanians were followers of Robert Sandeman, who spread the ideas of the Scottish Glasite church into England. William Godwin was at one time a Sandemanian.

13 *Charity begins at home*: The earliest example noted in Burton Stevenson, *Stevenson's Book of Proverbs, Maxims and Familiar Phrases* (Routledge and Kegan Paul, 1949), comes from Thomas Fuller, *The Appeal of Injured Innocence* (1659): 'Charity begins, but doth not end, at home.' Stevenson also notes that Horace and James Smith invert the cliché in their *Horace in London* (1813): 'Our charity begins at home, / And mostly ends where it begins' (book 2, ode 15).

14 **carry their religion**: TLP's footnote quotes at length from Milton's *Speech for the Liberty of Unlicensed Printing* – that is, *Areopagitica; A Speech of Mr. John Milton for the Liberty of Unlicenc'd Printing, to the Parliament of England* (1644). See *Complete Prose Works of John Milton*, gen. ed. Don M. Wolfe, vol. 2, ed. Ernest Sirluck (New Haven CT and London: Yale

University Press, 1959), pp. 543–5. Milton argues against restrictions upon expression on the ground that 'our faith and knowledge thrives by exercise, as well as our limbs and complexion' (p. 543).

15 **Abdiel among the fiends**: John Milton, *Paradise Lost* (1667), book 5, lines 803–907; book 6, lines 111–98, 369–72 (*Paradise Lost*, ed. Alastair Fowler, rev. 2nd ed., Longman Annotated English Poets (Harlow: Pearson/Longman, 2007)). Immediately after TLP quotes one of Milton's tracts in order to buttress Sir Telegraph's observations about where men carry their religion, Forester alludes to Milton's epic poem in order to endorse emulating Abdiel, who did not cooperate with the rebel angels.

16 **an allegory from Homer**: In *Iliad*, book 24, lines 527–33, Achilles refers to Zeus's two urns, one of which contains bad fortune, the other good. In *GG*, ch. 28, the Spirit-Rapper paraphrases the passage thus: 'Good without evil is not given to man. / Jove, from his urns dispensing good and ill, / Gives ill unmixed to some, and good and ill / Mingled to many, good unmixed to none.' TLP's footnote in *GG* observes that Alexander Pope's famous translation of *The Iliad* reflects a misinterpretation, insofar as Pope's Achilles indicates that some people receive unmixed good. Forester reverses Homer's allegory: rather than Zeus's two urns being the source of the good and evil experienced by human beings, the urns are receptacles into which people pour 'fluid', itself neither good nor evil, that each person has received from his or her 'natal genius'.

17 **Gad**: There may be no significance in Sir Telegraph's use of 'Gad', which is a form of 'God', dating back to 1608 (*OED*).

18 **the ornaments of their age, and the lights of the world**: Jesus, in the Sermon on the Mount says, 'Ye are the light of the world. A city that is set on an hill cannot be hid' (Matthew, ch. 5, v. 14). The title of ch. 40 of *Mel* is 'The Hopes of the World'.

19 **the Anti-saccharine Society**: It is not clear that this society is meant to evoke any particular organization active in TLP's day.

20 **inside passengers**: People who ride inside the barouche because of their age, rank or gender. Sir Telegraph is probably thinking of Mrs Pinmoney and Miss Danaretta Contantina, who do indeed attend.

CHAPTER 6

1 **the Indians of South America**: According to Forester, Sir Oran is the kind of 'wild man' that the people of Angola call a 'pongo' and the people of 'South America' call an 'Oran Outang', so his implication is that this one species is found in different continents. However, there are no anthropoid apes of any kind native to the Americas. Nicholas A. Joukovsky observes that TLP knew from Monboddo that the oran outang 'was native to the East Indies', and 'it seems likely that the compositor of the first edition misread the unfamiliar "Sumatra" as "S. America"' (TLP never revised the text of *Melincourt*)'; 'Peacock's Sir Oran Hautton', p. 173. If TLP did write 'Sumatra', then the presence of 'South America' in the published text suggests that he sometimes proofread carelessly or that some of his proof corrections were disregarded. In the French translation of *Mel*, the wild man of the woods is called 'Oran-Outang' in 'tout le midi de l'Amérique' (*Paris-1818*, 1.56).

2 **the natural and original man**: TLP's footnote here, the first of many that provide authorities for Sir Oran's traits and actions, quotes, in succession, from the third volume of Monboddo's *AM* (1784), from Jacobus Bontius (Jakob de Bondt) – by way of the *Histoire Naturelle* of the French naturalist George Louis LeClerc, Comte de Buffon – and from the first volume of Monboddo's *Origin* (1773).

3 [Footnote:] **'I think I have . . . testimony'**: *AM* refers to 'the Oran Outang, whose humanity, I think, I have established by proof, that ought to satisfy every one who gives credit to human testimony' (3.40). The 'proof' to which Monboddo refers is that

provided in his earlier *Origin*, vol. 1, although he proceeds in *AM* to supply new evidence of which he had become aware in the intervening eleven years (3.40–4).

4 [Footnote:] **'I have brought myself . . . any of us'**: Monboddo writes that 'By this way of reasoning, I have brought myself to a perfect conviction, that the Oran Outang is a human creature, as much as any of us' (*AM*, 3.133). His method of reasoning involves assessing the reliability of writers on natural history, a method he contrasts with the arguments *a priori* used by the French naturalist Buffon (3.131–3). Buffon, whose *Histoire Naturelle* originally was published in French from 1749 to 1767, believed that human beings and anthropoid apes had no ancestors in common. Joukovsky writes that TLP 'evidently read Buffon's *Histoire Naturelle* in the greatly expanded edition of C. S. Sonnini (127 vols., Paris, [1799]–1808)'. This edition 'was probably among the books that Shelley had left at Marlow, some of which TLP had used to fill his shelves' (*Letters*, 1.142 n. 44). I have traced all Buffon quotations to the 1799–1808 edition ('*Buffon 1799*').

5 [Footnote:] **'Nihil . . . loquelam'**: This quotation from Jacobus Bontius (Jakob de Bondt) TLP evidently borrows from Buffon, who wrote that Bontius had seen examples of 'pongo ou grand orang-outang' in the East Indies (*Buffon 1799*, 35.81), including a female who performed many 'actions humaines, de manière qu'il sembloit que rien ne lui manquât que la parole' (*Buffon 1799*, 35.82). Buffon quotes Bontius' Latin: the female oran outang 'humanos actus exprimentem, ut nihil humani ei deesse diceres præter loquelam' (*Buffon 1799*, 35.82n).

6 [Footnote:] **'The fact truly is . . . we now see him'**: In this quotation from *Origin*, TLP's 'shape as ours' replaces Monboddo's 'shape with ours' (*Origin*, 1.357). TLP's ellipsis after 'ours', and before 'according to' replaces this: 'at least in the large kind, (for there is among them variety of sizes, as well as among us)' (*Origin*, 1.357). TLP's italicized, parenthetical 'that all animals thrive best in their natural state' is his own interpolation. TLP's

ellipsis after 'woods' marks the removal of a long section that appears in Monboddo (*Origin*, 1.357–9), and the ellipsis after 'come' marks the omission of another long passage (*Origin*, 1.359–60). TLP's 'in which the oran outang is' is Monboddo's 'in which the Orang Outang lives' (*Origin*, 1.361).

7   **a degenerated man**: The French philosopher who called the oran outang 'a degenerated man' (Forester's translation and paraphrase) was Jean-Baptiste-Claude Izouard, also known as Delisle de Sales; the quotation in the footnote comes from *De la philosophie de la nature, ou, Traité de morale pour le genre humaine: tiré de la philosophie et fondé sur la nature*, 7th ed., 10 vols. (Paris: Gide Libraire, [1804]), vol. 5, p. 400. 'Le Pline de la nation' was Buffon, and Delisle de Sales quotes (pp. 401–2) a passage from *Histoire Naturelle* (see *Buffon 1799*, 35.93–4, from 'J'ai vu' to 'souvent de lui-même'), the beginning of which TLP quotes later in *Mel* (see ch. 15, n. 22). TLP also draws on Delisle de Sales in the notes to *The Philosophy of Melancholy* (1812), part 3, and 'The Spirit of Fire' (see Halliford, 6.239–40, 259).

8   **his gentleness and sweet temper**: TLP's footnote quotes two passages from Monboddo's *Origin* (1.289, 280), in modified form. Monboddo wrote that reports reveal 'that the Orang Outang is an animal of the human form, inside and outside'; one sign of the oran outang's humanity is 'That he has a disposition of mind, mild, docile, and humane' (*Origin*, 1.289). TLP quotes Monboddo stating that 'The oran outang whom Buffon himself saw was of a sweet temper'; Monboddo wrote that Buffon 'says, *Pag.* 53. that he saw one of the small kind, who walked always upon two; and, in that, and all his movements, was grave and composed. He was of a sweet temper, and, in that respect, very different from the ape or monkey kind' (*Origin*, 1.280). This quotation from Monboddo contains TLP's first reference to Buffon by name. Monboddo used the 1766 edition of Buffon; the passage that Monboddo attributes to p. 53 of *Histoire Naturelle, Générale et Particulière, Avec la Description Du*

Cabinet du Roi, vol. 14 (Paris: L'Imprimerie Royale, 1766) can be found in *Buffon 1799*, 35.93–4.

9 **Captain Hawltaught**: TLP's granddaughter Edith Nicolls indicated that Hawltaught is modelled on the author's maternal grandfather, Thomas Love (d. 1805): 'As a boy, in his holidays, he would listen for hours with intense interest to his old sailor grandfather's vivid descriptions of the great naval battles in which he had fought, and the meeting of the ships after the "Mutiny at the Nore." This grandfather is brought into the novel "Melincourt" as old Captain Hawltaught'; Nicolls, 'Biographical Notice', in *The Works of Thomas Love Peacock, Including His Novels, Poems, Fugitive Pieces, Criticisms, Etc.*, ed. Henry Cole, with a preface by Lord Houghton, and a Biographical Notice by Edith Nicolls, 3 vols. (R. Bentley, 1875), vol. 1, p. xxvi. 'Haul' is a nautical term meaning 'To trim the sails, etc. of a ship so as to sail nearer to the wind (also **to haul up**); hence more generally, to change or turn the ship's course; to sail in a certain course' (*OED*; earliest example 1589).

10 **the contemplative cast of Sir Oran's countenance**: TLP's footnote quotes *Origin*, changing Monboddo's 'resemble ours' to 'resemble man's' and Monboddo's 'gait and behaviour' to 'gait or behaviour'.

11 **he wept bitterly**: TLP's footnote quotes from *Origin*, 'book ii. chap. 4' (sic; actually ch. 5, 1.344). The only change in substantives is that Monboddo's 'an Orang Outang, which was on board' (*Origin*, 1.344) becomes 'an oran outang on board'. The fact that Hawltaught *buys* Sir Oran may be significant in a book in which the slave trade is often discussed. TLP does not quote Monboddo's next sentence, concerning the oran outang enslaving boys and girls, although later in ch. 6 (see n. 50) he does quote a passage from *AM* asserting that the oran outang, 'instead of killing men and women, as he could easily do, takes them prisoners, and makes servants of them' (*AM*, 3.42). In vol. 3 of *Mel*, TLP refers back to a footnote at 'vol. i. p. 73' (ch. 33; *1817*,

3.63 n.) although there are two footnotes on page 73 of vol. 1 of the first edition. This note, the first of the two, is clearly the one TLP meant.

12 **his life was despaired of**: A legal formula employed when someone supposedly was wounded severely in an assault. In [John Anstey], *The Pleader's Guide, A Didactic Poem in Two Books, Containing the Conduct of a Suit at Law, with the Arguments of Counsellor Bother'em and Counsellor Bore'em in an Action Betwixt John-a-Gull, and John-a-Gudgeon, for Assault and Battery at a Late-Contested Election. By the Late John Surrebutter Esq. Special Pleader, and Barrister-at Law* (1796), the bill of complaint asserts that John-A-Gull '*did . . . much discompose / Said Gudgeon's mouth, eyes, ears, and nose, / Back, belly, neck, thighs, feet, and toes, / By which, and other wrongs unheard of, / His clothes were spoil'd, and life despair'd of*'; *The Pleader's Guide*, 2nd ed. (T. Cadell and W. Davies, 1803), p. 178. TLP's footnote here quotes from 'book ii. chap. 4' of *Origin* (specifically, from 1.287), changing Monboddo's 'One of themselves' to 'One of them'.

13 **in ordinary**: The term 'ordinary' refers to 'A part of a fleet which is laid up or out of service. Chiefly in *in ordinary*: (of a ship) out of commission, not in service' (*OED*).

14 **half-pay and the produce of his prize-money**: Retired officers of the British army and navy received half the salary to which they would be entitled if they were in active service; naval men were entitled to 'prize money' for the ships that they participated in capturing.

15 **a little village in the West of England**: Soon Forester mentions that he visited Hawltaught in Devonshire.

16 **honourable houses**: The phrase plays on the conventional term for the House of Lords and House of Commons.

17 **vapouring**: 'The action of talking or acting in a high-flown or pretentious manner' (*OED* 'vapouring', 2, first example 1656).

18 **on the flute and French horn**: The footnote quotes *Origin*, 1.346–7. Monboddo explains why oran outangs do not acquire

speech from contact with human beings, even though they are (according to Monboddo) capable of speech and they clearly learn music from human beings. Where *Origin* reads 'circumstances; and it shall be shewn, in the sequel, that men, living' (346), TLP leaves out Monboddo's glance forward, printing 'circumstances; and men, living'. TLP conceals the fact that he begins quoting in the middle of one of Monboddo's sentences, and cuts off the end: TLP's 'acquired than speech' is Monboddo's 'acquired than even speech' – and Monboddo's sentence continues from there (p. 347).

19 **en passant**: This French phrase, 'in passing', is familiar from chess, and later in *Mel* the characters participate in the Chess Dance (ch. 28).

20 **speech**: In *1817* there is a superfluous asterisk after 'speech', an interesting example of careless printing and proofreading. There is only one footnote on this page in *1817* (1.75), and the footnote clearly applies to the asterisk higher on the page, at the phrase 'French horn'.

21 **grog**: 'A drink consisting of spirits (originally rum) and water' (*OED* 'grog', 1.a., first example 1770).

22 **to sympathize in this taste**: TLP's footnote quotes Buffon quoting 'M. de la Brosse' (*Buffon 1799*, 35.96), a man 'qui a écrit son voyage à la côte d'Angole en 1738, et dont on nous a communiqué l'extrait' (*Buffon 1799*, 35.90). TLP emends the quotation to indicate that the 'il' to whom Buffon refers is de la Brosse. The misprint 'de conteau' in Buffon becomes 'du couteau'; Buffon's 'pour couper et prendre' becomes 'pour prendre et couper'; and Buffon's 'qu'on leur sert sur' becomes 'qu'on sert sur'. *1817* also omits the circumflex from 'portâmes'. Most important, TLP italicizes Buffon's 'ils boivent du vin et d'autres liqueurs'. Later in this chapter TLP quotes Monboddo referring to de la Brosse and Buffon.

23 **Rule Britannia, True Courage, or Tom Tough**: 'True Courage' and 'Tom Tough' are both songs by Charles Dibdin. See *The*

Professional Life of Mr. Dibdin, Written by Himself, with the Words of Six Hundred Songs, 4 vols. (published by the author, 1803).

24 **rencontre**: A chance encounter (French). Forester was surprised to meet an oran outang in Devon.

25 **philosophical education**: TLP's footnote, drawing upon *AM*, quotes the middle of Monboddo's sentence. Monboddo's 'one of the great kind, seven feet high' is simplified into 'an oran outang of the great kind'. Monboddo, continuing, explains that he wishes the oran outang will be educated, 'for, being of the large kind, and no more than seven feet high, I suppose he is but young, and therefore may, with proper pains, be taught to speak, which will convince the most credulous of his humanity, even those who believe that the faculty of speech is essential to Man' (*AM*, 3.40).

26 **villany**: The spelling 'villanous' occurs later in *1817* (ch. 13; *1817*, 1.187). Both 'villany' and 'villanous' were legitimate alternative spellings in 1817, and each is retained in *1856* (pp. 39, 92).

27 *Nothing like Grog, Saturday Night,* **or** *Swing the flowing Bowl*: Three drinking songs composed for the London stage by Charles Dibdin (see n. 23).

28 **the elixir of life**: The mythical drink that would make a person immortal. Its most notable appearance in Romantic literature is in William Godwin's novel *St. Leon: A Tale of the Sixteenth Century*, 4 vols. (G. G. and J. Robinson, 1799).

29 **bumper**: 'A cup or glass of wine, etc. filled to the brim, *esp.* when drunk as a toast' (*OED* I, first example 1677). Grose's *Dictionary of the Vulgar Tongue* (1785) defines a 'bumper' as 'a full glass, in all likelihood from its convexity or bump at the top; some derive it from a full glass formerly drank to the health of the pope, *a la bon pere*'. This definition also appears in the 1811 revised edition of Grose, *Lexicon Balatronicum: A Dictionary of Buckish Slang, University Wit, and Pickpocket Eloquence*, which was 'Compiled Originally by Captain Grose. And now considerably altered

and enlarged, with the modern changes and improvements, by a Member of the Whip Club. Assisted by Hell-Fire Dick, and James Gordon, Esqrs. of Cambridge; and William Soames, Esq. of the Hon Society of Newman's Hotel' (C. Chappel, 1811).

30 **stave**: *OED* 'stave', III.5.a: 'A "verse" or stanza of a poem, song, etc.'. Earliest example 1659.

31 **he would infallibly die of a broken heart, as has been seen in some of his species**: TLP's footnote directs the reader to *Origin*, book 2, ch. 4, in which Monboddo provides two stories of African oran outangs (one an 'impungu', one a 'chimpenza') dying of humiliation. Though the 'impungu' had lived happily amid humans, 'when he was brought into the town, such crowds of people came about him to gaze at him, that he could not bear it, but grew sullen, abstained from food, and died in four or five days' (*Origin*, 1.287). Chimpenzas seem 'to have the same sense of honour': the natives informed the Bristol merchant on whom Monboddo relies that when chimpenzas 'are laughed at, they take it so much to heart, that they languish and die', and the merchant 'had one of them . . . aboard his ship, who died, as he imagines, for that reason, in three months' (*Origin*, 1.287). Monboddo reproduces the merchant's letter that is his source for both anecdotes (*Origin*, 1.281–6; see specifically 282n, 284n). The merchant, learning that chimpenzas can die if laughed at, responds, 'if that was the case, they must die; for it was impossible to look at them without laughing' (1.284n). People have a 'propensity to laugh' when they first see Sir Oran.

32 **I have purchased him a baronetcy**: The implication is that Forester paid someone in government in order to acquire this honour for Sir Oran. A baronetcy is granted by the crown, and it is hereditary, unlike a knighthood (and like a title of nobility). Sir Telegraph is also a baronet (ch. 16).

33 **the Duke of Rottenburgh**: A 'rotten borough' is 'a borough whose constituency has dwindled severely or (in certain cases) ceased to exist altogether, but which retains the power to elect a

Member of Parliament' (*OED*; earliest example 1765). A rotten borough differs from a 'pocket borough', which is 'A borough in which the election of political representatives was controlled by one person or family' (*OED*, with the earliest example dating from 1783). On rotten and pocket boroughs, see Introduction.

34 **Mr. Christopher Corporate**: Corporation boroughs 'were among the most manageable boroughs, with circumscribed electorates'; they could easily be controlled by a single person or family. Of these boroughs, 'The largest, Helston, where in theory the corporation could create an unlimited number of freemen entitled to vote, had no more than about 70 voters'; Thorne, *History of Parliament*, vol. 2, p. 34.

35 *finish his education*: This phrase appears repeatedly in TLP's early fiction. In *NA*, Scythrop is 'sent home like a well-threshed ear of corn, with nothing in his head: having finished his education to the high satisfaction of the master and fellows of his college'. See *HH*, ch. 4; *CC*, ch. 9; *Mel*, chs. 13, 23, 24. A similar phrase appears in TLP's *Sir Proteus* (1814); Halliford, 6.286. Forester later summarizes TLP's view: 'Great, indeed, must be the zeal for improvement, which an academical education cannot extinguish' (ch. 8).

36 **'large body corporate of one'**: George Colman the Younger's poem 'An Ode to We, A Hackney'd Critic' begins, 'HAIL, Plural Unit! who would'st be / A Junto o'er my Muse and me, / With dogmas to control us; / Hail, mystick WE! grand Next-to-None! / Large Body Corporate of One!'; *Poetical Vagaries; Containing An Ode to We, A Hackney'd Critic; Low Ambition, or the Life and Death of Mr. Daw; A Reckoning with Time; The Lady of the Wreck, or Castle Blarneygig; Two Parsons, or the Tale of a Shirt*, 2nd ed. (Longman, Hurst, Rees, Orme and Brown, 1814) p. [1]. With this allusion, Sir Telegraph and TLP compare Christopher Corporate's 'virtual representation' of thousands to the practice of individual literary critics referring to themselves in the plural. This Colman poem is quoted later; see ch. 21, n. 26; ch. 22, n. 38.

37 *as notorious as the sun at noon-day*: The italicized phrase reappears in chs. 13 (used by Mr Vamp), 16 (Mr Feathernest), 21 (Mr Sarcastic) and 22 (Sarcastic again). This phrase, which Cicero used in condemning Catiline (*In Catilinam* 1), was frequently applied in the late eighteenth and nineteenth centuries to political corruption. TLP may have had it in mind because in Oct. 1816, as he was writing *Mel*, Cobbett recalled that when the Commons debated 'the case of Quintin Dick' some members stated 'that the traffic in seats was as notorious as the Sun at noon-day' (*WPR*, 12 Oct. 1816, p. 449). That debate, on 11 May 1809, concerned a possible inquiry into ministerial influence over elections. Lord Archibald Hamilton claimed that George Tierney said that the accusation involved a practice that 'had long been as open and broad as the sun at noon-day' (*Times* (12 May 1809)). Cobbett was not alone in recalling the 1809 debate. On 28 Nov. 1816, the London Court of Common Council condemned the 'shameful traffic in seats' that was 'avowed in Parliament, in a transaction in which . . . a motion for enquiry [was] rejected, on the ground of the notoriety of the practice' (*The Examiner* (1 Dec. 1816), 765).

38 **Linnæus**: The Swedish botanist and zoologist Carl von Linné, or Linnaeus, whose system of classifying and naming forms of life was hugely influential. He focused less than Buffon did on the development of species.

39 **Linnæus has . . . be its sovereign**: When TLP's footnote quotes from Linnaeus, he evidently relies exclusively upon Monboddo, who quotes this Linnaeus passage in a footnote (see *Origin*, 1.305n). Forester's comments provide a rough translation of Linnaeus.

40 **Valentine and Orson**: Twin brothers in the Carolingian romance *Valentine and Orson*. Valentine is raised at court, while Orson is raised by bears. On this romance, see Jerome Mitchell, *Scott, Chaucer, and Medieval Romance: A Study in Walter Scott's Indebtedness to the Literature of the Middle Ages* (Lexington: University Press of

Kentucky, 1987), p. 23. A version of this work, titled 'Valentine and Ursine', appears in Thomas Percy, *Reliques of Ancient English Poetry: Consisting of Old Heroic Ballads, Songs, and Other Pieces of Our Earlier Poets. (Chiefly of the Lyric Kind): Together with Some Few of Later Date*, 3 vols. (Robert and James Dodsley, 1765), vol. 3, pp. 260–77, a compilation mentioned later in *Mel.*

41 **'No waiter, but a knight templar'**: From 'The Rovers; or the Double Arrangment', George Ellis and George Canning's parody of German drama, first published in the newspaper *The Anti-Jacobin* and then included in the compendium *The Poetry of the Anti-Jacobin* (J. Wright, 1799). When TLP died, his library included an 1801 edition of *Poetry of the Anti-Jacobin* (*Sale Catalogue* 665). In 'The Rovers', a character is revealed to be 'No Waiter, but a *Knight Templar*' (p. 196). The punctuation in *Mel* suggests that Sir Telegraph is aware that he is quoting. TLP was not the only second-generation Romantic writer to recall this phrase from 'The Rovers'. In the fourth edition (Sept. 1812) of cantos 1 and 2 of *Childe Harold's Pilgrimage*, Lord Byron wrote that the title character of his poem 'was so far perfectly knightly in his attributes—"No waiter, but a knight templar"'; *The Complete Poetical Works*, vol. 2 (1981), p. 5.

42 **the very words . . . human nature**: TLP's footnote quotes three passages from Buffon's *Histoire Naturelle* (see *Buffon 1799*, 35.7–8, 40–1, 116); then a passage from Delisle de Sales' *De la philosophie de la nature*, vol. 10, p. 196. Buffon's 'ses bras' (*Buffon 1799*, 35.7) becomes 'que ses bras', and Buffon's 'et qu'il marche' (35.7) becomes 'il marche'. For sense, TLP omits the word 'également' from Buffon's phrase 'pourroit également regarder' (35.40); TLP clarifies Buffon's 'cet animal' (35.40) as 'l'oran outang' and 'ce singe' (35.116) by printing 'l'oran outang'; later, Buffon's 'ce singe' (35.116) becomes just 'il'.

43 **Pongos, Mandrills, and Oran Outangs . . . Fauns and Satyrs, Silenus and Pan**: TLP's footnote first supplies the passage from Rousseau's *Discours sur l'Origine et les Fondemens de l'Inégalité*

Parmi Les Hommes that Forester echoes; see *Œuvres complètes*, vol. 3, p. 211. 'Without ceremony our travelers take for beasts, under the names *Pongos, Mandrills, Orangutans,* the same beings that the ancients, under the names *Satyrs, Fauns, Sylvans,* took for Divinities. Perhaps, after more precise research, it will be found that they are neither animals nor god, but men'; Jean-Jacques Rousseau, *Discourse on the Origins of Inequality (Second Discourse); Polemics, and Political Economy,* The Collected Writings of Rousseau, vol. 3, ed. Roger D. Masters and Christopher Kelly, trans. Judith R. Bush, Roger D. Masters, Christopher Kelly and Terence Marshall (Hanover, NH: University Press of New England, 1992), p. 83. TLP's footnote next quotes from Delisle de Sales' *De la philosophie de la nature,* vol. 5, pp. 406–8, although after the words 'l'origine que des oran outangs', a phrase in Delisle de Sales has been omitted: 'leur nez aplati, leur vigueur et leur libertinage, sont des traits caractérisques, qui déposent en faveur de cette généalogie' (p. 407). The only other changes in substantives are that TLP omits the 'jusque' after 'l'apperçoit', and Delisle de Sales' 'épicycles à Ptolomée, pour rendre raisonnable son systême planétaire' becomes 'épicycles dans le systême planétaire de Ptolomée'. The word 'temps' is misspelled 'tems' in *1817.*

44 **a learned mythologist**: This mythologist has been associated with Thomas Taylor (see Van Doren, *Life,* p. 102; Garnett, *Novels,* 1.135), though the connection was not mentioned in print in TLP's lifetime. David Garnett writes that 'Thomas Taylor embraced the Pythagorean doctrine of metempsychosis, kept a small menagerie of animals which he treated with profound respect, and was the author of a *Vindication of the Rights of Brutes,* imitated from the *Vindication of the Rights of Women* [sic] by Mary Wollstonecraft, who had lodged in his house' (Garnett, *Novels,* 1.136). See also *Thomas Taylor, the Platonist: Selected Writings,* ed. and introd. Kathleen Raine and George Mills Harper (Princeton: Princeton University

Press, 1969). Taylor may have been the model for the 'modern Platonist' in Isaac D'Israeli's anti-Jacobin satirical novel *Vaurien, or Sketches of the Times* (T. Cadell and W. Davies, and J. Murray and S. Highley, 1797), ch. 26, 'The Platonist', vol. 2, pp. 165–82).

45 βακχευτα: The footnote, citing 'Orphica, Hymn. XI. (X. Gesn.)', refers to an edition of the Orphic Hymns that was prepared by Johann Matthias Gesner and published posthumously. TLP at the time of his death owned *Orphica. Cum notis H. Stephani, A. Chr. Eschenbachii, J. M. Gesneri, Th. Tyrwhitti; recensvit Godofredus Hermannus*, 2 vols. (Leipzig: C. Fritsch, 1805) (*Sale Catalogue* 468). Ode 11 (also numbered 10), the ode to Pan, appears on pp. 270–2, and the 'learned mythologist''s salutation combines the beginning of line 4, the end of line 5, line 6, the first word of line 11 and a word from line 21. Thomas Taylor's translation of this hymn, titled 'To Pan', appeared in his *The Mystical Initiations; or Hymns of Orpheus Translated from the Original Greek: with a Preliminary Dissertation on the Life and Theology of Orpheus* (for the author, 1787), pp. 130–3. Taylor used iambic pentameter couplets, not the 'learned mythologist''s hudibrastics. One oddity in *1817* is that the Greek letter rho in 'κρεκων' is different from the four rho's that precede it and the two that follow it.

46 *et id genus omne*: 'and all of that family' (Latin).

47 **the Troglodyte of Linnæus . . . *he will again be its sovereign***: See the passage from Linnæus that TLP quoted in an earlier footnote (ch. 6, n. 40), beginning 'Homo nocturnus'. As Forester said, Linnæus thought that the oran outang was human, and 'he describes him as having a hissing speech, thinking, reasoning, believing that the earth was made for him, and that he will one day be its sovereign'.

48 *iterum fore telluris imperantem*: Echoing the phrase from Linnæus: he will once again be the sovereign of the earth.

49 *non compos*: 'Of unsound mind' (Latin).

50 *Now I will only observe … from the man of art*: Most of Forester's speech here is put in italic font, and TLP's footnote (two pages later in the first edition) explains that the italicized words are taken from Monboddo's *AM*, 3.41, 42. Indeed, all the words in roman type are TLP's or Forester's interpolations. Monboddo's 'I will only add further' (*AM*, 3.41) becomes TLP's 'Now I will only observe'. TLP inserts a passage ('which is shown by breaking his heart, if laughed at, or made a show, or treated with any kind of contumely') and he inserts the word 'from' after Monboddo's 'monkey', and changes 'attachments' to 'attachment'. Monboddo's 'which the monkey is altogether incapable of' becomes 'of which the monkey is altogether incapable'. Whereas Monboddo's oran outang 'learns, not only to do the common offices of a menial servant, as the Oran Outan did whom I saw stuffed in the French King's cabinet of curiosities, but also to play upon the flute'; Forester's oran outang *'learns not only to do the common offices of life, but also to play on the flute and French horn'*. Monboddo's 'Animal is not a Man', becomes TLP's *'animal be not a man'*.

51 [Footnote:] **'The words in italics … by their actions'**: When TLP quotes what 'Monboddo adds' in *AM* (3.42–3 – TLP does not provide the page numbers), he never departs from Monboddo's text in substantives. TLP's footnote next quotes Rousseau's *Discours sur l'Inégalité* (*Discourse on the Origins of Inequality*), 'note 8'; see *Œuvres complètes*, vol. 3, p. 210. Rousseau criticizes those who have acknowledged humanity too narrowly, and comments that speech is a poor criterion for inclusion: 'although the organ of speech is natural to man, speech itself is nonetheless not natural to him, and who knows to what point his perfectibility can have raised Civil man above his original state'; Rousseau, *Discourse on the Origins of Inequality*, vol. 3, p. 82. Finally, TLP quotes twice from *AM*. He modifies the first quotation; Monboddo is responding to an anatomist who failed to find organs of speech when he dissected oran outangs, and Monboddo says that this anatomist's

oran outangs 'were all from the Island of Borneo; whereas the Oran Outan, so accurately dissected by Tisson, who says that he had exactly the same organs of voice that a Man has, was from Angola' (*AM*, 3.44). 'Tisson' (sometimes 'Tysson' in Monboddo's spelling) is Edward Tyson, author of *Orang-Outang, sive homo sylvestris, or, The Anatomy of a Pygmie Compared with That of a Monkey, An Ape, and a Man* (1699). TLP's quotation from *AM* 3.40 involves no changes in substantives.

52 **fish and partridge**: The footnote quotes *Origin*, 1.297. Spelling, capitalization and punctuation are modified, and Monboddo's first 'betwixt' is changed to 'between', though not his second. TLP does not indicate that he begins quoting in the middle of a sentence, or that he stops quoting in the middle of a sentence.

53 ***With regard to his ... civilized countries***: TLP's footnote attributes the italicized words to *AM*, 4.55, where Monboddo says of the oran outang that 'He is social too, and lives in herds; so that with regard to his character, he is undoubtedly a man, and a much better man than many that are to be found in civilized countries'.

54 **you will readily acknowledge**: TLP's note, *1817*, 1.96–7, quotes the conclusion of n. 8 from Rousseau's *Discours sur l'Inégalité* (*Discourse on the Origins of Inequality*); see *Œuvres complètes*, vol. 3, pp. 213–14. Rousseau explains that if observers of the calibre of 'a Montesquieu' were to visit these various nations (Turkey, Egypt and so on), then 'when such Observers will affirm of a given Animal that it is a man and of another that it is a beast, they will have to be believed'. However, 'it would be too credulous to defer to crude travelers about whom one would sometimes be tempted to ask the very question that they meddle in resolving concerning other animals'; Rousseau, *Discourse on the Origins of Inequality*, vol. 3, p. 86.

55 **the iron tongue of midnight**: Theseus in *A Midsummer Night's Dream* says that 'The iron tongue of midnight hath told twelve' (act 5, scene 1, line 363).

CHAPTER 7

1   **The Principle of Population:** The title of the chapter obviously
    alludes to *An Essay on the Principle of Population, as It Affects the
    Future Improvement of Society. With Remarks on the Speculations of
    Mr. Godwin, M. Condorcet, and Other Writers* by Thomas Robert
    Malthus. This work was first published in 1798, in one volume,
    without Malthus's name, and it was significantly expanded in
    later editions, which were signed. TLP cites Malthus's *Essay*
    twice later in *Mel* – once when Fax echoes Malthus (ch. 40),
    once to provide context for an observation of the narrator (ch.
    42). The latter instance reveals that TLP had access to the 2nd
    ed., an 1803 quarto (see ch. 42, n. 16, and List of Abbreviations).
    References in these explanatory notes use the 1803 edition.
    Malthus is famous for the proposition that population naturally
    increases geometrically while food supplies do not, and there-
    fore population growth, when unchecked, will bring suffering.
    In *Cal* the inhabitants of Terra Incognita are 'exempt from age
    and mortality: but they did not, as a great philosopher has con-
    jectured that persons similarly circumstanced would do, "cease
    to propagate"'. Merlin, 'assuming . . . the figure of Mr. Malthus,
    made them an oration on the evils that might result from a too
    rapid increase of population, in an island where no one could
    die' – to no avail (Halliford, 8.327). On Malthus in *Mel*, see
    Introduction.

2   **a post-chaise:** 'A horse-drawn, usually four-wheeled carriage (in
    Britain usually having a closed body, the driver or postillion rid-
    ing on one of the horses) used for carrying mail and passengers,
    esp. in the 18th and early 19th centuries' (*OED*). Mr Fax's mode
    of transport is appropriately efficient and practical.

3   **Mr. Fax:** Forester's initial description of Mr Fax, and the name
    'Mr Fax' itself, could apply to many political economists, but
    Fax's opinions most often resemble those professed by Malthus.
    Mr Fax's physical appearance connects him to Mr Escot in

HH, who is 'more pale and saturnine' than Mr Foster (ch. 1); Fax is 'tall, thin, pale' and 'grave-looking', and both his general appearance (ch. 15) and his complexion (ch. 12) are perceived as 'saturnine'.

4 **weather-stain**: The second example of 'weatherstain' in the *OED*, the first coming from Walter Scott's *Guy Mannering* (1815).

5 **the Squire of Dames**: The Squire of Dames appears in book 3, canto 7 of Edmund Spenser's *The Faerie Queene*. The woman the squire loved demanded that he pursue women until he has been rejected 300 times, but he has been rejected by only three (canto 7, stanzas 56–60).

6 **in my mind's eye**: Shakespeare's Hamlet says he has seen his late father 'In my mind's eye' (act 1, scene 2, line 185).

7 **Bachelors and spinsters I decidedly venerate**: In the final chapter of *Mel*, TLP quotes from Malthus's most explicit endorsement of celibacy, which appeared in the expanded 1803 edition of the *Essay* (see pp. 549–52) but was omitted from subsequent editions.

8 **featherless bipeds**: This is the term used in Plato's *Politicus* to refer to human beings. In *HH*, Mr Cranium observes that although a philosopher has 'defined [man] to be a *featherless biped*', this definition 'is equally applicable to an unfledged fowl' (ch. 12); the word also occurs in ch. 9, in a paraphrase of Mr Escot's thoughts. On 8 May 1817, not long after *Mel* appeared, Percy Shelley jokingly used the phrase to refer to his son (*Shelley and His Circle*, 5.214).

9 **More men than corn ... famine**: A proposition found throughout Malthus's writings.

10 **Some must marry, that the world may be peopled**: In Shakespeare's *Much Ado about Nothing*, Benedick says that one argument in favour of marrying is that 'the world must be peopled' (act 2, scene 3, line 242).

11 **attribute it, with the Manicheans, to a mythological principle**: In *NA*, the 'Manichæan Millenarian' Mr Toobad believes that the world is now ruled by 'the Evil Principle' (ch. 1).

12 **the tendency of population to increase beyond the means of sustinence**: Malthus, identifying 'the causes that have hitherto impeded the progress of mankind towards happiness', emphasizes 'the constant tendency in all animated life to increase beyond the nourishment prepared for it' (*Essay*, pp. [1]–2). Malthus held that 'It is clearly the duty of each individual not to marry till he has a prospect of supporting his children' (*Essay*, pp. 492–3). For families having six children, see *Essay*, p. 595.

13 **Drury Lane**: The Theatre Royal in Drury Lane is used as synecdoche or metonymy for works of the human imagination. Along with Covent Garden, Drury Lane was one of the two theatres in the West End that were authorized to perform plays, as distinguished from operettas and pantomimes.

14 **prospiciencies**: This is the first occurrence of 'prospiciency' after 1681 that is noted in the *OED*, which defines the word as 'The action or quality of looking forward, foresight; an instance of this'. TLP's 'prospicient', later in *Mel* (ch. 16), is the first occurrence of that word after 1654 that the *OED* acknowledges.

15 **'When unrevenged stalks Cocker's injured ghost'**: David Garnett (*Novels*, 1.142) calls this quotation a 'witty embroidery on' Samuel Butler, *Hudibras*, part 1 (1663), canto 2, lines 494–8:

> What Rage, O Citizens! what Fury
> What *Oestrum*, what Phrenetick Mood
> Makes you thus lavish of your Blood,
> While the proud *Vies* your Trophies boast
> And unreveng'd walks —— Ghost?

TLP's embroidery entails replacing Butler's '——' with the name of Edward Cocker, author of *Cocker's Arithmetick* (1677). According to John Wilders' edition of *Hudibras*, the '——' probably would suggest Sir Hardress Waller; Samuel Butler, *Hudibras*, ed. introd. and comm. John Wilders (Oxford: Clarendon Press, 1967), p. 350. *Hudibras* is quoted by Forester (ch. 7), Feathernest (ch. 16), Sarcastic (ch. 21) and the narrator (chs. 23, 28); in one instance, *Hudibras* is quoted by the narrator when describing Feathernest's thoughts (ch. 17). Butler is the source of the title-page epigraphs of *NA* and *GG*, the epigraphs to chs. 3 and 4 of *MM*, and the epigraphs for the title page and chs. 2, 6 and 7 of *CC*.

16 **the torch of Prometheus**: Writers of TLP's generation were fascinated by the figure of Prometheus; while TLP was writing *Mel*, Mary Wollstonecraft Shelley was working on *Frankenstein; or, The Modern Prometheus* (1818), and Percy Shelley went on to write *Prometheus Unbound* (1820).

17 **a degenerate race**: In general, *Mel* relates human degeneration to the theories of Monboddo. In ch. 25, Forester says that living amid mountains may protect 'a few favoured mortals from the vortex of that torrent of physical and moral degeneracy, which seems to threaten nothing less than the extermination of the human species', and TLP's footnote cites Monboddo, *AM*, 5.237–8.

18 **'with hearts in our bodies, no bigger than pins' heads'**: Shakespeare's Falstaff says that 'I press'd me none but such toasts-and-butter, with hearts in their bellies no bigger than pins' heads' (*1 Henry IV*, act 4, scene 2, lines 20–2).

19 **the baleful influence of the poor laws**: The main poor law was 43 Eliz. c. 2, which decreed that every parish would have overseers of the poor, who were 'first, to raise competent sums for the necessary relief of the poor, impotent, old, blind, and such other, being poor and not able to work: and secondly, to provide work for such as are able, and cannot otherwise get employment' (Blackstone, *Commentaries*, vol. 1, p. 360). One means of providing such work was the workhouses to which Fax refers. Malthus argued that 'if the poor laws had never existed in this country . . . the aggregate mass of happiness among the common people

would have been much greater than it is at present' (*Essay*, p. 413). The poor laws 'tend[ed] to depress the general condition of the poor in . . . two ways': first, they 'increas[ed] population without increasing the food for its support' (p. 409); second, 'the quantity of provisions consumed in workhouses . . . diminishe[d] the shares that would otherwise belong to more industrious and more worthy members, and thus, in the same manner, force[d] more to become dependent' (p. 410). '[A]ll systems of this kind' tend 'to increase population, without increasing the means for its support, and, by thus depressing the condition of those that are not relieved by parishes, to create more poor' (p. 413). Moreover, the poor laws were 'calculated to eradicate' the 'spirit of independence' that 'still remains among the peasantry' (p. 410).

20 **Those four horses . . . amusement of one:** Malthus wrote that 'waste among the rich' and 'land remaining uncultivated', contrary to what many have argued, 'have little or no influence on what may be called the average pressure of distress on the poorer members of society. If our ancestors had been so frugal and industrious, and had transmitted such habits to their posterity, that nothing superfluous was now consumed by the higher classes, no horses were used for pleasure, and no land was left uncultivated, a striking difference would appear in the state of the actual population; but probably none whatever, in the state of the lower classes of people, with respect to the price of labour, and the facility of supporting a family (*Essay*, 477–8).

21 **'This is vanity, and a great evil':** 'For there is a man whose labour is in wisdom, and in knowledge, and in equity; yet to a man that hath not laboured therein shall he leave it for his portion. This also is vanity and a great evil' (Ecclesiastes, ch. 2, v. 21).

22 **He had . . . came away:** In *NA*, Scythrop 'had had some taste for romance-reading before he went to the university, where, we must confess, in justice to his college, he was cured of the love of reading in all its shapes' (ch. 2).

CHAPTER 8

1 **Mr. Hippy**: Sir Telegraph is welcomed not by Anthelia but by the man she invited to serve as 'a lord seneschal' (ch. 3). Hippy has assumed (as we soon read) 'the character of lord of the mansion'.

2 **outré**: 'Beyond the bounds of what is usual or considered correct and proper; unusual, peculiar; eccentric, unorthodox' (*OED*). The narrator adopts the French term that Mrs Pinmoney would use to mean unconventional. The word is italicized when it appears in *NA* (ch. 3).

3 **Lord Anophel Achthar**: As TLP's footnote explains, the name connotes ανωφελον αχθος αρουρας, meaning '*Terræ pondus inutile*', a useless product of the earth. The form of Lord Anophel's name is implausible, as George Saintsbury seems to be the only critic to have noticed: 'how with that title he came to be heir-apparent to a marquis Peacock does not explain'; Saintsbury, introd., *Melincourt; or, Sir Oran Haut-ton*, ill. F. H. Townsend (London and New York: Macmillan, 1896, p. xii). The character is continually referred to as 'Lord Anophel', and therefore 'Anophel' is his first name and 'Achthar' his family's name, but the 'son and heir' of a marquess would be known by one of his father's lesser titles. For example, when *Mel* was written, the Marquess of Londonderry's eldest son used the courtesy title 'Viscount Castlereagh' or 'Lord Castlereagh'. Only a marquess's younger sons would be known as 'Lord Firstname Lastname', or would be referred to as 'Lord Firstname' (the conventional style for younger sons of dukes, as well). In ch. 42, Lord Anophel presses Anthelia to become 'Lady Achthar', although the wife of a 'Lord Anophel' who is a marquess's son would usually be styled 'Lady Anophel'. The fact that in *CC* the Earl of Foolincourt's eldest son is styled Lord Bossnowl shows that in 1830 TLP was aware of the conventions governing courtesy titles.

4   **the Marquis of Agaric**: TLP's footnote explains that 'agaricus' is 'a genus of plants' that includes 'the mushroom, and a copious variety of toadstools'.

5   **the**: The quotation marks in *1817* before 'The young lord' cannot be correct, as this sentence and the rest of the paragraph clearly are in the narrator's voice, and Mrs Pinmoney is not being quoted directly. Later in the paragraph, *1817* puts double quotation marks around the phrase 'to all the crowned heads in Europe' and puts single quotation marks around 'Whatever is at court, is right', with double quotation marks at the end. The obvious conclusion is that the compositor became confused as to which words were uttered by Mrs Pinmoney. *1856* punctuates as if the entire paragraph beginning with 'the young lord' is spoken by Mrs Pinmoney.

6   **Grovelgrub**: As in grovelling for grub.

7   **Mr. Feathernest**: A character reminiscent of Robert Southey, poet laureate since 1813. Once the most radical of the Lake Poets, he now supported the ministry and voiced his antipathy toward views he considered subversive. The Marquis of Agaric has given Feathernest 'a place in exchange for his conscience'; Southey received £300 a year from the government – £100 as poet laureate, £200 in the form of a pension. See e.g. John Wade, *The Black Book; or, Corruption Unmasked!* (John Fairburn, 1820), p. 78. Roderick Sackbut's name in *NA* makes the reader think of the poet laureate's compensation from the crown (see ch. 1, n. 10).

8   **Odes to Truth and Liberty**: An allusion to the political poetry Southey wrote in the 1790s. In Dec. 1816, Leigh Hunt reminded *The Examiner*'s readers of 'the Jacobinical doctrines exalted in *Joan of Arc* [1796], a poem by Mr. SOUTHEY, now one of the most canting of the *Quarterly Reviewers*; —see also passages in his *Odes to Horror*, his *Botany Bay Eclogues*, and a hundred other excitements of popular irritability' (*The Examiner* (7 Dec. 1816), 769). In Aug. and Sept. 1816, *The Examiner* reprinted a series of

early Southey poems under the title 'Acanthologia. Specimens of Early Jacobin Poetry' (see *The Examiner* (11 Aug. 1816), 504; (18 Aug. 1816), 521; (25 Aug. 1816), 538; (1 Sept. 1816), 552; (15 Sept. 1816), 586). The specimen that appeared on 25 Aug., Southey's 'Inscription for a Monument at Old Sarum', was reprinted on 30 Aug. by the *Morning Chronicle*.

9 **Panegyrical Addresses 'to all the crowned heads of Europe'**: The jibe is directed towards the poems Southey composed as poet laureate, extolling not only British royalty but also the Continental monarchs who had triumphed over Napoleon. See 'Robert Southey, Esq. Poet Laureat', *Odes to His Royal Highness the Prince Regent, His Imperial Majesty the Emperor of Russia, and His Majesty the King of Prussia* (Longman, Hurst, Rees, Orme and Brown, 1814). Roderick Sackbut in *NA*, ch. 5, is author of *An Ode to the Red Book*, the 'red book' being 'A register or directory of the British court, nobility, members of the government, and other socially important people; *spec.* (a name for) the *Royal Kalendar, or Complete and Correct Annual Register*, an annual directory published from 1767 to 1893' (*OED* 'red book', 4). In *CC*, Lady Clarinda says that Mr Skionar, who resembles Coleridge, 'has got an ill name by keeping bad company'; the bad company includes two figures meant to suggest Wordsworth and Southey: 'Mr. Wilful Wontsee, and Mr. Rumblesack Shantsee' are 'poets of some note, who used to see visions of Utopia, and pure republics beyond the Western deep: but, finding that these El Dorados brought them no revenue, they turned their vision-seeking faculty into the more profitable channel of espying all sorts of virtues in the high and the mighty, who were able and willing to pay for the discovery' (ch. 5). *Mel*'s version of Wordsworth, Mr Paperstamp, does not appear until ch. 28, at the end of the second volume.

10 **'Whatever is at court, is right'**: An obvious parody of Pope's 'Whatever is, is right', from *An Essay on Man* (1733–4), Epistle I, line 294. Later Feathernest says that material benefits have

persuaded him that 'all is right, especially at court' (ch. 16). In *CC*, Dr Folliott assumes that 'whatever had been in Greece, was right' (ch. 7). *The Twickenham Edition of the Poems of Alexander Pope*, ed. John Butt et al., 11 vols. (London: Methuen; New Haven, CT: Yale University Press, 1939–69), vol. 3(i): *An Essay on Man*, ed. Maynard Mack (1950; repr. 1964).

11 **inmate**: 'In relation to other persons: One who is the mate or associate of another or others in the same dwelling; one who dwells with others in a house' (*OED* 'inmate', A.1.a).

12 **composed him in the Roman sense**: 'To lay out (a dead body)' (*OED* 'compose', 15.b.). The *OED* notes this word's appearance in Southey's *Roderick, the Last of the Goths* (1814).

13 **The fashionable attractions of Low-wood and Keswick**: In late 1813 TLP and Percy Shelley travelled to the Lake District, and they visited the Lowwood Inn, on the eastern shore of Windermere. *A Picturesque Tour of the English Lakes* (R. Ackermann, 1821) explained that 'Few inns on the lake have, on the whole, so many attractions for the traveller.' Noting that the Lowwood Inn 'commands a view of the whole of the upper part of the lake, upon the margin of which it stands', the *Picturesque Tour* explained that 'a scene opens to the eye, of which no description can give an adequate idea', as 'The lake spreads out into an immense plain of shining water, curiously indented along the opposite shore, where the hills gradually sloping, display a mixture of woodlands and beautiful farms' (pp. 69–70).

14 *logement*: In military terminology, this French word meant a position that an attacking force gains on the enemy's ground, and from which subsequent attacks may be launched.

15 **Harum O'Scarum, Esquire**: Francis Grose's *Classical Dictionary of the Vulgar Tongue* (S. Hooper, 1785) defines 'harum scarum' thus: 'he was running harum scarum, said of any one running or walking carelessly and in a hurry, after they know not what'. This definition also appears in the 1811 edition of Grose, *Lexicon Balatronicum*.

16 **Mr. Derrydown**: Derrydown is one of TLP's more ambiguous creations. The *British Critic* thought Derrydown was
Wordsworth (new ser., vol. 8 (Oct. 1817), 441), but the *North
American Review* identified him as Walter Scott (vol. 5 (Sept.
1817), 437); David Garnett and Ian Jack agreed (Garnett, *Novels*,
1.145; Jack, *English Literature*). Carl Dawson called Derrydown
'a curious mixture of Scott and Burns', whereas Howard Mills
wrote that Derrydown 'reminds us partly of Scott, partly of
Coleridge'; Dawson, *His Fine Wit*, p. 198, and Mills, *Peacock*, p.
123. Derrydown perhaps is best understood as TLP's means of
reflecting upon broad trends in literary and antiquarian culture.

17 **the central opacity of utter darkness**: In *NA*, Flosky 'plunged
into the central opacity of Kantian metaphysics' (ch. 1). In ch.
31 of *Mel*, Mystic 'take[s] a very opaque and tenebricose view'.

18 **'that all human learning is vanity'**: Ecclesiastes states repeatedly that 'All is vanity', yet the verse most applicable to 'human
learning' is that which Fax quoted a few pages earlier, in ch. 7:
'there is a man whose labour is in wisdom, and in knowledge,
and in equity; yet to a man that hath not laboured therein shall
he leave it for his portion' (ch. 2, v. 21).

19 **Reliques of Ancient Poetry**: Thomas Percy's *Reliques of Ancient
English Poetry* (see ch. 6, n. 40) was reprinted many times; TLP
owned an 1839 edition at the time of his death (*Sale Catalogue*
183). He also owned George Ellis's *Specimens of Early English
Metrical Romances*, 3 vols. (Longman, Hurst, Rees and Orme,
1805) (*Sale Catalogue* 159).

20 **glimpses of the truth of things**: In Wordsworth's 'Lines Written
a Few Miles above Tintern Abbey, On Revisiting the Banks of
the Wye During a Tour, July 13, 1798', first published in *Lyrical
Ballads, with a Few Other Poems* (1798), 'We see into the life of
things' (line 49).

21 **a travelling chariot**: On chariots, see ch. 2, n. 2, and ch. 3, n. 10.

22 **some good livings**: Grovelgrub is understandably interested
when he learns that Sir Telegraph controls appointments to

some lucrative benefices. In an age when clergy in the Church of England could hold and enjoy the income from several parishes at once, receiving patronage of this kind would not inhibit any of Grovelgrub's other activities.

23 **Strephons**: See ch. 2, n. 5.

24 **the suitors of Penelope**: Another of many references to Homer's *Odyssey* in *Mel*. However, Anthelia, unlike Penelope, has no Odysseus whose return might be anticipated.

25 **the usual cant**: 'Cant' here seems to mean 'A pet phrase, a trick of words; *esp.* a stock phrase that is much affected at the time, or is repeated as a matter of habit or form' (*OED* 'cant', *n.*[3] 5.b.) or 'Phraseology taken up and used for fashion's sake, without being a genuine expression of sentiment; canting language' (6.a.).

26 **the spirit . . . modern life**: On the distinction between chivalry's spirit and the specific forms it might take in different periods, see the writers quoted in ch. 2, n. 43, such as Charles Mills, who observed that the 'spirit, though not the form, of the chivalric times has survived to ours' (*The History of Chivalry*, vol. 2, p. 360).

27 *ami du prince*: 'Friend of the prince' (French). TLP is probably thinking of the passage from Voltaire's *La Pucelle d'Orléans* that he later quoted in *MM*, ch. 9, in regard to Prince John's 'travelling minstrel, or laureate', Harpiton. In Voltaire's poem, Bonneau, at court, is said 'être l'ami du prince', but 'qu'à la ville, et surtout en province, / Les gens grossiers ont nommé maquereau' (lines 58–60); *La Pucelle d'Orléans*, ed. Jeroom Vercruysse, *Les Œuvres complètes de Voltaire*, vol. 7 (Geneva: Institute et Musée Voltaire, 1970), p. 261. Bonneau 'Is commonly esteem'd the prince's friend; / But, in the town, and where vile peasants live, / *Pimp* is the name, such vulgar people give'; W. H. Ireland, trans., *The Maid of Orleans, or La Pucelle of Voltaire. Translated into English Verse*, 2 vols. (John Miller and W. Wright, 1822), 1.3–4.

28 **the horns of a dilemma**: *ODEP* explains expressions involving the 'horns of a dilemma' by referring to 'Each of the alternatives

of a dilemma—in scholastic Lat. *argumentum cornutum*—on which one is figured as liable to be caught or impaled'.

29 **Mr. Mystic**: Mystic is one of TLP's visions of Coleridge, alongside Mr Flosky in *NA* and Mr Skionar in *CC*. (Another is 'Mr. Crocodile, the lay-preacher', who a bookseller in the unfinished *Cal* says 'looks in upon me now and then, and talks a great deal about old philosophy'; Halliford, 8.340.) TLP wrote in 'The Four Ages of Poetry' that 'Mr. Coleridge . . . superadds the dreams of crazy theologians and the mysticisms of German metaphysics' (*NA*, p. 152). In 'Coleridge's Lay Sermon', a review of *The Statesman's Manual* published in the *Edinburgh Review*, vol. 27, no. 54 (Dec. 1816), Hazlitt referred to Coleridge as 'Our mystic'; *The Complete Works of William Hazlitt*, ed. P. P. Howe, 21 vols. (London and Toronto: J. M. Dent and Sons, 1930–4), vol. 16, pp. 99–114. In *Academical Questions*, a book TLP cites later in *Mel* to illuminate Mr Mystic's Kantianism, Sir William Drummond refers to 'the mystical system of the transcendental critics', to 'the transcendental mystagogue' and to 'the modern mystics of the sect of Kant'; Drummond, pp. 353, 370, 372. TLP still owned a copy of *Academical Questions* when he died (*Sale Catalogue* 304). In TLP's *Paper Money Lyrics*, 'The Wise Men of Gotham' is attributed to 'S. T. C., Esq., Professor of Mysticism' (Halliford, 7.119).

30 **Cimmerian Lodge**: Named after the *Kimmerioi* in Homer's *Odyssey*, who live in a land of darkness caused by mists and clouds (see *Odyssey*, book 11, lines 13–19). The dedication to TLP's early poem *Sir Proteus* (1814) states that Byron's poems are 'enveloped in all the Cimmerian sublimity of the impenetrable obscure' (Halliford, 6.279). The typical modern poet, according to TLP's 'The Four Ages of Poetry', is like Mr Mystic: 'The brighter the light diffused around him by the progress of reason, the thicker is the darkness of antiquated barbarism, in which he buries himself like a mole, to throw up the barren hillocks of his Cimmerian labours' (*NA*, p. 153).

31 **transcendental philosophy**: In Kant's philosophy, 'transcendental' means 'Not derived from experience, but concerned with the presuppositions of experience; pertaining to the general theory of the nature of experience or knowledge, *a priori*; critical' (*OED* 'transcendental', 2.b.). According to the *OED*, 'transcendental' was first used in this sense in English in A. F. M. Willich, *Elements of the Critical Philosophy: Containing a Concise Account of its Origin and Tendency; A View of All the Works Published by its Founder, Professor Immanuel Kant; and a Glossary for the Explanation of Terms and Phrases* (T. N. Longman, 1798). In *Sir Proteus* TLP calls Coleridge 'the profound transcendental metaphysician of the *Friend*' (Halliford, 6.290). When Skionar in *CC* offers to discuss 'the transcendental philosophy' with Fitzchrome, Fitzchrome is 'about to protest that he had never heard the word transcendental before' (ch. 4), which would be odd in 1831, the year in which *CC* was published.

32 **ponderous jargon**: According to Drummond, 'The young and ignorant disputant' who takes up 'the mystical system of the transcendental critics' will be able to enjoy 'overwhelming his astonished adversaries with a pedantic and cumbrous jargon, and in maintaining controversies, where reason is fatigued, before definition can be finished'. A real philosopher, in contrast, 'will not be so easily deceived by the shallow seeming of verbal phantoms', but 'will say, that mystecism [sic] is not congenial with philosophy' (p. 353).

33 **a decent pretext for picking a quarrel**: TLP here evokes the stereotype of Irish gentlemen as prone to duels. See, for example, Sir Kit in Maria Edgeworth's *Castle Rackrent* (1800).

34 **Major O'Dogskin**: The significance of associating this character with items made of dog's leather is not clear.

35 **my lady of the lake**: A phrase that in 1817 would point in particular to Walter Scott's *The Lady of the Lake* (1810). By 1866 TLP owned a copy of the first edition (*Sale Catalogue* 555).

36 **Ulleswater**: It is unusual to see this spelling of the name of Ullswater, the lake that formed part of the border between Westmorland to the south and Cumberland to the north in the Lake District.

37 **pinnace**: 'A small light vessel, usually having two schooner-rigged (originally square-rigged) masts, often in attendance on a larger vessel and used as a tender or scout, to carry messages, etc'. The word is 'Chiefly *hist.* and *poet.* after 18th cent' (*OED* 'pinnace', I.1). Also in *CC*, ch. 9.

38 **A four-in-hand race**: A race in which each driver had to manage four horses, as Sir Telegraph does when he drives his barouche. See ch. 2, nn. 49–50.

39 **neck or nothing**: A phrase meaning to act without regard for consequences. *Stevenson's Book of Proverbs* (p. 1670) and *ODEP* (p. 559) cite examples going back to 1678, including this from Edward Daniel Clarke's *Travels in Various Countries of Europe, Asia, and Africa* (1810): 'She rides, to use the language of English sportsmen, "neck or nothing"' (p. 333).

CHAPTER 9

1 **circumvallation**: 'The making of a rampart or entrenchment round a place, *esp.* in besieging' (*OED*, first example 1655).

2 **Chevy Chase**: Two versions of this well-known traditional ballad appear in Percy's *Reliques of Ancient English Poetry*, the compendium that inspires Derrydown to begin collecting ballads: 'The Ancient Ballad of Chevy-Chase', *Reliques*, vol. 1, pp. [1]–18; 'The More Modern Ballad of Chevy Chace', *Reliques*, vol. 1, pp. [231]–46. This ballad was praised, notably, by Addison in *Spectator* 70 and 74; see *The Spectator*, ed. Donald F. Bond, 5 vols. (Oxford: Clarendon Press, 1965), vol. 1, pp. 297–303, 315–22. In TLP's *Sir Proteus*, Neptune utters 'A wondrous speech, and all in rhyme, / As long as *Chevy Chase*' (Halliford, 6.303).

3 **your protection**: That is, O'Scarum would violate decorum if he were to challenge a clergyman to a duel. In *CC*, Mr Eavesdrop tells Dr Folliott that 'Your cloth protects you, sir' (ch. 6).

4 **Old Robin Gray**: 'Auld Robin Gray' was first published, untitled and anonymous, in [David Herd, ed.], *Ancient and Modern Scottish Songs, Heroic Ballads, Etc.*, 2nd ed., 2 vols. (Edinburgh: James Dickson and Charles Elliot, 1776), vol. 2, pp. 196–7. Though Derrydown does not say whether he considers 'Auld Robin Gray' an 'ancient' or a 'modern' ballad, it was in fact the work of Lady Anne Lindsay (1750–1825), whose authorship of the poem had been revealed in print by the time TLP wrote *Mel*; see John Gilchrist, *A Collection of Ancient and Modern Scottish Ballads, Tales, and Songs: with Explanatory Notes and Observations*, 2 vols. (Edinburgh: Blackwood, 1815), vol. 2, p. 268. As Derrydown's explication shows, 'Auld Robin Gray' is relevant to the theme of mercenary marriage that runs through *Mel*.

5 **the heterodox kirk of the north**: The Church of Scotland, the Presbyterian and Calvinist 'heterodoxy' of which provokes a reaction from the Anglican Grovelgrub.

6 **poverty coming in at the door**: *Stevenson's Book of Proverbs* cites a range of examples, the earliest being from Richard Brathwait's *The English Gentlewoman* (1631): 'It hath beene an old maxime; that as poverty goes in at one doore, love goes out at the other.' Later in *Mel*, Forester says that in the case of Desmond and his wife, 'Poverty has certainly come in at the door, but Love does not seem to have flown out at the window' (ch. 14).

7 **as Captain Bobadil . . . Matthew?'**: In Ben Jonson's *Every Man in His Humour* (1598), Bobadil says, 'Should your adversary confront you with a pistol, 'twere nothing, by this hand; you should, by the same rule, control his bullet in a line, except it were hail-shot, and spread. What money ha' you about you, Master Matthew?' (act 1, scene 5, lines 134–7; *The Cambridge Edition of the Works of Ben Jonson*, gen. ed. David Bevington, Martin Butler, Ian Donaldson, vol. 4 (Cambridge: Cambridge University Press,

2012). In 1816, Jonson's play was revived at Drury Lane, with Edmund Kean as Kitely and John Harley as Bobadil. William Gifford's edition of *The Works of Ben Jonson* was published the same year, and TLP owned a copy when he died (*Sale Catalogue* 267), although he may not have acquired it until after he wrote *Mel*: when Percy Shelley recommended a quotation from *Every Man in his Humour* to TLP on 25 July 1818, he copied the passage because 'I do not think you have these plays at Marlow' (*PBS Letters*, 2.27).

8 **Will the love . . . kitchen**: From the nursery rhyme beginning 'There was a little man, / And he wooed a little maid'; see Iona Opie and Peter Opie, *The Oxford Dictionary of Nursery Rhymes*, 2nd ed. (Oxford: Oxford University Press, 1997), pp. 341–3. Horace Walpole printed a version of this ballad in 1764, and recorded that it was the work of 'Sʳ Ch. Sidley', which would be either Sir Charles Sedley (c. 1639–1701) or his great grandson who had the same name (c. 1721–78).

9 **'God prosper . . .'**: The opening lines of 'The More Modern Ballad of Chevy Chace', Percy, *Reliques*, vol. 1, pp. [231]–46: 'GOD prosper long our noble king, / Our lives and safetyes all; / A woful hunting once there did / In Chevy-Chace befall' (vol. 1, p. 235).

10 **the sword of Orlando**: In Boiardo's *Orlando Innamorato*, 'The king of Sericana declared war on Charlemagne to obtain Orlando's sword, Durindana' (Garnett, *Novels*, 1.153).

11 **the girdle of Florimel**: In Spenser's *Faerie Queene*, book 4, canto 5, Amoret is the only woman who is chaste, and thus the only one who can wear this girdle.

CHAPTER 10

1 **a flight of rugged steps**: In ch. 41, Anthelia is kidnapped after she descends these 'rocky steps' into the dingle; the kidnappers had to know of the existence of this secret exit.

2 **the genius of the scene**: A 'genius loci' is 'A guardian spirit or god associated with a place' (*OED* 1).

3 **energies of nature, energies of liberty and power**: In ch. 1, the narrator records how Anthelia's personality was shaped by 'the spirit of mountain liberty'. However, in ch. 37, 'The Mountains', Fax rejects the familiar association of nature with liberty.

4 *the nearness of the paths of night and day*: The Greek quotation in TLP's footnote comes from *Odyssey*, book 10, line 86.

5 **Anthelia had never seen so singular a physiognomy**: This is another instance of people failing to see that Sir Oran might not be human.

6 **Ils sont . . . book ii. c. 4**: The first quotation in the footnote comes from Rousseau's *Discours sur l'Inégalité* (*Discourse on the Origins of Inequality*); see *Œuvres complètes*, vol. 3, p. 209. Rousseau writes that 'Pongos are never taken alive because they are so robust that ten men would not suffice to stop them'; Rousseau, *Discourse on the Origins of Inequality*, vol. 3, p. 81. TLP attributes the statement that 'The oran outang is prodigiously strong' to *AM*, referring to 'vol. iv. p. 51' and 'vol. v. p. 4', but the quotation is not precise. In volume 4 of *AM*, Monboddo writes that 'of the Ourang Outangs . . . there are three kinds, very different in their size', and '[t]he first, which are called Pongos or Impongos, are of very great size, betwixt seven and nine feet high, and prodigiously strong' (*AM*, 4.51). In volume 5, Monboddo writes that 'those they call Chimpenza's . . . are only about five or six feet when they are erected', but 'the Pongos, or Impongos, are of very great size, betwixt seven and nine feet high, and prodigiously strong' (*AM*, 5.4) – a note directs the reader back to *AM*, 4.51. In TLP's quotation from *Origin*, Monboddo's 'heard them say' becomes 'heard the natives say'; Monboddo's 'that it can throw down' becomes TLP's 'he can throw down'; and Monboddo's 'its amazing' becomes TLP's 'his amazing'. Monboddo quotes the Bristol merchant saying that an oran outang will pull up a palm tree when he wants palm wine, but wine is not Sir Oran's motive.

7 **quizzing-glass**: 'A single eyeglass, with or without an attached handle; a monocle' (*OED*, the first example dating from 1802).

8 **with gestures as well as words**: After Anthelia invites Sir Oran to dinner, Hippy supplements the invitation with gestures, though he does not learn until later that Sir Oran cannot speak.

9 **Orlando Furioso**: Meeting Sir Oran, Mr Hippy instantly compares him not only to Hercules but also to the protagonist of Ariosto's epic poem, *Orlando Furioso* (1516), as though Sir Oran is obviously a character out of romance, or Hippy is aware of the romance theme of the novel in which he is a character.

10 **a mushroom**: Lord Anophel, hearing that Sir Oran pulled up a pine just as he would pull up a mushroom, responds that he has 'nothing to do with mushrooms' (I, 152), using 'mushroom' to mean someone who is newly wealthy. Lord Anophel seems unaware that his own name alludes to mushrooms – a joke at Lord Anophel's expense.

11 **gentlemanly satisfaction**: Lord Anophel acknowledges that Sir Oran is a gentleman, a 'man of consequence'. Therefore, in order to receive satisfaction, Lord Anophel must challenge him, rather than call upon the law.

CHAPTER 11

1 **Ratstail**: The solicitor's name evokes primarily '(in *singular*) a thin plait or tail of hair' (*OED* 2.a.), although it also evokes the literal tail of a rat.

2 **a notice**: a parody of the 'absurdities of special pleading' that Charles Knight remembered (writing in 1864). In this mode of pleading, 'John Brown, complainant in an assault which consisted in lifting a finger against him, [would] be made to declare that William Smith, "with a certain stick, and with his fists, gave and struck the said John a great many violent blows and strokes on and about his head, face, breast, back, shoulders, arms, legs, and divers other parts of his body; and also, then and there, with

great force and violence, shook and pulled about him the said John, and cast and threw him, the said John, down to and upon the ground, and then and there violently kicked the said John, and gave and struck him a great many other blows and strokes; and also, then and there, with great force and violence, rent, tore, and damaged the clothes and wearing apparel, to wit, one coat, one waistcoat, one pair of breeches, one cravat, one shirt, one pair of stockings, and one hat, of the said John'"; Knight, *Passages of a Working Life During Half a Century: with a Prelude of Early Reminiscences* (Bradbury & Evans, 1864), vol. 2, p. 71. The reader may wonder how Ratstail or his client knew that the mysterious stranger was Sir Oran, or knew that Sir Oran can receive mail at Redrose Abbey.

3 **an action:** An action at law for trespass, which is 'an entry on another man's ground without a lawful authority, and doing some damage, however inconsiderable, to his real property'; Blackstone, *Commentaries*, vol. 3, p. 209.

4 **Muckwormsby:** A muckworm is literally 'A worm or grub that lives in manure', but figuratively it meant 'A miser, a money-grubber' (*OED*). In Cobbett's *Paper Against Gold*, 'Messrs. Muckworm and Co.' lend money to the government; *Paper Against Gold and Glory Against Prosperity*, 2 vols. (printed J. M'Creery, 1815), vol. 1, p. 28.

5 **staves:** This archaic word for staffs, spears or lances was conventional in English law. In John Anstey's *The Pleader's Guide*, 'The Pleadings state, *'that* JOHN-A-GULL / *With envy, wrath, and malice full, / With swords, knives, sticks, staves, fist and bludgeon, / Beat, bruis'd, and wounded* JOHN-A-GUDGEON' (p. 177).

6 **will appear hereafter:** The reasons appear in ch. 24.

7 *beau idéal:* French, the 'perfect type and model' (*OED*).

8 **archetype:** 'The original pattern or model from which copies are made; a prototype' (*OED* 'archetype', 1.).

9 **chimæra:** The sense here is 'An unreal creature of the imagination, a mere wild fancy; an unfounded conception' (*OED* 3.b.) – which

the *OED* identifies as 'The ordinary modern use'. The word occurs again in *Mel* in chs. 13, 15, 16 and 24, and the adjective 'chimerical' appears in chs. 30, 31, 33 and 39.

10 **sentiment of Voltaire**: The three lines quoted are the final lines (lines 427–9) of Voltaire's 'Ce Qui Plait aux Dames' (1764), where the poet says that though reason rules and we still seek truth, error has its advantages. See *Les Œuvres complètes de Voltaire*, vol. 57B, ed. Nicholas Cronk (Oxford: Voltaire Foundation, 2014), p. 62.

11 **I hope not:** See Malthus, ch. 9, 'Of the Direction of Our Charity' (*Essay*, 558–66).

12 **Every species of falsehood . . . should be abhorrent to her**: Godwin wrote in his *Enquiry Concerning Political Justice* that a person who, 'having laid down to himself a plan of sincerity, is guilty of a single deviation, infects the whole' and 'contaminates the frankness and magnanimity of his temper (for fortitude in the intrepidity of lying is baseness)' (vol. 1, p. 246). Oddly enough, Forester's description of his ideal mate resembles the description of Kant's character given by Thomas Wirgman in an encyclopedia article that TLP cites in ch. 31 (see ch. 31, n. 22): 'He was a most decided enemy to falsehood of every kind. He never could endure to hear an untruth even in jest; and in his own language, he was scrupulous to avoid every thing that could convey a false idea of himself'; Wirgman, 'Kant', *Encyclopædia Londinensis: or, Universal Dictionary of Arts, Sciences, and Literature*, ed. John Wilkes, 24 vols., vol. 11 ('for the proprietors', 1812), p. 605.

13 καλος κ'αγαθος: 'the beautiful and the good' (Greek). Forester believes 'that beauty and goodness are inseparable'; in *NA*, Mr Toobad says that 'Good men and true' was the 'common term' of earlier generations of Englishmen, much 'like the καλος καγαθος of the Athenians' (ch. 11). Monboddo says that this Greek term means 'a man who has worth and goodness, and at the same time, a high sense of what is beautiful and becoming in sentiments and actions, without which no character can be perfect' (*AM*, 4.205).

14 **Louvet and his Lodoiska**: TLP's footnote directs us to 'Louvet's "Récit de mes Périls"', meaning *Quelques notices pour l'histoire, et le récit de mes périls depuis le 31 Mai, 1793* (1795) by Jean-Baptiste Louvet de Couvrai (1760–97), a memoir in which Louvet, a Girondist, described his tribulations and those of his wife, whom he called 'Lodoiska' after the heroine of the fictional romances he composed that were collected as *Vie du Chevalier de Faublas*.

15 **his reversion**: Forester's heir presumptive would lose his claim to inherit Forester's property (the 'reversion') only if this heir presumptive were displaced by a legitimate child.

CHAPTER 12

1 *in terrorem*: 'as a warning, in order to terrify or deter others' (*OED*). In *Sir Proteus*, literary criticism can 'operate *in terrorem* on the side of common sense' (Halliford, 6.300n).

2 **political economy**: 'Political economy', a coinage of the eighteenth century, was used to mean 'The branch of knowledge ... that deals with the production, distribution, consumption, and transfer of wealth; the application of this discipline to a particular sphere; (also) the condition of a state, etc., as regards material prosperity; the financial considerations attaching to a particular activity, commodity, etc.' (*OED*, 'political economy'). The phrase 'political economists' appears in ch. 24.

3 **because both began with an M**: In Shakespeare's *Henry V*, Fluellen says that Macedon and Monmouth have similar 'situations': 'There is a river in Macedon, and there is also moreover a river at Monmouth'; moreover, 'there is salmons in both' (act 4, scene 7, lines 25–8, 31). In *NA*, Marionetta alludes to Fluellen's contention (ch. 7).

4 **let all possible calamities...disunion of hearts**: As TLP's footnote mentions, the source is book 5 of Rousseau's *Émile, ou de L'Éducation* (1762), from which the author quoted in the

original French on all three title pages of *Mel*. See *Œuvres complètes*, vol. 4, pp. 755–6; *Emile*, p. 581.

5 **in your mind's eye**: Fax uses the trope from *Hamlet* that Forester employed earlier (see ch. 7, n. 6).

6 **Our indiscretions . . . do pall**: Hamlet says that 'Our indiscretion sometime serves us well / When our deep plots do pall, and that should learn us / There's a divinity that shapes our ends' (act 5, scene 2, lines 8–10).

7 [Footnote:] **L'issuë aucthorise . . . chap. 8.**: When Forester quotes Shakespeare, TLP quotes one of Shakespeare's contemporaries; the author's footnote combines four passages from an essay by Michel de Montaigne: 'The event often justifies very foolish conduct. Our interposition is as it were but a thing of course, and more commonly a consideration of use and example than of reason' (*The Essays of Michael Seigneur de Montaigne, Translated into English*, 8th ed., 3 vols. [J. Pote et al., 1776], vol. 3, p. 194); 'Good fortune and ill fortune are, in my opinion, two sovereign powers. It is a folly to think that human prudence can play the part of fortune; and vain is his attempt who presumes to comprehend causes and consequences, and to lead the progress of his design, as it were, by the hand . . .' (p. 195); 'If we but observe who are the men of the greatest sway in cities, and who do their own business best, we shall commonly find that they are men the least qualified. . . . We ascribe the effects of their good fortune to their prudence' (p. 196); 'Wherefore I make no manner of scruple to declare, that events are slender proofs of our worth and capacity' (p. 196).

8 **'Where there is prudence . . . fortune is powerless'**: Juvenal says that 'nullum numen habes, si sit prudentia: nos te, / nos facimus, Fortuna, deam caeloque locamus' (*Satires*, 10.365–6); 'You would not be divine, Fortune, if we only had wisdom; we make you into a goddess, and put you in the skies.' In this instance, a character in *Mel* quotes a classical author in translation and names the author, but TLP provides neither a specific attribution nor the Latin original.

9 **one of the greatest poets and philosophers of antiquity**: Forester quotes Ecclesiastes, ch. 4, vv. 8–10, omitting a few phrases.

CHAPTER 13

1 **Desmond**: On the similarities between Desmond and the young TLP, Joukovsky writes, 'Whether or not there was any autobiographical basis for Desmond's experiences with Mr Vamp and Mr Dross—and there may well have been—Peacock clearly shared Desmond's predicament: that of a poor but well educated young man who wanted to employ his literary talents without sacrificing his independence or compromising his integrity'; Joukovsky, 'Peacock before *Headlong Hall*, 39. A character named Desmond appears in a draft of a play in the same MS volume as TLP's draft of *The Three Doctors* ('Peacock before *Headlong Hall*, 29).

2 **machiavelism**: The *OED* entry for 'Machiavellism' (earliest example 1592) directs us to 'Machiavellianism', which means 'The principles and practice of Machiavelli or of Machiavellians; cunning, unscrupulousness, or duplicity in behaviour (*esp.* in politics); an instance of this' (earliest example 1607). It is unlikely that Desmond or TLP intends any reference to the actual writings of Niccolò Machiavelli.

3 **a single blow . . . imposture**: Using trees to represent political institutions, whether healthy or unhealthy, was common in TLP's lifetime. One source is Matthew, ch. 3, v. 10: 'And now also the axe is laid unto the root of the trees: therefore every tree which bringeth not forth good fruit is hewn down, and cast into the fire.'

4 **'The children . . . favoured more'**: The opening of section 6 of Robert Southey's poem *Madoc* (1805): the high priest of the Native Americans 'With reverential awe accosted us, / For we, he weened, were children of a race / Mightier than they, and wiser, and by heaven / Beloved and favoured more'; *Madoc*, 2

405

vols. (Longman, 1807), vol. 1, p. 54. Desmond suggests that the multitude submit to 'the hired misleaders of society' much as Southey's native Americans supposedly revere the Welsh prince Madoc and his countrymen.

5   **the *igneus vigor et cœlestis origo***: Virgil's Anchises says to Aeneas that 'igneus est ollis vigor et caelestis origo / seminibus' (*Aeneid*, book 6, lines 730–1); 'Fiery is the vigour and divine is the source of those seeds of life.'

6   **Lycophron**: Lycophron (third century BC). According to John Lemprière's standard *Classical Dictionary*, 'The only remaining composition of this poet is called *Cassandra* or *Alexandra*', and its 'obscurity has procured the epithet of *Tenebrosus* to its author'; J. Lemprière, *Classical Dictionary; Containing A Copious Account of All the Proper Names Mentioned in Ancient Authors: with the Value of Coins, Weights, and Measures, Used among the Greeks and Romans; and a Chronological Table*, 8th ed. (T. Cadell and W. Davies, 1812), n. p.

7   *difficiles nugæ* and *labor ineptiarum* . . . **adytum**: 'Turpa est difficiles habere nugas / et stultus labor est ineptiarum' (Martial, *Epigrams*, 2.86–7); 'to work on difficult trifles is degrading, and the effort spent on puerilities is foolish'. The phrases also appear in *Sir Proteus* (Halliford, 6.287). An 'adytum' is 'a small sanctuary in the cella reserved for oracles, priests, or priestesses' (*OED*), so Desmond contrasts the exterior of knowledge, its vestibule, from its interior. 'Adytum' also appears in *CC*, ch. 7.

8   **noometry**: TLP coins the term 'noometry' to mean 'measurement of the mind', appropriating the Greek *nous* (mind) and *metros* (measurement). The appearance of 'noometry' in *Mel* is the only instance given in the *OED*, which compares 'noometry' to 'noology', first used by Jeremy Bentham in his *Chrestomathia*, published in the same year as *Mel*.

9   **Bond Street**: Several important booksellers were located in Bond Street in 1817, including TLP's publisher, Hookham (at 15 Old Bond Street).

10 **offered the copyright**: Desmond wishes to sell the entire copyright, so that he would receive all his payment up front, rather than, for example, accepting a percentage of the profits.

11 **Mr. Vamp**: The verb 'vamp' meant 'To provide or furnish with a (new) vamp [i.e. part of a stocking]; to mend or repair with or as with patches; to furbish up, renovate, or restore' (*OED* verb[1], I.1.a, first example 1599). The term came to be applied to 'literary compositions' (I.1.b., *trans.* and *fig.*), with the *OED*'s first example dating from 1741 ('vamping up an old Play or two of Massinger and Decker'). 'Vamp' also meant 'To make or produce by or as by patching; to adapt, compile, compose, put together (a book, composition, etc.) out of old materials; to serve up (something old) as new by addition or alteration' (2.a, *transf.*).

12 **pair of scissars**: That is, Vamp is literally vamping; see previous note.

13 **Mr. Foolscap**: The primary connotation of this name is clearly 'A long folio writing- or printing-paper, varying in size' (*OED* 'fool's cap/foolscap', 3). The speech Vamp addresses to Desmond is TLP's caricature of the editorial policy of the *Quarterly Review*; Vamp might make a reader think of William Gifford (who edited the *Quarterly* from 1809 to 1824). Although Vamp does not, like Gifford, write poetry or carry out literary scholarship, he does have a pension; Gifford received £600 as Comptroller of the Lottery Office and £300 as Paymaster of Gentlemen Pensioners (Wade, *The Black Book*, p. 43). See TLP's 'An Essay on Fashionable Literature', where he argues that the *Quarterly* differs from the *Edinburgh Review* insofar as its 'contributors are more in contact being all more or less hired slaves of the Government and for the most part gentlemen pensioners clustering round a common centre in the tangible shape of their paymaster Mr Gifford'. TLP adds that the *Quarterly* 'contains more talent and less principle than it would be easy to believe coexistent' (*NA*, p. 113). (TLP elsewhere in his fiction focuses

on the *Edinburgh Review*; see *CC*, ch. 4.) Later in *Mel* we learn that the name of Vamp's periodical is *The Legitimate Review* (ch. 17); in *Cal*, rumours report that the philosopher who accompanies Calidore back to Terra Incognita will 'sit down for life as an Honorable Gentleman Pensioner, with such a pension in his single person as in this more economical nation would keep in pay two whole gangs of Legitimate Reviewers' (Halliford, 8.340). Cf. also *The Downing-Street Review* in *NA*, 'a popular Review, of which the editor and his co-adjutors were in high favour at court, and enjoyed ample pensions for their services to church and state' (ch. 5).

14 **to do away**: '*trans.* To put an end to, abolish, destroy, undo' (*OED* 2.a.). Examples cited by the *OED* include Southey's *Wat Tyler* (1794), act 2, scene 3: 'Your grievances shall all be done away.'

15 **villanous**: See ch. 6, n. 26.

16 *persuasion in a tangible shape*: This phrase or a variant recurs later in *Mel*, three times in ch. 13 and again in chs. 16, 17 and 22 (twice). In *Sir Proteus*, John Bull has suffered because of 'the selfish and mercenary apostacy' of men like Southey, and 'The spell which Armida [in Tasso's *Gerusalemme Liberata*] breathed over her captives was not more magically mighty in the operation of change, than are the golden precepts of the language politic, when presented in a compendious and tangible shape to the "sons of little men"' (Halliford, 6.289n).

17 *as notorious as the sun at noon-day*: See ch. 6, n. 37.

18 **a gentleman high in office . . . several thousands per annum**: The *Quarterly Review* had several contributors with high offices who made large incomes from the public purse, the most prominent being John Wilson Croker, who received £3,000 annually as First Secretary to the Admiralty and £250 as First Secretary to the Widows' Charity (Wade, *The Black Book*, p. 32).

19 **a Jacobin**: The term 'Jacobin', common in British political discourse of the 1790s, had been revived in the Regency and applied to a range of reformists and radicals.

20 **Mr. Dross**: 'Dross' here means useless matter left over from some process, or impurities.

21 **a tun of man**: 'a tun of man is thy companion' *1 Henry IV*, act 2, scene 4, line 448). A tun is 'a large cask or barrel, usually for liquids, esp. wine, ale, or beer, or for various provisions' (*OED* 'tun', 1.a.).

22 **respectable people**: As Lady Clarinda in *CC* says, sarcastically, 'Respectable means rich, and decent means poor' (ch. 3).

23 **poor-rates**: The poor rates were the parish's assessments for support of the local poor. (On the poor laws, see ch. 7, n. 19). Cobbett contrasted the poor rates, which aided deserving members of the community, with government taxes, some of which went to support sinecurists. In response to a proposal to end parish relief of the poor, Cobbett wrote that some 'would deny the poor man, who cannot find work, bread to save him from starving, but not one penny do they propose to take from the enormous sinecures of Lord Camden, Lord Ellenborough, Lord Melville, Lord Grenville, or any of the rest of them' (*WPR*, 28 Sept. 1816, p. 399).

24 **the main chance**: TLP introduces the phrase 'main chance', which is picked up again later, in the visit to 'Mainchance Villa'. The term means 'Something which is of principal importance in life; a livelihood; (now) *esp.* the opportunity of enriching or otherwise benefiting oneself' (*OED* 'main chance', n, II; first example 1584).

25 **a *tutorer***: A rare form of 'tutor'. The *OED* gives examples from 1702, 1824 and 1841.

26 **like Mahomet's coffin**: This phrase was used by Hazlitt in his anticipatory review of *The Statesman's Manual*, 'Mr. Coleridge's Lay Sermon', *The Examiner* (8 Sept. 1816), 571–3: 'This Lay-Sermon puts us in mind of Mahomet's coffin, which was suspended between heaven and earth, or of the flying island at Laputa, which hovered over the head of Gulliver'; *The Selected Writings of William Hazlitt*, ed. Duncan Wu, 9 vols. (Pickering

& Chatto, 1998), vol. 4, p. 107. (This *Examiner* article should not be confused with 'Coleridge's Lay Sermon', Hazlitt's review of *The Statesman's Manual* published in the *Edinburgh Review* in Dec. 1816.)

27 **Télémaque**: The didactic prose romance *Les Aventures de Télémaque* (1699), by François Fénelon. It is odd that TLP contrasts Fénelon's writings with those of central Enlightenment figures such as Rousseau and Voltaire, as *Télémaque* was hardly reactionary. Indeed, in *Political Justice* Godwin argued (notoriously) that Fénelon's works were so beneficial that a virtuous man must prefer saving Fénelon's life to that of the man's own wife or mother (vol. 1, pp. 82–3). Rescuing Fénelon 'at the moment when he was conceiving the project of his immortal Telemachus' would 'promot[e] the benefit of thousands, who have been cured by the perusal of it of some error, vice and consequent unhappiness' (vol. 1, p. 82).

28 **moveables**: Personal property, as opposed to real property.

29 **embarrassed**: In debt.

30 **'The valiant by himself, what can he suffer?'**: In James Thomson's play *Edward and Eleonora*, act 4, scene 7, Edward asks rhetorically, 'The Valiant, by himself, what can he suffer?', while emphasizing that when the valiant man has children, 'O then! he feels / The Point of Misery festring in his Heart'; Thomson, *Edward and Eleonora. A Tragedy. As it was to have been Acted at the Theatre-Royal in Covent-Garden* (Dublin: G. Faulkner, 1739), p. 47.

31 **Cincinnatus:** Lucius Quinctius Cincinnatus (520–430 BC), who left his humble farm to serve as dictator and lead the Roman armies, then returned to his farm when the war was done (see Livy, *Ab Urbe Condita*, 3.26–9). In the eighteenth and nineteenth centuries, he exemplified the republican ideal of the citizen who took up arms when needed.

32 **We will cultivate our garden**: A phrase famously adopted by the main characters at the conclusion of Voltaire's *Candide*. Their

desire merely to escape is notably different from Cincinnatus' virtuous renunciation (see previous note).

33 **any metamorphosis in Ovid**: In Ovid's *Metamorphoses*, which is quoted in ch. 40.

34 **Pythagoreans**: The followers of Pythagoras, the sixth-century BC philosopher, practised restraint in diet, perhaps including vegetarianism, and 'Pythagorean' is used here to mean a vegetarian. Percy Shelley's *A Vindication of a Natural Diet* (1813), *Queen Mab* (1813) and *On the Vegetable System of Diet* (1814–15) all drew upon a book by Shelley's and TLP's friend John Frank Newton, *Return to Nature, or Defence of Vegetable Regimen* (1811), as well as upon Joseph Ritson's *An Essay on Abstinence from Animal Food, as a Moral Duty* (1802). See in particular *Queen Mab*, n. 17, *The Complete Poetry of Percy Bysshe Shelley*, vol. 2, pp. 295–312 (for the editorial commentary, see pp. 650–70). In 1813 TLP visited Percy Shelley at Bracknell, where 'Shelley was surrounded by a numerous society, all in a great measure of his own opinions in relation to religion and politics, and the larger portion of them in relation to vegetable diet' (Halliford, 8.70–1).

CHAPTER 14

1 *en bonne odeur*: 'In good odour' (French), here used to mean in favour; later, Feathernest says he is 'in good odour at Court' (ch. 16).

2 *he . . . indulge in*: William Paley (1743–1805). At the time of the controversy at Cambridge University over subscription to the Thirty-Nine Articles of the Church of England, 'Mr. Paley, though personally attached to many of the reforming party, and, from the known liberality of his sentiments, considered favourable to their claims, did not sign the clerical petition for relief, which was presented to the House of Commons in 1772, alleging jocularly to Mr. Webb, as an apology for his refusal, that "he could not afford to keep a

conscience'"; G. W. Meadley, *Memoirs of William Paley, D.D.* (Sunderland: for the author, 1809), pp. 47–8. Meadley's footnote directs us to *The Works Theological, Medical, Political, and Miscellaneous, of John Jebb, M.D. F.R.S. with Memoirs of the Life of the Author; by John Disney, D.D. F.S.A.*, 3 vols. (Cadell, 1787), vol. 2, when the editor in a footnote quotes the phrase 'could not afford to keep a conscience' without naming the cleric of the Established Church who said it (vol. 2, p. 127n). The phrase about affording to have a conscience recurs in *Mel*, in chs. 16 and 24.

3 **'Ye'll voind them'**: The first appearance of dialect in *Mel*. David Garnett comments that 'Peacock's peasantry speak in the dialect of his native Dorset even when they are met in Westmorland' (*Novels*, 1.180).

4 **Poverty...window**: Forester adopts the proverb that Derrydown used in ch. 9, in a conversation for which Forester was not present.

5 **A picturesque tourist**: See ch. 1, n. 8.

6 **Democritus himself could have done**: Democritus, according to Seneca (*De Ira* 2.10) 'never appeared in public without laughing; so little did the serious pursuits of men seem serious to him'. According to TLP's granddaughter, in later life 'he was always so agreeable and so very witty that he was called by his most intimate friends the "Laughing Philosopher"'; Nicolls, 'Biographical Notice', in *The Works of Thomas Love Peacock* (1875), vol. 1, p. xlix.

7 **the nation of the Orans**: An odd construction, treating 'oran' as shorthand for 'oran outang'.

8 **a barbarous nation...speech**: Oran outangs are, 'according to my hypothesis, a barbarous nation, which has not yet learned the use of speech' (*Origin*, 1.270).

9 [Footnote:] **'I have ... articulate sounds'**: This quotation from *Origin*, 1.298–9, involves no changes in substantives.

10 **Xerxes on the shores of Salamis**: The reference is to the reaction of the Persian king Xerxes to the defeat of his fleet at the battle of Salamis. See Herodotus, book 8, chs. 88–90.

11 *Better is a poor and wise child, than a foolish king that will not be admonished*: Ecclesiastes, ch. 4, v. 13.

12 **mantua-makers**: A 'mantua-maker' was 'Originally: a person who made mantuas. Later more generally: a dressmaker' (*OED*). The first example cited comes from 1694. A 'mantua' was 'A kind of loose gown worn by women, fashionable esp. in the late 17th and early 18th centuries' (*OED* 'mantua', n.^{II}).

13 *Testaceous Mollusca*: Mollusks with shells (Latin).

14 **the noblest of human pursuits**: In *Frankenstein; or, The Modern Prometheus* (1818), which Mary Shelley was writing when TLP was working on *Mel*, Elizabeth Lavenza praises farming by contrasting it with the work of a lawyer: 'it is certainly more creditable to cultivate the earth for the sustenance of man, than to be the confidant, and sometimes the accomplice, of his vices' (vol. 1, ch. 5).

CHAPTER 15

1 **shook his head significantly**: With this ambiguous gesture, Forester permits Hippy to infer that Sir Oran is a mute man, instead of telling Hippy that Sir Oran is an oran outang.

2 **Anthy**: Anthelia's name is abbreviated this way only in this scene, and only by Hippy.

3 **Corydons**: Earlier the narrator sarcastically referred to Anthelia's suitors as 'her Strephons' (ch. 8); by calling these men 'Corydons', Hippy resorts to another name that in pastoral literature was conventional for a lover (see ch. 2, n. 8).

4 *Love's Labour Lost*: An allusion to Shakespeare's *Love's Labour's Lost*, a play that was not performed publicly in TLP's lifetime before 1839. In the First Folio, the title is *Loves Labour's Lost*; in the 1813 Johnson-Steevens edition, a copy of which TLP owned at the time of his death (*Sale Catalogue* 562), it is *Love's Labour's Lost*.

5 **love and wine**: The Latin proverb says that 'sine Cerere et Baccho friget Venus', meaning that love freezes when deprived of bread and wine. In *Confessions of an English Opium-Eater* (1821), Thomas De Quincey described his interactions with London prostitutes and said, 'not to remind my classical readers of the old Latin proverb—'*Sine Cerere*', &c., it may well be supposed that in the existing state of my purse, my connexion with such women could not have been an impure one'; *The Works of Thomas De Quincey*, gen. ed. Grevel Lindop, 21 vols. (Pickering and Chatto, 2000–3), vol. 2, pp. 24–5. Hippy goes on to say that he gives the suitors wine because Anthelia denies them love.

6 *Men die, and worms eat them,* **as usual,** *but not for love*: Rosalind in Shakespeare's *As You Like It* says 'men have died from time to time, and worms have eaten them, but not for love' (act 4, scene 1, lines 106–8).

7 **'Folly and mischief . . . are very nearly allied'**: An echo of John Dryden, *Absalom and Achitophel* (1681): 'Great wits are sure to madness near allied, / and thin partitions do their bounds divide', lines 162–3; see *The Works of John Dryden*, 20 vols., gen. eds. E. N. Hooker, H. T. Swedenberg, Jr and Alan Roper (Berkeley and Los Angeles: University of California Press, 1956–2000), vol. 2: *Poems 1681–1684*, ed. H. T. Swedenberg (1972), p. 10.

8 **Tasso**: The poetry of Torquato Tasso was very popular in the Romantic Period. Goethe's *Torquato Tasso* appeared in 1790, and Lord Byron's *The Lament of Tasso* was written and published in 1817.

9 **a mansion . . . harmonies**: In 'Tintern Abbey' Wordsworth imagines a time when his sister's 'mind / Shall be a mansion for all lovely forms', and her memory will 'be as a dwelling-place / For all sweet sounds and harmonies' (lines 140–3). Forester applies this sentiment to women's minds in general.

10 **If women are treated only as pretty dolls**: Scythrop in *NA* says that the 'artificial education' to which women are subjected 'studiously models them into mere musical dolls, to be set out

for sale in the great toy-shop of society' (ch. 1). Wollstonecraft wrote that women's 'rank in life' often 'necessarily degrades them by making them mere dolls'; *A Vindication of the Rights of Woman*, p. 331.

11 **intellectual beauty**: The phrase 'intellectual beauty' is commonly associated with Percy Shelley's 'Hymn to Intellectual Beauty', written in summer 1816 and published in *The Examiner* on 19 Jan. 1817 (41). 'Intellectual' in this context means incorporeal or ideal, and it is awareness of this kind of beauty that women were discouraged from cultivating. The phrase is used by Monboddo in *Origin and Progress of Language* in discussing Plato's philosophy of beauty (see *Origin*, 1.106), and Robert Forsyth employs it in his *Principles of Moral Science*, a book cited later in *Mel*, in ch. 21: some inquirers are 'continually discovering new and deep treasures of reason and of truth; and unknown regions of moral and intellectual beauty and excellence are continually rising to their view'; Forsyth, *The Principles of Moral Science*, 2 vols. (Edinburgh: Bell and Bradfute, 1805), vol. 1, pp. 513–14. The most notable application of this phrase to mental attainments in women occurs in Wollstonecraft's *Vindication of the Rights of Woman*: 'a German writer' (Kant) has said 'that a pretty woman, as an object of desire, is generally allowed to be so by men of all descriptions; whilst a fine woman, who inspires more sublime emotions by displaying intellectual beauty, may be overlooked or observed with indifference, by those men who find their happiness in the gratification of their appetites' (p. 97).

12 **the valleys and fountains of Ida, and by the banks of the edifying Scamander**: TLP's footnote directs the reader to Homer's *Iliad*, and Forester refers to Mount Ida in Asia Minor and to the plain of the Scamander River, where the Greeks and Trojans battled (on the Scamander, see *CC*, ch. 1). Forester's list of images that occur in certain Greek epics or tragedies is intriguing not only for the specific choices but also because TLP provides so many footnotes to identify his sources.

13 **the island of Calypso and the gardens of Alcinous**: In Homer's
Odyssey, to which TLP's footnote refers, Odysseus is imprisoned
by Calypso for seven years on Ogygia (see book 5); and he visits
Alcinous' gardens (see book 7, lines 112–32).

14 **the rocks of the Scythian desert**: The footnote refers to 'The
Prometheus of Æschylus'; in *Prometheus Bound* Prometheus is
chained to a rock in an uninhabited part of Scythia.

15 **the caverned shores of the solitary Lemnos**: TLP's footnote mentions Sophocles' *Philoctetes*, in which Odysseus and
Neoptolemus have travelled to the island of Lemnos.

16 **the fatal sands of Trœzene**: In Euripides' play *Hippolytus* (mentioned in TLP's footnote), Hippolytus, the son of Theseus and
Phaedra, is wounded fatally when a bull comes out of the sea and
startles his horses. TLP translated excerpts from various Greek
dramas in 1812 or 1813 (see *Letters*, 1.392), and in 1814 the
Morning Chronicle published his letter translating one passage
from *Hippolytus* and observing that it 'bears a striking resemblance to a part of Hamlet's soliloquy' (*Letters*, 1.107).

17 **Like the ... tribe**: Shakespeare's Othello refers to himself as 'one
whose hand / (Like the base [Indian]) threw a pearl away / Richer
than all his tribe' (act 5, scene 2, lines 346–8); Forester here uses
Shakespeare's Moor to exemplify patriarchal husbands. Forester
changes 'threw' to 'throw' in order to maintain present tense, but
TLP uses quotation marks as if the quotation were verbatim.
The 1813 Johnson-Steevens edition prints not the 1622 quarto's
'Indian' but the 'Judean' of the First Folio (19.518).

18 **a general election**: Sir Oran has been obliged to wait for a general election in order to gain the seat that Forester purchased for
him. Although the voting at Onevote (in ch. 22) is a crucial episode, the general election is never mentioned again, the narrative
ignoring the other contests that would be occurring at about the
same time.

19 **a good estate**: Cf. Desmond's earlier remarks about 'what the
world calls respectable people' (ch. 13), and Lady Clarinda's

observation in *CC* that 'Respectable means rich, and decent means poor' (ch. 3).

20 **remarkably ugly gentleman**: Mrs Pinmoney's description shows, again, that people cannot recognize Sir Oran as an ape unless they are enlightened by Forester. Her reference to Sir Oran's height confirms that TLP visualizes Sir Oran as looking like one of the African oran outangs Monboddo describes, and not like an actual gorilla or orangutan. In *AM* Monboddo, discussing human physical degeneration, points to the 'great oran outang' as revealing 'the size of Men in the perfect natural state' (3.135): the oran outang is 'betwixt eight and nine feet of height when he is come to maturity' (3.136).

21 **something very French in his physiognomy**: When Frenchman Louis Simond visited Britain in 1810–11, he observed that caricaturists depicted men of his nation 'as diminutive, starved beings, of monkey-mien, strutting about in huge hats, narrow coats, and great sabres'; see *Journal of a Tour and Residence in Great Britain, during the Years 1810 and 1811, by a French Traveller: with Remarks on the Country, its Arts, Literature, and Politics, and on the Manners and Customs of its Inhabitants*, 2 vols. (Edinburgh: Constable, 1815), vol. 1, p. 21. In *NA*, Scythrop says that 'A Frenchman is a monstrous compound of monkey, spaniel, and tiger' (ch. 11), and Scythrop elaborates on Voltaire's well-known saying that Frenchmen are 'half tiger and half monkey' (ch. 11, n. 18).

22 **Je l'ai vu . . . *Oran-Outang***: TLP quotes from Buffon's '*H. N. de l' Oran-Outang*', that is, from the section of *Histoire Naturelle* dealing with the oran outang (see *Buffon 1799*, 35.93). Buffon's 'J'ai vu cet animal présenter' becomes TLP's 'Je l'ai vu présenter.'

CHAPTER 16

1 **a heeltap**: On 'heeltap', see ch. 5, n. 1.

2 **Of mithridate...crystals**: TLP's footnote points the reader to the play *The Sea Voyage* (1622) by John Fletcher, and these lines

appear in act 5, scene 2. The edition TLP owned at his death – *The Works of Beaumont and Fletcher*, introd. and notes Henry Weber, 14 vols. (Edinburgh: F. C. and J. Rivington et al., 1812) (*Sale Catalogue* 53) – does not number lines, but those which appear in *Mel* are lines 27–34 in *The Dramatic Works in the Beaumont and Fletcher Canon*, gen. ed. Fredson Bowers, 10 vols. (Cambridge University Press, 1966–96), vol. 9, p. 70. TLP may have owned Weber's edition at the time he wrote *Mel*, given that, three years before it appeared, he asked Edward Thomas Hookham, 'Has Gifford undertaken to edit Beaumont and Fletcher? Or is any new edition of those dramatists in contemplation?' (10 Feb. 1809; *Letters*, 1.27). *1817* omits the phrase 'though cerus'd o'er' after 'cheek', omits the word 'too' after 'sparkles' and replaces 'That number' with 'Who number'. The line that in Weber's edition reads 'They are poor drunkards, and not worth thy favours' becomes 'Mistress of merry hearts, they are not worth thy favours' in *1817*. Weber argued that *The Sea Voyage* 'was the work of Fletcher solely' (7.[339]), but the current view is that '*The Sea Voyage* is the joint work of Fletcher and Massinger, and the basic nature of their collaboration is clear enough: Fletcher wrote Acts I and IV, Massinger wrote Acts II, III, and V' (Bowers, vol. 9, p. 5). Hippy's knowledge of early modern drama is impressive.

3   **prospicient**: This is the first occurrence of 'prospicient' noted in the *OED* that dates from after 1654. Earlier in *Mel*, TLP's 'prospiciencies' was that word's first appearance since 1681 recorded in the *OED*; see ch. 7, n. 14.

4   **says St. Augustine**: Quotation not traced to St Augustine, but in François Rabelais' *Gargantua and Pantagruel*, book 1, ch. 5, a character says that *The Soul never dwells in a dry place*; *The Works of Francis Rabelais, M.D. . . . Now carefully revis'd*, ed. John Ozell [revision of Urquhart-Motteux translation], 5 vols. (J. Brindley and C. Corbett, 1737), vol. 1, p. 151. See also François Rabelais, *Œuvres complètes*, ed. Mireille Huchon, with François Moreau, Bibliothèque de la Pléiade, new ed. (Paris: Gallimard, 1994), p. 18.

5 **hepatic, phlogistic, and exanthematous**: 'Hepatic' means 'of or pertaining to the liver' (*OED* 1) or good for the liver (*OED* 3). 'Phlogistic' probably means 'inflammatory' in this context. 'Exanthematous', according to Johnson's *Dictionary* (1755), means 'pustulous; efflorescent; eruptive'; Johnson is the earliest example noted in the *OED*.

6 **archiepiscopal**: 'Of, pertaining to, or of the nature of, an archbishop' (*OED*).

7 **Bacchus is said to have conquered the East**: In *Gargantua and Pantagruel*, book 1, ch. 5, which Portpipe may have just echoed (see n. 4), a character refers to Bacchus conquering India (Rabelais, *Œuvres complètes*, p. 19).

8 **'Marry how? tropically'**: When Claudius asks the name of the play that the court is watching, Hamlet replies '"The Mousetrap." Marry, how? tropically' (act 3, scene 2, lines 237–8).

9 **sublimated**: 'To act on (a substance) so as to produce a refined product' (*OED* 'sublimate', 2.b.; earliest example 1601).

10 **You were not always so fond of wine**: Part of the poet laureate's salary was an annual cask of wine (see ch. 1, n. 10). By asking this question, Lord Anophel draws attention to Feathernest's 'youthful errors', just as Forester does.

11 **Demosthenes . . . expense of others**: Not traced.

12 **a devilled biscuit or an anchovy toast**: 'devilled': 'Of food, esp. meat or nuts: prepared with spicy seasonings or condiments such as pepper, paprika, or mustard, and (often) grilled or fried' (*OED* 2). The earliest occurrence in the *OED*, from *The Morning Post* in 1796, refers to a 'deviled biscuit'. 'Anchovy toast' is simply 'toast, or a slice of toast, spread with anchovy paste, typically eaten as an appetizer' (*OED*, first occurrence 1769).

13 **Odes to Truth and Liberty**: See ch. 8, n. 8.

14 **'Ah, no more of that, an thou lovest me'**: Falstaff says 'Ah, no more of that, Hal, and thou lovest me!' (*1 Henry IV*, act 2, scene 4, line 283). While *The Riverside Shakespeare* has 'and', Johnson-Steevens has 'an' (11.293).

15 **pipe of wine**: Although Feathernest does not appear to be literally poet laureate of the United Kingdom, as Southey was, here he is using the laureate's traditional compensation to represent the rewards he receives. On 'pipe' as a unit of measure, see ch. 1, n. 10.

16 **dithyrambics**: A genre of Greek poetry paying tribute to Dionysus, who is, appropriately in the case of a poet laureate, the god of wine.

17 **'to all the crowned heads in Europe'**: See ch. 8, n. 9.

18 **all is right, especially at court**: See ch. 8, n. 10.

19 **Then I saw darkly through a glass—of water**: St Paul writes, 'When I was a child, I spake as a child, I understood as a child, I thought as a child: but when I became a man, I put away childish things'; similarly, 'now we see through a glass, darkly' but we will see 'face to face' (1 Corinthians, ch. 13, vv. 11–12).

20 **apostacy**: The first occurrence of this term in *Mel*; it is surprising it took so long to make its appearance, given how frequently 'apostate' was applied to Southey and some of his allies. See e.g. 'Literary Notices. No. 19. Illustrations of the Times Newspaper. On Modern Apostates', *The Examiner* (15 Dec. 1816), 785–7, which discusses Southey and Coleridge. Later in *Mel*, Forester notes that some have called Edmund Burke 'a pensioned apostate'. In *Sir Proteus*, TLP notes 'the selfish and mercenary apostacy' evident when 'The antique enemies of "the monster Pitt" are now the panegyrists of the immaculate Castlereagh' (Halliford, 6.289 n.).

21 **_The gradual falling off . . . reprobation_**: As TLP's footnote explains, this is a quotation from the *Edinburgh Review*, vol. 27, no. 53, 10 (from an article on Walter Scott's edition of Swift). This number of the *Edinburgh Review* was dated Sept. 1816, but it was not published until 12 Nov.; see Joukovsky, 'Composition', 22, noting an advertisement in the *Morning Chronicle*. Joukovsky notes that Fax's quotation of the *Edinburgh Review* 'may or may not have been a late addition'.

22 **in good odour at court**: Feathernest says he is 'in good odour at Court', an echo of Fax's observation that an unnamed divine (Paley) was '*en bonne odeur*' by the time of his death (ch. 14, nn. 1–2).

23 **Non cuivis homini contingit adire Corinthum**: 'It is not every man's lot to reach Corinth' (Horace, *Epistles,* book 1, epistle 17, line 36). In Horace's poem, arriving in Corinth is metonymy for winning the praise of prominent men; Horace, if not Feathernest, assumes these prominent men are good judges of virtue.

24 **two or three others got in at the same time**: Presumably one of these two or three men is Mr Paperstamp (see ch. 28). Wordsworth became Distributor of Stamps for Westmorland in 1813.

25 ***If you could live on roots . . . nothing to do with roots***: Diogenes Laertius, *Lives of the Eminent Philosophers,* 2.68. The story is repeated by Horace, *Epistles,* 1.17.13–15.

26 **stave**: As in ch. 6 (see n. 30), the meaning is 'A "verse" or stanza of a poem, song, etc' (*OED* 'stave', III.5.a). The stave Derrydown quotes originates in [Isaac Bickerstaff{e}], *Love in a Village: A Comic Opera. As It is Performed at the Theatre Royal in Covent Garden* (Dublin: W. Smith, 1763), act 3, scene 1, air 32. David Garnett claims (*Novels,* 1.195) that Bickerstaffe's 'lines clearly inspired' the epigram that Byron included in a letter to Thomas Moore on 22 June 1821: 'The world is a bundle of hay, / Mankind are the asses who pull, / Each tugs it a different way,— / And the greatest of all is John Bull!'; *Byron's Letters and Journals,* ed. Leslie A. Marchand, 13 vols. (Cambridge: Harvard University Press, 1973–94), vol. 8, p. 141.

27 **Buz the bottle**: *OED* 'buz', v.[II] 'To finish to the last drop in the bottle.' The only example preceding *Mel* in the *OED* comes from Grose, who adds in his 1785 *Classical Dictionary of the Vulgar Tongue* that this command 'is commonly said to one who hesitates to empty a bottle that is nearly out'. This definition does not appear in *Lexicon Balatronicum,* the 1811 revision of Grose.

28 *afford to have a conscience*: Echoing William Paley (see ch. 14, n. 2).

29 **'give God thanks, and make no boast of it'**: Dogberry in *Much Ado about Nothing* (act 3, scene 3, lines 19–20).

30 *cæteris paribus*: 'Other things being equal, other conditions corresponding' (*OED*; Latin).

31 **chapmen**: in this context, pedlars.

32 *as notorious, Sir, as the sun at noon-day*: See ch. 6, n. 37. Although elsewhere in *Mel* this simile is applied to political corruption, such as the sale of seats in the Commons or the sale of one's vote in parliament, here Feathernest applies it to the proposition 'that theory and practice are never expected to coincide'.

33 **the Algerines**: In Aug. 1816 a British fleet led by Lord Exmouth defeated the Algerine pirates in a single day.

34 **'What makes . . . more'**: Samuel Butler, *Hudibras*, part 3, canto 1, lines 1277–80: '*What makes all Doctrines plain and clear? /* About two hundred Pounds a Year. / *And that which was prov'd true before, / Prove false again?*—Two hundred more'.

35 **a glee**: 'A musical composition, of English origin, for three or more voices (one voice to each part), set to words of any character, grave or gay, often consisting of two or more contrasted movements, and (in strict use) without accompaniment' (*OED* 2.c.).

36 **'O list!'**: Quoting the Ghost in *Hamlet*, act 1, scene 5, line 22.

37 **Man under the influence . . . deteriorated in strength**: See ch. 4, n. 8.

38 *that man has fallen never to rise again*: TLP's footnote directs us to 'the preface to the third volume of the Ancient Metaphysics', where Monboddo explains that volume 3 is meant to show how 'History and Philosophy', not only religion, demonstrate 'THAT Man is fallen, and is not to rise again in this life'. Monboddo adds that he feels 'singular pleasure, to find that my Philosophy agrees so perfectly with Christianity' (*AM*, 3.[i]). Monboddo's 'Christianity' becomes Forester's 'superstition'. TLP's footnote also directs us to 'Rousseau's Discourse on Inequality, and that

on the Arts and Sciences'; he quoted from *Discours sur l'Inégalité* earlier; see ch. 6, nn. 43, 51, and 54; ch. 10, n. 6.

39 **the foliage of the Pierian laurel**: The Pierian shade is the grove of the Muses.

40 **chaplet**: 'A wreath for the head, usually a garland of flowers or leaves, also of gold, precious stones, etc.; a circlet, coronal' (*OED* 1.a).

41 **'If you see no glimpse of coin . . . a barber or an auctioneer'**: A loose translation of Juvenal, *Satires*, 7.8–10: 'nam si Pieria quadrans tibi nullus in umbra / ostendatur, ames nomen victumque Machaerae / et vendas potius commissa quod auctio vendit / stantibus, oenophorum tripedes armaria cistas' (lines 8–11). Forester earlier in the chapter said that he had been (figuratively) up for sale at an auction.

42 **in the suds**: A pun: 'in the suds' can mean both being 'In difficulties, in embarrassment or perplexity' (*OED* 'suds', 5.a.) and 'Being lathered', as if by a barber (5.e.).

43 **'most sweet voices'**: *Coriolanus*, act 2, scene 3, line 112.

CHAPTER 17

1 **The Flower of Love**: Set to music and published as *The Flower of Love, a Song, from Melincourt, The Music Composed by G. Kiallmark* (C. Chappell and Co. [1817]).

2 **Ballad Terzetto**: A 'terzetto' is 'A (small) trio, esp. vocal' (*OED*). The word occurs in *HH*, ch. 13.

3 *Nil desperandum*: 'As an exhortation: "do not despair!", "never despair!"' (*OED*, Latin).

4 **edition of Tasso, printed by Bodoni at Parma**: Bodoni published editions of the *Aminta* (1789) and *La Gerusalemme Liberata* (1794). At his death TLP owned a Bodoni edition of Virgil's works (*Sale Catalogue* 741).

5 **Chapman's Homer . . . Taylor's Holy Living**: Translations of *The Iliad* and *The Odyssey* by George Chapman were published

between 1598 and 1615. They were later eclipsed by the Homer translations of Alexander Pope. Keats's famous sonnet 'On First Looking into Chapman's Homer' appeared in *The Examiner* on 1 Dec. 1816, when TLP was writing *Mel*. The religious writings of the Anglican cleric Jeremy Taylor, whose *Holy Living* appeared in 1650, were admired by Coleridge and Charles Lamb. In *Cal* the vicar is 'Jeremitaylorically pathetic' (Halliford, 8.315), and in *NA*, ch. 8, Flosky speaks in 'a tone of ruefulness most jeremitaylorically pathetic'. In 'The Four Ages of Poetry' TLP wrote that Coleridge combined 'the quadruple elements of sexton, old woman, Jeremy Taylor, and Emanuel Kant' (*NA*, p. 152).

6 **duplex**: This is the first occurrence recorded in the *OED* of 'duplex', here an adjective meaning 'Composed of two parts or elements; twofold'. The *OED* does not record the word's use as a noun before 1922.

7 **Dennis and Colley Cibber**: John Dennis, literary critic and enemy of Pope, and Colley Cibber. Although both men wrote in several genres, and Cibber was a famous actor and theatre manager, they appear here as a representative bad critic and a representative bad writer. Cibber was one of Southey's predecessors as poet laureate, serving from 1730 to 1757.

8 *genus irritabile*: 'the irritable or over-sensitive race or class (of poets)' (*OED*, citing Horace, *Epistles*, book 2, epistle 2, line 102).

9 **'To prove his . . .knocks'**: Butler's *Hudibras*, part 1 (1663), canto 1, from the introductory description of Sir Hudibras, one of those 'Errant Saints', who 'build their Faith upon / The holy Text of *Pike* and *Gun*', 'prove their Doctrine Orthodox / By Apostolick *Blows* and *Knocks*' (lines 193, 195–6, 199–200). TLP applies Butler's description of sectarians to an Anglican clergyman. Part of this section of *Hudibras* is echoed in ch. 28 (see n. 17).

10 **are all the articles . . . Legitimate Review**: In *NA*, ch. 5, Flosky reads a number of *The Downing-Street Review* in which the first article concerns 'An Ode to the Red Book, by Roderick Sackbut, Esquire'; Sackbut's 'own poem [is] reviewed by himself'.

11 **the 'Tickle me Mr. Hayley' principle**: In his 'Essay on Fashionable Literature', TLP wrote that in the monthly periodicals, 'the mutual flattery of "learned correspondents" to their own "inestimable miscellany" carries the "Tickle me Mr Hayley" principle to a surprising extent' (*NA*, p. 115). The allusion is to the poem 'On the Reciprocal Blandishments of Mr. Hayley and Miss Seward', satirizing Anna Seward and William Hayley, a poem first published in *The World* in Feb. 1790:

> 'TICKLE *me*', says Mr. HAYLEY,
> 'TICKLE *me*, Miss SEWARD, do!—
> 'Depend upon't, then I'll not fail ye,
> 'But, in my turn, will *tickle* you'.
>
> To it then they fall a *tickling*—
> SHE. 'Sir, your Poems are divine!'
> HE. 'MA'AM, I'll aver it, without stickling,
> 'YOU, alone, are all the NINE!'

The Poetry of the World. Vol. III (James Ridgway, 1791), p. 41.

12 **bankrupt gazettes**: English bankruptcies were announced in the *London Gazette*. In *CC*, 'The great firm of Catchflat and Company figured in the Gazette, and paid sixpence in the pound' (Conclusion).

13 **gang**: 'A set of tools, instruments, or devices arranged to work in unison or coordination' (*OED* 7.b.) or 'A company of workers' (9.a.).

14 **outrageous**: 'Excessive or unrestrained in action; violent, furious' (*OED* 2.a.).

15 **'Oh that mine enemy had written a book!'**: 'Oh that one would hear me! behold, my desire is, that the Almighty would answer me, and that mine adversary had written a book' (Job, ch. 31, v. 35).

16 **ebullitions**: 'A sudden outburst or boiling or bubbling over' (*OED* 'ebullition', 4). The word is repeated two chapters later.

CHAPTER 18

1 **Mrs. Pinmoney's request to Anthelia**: See ch. 17 for Mrs Pinmoney's request that Anthelia join them in the excursion to Novote.

2 **the ninth chapter**: This reference, in volume two of *1817*, refers back to the first volume, 1.121–37 (G1r–G9r); specifically, to 1.121–2.

3 *coup-de-main*: 'a sudden and vigorous attack, for the purpose of instantaneously capturing a position' (*OED* 'coup', *n.³* 5.f.).

4 **confidential**: 'Enjoying the confidence of another person; entrusted with secrets; charged with secret service' (*OED* 'confidential', 4).

5 **adoperation**: 'The application or employment of something; an instance of this' (*OED*); both obsolete and rare. Used by Bacon in 1608 and TLP in 1817.

6 *pedetentim*: Step-by-step, cautiously (Latin).

7 *peirastically*: 'By experiment, tentatively' (*OED*). The word's appearance in *Mel* is the earliest noted in the *OED*, although the adjective 'peirastic' dates back to 1656. 'Peirastically' also occurs in *CC*, ch. 7.

8 [Footnote:] **'They use . . . chap. 4.'**: Cf. *Origin*, 1.290. TLP begins quoting in the middle of Monboddo's sentence, and therefore inserts 'they' in front of 'use'. There are no other modifications in substantives.

9 **natural justice**: A term that is again applied to Sir Oran's actions in chs. 38 and 42.

10 *quantum sufficit*: A sufficient quantity. The Latin phrase was commonly abbreviated 'q. s.'.

11 [Footnote:] **'There is a story…'**: Cf. *Origin*, 1.287–8. Monboddo writes not 'There is a story' but 'And he tells a story' (with 'he' being one of the author's informants). TLP also changes Monboddo's 'Chimpenza' to 'oran'.

12 **post-boys**: See ch. 2, n. 12. In ch. 2, the word is printed 'postboys'.

13 **Sir:** The word 'Sir' is missing from the first edition, with a space where it should be, at the end of the last line on the page (*1817*, 2.62).

CHAPTER 19

1 *pas de deux*: In ballet, a dance for only two dancers (French).

2 *La Belle Laitière*: A well-known ballet, with music by Daniel Steibelt, that premiered at the King's Theatre, Haymarket, in 1805.

3 **Mr. Forester produced the Abbot's skull:** TLP's footnote directs the reader to ch. 4, in the first volume, specifically *1817*, 1.38–50 (that is, C7v–D1v). The precise passage to which TLP alludes can be found in *1817*, 1.43 (C10r).

4 **Homer:** TLP's footnote quotes at length from *AM*, 3.146, which deals with the evidence provided by *The Iliad*. Monboddo's footnotes alert his reader that the 'Prospect from the Walls' (*AM*, 3.146) is found at *Iliad*, book 3, line 121, and that the passage cited from Lucius Flavius Philostratus can be found in the *Heroicus* 'Prooem. Cap. i. N. 2.'. For clarity, TLP modifies Monboddo's initial 'He has said' to 'Homer has said', but makes no other changes in substantives.

5 **Herodotus:** TLP's long footnote quotes *AM*, 3.146–8 (though he cites only 3.146), and *AM*, 3.150–1 (he cites 3.150). In the first quotation, TLP italicizes all words from 'believing that' to 'the present'. Monboddo attributes the story 'pleasantly told by Herodotus' to book 1, chs. 67–8 of that author (*AM*, 3.148n). The passage TLP quotes from *AM*, 3.146–8 (beginning 'It was only') follows immediately upon Monboddo's discussion of *The Iliad* that TLP had quoted in the preceding footnote. In the passage that TLP quotes from *AM*, 3.150–1, Monboddo includes a footnote (150n) at the word 'prodigiously' which cites Lucian's *De Saltatione*, and TLP's parenthesis ('and I . . . whole people', II, 70–1n) is adapted from this same Monboddo footnote.

6 **Arrian**: Monboddo relies on Arrian of Nicomedia's *Expedition of Alexander*, Book V, for the information that 'The stature of the people in [India], at the time of Alexander the Great, was five cubits, that is, seven feet and a half' (*AM*, 3.145).

7 **Plutarch**: According to Monboddo, 'Plutarch, in the beginning of his life of Theseus, relates it as a fact most certain, that there were in those days men of extraordinary prowess, and of wonderful strength of body and swiftness of foot' (*AM*, 3.149–50).

8 **Philostratus, Pausanias**: Lucius Flavius Philostratus' *Heroicus* is cited in Monboddo's discussion of Homer, *AM*, 3.146, quoted by TLP (see ch. 19, n. 4, above). In *AM* (3.148), immediately after the discussion of Orestes' bones that TLP quoted, Monboddo compares the accounts of Ajax's body provided by Philostratus and Pausanias (second century AD).

9 **Solinus Polyhistor**: Monboddo writes that the physical diminution of the later Romans 'was observed by one of their learned men, Solinus Polyhistor, who speaks of it as a thing quite certain' (*AM*, 3.156). Solinus (third century AD) wrote the work usually known as *Polyhistor*. This passage occurs in *AM* immediately before that which TLP quotes in the next footnote (*1817*, 2.71–3).

10 **ten inches in length**: TLP's footnote quotes *AM*, 3.156 (actually, 3.156–7), which is reproduced on pp. 2.71–3n, and then quotes *AM*, 3.161 (actually, 3.161–2), reproduced on 2.73–4n. The first part of the quotation from *AM*, 3.156–7 is transferred faithfully to *1817* (2.71–2n), with no differences in substantives, except that Monboddo's 'had in those days, could have' becomes 'had, could have'; Monboddo's 'set upon end' becomes 'set up on end'; Monboddo's 'upon the top' becomes 'on the top'; and Monboddo's 'the passage which is quoted at the bottom of the page' becomes TLP's 'the following passage'. One curiosity of the form that Monboddo's quotation from 'Elyote' takes in *1817* (2.72–3n) is that TLP's printer modernized some of the archaic English: Monboddo's 'myselfe' becomes 'myself', 'Monasterye'

becomes 'monastery', 'Chanons' becomes 'canons', 'greatte' becomes 'great', 'bycause' becomes 'because', 'somme' becomes 'some' and so on. In the quotation from *AM*, 3.161–2 that appears on *1817*, 2.73–4n, Monboddo's 'nations civilized and barbarous, can' is simplified to 'nations can'. After 'the greater part worse', TLP quotes *Odyssey*, book 2, line 227, then adds, 'And this he puts into the mouth of the Goddess of Wisdom'; after a double ellipsis, TLP resumes quoting Monboddo ('But when I speak'). At 'worse', Monboddo has a footnote which quotes that line from Homer, with the comment, 'This he puts into the mouth of the Goddess of Wisdom.' The main text goes on to refer to Horace *Odes* 1.15 (that passage whose omission was marked by TLP's ellipsis), and then proceeds: 'But, when I speak'. That is, TLP shifts Monboddo's footnote (*AM*, 3.161, n. '‡') into Monboddo's text (*1817*, 2.74n); otherwise, he would have a footnote within a footnote. TLP omits some of Monboddo's other notes: at 'Domestic Gods', Monboddo cites Passerius, *De Laribus*; quoting Hesiod, he cites 'Operae et Dies, V. 123' (*AM*, 3.161).

11 **Sir Telegraph Paxarett . . . left at Melincourt**: Sir Telegraph's barouche accommodates twelve people. While the three women and the older man sit inside, the outside passengers include the younger gentlemen and an oran outang (among this group, two baronets), as well as four servants (two Sir Telegraph's, one Mr Hippy's, one Anthelia's). Mrs and Miss Pinmoney make do without servants. Sir Oran sits beside the driver, Sir Telegraph. Because Sir Telegraph's two grooms have squeezed out his coachman, no one but Sir Telegraph is available to drive.

12 **Pindar**: The conclusion of the sentence (and later references) make clear that Pindar is Sir Telegraph's choice because several of his odes celebrate chariot races.

13 **tethrippharmatelasipedioploctypophilous**: This word 'is Peacock's own coinage, meaning "driving a chariot of four horses with hoofs striking the ground", an explanation which he leaves

his readers to work out for themselves from their knowledge of Greek' (Madden, *Thomas Love Peacock*, p. 99). Cf. 'philotheoparoptesism' in *MM*, ch. 5, which, according to TLP's footnote, means 'Roasting by a slow fire for the love of God'.

14 **almost at the extremity of the kingdom**: Most of *Mel*'s original readers probably thought specifically of the borough of Old Sarum, which lay in Wiltshire, 'at the extremity of the kingdom' for a person who travelled there from Cumberland.

15 **'the poet's page…the rest'**: William Cowper's *The Task* (first published 1785), book 4, 'The Winter Evening'. 'The poet's or historian's page, by one / Made vocal for th' amusement of the rest' is one of the things that 'Beguile the night, and set a keener edge / On female industry', so that 'the threaded steel / Flies swiftly, and unfelt the task proceeds' (lines 158–9, 164–6); see *The Poems of William Cowper*, ed. John D. Baird and Charles Ryskamp (Oxford: Clarendon Press, 1995), vol. 2, p. 191.

16 **a little excursion on the lake**: Ackermann's *Picturesque Tour of the English Lakes* noted that 'At a short distance from [the Lowwood] inn, there is a commodious pier for embarking on a voyage down the lake; and a cannon is kept at the place to gratify visitors with the surprising reverberations of sound which follow its discharge in these romantic vales' (p. 70).

17 **TERZETTO**: See ch. 17, n. 2.

18 **a six-bottle cooper**: 'A six- (or twelve-) bottle basket, used in wine-cellars' (*OED* 'cooper', 3). This is the first occurrence of the word with this sense that is noted in the *OED*.

19 **our Thalia**: Thalia is the muse of comedy; the epigraph on the half-titles of each volume announce that *Mel* is comedy, albeit comedy that sometimes sounds like tragedy.

20 **veridicous**: From the Latin *veridicus*, 'truthful'. TLP is the only user of 'veridicous' recognized in the *OED* (the word appears again in *CC*, ch. 17). The standard English term is 'veridical'.

21 **The heroes and heroines of Homer used to eat and drink all day till the setting sun**: TLP's footnote quotes Homer, *Odyssey*,

book 9, lines 161–2, where Odysseus says that he and his men sat feasting on plentiful meat and sweet wine until sunset.

22 **necessitated, like Penelope, to sit up all night**: In Homer's *Odyssey*, Penelope weaves a shroud for Laertes during the day, but unravels her weaving each night. See book 2, lines 103–5; book 19, lines 148–55; book 24, lines 138–40.

CHAPTER 20

1 **like a Nereid to Triton's shell**: Like a sea nymph listening to the sound of the shell-trumpet of Triton.

2 **'when nature's self is new'**: Not traced.

3 **Tempe**: As Lemprière's *Classical Dictionary* explains, Tempe, 'a valley in Thessaly', has been described by poets 'as the most delightful spot on the earth, with continually cool shades, and verdant walks, which the warbling of birds rendered more pleasant and romantic, and which the Gods often honored with their presence'.

4 **Pensa che questo di mai non raggiorna!**: Virgil's admonition to Dante as they are in purgatory: 'Remember that this day will never return' (*Purgatorio* 12.84). At his death TLP owned *Divina Commedia, col comento del P. Venturi*, 4 vols. (Lucca, 1811) (*Sale Catalogue* 146).

5 **Achilles and Thetis**: See *Iliad*, book 1, lines 357–430.

6 **the ambassadors of Agamemnon**: In *Iliad*, book 9, Agamemnon sends Phoenix, Ajax and Odysseus to plead with Achilles to rejoin the main Greek force (they are unsuccessful).

7 **Comparatio non urgenda, as I think Heyne used to say**: 'The comparison should not be pressed.' TLP, when he died, owned several texts edited by Christian Gottlieb Heyne: *P. Virgilii Maronis Opera, varietate lectionis et perpetua adnotatione illustrata a C. G. Heyne*, 4 vols. (T. Payne, 1793) (*Sale Catalogue* 614); *Homeri Ilias, cum brevi annotatione curante C. G. Heyne*, 2 vols. (Leipzig: Weidmann, 1804) (*Sale Catalogue* 236); *Homeri Ilias*,

cum brevi annotatione C. G. Heyne, 4 vols. (J. B. Whittaker and G. Cowie, 1817) (*Sale Catalogue* 237). See also *CC*, pp. 212–13. In *GG*, ch. 28, TLP quotes Heyne on Homer. Again, it is remarkable how much classical learning Sir Telegraph acquired.

8 **if you call me Achilles, solacing my mind with music,** φρενα τερπομενον φορμιγγι λιγειη: *Iliad*, book 9, line 186.

9 **Pindar himself:** In ch. 19 the narrator said that Sir Telegraph never looks at his Pindar.

CHAPTER 21

1 **large and populous city . . . the ancient and honourable borough of Onevote:** On the connotations of Novote, Onevote and their proximity, see Introduction.

2 **virtually supplied:** The narrator alludes to 'virtual representation'. This phrase, which dated back to debates over parliamentary representation in the 1760s, meant 'political representation of a group or constituency who have not voted, or are not permitted to vote, for those who represent them; the (theoretical) political representation of people who are disenfranchised' (*OED*). In 'On the Game Laws', written between Mar. 1816 and Feb. 1818 (*PBS Prose*, 487), Percy Shelley wrote: 'It is said that the House of Commons tho' not an actual, is a virtual representation of the people', but 'such cannot be the case' because members of the Commons 'virtually represent none but the powerful and the rich' (p. 280). See TLP's contrast between the past and present in *ME*, ch. 6: in the sixth century, 'The blessings of virtual representation were not even dreamed of'.

3 **burgess:** An inhabitant of a borough, or, more specifically, a man entitled to vote in a parliamentary burgage borough. In England there were 30 such boroughs, where the right of voting was attached to the tenancy of a house or property designated as a 'burgage' for parliamentary elections (Thorne, *History of Parliament*, vol. 2, p. 37).

4 **the learned author of *Hermes* calls *a method of supply by negation***: In *Hermes, or, A Philosophical Inquiry Concerning Universal
Grammar* (1751), James Harris observed that Greek has no
equivalent to the English indefinite article 'a', so Greek speakers and writers 'supply its place' by omitting the definite article
(p. 217). J. H., *Hermes: or, A Philosophical Inquiry Concerning
Language and Universal Grammar* (J. Nourse and P. Vaillant,
1751). At his death, TLP owned a 1794 edition of *Hermes* (*Sale
Catalogue* 222).

5 **signalized**: 'To point out, note or mention specially, draw attention to. Now *rare*' (*OED* 'signalize', 3).

6 ***See the conquering hero comes!***: Sir Oran probably heard this
famous chorus of Handel's while in London with Forester (as
related in ch. 6).

7 **huzzaing**: The *OED* defines the noun 'huzza' as 'A shout of
exultation, encouragement, or applause; a cheer uttered by a
number in unison; a hurrah'. The earliest example noted dates
from 1682, with the first instance of 'huzza' (as a verb meaning
'To shout huzza') dating from 1683.

8 **the admirable doctrine . . . fifty thousand**: See ch. 21, n. 2, for
'virtual representation'.

9 **They**: The apparent antecedent of 'they' is 'inhabitants', although
TLP obviously means to refer to the newly arrived Forester and
company. The *Monthly Review* found a similar ambiguity at the
opening of ch. 40 (see ch. 40, n. 1).

10 ***corps d'hôtel***: A 'corps' here is 'A body or company of persons
associated in a common organization, or acting under a common
direction' (*OED* 3.a.), and TLP's French phrase is created by
analogy with terms like *corps de ballet*.

11 **landlady in the van, and Boots in the rear**: The phrase 'the van'
means 'the vanguard'. The 'van' is 'The foremost portion of, or
the foremost position in, a company or train of persons moving,
or prepared to move, forwards or onwards' (*OED* 2.a.), and the
term was also '*fig*., esp. in the phrases ***to lead (bear, have) the van***,

and *in the van'* (2.b.). See *CC*, chs. 1 and 18. Byron was fond of the term: in *Don Juan*, General Suwarrow (Suvorov) 'was come to lead the van' (canto 7, st. 7, line 8); the Tartar Khan 'fought with his five children in the van' (canto 8, st. 105, line 8); no one 'could lead the van' like Tom (canto 11, st. 19, line 3); Juan does not dance 'like a ballet-master in the van / Of his drill'd nymphs' (canto 14, st. 38, lines 7–8); and Lord Henry is suited 'to lead the courtly van' (canto 14, st. 70, line 5).

12 **to *peel***: 'To take off one's outer garments; to undress, strip (originally in preparation for a fight)' (*OED*). The earliest appearance to which the *OED* points is Grose's *Classical Dictionary of the Vulgar Tongue* (1785), which defines 'to peel' as 'to strip, allusion to the taking off the coat or rind of an orange or apple'. This definition also appears in the 1811 revision of Grose, *Lexicon Balatronicum*.

13 **four *benjamins***: Sir Telegraph wears four coats designed for driving. The *OED* defines 'benjamin' simply as 'An overcoat of a particular shape formerly worn by men', and cites as the earliest instance a passage in the *Sporting Magazine* in 1810. *NA* has 'upper benjamin' (ch. 13). The word does not appear in the 1785 edition of Grose, but is there in the 1811 revision (*Lexicon Balatronicum*).

14 **A man who 'will go through fire and water to serve a friend'**: *Stevenson's Book of Proverbs* notes examples dating back to the sixteenth century.

15 **Sir Oliver Oilcake**: 'Oilcake' is 'The mass of fibrous vegetable matter left after seeds such as rapeseed, linseed, or cotton-seed have been pressed for their oil'; oilcake is 'used as fodder for livestock and as manure' (*OED*).

16 **notorious as the sun at noon-day**: See ch. 6, n. 37.

17 **restoring the Great Lama . . . Mahomet's mother**: Sarcastic's and TLP's jibe at the British role in restoring Continental monarchies. Cobbett complained that 'the Bourbons and the Inquisition and the Pope and the Jesuits have been restored . . .

the Republics of Europe have been destroyed, and . . . a holy alliance has been solemnly concluded between all the principal sovereigns' (*WPR*, 8 Feb. 1817, p. 162). Sarcastic replaces French Catholicism, Prussian Protestantism and Russian Orthodoxy with Tibetan Buddhism and Islam; the point is that the parliament representing freedom-loving Britons could support even 'Oriental despotism'.

18 **shiploads of turtle**: turtle here is 'The flesh of various species of turtle used as food; also short for *turtle-soup*' (*OED*). Turtle is 'Often mentioned or alluded to as a feature of civic banquets'.

19 **swinish multitude**: Like the statement that 'the age of chivalry is gone' (ch. 2), this phrase was made famous or notorious by Burke's *Reflections on the Revolution in France*, in which he predicted that 'Along with its natural protectors and guardians, learning will be cast into the mire, and trodden down under the hoofs of a swinish multitude'; *The Writings and Speeches of Edmund Burke*, vol. 8, p. 130. See Introduction. Burke's phrase had not been forgotten when *Mel* was composed: Cobbett, for example, wrote that 'There may be, as there have been, men to call us the "*Swinish Multitude*"' (*WPR*, 1 Feb. 1817, p. 150). The phrase recurs twice in the third volume of *Mel* (chs. 31, 39), and, in *Cal*, written shortly afterwards, King Arthur learns (evidently in the 1790s) 'that all Europe was in an uproar; that the swinish multitude had broken loose, and was playing at cup and ball with sceptres and crown' (Halliford, 8.334). The phrase appears three times in *MM* (twice in ch. 9, once in ch. 11).

20 **draff and husks**: The Prodigal Son in the parable Jesus relates was so hungry that he would eat the husks given to the pigs he tended (Luke, ch. 15, v. 16); 'draff' is pigs' swill. In *1 Henry IV*, Falstaff compares his soldiers to 'prodigals lately come from swine-keeping, from eating draff and husks' (act 4, scene 2, lines 34–5).

21 *laying herself out* **for** *a good match*: According to the *OED*, 'to lay out' can mean 'To exert oneself *in*, *upon* (*obs.*); to take measures,

435

frame one's conduct with a view to effecting a purpose or gaining an object' (*OED*, 'to lay out', 5). The earliest instance cited is from 1659. TLP repeatedly refers to women's pursuit of a *'good match'* (chs. 39, 42), always italicized to indicate that the phrase is a sentimental euphemism for marrying a rich, well-situated man. 'Laying herself out' is italicized as if this, too, is a phrase Miss Pennylove would use.

22 **Christie**: The famous auction house of James Christie and his son, also James Christie, in Pall Mall in London. In *HH*, Miss Philomela Poppyseed's novels teach young women 'to consider themselves as a sort of commodity, to be put up at public auction, and knocked down to the highest bidder' (ch. 6); see *Mel*, ch. 2, n. 6. In ch. 16, Forester describes himself and his poetic skills having been sold at auction.

23 **the Reverend Doctor Vorax**: The Latin adjective 'vorax', meaning consuming or eating greedily, is the root of the English 'voracious'; Vorax is another of TLP's gluttonous clergy, a man who would rate other clerics on the quality of their wine and their food.

24 **Intrusted under solemn vows...to disperse**: TLP's footnote identifies the source as Butler's *Hudibras*, part 3 (published 1678), canto 2, where the poet sarcastically advises his auditor to 'Intrust it under solemn Vows / Of *Mum*, and *Silence*, and the *Rose*, / To be retail'd again in Whispers, / For th' easy Credulous to disperse' (lines 1493–6).

25 **free, fat, and dependent**: A parody of the conventional way of referring to a member of parliament as 'free and independent'. See also ch. 22, n. 26.

26 **'plural unit'**: Mr Sarcastic, like Sir Telegraph in ch. 6, alludes to George Colman the Younger's 'An Ode to We', which begins, 'Hail, Plural Unit'. See ch. 6, n. 36; ch. 22, n. 38.

27 **Verba animi proferre, et vitam impendere vero**: TLP does not provide a footnote to identify the source, which is Juvenal. One of the Emperor Domitian's advisors, Crispus, was not

willing 'libera . . . verba animi proferre et vitam impendere vero' (Juvenal, *Satires*, 4.90–1), 'to speak freely the thoughts of his heart, and stake his life upon the truth'. Forester might as well have quoted Godwin, who wrote in *Political Justice* that 'If there be any meaning in courage, its first ingredient must be the daring to speak the truth at all times, to all persons, and in every possible situation' (vol. 1, p. 96; see also vol. 2, pp. 494–5, 648). In *HH* Escot says, 'I make a point of speaking the truth on all occasions; and it seldom happens that the truth can be spoken, without some stricken deer pronouncing it a libel' (ch. 5).

28 **the *passion for reforming the world***: As TLP's footnote observes, the allusion is to Forsyth's *The Principles of Moral Science*; see ch. 16, 'Of the Passion for Reforming the World' (pp. 283–93). In *NA*, ch. 2, Scythrop becomes 'troubled with the *passion for reforming the world*', and TLP's footnote refers to Forsyth's book. *The Principles of Moral Science* was a favourite of TLP's, one he publicized much as he did Drummond's *Academical Questions* (see ch. 8, n. 29). In a 10 Feb. 1809 letter to Edward Thomas Hookham, TLP asked for Forsyth's *Principles* (*Letters*, 1.27), and on 13 Mar. he said he had 'been very busy with' it (*Letters*, 1.29). In *Cal*, Ellen's father, a vicar, 'detected her in the fact of reading a wicked book called *Principles of Moral Science*, which, with his usual sweet temper, he put, without saying a word, behind the fire'. Her father, she reports, 'says liberal opinions are only another name for impiety' (8: 314).

29 [Footnote:] **'Il buvoit du vin'**: Buffon wrote of the oran outang he saw in Paris that 'il buvoit du vin, mais en petite quantité, et le laissoit volontiers pour du lait, du thé ou d'autres liqueurs douces' (*Buffon 1799*, 35.94). By omitting the phrase 'en petite quantité', TLP conceals the fact that Buffon's oran outangs do not drink as freely as Sir Oran does.

30 **paper-money**: Banknotes, whether issued by the Bank of England or by other banks. (The *OED* defines 'paper money' simply as 'Negotiable documents used instead of coins; *spec.*

legal tender in the form of banknotes', the earliest example from 1691.) See TLP's *Paper Money Lyrics*. In 1797 the Bank of England suspended cash payments, so their banknotes could no longer be exchanged for gold; payments had not been resumed when *Mel* was published (see Introduction). In *ME*, TLP comments that the twelfth century did not have 'the safe and economical currency, which is produced by a man writing his name on a bit of paper, for which other men give him their property, and which he is always ready to exchange for another bit of paper, of an equally safe and economical manufacture, being also equally ready to render his own person, at a moment's notice, as impalpable as the metal which he promises to pay' (ch. 6). When Mr Chainmail in *CC* discovers that Susanna's father is a banker who absconded, he rationalizes that 'I have always understood, from Mr. Mac Quedy, who is a great oracle in this way, that promises to pay ought not to be kept; the essence of a safe and economical currency being an interminable series of broken promises' (ch. 16).

31 **places either found or made for the useful dealers in secret services**: Cobbett wrote that a 'reformed parliament', one that was 'elected by the people themselves' and 're-chosen *yearly*', would 'want no "*secret-service money*"'. Having no reason to fear '*secret* enemies of the government', such a parliament 'would need no hired scoundrels to inform against this man or that man' and would never countenance the 'disgraceful spy-work' currently in place. Furthermore, such a parliament 'could have no idea of expending money for any *secret* purpose', but 'would openly avow all its objects' (*WPR*, 12 Oct. 1816, pp. 461, 463).

32 **a consummation devoutly to be wished**: Echoing Hamlet's sentiment that ending the sufferings endemic to life is 'a consummation / Devoutly to be wish'd' (act 3, scene 1, lines 62–3).

33 **'the hope of personal advantage, and the dread of personal punishment'**: Forester is quoting Drummond's *Academical Questions*: 'Let his interests change, and man will take as many

colours as the cameleon: cruel or gentle, insolent or meek, mean or generous, and only constant to the love of self, and, therefore, only consistent in his aim to deceive, he is always guided by the hopes of individual advantage, or by the dread of personal punishment' (p. 227). This passage in Drummond was reproduced at greater length, and attributed to *Academical Questions*, in *HH*, where Escot comments that self-love is rarer 'among savage than civilized men, who, *constant only to the love of self, and consistent only in their aim to deceive, are always actuated by the hope of personal advantage, or by the dread of personal punishment*' (ch. 5). Forester's quotation is the first direct appearance in *Mel* of Drummond's book, which TLP names in two footnotes in volume 3 – once as an authoritative source on Kant (ch. 31), and once to identify the work that Forester echoes (ch. 40).

34 **Plato proposed**: Plato, *Republic*, book 8.

35 **Heraclitus the Ephesian**: The philosopher Heraclitus (c. 525–475 BC), whose works survive only in fragments.

CHAPTER 22

1 *éclat*: The narrator repeats the word that Sarcastic used when he said he aimed to give the election some '"Lustre" of reputation; social distinction; celebrity, renown' (*OED 'éclat'*, 3.a.) or 'Conspicuous success; universal applause, acclamation' (3.b.).

2 *dearly beloved brethren*: Edward Bulwer wrote in his preface to *The Siamese Twins: A Satirical Tale of the Times* (1831) that 'Every one knows the story of a certain Divine, who, on beginning the church service, found himself without a congregation; and turning to his clerk Roger, addressed him with "Dearly beloved Roger", &c.'; [Bulwer], *The Siamese Twins: A Satirical Tale of the Times: With Other Poems* (Henry Colburn and Richard Bentley, 1831), p. vii.

3 *a respectable body of constituents*: In 'An Essay on Fashionable Literature', TLP commented on the effect periodicals created

by using the pronoun 'we': 'The mysterious *we* of the invisible assassin converts his poisoned dagger into a host of legitimate broadswords', much as 'The solitary quack becomes a medical board'; 'The solitary play-frequenter becomes a committee of amateurs of the drama'; and, yes, 'The elector of Old Sarum' becomes 'a respectable body of constituents' (*NA*, p. 113). Cf. TLP's use of George Colman the Younger's poem 'An Ode to We' (ch. 6, n. 36 and ch. 22, n. 38).

4 **'venerable** *feature*' . . . **rotten borough**: Robert Stewart, who, as the marquess of Londonderry's heir, was styled Viscount Castlereagh until Apr. 1821, served as foreign secretary and the ministry's primary spokesman in the Commons from 1812 to 1822. TLP again refers to Castlereagh as 'Lord C.' in *NA*, ch. 10, where the home secretary, Lord Sidmouth, is 'Lord S.' Castlereagh was a poor speaker, prone to awkward rhetoric. At about the time when *Mel* was published, *The Examiner* observed that 'You might make an almanack of [Castlereagh's] absurdities, week after week'; he often abused figurative language: if 'on Tuesday, he will be metaphorical, and take a view of the "features of foundations"', it is likely that 'on the Friday, he gets metaphorical again, and hopes that "the people will not turn their back on themselves"; and on the Saturday, still metaphorical', he will rejoice 'that "England does not stand in the same prostrate situation as the nations of the Continent"' (*The Examiner* (9 Mar. 1817), 145). Castlereagh's figures of speech were often the target of satirists, such as Thomas Moore in *The Fudge Family in Paris* (1818). In *NA*, Mr Listless suggests that 'blue devils' are 'the fundamental feature of fashionable literature'; see ch. 6, n. 8.

5 **adhibition**: In this context, 'adhibition' means 'application' ('adhibit' means 'make use of; to use, apply, deploy', *OED* 'adhibit', 1.a.). In *HH*, Mr Nightshade recalls that 'The Romans were in the practice of adhibiting skulls at their banquets, and sometimes little skeletons of silver, as a silent admonition to

the guests to enjoy life while it lasted' (ch. 5); later, Headlong encourages Cranium to 'adhibit' his consent to Cephalis' marriage with Escot (ch. 14).

6 *frothy rhetoric*: Whether or not TLP had a specific occurrence of this phrase in mind, the adjective 'frothy' (*OED* 3: 'Vain, empty, unsubstantial, trifling') was apt to be applied to public speakers. The *OED* cites Samuel Foote's play *The Orators*, where orators can be divided into 'the choleric, the placid, the voluble, the frigid, the frothy, the turgid, the calm, and the clamourous'; *The Orators, As it is now performing at the New Theatre in the Hay-Market. Written by Mr. Foote* (J. Coote, 1762), p. 59. In 1783 Hugh Blair wrote that 'a frothy and ostentatious harangue, without solid sense and argument' will not prevail, and speakers must not 'follow the track of those loose and frothy Declaimers, who have brought discredit on Eloquence'; Hugh Blair, *Lectures on Rhetoric and Belles Lettres*, 2 vols. (W. Strahan and T. Cadell, 1783), vol. 2, p. 49.

7 **The borough of Onevote . . . in existence**: See ch. 19, n. 14. Like Onevote, Old Sarum lay in the middle of open ground. In this, the smallest of England's burgage boroughs, the '11 parchment burgages' were 'conveyed for electoral purposes to friends by its successive proprietors, Lords Camelford and Caledon' (Thorne, *History of Parliament*, vol. 2, p. 38). In 1817 the proprietor was Caledon, who had purchased it in 1802 for £43,000 (*History of Parliament*, vol. 2, p. 425). The number of actual voters in Old Sarum in this period was fewer than eleven (*History of Parliament*, vol. 2, p. 424).

8 **pedestrians and equestrians**: In TLP's previous novel, transporting the guests to Squire Headlong's Christmas ball requires 'every chariot, coach, barouche and barouchette, landau and laudaulet, chaise, curricle, buggy, whiskey, and tilbury' to be found in three counties (ch. 11); the people of Novote travel to Onevote using a wider assortment of methods, including a stagecoach and a range of horses.

9 **chariots**: A chariot, technically, was a vehicle holding two people, differentiated from a post-chaise in that the chariot had a coach box (see ch. 2, n. 2), but evidently the word is being applied here to a wide range of vehicles.

10 **hunter**: That is, a horse suitable for hunting – perhaps an unexpected choice for a farmer.

11 **hack**: A hackney, a horse used for ordinary transportation, rather than for special uses such as hunting.

12 **chaise**: Even if the grocer's chaise is the size of a post-chaise (see ch. 2, n. 2; ch. 3, n. 10; ch. 7, n. 2), it would be small for six passengers. This chaise presumably has only one horse, upon which the driver sits.

13 **tilbury**: 'A light open two-wheeled carriage, fashionable in the first half of the 19th c.' (*OED* 1; first occurrence noted 1814). According to D. J. M. Smith, 'The tilbury was a 'Gig designed by the Hon. Fitzroy Stanhope, although named after its builder [the London firm of Tilbury]'. The tilbury 'was much heavier than the original Stanhope Gig, although appearing at roughly the same period (early 19th century). . . Large numbers were exported to all parts of Europe where badly made roads and mountain passes made extra springs necessary' (Smith, *Dictionary of Horse-Drawn Vehicles*, p. 161). A gig was 'Normally a two-wheeled passenger vehicle used mainly in country districts, but—in later years—for town driving' (*Dictionary of Horse-Drawn Vehicles*, p. 85).

14 **tandem**: Grose's *Classical Dictionary of the Vulgar Tongue* (1785) defines a 'tandem' as 'a two wheeled chaise, buggy, or noddy, drawn by two horses, one before the other, that is *at length*' (the first occurrence of this meaning noted in the *OED*). Presumably the point is that the banker uses two horses while the dancing-master uses only one. A 'tandem cart' was a 'Two-wheeled dogcart, kept mainly for show purposes'; the horses were arranged in tandem, and 'The rear seat, occupied by a groom, was on a slightly lower level than the driving seat' (Smith,

Dictionary of Horse-Drawn Vehicles, p. 159). In *NA*, Scythrop's fellow students 'drove tandem and random in great perfection' (ch. 1).

15 **mantua-makers**: See ch. 14, n. 12, above.

16 **men-milliners**: 'A male milliner. Hence *derogatory*: a vain, trifling, or effeminate man (*rare* in later use)' (*OED*, first example 1787). A man-milliner sells women's clothes and accessories.

17 **the stage ... six inside and fourteen out**: Whereas mantua-makers and servant-maids must travel in the humble waggon, the pastry-cooks, men-milliners and journeymen tailors travel in a stagecoach, although most are riding uncomfortably on the outside.

18 **the bumpkin in his laced boots and Sunday coat, trudging through the dust with his cherry-cheeked lass on his elbow**: Cf. Robin Ruddyface and Susan in ch. 35.

19 **his box**: Both the gentleman driver (on the model of Sir Telegraph) and 'his painted charmer' fit on the coach box.

20 **half-starved Rosinante**: The name of the horse Miguel Cervantes gives to his protagonist Don Quixote.

21 **carriage and six**: A carriage (of an unspecified kind) that is drawn by six horses, whereas Sir Telegraph's barouche is drawn by only four.

22 **Death in the Revelations**: 'I looked, and behold a pale horse: and his name that sat on him was Death, and Hell followed with him. And power was given unto them over the fourth part of the earth, to kill with sword, and with hunger, and with death, and with the beasts of the earth' (Revelations, ch. 6, v. 8). The irony is that a medical doctor looks like Death, just as it is ironic for a physician to be named 'Dr. Killquick' (ch. 8).

23 **the devil in the Wild Huntsmen**: Walter Scott's translation of Gottfried Bürger's ballad *Der Wilde Jäger* appeared in 1796.

24 **barrel organs**: 'A musical instrument of the organ type, the keys of which are mechanically acted on by a revolving barrel or cylinder studded with metal pins' (*OED* 'barrel-organ').

25 **the hustings**: The stand upon which candidates stood to address the crowd, such as was erected in Covent Garden for elections for the populous borough of Westminster (see Introduction).

26 **Free, fat, and dependent**: See ch. 21, n. 25.

27 **a three-hundredth part of the whole elective capacity of this extensive empire**: Beginning in 1801, the House of Commons had 658 members, representing England, Wales, Scotland and Ireland; therefore Christopher Corporate would comprise one three hundred and twenty-ninth of 'the whole elective capacity' of the United Kingdom.

28 **eleven millions**: Although Sarcastic refers to the 'extensive empire', his estimate of the population is most plausible for Great Britain, excluding Ireland. According to the 1811 census, the population of England, Scotland and Wales was 12.2 million, while the population of Ireland was about 6 million (Ireland was not included in a census until 1821); Norman Gash, *Aristocracy and People: Britain, 1815–1865* (Cambridge, MA: Harvard University Press, 1979), p. 364.

29 **Stentor**: In *Iliad*, book 5, lines 785–6, Stentor speaks with a huge voice. The adjective 'Stentorian', which occurs later in this chapter, dates back to 1606 (*OED*).

30 **the voice of Harry Gill**: In Wordsworth's 'Goody Blake, and Harry Gill, A True Story', first published in *Lyrical Ballads, with a Few Other Poems* (1798), Harry's 'voice was like the voice of three' (l. 20). TLP contrasts the larger-than-life world of Homeric epic with the mundane world that Wordsworth presents. It is also notable that Sarcastic has read Wordsworth. In *NA*, Mr Larynx says, 'I'll be Harry Gill, with the voice of three' (ch. 11); in *Cal*, King Arthur's butler shouts 'with a voice like the voice of three' (Halliford, 8.326).

31 *'he is himself an host***, and that** *none but himself can be his parallel'*: The first phrase translates Virgil's 'quantum instar in ipso est' (*Aeneid*, book 6, line 865); the second comes from Lewis Theobald, *Double Falshood; or, The Distrest Lovers. A Play, as It is*

Acted at the Theatre-Royal in Drury Lane (pr. J. Watts, 1728), act 3, scene 1, where Julio says of another character's treachery that 'None but Itself can be its Parallel' (p. 25).

32 **Most potent, grave, and reverend Signor!**: Shakespeare's Othello addresses the Venetian senators as 'Most potent, grave, and reverend signiors' (act 1, scene 3, line 76).

33 **vapouring**: See ch. 6, n. 17.

34 *monied interest*: Cobbett believed that 'Amongst the great and numerous dangers to which this country, and particularly the monarchy, is exposed in consequence of the enormous public debt, the influence, the powerful and widely-extended influence, of the monied interest is, perhaps, the most to be dreaded, because it necessarily aims at measures which directly tend to the subversion of the present order of things' (*WPR*, 8 Sept. 1804, p. 370). By the 'monied interest' he meant 'the numerous and powerful body of loan-jobbers, directors, brokers, contractors and farmers-general, which has been engendered by the excessive amount of the public debt, and the almost boundless extension of the issues of paper money'. The monied interest was 'hostile alike to the land-holder and to the stock-holder, to the colonist, to the real merchant, and to the manufacturer, to the clergy, to the nobility and to the throne' (pp. 370–1).

35 *as the sun at noon-day*: See ch. 6, n. 37.

36 *tangible a shape*: On the italicized examples of 'parliamentary rhetoric' here (the phrase occurs in TLP's footnote), see ch. 22, n. 4.

37 **marketable value**: Having bought his place in the House of Commons, Sarcastic will now sell his votes. At the end of ch. 24, Sir Telegraph lists events that must occur before he will give up his barouche, and he will not surrender it until 'borough-electors will not sell their suffrage, nor their representatives their votes'.

38 *plural unity*: Another allusion to the opening of George Colman the Younger's 'An Ode to We' (see ch. 6, n. 36; ch. 21, n. 26).

39 **the distribution of secret service money**: See ch. 21, n. 31.

40 **foreign legitimacy**: That is, the restoration and maintenance of monarchs in Continental Europe (see ch. 21, n. 17). In ch. 39, Anyside Antijack says that the British victory against France has benefited 'legitimacy, divine right, the Jesuits, the Pope, the Inquisition, and the Virgin Mary's petticoat'.

41 **the car of Jaggernaut**: In Hindu belief, the chariot of Juggernaut would carry statues of gods, and people killed themselves by throwing themselves under the wheels. TLP and many of his readers would know the account provided in Southey's *The Curse of Kehama* (1810), book 14: 'Prone fall the frantic votaries in its road, / And, calling on the God, / Their self-devoted bodies there they lay / To pave his chariot-way. / On Jaga-Naut they call, / The ponderous Car rolls on, and crushes all'; *The Curse of Kehama* (Longman, 1810), p. 147.

42 **The constitution says that no man shall be taxed but by his own consent**: Cobbett repeatedly made this point at about the time when TLP was finishing *Mel*. 'Magna Charta says, that Parliament shall be *annual*, and that *no man shall be taxed without his own consent*', he wrote (*WPR*, 25 Jan. 1817, p. 121), and he mentioned a month later that 'It is . . . a well-known maxim of the Constitution, that no man shall be *taxed without his own consent*' (*WPR*, 22 Feb. 1817, p. 234). For a summary of the law on these principles of taxation, see Blackstone, *Commentaries*, vol. 1, pp. 140–0a.

43 **a lancet**: Medical instrument used to bleed patients, at a time when bloodletting ('phlebotomy') was standard treatment for many maladies.

44 **all feeling is founded on sympathy**: See Adam Smith, *The Theory of Moral Sentiments* [1759], ed. Knud Haakonssen, Cambridge Texts in the History of Philosophy (Cambridge: Cambridge University Press, 2002), esp. pp. 26, 53, 87–9, 264.

45 *sang-froid*: French for 'cold blood', this term means 'Coolness, indifference, absence of excitement or agitation' (*OED*). The first instance in the *OED* dates from 1750.

46 **a *full* Gazette**: The *London Gazette*, issued by the government, announced not only bankruptcies (see ch. 17, n. 12) but also appointments and promotions in the government and the military.

47 **the *quidnunc***: A 'quidnunc' is 'A person who constantly asks: "What now?"; an inquisitive or nosy person; a gossip' (*OED*). The earliest example in the *OED* dates from 1709. In *Biographia Literaria*, published a few months after *Mel*, Coleridge recalled that he was spied upon in 1796 because of reports that 'some zealous Quidnunc' had submitted to the Home Office; *Biographia Literaria: or Biographical Sketches of My Literary Life and Opinions*, ed. James Engell and W. Jackson Bate, 2 vols. (Princeton: Princeton University Press, 1983), vol. 1, p. 193.

48 **as long as the cry of *Question* is a satisfactory *answer* to an argument**: That is, when a member of parliament 'calls the question', demanding a vote on the motion that is being discussed.

49 **neither poll nor scrutiny being demanded**: 'If the electors are unanimous, or but a few dissent from the choice of the larger number, it is easy to determine the election upon the view', but any 'party interested in the competition . . . is entitled to try the question by the numeration of voices', regardless of how 'clear the majority of the view is in favour of the rival candidate', and 'Taking the voices, or numbering the votes man by man . . . is called the "poll"'; *A Treatise on the Law of Elections, in All its Branches*, 2nd ed. (J. Butterworth, 1795), pp. 155–6.

50 **Chair**: 'To place in a chair or on a seat, and carry aloft in triumph, as an honour to a favourite, a successful competitor, and formerly often to the successful candidate at a parliamentary election' (*OED* 'chair', 1.b., first example 1761).

51 **'large body corporate of one'**: From George Colman the Younger's 'An Ode to We, A Hackney'd Critic'; see ch. 6, n. 36.

52 **into a committee**: Sarcastic appropriates the term that normally referred to a legislative body reconstituting itself (for example, the House of Commons transforming itself into a committee of

supply) and applies it to the emergence of multiple Christopher Corporates.

53 **like Artegall's Iron Man, or like Ajax among the Trojans, or like Rhodomont in Paris, or like Orlando among the soldiers of Agramant:** The 'iron man', Talus, assists Artegall in *The Faerie Queene*, book 5, canto 1; for Rhodomont's role in the attack on Paris in *Orlando Furioso*, see cantos 14–15; for Orlando, see cantos 40–2. Sir Oran was compared to Homer's Ajax earlier in *Mel* (by Sir Telegraph, in ch. 20).

54 *sanctum sanctorum:* 'the holy of holies' (Latin).

55 **Hesperian liquor:** 'Hesperian' in this context meant primarily having to do with the Hesperides (*OED* 2). The 'Hesperides' were the daughters of Hesperus who guarded the garden of the golden apples, on the Isles of the Blest, in the west, but the term also referred to the garden itself.

56 **Hats and wigs:** Some men of Novote wear wigs, although wigs were out of style by 1817.

57 **immortal guy:** At the annual 5 Nov. ceremonial burning of effigies of Guy Fawkes. The narrator implicitly makes an analogy between burning the cottage that represents 'the ancient and honourable borough of Onevote' and burning in effigy a man who committed treason by conspiring to blow up the House of Lords.

CHAPTER 23

1 **whom we left:** At the end of ch. 18.

2 **as Hudibras and Ralpho in their 'wooden bastile':** In Butler's *Hudibras*, Hudibras '*encounters* Talgol, *routs the* Bear, / *And takes the* Fidler *prisoner,* / *Conveys him to inchanted Castle,* / *There shuts him fast in Wooden* Bastile' (the 'Argument' of part 1, canto 2).

3 *quæritur:* 'it is asked' (Latin), meaning, in this context, the question at issue.

4 **beaten black and blue in the capacity of *fag*:** A 'fag' was a younger boy assigned to serve an older one at elite schools ('our public seminaries'); see *OED* 'fag', *n.¹*, 2.a.

5 **The race is not always to the swift, nor the battle to the strong**: 'I returned, and saw under the sun, that the race is not to the swift, nor the battle to the strong, neither yet bread to the wise, nor yet riches to men of understanding, nor yet favour to men of skill; but time and chance happeneth to them all' (Ecclesiastes, ch. 9, v. 11).

6 **incipiency**: 'The quality or state of being incipient; incipience' (*OED*). This is the first occurrence recorded in the *OED* of this derivative of 'Incipient', an adjective meaning 'Beginning; commencing; coming into, or in an early stage of, existence; in an initial stage'.

7 **Though with pistols...action?**: This quotation has perplexed R. L. Moreton (see *Notes and Queries*, ser. 10, 7 [8 June 1907], p. 448), David Garnett (*Novels*, 1.235), and the present editor.

8 **none are so dumb as those who won't speak**: Grovelgrub's parody of the proverb that appears later in *Mel* as 'None are so blind as those who won't see' (ch. 31). *Stevenson's Book of Proverbs* (p. 198) and *ODEP* (67) cite examples of this proverb dating back to 1546.

9 **People crossed in love, Saint Chrysostom says, lose their voice**: Grovelgrub may be misremembering the homily of St John Chrysostom (c. 347–407) in which that church father discusses the effects of his love for his congregation; see St John Chrysostom, *On Repentance and Thanksgiving*, trans. Gus George Christo (Washington, DC: The Catholic University of America Press, 1998), pp. 1–2.

10 **Alga Castle**: 'Alga' means seaweed; by giving the castle this name, TLP continues the association of Lord Anophel and his family with useless plants such as toadstools (see ch. 8, n. 4).

11 **'First, catch your carp'**: As early as the thirteenth century Henry de Bracton testified that 'It is a common saying that it is best first to catch the stag, and afterwards, when he has been caught, to skin him' (*De Legibus et Consuetudinibus Angliae*, book 4, ch. 31, sec. 4, cited in *Stevenson's Book of Proverbs*). In 1814, a

letter to the editor of *The Times* by 'Verax' commented that 'the Chemist's Friend''s description of his experiment 'reminds me forcibly of the receipt for dressing carp in a celebrated treatise on cookery, which opens with the salutary advice, "First catch your Fish"' (*Times* (24 Dec. 1814)). The gas explosion in ch. 31 suggests that TLP was aware of the series of letters in *The Times* to which Verax was contributing; see ch. 31, nn. 70–1.

12 **let me be devilled like a biscuit after the second bottle, or a turkey's leg at a twelfth night supper**: For 'devilled', see ch. 16, n. 12.

13 **there is a passage in Æschylus, very applicable to our situation**: As we soon see, a passage in Aeschylus' *Hiketides*, or *The Supplicant Maidens* ('Supplices' is the Latin title). The fifty Danaids have fled to avoid being forced to marry King Aegyptus' sons. Grovelgrub says that the chorus wishes to be in a place like that where he and Lord Anophel find themselves, but he does not mention that the Danaids would prefer to be there only because the sole alternative is a forced marriage. In light of Lord Anophel's recent schemes, it is ironic that Grovelgrub quotes a woman who flees an unwanted suitor, although Grovelgrub evidently cannot see the irony. In 1851 TLP set to work on a translation of this Aeschylus play (*Letters*, 2.336–7, 355, 359, 438). TLP cites 'Supplices. 807. Ed. Schutz.'; 'Æschyli Tragœdiæ, Gr. edidit C. G. Schutz, 3 vol. *ib. Halæ-Sax.* 1799–1801' was in his library when he died (*Catalogue* 159). When Grovelgrub translates Aeschylus, he uses the same Latinate adjective, 'precipitous', that TLP used in ch. 18 to describe the rock where Grovelgrub and Lord Anophel were placed by Sir Oran.

14 *dumetum*: a thicket of bushes (Latin).

15 ***Dumosâ pendere procul de rupe videbor!***: Virgil, *Eclogues* 1.76 (with 'videbo' changed to 'videbor'): literally, to be seen hanging from a bushy crag.

16 **a firm *appui***: 'Support, stay, prop' (*OED* 'appui', 1). Citing examples from 1573 and 1601, the *OED* records that the word is 'Now treated as French, though formerly naturalized'.

CHAPTER 24

1 THE **morning after the election**: And *before* the events narrated at the end of ch. 22, where the reader is informed that Onevote was rebuilt within a few days.

2 *things as they are*: From the 1790s onwards, the phrase TLP italicizes was frequently used to contrast regrettable reality with possible improvements (see Introduction, pp. cxxxiv–cxxxv). In *Enquiry Concerning Political Justice* (1793), Godwin warned of the dangers if the public hears only 'the praise of things as they are' (vol. 2, p. 643). The phrase was most familiar to TLP's generation from Godwin's *Things as They Are; or, The Adventures of Caleb Williams* (1794), a novel that, as the preface explained, was designed to reflect on 'The question now afloat in the world respecting THINGS AS THEY ARE'; *Caleb Williams*, vol. 1, p. 1. In 1809 TLP received a copy of *Political Justice* from E. T. Hookham (*Letters*, 1.36). The phrase reappears in ch. 39 of *Mel*, when Mr Anyside Antijack claims that virtue consists of appropriating public money and defending this practice. Whereas *Mel* associates the phrase 'things as they are' with complacency about the current state of society, *NA* reveals how reactions against things as they are must be inefficacious if they are irrational: Scythrop proclaims that 'Ardent spirits cannot but be dissatisfied with things as they are; and, according to their views of the probabilities of amelioration, they will rush into the extremes of either hope or despair—of which the first is enthusiasm, and the second misanthropy' (ch. 7). In 'An Essay on Fashionable Literature', TLP writes: 'Young ladies' prefer works of the imagination that 'implicitly acquiesce in all the assumptions of worldly wisdom' and are 'well-seasoned with petitiones principii in favor of things as they are' (*NA*, p. 119). In 'Nehemiah Nettlebottom, Esq., Collector and Arranger', *The Fudge Family in Edinburgh, in a Series of Poetical Epistles* (Edinburgh: J. Dick, 1820), we read that after Prince Leopold visited the Scottish

capital, 'The rulers and people' are 'further enamour'd of *things as they are!*' (p. 171).

3 **defalcation**: Reduction.

4 **they know not what they do**: An allusion to Luke, ch. 23, v. 34: 'Then said Jesus, Father, forgive them; for they know not what they do.'

5 *Do as ye would be done by*: 'Therefore all things whatsoever ye would that men should do to you, do ye even so to them: for this is the law and the prophets' (Matthew, ch. 7, v. 12); 'And as ye would that men should do to you, do ye also to them likewise' (Luke, ch. 6, v. 31).

6 *Inasmuch . . . unto me*: 'And the King shall answer and say unto them, Verily I say unto you, Inasmuch as ye have done it unto one of the least of these my brethren, ye have done it unto me' (Matthew, ch. 25, v. 40).

7 *Behold a man . . . sinners*: Attributed by TLP's footnote to Matthew, ch. 11, v. 19, which reads: 'The Son of man came eating and drinking, and they say, Behold a man gluttonous, and a winebibber, a friend of publicans and sinners. But wisdom is justified of her children.'

8 **poor Lazarus**: 'There was a certain rich man, which was clothed in purple and fine linen, and fared sumptuously every day: And there was a certain beggar named Lazarus, which was laid at his gate, full of sores, And desiring to be fed with the crumbs which fell from the rich man's table: moreover the dogs came and licked his sores' (Luke, ch. 16, vv. 19–21). The rich man died, 'And in hell he lift up his eyes, being in torments, and seeth Abraham afar off, and Lazarus in his bosom' (Luke, ch. 16, v. 23).

9 **like Dives that lived in purple**: TLP's footnote quotes from Milton's *Of Reformation Touching Church-Discipline in England: And the Causes that Hitherto have Hindered It* (1641). See *Complete Prose Works of John Milton*, gen. ed. Don M. Wolfe, vol. 1, ed. Wolfe (New Haven CT and London: Yale University

Press, 1953), pp. 548–9. No edition of Milton's prose works is mentioned in *Sale Catalogue*; *Of Reformation* was reprinted only four times between 1641 and 1817.

10 **'forgotten what the inside of a church is made of'**: In Shakespeare's *1 Henry IV*, Falstaff says he has 'forgotten what the inside of a church is made of' (act 3, scene 3, lines 7–8). This statement is also quoted by the narrator in *HH*, ch. 9.

11 *It is easier ... heaven*: Forester's quotation is imprecise. 'It is easier for a camel to go through the eye of a needle, than for a rich man to enter into the kingdom of God' (Matthew, ch. 19, v. 24); see also Mark, ch. 10, v. 25 and Luke, ch. 18, v. 25.

12 **the chimæra of an agrarian law**: When Fax refers to this 'revolutionary doctrine of an equality of possession', TLP seems to be thinking of the Spenceans, who were followers of agrarian reformer Thomas Spence. On the Spenceans, see David Worrall, *Radical Culture: Discourse, Resistance, and Surveillance, 1790–1820* (Detroit: Wayne State University Press, 1992). In ch. 39 Forester dismisses 'the Spencean theory' as 'the impracticable chimæra of an obscure herd of fanatics', but Southey held (in the *Quarterly Review* article to which TLP repeatedly refers in that chapter) that the Spencean 'Agrarian system' was not 'so foolish, or so devoid of attraction, that it may safely be despised'; 'Parliamentary Reform', *Quarterly Review*, vol. 16, no. 31 (Oct. 1816), 225–78, at 271. The phrase 'agrarian law' refers primarily to the *lex sempronia agraria* advocated by Tiberius Gracchus in Rome (second century BC). TLP may also be remembering Monboddo, who wrote that the practice 'by which the smaller gentry are, as it were, devoured by the greater' was 'so much increased in Scotland, of late years, that if it is not put a stop to by some kind of Agrarian law, the land of Scotland is in hazard of being monopolised by a few great proprietors' (*AM*, 5.303).

13 **the American laws**: Forester's reference to 'the American laws' that limit 'the fortune of a private citizen to twenty

thousand a year' is mysterious. Joukovsky suggests (private communication) that TLP wrote 'Agrarian laws', a phrase Fax just used.

14 **I keep none myself**: On Forester's keeping no 'pleasure-horses', TLP's footnote tells the reader to 'See Vol. I. page 156.' – that is, H6v of the first volume, where the narrator reveals that Forester 'kept no horses himself, for reasons which will appear hereafter' (see ch. 11, n. 6). TLP had evidently seen proofs of volume 1, signature H, when he wrote this, or by the time he read the proofs. Falconer in *GG* does not keep horses, but he does own a 'travelling chariot' (ch. 22).

15 **trammels**: A trammel is 'A hobble to prevent a horse from straying or kicking' or 'a contrivance for teaching a horse to amble', but the word (particularly when plural) can mean 'Anything that hinders or impedes free action; anything that confines, restrains, fetters, or shackles' (*OED*).

16 **Pindar**: See ch. 19, n. 12; ch. 20, n. 9.

17 **Anacreon**: Anacreon, whose odes often celebrate wine, was a cultural force in the late eighteenth and early nineteenth centuries, as represented in particular by Thomas Moore's *The Odes of Anacreon* (1800), one of the subscribers to which was the Prince of Wales. However, Henry Brougham wrote in a review of Moore's book that 'we believe it would be difficult to point out any classical writer, whose pen has done smaller service to the cause of virtue or good citizenship' (*Edinburgh Review*, vol. 2, no. 4 (July 1803), 462–76, 463). Anacreon was suspect because of his erotic (and homoerotic) emphasis, his celebration of dancing and drinking, and, perhaps above all, his service as a court poet to tyrants. Moore should have known better than to believe that the Greek poems he translated were the work of Anacreon, who lived in the fifth century BC; scholars had shown that these poems, commonly called the *Anacreontea*, were actually written about a thousand years later.

CHAPTER 25

1 **heartless fops . . . mountains**: Forester's views are supported with a footnote that quotes Gilpin's *Picturesque Observations on Cumberland and Westmoreland*, vol. 2, p. 67. Gilpin's text reads 'philosophy——or, if that could be hoped, to adore the great Creator in these his sublimer works—if, in their passage'. TLP omits the middle phrase. He also changes Gilpin's 'these scenes' to 'these parts', 'a lake' to 'the lake', and 'soonest arrives' to 'arrives soonest'. On Gilpin, see ch. 1, n. 2.

2 **deaf as the adder to the voice of the charmer**: See Psalms, ch. 58, v. 4: 'they are like the deaf adder that stoppeth her ear'. *Stevenson's Book of Proverbs* and *ODEP* (p. 172) cite many examples of someone being as deaf as an adder; the earliest example of the adder being deaf to a snake-charmer comes from Ariosto's *Orlando Furioso*. TLP's phrasing, 'deaf as the adder to the voice of the charmer', also appears in Walter Scott's *The Pirate* (1821), perhaps suggesting a common source. The Edinburgh Edition of the Waverley Novels, vol. 12: *The Pirate*, ed. Mark Weinstein and Alison Lumsden (Edinburgh: Edinburgh University Press, 2001), vol. 3, ch. 1, p. 60.

3 **quadrates**: 'To cause (a theory, practice, observation, etc.) to conform, correspond, or agree (*to* or *with* something)' (*OED* 'quadrate', 2.b.). The *OED* cites *Mel*, after noting two examples from the seventeenth century.

4 **Lochinvar**: A disappointed suitor in 'Lady Heron's Song', in Scott's *Marmion* (1808), canto 5, who says that 'There are maidens in Scotland more lovely by far, / That would gladly be bride to the young Lochinvar' (p. 259). In *NA*, Scythrop Glowry concedes to his father that 'there are yet maidens in England' (ch. 15).

5 **Fabricius under his oak**: The first of the 'fathers of the Roman republic' Forester mentions is Gaius Fabricius Luscinus Monocularis, third century BC. See Livy 9.43, Plutarch *Pyrrhus* 18, Valerius Maximus 4.3.6.

6 **Curius in his cottage**: Manius Curius Dentatus, d. 270 BC, Roman statesman and general, greeted the Samnite emissaries while boiling vegetables in his humble cottage, and he rejected the gold with which they tried to bribe him; Valerius Maximus, *Factorum ac dictorum memorabilium libri*, 4.3.5.

7 **Regulus**: Marcus Atilius Regulus, consul 267 and 256 BC, who fought in the First Punic War, which lasted from 264 to 241.

8 ***Rome, the seat of glory and of virtue, if ever they had one on earth***: TLP's italics demarcate Forester's quotation from Rousseau, *Emile*, book 5, which the footnote reproduces in the original (see *Œuvres complètes*, vol. 4, p. 742). The context in *Emile* is Rousseau's discussion of female virtue, as Rousseau understands it. Rousseau writes that 'All peoples who have had morals have respected women. Look at Sparta; look at the ancient Germans; look at Rome—Rome, home of glory and of virtue if ever they had one on earth' (Rousseau, *Emile*, p. 570).

9 **in those dear books . . . lore**: Anthelia quotes 'The Ruined Cottage', the sixth of the 'English Eclogues', included in *Poems, by Robert Southey . . . The Second Volume* (Bristol: Longman and Rees, 1799). Anthelia has read Southey, just as Forester has read Wordsworth (ch. 15, n. 9). Southey's poetic speaker relates that he led Charles to his 'favourite walk even [sic] since I was a boy' where there is a ruin which he remembers as 'The neatest comfortable dwelling place'. He goes on to say:

> when I read in those dear books that first
> Woke in my heart the love of poesy,
> How with the villagers Erminia dwelt,
> And Calidore for a fair shepherdess
> Forgot his quest to learn the shepherd's lore;
> My fancy drew from this the little hut
> Where that poor princess wept her hopeless love,
> Or where the gentle Calidore at eve
> Led Pastorella home. (p. 227)

This edition emends *1817*'s 'his guest' to Southey's 'his quest' on the grounds that 'guest' must be a printer's error (reproduced in *1856*). Erminia dwells with villagers in Tasso's *La Gerusalemme liberata*, and Calidore settles with Pastorella in Spenser's *The Faerie Queene*, book 6. (TLP wrote *Cal* in early 1817, shortly after finishing *Mel*.) Whereas Southey's speaker remembers a time when the hut could serve as a location found in Spenser or Tasso, Anthelia regrets she has never been able to perceive Spenser's and Tasso's pictures embodied in the people of the English countryside.

10 **extrema per illos ... VIRG.**: Virgil, *Georgics*, book 2, lines 473–4, on the life of farmers. Forester paraphrases these lines closely when he says that 'primæval Justice departed from the earth, her last steps were among the cultivators of the fields'.

CHAPTER 26

1 **what was in Scotland called a *cottar town***: TLP's footnote directs the reader to *AM*, vol. 5, book 4, ch. 8, where Monboddo, writing of Scotland in the 1790s, argues that decades earlier 'the country must have been very well peopled; for the farms ... were not large, not near so large as they are now; and they were cultivated chiefly by cottagers, who lived upon the farm, in a little village called a *cottar-town*' (*AM*, 5.301).

2 **exorbitant taxation . . . paper-credit**: Forester sounds like Cobbett when he says that 'the labouring classes' suffer most from high taxes and that 'the imaginary riches of paper credit' threaten national prosperity. Part of TLP's point is that what happened to Scotland is now happening to England.

3 **Large farms . . . depopulating their estates**: Again, TLP's footnote points to *AM*, vol. 5, book 4, ch. 8, where Monboddo writes, 'I am persuaded I could more than double the rent of their land by letting it off to one tenant: But I should be sorry to increase my rent by depopulating any part of the country; and I keep these small tenants as a monument of the way in which, I

believe, a great part of the low lands of Scotland was cultivated in antient times' (*AM*, 5.307–8).

4 **according to the definition of Socrates**: In Xenophon's *Oeconomicus*, a dialogue between Socrates and Critobulus, Socrates says that his property is enough to satisfy his needs.

5 **subsidium**: 'A thing (or occas. a person) that provides support or assistance; a help, an aid' (*OED*, earliest example 1640; *Mel* is also cited).

6 **desire to be quit of them**: TLP again cites *AM*, vol. 5, book, 4, ch. 8, where Monboddo writes, 'I think, therefore, that my farm is very well peopled, very much better than most farms in Scotland are now-a-days; though, I believe, not so well as they were in antient times. There are many proprietors, I know, who think that the number of cottagers on their land is a grievance, and they desire to be quit of them; but, for my part, I am fond of them, and call them *my people;* and have a pleasure in numbering them and seeing them increase, and am sorry when any of them leaves my land' (*AM*, 5.308–9).

7 **ploughed . . . Cincinnatus**: On Cincinnatus, see ch. 13, n. 31. TLP's footnote observes that Forester adopts two lines from Juvenal: 'if you alone possess as many acres of good land as the Roman people tilled in the days of Tatius' (Juvenal, *Satires*, 14.159–60; Tatius lived in the eighth century BC).

8 **The three great points . . . any considerable time**: In the chapter that TLP's footnote mentions, Monboddo writes, after noting that the British population has decreased, that 'population is the most material part of the political system, so material, that without it, the system cannot subsist. Of that system, as I have observed in a preceeding [sic] part of this work, there are three capital articles, the *health*, the *morals*, and the *numbers* of the people. Without health and morals the people cannot be happy; but without numbers they cannot be a great and powerful nation, nor even exist for any considerable time' (*AM*, 5.312–13). TLP uses no italics to indicate quotation, as though Forester is Monboddo.

CHAPTER 27

1 *michin malicho,* **which means mischief:** Shakespeare's Hamlet
tells Ophelia that the dumb show is '[miching] mallecho, it
means mischief' (act 3, scene 2, lines 137–8). The word 'miching'
is in brackets in *The Riverside Shakespeare* because it is supplied
from the First Folio; Johnson-Steevens has 'miching mallecho'
(18.200). A character named Lord Michin Malicho appears in
GG, chs. 8, 18.

2 **a worthy Alderman and Baronet:** This alderman is identified in
the next chapter as Sir Gregory Greenmould; perhaps TLP realized that the character was too important to remain nameless.
Greenmould has 'been studying the picturesque at Low-wood
Inn'; this is another among many references to travellers' seeking
picturesque sights (see ch. 1, n. 8). TLP may have been thinking
of the most notable conservative member of parliament for the
City of London, Sir William Curtis, who represented the city
from 1790 to 1818 and from 1820 to 1826, and whom TLP
called 'Alderman Curtis' (*Letters*, 1.77). On Curtis, see Thorne,
History of Parliament, vol. 3, pp. 545–8. Curtis's support for suspension of habeas corpus early in 1817 was a factor when he lost
his seat the next year, and TLP refers to Curtis's defeat in a letter
to Percy Shelley (*Letters*, 1.130–1). In Dec. 1817, William Hone
observed during one of his blasphemy trials that no one was
a subject of parody more often than Curtis; *The Third Trial of
William Hone, on an Ex-Officio Information. At Guildhall, London,
December 20, 1817, Before Lord Ellenborough and a Special Jury,
For Publishing a Parody on the Athanasian Creed, Entitled 'The
Sinecurist's Creed'*, 2nd ed. (William Hone, 1818), p. 35.

3 *toujours prêt:* 'Always prepared' (French).

4 *coup-d'œil:* Like 'toujours prêt', 'coup-d'œil' (French), meaning a
glance, has military connotations.

5 **compotatory:** This is the earliest citation for this adjective
in the *OED*; it means 'Pertaining or addicted to compotation'. 'Compotation' (first example 1593) means 'A drinking or

tippling together, drinking-bout, carouse, symposium'. The fact that Cicero uses *compotatio* to translate the Greek *symposion* suggests that TLP's 'compotatory' means specifically 'having to do with a symposium'.

6 **wave**: I have retained the unusual *1817* (1.188) and *1856* (201) spelling of 'waive', a word used here to mean 'To refrain from insisting upon, give up (a privilege, right, claim, etc.); to forbear to claim or demand' (*OED* 5.b.) or 'To forbear persistence in (an action or course of action); to refrain from pressing (an objection, a scruple, an argument)' (*OED* 5.c.).

7 **Slaves cannot breathe in the air of England: 'They touch our country, and their fetters fall'**: See William Cowper's *The Task* (1785), book 2, 'The Time-Piece', lines 40–2: 'Slaves cannot breathe in England; if their lungs / Receive our air, that moment they are free, / They touch our country and their shackles fall' (*The Poems of William Cowper*, vol. 2, p. 140). Forester switches from paraphrasing Cowper to quoting him, although he substitutes 'fetters' for the poet's 'shackles'. Cowper's immediate source would appear to be the argument that the distinguished lawyer Francis Hargrave made in 1772 on behalf of the former slave James Somerset. Hargrave informed the Court of King's Bench that in 1568 or 1569 'one Cartwright brought a slave from Russia, and would scourge him; for which he was questioned; and it was resolved, that England was too pure an air for a slave to breathe in'. The obvious conclusion, Hargrave argued, was that 'the slave was become free by his arrival in England' (Howell, ed., *A Complete Collection of State Trials*, vol. 20, p. 51).

8 [Footnote:] **Pochi compagni ... Petrarca**: Petrarch, *Canzoniere*, canto 7, lines 12–14 (slightly misquoted): 'You will have little company on that other road: / So I beg you all the more, gentle spirit, / not to abandon your great undertaking.' That is, do not abandon the pursuit of 'laurel and myrtle' (representing glory and love) in favour of material profit. See Petrarch, *The Canzoniere or Rerum vulgarium fragmenta*, ed. and trans.

Mark Musa (Bloomington and Indianapolis: Indiana University Press), p. 8.

9 **Do you consider that Custom is the great lord and master of our conduct?**: TLP's footnote quotes Milton's *The Doctrine and Discipline of Divorce* (1643). See *Complete Prose Works of John Milton*, vol. 2, pp. 222–4. Sarcastic, arguing that custom reigns supreme, quotes a tract in which Milton announces that he will fight against custom as 'the sole advocate of a discountenanced truth'.

CHAPTER 28

1 **a fanciful scheme**: This dance resembles that which occurs at the court of the Queen of Quintessence in book 5, chs. 23–4 of Rabelais' *Gargantua and Pantagruel*, although a key difference is that TLP has many of his characters serve as dancer-chesspieces. Marilyn Butler observes that TLP's Chess Dance 'is a stylised representation of the characters with whom Anthelia does not really wish to consort, a mime of the hard and rather meaningless elegance of fashionable life'; *Peacock*, pp. 85–6.

2 **Mr. Hermitage and Mr. Heeltap**: 'Hermitage' is 'a French wine produced from vineyards on a hill near Valence; so called from a ruin on the summit supposed to have been a hermit's cell' (*OED* 2). The first of TLP's two country squires is named after a kind of wine; the second, Mr Heeltap, after the dregs left in a bottle or glass (see ch. 5, n. 1).

3 **Sir Gregory Greenmould**: The narrator names the 'fat alderman' who appeared in the previous chapter (see ch. 27, n. 2).

4 **Mr. Paperstamp**: In 1813 Wordsworth was appointed Distributor of Stamps for Westmorland, a sinecure that paid him £400 annually. One of TLP's *Paper Money Lyrics*, written in 1825–6, is 'A Mood of My Own Mind, Occurring During a Gale of Wind at Midnight, While I was Writing a Paper on the Currency, by the Light of Two Mould Candles. By W. W., Esq.,

Distributor of Stamps' (Halliford, 7.113–17). Mr Paperstamp's waistcoats are 'duffil grey' because of the duffel-grey cloak that the poetic speaker in Wordsworth's 'Alice Fell; or, Poverty' buys for young Alice. In ch. 3 TLP mentioned that Mr Hippy's servant, Harry Fell, was related to Alice.

5 **Mr. Killthedead**: An allusion to John Wilson Croker; see ch. 13, n. 18. Killthedead is 'a great compounder of narcotics, under the denomination of BATTLES', referring mainly to Croker's *The Battles of Talavera* (1809).

6 **He fought the BATTLE o'er again…slew the slain**: John Dryden, *Alexander's Feast; or the Power of Musique. An Ode, In Honour of St. Cecilia's Day* (1697), lines 67–8; see *The Works of John Dryden*, 20 vols., gen. eds. E. N. Hooker, H. T. Swedenberg, Jr and Alan Roper (Berkeley and Los Angeles: University of California Press, 1956–2000), vol. 7: *Poems 1697–1700*, ed. Vinton A. Dearing (2000), p. 5. In TLP's *Sir Proteus*, 'a voice of thrilling force' describes 'Oblivion's cave' thus: 'Here Cr—k—r fights his battles o'er, / And doubly kills the slain' (Halliford, 6.311).

7 **the *King's Rook***: The word 'rook' might mean not only the chess piece (*OED* 'rook' *n.²*) but also 'A foolish person, a gull' (*OED* 'rook', *n.¹* 2.c.).

8 *mauvaise plaisanterie*: A bad joke (French).

9 **full canonicals**: That is, in full ecclesiastical dress.

10 **dazzling helm, and nodding crest**: In Alexander Pope's translation of *Iliad*, book 6, lines 596–7, Hector reaches for his son, Astyanax, and 'The Babe clung crying to his Nurse's Breast / Scar'd at the dazzling Helm, and nodding Crest'; *The Iliad of Homer: Books I–IX*, ed. Maynard Mack (New Haven CT and London: Yale University Press, 1967), vol. 7 of *The Twickenham Edition of the Poems of Alexander Pope*, ed. John Butt et al., 11 vols. (1939–69), p. 356.

11 **mural robe**: 'Designating a crown or (later also) a garland, wreath, etc., conferred as a mark of honour (originally by the ancient Romans) on the first soldier to scale the walls of a

besieged town. In extended use: designating any similar crown, esp. in heraldic depictions or as worn by the goddess Cybele' (*OED* 'mural', adj., 1). Cf. 'mural artillery', below.

12 **the walking wall in Pyramus and Thisbe**: See *A Midsummer Night's Dream*, act 5, scene 1.

13 **Celandina Paperstamp**: Her first name connotes the three poems in Wordsworth's *Poems in Two Volumes* (1807) that deal with the flower called the lesser celandine.

14 **'fought and conquered ere a sword was drawn'**: In John Home's well-known verse tragedy *Douglas* (1756), act 2, scene 1, the Stranger says, 'The pursuit I led, / Till we o'ertook the spoil-encumber'd foe. / We fought and conquer'd. E're a sword was drawn, / An arrow from my bow had pierc'd their chief, / Who wore that day the arms which now I wear' (*Douglas: A Tragedy. As It is Acted at the Theatre-Royal in Covent-Garden* [A. Millar, 1757], p. 14). TLP at his death owned a Bell's *British Theatre*, 30 vols. (1791–3) (*Sale Catalogue* 82), and Bell included *Douglas*.

15 **TRIPUDII PERSONÆ.**: Persons of the ritual dance, on analogy with the familiar Latin phrase 'dramatis personae'.

16 **NOLO EPISCOPARI!**: 'I do not wish to be a bishop' (Latin).

17 **the true church militant**: Another echo of Butler's *Hudibras*. The 'Errant Saints, whom all men grant / To be the true Church *Militant*', are the ones who (in a passage quoted earlier in *Mel*) 'prove their Doctrine Orthodox / By Apostolick *Blows* and *Knocks*' (part 1, canto 1, lines 193–4, 199–200). See ch. 17, n. 9.

18 *The Triumph*: A well-known country dance.

19 **'till the toil-drops fell from his brows like rain'**: The opening lines of canto 2, stanza 18 of Walter Scott's *The Lay of the Last Minstrel* (1805): 'With beating heart, to the task he went; / His sinewy frame o'er the grave-stone bent; / With bar of iron heaved amain, / Till the toil-drops fell from his brows like rain'; *The Lay of the Last Minstrel: A Poem* (Longman, Hurst, Rees and Orme, 1805), p. 47.

20 **advance two squares**: TLP gives the reader the first six moves of the game-dance: 1. e4 e5 2. Bc4 Bc5 3. c3 Nf6 4. d4 exd4 5. cxd4 Bb6 6. Nc3 0-0. These moves replicate those in the game described in the article on chess in vol 4. (1810) of the *Encyclopædia Londinensis* (p. 414), an encyclopedia that TLP cites in *Mel* as one of his sources on Kant's philosophy (see ch. 31, n. 22). The *Encyclopædia Londinensis* takes this game from a treatise on chess by François-André Danican Philidor.

21 *hors de combat*: 'Out of fight, disabled from fighting' (*OED*), from the French; first use 1757.

22 **a friendly parle**: 'A debate or conference; discussion; negotiation; *spec.* a meeting between enemies or opposing parties to discuss the terms of an armistice; a parley' (*OED*). In book 6 of *The Iliad*, the Greek Diomedes and the Trojan Glaucus meet in the area between the two armies, discover that their fathers were friends, and pledge not to fight each other.

23 *ad libitum*: A Latin phrase used to mean 'At one's pleasure or discretion; at will, as one pleases' (*OED* A.1.).

24 **minuet**: The black king, passing the king's rook in the act of castling, makes a movement characteristic of this dance.

25 **a great refresher in the toils of war**: TLP's footnote directs us to Homer, *Iliad*, book 6, line 261, where Hecuba tells Hector that wine refreshes a weary man. This line occurs shortly after the parle between Glaucus and Diomedes to which TLP just referred.

26 **locomotion**: It is mysterious that the black king, O'Dogskin, bows and admits defeat because of his 'incapacity of locomotion', given the fact that English chess-players in 1817 either accepted the European rule that a stalemate was a draw, or persisted with the traditional English rule that the stalemated player was the winner. See H. J. R. Murray, *A History of Chess* (Oxford: Clarendon Press, 1913), p. 391; see also J. H. Sarratt, *A Treatise on the Game of Chess; Containing a Regular System of Attack and Defence*, 2 vols. (William Miller, 1808), vol. 1, p. 9. According to

the *Encyclopædia Londinensis* (see n. 20, above), the player who was stalemated won (vol. 4, p. 413).

27 **Waltzes**: 'No event ever produced so great a sensation in English society as the introduction of the German waltz in 1813', Thomas Raikes recalled in 1835. Before then, dancing was limited to 'the English country dance, Scotch steps, and an occasional Highland reel'; *Personal Reminiscences by Cornelia Knight and Thomas Raikes*, ed. Richard Henry Stoddard (New York: Scribner, 1875), p. 284. Anthelia and Forester oppose waltzing; the latter associates it with foreign decadence. They were not alone, at a time when (as Raikes recalled) 'the taste for continental customs and manners became the order of the day' (*Personal Reminiscences*, p. 285). In Byron's poem *Waltz: An Apostrophic Hymn*, published in 1813 as the work of 'Horace Hornem, Esq.', Hornem, a gentleman from the country newly arrived in London with his family, is startled by the popularity of waltzing and disturbed by the physical contact that this dance involves. The *Monthly Review* expressed a wish that Byron's poem 'would have the effect of banishing the loose Waltz from the British' (*Monthly Review*, vol. 70, no. 4 (Apr. 1813), 432); the *Critical Review* 'declare[d] that, as husbands and fathers, we should, positively and imperiously, prohibit our wives and daughters from *showing off in the Waltz*' (*Critical Review*, ser. 4, vol. 3, no. 3 (Mar. 1813), 331). According to Rees-Howell Gronow, as late as 1814 'the dances at Almack's were Scotch reels and the old English country-dance', but in about 1815 the waltz was introduced, and soon, 'in course of time, the waltzing mania, having turned the heads of society generally, descended to their feet, and the waltz was practised in the morning in certain noble mansions in London with unparalleled assiduity' (*The Reminiscences and Recollections of Captain Gronow, Being Anecdotes of the Camp, Court, Clubs, and Society 1810–1860*, 2 vols. (John Nimmo, 1892), vol. 1, pp. 32, 133). The Prince Regent's fête on 12 July 1816 was the first occasion on which there was

waltzing at court; for criticisms of this innovation, see *The Times* (16 July 1816) (reprinted in *The Examiner* (21 July 1816), 458), and Syntax Sidrophel, F.S.A., *Napoleon and the Spots in the Sun; or, the R——t's Waltz; and Who Waltzed with Him—and Where. A Poetical Flight, with Notes Variorum* (William Hone, 1816). In *HH* Escot dances, although dancing is 'contrary to my system' (ch. 13).

28 **quadrilles**: Quadrilles were introduced to England at about the same time as waltzing (see Gronow, *Reminiscences and Recollections*, vol. 1, pp. 32–3). See Cheryl A. Wilson, *Literature and Dance in Nineteenth-Century Britain: Jane Austen to the New Woman* (Cambridge: Cambridge University Press, 2009), ch. 4, "Social Circles and Dance Squares: The Quadrille" (pp. 104–31).

29 *figurante*: Ballet-dancer (Italian).

30 **Doric column**: Used here to represent noble simplicity.

31 **An Englishman in stays**: In the second decade of the nineteenth century, men's clothes became increasingly affected, as 'Padding was often added to the breast, and the use of stays by Exquisites excited many comments'; Cunnington, *Handbook of English Costume*, p. 77 ('Exquisites' were coxcombs or dandies). In *NA*, Mr Toobad lists 'men in stays' as one sign of contemporary degeneration (ch. 11), and Mr Listless loosens his stays after dinner (ch. 12). In 'An Essay on Fashionable Literature', TLP writes that 'The fashionable metropolitan winter' sees 'the levy *en masse* of gentlemen in stays and ladies in short petticoats against the arch enemy Time' (*NA*, p. 107).

32 **treble-flounced short petticoats**: For TLP on women's short petticoats, see the preceding note. A 'flounce' is 'An ornamental appendage to the skirt of a lady's dress, consisting of a strip gathered and sewed on by its upper edge around the skirt, and left hanging and waving' (*OED* n² 1).

33 **Alfred . . . the barons of Runnymead**: Forester's representatives of the virtuous simplicity of England's past are Alfred the Great, who ruled 871–99; Edward III, who ruled 1327–77;

John Hampden (1595–1643), republican leader; Sir Philip Sidney (1554–86); and the barons who compelled King John to endorse the Magna Carta. Hampden is invoked as an exemplary champion of liberty later in *Mel*, by Forester (ch. 37) and by Feathernest (ch. 39).

34 **THE MORNING OF LOVE**: Set to music and published as *The Morning of Love, a Song, from Melincourt, The Music Composed & Dedicated to Miss Gale, by G. Kiallmark* (Chappell, [1817]).

CHAPTER 29

1 **The course . . . as smooth**: Lysander in Shakespeare's *A Midsummer Night's Dream* says that 'The course of true love never did run smooth' (act 1, scene 1, line 134). Quoted (accurately) by Lady Clarinda, *CC*, ch. 10.

2 **that which we have detailed in the eighteenth Chapter**: This is the fourth occasion in *Mel* on which the narrator directs the reader to an earlier volume. The absence of a volume number and page number suggests that when TLP wrote ch. 29 he did not have access to the proofs of volume 2, signature D, which contains ch. 18 (and that he never made use of later opportunities to supply this information). The adventure in ch. 18 is the attempted abduction of Anthelia.

3 **his ignorance of the actors on that occasion**: Forester does not know who the perpetrators were; although Sir Oran unmasked Lord Anophel and Mr Grovelgrub just as Forester wished, Sir Oran did so in such a manner that only he saw their faces.

4 **perlustration**: 'The action or an act of inspecting, surveying, or viewing a place thoroughly; a comprehensive survey or description' (*OED*). This Latinate word recurs in the first sentence of ch. 32, when Forester, Fax and Sir Oran resume 'their perlustration'. The effect of Fax's proposal is that he, Forester and Sir Oran will re-enact the many walking tours of the Lake District. 'Perlustrations' also appears in *CC*, ch. 9.

5 **a bit of neat turf**: That is, by fighting a duel with pistols.

6 **muzzy**: 'Affected by alcohol; dazed or fuddled from drinking' (*OED* 2). The *OED* lists two occurrences in 1795.

7 **it is water in the desert, and manna in the wilderness**: The manna is the food that God provided to the Israelites in the Wilderness; see Exodus, ch. 16, vv. 11–15. For water, see Exodus, ch. 15, vv. 5–6.

8 **Och!**: 'Originally: expressing sorrow or regret. Later: expressing annoyed dismissal or disregard, exasperation, etc.' (*OED*). Major O'Dogskin uses a word that is 'chiefly Scottish and Irish English'.

CHAPTER 30

1 **Gullgudgeon**: A 'gull' is 'a simple credulous fellow, easily cheated'; 'gulled' means 'deceived, cheated, imposed on'; a 'gudgeon' is 'one easily imposed on'; and 'to gudgeon' is 'to swallow the bait, or fall into a trap, from the fish of that name, which is easily taken' (Grose, *Classical Dictionary of the Vulgar Tongue*; these definitions are also in *Lexicon Balatronicum*). John Anstey's *The Pleader's Guide* (see ch. 6, n. 12, above) recounts 'an Action Betwixt John-a-Gull, and John-a-Gudgeon'. 'Gullgudgeon' may suggest either 'gulls and gudgeons' or 'to gull a gudgeon'. The younger Crotchet in *CC* works for 'the eminent loan-jobbing firm of Catchflat and Company' (ch. 1) – 'flat' being nearly synonymous with 'gull' or 'gudgeon' – and Dr Folliott comments, 'Never did angler in September hook more gudgeons.' In one of TLP's *Paper Money Lyrics*, financial merit 'means the art of robbing / By huckstering and jobbing, / And sharing gulls and gudgeons / Among muckworms and curmudgeons' (Halliford, 7.102). For 'muckworms', see ch. 11, n. 4.

2 **Messieurs Smokeshadow, Airbubble, Hopthetwig, and Company**: 'Hop the twig' was slang for 'run away' (Grose, *Classical Dictionary of the Vulgar Tongue*, and *Lexicon Balatronicum*). In

CC, the bank for which the younger Crotchet works, Catchflat and Company, stops payments (ch. 18). In that same novel, Timothy Touchandgo prospers as a 'paper-money manufacturer' in the United States, assisted by Roderick Robthetill (ch. 11). In the 1818 French translation of *Mel*, the bank's name becomes 'messieurs Suw-Kesladow, Airbubble, Hopthulwig et compagnie' (*Paris-1818*, 2.78).

3 **shoaling in**: 'Of persons, birds, things: To crowd together, assemble in swarms' (*OED* 'shoal, *v.*' 2). *Mel* provides the *OED*'s earliest example of 'shoal' in this sense that postdates Milton's *Paradise Lost* (1667).

4 *promises to pay*: That is, banknotes. The reader soon learns that on one such note Henry Hopthetwig promises to pay £5 'to Mr. Gregory Gas, or bearer', just as the title character in TLP's *Cal* is handed a note on which John Figginbotham promises to pay Henry Hare £1,000 (Halliford, 8.337). Calidore is given the explanation that 'promises are of two kinds, those which are meant to be performed, and those which are not'; Figginbotham's is one of the latter kind (8.338). In *MM*, TLP writes that the 'unenlightened days' of the twelfth century 'were ignorant of the happy invention of paper machinery, by which one promise to pay is satisfactorily paid with another promise to pay, and that again with another in infinite series, they would not, as their wiser posterity has done, take those tenders for true pay which were not sterling' (ch. 5). TLP's most vivid analogy between different kinds of promise appears in *NA*, ch. 8, where Flosky says he has written 'seven hundred pages of promise to elucidate' the relation between fancy and imagination, 'which promise I shall keep as faithfully as the bank will its promise to pay'. Hazlitt said in his *Edinburgh Review* commentary on *The Statesman's Manual* that Coleridge 'is always promising great things, in short, and performs nothing' (*Complete Works*, vol. 16, p. 101).

5 **cash**: The Rev. Mr Peppertoast (who has not yet been named) uses 'cash' to mean banknotes that can be exchanged on demand

for gold or silver coins, but, as Forester hints, the term had been a misnomer for 'a Threadneedle Street note' ever since the Bank of England suspended cash payments (on using Threadneedle Street or 'the old lady' as metonymy for the Bank of England, see ch. 2, n. 9).

6 **a Jacobin rascal**: Upon arriving in London, Calidore attempts to exchange 'gold Arthurs' (Halliford, 8.335) – coins named after his homeland's ruler, King Arthur – but when he asks for 'gold coin' in return, he is accused of being 'a disaffected man and a Jacobin' (336).

7 **day of reckoning**: In the preface to *Paper Money Lyrics*, TLP says that the 'influenza to which the beautiful fabric of paper-credit is periodically subject' is termed 'commercial panic by citizens, financial crisis by politicians, and day of reckoning by the profane' (Halliford, 7.99). Obviously, TLP believes that the profane are correct.

8 **Peppertoast**: The term 'pepper toast' may be a coinage of TLP's; note the earlier 'anchovy toast', ch. 16, n. 12.

9 *lucus à non lucendo*: Quintilian's example in *Institutio Oratoria* (1.6.34) of an absurd etymological derivation is the contention that *lucus*, meaning a grove, comes from *non lucendo*, meaning that something fails to admit light.

10 **golden guineas**: The fisherman received £27 in banknotes for his 20 guinea coins, though the nominal equivalent of 20 guineas would be £21.

11 Ρεχθεν δε τε νηπιος εγνω: In *Iliad*, book 17, line 32, Menelaus tells Euphorbus that after a predictable event has occurred, even a fool can recognize that it was predictable.

12 *We ought now to be convinced … might have been prevented*: 'The words in italics are Lord Monboddo's,' as TLP's footnote states, though there are changes in capitalization and punctuation. In the preface to the third volume of *AM*, Monboddo writes that 'We ought now to be convinced, if not before, that what Plato has said is strictly true,——That there will be no end of human

misery till Governors become Philosophers, or Philosophers Governors;——and that our present humiliating state is owing to the want of Philosophy and true political Wisdom in our Rulers, by which they might have seen things in their causes, not felt them only in their effects, as every [sic] the most vulgar man does; and by which foresight, all the mischiefs that have befallen us might have been prevented' (*AM*, 3.lxxix). Forester suspends his quoting in order to replace Monboddo's 'our present humiliating state' with an 1817 equivalent: paper money. (Forester also revises Monboddo's 'mischiefs that are befalling us' to 'mischiefs that have befallen us'.) When Monboddo mentions that even 'the most vulgar man' can perceive dangers after they have caused injury, he appends a footnote quoting the same proverb from *The Iliad* that Fax quotes, Ρεχθεν δε τε νηπιος εγνω; that is, Fax echoes *The Iliad*, and Forester then quotes a writer, Monboddo, who exploits the same proverb from that poem.

13 **walk blindfold on the edge of a precipice, because it is too much trouble to see**: A continuation of the blindness and sight metaphor, which will dominate the next chapter, taking place at 'Cimmerian Lodge'.

14 **a voive-and-zixpenny dollar**: The word 'dollar' could refer in 1817 to several different foreign coins (*OED* 'dollar', 1–3); at some point, the word came to be slang for 'A five-shilling piece; a crown' (*OED* 4.b.).

CHAPTER 31

1 **poeticopolitical**: This portmanteau of 'poetical' and 'political' is not in the *OED*.

2 **rhapsodicoprosaical**: This adjective, combining 'rhapsodic' and 'prosaical', is not in the *OED*.

3 **deisidæmoniacoparadoxographical**: *Deisidaimonia* is Greek for fear of the gods; 'paradoxography' is 'A literary genre, originating in early Alexandrian Greece, in which (natural or man-made)

phenomena considered remarkable or fantastic are described'
(*OED*). The meaning of 'deisidæmoniacoparadoxographical'
would seem to be 'devoted to cataloguing superstitions'. In ch. 8
of *NA*, Flosky disavows 'hyperoxysophical paradoxology'.

4 **pseudolatreiological**: *Latreia* is Greek for service or worship of
the gods. Again, TLP associates Mystic with superstition.

5 **transcendental**: See ch. 8, n. 31, above.

6 **meteorosophist**: TLP's invented word, derived from Greek,
means 'knowledgable about lofty things'.

7 **Moley Mystic, Esquire**: On Mystic's surname, see ch. 8, n. 29.

8 **Cimmerian Lodge**: On 'Cimmerian', see ch. 8, n. 30. The 1818
French *Mel* translates the second part of this sentence in such a
way as to slight TLP's wordplay: 'Sir Fax reconnut immédiate-
ment en lui sir Mystic de Cimmerian, homme unique dans la
science des lumières obscures, c'est-à dire, dans l'art de raisonner
profondément sur des inepties' (*Paris-1818*, 2.90). After making
no attempt to translate or reproduce terms like 'deisidæmoniacoparadoxographical', the translator disregards the remainder
of TLP's paragraph and its allusions to 'the system of Kantian
metaphysics'.

9 **'That Moly, / Which Hermes erst to wise Ulysses gave'**:
Milton's *Comus*, lines 636–7 (in *Complete Shorter Poems*, ed.
John Carey, rev. 2nd ed., Longman Annotated English Poets
(Harlow: Pearson/Longman, 2007)), alluding to book 10, lines
302–6 of *The Odyssey*, translated thus by William Cowper:

> So spake the Argicide, and from the earth
> That plant extracting, placed it in my hand,
> Then taught me all its pow'rs. Black was the root,
> Milk-white the blossom; Moly is its name
> In heav'n; not easily by mortal man
> Dug forth, but all is easy to the Gods.

(Cowper, *The Iliad and Odyssey of Homer, Translated into English
Blank Verse* (J. Johnson, 1791), vol. 2, p. 232)

The passage is allegorical, the black root representing the difficulties of instruction and the white flower its benefits.

10 **a *pure*... Kantian metaphysics**: The first direct reference in *Mel* to Immanuel Kant, who is central to TLP's views of Coleridge. In *NA*, Mr Flosky, who has named his son 'Emanuel Kant Flosky' (ch. 6), exposes Scythrop to the writings of the philosopher of Königsburg (ch. 2); Mr Skionar in *CC* proclaims that 'the true road of metaphysics' has been found by 'the sublime Kant, and his disciples' (ch. 2). Drummond is one of the sources TLP acknowledges for 'the words and phrases marked in italics' in a footnote in ch. 31, and 'pure anticipated cognition' is Drummond's term for a concept of Kant's; see Drummond, p. 352. In *Cal*, Merlin makes Malthusian arguments 'by means of a pure anticipated cognition, as the transcendentalists express it' (Halliford, 8.327); in *NA* Scythrop has had 'many *pure anticipated cognitions* of combinations of beauty and intelligence' (ch. 3). Hazlitt's 'Coleridge's Lay Sermon', a review of *The Statesman's Manual* in the *Edinburgh Review*, vol. 27, no. 54 (Dec. 1816), may have encouraged TLP to relate Coleridge to Kant. Hazlitt discerned in *The Statesman's Manual* the misconceived idealism that Drummond and others attributed to the Prussian philosopher: 'the mob-hating Mr. Coleridge' imagines the common people 'intuitively to perceive the cabalistical visions of German metaphysics' (Hazlitt, *Complete Works*, vol. 16, p. 110). Whereas Coleridge refers to Kant by name just once in *The Statesman's Manual*, Kantian elements were on the surface in his *Biographia Literaria*, published in July 1817; Hazlitt claimed that in that book Coleridge was 'floating or sinking in fine Kantean categories', even though Kant's 'system appears to us the most wilful and monstrous absurdity that ever was invented' (*Complete Works*, vol. 16, pp. 118, 123).

11 **the *luminous obscure***: See Hazlitt's anticipatory review of Coleridge's *Statesman's Manual*, published in *The Examiner* on 8 Sept. 1816: Coleridge 'would persuade you that Sir Isaac

Newton was a money-scrivener, Voltaire dull, Bonaparte a poor creature, and the late Mr Howard a misanthrope; while he pays a willing homage to the Illustrious Obscure, of whom he always carries a list in his pocket' (*Selected Writings*, vol. 4, p. 109).

12 *dark root . . . a white flower . . . it was called Moly by the Gods*: See ch. 31, n. 9.

13 **under the stone of doubt . . . root of human science**: Mortals had trouble digging up Homer's 'moly' (see ch. 31, n. 9); TLP combines this image with metaphors found in expositions of Kant. Charles de Villers in his *Philosophie de Kant* (to which TLP refers in a footnote) uses the phrases 'la pierre du doute' and 'racines des connoissances humaines'; Villers, *Philosophie de Kant, ou Principes Fondamentaux de la Philosophie Transcendentale* (Metz: Collignon, 1801), p. 61. Drummond commented that a 'sceptic may not very well understand these mysterious metaphors', and may be surprised 'that the aspirant should search for the *roots of human knowledge* under the *stone of doubt*; and that he should be able to assist at the mysteries of their formation, until this stone be removed' (p. 371). According to Drummond, the truth of Villers' contentions is obscure to anyone who has 'not yet had the advantage of beholding a vision of pure reason' (p. 371); in *NA*, Flosky mentions having had 'a vision of pure reason' (ch. 8).

14 **the opinion of some naturalists that the mole has eyes**: The source for this information does not seem to be Buffon, as one might expect. However, see Oliver Goldsmith, *An History of the Earth, and Animated Nature*, 8 vols. (J. Nourse, 1774): 'Anatomists mention' that the eyes of moles have an advantage 'that contributed to their security; namely, a certain muscle, by which the animal can draw back the eye whenever it is necessary or in danger' (vol. 4, p. 94). TLP at his death owned an 1819 edition of Goldsmith's *History* (*Sale Catalogue* 321).

15 **None are so blind as those who won't see**: This proverb appeared in modified form in the previous volume of *Mel*, when Grovelgrub observed that 'none are so dumb as those who won't

speak'; see ch. 23, n. 8. Commenting on *The Statesman's Manual* in the *Edinburgh Review*, Hazlitt wrote that 'Our Lay-preacher, in order to qualify himself for the office of a guide to the blind, has not, of course, once thought of looking about for matters of fact, but very wisely draws a metaphysical bandage over his eyes, sits quietly down where he was, takes his nap, and talks in his sleep—but we really cannot say very wisely' (*Complete Works*, vol. 16, p. 100). 'Wilful blindness' is 'most happily characteristic of a transcendental metaphysician' like Mr Mystic; Flosky in *NA* 'lay *perdu* several years in transcendental darkness, till the common daylight of common sense became intolerable to his eyes' (ch. 1).

16 *Ocean of Deceitful Form . . . Island of Pure Intelligence*: In a subsequent footnote, TLP mentions Friedrich Gottlob Born, trans., *Immanuelis Kanti Opera ad Philosophiam Criticam*, 4 vols. (Leipzig: Schwickert, 1796–8), as one of his sources (see ch. 31, n. 22); Drummond, translating into English Born's Latin translation of Kant, refers to '*a vast and stormy ocean, the proper seat of deceitful form*'. In Drummond's version of Born, 'the region of pure intelligence' is 'an island' amid this ocean (p. 380). 'Intelligence' is Thomas Brown's equivalent for Kant's *Verstand*, which is usually rendered 'understanding'; [Brown], rev. of Charles Villers, *Edinburgh Review*, vol. 1, no. 2 (Jan. 1803), 253–80 (259 n.) – an article that TLP also noted as a source. In *NA*, Scythrop tells Marionetta that if they drink their own blood, they will 'soar on the wings of ideas into the space of pure intelligence' (ch. 3).

17 *topography of the human mind*: This phrase does not appear in TLP's acknowledged sources for Kant.

18 **'darkness visible'**: The most famous use of this phrase occurs in *Paradise Lost*, where Hell has no light but only 'darkness visible' (book 1, line 63).

19 **opticothaumaturgical**: The prefix 'optico-' obviously refers to eyesight, and 'thaumaturgical' is a variant of 'thaumaturgic', an

adjective describing something 'That works, or has the power of working, miracles or marvels; wonder-working' (*OED* 1).

20 **transcendentalising a *cylindrical mirror*:** The immediate source of Mystic's example of the cylindrical mirror is Drummond, pp. 373–8, who relies upon Villers, *Philosophie de Kant*, pp. 111–16. See also Brown's review of Villers, p. 266. The *OED*'s earliest example of 'transcendentalize', meaning either 'To render transcendent' or 'To render transcendental; to idealize' (*OED*) dates from 1846, twenty-nine years after *Mel*; there is no *OED* entry for 'transcendentalising'.

21 **the difference between *objective* and *subjective* reality:** Drummond examines Villers' 'explanation of the distinction between what is *objective*, and what is *subjective*'. This is 'the most sublime, we are told, and the most extravagant, we think, of the doctrines of Kant. It is now, that [Villers] draws from beneath his philosopher's robe, *a camera oscura* [sic], *a seal-ring, and three pocket mirrors*' (pp. 372–3). In the *Edinburgh Review*, Brown noted that Villers 'adduce[d] the probable reflections of a camera obscura, which . . . he has endowed with animation', and commented that 'there is something so ludicrous in the conception, that an author, who designed it only for illustration, would have been very cautious of repeating it'. Indeed, a reader of Villers might suspect that he intends to satirize 'the follies of metaphysics'; one 'passage is surely more in the manner of Voltaire, than of the grave Professor of Königsburg' ([Brown], rev. of Charles Villers, 265).

22 [Footnote:] **the mysteries of the words and phrases marked in italics in this chapter:** TLP's footnote lists several of the most substantial sources on Kant's thought that were available in 1817 to a reader who, like TLP, knew no German: Born, trans., *Immanuelis Kanti Opera ad Philosophiam Criticam* (see ch. 31, n. 16); Villers, *Philosophie de Kant* (see ch. 31, n. 13); [Brown], rev. of Villers (see ch. 31, n. 16); Wirgman, 'Kant', *Encyclopædia Londinensis* (see ch. 11, n. 12); and Drummond's

Academical Questions (see ch. 8, n. 29). On TLP's ignorance of German, see *Letters*, 2.284, 285 n. 4. TLP, however, apparently relied upon Drummond's critique of Kant for most of 'the words and phrases marked in italics', even when Drummond in turn relied upon Born or Villers. On Drummond's discussion of Kant, see René Wellek, *Immanuel Kant in England, 1793–1838* (Princeton: Princeton University Press, 1931), pp. 38–40. Some prominent sources on Kant are absent, such as Madame de Staël's *De D'Allemagne*, first published in Britain as *Germany*, 3 vols. (John Murray, 1813), vol. 3, pp. 70–98; and the review of de Staël that appeared in the *Edinburgh Review*, vol. 22, no. 43 (Oct. 1813), 198–238; see 235–8. TLP may also have drawn in *NA* upon de Staël's account of Kant. Some of the sources TLP acknowledged were unreliable. In 1830, Thomas De Quincey claimed that Brown's *Edinburgh Review* article was 'mere nonsense, in a degree possible only to utter and determined ignorance of the German language' (Brown admitted he had not read Kant). De Quincey observed that Wirgman produced 'so close a translation of the *ipsissima verba* of Kant, as to offer no sort of assistance to an uninitiated student'; *The Works of Thomas De Quincey*, gen. ed. Grevel Lindop, 21 vols. (Pickering and Chatto, 2000–3), vol. 7, p. 48; and, indeed, some of the more densely technical phrases that TLP italicized in this chapter he seems to have extracted from Wirgman in exasperation. Drummond evidently knew Kant primarily through Villers's treatise, secondarily through Born's Latin translation, and he misunderstood the philosopher's ideas. Drummond believed, for example, that philosophers who refer to truths that are known *a priori* refer to innate knowledge, but not all knowledge *a priori* is innate: although Drummond knew *a priori* that no bachelors are married, he would not know the meaning of the word 'bachelor' if he had never learned it. Mr Mystic continually echoes Kant; the obvious import is to depict Coleridge as a follower of the Prussian philosopher, but Kant is barely mentioned in *The Statesman's Manual*. Probably the obscurity of *The Statesman's Manual* and its distaste for the 'reading public' provoked TLP into associating its author with Kant, whose philosophy Drummond and Augustin de Barruel saw as the esoteric discourse of a secret society. Because TLP wrote *NA* after the publication of the *Biographia Literaria*, in which Coleridge praises Kant in detail, it is predictable that the Coleridgean character in that novel names his son 'Emanuel Kant Flosky'. In *NA*, Scythrop is also a devotee of Kant, and TLP's view of Kant expressed in that novel appears to have been influenced by the caricature of Kantians as a secret society that appeared in Barruel's *Memoirs, Illustrating the History of Jacobinism*, translated by Robert Clifford (1797–8).

23 **sub Jove frigido**: Under the cold sky (Latin).

24 **The reader who is deficient in *taste for the bombast*, and is no *admirer of the obscure*, may as well wait on the shore till they return**: Drummond, after quoting one of the 'excursions, which the transcendental philosopher occasionally makes into the regions of pure intelligence' (p. 369), writes that those who find the excursion unintelligible must be unfamiliar with Kant's 'usual diction'; 'They must be without taste for the bombast—they cannot be admirers of the obscure.' 'The candid reader will, however, recollect, that the language of mystecism [sic] is generally both obscure and figurative. The initiated alone can discover its latent beauties. We have not yet penetrated to the *adytum*.' (On 'adytum', see ch. 13, n. 7.) Drummond then writes, 'Let us follow the transcendental mystagogue' (p. 370); TLP picks up on this metaphor when he suggests that his readers may prefer to 'wait on the shore'.

25 **But we must not enter the regions of mystery without an Orphic invocation**: TLP's 'Orphic invocation' seems to combine phrases from several of the Orphic Hymns.

26 [Footnote:] *Πρωτευς Ολβοδοτης, Proteus the giver of riches*: The Greek here echoes the last line of the 'Orphic invocation'.

27 [Footnote:] **the *Lares* of every poetical and political turncoat**: 'Lares' are 'The tutelary deities of a house; household gods' (*OED* 'lar', 1.a.). Byron called Southey a 'turncoat' in *Don Juan* (canto 11, stanza 56), and in the appendix to *The Two Foscari* he referred to Southey's 'shifting and turncoat existence'; *The Complete Poetical Works*, vol. 6 (1991), p. 224.

28 **consentaneous to**: 'Suited to'. The first use of 'consentaneous to' noted in the *OED* in this sense dates from 1625.

29 **'that Experience was a Cyclops, with his eye in the back of his head'**: The source is Coleridge's *The Statesman's Manual*: 'Without [an 'Idea'], Experience itself is but a cyclops walking backwards, under the fascination of the Past' (*LS*, 43).

30 ***on a new principle***: The most obvious allusion is to Coleridge's preface to 'Christabel' (1816) in which he asserts that the poem's meter is founded on a 'new principle'. Cf. the parody *Christabess* (1816), by 'S. T. Colebritche, Esq.': 'I have, out of my profundity of genius, entirely created a new system of my own,—namely, that of measuring the lines by length, rather than by their harmony of syllables'; John Strachan, gen. ed., *British Satire, 1785– 1840*, 5 vols. (Pickering, 2003), vol. 2, p. 136. In 'The Four Ages of Poetry' TLP says that the Lake Poets 'wrote verses on a new principle' (see ch. 1, n. 2), and Coleridge's poetry is 'constructed on what [he] calls a new principle (that is, no principle at all)' (*NA*, p. 152). In *NA*, Mr Listless remarks that he 'cannot exactly see the connexion' between Flosky's ideas; Flosky responds, 'I pity the man who can see the connexion of his own ideas'; he also pities the man 'the connexion of whose ideas any other person can see' (ch. 6). The abstract of Kant's philosophy that Wirgman reproduces says that Kant's 'science will be found to be entirely new, in the strictest sense of the word' ('Kant', p. 605).

31 **the Stygian pool**: The pool of the river Styx in Hades.

32 **the Aristophanic symphony of *Brek-ek-ek-ex! ko-ax! ko-ax!***: TLP's footnote directs the reader to Aristophanes' Βατραχοι, *The Frogs*. When Charon ferries Dionysus across the river Acheron,

the frogs' chorus annoys Dionysus. TLP quotes and translates this chorus in a footnote in *Sir Proteus*, Halliford, 6.282–3 n.

33 **as Charon did Æneas and the Sibyl**: TLP's footnote quotes the relevant line from the *Aeneid*: 'Informi limo glaucâque exponit in ulvâ' (book 6, line 416); Charon transports Aeneas across the Styx and lands him on the ugly mire and grey sedge. TLP juxtaposes diverse accounts of a ride with Charon: a comic account from Aristophanes and a serious account from Virgil.

34 **'The fog . . . around'**: A parody of lines from Coleridge's 'Rime of the Ancient Mariner': 'The Ice was here, the Ice was there, / The Ice was all around.'

35 *adytum*: See ch. 13, n. 7.

36 LUMINOUS OBSCURE: It is unclear why the first edition prints the phrase 'luminous obscure' in small capitals, rather than the italic font used for the phrase earlier in ch. 31.

37 *synthetical torch*: De Staël wrote that 'Kant is frequently guided by a very obscure system of metaphysics; and it is only in those regions of thought where darkness prevails in general, that he displays the torch of light' (*Germany*, vol. 3, p. 96). 'Synthetical' is the adjective for Kant's synthesis employed by Wirgman, who refers to '*synthetical unity*' ('Kant', p. 610).

38 *shed around it the rays of transcendental illumination*: Drummond objects to the pretensions of 'transcendental philosophers' by saying that 'It is . . . a little extraordinary that all mankind should have been gifted with intuition, without ever suspecting it; and that so many of us should still continue to affirm, that we are in the dark, even after the disciples of Kant have shed around us the rays of transcendental illumination' (pp. 357–8). In *NA*, Scythrop promises Marionetta that by drinking their own blood they can 'see visions of transcendental illumination' (ch. 3).

39 **nubilous**: 'Lacking precise definition; vague, obscure' (*OED* I). *Mel* is the second example cited, the first dating from 1533.

40 *'la pale lueur du magique flambeau'*: In Voltaire's *Henriade*, 'la pâle lueur d'un magique flambeau', the pale light of a magic

torch, illuminates a tomb; canto 5, line 223; *La Henriade*, ed. O. R. Taylor, *Les Œuvres complètes de Voltaire*, vol. 2 (Geneva: Institute et Musée Voltaire, 1970), ed. Theodore Besterman et al., p. 478. It appears that Fax and Forester do not actually quote Voltaire, but rather that this quotation is the narrator's embroidery upon the comments that the two men address to Mystic.

41 **a *Spontaneity free from Time and Space***: This does not appear to be a direct quotation from any of TLP's sources on Kant.

42 **at the point of *Absolute Limitation***: One of 'the primary Ideas of Reason' is 'Absolute Limitation', and 'Absolute Limitation gives the following judgment: *All intensive quantities of the Phenomena, when viewed by Reason, are unconditioned*. Moreover, 'Intensive quantities are the events that are in Time, and not in Space; that have breadth nor height, yet arise and vanish' (Wirgman, 'Kant', p. 618). It is easy to see why De Quincey complained that Wirgman 'offer[ed] no sort of assistance to an uninitiated student' (see ch. 31, n. 22).

43 ***the categories . . . absolute necessity***: As Brown explained in his review of Villers, one of Kant's categories, or 'necessary forms of intelligence', was 'modality', which included '*possibility* and *impossibility*', '*existence* and *nonexistence*', and '*necessity* and *contingence*' (Brown, pp. 260–1). Wirgman wrote that 'Absolute Necessity' is one of the 'primary Ideas of Reason' ('Kant', p. 618).

44 **flew into a rage**: Drummond writes that Villers, an admirer as well as an expositor of Kant, 'grows angry, when people speak of clear ideas' (p. 367).

45 ***empirical psychologists***: For Kant's followers, 'Plato is a mere *noologist*, Aristotle an *empiric*, Leibnitz a *purist*, and Condillac an *experimental psychologist*', according to Drummond (p. 351). If you decline to be 'initiated in the mysterious doctrines of Kant', then 'his disciples will give you hard names; and will assert, upon the faith of their own critical illuminations and transcendental

visions, that you are equally ignorant of logic and philosophy' (p. 353).

46 **slaves of definition, induction, and analysis**: Drummond wrote that 'The advantage of definition was formerly admitted by all philosophers, who had occasion to employ new terms, or to change the signification of those already in use', but 'The transcendental philosophers are not partial to definition' (p. 365). In *CC*, 'Mr. Skionar contended with Mr. Mac Quedy for intuition and synthesis, against analysis and induction in philosophy' (ch. 10).

47 **as Lord Peter treated his brothers**: Mr Fax thinks Mystic may serve invisible food, much as Peter in Section IV of Swift's *A Tale of a Tub* (1704) serves his brothers bread and tells them it is mutton and wine. See The Cambridge Edition of the Works of Jonathan Swift, *The Tale of a Tub and Other Works*, ed. Marcus Walsh (Cambridge: Cambridge University Press, 2010), pp. 74–6.

48 **pure idea of absolute substance**: According to Wirgman, 'Reason, which requires totality in a series of depending properties, forms *the idea of an absolute substance*' ('Kant', p. 617). Later, Wirgman writes that 'The sole business of Rational Psychology is to investigate the Idea of *absolute substance*, or that which thinks; i.e. the Soul' (p. 619). Regarding the phrase 'pure idea', Brown explains in the *Edinburgh Review* that 'The system of our world' in Kant's philosophy is 'pure *idealism*, but an idealism in which we may safely confide' ([Brown], rev. of Charles Villers, 258).

49 **relation of determinate co-existence**: Another phrase taken from Wirgman's paraphrases of Kant: 'The Schema of the Category, Action and Re-action, is the conception of an assemblage of Substances mutually determining each other's place in space; that is, a *Determinate Co-existence*' ('Kant', p. 611); 'Experience viewed by the understanding discovers a determinate co-existence, consequence, and duration' (p. 618).

50 *objective phænomenon*: This phrase combines two words that never occur together in TLP's sources for Kant's ideas.

51 **a four-branched gas lamp**: Indoor gaslighting was new and rare in 1817. The Gas Light and Coke Company had been chartered as recently as 1812; see Trevor I. Williams, *A History of the British Gas Industry* (Oxford: Oxford University Press, 1981), p. 9. Rudolph Ackermann's Repository of Arts and his house had been lit entirely by gas since about 1811; see Fredrick Accum, *A Practical Treatise on Gas-Light* (R. Ackermann, 1815), pp. 86–7.

52 *ex fumo dare lucem*: Ironically, this phrase from Horace's *Ars Poetica*, meaning 'to give light from smoke', was the inscription on the medal which the Royal Society presented to gaslight pioneer William Murdock in 1808 (Williams, *History*, p. 7); it was also the epigraph to Accum's *Practical Treatise on Gas-Light*.

53 **fuliginous**: For this word, which means 'Pertaining to, consisting of, containing, or resembling soot; sooty', the *OED* cites several seventeenth-century occurrences, and notes that it was used by Charles Lamb in 1823.

54 **smoked glass**: The adjective 'smoked' has a double meaning here. Among the senses that the *OED* notes for 'smoked' are 'Obscured, made dark, by smoke' (*adj.* 2) and 'Of a smoke colour' (*adj.* 4); the *OED* cites the same two occurrences as the earliest examples of each meaning: one quotation from 1755, and one from 1819, the latter originating in Percy Shelley's *Swellfoot the Tyrant*.

55 **sphereoid**: A spheroid is 'A body approaching in shape to a sphere, *esp.* one formed by the revolution of an ellipse about one of its axes' (*OED*).

56 **tenebricose**: From the Latin *tenebricus*, meaning dark and gloomy. This is one of only two occurrences of this word noted in the *OED*, the first from 1730.

57 **sphereoidical**: A form of the more common 'spheroidal' (*OED*).

58 **This point of view is *transcendentalism***: On the cylindrical mirror and sphere, see ch. 31, n. 20. *Mel* here provides the second

483

appearance of the term 'transcendentalism' noted in the *OED*, the first occurrence being in Brown's review of Villers (see p. 265).

59 **on a new principle**: See ch. 31, n. 30.

60 **General discontent . . . steadfast frame of hope**: TLP's two footnotes cite p. 10 of the first edition of 'Coleridge's Lay Sermon', meaning *The Statesman's Manual*, the only one of Coleridge's two 'lay sermons' that appeared before TLP finished *Mel*. Coleridge wrote that 'the habit of thoughtfully assimilating the events of our own age to those of the time before us' was the only possible antidote for 'that restless craving for the wonders of the day, which in conjunction with the appetite for publicity is spreading like an efflorescence on the surface of our national character'. This habit is also the only plausible 'means for deriving resignation from general discontent' or 'means of building up with the very materials of political gloom that stedfast frame of hope which affords the only certain shelter from the throng of self-realizing alarms' (*LS*, 8–9).

61 **The main point . . . synthetical and oracular**: TLP's footnote refers to p. 21 of the first edition of *The Statesman's Manual*. Coleridge wrote that the nature of certain 'universal principles' found in the Bible is that 'they are understood in exact proportion as they are believed and felt. . . . For the words of the apostle are literally and philosophically true: WE (that is, the human race) LIVE BY FAITH. Whatever we do or know, that in kind is different from the brute creation, has its origin in a determination of the reason to have faith and trust in itself' (*LS*, 17–18).

62 **The contradictory interests of ten millions may neutralize each other**: TLP's footnote refers to p. 25 of the first edition of *The Statesman's Manual*, where Coleridge wrote, 'By the happy organization of a well-governed society the contradictory interests of ten millions of such individuals may neutralize each other, and be reconciled in the unity of the national interest' (*LS*, 21).

63 **the spirit of Antichrist is abroad**: TLP's footnote directs the reader to p. 27 of *The Statesman's Manual*, where Coleridge called David Hume the 'heartless atheist who, in this island, was the main pioneer of that atheistic philosophy, which in France transvenomed the natural thirst of truth into the hydrophobia of a wild and homeless scepticism'. Hume is 'the Elias of that Spirit of Anti-christ, which

———still promising
Freedom, itself too sensual to be free,
Poisons life's amities and cheats the soul
Of faith, and quiet hope and all that lifts
And all that soothes the spirit! (*LS*, 22)

Coleridge quotes his own poem 'Fears in Solitude', lines 142–6.

64 **The public, the public in general, the swinish multitude, the many-headed monster, actually reads and thinks**: TLP's footnote refers to pp. 45 and 46 of the first edition of *The Statesman's Manual*, where Coleridge explained that his tract is not intended for 'a promiscuous audience', but rather is addressed 'to men of *clerkly* acquirements, of whatever profession', and that he wishes 'the greater part of our publications could be thus *directed*, each to its appropriate class of Readers'. However, now there exists 'a READING PUBLIC—as strange a phrase, methinks, as ever forced a splenetic smile on the staid countenance of Meditation; and yet no fiction! For our Readers have, in good truth, multiplied exceedingly, and have waxed proud' (*LS*, 36–8). He concluded, 'From a popular philosophy and a philosophic populace, Good Sense deliver us!' (38). On the 'reading public', see *CC*, ch. 15. Hazlitt quoted Coleridge's diatribe against the 'reading public' in both of his reviews of *The Statesman's Manual*, in *The Examiner* (*Selected Writings*, vol. 4, pp. 116–17) and the *Edinburgh Review* (*Complete Works*, vol. 16, pp. 106, 113). Hazlitt commented that Coleridge would 'impose upon us, by force or fraud, a complete

485

system of superstition without faith, of despotism without loyalty, of error without enthusiasm, and all the evils, without any of the blessings, of ignorance' (*Complete Works*, vol. 16, p. 106). Coleridge's 'first horror is, that there should be a reading public: his next hope is to prevent them from reaping an atom of benefit from "reflection and stirrings of mind, with all their restlessness"' (*Complete Works*, vol. 16, p. 113). See ch. 21, n. 19 regarding the phrase 'swinish multitude', which does not appear in *The Statesman's Manual*.

65 [Footnote:] **the reader may find in a note the two worst jokes that ever were cracked**: In the footnote on pp. 45–7 of Coleridge's first edition (see *LS*, 36–8) 'one of the READING PUBLIC' makes an inadvertent pun with 'dey-monstered' (*LS*, 37n), and a Dutchman, having encountered 'The Learned Pig' at a 'showman's caravan', understands the phrase 'Reading Fly' to mean an insect that reads, rather than a coach to the town of Reading (*LS*, 37–8n).

66 **Can it make them bloom where it has placed them in its classification**: TLP's footnote refers to *The Statesman's Manual*, p. xvii of the first edition: 'Man of understanding, canst thou command the stone to lie, canst thou bid the flower bloom, where thou hast placed it in thy classification?—Canst thou persuade the living or the inanimate to stand separate even as thou hast separated them?' (*LS*, 77).

67 **talked for three hours without intermission**: Accounts of Coleridge's conversational energy were ubiquitous.

68 *the infinite divisibility of time*: According to Kant, time is 'divisible *in infinitum*—and infinite' (Wirgman, 'Kant', p. 608).

69 [Footnote:] **Some travellers speak**: Monboddo cites 'Buffon. Nat. Hist. Vol. xiv. p. 49' here, though TLP does not include Monboddo's acknowledgment of a debt to Buffon. Monboddo was using the 1766 edition of Buffon, and the passage in question is in *Buffon 1799*, 35.87.

70 **the gas-tube in Mr. Mystic's chamber had been left unstopped**:
See the letter by 'Civis', *Times* (4 Nov. 1814). Concerned about
'preparations now making for the introduction of Gas Lights
into use, both within doors and without', Civis informed readers
of *The Times* that if a flame somehow is blown out in a closed
room, the gas will collect, and 'such a mixture of the gas with the
air of the room will soon take place, as to explode the instant a
lighted candle is brought into the room; with the probable effect
of blowing out the windows; setting fire to any thing that is combustible; and, what is worse, of destroying, or at least, endanger-
ing the life of the person present'. Civis commented that such
accidents are inevitable 'till a remedy is found for ignorance and
carelessness in servants' (*Times* (4 Nov. 1814)). In Dec. 1814,
The Times reported that an explosion at a factory in Shrewsbury
had blown off the roof and injured a man after he entered a
gas-filled chamber with a candle (*Times* (26 Dec. 1814)). The
explosion in Mystic's chamber is not the only physical disaster
in TLP's fiction brought about by negligence: note the explosion
in *HH*, ch. 8, that frightens Mr Cranium and nearly leads to his
drowning, and the flooding of Gwaelod in *ME*. The meteorol-
ogist in *CC* is named Mr Firedamp (ch. 2), and firedamp is a
combustible gas.

71 **the apartment being perfectly air-tight**: According to one of the
responses to 'Civis' that were published in *The Times*, Civis' sce-
nario is possible only if the room is airtight, yet rooms seldom are
airtight, and danger may be prevented by making certain that air
circulates freely (letter by 'Common Sense', *Times* (14 Jan. 1815)).

72 **an infallible omen of evil**: James Mulvihill has suggested that
TLP may have recalled one of Coleridge's essays from *The
Friend* (1809) in which he attacks 'deceit and superstition',
whose reaction to truth resembles 'a fire which bursts forth from
some stifled and fermenting mass on the first admission of light
and air'; James Mulvihill, 'A New Coleridge Source for Peacock's

Melincourt, *Notes and Queries*, 230 (1985), 344–5. The quotation appears in *The Friend*, ed. Rooke, vol. 2, p. 55.

73 **blown up by his own smoke**: There is no source for this phrase in *ODEP* or *Stevenson's Book of Proverbs* (although *ODEP* does note 'hoist with his own petard', which occurs in Shakespeare's *Hamlet*, act 3, scene 4, line 105.6).

74 **for smoke to be too thick**: There is no source for this phrase in *ODEP* or *Stevenson's Book of Proverbs*.

CHAPTER 32

1 **the index**: 'The hand of a clock or watch; also, the style or gnomon of a sun-dial' (*OED* 'index', 3.a.). The first example given dates from 1594 (*Mel* is also cited).

2 **dialled brass**: The earliest occurrence of the adjective 'dialled' noted in the *OED*, in which the word clearly means 'Marked with, or provided with, a dial' (the *OED* acknowledges that the example from 1625 is ambiguous).

3 **the tax-gatherers**: A favourite term of Cobbett's, who complained, for example, that 'the Taxgatherer . . . takes a large part of [the "Country Gentlemen"'s] incomes and hands it over to the Placemen, the Pensioners, the Grantees, the Fundholders, and the Army' (*WPR*, 21 Dec. 1816, p. 783). Cobbett argued for reductions in expenditures by which 'a million of pounds a year would . . . be left in the pockets of the people, instead of that sum being annually taken from them by the tax-gatherers' (*WPR*, 12 Oct. 1816, pp. 468–9).

4 **every vifty . . . real money**: Such comparisons were common. Cobbett noted, for example, that a pound in 'paper-money' often had been 'worth from *thirteen* to *fifteen* shillings', rather than twenty shillings (*WPR*, 1 Feb. 1817, p. 142).

5 **a vundholder**: Someone who had invested in 'the funds', government bonds. The first example of 'fund-holder' in this sense recorded in the *OED* dates from 1797.

6 **a cottage-horny**: A 'cottage orné' was 'A house built in a rural setting to a consciously picturesque or rustic design, typically with some decorative features such as ornate woodwork. Sometimes more generally: a house in any setting having some of these features' (*OED*). The first example in the *OED* dates from 1774. In *CC*, Lady Clarinda Bossnowl says that 'love in a cottage is very pleasant; but then it positively must be a cottage ornée: but would not the same love be a great deal safer in a castle, even if Mammon furnished the fortification?' (*CC*, ch. 3; see *CC*, ch. 3, n. 14).

7 **gimcrack boxes**: When used as a noun, 'gimcrack' is 'Now usually applied to a showy, unsubstantial thing; esp. to a useless ornament, a trumpery article, a knick-knack' (*OED*); when used as an adjective, it means 'Trivial, worthless; showy but unsubstantial; trumpery'.

8 **zixes and zevens**: The *OED* notes that 'six and seven' or 'sixes and sevens', which 'originally denot[ed] the hazard of one's whole fortune, or carelessness as to the consequences of one's actions', later came to mean 'the creation or existence of, or neglect to remove, confusion, disorder, or disagreement' ('six', 5). Grose's *Dictionary of the Vulgar Tongue* (1785) recorded that 'left at sixes and sevens' meant 'in confusion' and was 'commonly said of a room where the furniture, &c., is scattered about, or of a business left unsettled'.

9 **the great house in Lunnun**: Cash payments by the Bank of England were suspended in 1797 (see ch. 21, n. 30); in 1816, the question of resuming payments arose, but the Chancellor of the Exchequer, Nicholas Vansittart, and others opposed it because of the war debt.

10 **a little vreehold varm**: A freehold farm is a farm owned in fee simple, in fee tail or for term of life; Hawthorne's farm, having belonged to his family since the twelfth century, is presumably owned in fee tail. The main point is that Hawthorne is not a wealthy man's tenant.

CHAPTER 33

1 **the opera being open:** Here TLP reminds readers that the action takes place in Jan., and perhaps reveals that he wrote this sentence at about that time of year. The opera at the King's Theatre, Haymarket, opened its 1817 season on 11 Jan., with Cimarosa's *La Penelope* (*Times* (11 Jan. 1817)). Readers of *Mel* learned in ch. 6 that Sir Oran is devoted to opera.

2 **the Argand lamp:** Instead of the gaslight of Mystic's Cimmerian Lodge, Anthelia's library has the powerful oil lamp developed by François-Pierre-Ami Argand. See Michael Schrøder, *The Argand Burner: Its Origin and Development in France and England, 1780–1800* (Odense: Odense University Press, [1969]); John J. Wolfe, *Brandy, Balloons & Lamps: Ami Argand, 1750–1803* (Carbondale: Southern Illinois University Press, 1999).

3 **a posthumous work of the virtuous and unfortunate Condorcet:** *Esquisse d'un Tableau historique des Progrès de l'Esprit humain* (written 1794, published 1795) by Marie Jean Antoine Nicolas de Caritat, Marquis de Condorcet (1743–94), a book translated as *Sketch for a Historical Picture of the Progress of the Human Mind* (1795).

4 **took a candle in his hand:** Sir Oran's hands are such that he can grasp a candle.

5 **great abundance:** TLP's footnote refers to the first of the two notes on p. 73 of volume 1 of the first edition, the note that quotes Monboddo's *Origin* on how the oran outang 'is capable of the greatest affection, not only to his brother oran outangs, but to such among us as use him kindly' (see ch. 6, n. 11). TLP evidently had access to signature E of volume 1 (to be precise, E1r) when he wrote this footnote in volume 3 or when he read the proof.

6 **no uncommon effect . . . absence:** In this conversation, both Fax and Forester echo *The Principles of Moral Science*, cited by TLP in ch. 21 of *Mel* (see ch. 21, n. 28). Forsyth, offering explanations for concepts of immortality, wrote that 'The illusions produced by ardent affection have often been known to present to the fancy the

image or appearance of the departed' (p. 473). 'Even in health, a dream is sometimes mistaken for a waking perception, particularly by the weary, the anxious, or the solitary—a circumstance which will probably account for some visions or preternatural events recorded in history, such as the appearance of his evil genius to Brutus before the battle of Philippi, and the conversation of Balaam with his ass, recorded in the sacred scriptures' (p. 474).

7 **tales of apparitions**: See the discussion of apparitions in *NA*, ch. 12.

8 **Petrarch's beautiful pictures of the Spirit of Laura on the banks of the Sorga**: In *GG*, Falconer imagines Petrarch's Laura 'ris[ing] from one of the little pools . . . to seat herself in the shade', and TLP quotes from Petrarch's sonnet 240, in which Laura emerges from the Sorga and sits on its bank.

9 **Brutus saw the spirit of Cæsar**: Forsyth cited Brutus in his discussion of apparitions quoted above, in n. 6. Caesar's ghost is referred to again in ch. 39 of *Mel*, when Forester quotes from Shakespeare, *Julius Caesar*, act 4, scene 2 (Shakespeare drew upon Plutarch). In fact, there are at least four allusions to *Julius Caesar* in volume 3 of *Mel*.

10 **the ghost of Banquo, for example, and that of Patroclus**: In *Macbeth*, act 3, scene 4, the Ghost of Banquo appears twice, to Macbeth's distress. In book 23 of *The Iliad*, Patroclus' ghost appears to his comrade Achilles, and tells Achilles that he will die in battle (lines 65–98).

11 **call a spirit from the vasty deep**: Glendower in Shakespeare's *1 Henry IV* claims that 'I can call spirits from the vasty deep' (act 3, scene 1, line 51).

CHAPTER 34

1 **knock them off**: The earliest occurrence noted in the *OED* of 'to knock off' in the sense of 'To dispatch, dispose of, put out of hand, accomplish; to complete or do hastily; *spec.* to write, paint, etc., in a hurried and perfunctory fashion'.

2 **a few bottles of London Particular**: Though 'particular' can be colloquial for 'A thing specially characteristic of a place or person; a person's special choice or favourite thing', Portpipe uses the word to mean 'a kind of Madeira' (*OED*). The first example of this narrower meaning noted in the *OED* ('2 pipes of Old particular Madeira Wine £76') dates from 1794.

3 **Custom has rendered them alike indifferent to him**: See the discussions of 'custom' in chs. 16, 21 (where Sarcastic calls custom 'the pillar round which opinion twines') and 27 (where Sarcastic says that 'Custom is the great lord and master of our conduct'). Here Forester and Fax discuss the effects of 'custom' on human sensibilities, and Forester makes the point that this insensitivity can be valuable.

4 **The sexton 'sings at grave-making'**: Shakespeare's Hamlet asks, 'Has this fellow no feeling of his business? / He sings at grave-making' (act 5, scene 1, lines 61–2), and Horatio responds that 'Custom hath made it in him a property of easiness' (line 63).

5 **'in the imminent deadly breach'**: Othello informs the senators that he told Desdemona of his adventures, including 'hairbreadth scapes i' the imminent deadly breach' (act 1, scene 3, line 135). After Fax quotes *Hamlet*, Forester quotes *Othello*.

6 **writs and executions**: Writs and executions are legal documents. A 'writ' is issued by a court, 'commanding something to be done touching a suit or action, or giving commission to have it done', according to Giles Jacob, comp., *The Law-Dictionary: Explaining the Rise, Progress, and Present State, of the English Law, in Theory and Practice; Defining and Interpreting the Terms or Words or Art; and Comprising Copious Information, Historical, Political, and Commercial, on the Subjects of our Law, Trade, and Government*, rev. T. E. Tomlins, 2 vols. (Longman, et al., 1797). An 'execution' is a kind of judicial writ that is 'grounded on the judgment of the court from whence it issues'.

7 **as sound as that of Epimenides, or of the seven sleepers of Ephesus**: The Cretan Epimenides fell asleep in a cave and did

not awaken for fifty-seven years (see Diogenes Laertius, *Lives of the Eminent Philosophers* 1.109–15); seven young men who had hid in a cave near Ephesus slept for two hundred and thirty years. When Fax invokes Aristotle as authority for the principle that those who wake 'had always the capacity of waking', he may be thinking of Aristotle, *Physics* 4.11.

8 **the faults of the dead . . . longer lived**: Mark Antony in *Julius Caesar* says that 'The evil that men do lives after them, / The good is oft interred with their bones' (act 3, scene 2, lines 75–6).

9 *Sa mémoire expira avecques le son des cloches qui carillonarent à son enterrement*: At the end of book 4, ch. 12, of Rabelais' *Gargantua and Pantagruel*, Panurge says of a 'Chiquanou' that 'the Memory of it was lost with the Sound of the Bells that rung for Joy at his Funeral' (Ozell, *The Works of Francis Rabelais*, vol. 4, p. 51; see Rabelais, *Œuvres complètes*, p. 567).

CHAPTER 35

1 **Miss Simper**: Her name connotes 'An affectedly coy or bashful smile; a smile expressive of, or intended to convey, guileless pleasure, childlike innocence, or the like; a smirk; an act of simpering' (*OED* 'simper', n. 1). A 'Miss Simper' is discussed by characters in Richard Brinsley Sheridan, *The School for Scandal* (1777), act 2, scene 2.

2 **a Methody preacher**: Fax is surely disappointed to learn that Robin thinks of rural Methodist preachers when he hears an appeal to 'authority' that relies upon truth and benevolence. Robin has come to be married in the 'earthy-ducks' (orthodox) Church of England.

3 **Book o' Common Prayer**: According to 'The Form of Solemnization of Matrimony' in *The Book of Common Prayer*, one of 'the causes for which Matrimony was ordained' is providing 'a remedy against sin, and to avoid fornication; that such

persons as have not the gift of continency might marry, and keep themselves undefiled members of Christ's body'. The other causes are 'the procreation of children' and 'the mutual society, help, and comfort, that the one ought to have of the other, both of prosperity and adversity'; *The Book of Common Prayer, and Administration of the Sacraments and Other Rites and Ceremonies of the Church, According to the Use of the United Churches of England and Ireland: Together with the Psalter, or Psalms of David, Pointed as They Are to be Sung or Said in Churches* (John Reeves, 1810).

4   **Anan?**: 'Anan' or 'anon', which is 'A mode of expressing that the hearer has failed to catch the speaker's meaning', is 'Widely diffused throughout the dial[ect] of' the British Isles and America; Joseph Wright, ed., *The English Dialect Dictionary: Being the Complete Vocabulary of all Dialect Words Still in Use, or Known to Have Been in Use During the Last Two Hundred Years,* 6 vols. [1898] (Oxford: Oxford University Press, 1970), vol. 1, p. 61.

5   **our look-out**: 'Lookout' can be a colloquial term, used 'With possessive adjective or genitive', to mean 'One's own responsibility or concern, which others are not obliged to consider' (*OED* 5). The *OED*'s earliest example comes from 1795 ('it was not his look out'). TLP introduced a character named 'Mr. Lookout' in ch. 30, where the word has the more common sense of 'A person stationed to keep watch, esp. for danger or trouble, or (less commonly) sent out to reconnoitre' (*OED* 3.a.).

6   **the parish must do it for you**: By means of the poor rates; see ch. 13, n. 23.

7   **salt-box and trencher**: 'Salt-box' here seems to mean simply 'A box for keeping salt for domestic use' (*OED* 1.a.), and 'trencher' seems to mean either 'A flat piece of wood, square or circular, on which meat was served and cut up; a plate or platter of wood, metal, or earthenware, *arch.* and *Hist*'. (*OED* II.2) or 'A trencher and that which it bears; a supply of food' (4.a.).

CHAPTER 36

1 **'press of business':** The narrator puts quotation marks around this phrase because Portpipe used it in the previous chapter to refer to the duties he needed to perform.

2 **ramifications:** 'A division or single part of (something with) a branched structure, as a plant, blood vessel, nerve, river, etc.; a branch' ('ramification', *OED* 2.a.).

3 **Tillotson, Atterbury, and Jeremy Taylor:** The writings of High Church Anglican divines John Tillotson, Archbishop of Canterbury 1691 to 1694, Francis Atterbury, Bishop of Rochester, and Taylor (see ch. 17, n. 5) would be suitable reading for a clergyman of the Established Church.

4 **a translation of Rabelais and the Tale of a Tub:** Portpipe may go to Tillotson, Atterbury and Taylor for 'materials of exhortation and ingredients of sound doctrine', but when he reads for pleasure, he reaches for heterodox texts such as Rabelais' works and Swift's *A Tale of a Tub*. He does not read Rabelais in French, however.

5 *Multum in parvo:* 'much in a small space' (Latin).

6 **a curious bone that was found in a hill just by, invested with stalactite:** The word 'stalactite' is used here to mean limestone from one of the geological formations commonly known as stalactites. The first instance the *OED* notes of 'stalactite' being used in this sense dates from 1794.

7 **the Patagonians:** Forester's subsequent speech affirming the Patagonians' existence ends with a footnote directing the reader to 'Ancient Metaphysics, vol. iii. p. 139', but this speech draws on much of Monboddo's discussion of the Patagonians (*AM*, 3.137–43). Monboddo wrote that 'The Patagonians are not so much in the state of Nature as the Oran Outans; but they are not far removed from it' (*AM*, 3.137).

8 **Mr. Byron:** Admiral John Byron, grandfather of the poet, author of *The Narrative of the Honourable John Byron (Commodore in a Late Expedition Round the World) Containing An Account of*

the Great Distresses Suffered by Himself and His Companions on the Coast of Patagonia, from the Year 1740, Till Their Arrival in England, 1746 (S. Baker and G. Leigh, 1768). TLP appears to rely not on Byron's book, however, but on the testimony recounted by Monboddo, who depended entirely upon other sources: 'a sailor, who was aboard Mr. Byron's ship', 'an account taken down in writing, from a gentleman, who had it from the mouth of Mr. Byron', and a letter by Charles Clarke, one of Byron's officers, that appeared in *The Transactions of the Royal Society* in 1767 (*AM*, 3.137–8).

9 **M. de Guyot . . . arrived in Europe**: Forester's wording is Monboddo's: Guyot 'brought from the coast of Patagonia a skeleton of one of these great men, which measured betwixt twelve and thirteen feet. This skeleton he was bringing to Europe; but, happening to be catched in a great storm, and having aboard a Spanish bishop, (the Archbishop of Lima), who was of opinion that the storm was caused by the bones of this Pagan which they had on board, and having persuaded the crew that this was the case, the Captain was obliged to throw the skeleton over board. The bishop died soon after, and was thrown over board in his turn. I could have wished that he had been thrown over board sooner, and then the bones of the Patagonian would have arrived safe in France' (*AM*, 3.138–9). Monboddo's source for the story of Guyot is 'Dom Pernety, Abbe of the Abbacy of Burgel, who has written a dissertation upon America and the Americans' (*AM*, 3.139n).

10 **the sons of Anak, and the family of Goliah**: The Anakites were giants who lived in Canaan when the Hebrews arrived (see Numbers, ch. 13, v. 33). For Goliah, or Goliath, see 1 Samuel, ch. 17. Portpipe unwittingly continues the chain of allusions to Monboddo, who wrote that 'The Sons of Anak, and the family of Goliah, we believe, did once exist, though their race has been long ago extinct' (*AM*, 3.140). The Reverend Doctor Gaster in *HH* (ch. 5) also commends the orthodoxy of an account taken from Monboddo.

11 **The multiplication of diseases . . . destroyed by the change**:
TLP's footnote refers to this passage in Monboddo: 'If vices
and diseases, and an unnatural way of living, must necessarily
weaken men, though living in the country and in single houses,
or in hamlets and small villages, much more must it do so in
great towns, where trade and sedentary arts are carried on. In
such towns, the air, fouled with the breath of so many animals,
and impregnated with exhalations from the dead, the dying, and
things corrupted of all kinds, must be little better than a slow
poison, and so offensive, as to be perceptible by the sense of those
who are not accustomed to it; for it is said, that the wandering
Arabs will smell a town at the distance of several leagues. In this
country it is well known that our cottagers, who are driven, by
the avarice of landlords and great tenants, into towns, to seek for
a livelihood there, are very soon destroyed by the change of air
and manner of life' (*AM*, 3.193). In paraphrasing Monboddo,
TLP again uses the rare, Latinate word 'coacervation' (see ch. 5,
n. 5).

12 **And this hiving . . . diseases of all**: TLP's footnote refers to
the passage in *Antient Metaphysics* where Monboddo, arguing
that venereal disease travelled to Europe from Africa, cites
'Monsieur Jussieu' to the effect that 'it was by the Portuguese
brought into Europe, and by the negro slaves carried to the
West Indies and America; from whence, no doubt, it would be
brought back to Europe; for it is the effect of commerce to keep
up a constant circulation of vice and disease, and to make the
vices and diseases of one country the vices and diseases of all'
(*AM*, 3.191).

13 **Consider . . . devised by them**: Monboddo, after discussing
sodomy and masturbation, notes 'another thing peculiar to
these times' that is 'still more pernicious, as the influence of
it is much more extensive, especially among the lower sort of
people': namely, 'the use of spiritous liquors; a thing so ruinous
and destructive to the human species, that, if all the devils were

again to be assembled in Pandemonium, to contrive the ruin of the human species, nothing so mischievous could be devised by them' (*AM*, 3.181). In *HH* Escot says that 'The use of vinous spirit has a tremendous influence in the deterioration of the human race' (ch. 5).

14 **but which . . . vices of the people**: After noting that the Gin Act of 1736 restricted the flow of gin, Monboddo writes that 'money was wanted; and, according to our method of raising money upon the vices of the people, a great part of the duties was taken off, that the people might be enabled to purchase it; and so the vice was restored, and now continues, and is increasing, not only in London and its suburbs, but all over the country'. Not surprisingly, Monboddo was concerned that drinking gin had become so common 'that, if a remedy is not applied, it will not only shrivel and contract the size of the human body, but will absolutely extinguish the race, in not many generations' (*AM*, 3.182–3).

15 *mens sana in corpore sano*: Juvenal concluded that the only goal which is worthwhile is possessing 'mens sana in corpore sano', a sound mind in a sound body (*Satires*, 10.356).

16 **a heavier mass than that which Hector hurled from his unassisted arm against the Grecian gates**: In book 12 of *The Iliad*, Hector breaks open the gates of the Greek camp using a stone which is so heavy that two strong men of Homer's own day, well after the Trojan War, would have difficulty handling it (lines 445–62). Homer, like Forester, contrasts the past to the degenerate present. In ch. 4 of *HH*, Foster and Escot debate human progress, and when Foster asks what 'degree of improvement' has 'taken place in the character of a sailor, from the days when Jason sailed through the Cyanean Symplegades, or Noah moored his ark on the summit of Ararat', Escot responds that 'If you talk to me . . . of mythological personages, of course I cannot meet you on fair grounds.'

CHAPTER 37

1 **A modern poet**: Wordsworth, in 'Thoughts of a Briton on the Subjugation of Switzerland', *Poems in Two Volumes*, vol. 1, p. 138, wrote that 'Two Voices are there; one is of the Sea, / One of the Mountains; each a mighty Voice: / In both from age to age Thou didst rejoice, / They were thy chosen Music, Liberty!' (lines 1–4).

2 **the genius of liberty**: At the beginning of *Mel*, the narrator stated that Anthelia was nurtured by 'the spirit of mountain liberty' (ch. 1).

3 **the cant of the new school of poetry**: On 'cant', see ch. 8, n. 25. In 'An Essay on Fashionable Literature', TLP complained of the 'systematical cant in criticism which passes with many for the language of superior intelligence' (*NA*, p. 115). Byron repeatedly condemned 'cant', commenting in his *Letter to John Murray Esq.* (1821) that 'The truth is that in these days the grand 'primum mobile' of England is *Cant*—Cant political—Cant poetical—Cant religious—Cant moral—but always *Cant*—multiplied through all the varieties of life'; *Complete Miscellaneous Prose*, ed. Andrew Nicholson (Oxford: Clarendon Press, 1991), p. 128. The 'new school' is the Lake Poets (see ch. 1, n. 2); on the emergence of the 'Lake School' as a concept, see David Perkins, *Is Literary History Possible?* (Baltimore: Johns Hopkins University Press, 1992), pp. 88–91. In 'The Four Ages of Poetry' TLP imagined the poets of his age announcing that 'Society is artificial, therefore we will live out of society. The mountains are natural, therefore we will live in the mountains.' TLP comments that 'To some such perversion of intellect we owe that egregious confraternity of rhymesters, known by the name of the Lake Poets' (*NA*, p. 149).

4 **'sent forth a voice of power'**: In *The White Doe of Rylestone; or the Fate of the Nortons*, canto 1, Wordsworth writes that, although the 'courts' of Bolton Priory 'are ravaged', 'the tower / Is standing

499

with the voice of power, / That ancient voice which wont to call / To mass or some high festival' (lines 21–4).

5 **Hampden and Milton**: The family seat of John Hampden (see ch. 28, n. 33) was Hampden House, Great Hampden, Buckinghamshire, and in 1665–6 Milton lived in Chalfont St Giles, Buckinghamshire, in the building today known as 'Milton's Cottage'. Both locations are within a day's walk of Great Marlow, where TLP wrote *Mel.*

6 **a little horde of poets**: Returning to the subject of the Lake Poets, Forester emphasizes their relocation from the 'vales' of southern England to Westmorland and Cumberland (of the three major Lake Poets, only Wordsworth was a native of the north).

7 **every great man's door**: Fax is thinking of Swiss personal body-guards, such as the Papal Swiss Guards.

8 **Wild the . . . full growth**: Forester quotes from lines 74–9 of Southey's 'To A. S. Cottle', a prefatory poem to A[mos] S[imon] Cottle, *Icelandic Poetry, or The Edda of Saemund, Translated into English Verse* (Bristol: Joseph Cottle, 1797), pp. xxxv–vi. At TLP's death, his library included a copy of Cottle's book (*Sale Catalogue* 547). In 'The Last Day of Windsor Forest' (1862), TLP quoted lines 85–92 of 'To A. S. Cottle' and commented that 'It is strange that this Epistle was not included in Southey's collected works. It is one of the best of his minor poems, and would alone suffice to show, that he had "looked on nature with a poet's eye"' (Halliford, 8.148n). TLP quoted lines 74–113 from this Southey poem, 'from memory', in his letter to Mary Shelley, 29 July 1847, having quoted from lines 90–2 in his previous letter to her, 26 July 1847 (*Letters*, 2.295–8). He quoted lines 85–92 in his 'Memoirs', Part II (1860), Halliford, 8.94.

9 **lying panegyrics**: Compare Fax's comments on 'fulsome flattery of the chieftain' to TLP's observations in 'The Four Ages of Poetry' and in *ME*. In 'The Four Ages of Poetry', TLP wrote that in the 'iron age of poetry . . . rude bards celebrate in rough

numbers the exploits of ruder chiefs' (*NA*, p. 136). 'The successful warrior becomes a chief; the successful chief becomes a king: his next want is an organ to disseminate the fame of his achievements and the extent of his possessions; and this organ he finds in a bard, who is always ready to celebrate the strength of his arm, being first duly inspired by that of his liquor' (*NA*, p. 137). Fax describes the poet as the chieftain's 'laureat' – another swipe at Robert Southey. In *MM*, Prince John's 'travelling minstrel, or laureate', Harpiton, is 'always ready, not only to maintain the cause of his master with his pen, and to sing his eulogies to his harp, but to undertake at a moment's notice any kind of courtly employment, called dirty work by the profane, which the blessings of civil government, namely his master's pleasure, and the interests of social order, namely his own emolument, might require' (ch. 9). The most vivid portrait of an obsequious court bard from the period appears in canto 3, stanzas 78–87 of Byron's *Don Juan* (cantos 3–5 were published in 1821). For a parody of a 'rhapsody rejoicing in carnage', see 'The War Song of Dinas Vawr' in *ME*, ch. 11.

CHAPTER 38

1 **benighted**: Here used to mean 'To be overtaken by the darkness of night (before reaching a place of shelter)' (*OED* 'benight', 1.a.). In ch. 40, 'benighted' has the more common meaning of 'To involve in intellectual or moral darkness, in the "night" of error or superstition' (2.b.).

2 **Gretna**: Gretna Green, the village just beyond the Scottish border where English couples went to marry if one or both were under 21 and they could not get the necessary parental consent.

3 **a rap of the ready**: The word 'rap' can be 'Used as a type of the coin of the least possible value' (*OED*, first example 1778). See canto 11 of Byron's *Don Juan*, published in 1823: 'I have seen

the landholders without a rap' (stanza 84, line 1). According to Grose's *Classical Dictionary of the Vulgar Tongue* (1785 and 1811), 'rap' can mean specifically 'an Irish halfpenny'. 'Ready' here means 'ready money, cash' (*OED*). In ch. 2, the reader learned that Miss Danaretta Contantina Pinmoney's given names are derived from '*danaro contante*, signifying *ready money*'.

4   **five hundred a year**: For comparison, Percy Shelley received an annuity of £1,000 beginning in 1815; from that annuity, he gave TLP £120 a year.

5   **Sir Bonus Mac Scrip**: Given TLP's focus upon political corruption, the primary meaning of 'bonus' here would not be 'Money or its equivalent, given as a premium, or as an extra or irregular remuneration, in consideration of offices performed, or to encourage their performance', but 'a euphemism for *douceur, bribe*' (*OED* 'bonus', a). Given TLP's focus on the dangers presented by paper money, the primary meaning of 'scrip' here would be 'A certificate of indebtedness issued as currency or in lieu of money' (*OED* 'scrip', n.³, 3.b.).

6   **myrmidons**: The obvious meaning may be 'A member of a bodyguard or retinue; a faithful follower; one of a group or team of attendants, servants, or assistants' (*OED* 2). The word occurs in ch. 2 of *HH*, when Headlong's butler serves as his 'myrmidon'; the *OED* takes the word there to mean 'A member of a gang or army adhering to a particular leader; a hired ruffian or mercenary' (*OED* 3.a.), although that interpretation is disputable. In Homer's *Iliad*, the Myrmidons are led by Achilles.

7   **irruption**: 'The action of bursting or breaking in; a violent entry, inroad, incursion, or invasion, esp. of a hostile force or tribe' (*OED*; earliest example 1577).

8   **various green wounds and bloody coxcombs**: In *Henry V*, Fluellen says, 'Bite, I pray you, it is good for your green wound and your ploody coxcomb' (act 5, scene 1, lines 41–3).

9   **coverts**: A covert is 'That which serves for concealment, protection, or shelter; a hiding-place' (*OED*).

CHAPTER 39

1 **Mainchance Villa**: On the phrase 'main chance', see ch. 13, n. 24. Even if TLP's Mainchance Villa is not meant to represent Rydal Mount, to which Wordsworth moved in 1813, Paperstamp's acquisition of his new residence certainly evokes Wordsworth's recent prosperity. In 1813, he was granted £400 a year as Distributor of Stamps for Westmorland. In the 1818 French translation of *Mel*, ch. 39 is titled 'La Maison de Campagne de Mainchance' (*Paris-1818*, 2.156), with 'Mainchance' left in English.

2 **perquisitions**: 'A thorough or diligent search, *esp.* one made officially; careful investigation or inquiry; (*Law*) a search of property to find a person, incriminating documents, etc.' (*OED*).

3 **the middle of winter**: Although the quest for Anthelia has been helped by fair weather so far, TLP reminds the reader that these conditions could not last.

4 **Peter Paypaul Paperstamp, Esquire**: The reader learns Paperstamp's full name. The *ODEP* gives examples for 'To rob Peter to [give to, clothe] pay Paul' dating back to the fourteenth century; by alluding to this proverbial phrase, TLP implies that when Wordsworth accepted a sinecure he robbed the people in order to meet some other obligation.

5 **whom we introduced to our readers in the twenty-eighth Chapter**: Again, TLP directs the reader to an earlier volume; the absence of a page number suggests that when TLP wrote ch. 39, he could not consult the proofs of volume 2, signature K, which contains ch. 28.

6 **placing his affections where they would be more welcome**: In the chess dance (ch. 28), Celandina was the black queen and Derrydown the black queen's knight.

7 **a very *good match***: Earlier, Miss Pennylove was '*laying herself out* for a *good match*' (ch. 21); later, we learn that 'making a *good match*' is Miss Danaretta Contantina Pinmoney's 'principal object' (ch. 42).

8 **Mr. Anyside Antijack**: Encountering this 'very important personage just arrived from abroad', readers in early 1817 would think of George Canning, who contributed to *The Anti-Jacobin* in the 1790s (see ch. 6, n. 41), and who had returned in May 1816 from Lisbon, where he had been ambassador, in order to become President of the Board of Control. In June 1816, Leigh Hunt, writing in *The Examiner*, accused Canning of political inconsistency (*The Examiner* (23 June 1816), 385–6), but TLP emphasizes the consistency of Canning's anti-Jacobinism. Ironically, Canning, as President of the Board of Control, became 'the main arbiter of Peacock's future career' in the East India Office (Sylva Norman, 'Peacock in Leadenhall Street', *Shelley and His Circle*, 6.720).

9 **a letter from Mr. Mystic**: To some extent, Mystic's 'letter' represents Coleridge's *Statesman's Manual*, published in Dec. 1816.

10 **Margery Daw**: On Margery Daw, see Opie, *The Oxford Dictionary of Nursery Rhymes*, pp. 350–2. TLP made use of this nursery rhyme again in his *Paper Money Lyrics*, one of which is 'Margery Daw', spoken by 'A Chorus of Paper Money Makers' (Halliford, 7.141–6): 'Margery Daw was our prototype fair: / She build the first bank ever heard of: / Her treasury ripened and dried in the air, / And governments hung on the word of / Margery Daw, Margery Daw, / Who spent all her gold and made money of straw' (7.141).

11 **Tommy with his Banbury cake**: It is not certain when *The History of a Banbury Cake: An Entertaining Book for Children* (Banbury: J. G. Rusher) was first published.

12 **Jack and Jill**: See Opie, *The Oxford Dictionary of Nursery Rhymes*, pp. 265–7. In *Sir Proteus*, the first of the 'three wise men' 'chatter[s]' meaninglessly about Jack and Jill, as well as about Wordsworth's Harry Gill and Alice Fell (see ch. 3, n. 6 and ch. 22, n. 30). In a footnote, TLP compares these Wordsworth poems to such verse for children (Halliford, 6.290).

13 **the famous house that Jack built**: Opie, *The Oxford Dictionary of Nursery Rhymes*, pp. 269–73. This nursery rhyme was the

basis of William Hone's satire *The Political House that Jack Built* (1819), illustrated by George Cruikshank.

14 **Dickory Dock**: Opie, *The Oxford Dictionary of Nursery Rhymes*, p. 244.

15 **little Jack Horner**: 'Little Jack Horner / Sat in the corner, / Eating a Christmas pie; / He put in his thumb, / And pulled out a plum, / And said, What a good boy am I!' (Opie, *Oxford Dictionary of Nursery Rhymes*, pp. 275–7). Iona Opie and Peter Opie point out that 'The figure of Jack Horner has frequently been used metaphorically, as by Swift in "A Christmas Box", by Byron in *Don Juan* [canto 11, stanza 69, line 4], by the Member for Farnham in the House of Commons, 22 Apr. 1947', and by Charles Lamb, who 'put the rhyme into Latin in a letter [dated] 30 Apr. 1831'; Opie, *The Oxford Dictionary of Nursery Rhymes*, p. 279. TLP's *Paper Money Lyrics* include 'Prœmium of an Epic Which Will Appear Shortly in Quarto, under the Title of "Fly-by-Night", by R— S—, Esq., Poet Laureate', in which Jack Horner 'Sate sulking in the corner, / And in default of Christmas pie / Whereon his little thumb to try, / He put his finger in his eye, / And blubbered long and lustily' (Halliford, 7.112).

16 **'taking care of number one'**: This catch-phrase goes back to at least the early eighteenth century. *Stevenson's Book of Proverbs* mentions an example from 1704 – ''Tis very careful of number one, and looks no further' (p. 1718). William Betagh, in *A Voyage Round the World. Being an Account of a Remarkable Enterprize, Begun in the Year 1719 Chiefly to Cruise on the Spaniards in the Great South Ocean* (T. Combes, 1728), writes: 'But now 'tis damn them; and for his part he would take care of number one' (p. 17).

17 **'Go, and do thou likewise!'**: Jesus said that his disciples should emulate the behaviour of the Good Samaritan (Luke, ch. 10, v. 37), behaviour quite unlike the greed that Paperstamp and his allies value in the story of Little Jack Horner.

18 **Mr. Mystic's synthetical logic**: At the time *Mel* was written, *The Statesman's Manual* had just been published; Southey had not yet had time to draw upon Coleridge in his published writings.

19 **Jack the Giant-killer, whose *coat of darkness***: See Iona Opie and Peter Opie, *The Classic Fairy Tales*, 2nd ed. (Oxford: Oxford University Press, 1992), pp. 47–65. Jack receives this magical tool from the giant himself (see p. 57). In *NA*, Scythrop 'wear[s] his coat of darkness with an air of great discomfort' (ch. 8).

20 **'Sherris sack'**: A name for sherry, which is sack imported from the Spanish city of Xeres or Jerez (see Falstaff's comments in *2 Henry IV*, act 4, scene 3, line 96). Once again, Feathernest is associated with the poet laureate's butt of wine.

21 **criticopoetical**: *Mel* is the only work cited in the *OED* as using 'critico-poetical' (printed 'criticopoetical' in *1817*). The word 'criticopoeticopolitical' appears in *NA* (ch. 10).

22 ***supplied by negation***: In the previous volume, TLP referred to 'a method of supply by negation' and attributed the concept to James Harris's *Hermes, or, A Philosophical Inquiry Concerning Universal Grammar* (see ch. 21, n. 4).

23 **œnogen**: This word, combining the Greek term for 'wine' ('œno-') with the suffix '-gen', is another of TLP's nonce words, and one that did not catch on: this is the only occurrence recorded in the *OED*. Responsibility for this word belongs to Derrydown, whose thoughts the narrator is summarizing.

24 **labial valve**: TLP's Latinate mode of referring to the lips.

25 **'Thus in dregs ... speech.'**: A quotation from Cottle's *Icelandic Poetry*, upon which TLP drew two chapters earlier (see ch. 37, n. 8). TLP's footnote observes that Cottle's work imitates rather than translates the original.

26 **one or two honest men among our opposers**: TLP supplies the first of his twenty-three footnotes that direct the reader to 'exquisite passages' in Southey's 'Parliamentary Reform'. This unsigned article of Southey's reviewed various publications that examined the state of the nation and that called

for reform, among them Cobbett's *Political Register*. In early Mar., Hazlitt named Southey as the author (*The Examiner* (9 Mar. 1817), 157). Though Southey's article was published at a moment (11 Feb. 1817) when TLP had probably written most of *Mel*, he relies on it in the Mainchance Villa scene as though it encapsulates views he has been satirizing in the preceding thirty-eight chapters. He puts Southey's sentiments into the mouths of no fewer than five characters – Antijack, Vamp, Feathernest, Killthedead and Paperstamp – as if Southey's views would be shared by Canning, Gifford, Croker and Wordsworth. Antijack dominates among the five, however, and his prominence suggests that TLP saw Canning as central to the forces of reaction. One factor in TLP's thinking was probably the speech Canning made in the Commons on 29 Jan. 1817, when acting as spokesman for the ministry because Castlereagh was abroad. In the passage cited by this footnote and by the next, Southey offered mixed praise of people who, like himself, initially opposed Great Britain's war against France: 'There was a deep, though mistaken principle in the opposers of the anti-jacobine [sic] war,—a passionate persuasion that England was engaged in a bad cause' ('Parliamentary Reform', 236–7). When the Peace of Amiens ended, in 1803, these same men favoured resumption of war; because they 'loved liberty', they 'could have no other wish' than to see Napoleon defeated (p. 237).

27 **ill read in history, and ignorant of human nature**: Southey wrote that the men who believed that 'England was engaged in a bad cause' were 'ill-read in history and ignorant of human nature' (p. 237). When Antijack criticizes Paperstamp (Wordsworth) and Feathernest (Southey), he is echoing an article written by Southey. In 'The Four Ages of Poetry', TLP stated that 'the Lake Poets' while they 'saw rocks and rivers in a new light', nonetheless 'remain[ed] studiously ignorant of history, society, and human nature' (*NA*, p. 149).

28 **the sublime Burke altered his mind, from the most disinterested motives**: In the passage to which TLP's footnote directs the reader, Southey wrote that all advocates of reform relied upon the principle which lay behind 'Mr. Dunning's or Mr. Burke's famous motion, that the influence of the crown has increased, is increasing, and ought to be diminished' (p. 252). (John Dunning, later the first Baron Ashburton, made this motion in Apr. 1782.) However, even if that principle was valid at one time, it 'had ceased to be so at the beginning of the French revolution in Mr. Burke's judgment, we know; he himself having recorded his opinion in works which will endure as long as the language in which they are written; and the converse of that proposition is now distinctly and decidedly to be maintained'. Anyside Antijack's word 'sublime' hints at the title of Burke's *A Philosophical Enquiry Concerning the Origin of Our Ideas of the Sublime and the Beautiful* (1757).

29 **a pensioned apostate**: This is one of only two references in *Mel* to political apostasy by that name (the first was in ch. 21), but references to political pensions have been far more common, and it is not surprising that TLP alludes to Burke's pension. According to Cobbett, in the *WPR* dated 1 Feb. 1817, Burke in the early 1790s 'drew his quill against the Parliamentary Reformers, whom he designated by all sorts of foul appellations', and Burke 'soon afterwards became a great pensioner for life, with a reversionary pension to his wife, and on whose *executors*, for *three lives*, two large grants of the public money, annually paid out of the taxes, are settled' (p. 130). In *The Black Book*, John Wade commented that Burke's 'zeal against the French revolution' no longer seems 'so *insane*, as one might have inferred from the outrageous tenor of his writings', if one is aware that Burke, 'during his life, had a pension of £3000 a year; . . . his *executors* had a grant of £2500, and his wife a pension of £1200 a year; and . . . that but for the premature death of his son, he would have been elevated to the peerage' (p. 23). In *NA*, ch. 10, 'the whole honorable band of

gentlemen-pensioners has resolved unanimously, that Mr. Burke was a very sublime person, particularly after he had prostituted his own soul, and betrayed his country and mankind, for 1200*l.* a year' (authorial footnote).

30 **Every man . . . his neighbour's property**: Now Vamp instead of Antijack echoes Southey, who wrote that 'of all men, the smatterer in philosophy is the most intolerable and the most dangerous; he begins by unlearning his Creed and his Commandments, and in the process of eradicating what it is the business of all sound education to implant, his duty to God is discarded first, and his duty to his neighbour presently afterwards'. Even before the smatterer applies his new views to public matters, 'his neighbour's wife may be in some danger, and his neighbour's property also' (p. 227). TLP takes Southey's phrase 'the smatterer in philosophy' to apply to 'Every man who talks of moral philosophy'.

31 **The church is in danger!**: A catch-phrase frequently used by writers who claimed that the supremacy of the Church of England was imperilled, and a phrase that was attributed to them by their opponents. Eighteenth-century examples are legion. Mary Wollstonecraft wrote in her *Vindication of the Rights of Woman* that often a 'maxim deduced from simple reason, raises an outcry—the church or the state is in danger, if faith in the wisdom of antiquity is not implicit' (*Vindication*, p. 25). In *Mel*, 'Peacock satirizes the government's insistence that state religion was essential if social order was to be maintained', Marcus Wood writes; 'Mr Vamp's cynical belief that the church can be "infallibly" exploited to whip up solidarity in the political ranks relates to the state's recent harnessing of blasphemy charges to libel prosecutions' (Marcus Wood, *Radical Satire and Print Culture, 1790–1822* (Oxford: Clarendon Press, 1994), p. 102).

32 **Every moral philosopher discards the creed and commandments**: See ch. 39, n. 30, above.

33 **tocsin**: 'A signal, esp. an alarm-signal, sounded by ringing a bell or bells: used orig. and esp. in reference to France' (*OED*). The *OED* does not record 'tocsin' being applied in a figurative sense, as it is applied here, before 1794.

34 **The people read and think**: Forester echoes Mr Mystic, who stated (in ch. 31) that 'The public, the public in general, the swinish multitude, the many-headed monster, actually reads and thinks.'

35 **My friend Mr. Mystic holds that it is a very bad thing for the people to read**: Southey's *Quarterly Review* article does not mention his friend Coleridge's recent work *The Statesman's Manual*, but Southey's contribution to the next *Quarterly* shows its influence, when he mourns the day when 'We had not yet learned to talk of the reading public, or to call ourselves a thinking people'; 'The Rise and Progress of Popular Disaffection', 530.

36 **Oh for the happy ignorance ... to be so**: Only now does TLP's Southey avatar, Feathernest, step in to use the words of Southey himself, who wrote that 'a people who are ignorant and know themselves to be so, will often judge rightly when they are called upon to think at all, acting from common sense, and the unperverted instinct of equity'. According to Southey, if 'the present state of popular knowledge' were not 'a necessary part of the progress of society', then 'it might reasonably be questioned whether the misinformation of these times be not worse than the ignorance of former ages'; 'Parliamentary Reform', 226.

37 **An ignorant man ... misinformed**: See ch. 39, n. 36, above.

38 **There was a time ... honest and honourable feelings**: Southey wrote that 'the people', who favoured the Peace of Amiens in 1802, endorsed resuming the war a year later because 'they saw plainly that the experiment had failed', and 'when, therefore, the government, in perfect accordance with the sound judgment, the common sense, and the honest honourable feelings of the nation, determined upon renewing hostilities, the news was

welcomed in the city of London with huzzas' ('Parliamentary Reform', 236).

39 **they are only capable . . . they squint**: After commenting that the ignorant populace 'will often judge rightly' because they rely upon 'common sense' and an 'unperverted instinct of equity', Southey wrote that 'there is a kind of half knowledge which seems to disable men even from forming a just opinion of the facts before them—a sort of squint in the understanding which prevents it from seeing straightforward, and by which all objects are distorted' ('Parliamentary Reform', 226).

40 **They would . . . suffrage**: Southey 'appeal[ed] to every person who remember[ed] the beginning of the French Revolution, whether, if the question of peace or war had been referred to the people of England and decided by universal suffrage, Mr. Pitt would have found one dissentient voice in a thousand' ('Parliamentary Reform', 228).

41 **But they were in a most amiable ferment of intolerant loyalty**: According to Southey, in the 1790s 'The principle of loyalty was triumphant even to intolerance: in most parts of England the appellations of republican and jacobin were sufficient to mark a man for public odium, perhaps for personal danger, persecution and ruin' ('Parliamentary Reform', 228).

42 **Gagging Bills**: The two 'gagging bills' to which Forester refers were enacted in Dec. 1795: 'An Act for the Safety and Preservation of His Majesty's Person and Government against treasonable and seditious Practices and Attempts' (36 Geo. III. c. 7), which toughened punishment for sedition by authorizing transportation for a second conviction, and 'An Act for the More Effectually Preventing Seditious Meetings and Assemblies' (36 Geo. III. c. 8.). (Habeas corpus had already been suspended, in May 1794.) The title of Thomas Beddoes's *A Word in Defence of the Bill of Rights, Against Gagging Bills* (1795) is the earliest example of the phrase 'gagging bills' cited by the *OED*. During the Regency, Southey endorsed aggressive prosecutions of the

press: although he acknowledged that 'The press may combat the press in ordinary times and upon ordinary topics', he contended that 'in seasons of great agitation, or on those momentous subjects in which the peace and security of society, nay the very existence of social order itself, is involved, it is absurd to suppose that the healing will come from the same weapon as the wound'; 'Parliamentary Reform', 275. Hazlitt, writing in *The Examiner*, condemned Southey for 'recommending gagging bills against us' (*The Examiner* (30 Mar. 1817), 194; *Selected Writings*, vol. 4, p. 166). Cobbett, who responded promptly to Southey's call for prosecutions (*WPR*, 22 Feb. 1817, p. 253), had written earlier that 'the Courier and Times and their foolish and wicked supporters may call for GAGGING BILLS, but no Gagging Bills will be passed', for 'To suspend the *Habeas Corpus* must, in time of peace, be regarded as the establishment of a permanent military despotism' (*WPR*, 11 Jan. 1817, p. 55). Cobbett's optimism was not borne out: on 4 Mar., parliament suspended the right to habeas corpus in cases of 'high treason, suspicion of high treason, or treasonable practices', and this suspension remained in effect until the following Jan.; see A. Aspinall and E. Anthony Smith, ed., *English Historical Documents, 1783–1832* (Eyre & Spottiswoode, 1959), p. 329. On 31 Mar. a new Seditious Meetings Act was passed (see Aspinall and Smith, pp. 330–2). On 27 Mar., Sidmouth sent the Lord Lieutenants of the counties of England and Wales a circular letter reporting the opinion of the Attorney General and Solicitor General that a libeller might be held to bail before an indictment or information had been filed. See Gary Dyer, '1817: The Year Without Habeas Corpus', *Keats–Shelley Journal*, 66 (2017), 136–54, 139–40.

43 **domestic reform . . . incendiary**: TLP's footnote directs the reader to Southey, 'Parliamentary Reform', 273 (where Southey condemns Cobbett's and *The Examiner*'s observations about the Spa Fields riots) '*et passim*'. Southey continually depicts advocates of reform as ruffians, scoundrels and incendiaries. If it is

established 'that the representative must obey the instructions of his constituents', then '"chaos is come again", anarchy begins, or more truly an ochlocracy, a mob-government, which is as much worse than anarchy, as the vilest ruffians of a civilized country are more wicked than rude savages' (258–9). See 273 for Leigh Hunt of *The Examiner* as a preeminent 'scoundrel' and as a 'flagitious incendiary'; see 227 and 275 for other incendiaries.

44 **Rousseau and Voltaire . . . Hebert and Marat**: Southey wrote that 'men of real talents, when those talents are erroneously or wickedly directed, prepare the way for men of no talents, but of intrepid guilt, and more intrepid ignorance'. Illustrating this principle, Southey took swipes at both Leigh Hunt and Henry Hunt, the radical leader who spoke at the Spa Fields meeting: 'Marat and Hebert followed in the train of Voltaire and Rousseau; and Mr. Examiner Hunt does but blow the trumpet to usher in Mr. Orator Hunt in his tandem, with the tri-colour flag before him and his servant in livery behind' ('Parliamentary Reform', 248; misattributed to 258 by TLP's footnote). Cobbett complained that a newspaper or newspapers asserted that Henry Hunt travelled to Spa Fields 'with a Tri-coloured Flag', although Hunt had not 'known of the existence of any flag until his arrival on the spot'. Cobbett doubted that Hunt ought to have left 'merely because some whimsical persons *had hoisted a flag and a cap of liberty*' (*WPR*, 23 Nov. 1816, p. 653).

45 **And I'll hang…*dying day***: Not traced.

46 **I am happy to reflect . . . arises from them**: Here Anyside Antijack follows Southey verbatim: the House of Commons contains 'very few who sanction the silly question of Reform; but few as they are, the number would be lessened, if those among them who have come into parliament by means which that question attempts to stigmatize, were to abstain from voting upon it. Undoubtedly such practices are scandalous, as being legally and therefore morally wrong; but it is false that any evil to the legislature arises from them'; 'Parliamentary Reform', 257–8.

47 **madmen moreover, and villains**: After Antijack, Vamp and
Feathernest speak with Southey's voice, it is Killthedead's turn.
On the page to which TLP directs his reader, Southey wrote
that contemporary 'circumstances . . . render the multitude more
dangerous and more apt instruments for madmen and villains
to work with than they ever were in other ages' (249). Later in
this article, Southey claimed that 'Any man that is not either a
madman or a villain' would agree with him concerning remedies
for the economic distresses (274).

48 [Footnote:] **the fourth article of the same number**: A review
of Archibald Campbell's *A Voyage Round the World, from 1806
to 1812: in which Japan, Kamschatka, the Aleutian Islands, and
the Sandwich Islands, were Visited* (1816), probably written by
John Barrow, appeared in the same number of the *Quarterly*
as Southey's 'Parliamentary Reform', 69–85. 'Owyhee' is
Hawaii, and 'Wahoo' is Oahu. Barrow wrote that King
Tamaahmaah, 'though endowed by nature with more feeling,
more energy, and more steadiness of conduct, than savages
in general possess', nevertheless 'has done little, if any thing,
that we can find, to ameliorate the condition of his people'.
Tamaahmaah has 'prevented the recurrence of those horrid
murders which, till his reign, were so frequent as almost to
deter navigators from communicating with those islands; but
it is to be apprehended that the practice has been discontinued
more from personal fear, than from any new feeling or principle of justice or humanity which he has awakened in their
minds' (78). TLP responds that Tamaahmaah differs from
European kings in that he 'has neither put to death brave and
generous men, who surrendered themselves under the faith of
treaties, nor re-established a fallen Inquisition, nor sent those
to whom he owed his crown, to the dungeon and the galleys'.
Presumably one such brave and generous man is Marshal Ney
(1769–1815), Napoleon's general, who was executed under the
restored Bourbon monarchy.

49 [Footnote:] **the tenth article of the same number**: A review of William Warden's *Letters Written on Board His Majesty's Ship the Northumberland, and at Saint Helena* (1816), contributed by John Wilson Croker; *Quarterly Review*, vol. 16, no. 31 (Oct. 1816), 208–24. Warden, whom Croker termed a 'blundering, presumptuous and falsifying scribbler', had applied the term 'trash' to a pamphlet by a Lieutenant Bowerbank that was reviewed in an earlier *Quarterly*, a pamphlet that Warden was surprised the *Quarterly* 'should condescend to notice'. Warden 'assert[s], that some of the facts quoted in our XXVIIth Number from that pamphlet and other authentic sources, are mere silly falsehoods, and he endeavours to represent Bonaparte as concurring in this assertion'. Croker's opinion of Warden's judgment is so low that he is 'sorry to find he calls [the *Quarterly*] a respectable work' (p. 213).

50 **The insane and the desperate are scattering firebrands**: After asserting that 'the multitude' had become 'more dangerous and more apt instruments for madmen and villains to work with', Southey commented that '[w]e are treading upon gunpowder, and if we suffer the insane or the desperate to scatter firebrands,—it will be but a miserable consolation to know that the explosion by which we perish, will bury them also in the ruin which they produce'; 'Parliamentary Reform', 249. TLP observes in his footnote that 'The reader will be reminded of Croaker in the fourth act of the Good-natured Man.' When TLP quotes from *The Good-Natur'd Man*, Oliver Goldsmith's earliest play (finished 1767, first performed 1768), he combines three passages from two distinct speeches in which Croaker, having received a letter, misinterprets it as threatening physical violence; see Oliver Goldsmith, *Collected Works*, ed. Arthur Friedman, 5 vols. (Oxford: Clarendon Press, 1966), vol. 5, pp. 62–4. The name 'Croaker' can suggest John Wilson Croker, who wrote for the *Quarterly*. It is possible that TLP thought Croker had a hand in 'Parliamentary Reform' or in the review of Warden's *Letters*

Written on Board His Majesty's Ship the Northumberland, and at Saint Helena.

51 **the *Spencean* blunderbuss**: A 'blunderbuss' is 'A short gun with a large bore, firing many balls or slugs, and capable of doing execution within a limited range without exact aim' (*OED*). In *CC* Mac Quedy says that he 'would fain have a good blunderbuss charged with slugs' (ch. 18, p. 152). In 1816 and 1817 opponents of parliamentary reform associated reformers with the radical egalitarianism of the Spenceans (on the Spenceans, see ch. 24, n. 12). Southey emphasized the Spenceans' supposed role in agitation for parliamentary reform ('Parliamentary Reform', 263–71), as did the report of the parliamentary secret committees, which urged that habeas corpus be suspended (*The Examiner* (23 Feb. 1817), 118). On 29 Jan. 1817, Canning implied in the House of Commons that parliamentary reformers were Spenceans; this speech is the subject of TLP's footnote here.

52 **a pop-gun**: A toy air gun. Southey wrote in the *Quarterly* that 'if the [Spencean] system were taken up by some stronger hand . . . compared to all other weapons of discontent, it would be found as Thor's mallet to a child's pop-gun' ('Parliamentary Reform', 271).

53 **[Footnote:] the mouse and the mountain**: In *Ars Poetica*, Horace envisions a poet taking the Trojan War as his subject, only to demonstrate that 'parturient montes, nascetur ridiculus mus' (line 139); 'mountains will labour, to give birth to a ludicrous mouse'. Mary Shelley wrote to Percy on 5 Dec. 1816 applying Horace's metaphor to the events at Spa Fields: the *Morning Chronicle* 'does not make much of the riots which they say are entirely quieted and you would almost be enclined to say out of the mountain comes forth a mouse'. She commented, however, that 'poor Mrs Platt does not think so' (*MWS Letters*, 1.22); one Richard Platt had been injured. Southey would concur with Mary Shelley: he wrote that 'the existence of St. Paul's Church is not more certain than that an attempt was made to murder Mr.

Platt, whose recovery is at this moment doubtful'; 'Parliamentary Reform', 273.

54 [Footnote:] *Spence's Plan!*: According to *The Examiner*, Canning on 29 Jan. 'read an extract from a publication, entitled, "The Spencean Plan". Among other principles it was stated, "that the only security of freedom was the restoration of the land to the people; and without that even revolution would be unnecessary". Again it was declared, "that the people were the only proprietors of the soil"'. Canning asked 'How far did the plans of the moderate reformers fall short of these principles? and how were they sure that when they set the whirlwind in motion, they would be able to direct its course?' (*The Examiner* (2 Feb. 1817), 71; cf. *Times* (30 Jan. 1817)).

55 [Footnote:] **So having said . . . of public scorn**: *Paradise Lost*, book 10, lines 504–9.

56 [Footnote:] **the very foolishness of folly**: Cobbett took the view that 'The silly *Spenceans* have been going on with their nonsense for more than *ten years*', and 'Their notions are foolishness itself' (*WPR*, 1 Mar. 1817, p. 262).

57 [Footnote:] **'husk about it like a chestnut'**: See Goldsmith, *An History of the Earth, and Animated Nature*, ch. 4, 'Of Multivalve Shell-fish': 'To a slight view, the sea urchin may be compared to the husk of a chestnut; being like it round, and with a number of bony prickles standing out on every side' (vol. 7, p. 61). On Goldsmith's *History*, see ch. 31, n. 14.

58 [Footnote:] **Horridus, in jaculis, et pelle Libystidis ursæ!**: When Virgil's Acestes goes to greet Aeneas, he is 'bristling with weapons and the skin of a Libyan bear' (*Aeneid*, book 5, line 37).

59 **a paper pellet**: Benedick in *Much Ado about Nothing* asks, 'Shall quips and sentences and these paper bullets of the brain awe a man from the career of his humor?' (act 2, scene 3, lines 240–2).

60 **'Who in a kind of study sate'**: A 'brown study' is 'A state of mental abstraction or musing' (*OED*), and TLP quotes from George Colman the Younger, 'Mr. Champernoune', in *Eccentricities for*

Edinburgh (Edinburgh: John Ballantyne, 1802), which deals with Henry VIII: 'King Harry stroke'd his face so fat, / Next, gave his pincushion a pat, / And in a sort of study sate, / Denominated, brown' (p. 61).

61 **you will find it the mallet of Thor**: As noted in ch. 39, n. 52, Southey thought that the Spencean system might 'be found as Thor's mallet to a child's pop-gun'; 'Parliamentary Reform', 271.

62 **The Spenceans . . . intelligible system**: Southey wrote that the Spenceans were 'far more respectable' than the 'Ultra Whigs' and 'Extra-Reformers', because, unlike the 'factious crew who clamour they know not why, for they know not what', the Spenceans 'have a distinct and intelligible system; they know what they aim at and honestly declare it' ('Parliamentary Reform', 271). Southey thought that their 'Agrarian system' was not 'so foolish, or so devoid of attraction, that it may safely be despised' (271), whereas Cobbett found that the Spenceans' ideas were 'foolishness itself' (see n. 56 above).

63 *half-seas-over*: 'Half seas over' meant 'almost drunk' (Grose's 1785 *Classical Dictionary of the Vulgar Tongue*, as well as the 1811 revision of Grose, *Lexicon Balatronicum*). At the Christmas Ball in *HH*, 'a few servants and a few gentlemen' are 'not above *half-seas-over*' (ch. 14), and in *CC* Dr Folliott says that the men who attacked him imagined that he was 'half-seas-over' and therefore vulnerable (ch. 8).

64 **The members . . . least so**: TLP's footnote refers to the page where Southey wrote that members of the House of Commons who 'have made a direct purchase of their seats' were 'the most independent men in the House, as the mob-representatives are undoubtedly the least so'; 'Parliamentary Reform', 258. Much as TLP has Killthedead turn Southey's 'mob-representatives' into 'the representatives of most constituents', Southey's 'direct purchase[rs] of their seats' becomes 'The members for rotten boroughs', but the last two groups mentioned were not coextensive. While the only seats that might be bought directly were seats for

proprietary (or 'pocket') boroughs, not all proprietary boroughs were rotten, and some representatives for rotten boroughs did not pay for their seats or have the means to do so. If a borough was controlled by someone who was eligible to serve in the Commons, he could have himself elected; for example, Henry Bankes represented his family's borough, Corfe Castle (which had about fifty voters). The nature of pocket boroughs, whether rotten or not, meant that they could accommodate wealthy men who were 'independent', like David Ricardo (or Forester), just as they served wealthy men who sought government patronage.

65 **mob-representatives**: See the previous note. After Killthedead refers to 'the representatives of most constituents', he reinstates the phrase Southey actually used, 'mob-representatives'.

66 **We ... good men**: On the page that TLP's footnote mentions, Southey asked, 'what wise man, and what good one, but must perceive that it is the power of the Democracy which has increased, is increasing, and ought to be diminished?' ('Parliamentary Reform', 273). This was Southey's parody of Dunning's 'famous motion, that the influence of the crown has increased, is increasing, and ought to be diminished' (252); see ch. 39, n. 28.

67 **a good man**: On the meaning of the phrase 'a good man', see ch. 2, n. 10.

68 **'I am perfectly satisfied with things as they are'**: On the phrase 'things as they are', see ch. 24, n. 2. Antijack echoes Sir William Curtis, MP for the City of London (see Introduction; on Curtis, see also ch. 27, n. 2, above). On 28 Nov. 1816, London's Court of Common Council discussed 'the distressed state of the nation', and Curtis said that, if asked whether he supported parliamentary reform, he would respond that he was 'quite satisfied with things as they are' (*Times* (29 Nov. 1816)). On 7 Feb. 1817, Curtis spoke against Reform in the House of Commons (*The Examiner* (9 Feb. 1817), 86). One irony is that the constituency Curtis represented was noted for radicalism for much of the eighteenth century.

69 **to call the present public distress an awful dispensation**: Paperstamp is the fifth among the men at Mainchance Villa to draw upon Southey's *Quarterly Review* article. Southey asked, 'What . . . are the prospects of the country under the awful dispensation with which it is visited? and what is the course which the government and the parliament are bound, or competent to pursue?'; 'Parliamentary Reform', 276. Southey argued that 'Of distresses, such as now pervade the mass of the community, small indeed is the part which parliaments or governments either create or cure.' Unfortunately, the causes of the distresses 'either lie without the limits of human control, or have been carried beyond our reach by the tide of time', the causes being the weather and 'the pressure bequeathed us by a long and exhausted war' (276). Sir William Curtis (see ch. 39, n. 68) thought the people should recognize that their sufferings were 'a dispensation of Providence' (*Times* (29 Nov. 1816)); there were other instances of what Paperstamp terms 'pious cant' designed to counteract 'the dangerous and jacobinical propensity of looking into moral and political causes, for moral and political effects'.

70 **is the ghost of bullion abroad?**: Antijack follows Southey, who, after the Court of Common Council condemned 'A delusive paper currency', responded by asking, 'What! is the ghost of Bullion abroad?' Southey endorsed the view that 'the difficulty does not consist in there being *too much*, but *too little* money; that the sudden subtraction of so much paper currency has been a direct and obvious cause of the stagnation of industry'; and so one antidote would be 'an increase of the circulating medium to a great amount' ('Parliamentary Reform', 260).

71 **'I am thy evil spirit!'**: Forester exploits Southey's and Antijack's ghost metaphor by alluding to Shakespeare's *Julius Caesar*, in which Brutus demands of Caesar's ghost, 'Speak to me what thou art', and the ghost replies, 'Thy evil spirit, Brutus' (act 4, scene 3, lines 281–2). On Brutus' encounter with the ghost, see ch. 33, n. 9.

72 **the swinish multitude**: This catchphrase appeared earlier, in chs. 21 and 31. See ch. 21, n. 19.

73 **recruit the army and navy … Virgin Mary's petticoat**: Cobbett and *The Examiner*, among others, deplored some consequences of the Allies' victory over Napoleon. The British 'found the Pope dethroned, the Jesuits scattered, the Bourbons driven out, and the Inquisition put down', and then, according to Cobbett, '*our success* has caused them all to be *restored*' (*WPR*, 28 Dec. 1816, pp. 829–30). In order to reveal 'the precise nature of that "*venerable* institution*"*, which Napoleon abolished, and which has been restored in consequence of the successes of the war', Cobbett quoted at length from the *Encyclopaedia Britannica*'s articles on the Inquisition and the *auto-de-fé* (*WPR*, 28 Dec. 1816, pp. 824–30). Because of the Allies' triumph, 'the Republics of Europe have been destroyed' and 'a holy alliance has been solemnly concluded between all the principal sovereigns' (*WPR*, 8 Feb. 1817, p. 162). *The Examiner* asserted that Britain had 'purchased thrones for the Bourbons too dearly', for 'Napoleon is scarcely an equivalent, even with the Pope, the Jesuits, and the Inquisition, as make-weights' (*The Examiner* (19 Jan. 1817), 36). Southey thought that arguments like these ill befitted populist writers: in the case of the Inquisition, 'the people' were the ones 'who restored that accursed tribunal, spontaneously and tumultuously'; 'Parliamentary Reform', 276.

74 **the stream of Tendency**: The Pedlar in Wordsworth's *The Excursion* (1814), Book the Ninth, hopes that people as they age will become able 'to commune with the invisible world', and will 'hear the mighty stream of tendency / Uttering, for elevation of our thought, / A clear sonorous voice, inaudible / To the vast multitude' (lines 86–90); *The Excursion*, ed. Sally Bushell, James A. Butler and Michael C. Jaye (Ithaca: Cornell University Press, 2007), p. 278.

75 **a poet**: The poet whose 'fallen state' Forester laments is Wordsworth, and Forester quotes the final five lines of the last of Wordsworth's

twenty-six 'Sonnets Dedicated to Liberty', dated '26. November, 1806', which appeared in *Poems in Two Volumes* (1807), vol. 1, p. 152. In this sonnet, Britain, 'the land', is 'the last that dares to struggle with the Foe' (l. 4), namely Napoleon. Wordsworth's note says that the last two lines of the sonnet are taken 'from Lord Brooke's Life of Sir Philip Sydney [sic]' (vol. 1, p. 158).

76 **marks of inconsistency**: TLP's footnote points to Walter Scott's examination of Byron's *Childe Harold's Pilgrimage: Canto the Third* and *The Prisoner of Chillon* that appeared in the same number of the *Quarterly* as Southey's 'Parliamentary Reform' and the reviews of Archibald Campbell and William Warden. Scott, believing that Byron's political views required an apologia, relied upon the 'French author' who wrote *Le Censeur du Dictionaire des Girouettes, ou, Les Honnêtes gens Vengés* (Paris, 1815) – Charles Doris – for the insight that 'poets in particular are not amenable to censure, whatever political opinions they may express, or however frequently these opinions may exhibit marks of inconsistency'; *Quarterly Review*, vol. 16, no. 31 (Oct. 1816), 172–208 (192). The French author 'has undertaken the hardy task of vindicating the consistency of the actors in the late revolutions and counter-revolutions of his country'. TLP, who was probably unaware that Scott wrote this article, utilizes the *Quarterly*'s defense of a Whiggish poet as Feathernest's defense of himself. TLP employs Scott's phrase 'A French author' in the next sentence, when Feathernest gives his version of Scott's paraphrase of the author.

77 **a mere *étourdie*, a *folâtre***: An 'étourdie' is 'A thoughtless, irresponsible, or foolish woman' (*OED*); the French adjective 'folâtre', meaning 'playful', is used here as a substantive.

78 **from Hampden to Ferdinand, and from Washington to Louis**: The Muse may go from John Hampden (see ch. 28, n. 33) to Ferdinand VII, reigning King of Spain in 1817; or from George Washington, Commander-in-Chief of the Continental Army in the American War of Independence and first President of

the United States, to Louis XVIII, current King of France. Feathernest's invoking Hampden is ironic because Southey praised Hampden in an early poem that was reprinted in *The Examiner* when TLP was writing *Mel:* 'The rebel HAMPDEN' is a man 'at whose glorious name / The heart of every honest Englishman / Beats high with conscious pride'; 'Acanthologia. Specimens of Early Jacobin Poetry. . . Specimen I. Inscription for a Column at Newberry. By Robert Southey, Esq. Poet-Laureate' (*The Examiner* (11 Aug. 1816), 504).

79 **a merry-andrew**: 'A person who entertains people with antics and buffoonery; a clown; a mountebank's assistant' (*OED*); the term also appears in *CC*, ch. 4. Note Forester's earlier reply to Feathernest: poets should not be willing to serve any master who will pay them unless they are also 'content to announce themselves as dealers and chapmen' (ch. 16).

80 **'So are we all, all honourable men!'**: In Shakespeare's *Julius Caesar*, Antony says of Caesar's assassins, 'So are they all, all honorable men' (act 3, scene 2, line 83).

81 **'Turning, turning, turning, as the wheel goes round'**: From Richard Brinsley Sheridan's *The Camp: A Musical Entertainment* (1778), act 1, scene 1.

82 **war doth increase sa-la-ry, ry, ry**: Killthedead's reference to his salary 'was probably inspired by the debate in the House of Commons on 17 Feb. 1817 over John Wilson Croker's demand for a quarter's war salary as Secretary to the Admiralty during Lord Exmouth's expedition against the Algerine pirates ("the triumph of Algiers"), but the allusion is not absolutely certain since the question of Croker's salary had previously been raised in March 1816' (Joukovsky, 'Composition', 22). See *Times* (18 Feb. 1817). Croker's salary as first Secretary was £3,000 in time of peace, £4,000 in time of war, and the fight with Algerine pirates, led by Edward Pellew (1757–1833), first Viscount Exmouth, had been used to justify wartime salaries, even though the war lasted only two days.

83 **canting**: The term 'canting' seems to mean using 'stock phrase[s] that [are] much affected at the time, or [are] repeated as a matter of habit or form' (*OED* 'cant', *n.*³ 5.b.), or 'Phraseology taken up and used for fashion's sake, without being a genuine expression of sentiment' ('cant' 6.a.), much as it did earlier. On 'cant', see ch. 8, n. 25, and ch. 37, n. 3.

84 **patent smoke**: the adjective 'patent' here refers to 'a process, invention, commodity, etc.: protected by letters patent; made, used, or sold under the protection of letters patent; that has been patented' (*OED* I.3.a.); or perhaps to something 'to which a person has a proprietary claim' (I.3.b., first occurrence 1797).

85 **the loaves and fishes**: Alluding to the story of Jesus feeding multitudes with a few loaves of bread and a few fish (Matthew, ch. 14, vv. 17–21; Mark, ch. 6, vv. 38–44; Luke, ch. 9, vv. 13–17).

86 **CHRISTMAS PIE**: After Antijack's last speech, the 1818 French translation of *Mel* inserts this paragraph: 'L'orgie des cinq associés se prolongea fort avant dans la nuite, même après l'absence des nouveaux venus, qui se retirèrent de bonne heure, ainsi que sir Derrydown, pour pouvoir continuer le lendemain leurs recherches' (*Paris-1818*, 2.174).

CHAPTER 40

1 **they were compelled**: The *Monthly Review* found 'occasional inadvertencies' in *Mel* and pointed to this sentence, in which 'the reader is not obliged to know who is here meant, since even the persons who were last mentioned in the chapter preceding are certainly not among the travellers'; *Monthly Review*, new ser., vol. 83, no. 3 (July 1817), 323.

2 [Footnote:] **'To scatter praise or blame . . . 136'**: TLP quotes from Samuel Johnson, *The Rambler*, no. 136 (6 July 1751). Before the phrase 'What credit can he expect', TLP has omitted several sentences that deal with literary dedications, Johnson's immediate topic in this *Rambler* essay. See *The Rambler*, ed. W.

J. Bate and Albrecht B. Strauss (1969), vols. 3–5 of *The Yale Edition of the Works of Samuel Johnson*, vol. 4, pp. 355–6.

3 **Lucretius**: Mr Fax appears to use Lucretius (first century BC), the poet who wrote *De Rerum Natura*, to exemplify free inquiry.

4 **Tiberius**: Augustus was deified after his death, and when one Rubrius was accused of violating Augustus' sanctity, Tiberius observed sarcastically that 'deorum iniurias dis curae': 'gods must deal with their own injuries' (Tacitus, *Annales* 1.73).

5 *there is most indigence in the richest countries*: TLP's footnote, quoting at length from *AM*, reveals that the italicized words in Forester's speech are adapted from Monboddo. In TLP's footnote, Monboddo's 'will be still more surprised' becomes 'will be surprised'; Monboddo's 'maintained upon' becomes 'maintained on'; and Monboddo's 'who, therefore, may' becomes 'who may therefore'.

6 **almost all of them are new creations**: Readers may wonder which 'titled names' Forester and Fax might consider to be adornments of their age: perhaps Lord Erskine, formerly the barrister Thomas Erskine; and, conceivably, a traditional Whig politician like Earl Grey (whose father was raised to the peerage in 1801 and created an earl in 1806). Lord Byron's baronage dated to 1643, so it was not a new creation. Forester's hero, Lord Monboddo, was not actually a peer, even though he was 'titled'.

7 [Footnote:] **Omnia . . . erit**: As TLP explains, the source is Tacitus' *Annales* 11.24. The statement by the Roman Emperor Claudius that TLP quotes might be translated thus: 'All that is now thought of as extremely old was once new. Similarly, our innovations will be part of the past, and what we today support by examples from the past will be among the examples.' Given the attention paid to parliamentary reform in *Mel*, it may be significant that Claudius is endorsing the admission of Gauls into the Roman senate.

8 **only in minds . . .** *only for itself*: TLP's footnote directs us to the preface to *Academical Questions*, where Drummond writes that any writer who indulges in 'philosophical speculations' 'must be contented with seeking for his rewards and his recompenses . . . in the approbation of the few, who have courage enough to despise prejudice, and virtue enough to love truth only for itself' (p. iv).

9 **'Honourable Friends'**: The formula members of the House of Commons employed when referring to members on their own side of the chamber.

10 **an** *ignis fatuus*: 'A phosphorescent light seen hovering or flitting over marshy ground . . . popularly called *Will-o'-the wisp*', according to the *OED*, which also notes that 'the term is commonly used allusively or fig. for any delusive guiding principle, hope, aim, etc'. In *NA*, TLP writes that Flosky, after having lain 'in transcendental darkness, till the common daylight of common sense became intolerable to his eyes', 'call[s] the sun an *ignis fatuus*' (ch. 1).

11 **to find a man . . .** *blow over him*: Although the italics imply that Forester or TLP is quoting, the quotation is imprecise. Monboddo wrote that a man will despair of finding 'any man of worth and goodness fit to make a friend of; and, if he does find such a man, he will be doubly fond of him, and will love him, as Hamlet does Horatio in the play; and with him retiring, and getting, as it were, under the shelter of a wall, (to borrow a similitude from Plato), will let the storm of life blow over him' (*AM*, 3.280).

12 *amor sceleratus habendi*: Ovid's phrase, meaning 'the accursed love of possessing' (*Metamorphoses* 1.131).

13 *Money you must have . . .* **the heroic age**: Not traced.

14 *the monk Rubruquis . . . before they are married*: Malthus, commenting on the Tartars, wrote that 'as all wives are bought of their parents, it must sometimes be out of the power of the poorer

classes to make the purchase. The monk Rubruquis, speaking of this custom, says, that as parents keep all their daughters till they can sell them, their maids are sometimes very stale before they are married' (*Essay*, 100). Malthus cited 'Travels of Wm. Rubruquis in 1253' (*Essay*, 100n).

15 **the sword of Damocles**: Fax alludes to the myth in which Damocles, assuming the role of a king, sat with a sword hanging above him, secured with a single hair. See Cicero, *Tusculan Disputations*, 5.61–2.

16 **the *elegant* philosopher**: The apparent meaning of 'elegant' here is 'having superior taste or discernment' or 'performing the specified activity with refined discernment', as in the phrase 'elegant scholar' (*OED* 'elegant', 5.a.).

17 ***They are married, and cannot come!***: In one of Jesus' parables, a man has a 'great supper', and one of those invited makes the excuse that 'I have married a wife, and therefore I cannot come' (Luke, ch. 14, v. 20).

18 *Εψαυσας αλγεινοτατας εμοι μεριμνας*: In Sophocles' *Antigone*, the title character tells the chorus that 'You have touched on a subject that causes me great pain', the subject being the fate of her father, Oedipus. TLP attributes the quotation to line 850 in *Antigone* as edited by Karl Gottlob August Erfurdt (1780–1813). See *Sophoclis Tragoediae ad Optimorum Librorum Fidem Iterum Recensvit et Brevibus Notis Instruxit Car. Gottlob Aug. Erfurdt*, vol. 1 (Leipzig: Gerhard Fleischer, 1809), p. 98. At the time of his death, TLP owned another edition making use of Erfurdt's work, *Sophoclis Tragœdiæ, recens. et notis instruxit C. G. A. Erfurdt, cum adnotat. G. Hermanni*, 7 vols. (1823–5) (*Sale Catalogue* 578).

19 **everlasting talkers ... the harmonizing hints of moss, mildew, and stone-crop**: Fax here echoes the earlier comments on tourists in search of the picturesque (see ch. 1, n. 8).

20 **The Canadian savages ... half an one**: The footnote quotes Isaac Weld, *Travels through the States of North America and the*

Provinces of Upper and Lower Canada, during the Years 1795, 1796, and 1799 (J. Stockdale, 1799), p. 402, with TLP changing Weld's 'they are liberal' by identifying 'they' as 'the Indians'.

21 **a fiction of the northern mythology**: As TLP's footnote indicates, these mythological figures come from Scandinavian myths. According to Amos Cottle's note to the 'Song of Grimner' in his *Icelandic Poetry, or The Edda of Saemund, Translated into English Verse* (see ch. 37, n. 8), Yggdrasil 'is the greatest of all trees, its branches cover the surface of the earth, its top reaches to heaven, it is supported by three vast roots, one of which extends to the ninth world, or Hell. An Eagle, whose piercing eye discovers all things, perches on his branches. A Squirrel is continually running up and down to bring news; while a parcel of serpents, fastened to the trunk, endeavour to destroy him' (Cottle, p. 62n). Paul Henry Mallet says much the same thing when he describes Scandinavian religion in *Northern Antiquities: or, A Description of the Manners, Customs, Religion and Laws of the Ancient Danes, and Other Northern Nations; Including Those of Our Own Saxon Ancestors, with A Translation of the Edda, or System of Runic Mythology, and Other Pieces, From the Ancient Islandic [sic] Tongue*, 2 vols. (T. Carnan, 1770), vol. 1, p. 102: 'That Ash, says Jafnhar, is the greatest and best of all trees. Its branches extend themselves over the whole world, and reach above the heavens. It hath three roots, extremely distant from each other: the one of them is among the Gods; the other among the Giants, in that very place where the abyss was formerly; the third covers *Nistheim*, or Hell; and under this root is the fountain *Vergelmer*, whence flow the infernal rivers: this root is knawed upon below by the monstrous serpent *Nidhoger*' (Mallet, *Northern Antiquities*, vol. 2, p. 49). In *GG* Falconer uses 'Ratatosk at the roots of the Ash of Ygdrasil' as a simile, and Opimian responds by terming 'Scandinavian mythology . . . one of the most poetical of all mythologies' (ch. 32).

CHAPTER 41

1 **the rocky steps**: In ch. 10, the reader learned of this secret exit from the castle rock; Lord Anophel or Grovelgrub must have become aware of its existence when they and other visitors to Melincourt Castle were obliged to go in search of Anthelia.

2 **Gibbon and Rousseau . . . *Carnifex***: Burned in the forum of a city by an executioner. In ch. 13, Desmond said that Mrs Dross 'hated the names of Rousseau and Voltaire, because she had heard them called rascals by her father, who had taken his opinion on trust from the Reverend Mr. Simony, who had never read a page of either of them'.

CHAPTER 42

1 **there is one, at least**: When Anthelia says that at least one person will never abandon the search for her, Lord Anophel is uncertain whether the person she means is Forester or Sir Oran.

2 **the opening of the Honourable House**: Parliament opened on 1 Feb. in 1816, on 28 Jan. in 1817 (on the latter day, the Prince Regent's carriage was reportedly fired upon, as he returned after delivering the address). Searching for Anthelia, Sir Oran, MP for Onevote, has missed the beginning of the new session.

3 **Your Lordship's word is quite as good as the authority you have quoted**: That is, not good at all. On *The Morning Post*, see ch. 2, n. 1.

4 **'Dearly beloved'**: The opening words of a marriage ceremony in the Church of England (see ch. 35, n. 3).

5 **a system of uniform sincerity**: Such as the system advocated by William Godwin in his *Enquiry Concerning Political Justice* (see ch. 11, n. 12).

6 **Falstaff on Gads-hill**: In Shakespeare's *1 Henry IV*, act 2, scene 2, Harry and Poins, in disguise, attack Falstaff and company, who run off, leaving behind the money they stole.

7 **Mentor**: Grovelgrub, who a moment ago resembled Prince Hal's advisor, Falstaff, now is Telemachus' tutor, and it is ironic to see Lord Anophel as Odysseus' son.

8 *ad libitum*: TLP's second use of this phrase; see ch. 28, n. 23.

9 **overtaken the swift-footed Achilles**: Grovelgrub is not as swift as Achilles, though he proves to be as swift as Falstaff. TLP's footnote obscures the fact that he begins quoting in the middle of Monboddo's sentence, and he silently omits a quotation from Horace's *Ars Poetica* (which appeared in Monboddo between 'honorable' and 'and'). Monboddo's 'the civilized man will, from that sense of honour, submit' becomes TLP's 'The civilized man will submit', and Monboddo's 'the great Oran Outan of Angola' TLP shortens to 'the oran outang of Angola'. Monboddo has a footnote to *Iliad*, book 1, line 263. Monboddo's point is that only the uniquely human appreciation of honour would enable a man to outrun an Angolan oran outang, who is faster by nature; TLP's point is that Sir Oran's sense of honour raises him above his fellow oran outangs.

10 **'he would confess all'**: It is unclear if any specific source is meant here.

11 **durance**: 'Forced confinement, imprisonment; constraint' (*OED* 5; first example 1535).

12 **to make a mystical unit**: According to the marriage ceremony used in the Church of England, marriage 'is an honourable estate, instituted of God in the time of man's innocency, signifying unto us the mystical union that is betwixt Christ and his church'; see ch. 35, n. 3.

13 *voti compos*: 'having attained his wishes' (Latin).

14 **the Satyr in Fletcher forms for the Holy Shepherdess**: TLP's footnote provides three quotations from Fletcher's *The Faithful Shepherdess* (c. 1607–8), each of which conforms closely to the text in Henry Weber's *Works of Beaumont and Fletcher* (see ch. 16, n. 2). In *The Dramatic Works in the Beaumont and Fletcher Canon*, gen. ed. F. Bowers, *The Faithful Shepherdess* can be found

in vol. 3, pp. 483–612, where TLP's first quotation is act 1, scene 1, lines 57–67, the second is act 4, scene 2, lines 130–8, and the third is act 5, scene 5, lines 238–59. Marilyn Butler writes that Fletcher's Satyr and Spenser's Sir Satyrane (in the *Faerie Queene*) are 'rough but loyal creatures, who proved their native nobility by championing a woman and saving her from rape by a so-called civilised man. It is highly ironic that they should do this, since the satyr's partly bestial nature traditionally connoted lust' (*Peacock*, p. 69).

15 **to all humanity**: *The Faithful Shepherdess*, act 4, scene 2, lines 62–6 (line numbers from Bowers), with Henry Weber's 'term' becoming *1817*'s 'call' and Weber's 'brags' becoming *1817*'s 'boasts'.

16 **that lady had irrevocably determined on a single life**: TLP's footnote quotes Malthus's encomium to 'old maids' that was excised from *Essay on the Principle of Population* after the 1803 edition (see Malthus, *Essay*, 551).

17 **wearing the willow**: In Spenser's *Faerie Queene*, one of the trees that shelter the Redcrosse Knight and Una is 'The Willow worne of forlorne Paramours' (Edmund Spenser, *The Faerie Queene*, ed. A. C. Hamilton (Longman, 1977), book 1, canto 1, stanza 9, line 3).

18 **her principal object of making a *good match***: Earlier in *Mel*, Miss Pennylove was '*laying herself out* for a *good match*' (ch. 21), and Mr Paperstamp determined that Mr Derrydown would be 'a very *good match* for his daughter' (ch. 39).

19 **Lord Anophel Achthar**: After TLP's final sentence, the 1818 French translation adds: 'Le révérend Grovelgrub attend encore son évêché, sa tutelle étant achevée; mais toutes les promesses qui lui avaient été faites, sont encore à réaliser' (*Paris-1818*, 2.199).

SELECT BIBLIOGRAPHY

Place of publication is London unless stated otherwise.

PRIMARY SOURCES

Born, Friedrich Gottlob Born, trans., *Immanuelis Kanti Opera ad Philosophiam Criticam*, 4 vols. (Leipzig: Schwickert, 1796–8)

[Brown, Thomas,] rev. of Charles Villers, *Edinburgh Review*, vol. 2 (Jan. 1803), 253–80

[Buffon, George Louis LeClerc, Comte de,] *Histoire Naturelle Generale et Particuliere, par Leclerc de Buffon; Nouvelle Edition, accompagnée de Notes, et dans laquelle les Supplémens sont insérés dans le premier texte, à la place qui leur convient. . . . Redige par C. S. Sonnini, Membre de Plusieurs Sociétés Savantes*, 127 vols. (Paris: F. Dufat, [1799]–1808)

Butler, Samuel, *Hudibras*, ed. introd. and comm. John Wilders (Oxford: Clarendon Press, 1967)

Byron, George Gordon, Lord, *The Complete Poetical Works*, ed. Jerome J. McGann, 7 vols. (Oxford: Oxford University Press, 1980–93)

Cobbett, William, *Paper Against Gold and Glory Against Prosperity*, 2 vols. (printed J. M'Creery, 1815)

The Weekly Political Register

Coleridge, Samuel Taylor, *Lay Sermons*, ed. R. J. White (Princeton: Princeton University Press, 1972)

[D'Israeli, Isaac,] *Flim-Flams! or, the Life and Errors of My Uncle, and the Amours of My Aunt! with Illustrations and Obscurities, By Messieurs Tag, Rag, and Bobtail. With an Illuminating Index!*, 3 vols. (John Murray, 1805)

Drummond, William, *Academical Questions* (Cadell and Davies, 1805)

The Examiner

Garside, Peter, James Raven, and Rainer Schöwerling, gen. eds.,
　　The English Novel 1770–1829: A Bibliographical Survey of
　　Prose Fiction Published in the British Isles, 2 vols. (Oxford:
　　Oxford University Press, 2000)

Gilpin, William, *Observations, Relative Chiefly to Picturesque*
　　Beauty, Made in the Year 1772, On Several Parts of England;
　　Particularly the Mountains, and Lakes of Cumberland, and
　　Westmoreland, 2 vols. (R. Blamire, 1786)

Grose, Francis, *A Classical Dictionary of the Vulgar Tongue* (S.
　　Hooper, 1785)

Hazlitt, William, *The Complete Works of William Hazlitt*, ed. P. P.
　　Howe, 21 vols. (London and Toronto: J. M. Dent and Sons,
　　1930–4)

Malthus, T[homas] R[obert], *An Essay on the Principle of*
　　Population; or, A View of Its Past and Present Effects on Human
　　Happiness; with An Inquiry into Our Prospects Respecting the
　　Future Removal or Mitigation of the Evils Which It Occasions.
　　A New Edition, Very Much Enlarged (J. Johnson, 1803)

Milton, John, *Paradise Lost*, ed. Alastair Fowler, rev. 2nd ed.,
　　Longman Annotated English Poets (Harlow: Pearson/
　　Longman, 2007)

[Monboddo, James Burnett, Lord,] *Antient Metaphysics: or,*
　　The Science of Universals, 6 vols. (Edinburgh: J. Balfour,
　　1779–1799)

Monboddo, James Burnet (*sic*), Lord, *Of the Origin and Progress*
　　of Language, vol. 1, 2nd ed. (Edinburgh: J. Balfour and T.
　　Cadell, 1774)

Peacock, Thomas Love, *The Halliford Edition of The Works of*
　　Thomas Love Peacock, ed. H. F. B. Brett-Smith and C. E.
　　Jones, 10 vols. (Constable, 1924–34)

　　The Letters of Thomas Love Peacock, ed. Nicholas A. Joukovsky, 2
　　vols. (Oxford: Clarendon Press, 2001)

　　The Novels of Thomas Love Peacock, ed. David Garnett (Hart-
　　David, 1948; 2nd impression corrected in 2 vols. 1963)

　　The Works of Thomas Love Peacock, Including His Novels, Poems,
　　Fugitive Pieces, Criticisms, Etc., ed. Henry Cole, 3 vols. (R.
　　Bentley, 1875)

Percy, Thomas, *Reliques of Ancient English Poetry: Consisting of Old Heroic Ballads, Songs, and Other Pieces of Our Earlier Poets. (Chiefly of the Lyric Kind): Together with Some Few of Later Date*, 3 vols. (Robert and James Dodsley, 1765)

Rabelais, François, *Œuvres complètes*, ed. Mireille Huchon, with François Moreau, Bibliothèque de la Pléiade, new ed. (Paris: Gallimard, 1994)

The Works of Francis Rabelais, M.D. . . . Now carefully revis'd, ed. John Ozell [revision of Urquhart-Motteux translation], 5 vols. (J. Brindley and C. Corbett, 1737)

Rousseau, Jean-Jacques, *Discourse on the Origins of Inequality (Second Discourse); Polemics, and Political Economy*, The Collected Writings of Rousseau, vol. 3, ed. Roger D. Masters and Christopher Kelly, trans. Judith R. Bush, Roger D. Masters, Christopher Kelley and Terence Marshall (Hanover, NH: University Press of New England, 1992)

Emile, or On Education: Includes Emile and Sophie, or the Solitaries, The Collected Writings of Rousseau, vol. 13, trans. and ed. Christopher Kelly and Allan Bloom (Hanover, NH: University Press of New England, 2010)

Scott, Walter, *Count Robert of Paris*, ed. J. H. Alexander (Edinburgh: Edinburgh University Press, 2006), vol. 23a of *The Edinburgh Edition of the Waverley Novels*, ed.-in-chief David Hewitt, 25 vols. in 30 (Edinburgh: Edinburgh University Press, 1993–2012)

Shakespeare, William, *The Plays of William Shakspeare: In Twenty-One Volumes, With the Corrections and Illustrations of Various Commentators, to Which are Added Notes, by Samuel Johnson and George Steevens, Revised and Augmented by Isaac Reed with a Glossarial Index*, 6th ed. (J. Nichols and Son, 1813)

The Riverside Shakespeare: The Complete Works, ed. G. Blakemore Evans et al., 2nd ed. (Boston: Houghton Mifflin, 1997)

Shelley and His Circle, 1773–1822, ed. Kenneth Neill Cameron, Donald H. Reiman, and Doucet Devin Fischer, 10 vols. to date (Cambridge, MA: Harvard University Press, 1961–2002)

Shelley, Mary Wollstonecraft, *The Journals of Mary Shelley, 1814–1844*, ed. Paula R. Feldman and Diana Scott-Kilvert (1987; repr. Baltimore: Johns Hopkins University Press, 1995)
> *The Letters of Mary Wollstonecraft Shelley*, ed. Betty T. Bennett, 3 vols. (Johns Hopkins University Press, 1980–88)

Shelley, Percy Bysshe, *The Letters of Percy Bysshe Shelley*, ed. Frederick L. Jones, 2 vols. (Oxford: Clarendon Press, 1964)
> *The Prose Works of Percy Bysshe Shelley*, ed. E. B. Murray, vol. 1 (Oxford: Clarendon Press, 1993)

[Southey, Robert,] 'The Rise and Progress of Popular Disaffection', *Quarterly Review*, vol. 16, no. 32 (Jan. 1817), 511–52

Villers, Charles de, *Philosophie de Kant, ou Principes Fondamentaux de la Philosophie Transcendentale* (Metz: Collignon, 1801)

SECONDARY SOURCES

Brown, Laura, *Homeless Dogs and Melancholy Apes: Humans and Other Animals in the Modern Literary Imagination* (Ithaca: Cornell University Press, 2010)

Butler, Marilyn, *Peacock Displayed: A Satirist in His Context* (Routledge and Kegan Paul, 1979)

Cameron, Kenneth Neill, 'Shelley's Chariot', *Shelley and His Circle*, 3.153–78

Catalogue of the Library of the Late Thos. Love Peacock, Esq. . . . which will be Sold by Auction, by Messrs. Sotheby, Wilkinson & Hodge, the 11th of June, 1866, and Following Day, reprinted in *Sale Catalogues of Libraries of Eminent Persons*, ed. A. N. L. Munby, vol. 1 (Mansell, with Sotheby Parke-Bernet, 1971)

Cunnington, C. Willett, and Phillis Cunnington, *Handbook of English Costume in the Nineteenth Century*, 3rd ed. (Faber, 1970)

Dawson, Carl, *His Fine Wit: A Study of Thomas Love Peacock* (Berkeley: University of California Press, 1970)

Dyer, Gary, *British Satire and the Politics of Style, 1789–1832* (Cambridge: Cambridge University Press, 1997)

Jack, Ian, *English Literature, 1815–1832* (Oxford: Clarendon Press, 1963)

Joukovsky, Nicholas A., 'The Composition of Peacock's *Melincourt* and the Date of the "Calidore" Fragment', *English Language Notes*, 12 (1975), 18–25

    'The French Translation of Peacock's *Melincourt*', *Notes and Queries*, 23 (1976), 110–12

    'Peacock before *Headlong Hall*: A New Look at His Early Years', *Keats–Shelley Review*, 36 (1985), 1–40

    'Peacock's Sir Oran Haut-ton: Byron's Bear or Shelley's Ape?', *Keats–Shelley Journal*, 29 (1980), 173–90

Kelly, Gary, *English Fiction of the Romantic Period, 1789–1830* (Longman, 1989)

Madden, Lionel, *Thomas Love Peacock* (Evans Bros., 1967)

Mills, Howard, *Peacock: His Circle and His Age* (Cambridge: Cambridge University Press, 1969)

Opie, Iona, and Peter Opie, *The Classic Fairy Tales*, 2nd ed. (Oxford: Oxford University Press, 1992)

    The Oxford Dictionary of English Proverbs, 3rd ed. (Oxford: Clarendon Press, 1970)

    The Oxford Dictionary of Nursery Rhymes, 2nd ed. (Oxford: Oxford University Press, 1997)

Smith, D. J. M., *A Dictionary of Horse-Drawn Vehicles* (J. A. Allen, 1988)

St. Clair, William, *The Reading Nation in the Romantic Period* (Cambridge: Cambridge University Press, 2004)

Thorne, R. G., *History of Parliament: The House of Commons, 1790–1820*, 5 vols. (Secker and Warburg, 1986)

Topp, Chester W., *Victorian Yellowbacks and Paperbacks, 1849–1905*, 9 vols. (Denver: Hermitage Antiquarian Bookshop, 1993)

Van Doren, Carl, *The Life of Thomas Love Peacock* (Dent, 1911)